# THESE
# WERE GOD'S PEOPLE

## A Bible history

The story of Israel and early Christianity, based on the Holy Scriptures, ancient historical and religious documents, and the findings of archaeology.

### BY WILLIAM C. MARTIN, M.A., B.D.

*The Southwestern Company*

NASHVILLE, TENNESSEE

Biblical quotations, except where otherwise indicated, are from the Revised Standard Version of
the Bible, copyrighted 1946 and 1952 by the Division of Christian Education, National Council of
Churches, and are used by permission.

Brief quotations from extra-Biblical sources are
taken from James B. Pritchard, *Ancient Near Eastern Texts*, second edition, 1955, and are used with
the permission of the Princeton University Press.

The illustrations for this book have been produced
by Carole Stone Straughn. Mrs. Straughn received
her training at Abilene Christian College and Harvard University.

Copyright © 1966 by
THE SOUTHWESTERN COMPANY
Nashville, Tennessee
*All Rights Reserved*
Library of Congress Catalog Card No. 66-20336
Printed in the United States of America
R.R.D. 1-66

# Foreword

THE BASIC PURPOSES of this book, as set forth more fully on pp. 3–8, are: (1) to plunge the average layman into the fascinating world of the Bible in a way that will make its pages and its people and its central themes come alive with color and power and richness; (2) to treat the history of God's people in a chronological fashion rather than book by book, and to place that history in the larger world historical context; (3) to illuminate the Biblical narrative by reference to relevant archaeological discoveries; and (4) to provide some idea as to how the various parts of our Bible actually came to be written and collected into the form in which we now possess them. My desire to write such a book arose out of my own experience that one's understanding of the Holy Scriptures is immeasurably increased and deepened as a result of study along these lines. I have tried to present the material in a way that is easily understood by the layman without special training, but at the same time takes into account the findings of responsible Biblical scholarship.

I have written this book in the hope that it will prove useful to young people and adults who seek a fuller understanding of the Bible, whatever the nature and degree of their faith. Because all of us (whether we realize it or not) approach the study of the Bible with certain presuppositions, it is quite possible the reader may occasionally disagree with something the author has said. In fact, it would be most unusual if any one person agreed with every single thing found in this or any other humanly-produced book. I can make no claims to infallibility. I have written on the basis of what knowledge and understanding I do possess and must ask the reader to forgive whatever errors may be due to an insufficiency of either.

This book is in no way intended to serve as a substitute for the Scriptures themselves. On the contrary, it is intended to stimulate the reader to approach the Bible with a new vigor and enthusiasm, to see it as more than just a collection of lovely thoughts and thrilling stories, to see it as the inspired record of God's gracious revelation of himself to his people.

It would be difficult, if not impossible, to acknowledge my debt to all who have had a part in the writing of this book, for such a list would include all those who taught me the Bible as a child, who encouraged me to follow the calling of the Christian ministry, and who have deepened my love for and understanding of the Scriptures as I have grown older. But I feel obligated to express particular gratitude to the following for

## FOREWORD

their special role: to Dortch Oldham, president of the Southwestern Company, for his conviction that such a book should be written; to Michael Stancik, who supervised the design and production of the book, for his high degree of technical competence, his sympathy with my aims, and his patient readjustments of deadlines; to Carole Stone Straughn, the illustrator, for her tireless research and considerable talent, and for her remarkable ability to reproduce exactly what I had in mind, but could express in neither words nor pictures; to Willard Nelson, for his advice and direction in the preparation of the illustrations; to Professors LeMoine G. Lewis, Frank Pack, J. D. Thomas, G. Ernest Wright, Frank Moore Cross, Jr., and Amos Wilder, who have directed my advanced study of the Bible, for having enabled me to drink more deeply of the waters of life, and for being large enough to forgive any embarrassment this book may cause them; to the writings of William Foxwell Albright, Bernhard W. Anderson, John Bright, James L. Price, and G. E. Wright, to which I owe a deep and obvious debt; to Philip H. Summerlin and S. Scott Bartchy, for unselfish, extensive and invaluable assistance in the preparation of the material dealing with the New Testament; to Richard Penuel, for reading most of the original manuscript and offering helpful suggestions as to how it might be improved; and finally, though by no means last, to my best friend, Patricia, for her never-failing support and love, and to our sons, Rex and Jeffrey, for showing amazing understanding toward a father they had to share with a typewriter for longer than any of them wished.

WILLIAM C. MARTIN

*Wellesley, Massachusetts*
*October, 1965*

# Contents

# INTRODUCTION

# The Task Before Us

WHY ANOTHER BOOK about the Bible? Surely everything has been said by now. If we must have another book, why should it be a history? Can we not learn everything we need to know about Biblical history simply by reading the Bible itself? These are questions the reader is likely to ask, and he has every right to expect a satisfactory answer. They are questions the author has had to answer for himself before undertaking a book such as this.

It is true that countless books about the Bible have already been written. It is also true that the writing of this book will not mark the grand conclusion of that mighty stream. However, most books that deal with the material presented here are directed toward the scholar, or at least toward the student engaged in formal study of the Bible. They make difficult reading for those who have, at best, a limited amount of time to give to Bible study. It is the needs of this group that this book will attempt to meet. At the same time, it will not be our purpose merely to skip lightly over the pages of the Bible, touching down here and there to point out curiosities that may prick the reader's interest but which add little to his understanding of the Bible. It is, rather, designed to take the average layman and plunge him into the fascinating world of the Israelites and the early Christians, enabling him to sense God's presence in the escape from Egyptian bondage, to stand with the multitudes at the foot of Sinai as they enter into covenant with their God, to walk behind the Ark of the Covenant as it leads the armies of Israel into Holy War, to observe the idolatrous worship of the Canaanites, to gaze in wonder at the splendor of Solomon's temple, to hear and understand the penetrating message of the prophets, to long for the coming of the Messiah, to hear that Messiah tell of God's salvation, to visit the cities of Europe and Asia Minor with the great apostle Paul, and to sit at his side as he writes letters explaining more fully the gospel of Jesus Christ. In short, we want to show that these people—the people of God—were real people. We want to see how they were shaped by their environment and in what ways they differed from it. We want to try to understand their faith, that ours may become more meaningful.

Such a book must almost of necessity be a history book. Some feel that it cheapens religion to tie it to concrete events in history. For them, true religion is a personal relationship between God and man that is not dependent upon, and is little affected by, events which have taken place hundreds of years before. This idea is entirely foreign to

3

Biblical religion. The Bible does not tell us about God by setting forth a number of abstract statements concerning his nature. It tells us about God by reciting and interpreting the way in which he has acted in human history, the primary arena of his self-revelation. God is the Lord of nature, and the Bible concedes that one may learn something of him from the wonders of the physical universe (*Ps. 19; Rom. 1:18–25*). Yet it is not by gazing at the heavens and thinking about their vastness that men come to know God and to understand his will. Instead, they come to know God and understand his will by looking at and reflecting upon his working out his purposes through *real historical* people and *real historical* events. The various "attributes" of God, such as providence and love and the rest, have little meaning for us apart from the manner in which they are manifested in history. For example, we read of the *providence* of God, but this has meaning for us only as we reflect upon the way he has *provided* for his people in concrete situations in the past. The scriptures abound with affirmations of God's love, but we learn what true love is in a historical event—the giving of his only begotten son for the redemption of mankind.

Both Judaism and Christianity are religions with a deep sense of history. Both look back to concrete events at a particular place and time in history as determinative for their faith. Both take history seriously. The sacred books of both are, in a very real sense, history books. The history they contain differs from what we refer to as "objective" history in that it is history as interpreted by a community of faith—the community that experienced it, the people of God. This in no way implies that it is not *real* history with which we are dealing; it simply means that Israel understood history differently than did her neighbors because in each event she saw the hand of God at work. For instance,

the Exodus may have been viewed by the Egyptians as nothing more than the escape of a band of slaves, but the community of faith saw it as a mighty act of God, an unmistakable sign of his election of the people of Israel as the instrument through whom all nations of the earth would be blessed. One can see that this interpretation does not detract from the worth of the Biblical account of the event; on the contrary, it is this that causes us to regard the Bible, rather than the chronicles of the Egyptians, as the record of God's communication to men.

Although the primary reason for the writing of the Bible was a religious one rather than a simple desire for a narrative of historical events, it does deal with factual matter open to the investigation of any student of history, whatever his religious presuppositions may be. We need not hesitate to subject the Biblical records to the kind of examination one gives to any other historical document. If they will not stand this test, their fitness to guide us in religious matters must be questioned. On the other hand, if they truly contain the word of God, we have an obligation to use whatever methods and resources are available that may help us understand them better. One of the simplest tasks of this book is to provide the reader with a better perspective of Biblical history by dealing with people and events in something like the order in which they actually lived and occurred. It is virtually impossible to do this with absolute precision, simply because we do not always have adequate information, but we can clear up a lot of misunderstandings common to beginning Bible students. For instance, if one reads the books of the Bible in the order that they appear in our collection (the Jewish order is somewhat different), it is easy to get the idea that Israel was carried into Babylonian captivity and returned from it long before the appearance of any of the prophets except Elijah and Elisha. Such, of course, is far from the actual case, as a glance at the opening verses of most of the books of prophecy will show. To avoid this confusion we have treated the prophets right alongside the kings in whose reigns they prophesied, insofar as we are able to place them exactly. In this arrangement they are seen not as obscure poets whose only importance is derived from an occasional statement that has been interpreted to refer to Jesus, but as spokesmen of God vitally involved in the social and political affairs of the nation. But the reader could do this for himself, armed with a Bible and a little initiative. Of more importance is the effort to place the history contained in the Bible in the context of the larger history of the ancient Near East and to add flesh and life to the often sketchy historical skeleton found in the Bible. As we read the stories of the early patriarchs, or the chronicles of the events of the period of the monarchy, or even the accounts of the missionary journeys of Paul, we frequently forget that these events did not occur in a vacuum. They become much more real to us when we know something of the customs, the religion, the commerce, and the social structure of the environment in which they took place and when we are able to place them in relation to events and figures known to us from secular history.

Due to remarkable achievements in the field of archaeology, we are in a better position than ever before to realize this goal. Literally thousands of texts and inscriptions have been found that illuminate the biblical period far beyond what was once believed possible. The discovery of thousands of clay tablets in the ruins of the ancient Amorite city of Mari, dating from the eighteenth century B.C., and a similar discovery at the Hurrian city of Nuzi, dating from the fifteenth and fourteenth centuries B.C., have shed much light on the period

in which the patriarchs were wandering through Palestine. The Amarna Letters, unearthed at the site of the fourteenth century Egyptian capital, Akhetaten (Tell-el Amarna), provide valuable information on the political situation in Canaan before the invasion of the conquering Israelites. From Hittite documents we gain a deeper understanding of the significance of the covenant made at Sinai. And, most recently, the famous Dead Sea Scrolls have added a whole new dimension to our knowledge of religious thought in Palestine at the time of the ministry of Jesus. In addition, extensive excavations of ancient ruins have told us much of the religious and social customs at various periods of antiquity and of the fortunes of a number of cities and individuals prominent in Biblical literature.

Finally, it is our purpose to provide some idea as to how the various parts of our Bible actually came to be written and collected into the form in which we find them. In doing this, we shall analyze the different types of literature contained in the Bible and look for special theological interests of the writers which may give us clues to understanding them better.

If we are successful in this enterprise we shall have shown the Bible to be so much more than a few comforting passages and a handful of exciting stories. We shall see it as the inspired record of the divine revelation, the sacred book that for centuries has spoken to the hearts of men, saying, "This is God, and these were God's people."

## The History of Israel

The decisive event in the History of Israel was the Exodus from Egypt. When we tell our children about God, we frequently begin with the story of the Creation found in the opening chapters of *Genesis*. When an Israelite parent told his children about God, he began with the story of the creation of the community of Israel in the events connected with the Exodus. Everything prior to this served as a prologue to the main event. To the Hebrew, the Exodus was the supreme example of God's acting in history in a redemptive way and provided the key to understanding all of history. This is made clear in a number of Old Testament passages. When the prophet Amos delivered the word of the Lord to Israel, he described the nation as the "family which (God) brought up out of the land of Egypt" (*Amos 3:1*). Hosea spoke of God's love for Israel and his electing them as his people in these words:

> When Israel was a child I loved him,
> And out of Egypt I called my son.
> —*Hosea 11:1*

When a delegation of Jewish elders came to the prophet Ezekiel during the captivity in Babylon, he recalled to their minds the gracious acts of God in the following words:

> Thus says the Lord God: On the day when I chose Israel, I swore to the seed of the house of Jacob, making myself known to them in the land of Egypt, I swore to them, saying, I am the Lord your God. On that day I swore to them that I would bring them out of the land of Egypt into a land that I had searched out for them, a land flowing with milk and honey, the most glorious of all lands.
> —*Ezekiel 20:5-6*

The term "Exodus" is sometimes used as a shorthand way of referring to a whole set of events which are inseparably bound up with it. These include the promises to Abraham and the other patriarchs, the actual deliverance from Egypt, God's providential guidance during the period of wanderings in the wilderness, the making of the covenant at Mt. Sinai, and the entry into the promised land. The stories of these events were repeated again and again by the ancient Hebrews. They were commemorated by monuments and feast days. The religious calendar provided occasions for talking about them, and even for acting some of them out in a symbolical way, to impress upon the Israelites that all their blessings could be traced to God's ordaining them as his people and his mighty acts in their behalf. The classic example of the manner in which this was done is found in *Deuteronomy 26:5-10*. This passage, which contains a brief summary of the events that brought Israel into existence as a united people, forms a creed or confession of faith to be recited at the annual offering of the first fruits of the harvest:

> A wandering Aramean was my father; and he went down into Egypt and sojourned there, few in number; and there he became a nation, great, mighty, and populous. And the Egyptians treated us harshly, and afflicted us, and laid upon us hard bondage. Then we cried to the Lord the God of our fathers, and the Lord heard our voice, and saw our affliction, our toil, and our oppression; and the Lord brought us out of Egypt with a mighty hand and an outstretched arm, with great terror, with signs and wonders; and he brought us into this place and gave us this land, a land flowing with milk and honey. And behold, now I bring the first of the fruit of the ground, which thou, O Lord, hast given me.     —*Deuteronomy 26:5-10*

In all these ways, the traditions—and by "tradition" we mean simply *that which was handed down,* and in no way imply it is false or unreliable—were passed along until eventually they were collected and written down in the form in which we now have them.

## The Pentateuch

The heart of Israel's sacred history is contained in the first five books of the Bible, called the Pentateuch ("a five-fold book"). *Exodus* and *Numbers* tell of the exodus and the period of wilderness wanderings. The entry into and conquest of the promised land is recorded in the book of *Joshua,* which is frequently grouped together with the Pentateuch to form what is called the Hexateuch ("a *six*-fold book"). *Leviticus* is a collection of laws and regulations governing virtually every aspect of the life of the community. To most of us it is somewhat dull, but to the Jews it was a vital source of divine guidance. *Deuteronomy* may be characterized as "a second look at the Law." The book of *Genesis* serves as a fitting introduction to this history, telling us something of the creation of the world and the early adventures of mankind, and preparing the soil for the Exodus story by recalling the promises that God made to Abraham and his descendants and by tracing their fortunes from the departure of Abraham from Ur of the Chaldees to the migration of Jacob's family into the delta area of Egypt.

Traditionally, Moses has been regarded as the author of the material contained in the Pentateuch. Surprisingly, when we turn to the Bible itself, we find it makes no such sweeping claim. We are told in *Exodus 17: 14* that God commanded Moses to write an account of the defeat of the Amalekites at Rephidim. He was also instructed to write a list of the different locations used by the Israelites as camping places during the period of wilderness wanderings (*Num. 33:2ff*). And he was, of course, charged with the task of writing down the law that he received from the mouth of the Lord on Mt. Sinai (*Ex. 24:4–8; 34:27; Deut. 31:9, 24*). On several occasions Jesus referred to sections of the law as that which Moses "wrote," "said," or "commanded" (see, for example, *Matt. 8:4; 19:8; Mark 7:10; 12:26; Luke 5:14; 20:37; John 5:47; 7:19*). From these passages we can reach the following conclusion: Moses is definitely credited with having written a number of specific items contained in the Pentateuch. It is quite possible he wrote a great deal more than the Bible specifically gives him credit for. Nev-

ertheless a considerable amount of the material contained in the Pentateuch remains anonymous. The text of the book of *Genesis*, for example, gives no hint whatever as to its author. There is little point in spending an undue amount of time on the question of authorship, since a thorough study of the matter requires a good knowledge of the Hebrew language and other highly technical skills and since any conclusion we might reach must remain tentative, in view of the imperfect state of our knowledge. There are, however, several examples we may cite which indicate that others besides Moses may have had a hand in bringing these books to their final form. For one thing, Moses is consistently spoken of in the third person. This, of course, is not decisive, but the style certainly seems to be that of a man writing about another rather than about himself. This is especially true in passages such as *Numbers 12:3*, in which we are told that "the man Moses was very meek, more than all men that were on the face of the earth." We do not often hear a truly humble man describe himself in such terms. Another observation concerns the occurrence of the phrase "beyond the Jordan" (*Gen. 50:10; Num. 22:1; 32:32; 35:14; Deut. 1:1, 5; 3:8; 4:46*). Without exception this is used to refer to Transjordan, the area to the east of the Jordan River. The natural supposition is that the writer was on the west side of the Jordan, yet Moses never set foot in this region. The account of the death of Moses in *Deuteronomy 34* has, of course, long been recognized as an addition by a later hand, even by those who insist that Moses wrote virtually every word of the Pentateuch. The point of all this is not that the Bible claims anything for Moses that is not true. There is no good reason to disbelieve Moses wrote a good many things contained in the Pentateuch. The point is: the Bible itself never claims Moses wrote *all* of the Pentateuch nor that he was solely responsible for its final form. If we do so, we must turn to something other than scripture for our authority.

In recent years, Biblical scholarship has shed a great deal of light on the process by which materials of the type found in the Pentateuch were transmitted from generation to generation and how they eventually arrived at their present form. It seems reasonable to assume that the stories connected with Adam, Abraham, Joseph, and the other patriarchs, arose at different times, for the simple reason that these people lived at different times in history. It seems just as reasonable that people knew these stories long before they were written down in the form in which we now have them. When Moses came on the scene, men had already talked of Abraham and his descendants for hundreds of years. Stories that told of God's dealings with men were passed down from decade to decade and century to century. Often, several stories were handed down together until, finally, under the direction of God's Holy Spirit, they were woven together to form what we commonly call the "books of Moses."

Archaeological discoveries have disclosed that writing has been in use much longer than was once supposed; it has also shown, however, that it was used primarily for such purposes as the recording of contracts and covenants, the publication of codes of law and other official notices, correspondence between governments, and commercial record-keeping. It was seldom employed as a means of preserving those historical traditions that undergirded the religious, social, and moral institutions of a people. For this, ancient man used an instrument he considered to be fully as reliable as a written record—his memory. In all probability, much of the material contained in the Pentateuch passed through the centuries in substantially unchanged form without ever having been written down. This seems strange, even improbable, to modern man, who has crippled his memory by disuse and must depend on the ready availability of literary crutches. But ancient man would have scoffed at our underdeveloped memories, and his scorn would be justified. The epics of Homer were transmitted orally for generations before they were finally written down. The Jewish rabbis committed to memory an almost incredible amount of material. Even today, it is not uncommon to find a Muslim youth who has memorized the complete *Koran,* a work of approximately 300 pages. Still more impressive is the feat Hindus have been performing for thousands of years—the memorizing of the *Rig Veda,* the sacred poem whose 10,000 stanzas have a greater bulk than the *Iliad* and the *Odyssey* together. When we look at these examples, it is much easier to see how the Israelites preserved those traditions that helped them understand their role in history and supported their belief that God was with them. By the time Israel came into the promised land, after the Exodus from Egypt, she possessed a body of traditions of great depth and color, unparalleled by any other ancient people. As time passed this body of tradition continued to develop. To the stories of Abraham, Isaac, and Jacob were added the stories of Moses and Aaron. Law codes and lists of various kinds, some of which had been written down by Moses himself, were incorporated. Probably, not every tribe handed down exactly the same stories, but tended to emphasize those which dealt with its own tribal ancestors, or with locations within their tribal territory. Finally, writing came into more general use and the different collections of traditions were gathered together and worked into the form in which they have come down to us. Now let us turn to that completed work.

# PART ONE

## *Background to the History of Israel*

# 1

# The Prehistory of Israel

*The sinfulness of mankind*
*persistently thwarts*
*the grace of the Creator*

Based on content, the material in the book of Genesis seems to fall naturally into two sections:

*Chapters 1-11*
> The Early History of Mankind

*Chapters 12-50*
> The History of the Patriarchs

As has already been noted, the place that the book seems to fill in relation to others in the Pentateuch is that of a prologue, particularly to Exodus and Numbers, which contain the real heart of the Mosaic faith. Even though the "creed" recorded in *Deuteronomy 26:5–10* (see p. 6) alludes briefly to the material we have called "The History of the Patriarchs" (*chs. 12–50*), none of the books mention the events recorded in chapters 1–11. If we recall what has already been said concerning Israel's faith, this creates no problem. The event that created the people and religion of Israel was the Exodus from Egypt; therefore, anything prior to that is not properly a part of the History of Israel. For that reason, we have chosen to characterize *Genesis 1–11* as a *pre*history of Israel. The material contained in this section is not restricted to Israel but shows that the God of Israel is also the Creator and Lord of the entire universe and all that dwell therein. He is not just the Lord of Israel's history, but the Lord of all history.

## The Creation

The early chapters of Genesis tell a simple, yet profound, story whose themes are among the most basic—God's plans for mankind and his efforts to carry out those plans. The average man is probably more familiar with this material than any other in the Old Testament. Yet it is upon this "battlefield" that science and "scripture" have encountered one another countless times in the past century, as documented studies have overturned or seriously questioned much Christians had assumed until that time. Among these assumptions were that:

1. the earth has been in existence for only 6,000 years,
2. the earth was created in six literal 24-hour days,

---

*A scripture reference is given at the beginning of each chapter. This indicates only the primary source of the material of the chapter. Other books will be referred to in the body of the narrative.

3. the earth is the center of the universe and the sun rises and sets in its path around it.

Historically, the initial reaction of the church, or at least part of it, has been either to condemn those who set forth new views such as these and close the mind to further investigation or else to go into panic over the new discovery, feeling that everything will crumble if we are forced to change views that religious men have previously held. Neither of these reactions, however, is to any avail, for they do not change the facts, if they *are* facts. To use an example, in the 16th and 17th centuries, men were condemned as religious heretics for asserting that the earth was not the center of the universe, but merely a satellite around the sun. Rather than accept this "heretical" theory, which today is embraced universally, the church of that time became the object of ridicule. In attempting to determine the approach toward science that Christians of this age must take, we need to avoid two pitfalls:

1. An anti-scientific attitude that treats scientists as enemies of the faith. The scientist is seeking the truth about the world, basing his conclusions on the best information available to him. This should also be the desire of every student of the Bible. If the Bible is a hoax and the universe is not dependent on God, condemning the scientist will not change matters. On the other hand, if God does rule over it as sovereign Lord, we need not be afraid of anything we may learn about it.

2. The temptation to make elaborate, artificial efforts to "harmonize" science and the Bible. Numerous attempts along this line have been made—some of them fantastic, most of them incorrect. Many of these imply that statements in the Bible refer to modern scientific discoveries. Generally speaking, this is a ridiculous trend, for the Bible is not primarily interested in making scientific statements. That is simply not its purpose. Despite what some defenders of religion have claimed, the Bible has nothing to say about the expansion of the universe, nuclear physics, airplanes, submarines, or wireless telegraphy.

The fact that the Bible is a religious document, not a scientific textbook, is especially important to keep in mind when we read the account of the Creation in *Genesis 1–2*. The creation story is not an attempt to give a detailed, scientific account of the origin and development of the universe. Rather, it is an attempt to set forth, in a brief and orderly way, the conviction that back of the universe is God, that men are dependent on him for their existence, and that his purposes are good and entirely worthy of our trust.

Most civilizations possess a traditional account of the origin of the world. Israel's neighbors were no exception. Among the best known is the Babylonian creation myth, *Enuma elish*. In this story, the monster Tiamat, a personification of the dark primeval waters, or "deep," is slain by the sun-god Marduk. Her body is then split in half to form the heavens and the earth. This emphasis on water, this association of chaos with "the deep," is striking, for we find the same imagery used in the inspired word of *Genesis 1:1–2*. Here we are told that "When God began to create" (this is a more accurate translation of the Hebrew than the traditional "In the beginning God created...") , the earth was a formless mass covered by the dark waters of chaos. Out of this blackness, this void, this formlessness, God began to bring light, order, beauty.

From this beginning, the story proceeds in a neat, balanced fashion. The work of creation is divided into six days. The brief account of the activity of each day is capped by the formulaic statement, "And there was evening and there was morning, a . . .

day." It is extremely doubtful that the writer of these words understood the word "day" to mean anything more than we commonly understand it to mean—a twenty-four hour period. To him, fossils and remains of long extinct beasts were no problem. He was not using the word as a symbol for "age" or "aeon" or any period that lasted millions of years. We are almost certainly mistaken when we try to do this. Again, let us emphasize: this is a religious, and not a scientific, treatise.

The climax of this divine creative activity came on the sixth day, when God said, "Let us make man in our image, after our likeness . . . So God created men in his own image, in the image of God created he him; male and female created he them." (*Gen. 1:26–27*). Man was distinguished from the beasts, over which he was given dominion, by having stamped upon him the impress of "the image of God." Judging from the frequent Biblical references to God's hands, feet, eyes, mouth, etc.,* the primitive Israelite probably understood this term to mean that God has a bodily form not unlike that of human beings. The Hebrew did not conceive of the soul or spirit as the "real" man, existing apart from the body and using the body only as a convenient means of getting around. For him, there was no true existence apart from bodily form; therefore, it was natural to conclude that God, as the source of all existence, possessed a bodily form similar to that of a man. Even today, it is difficult for us to conceive of God as "spirit" without subconsciously attributing a bodily form to him. But the "image of God" surely implies much more than this. It doubtless has reference to what we sometimes call the

"spiritual capacity" of man—the capacity to think rationally, to communicate with other rational beings, and to examine ourselves and our motives almost as if we were some other person. We can never exhaust the implications of this rich term, but this seems to be its fundamental significance.

Inseparable from the creation of man is the creation of the home. Significantly, the Bible says, "God created man . . . male and female he created them." This attests to the fact that man without woman is incomplete man. From the beginning, marriage, the home, and the procreation of children are seen as something more than the result of blind instinct or animal craving. They are part of God's eternal purpose for mankind.

Frequently occurring in this account is the phrase, "And God saw that it was good" (*Gen. 1:10, 12, 13, 21, 25, 31*). This is important for us to keep in mind, for it reminds us that the evils present in the world cannot be blamed upon God nor upon the creation itself. Then what is the origin of sin and suffering? Where does the responsibility and burden of guilt lie? In *Genesis 3*, the profoundest of all answers is given.

## The Fall of Man

The story of the sin of Adam and Eve, commonly referred to as the Fall of Man, is an answer to many questions that men, whether primitive or modern, might ask themselves. Some are not too momentous: Why are men ashamed of their nakedness? Why must we toil for our bread? Why do husbands dominate their wives, at least theoretically? Why is there pain in childbirth? Why does the serpent creep on the ground? And why do men find him so repulsive? Primarily, however, it has to do with a question of fundamental importance—the question of the origin, the nature, and the result of sin. Adam and Eve were placed by God in a beautiful garden "in Eden, in the east" (*2:8*),

---

*These figures of speech are called "anthropomorphisms" from the Greek words, *anthropos* (man) and *morphos* (form). Thus, when one uses an anthropomorphism in speaking of God, he describes him in "manform."

with the responsibility of caring for it. The only restriction placed upon them was the prohibition against eating the fruit of the tree of the knowledge of good and evil. Into this idyllic situation came the force of evil, in the form of a serpent (who, incidentally, is never explicitly identified as the devil). He led Eve to suspect the divine goodness, to disbelieve the word of God, to attempt to break the limits God had set for Adam and her. Finally, Eve gave in to his seducing words, and persuaded Adam to taste the fruit also. Punishment for their sin came quickly and devastatingly. They became ashamed of their nakedness and tried, vainly, to hide themselves from the sight of God. They began to blame one another, and even God himself, for their failure. They were banished from the peace of the primeval garden to the tribulation of the world outside. The hope of immortality was crushed as they were cut off from the tree of life. Mankind was still a giant among the creatures of the world, but he was a giant with a wounded heel (3:15).

Why is this story important for us? How are we related to Adam? What effect does his sin have on our lives? A number of answers have been given to these questions. Some have said that Adam's sinfulness has been passed down to us in the act of procreation, and that we stand guilty before God because of the sin of Adam. Perhaps the best-known expression of this is the couplet that New England school children learned in their first primer:

> In Adam's Fall
> We Sinned All.

Others have denied that we stand guilty before God as a direct result of Adam's sin, but affirm that we have inherited a fallen nature which is incapable of sinlessness. With this fallen nature, we inevitably sin and *become* guilty, just as Adam became guilty. Still another view is that nothing has been "passed down" from Adam, but that men have continued to sin in imitation of Adam. We feel the fundamental value of this story is not that it informs us that we are regarded as evil in the eyes of God because someone before us did evil. Rather, its value lies in the fact that it holds a mirror up to our lives and enables us to see and understand our own sinful condition. Significantly, the word "Adam" means "Mankind." In Adam, we see ourselves—beings created "in the image of God," related to the rest of creation, yet rising above it through the freedom of spirit God has granted us. We are dependent on God for our existence—indeed, our life has no real meaning apart from him—yet we continually listen to the temptation to follow our own paths, abusing the freedom he has granted us in an effort to become independent of his control. When we allow this to happen, we forfeit the life of bliss and peace that God intended for us. We are filled with guilt and anxiety, ever aware of the sentence of death that hangs over us.

## Cain and Abel

The story of Cain and Abel in *ch. 4* provides a further example of the consequences of the sin of mankind. We cannot be sure why God preferred the offering of Abel to that of Cain. But we cannot fail to see how human relationships are marred by jealousy, suspicion, and hatred, and how, when we allow ourselves to be overcome by these emotions and seek to deny our responsibility for the welfare of our "brother," we become alienated from nature, from our fellowmen, and from God. This is the situation that is characteristic of so much of our "progressive" modern civilization.

## The "Founding Fathers"

Ironically, the beginnings of "civilization" are traced to Cain, the murderer—son of

14

Adam, the sinner. Cain himself is credited with having founded the first city, which he named for his son, Enoch. Among his descendants were Jabal, regarded as the first nomad, "the father of those who dwell in tents and have cattle," (4:20), Jubal the musician (4:21), and Tubal-cain the metalworker (4:22). The advances in culture which these names symbolize, however, were not without their dark side, as the brief story of Lamech shows, Here we see an example of the moral corruption that accompanies cultural and technological developments. Whereas Cain had experienced profound anguish as a consequence of his crime, Lamech felt only pride at a similar offence:

> I have slain a man for wounding me,
>   a young man for striking me.
> If Cain is avenged sevenfold,
>   truly Lamech seventy-sevenfold.
>   —*Genesis 4:23-4*

## The Flood

This downward spiral of degradation continued until

> the Lord saw that the wickedness of man as great in the earth, and that every imagination of the thoughts of his heart was only evil continually. And the Lord was sorry that he had made man on the earth, and it grieved him to his heart.        —*Genesis 6:5-6*

God's judgment against sinful humanity came in the form of a great deluge, or flood. The Bible tells us that all of mankind was destroyed except a small handful, the household of Noah, whom God preserved in the ark. Despite the claims of popular handbooks and article on the subject, archaeology has not provided conclusive proof of the accuracy of the *Genesis* narrative; consequently, it is pointless to specu-

**Gilgamesh, legendary hero of the Babylonian epic story of a great flood.**

late as to its exact nature and scope. Archaeologists and anthropologists have, however, performed a valuable service in bringing to light numerous ancient traditions of such a deluge in which a select, group was preserved from destruction, usually in some kind of ship. Most striking in its similarity to the Biblical account is the "Gilgamesh epic" of ancient Babylon. In this story, the gods, in a moment of caprice, decide to destroy mankind by sending a flood on the earth. As in the *Genesis* story, the only survivors were the family of a man who had been instructed by a deity to build a ship according to strict specifications. Although the Babylonian epic and the *Genesis* flood story may well be based on the same catastrophic event, the Biblical account makes it clear that the flood was not a manifestation of the capriciousness of many gods, but an act of judgment against sin by the One True God. Furthermore, in the Babylonian legend the mortal Utnapishtim was saved simply because he was a favorite of the God Ea. In *Genesis*, it is clear that the salvation of Noah was based on his righteous obedience to the will of God.

## The Covenant with Noah

The flood marked the end of a wicked civilization. As a basis for the new culture, God made a covenant with Noah. Man was assured that never again would the earth suffer from such a deluge, but that "while the earth remains, seedtime and harvest, cold and heat, summer and winter, day and night, shall not cease" (*8:22*). This verse expresses a belief of Israel which set her religion in sharp contrast with that of Canaan. Both the religion of Israel and that of her neighbors in the ancient Near East claimed control of agriculture processes for their God and acknowledged the hand of divinity in the storm and the volcano. But to discern the influence of God in the quiet changing of the seasons belonged distinctly to the people of Israel, the people of God.

The symbol of God's fidelity to his covenant was to be "a bow in the cloud" (*9:13*). The Hebrew word for "bow" has reference to a weapon. Thus, Israel did not view the rainbow as a charming celestial ornament fashioned as a reminder *to them* of the promise of God. Rather, they viewed it as a weapon of God's wrath which he had laid to rest, a reminder *to him* that it was never to be used again.

The portion of the covenant which applied to man consisted not so much in commandments as in regulations for the new attempt at life in harmony with God's will. According to *Genesis 2:29–31*, man was originally intended to be a vegetarian, but here, he is given the right to eat every living beast, the only stipulation being that the animal be properly bled before it was eaten and that the blood not be consumed. In later times this was viewed not as a law peculiar to the Hebrew religion, but as binding on all mankind. The "Jerusalem conference" described in *Acts 15* officially relieved Gentile Christians of the burden of keeping the law of Moses; nevertheless, the circular letter it sent to the Gentile churches admonished all Christians to abstain from "what is strangled and from blood" (*Acts 15:20, 28, 29*). Perhaps the most significant of the provisions of the Noachite covenant was that the taking of human life was to be punishable by death. Thus, the idea of capital punishment received an early religious sanction, although we are left in the dark as to who possessed the authority to carry out the prescribed punishment. Presumably, the agent of vengeance was the closest relative of the slain man.

Man's first attempt at civilization was a miserable failure. Now, on a somewhat different basis, he was to begin anew. Unfortunately, further study shows us that he was no more capable of obeying God under the new plan than he had been under the old.

## Failure of the New Beginning

The activities of Noah and his sons after leaving the ark made it clear that even the most righteous of men were infected with the fatal disease called sin. Noah could not enjoy the fruits of his vineyard without falling into a drunken stupor. His son, Ham, instead of showing proper respect for his father, or even embarrassment, made sport of his naked, unconscious condition. The curse that Noah pronounced when he awoke and learned of the shame to which his son had subjected him has been the occasion of much speculation and misuse. It is sometimes claimed that, because of Ham's impiety, God placed a curse on his descendants. sentencing them to a life of servitude. These descendants are then identified with the Negro. Thus, it is argued, God intended the Negro to hold an inferior position, to be a servant to his white superiors.

To begin with, it should be noted that the curse is not uttered by, or credited to, God. Its source was an angry, drunken old man. More important, the curse is not on all the descendants of Ham, but only on Ham's son Canaan. The nations listed as descendants of Ham in *Genesis 10:6–20* do contain some Negroid peoples, but Canaan is not among them. The Canaanites were of the same general ethnic stock as the Israelites themselves. Probably, this curse is to be understood as falling on the people of Canaan, personified in their ancestor, the son of Ham. This fits with the historical fact that the Canaanites were dispossessed from their land and made to serve the descendants of Shem and Japheth.

## The Tower of Babel

The Early History of Mankind reaches its climax and conclusion in the story of the Tower of Babel (*11:1–9*). A group of migrants had settled in the plain of Shinar, another name for Babylonia. They advanced beyond the stage of the unsophisticated nomad and sought to consolidate their strength and establish a great city. The capstone of their work was to be a monument in the form of a high tower. It is probable that the type of building to which this refers is the Babylonian *ziggurat*, a structure built in terraced stages with a rectangular temple serving as a platform for a tower, at the top of which was a small chapel. Ruins of such structures can still be seen in the land which was once Babylonia. The phrase, "with its top in the heavens," was merely a figurative way of expressing great height, and ought not to be taken to mean the people literally sought to build a tower reaching to the throne of God. Nevertheless, the whole attitude of these people was one of self-assertive independence and rebellion against God. They, like all the sons of Adam, desired to break any limitations that might be placed upon them. They felt that nothing could restrain them once they were joined together in a concerted effort. But God was still in charge. Looking back on all the evil the imagination of man had been able to devise, he "confused the language of all the earth; and from there the Lord scattered them abroad over the face of all the earth" (*11:9*).

This story serves as an explanation for the diversity of languages and nations, but its real significance goes beyond this. It confirms the lamentable fact that man is an incurable sinner. Indeed, this is the central theme of these first eleven chapters of the Bible. Note the progression of this primeval history. Adam was placed in a situation which should have satisfied every desire, but he disobeyed and was cast from God's garden. God did not abandon him, however, but immediately set about to assist him, fashioning clothes from animal skins. When Cain murdered Abel, he received severe punishment, yet God protected him from strangers by the mark placed upon him. Eventually, mankind became so perverse that God was sorry he had ever created him; yet he did not blot him out completely, but preserved the household of Noah. He then promised Noah, in solemn covenant, that the new order would not again be destroyed in such a manner, but could be counted on to endure. Now, in the plain of Shinar, man once more raises his fist in defiance of God. Again the Lord dashes him into the dust, but this time he leaves him there...or so it seems. We expect to read of some provision made for the redemption of scattered humanity, but instead, the focus of the narrative shifts from universal mankind to the adventures of one obscure nomad. As we read further, however, we come to realize that the hope for fallen humanity *is* bound up with the election of this nomad as the servant of God. Yes, as unrelated as they appear, we can correctly say that the call of Abraham is truly the sequel to the incident at Shinar. The first eleven chapters of *Genesis* impress upon us that all nations have sinned and are deserving of the wrath of God. Beginning with *ch. 12*, this despairing note is replaced by the redemptive theme that runs throughout the Bible—namely, that *through the few, God will bless the many*. In the calling of Abraham, God forms the foundation of a new nation, the nation that will become the bearer of his promise of blessings to *all* the nations. Thus, although this first section of Genesis is not, strictly speaking, an integral part of the history of Israel, it provides us with the key to understanding what follows.

# 2

# The Patriarchs

*The life and times of the
ancestors of Israel*

T HE HISTORY of Israel has its official beginning with *Genesis 12*. It is not proper to speak of Israel as a nation until the time of the exodus experiences; but, as the history of no nation is complete without some history of its ancestors, so a history of Israel without a history of the patriarchs is unthinkable. These chapters tell how God selected Abraham as the agent through whom he would bless all mankind and of the providential manner in which he guided the lives of this ancestor of Israel and his descendants, in order to bring his promises to fulfillment.

## The Sources of our Knowledge

For many years critics of the Bible maintained that the stories contained in these thirty-eight chapters were purely legend, having no historical validity whatever. It is true that none of the characters mentioned in this section can be definitely identified with any known figure in secular history. However, the science of archaeology has shed so much light on the history and culture of the ancient Near East that even the most skeptical of Biblical critics have been forced to look at the inspired record with new respect. The archaeologist's spade has uncovered cities and towns visited by Abraham and his descendants. It has confirmed the existence of such people as the Hittites, who were once believed to be a figment of the Biblical writers' imagination. Most important has been the discovery of an almost incredible number of legal, commercial, political, and religious documents which make it possible to reconstruct a fairly reliable picture of the world in which the patriarchs lived. These discoveries constitute a major, if not the greatest, contribution of archaeology to Old Testament studies in the last half-century. The two most important groups of these documents, as far as the patriarchal period is concerned, are those discovered at the Amorite city of Mari, dating from the eighteenth century B.C., and at the Hurrian town of Nuzi, dating from the fifteenth century B.C. We shall say more of the Amorites and Hurrians, but for now, it is sufficient to remember Mari and Nuzi, as these strange words will occur frequently in the course of this chapter.

## The World of the Patriarchs

The world of the patriarchs was rather small. Their activity was confined to the

19

A tablet of Nuzi, describing the custom of adoption of an heir by a childless man.

area known to schoolchildren as the "Fertile Crescent," that is, the area bounded by the Euphrates River on the east and extending westward to include Syria, Palestine, and Egypt (See map, p. 21). Biblical history is bound up with the rise and fall of the several nations that comprise this territory and with the successes and failures of invaders from Arabia and from the lands to the north and east.

The Bible itself does not provide us with the dates of the activity of the patriarchs. To make matters worse, none of the events or situations recorded in the Bible are readily identifiable with specific periods in known history. It is highly probable, however, for reasons we shall soon discuss, that the patriarchal period is to be placed within the years 2000-1700 B.C. Before we turn to the Biblical narratives themselves, let us get

a brief idea of what was going on in the Fertile Crescent during this period.

For the first two centuries of the second millenium B.C., the western part of the Crescent was under the rule of the Egyptian Pharaohs of the Twelfth Dynasty. This period was one of the most stable in Egypt's long history. Later generations looked back on it as a Golden Age. On the international level there was sea trade with such places as Syria, Cyprus, and Crete. Fortresses were erected along the borders to thwart invaders from the north and east. Copper mining was revived in the Sinaitic peninsula. At home, land was made arable by means of elaborate irrigation systems. Notable advances were made in various fields of literature and science. In short, it was a high water mark of ancient Egyptian culture.

By the middle of the eighteenth century,

this stable situation had begun to disintegrate. Rival dynasties contended for the throne left vacant by the fallen Twelfth Dynasty. It was this disunified situation which paved the way for the domination of Egypt by the foreign invaders known as Hyksos. But let us, postpone the story of the Hyksos until we discuss the descent of Joseph into Egypt.

In the East, at the beginning of this same period, control lay with the Sumerian rulers who had their capital at Ur. About 1950 B.C., this dynasty was overthrown by the Elamites (See map). In the period of political confusion and uncertainty which followed, hordes of Semitic peoples from the Arabian desert poured across the Crescent. In the Bible (*Gen. 14:7; Num. 13:29*), these invaders are known as the Amorites ("West-

erners"). Within two centuries these remarkable people had gained control of all the major centers of population in Mesopotamia. The most important of the Amorite captials was Mari, whose remarkable archives we have already mentioned. In about 1700 B.C. the great Babylonian king, Hammurabi, conquered Mari and incorporated it into a prosperous, though modest, empire which had its center in Babylon. In the section on the Tower of Babel, we described a type of temple-tower known as a *ziggurat*. During the reign of Hammurabi, a *ziggurat* was erected of such proportion and splendor that it became one of the great wonders of the ancient world. Hammurabi is best remembered, however, for the code of laws which he issued. The laws contained in this code were not the creation of Hammurabi

The Fertile Crescent of ancient civilization.

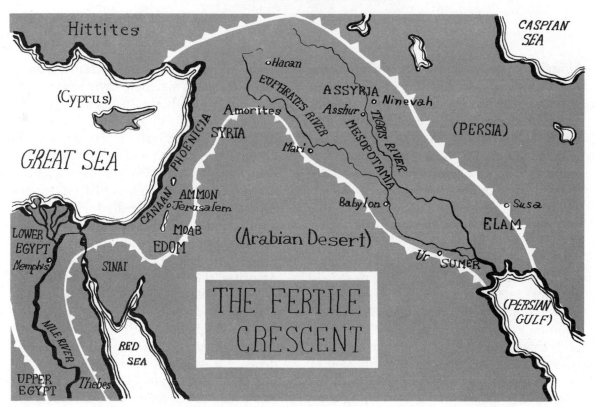

21

**Reconstruction of the Ziggurat of Ur.**

himself, but are a collection and adaptation of current laws and customs, codified in an effort to provide an official record of what was considered to be accepted law in the empire. Government officials in areas of the empire unfamiliar with Babylonian law could use this as a helpful guide. It was not necessarily binding on them, however. There are numerous parallels between this ancient law code and the law codes of Israel.

There is good reason to suppose that Abraham and his descendants were closely connected with—may even have been a part of—these Amorite peoples. There is frequent mention in the patriarchal narratives of the fact that Abraham and his descendants were of Aramean stock. The confession of faith in *Deuteronomy 26:5* begins with the words, "My father was a wandering Ara-

mean." When Isaac sought to find a wife for Jacob from among their own relatives, he sent him to the house of his uncle, who is characteristically described as Laban the Aramean (*Gen. 25:20; 31:20, 24;* see also *28:5*). The region to which Jacob went was known as Paddan-Aram ("The Field of Aram," *Gen. 28:2*). The chief city of this Aramean region was called Haran (*Gen. 28:10*), and was a known center of the new Amorite settlement. In addition to the close connection here between Arameans and Amorites, the very name of the city is significant. Bible students with a good memory may recall that Haran was the name of one of Abraham's brothers (*Gen. 11:31*). This might be dismissed simply as a coincidence if it were a unique example, but the fact is, archaeologists have established the existence of several towns that bore names identical with, or similar to, personal names found in the Bible. Among these are Nahor, the name both of Abraham's grandfather and brother (*Gen. 11:24, 26; 24:10*), Terah, Abraham's father (*Gen. 11:26*), and Peleg and Serug, both direct ancestors of Abraham (*Gen. 11:16, 20*). We cannot be sure as to how these towns came to be named. It is not unlikely they were named for the clan that founded or captured them, and that the leaders of these clans are the same men named in the Bible. Another possibility is that the Biblical characters took their names from the local towns. Even if neither of these suggestions is correct, the correspondence between the names is significant, for it lends support to the assertion we have made concerning the date of the patriarchs, since these names are known to have been current *only* in the three-hundred year period under discussion. The same holds true for the names Abraham, Jacob, Benjamin, Zebulun, Ishmael, and Levi, all of which were used as personal names among the Amorites.

### THE HABIRU

The texts of Mari and Nuzi, and other documents from the second millenium B.C. contain frequent references to a people known as *Habiru*. They were described in a variety of ways. Generally speaking, they were men without a country. They drifted across the Near Eastern lands in a fairly rootless manner, seldom really finding an established place in the social structure of the areas in which they roamed. In peacetime, they might subsist quietly on their flocks and herds, or hire themselves out in various capacities. The Nuzi texts reveal that, in hard times, they sometimes sold themselves as slaves. In unsettled periods, they might seek their living by raiding settled areas or by hiring themselves out as mercenary soldiers.

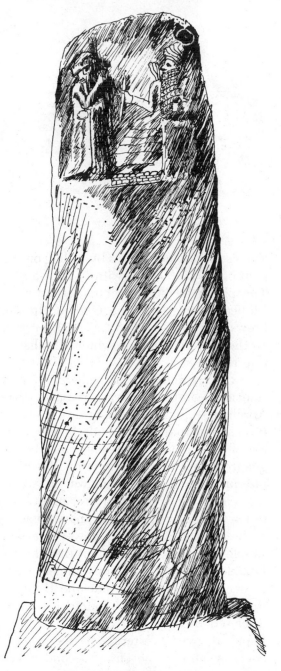

**The Code of Hammurabi.**

The similarity between the words *Habiru* and Hebrew makes it tempting to identify the ancestors of Israel with these unsettled wanderers. Certain items in the Bible support this identification. The *Habiru* some-

Egyptian wall painting of about 1900 B.C., depicting a caravan of Semitic nomads.

times sealed solemn oaths by calling on "the gods of the *Habiru*" to witness their action. This phrase has its exact counterpart in the Biblical expression, "the God of the Hebrews" (See *Ex. 3:18; 5:3; 7:16*). Further, on the only occasion on which Abraham is referred to as a Hebrew (*Gen. 14:13*), it seems he is regarded as something of an "outsider," and the situation is one in which Abraham rallies a fighting force of 318 trained men to do battle with the kings who had sacked Sodom and Gomorrah. The language of this account certainly allows the interpretation that Abraham was not wholly unaccustomed to such warfare, an interpretation that fits well with the known practice of the *Habiru*. We cannot, however, make a simple statement to the effect that the *Habiru* described in numerous ancient documents were none other than the Hebrews, the forerunners of Israel. Late evidence has disclosed the fact that *Habiru* were to be found all over Western Asia for a period covering almost the entire second millenium B.C. even after Israel had long since settled in Canaan. It is probably a mistake to conceive of the *Habiru* as a national or ethnic group. More likely, the name indicates an element of society, a layer of "displaced persons" without definite legal or social status. It is not implausible, however,

that the clans of Abraham and his descendants belonged to this unsettled layer and that their migration into Palestine was part of the larger movements that brought *Habiru* into this area in this period.

Thus, what we know of the Fertile Crescent in the first three centuries of the second millenium B.C. tends to confirm the trustworthiness of the Biblical naratives. To be sure, the stories preserved in *Genesis* reflect only a glimmer of the complex origins and activities of the numerous clans which made their way into Palestine at this time, but they contain nothing that contradicts what we have been able to learn from extra-Biblical sources. Instead, they help us fill out the Biblical account and give us a clearer and more detailed account of the type of life led by our spiritual forefathers.

## Life among the Patriarchs

We have spoken of the patriarchs as nomads. This word sometimes conjures up a picture of deserts and camels, but this is not the kind of nomad we have in mind. Widespread domestication of the camel did not occur for several centuries after this, and without camels, penetration of the desert is virtually impossible. The patriarchs' chief beast of burden was the ass; consequently, the wanderings of the patriarchs were re-

stricted to areas where vegetation was more likely to be available. Much of their time was spent wandering about Palestine seeking food and water for their families and their flocks. Actually, the term semi-nomad is a more accurate designation, for, although they often continued to move about, many of them remained stationary, dwelling in tents, or returned to the same area frequently enough to become associated with it. Abraham's main dwelling-place was near Hebron, south of Jerusalem, at the oaks of Mamre (*Gen. 13:18; 14:13*). Not far to the east was the field and cave of Machpelah, the family burial plot (*Gen. 23:17–20*). Isaac's primary headquarters seems to have been Beersheba (*Gen. 26: 23; 28:10*), in the extreme south of the habitable area of Palestine. Jacob is associated with several locations, particularly Bethel (*33:18*), Shechem (*35:1*), and Dothan (*37:17*). Archaeology has confirmed that these towns were major population centers in Palestine in the years between 2000 and 1700 B.C.

Naturally, some of these wanderers eventually founded cities or were assimilated into existing communities. At first, these cities were governed by true municipal law. There was no higher authority than the city council, composed of the elders of the city. The notion of a monarchy held little appeal for them. With the passage of time, powerful families sometimes came to dominate a city. An example of this is found in *Genesis 34*, in which the sons of Hamor are seen to be the ruling powers in Shechem. This story also illustrates another characteristic feature of early Canaanite culture, that of corporate guilt. As reflected here, an entire city (Shechem) could be held responsible for the crime (the rape of Dinah) by one of its inhabitants, especially if that individual was a prominent citizen (the prince of Shechem). The next stage in the political development of these cities was frequently the acceptance of a monarchy. These rulers gathered and commanded armies, built up the fortification of the cities, and, inevitably, levied taxes on the people in order to finance their projects.

### THE STRUCTURE OF THE FAMILY

Regardless of the particular stage of political development in the area in which the patriarchs found themselves, one element in the social structure remained fairly constant in this period—the family, the basic unit of Hebrew society. The very name by which we designate this period—patriarchal—furnishes us with a one-word description of the nature of the Hebrew family. The father was patriarch, the sole possessor and master of his goods, his property, and his

25

family. The family consisted of all who claimed kin to him. This included his wife (or wives), children, unmarried brothers and sisters, parents, and other relatives, as well as servants and concubines. In this circle, his rule was virtually absolute. His will was binding upon this community which attached itself to him. With this power and freedom, however, came the responsibility to instruct his household in the religious and social traditions of the family, the clan, and the nation.

In this male-dominated society the position of a woman was one of subordination and subjection to the men in her lives, her father and her husband. She married at the instruction and arrangement of her father and could be divorced by her husband at his pleasure, yet had little or no redress if she were wronged by him. Absolute faithfulness was required of her, but not of her husband, so long as he did not violate the rights of another husband. Yet, despite this inferior status, the relationship was often such as to allow her to retain her individuality, to enjoy a real personal relationship with her husband, and to experience the kind of love we commonly associate with marriage. Because of the importance attached to children, especially to sons who could carry on the strength and authority of the father, a woman could attain a position of respect and authority in the family through child-bearing. So great was the demand for offspring that, in *Genesis 38*, Tamar is pictured as a heroine for disguising herself as a prostitute to produce children to carry on the name of her dead husband! The practice of polygamy is also attributable to the desire for an abundance of heirs, rather than mere sexual passion.

## Summary

A comparison of the narratives contained in *Genesis 12–50* with what we know of the mode of life of the first three centuries of the second millenium B.C. indicates strongly that these narratives are more at home in this period than at any other in the history of the Fertile Crescent. Unfortunately, this does not mean we can assign dates to the activity of the patriarchs with anything approaching real precision. Neither does it mean we have found incontrovertible evidence that these stories are true. What it does mean is that the best of unbiased scholarship has done nothing to discredit the historical accuracy of these stories. On the contrary, it has confirmed them on point after point and has given us increased reason to believe that at some time in this period there was indeed a man named Abraham who, with the clan of which he was master, set out from Haran, "not knowing whither he went." Eventually, he came to Canaan, where he and his descendants spent their lives as semi-nomads. Probably, they were regarded by the settled inhabitants of the land as belonging to that unsettled class of people known as *Habiru*. Although they retained a strong feeling of kinship for their ancestors who had remained in Mesopotamia and for their neighbors of similar origins, there was intermarriage with local tribes and assimilation of local culture. The scriptures provide us with few details of this of this complex process, but the stories of Hagar and Ishmael, of Lot's place in the society of Sodom and Gomorrah, and of Esau's marriage to Hittite women surely reflect what was going on on a much wider scale among Israel's ancestors.

## The Religion of the Patriarchs

We have shown that the weight of the evidence indicates the patriarchs were real historical individuals. We have discussed briefly the type of lives they led. But our primary reason for studying them at all is to learn something of the nature of their religious beliefs and practices; it is to this subject that we now turn.

### THE GODS OF OUR FATHERS

It is a tendency of our age to think of God —when men think of him at all—as something utterly removed from the everyday affairs of humanity. We find just the opposite feeling among the patriarchs. The god they worshipped was considered a part of the family circle. The family or clan felt a real personal tie to their god. They conceived of God not so much as creator of the whole universe, but as their own personal deity, who was related to them in a special way. For example, when God is spoken of in a formal way, as in an oath, he is not simply called "God," but "the God of Abraham" (24:27), "the Mighty One of Isaac" (49:24), or "the God of Nahor" (31:53). In return for the devotion of the clan, which was thought of as his family, God was expected to protect them from harm and to see that they received those things necessary to their existence. He also served as witness to covenants they made with one another.

The names given to children illustrate this sense of closeness to the god of the family. The Hebrew syllable ab means "father," and when we find it as part of a name of a Bible character, it usually has reference to God. When the patriarchs and their descendants named their children Abiezer or Abimelech or Abiram, they were not simply picking out a name that sounded pleasant to them, as we commonly do in naming our children; rather, they were professing their belief that "My Father is a Helper" (Abiezer), or "My Father is my King" (Abimelech), or "My Father is Exalted" (Abiram). Another class of names expressive of faith in God are those which contain the syllable el. The original Hebrew text of our Bible makes it clear that El was one of the names by which the patriarchs addressed God. He is spoken of as El-Shaddai (translated "God Almighty,"* Gen. 17:1, etc.), El-Elyon ("God Most High," Gen. 14:19–22), and El-'Olam ("God the Everlasting," Gen. 21:33). Using this syllable, men named their children "God is my Helper" (Eliezer), "God is my King" (Elimelech), and, using both syllables we have noted, "God is my Father" (Eliab).

It is difficult to say whether or not the patriarchs were true monotheists, at least if we define monotheism as belief in the existence of one God and one God only. It is possible they were not too greatly concerned to identify the deity of their own clan with that of other clans. What was important to them was their relationship with the God whom they had undertaken to serve. He was the only God of any real consequence. Thus, even if they were not *theoretical* monotheists, they were *practical* monotheists.

### WORSHIP

The story of Rachel's theft of the household gods (31:19) leads us to suspect there may have been some use of images in the religion of the patriarchs. Lest we become shocked either by this suggestion, or the above statements concerning monotheism, it is well to remember that this was centuries before the giving of the Ten Commandments at Mt. Sinai. At this time, belief in the existence of a number of gods or worship utilizing a graven image violated no divine commandment of which we have any knowledge. On the other hand, what we know of the fertility cults and the orgiastic rites of the contemporary religions with which the patriarchs must have come in contact makes it clear that the worship of the God of the Fathers was of an entirely different order from that offered to other "gods."

---

*Actually, this is an improper translation. The correct rendering would be "God, the Mountain One," symbolic of the towering strength and majesty of God.

Teraphim: possessors of the household gods were guaranteed the family inheritance according to Amorite custom.

There was no special order of priests or other religious officials. The primary act of worship was the offering of animal sacrifices and this was performed by, or at the direction of, the patriarch, the head of the clan. There is evidence of the existence of ancient shrines at such places as Bethel, but patriarchal religion was not restricted to a particular locality. The God of the patriarchs was not a god of a particular shrine, but was a constant unseen traveling companion of the individual or clan with whom he had entered into covenant. He could be addressed in prayer or approached with sacrifice at any time and place. His temple could be found at whatever spot his worshipers built an altar. A second type of religious observance of which we read in *Genesis* is the erection of pillars (*28:18; 31:13; 35:14*). Ordinarily, these pillars consisted of a single stone or a heap of stones set up as a formal token of a vow (*31:13*) as a commemoration of an appearance of God (*35:14*), or as a reminder of a covenant made in the presence of God (*31:45*).

### ELECTION AND COVENANT

After the giving of the Law at Mt. Sinai, the religion of God's people underwent considerable change. Graven images were specifically forbidden. Detailed codes of law were given to guide Israel in every aspect of her life. The presence of God came to be more closely associated with a particular place—the tabernacle and, later, the temple. An official priesthood was ordained to perform all the duties connected with an elaborate sacrificial system. In view of all this, it is natural to ask if Israel was mistaken in looking back to Abraham as the ultimate ancestor of her faith. The answer is no. Despite whatever changes might have been made and whatever developments undergone, the religion of God's people was ever supported by the two foundation pillars of Election and Covenant. From the call of Abraham in *Genesis 12* to the close of the Old Testament, there is a constant affirmation of the belief that God had ordained Abraham and his descendants for a special relationship to him and a special task in the world, and that this elect people is bound to God in a solemn covenant.

The divine election was not based on God's having foreseen that Abraham and his descendants would be righteous. Indeed, even Abraham, the classic example of the man of saving faith, is seen to behave in such a way as to deserve reproach, as in his deception of Pharaoh (*12:10–20*) or his sending away of Hagar and Ishmael (*21:8–14*). Much of the Old Testament is a catalogue of the persistent sinfulness of the Israelites.

This helps us see that God did not choose them because they were better, but because he had a task he wanted them to perform. He chose the few for the sake of the many. He chose Abraham that through his seed all nations of the earth might be blessed.

This election was made effective by God's entering into covenant with those whom he had elected. In the covenant, God voluntarily bound himself to fulfill the promises he had made to Abraham, and men accepted the conditions of the covenant, signifying their acceptance of it by submitting to circumcision. During the patriarchal period, God renewed this covenant several times (*Gen. 15:5, 13–16; 18:18, 19; 26:2–4; 28:13 –15*), reaffirming his intention to bring to completion the great work for which he had chosen the family of Abraham. The covenant at Sinai, while in many respects different from the Abrahamic covenant, was still part of this same plan initiated by God for the redemption of fallen humanity.

In the patriarchal period, a man's righteousness could not be "measured'" by his obedience to an objective law, for there was no such religious law, no "Law of Abraham, Isaac, and Jacob." It was understood, of course, that God's people were expected to conform to the standard of morality generally accepted in the society in which they found themselves. But conformity to these standards did not make the patriarchs righteous before God. Righteousness was determined by faith—trust in God's promises and willingness to allow him to work out his purposes in his own good time. Conversely, lack of trust and patience constituted sin.

With this understanding of the religion of the patriarchs, together with what we have already learned of the time in which they lived and their mode of life, let us look more closely at the major figures in this second section of *Genesis*, which we have called The History of the Patriarchs.

## Abraham

At the close of chapter 1, it was noted that *Genesis 1–11* profoundly brings home the truth that hunmanity possesses a tragic flaw; that man, left to himself, invariably falls short of the goals for which he was created. The opening section of the Bible, which we called the Prehistory of Israel, ends dismally, as the once-proud builders of Babel wander abut the earth in confusion and frustration. With *ch. 12*, a new ray of hope appears on the horizon. The destruction of the world by water had brought little improvement, for Noah and his descendants picked up where those who had perished had left off. Now, God was to try something new. He would choose one man and make him the agent of his work of salvation. The man would not be expected to be perfect; he would simply be expected to believe what God told him and be willing to do whatever God required of him. The man God chose was Abraham, and "Abraham believed God, and it was reckoned to him as righteousness."

### FROM UR TO EGYPT

Abraham was, as we have already noted, a resident of Mesopotamia. He had come, with his father, Terah, from Ur to Haran, a chief city in Aram. After Terah's death, God confronted Abraham with these instructions and promises:

> Go from your country and your kindred and your father's house to the land that I will show you. And I will make of you a great nation, and I will bless you, and make your name great, so that you will be a blessing. I will bless those who bless you, and him who curses you I will curse; and by you all the families of the earth will bless themselves.
>
> —*Genesis 12:1-3*

No promise could be more meaningful to Abraham and his contemporaries than that of land and children. These were the dearest

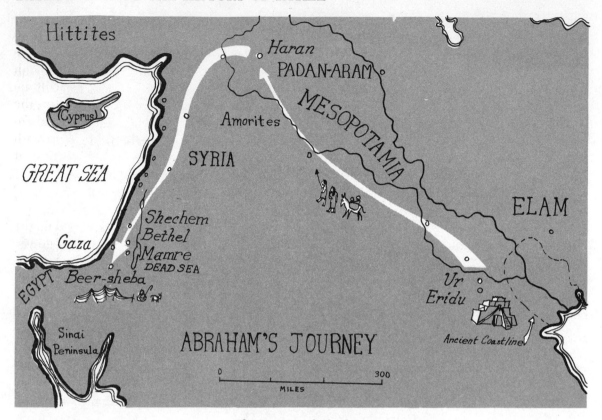

**The journies of Abraham.**

possessions a man could have. So, trusting in God, and encouraged by his promises, Abraham and a sizable clan left Haran for the land of Canaan. They wandered southward through Canaan, stopping briefly at the sacred Oak of Moreh, near Shechem, where God reaffirmed his intention to give him the land, then moving on through Bethel and Ai to the Negeb, the name applied to the desert region at the south of Palestine. In time of famine, Abraham followed a custom practiced by hungry neighbors for centuries, that of seeking relief in Egypt. There Abraham displayed a lack of trust in God's care for him. He feared that Pharaoh would kill him in order to gain his wife Sarah for his harem, so he said she was his sister and allowed her to be taken into Pharaoh's house. When Pharaoh learned of the deception, through afflictions that God brought upon

his house, he was angry with Abraham and ordered him to leave Egypt with all his possessions. The story Abraham had told Pharaoh was a half-truth. Sarah was his half-sister (*Gen. 20:12*). But it was also a half-lie, and we cannot admire this failure of Abraham to rely upon the hand of God to preserve him and his family from harm.

### THE SEPARATION FROM LOT

Let us emphasize once more that it is a mistake to conceive of the families of the patriarchs as closely akin to our modern families, with a mother, a father, a few children, and perhaps a mother-in-law or father-in-law. They included a wide range of relatives and a proportionate number of male and female servants. The clan traveling with Abraham was so numerous, and his flocks and herds so large, that it became necessary for the family of Lot, which before this had been a subdivision of Abraham's family, to separate and find another region in which to live. In this incident we see a much nobler side to Abraham than in his behavior before Pharaoh. To avoid strife, Abraham offered Lot his choice of all the land about them, agreeing to take for himself whatever was left—a most generous offer. Lot, a symbol of the man who seeks the easy path, chose the Jordan valley, leaving for Abraham the rough hills of Canaan. The Jordan contained grassy, well-watered land, and the cities of Sodom and Gomorrah. At first glance, it appears Lot got the better of the bargain, but we cannot miss the note of foreboding in the writer's summary of the transaction:

> Abram dwelt in the land of Canaan, while Lot dwelt among the cities of the valley and moved his tent as far as Sodom. Now the men of Sodom were wicked, great sinners against the Lord. —*Genesis 13:12-13*

This is immediately followed by an account of God's appearing to Abraham and assuring him that all the land he could see would be given to his descendants and they, though he was now childless, would eventually be as numberless as the grains of sand on the earth. His faith thus reinforced, Abraham moved his family to Hebron, the area with which he was to be associated for most of the remainder of his life.

### ABRAHAM AND MELCHIZEDEK

Some time after Lot settled in Sodom, the cities of the Jordan Valley banded together to throw off the yoke of Elamite oppression. Unfortunately, they were poorly prepared to carry their rebellion through and were crushed by a coalition of Eastern kings led by Chedorlaomer king of Elam. In the process Sodom and Gomorrah were sacked and the family of Lot was taken captive. When Abraham learned of this, he quickly

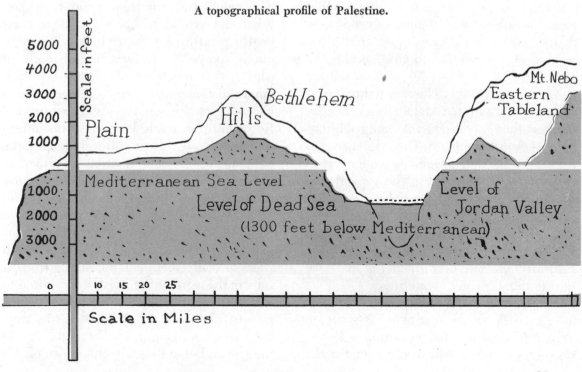

A topographical profile of Palestine.

31

gathered a fighting force of over three hundred men, indicating the considerable size of his clan, and pursued the Easterners all the way to Damascus, where he routed them and rescued Lot. At the same time, he recovered the goods which had been taken from the looted cities.

As Abraham returned home, he was met by Melchizedek, king of Salem (probably Jerusalem) and priest of God Most High (*El-Elyon*), and by the king of Sodom. To Melchizedek he gave a tenth of all he had taken in battle. This is the first record we have of the giving of a tithe to a priest of God, but it seems to represent a religious practice which was common long before it became institutionalized in the Law of Moses. In the New Testament (*Hebrews 5:5–10; 6:20; 7:1–19*) Jesus is spoken of as a priest after the order of Melchizedek," in the sense that he is "without father or mother or genealogy, and has neither beginning of days nor end of life, but . . . continues a priest for ever" (*Heb. 7:3*). The purpose of these passages is to point out that Jesus' priesthood was of another order than that of the Levitical priesthood, that it depended on his relation to God, as did the priesthood of Melchizedek, and not upon his earthly parentage. They are not to be understood to mean that Melchizedek literally fulfilled these conditions of being without parents or birth or death. The reference is to the record of Melchizedek as we have it in *Genesis 14*. In contrast to the typical Old Testament practice of tracing a man's lineage backwards and forwards and mentioning his birth and death, the writer simply introduces Melchizedek into the narrative and, after he has performed his task, we hear nothing further about him.

The interview with Melchizedek ordinarily overshadows the rest of what went on here, but Abraham's conversation with the King of Sodom is also instructive. Just as the rules of warfare gave Chedorlaomer the right to the spoils and captives of the cities he took, they also gave Abraham the right to that which he regained from Chedorlaomer. Thus, when the king of Sodom suggested Abraham keep the goods but return the people, he was not being especially generous, but was asking a favor of Abraham. Abraham had entered the battle to free his kinsman Lot, not as an opportunity for personal gain. He refused to take any of the goods, except that which his troops had used, intending to make it clear he was dependent on no one other than God for his existence. He did, however, see to it that his neighbors from Hebron received a fair share of the goods in payment for their time and efforts.

### HAGAR AND ISHMAEL

At this time, Abraham and Sarah were still childless. The only heir to Abraham's possessions was a slave, Eliezer. We have learned from the Nuzi texts that it was customary for a childless couple to adopt a son, who would care for them as long as they lived and attend to their burial at their death, in return for the right to inherit the family property. It was understood, of course, that the birth of a male heir nullified the agreement. Apparently, Abraham had adopted Eliezer for just this purpose. But again God made known his full intention to abide by his promises, renewing the covenant by the sacred ritual described in *Genesis 15*. Still, Abraham and Sarah found it almost impossible to believe they would actually become the natural parents of a child, since Sarah was well beyond the normal age for childbearing. It seems Sarah was especially skeptical. So, failing to trust fully in the word of the Lord, she resorted to a legal device which, according to the Nuzi tablets, was a customary practice. She gave her handmaid, Hagar, to Abraham, the arrangement being that any child born of this union would be counted as Sarah's. Both Abraham and Sarah were soon to regret their lack of faith. Hagar became pregnant, according to plan, but soon, perhaps as a result of Abraham's pride at the prospect of becoming a father, she began to treat Sarah rather contemptuously. The common law of this period forbade Abraham's sending Hagar away, but, under pressure from his jealous wife, he allowed her to be driven from the camp. At a spring in the wilderness, an angel of the Lord directed Hagar to return to her mistress, and to display a more submissive attitude. When she returned, she bore a son whom she named Ishmael. But Ishmael was not to be the child of promise.

### THE SIGN OF THE COVENANT

For thirteen years, Abraham looked for the fulfilling of the promise God had made to him. On one occasion, after having heard another of the several assurances that Sarah should bear him a son, Abraham collapsed in laughter (*Gen. 17:17; cf. 18:12*) and tried to persuade God to recognize Ishmael as his rightful heir. But the Lord refused to change his plan. Not only did he solemnly reaffirm his part of the covenant agreement, but he commanded Abraham to submit to the rite of circumcision as a token of his full acceptance of this covenant. We sometimes think of circumcision as a purely Jewish institution. Actually, it seems to have been widely practiced among the Egyptians and most ancient Semitic peoples, with the exception of the Babylonians and Assyrians. All of the peoples of Palestine practiced it except the Philistines, who were scornfully referred to by the Israelites as "the uncircumcised" (*Judges 14:3; 15:18; I Sam. 14:6; 17:26, etc.*). Although it was sometimes performed for the sake of general hygiene, it was ordinarily associated with initiation into puberty or with full acceptance into the religious and civil affairs of the community.

Nevertheless, in the religion of Israel, and that of the patriarchs, it held a distinctive place. Here, it was performed not at puberty, but in infancy. As in other societies, it signified acceptance into membership in the tribe or nation, but this was subordinated under its primary role as a token of consecration and dedication to God.

### SODOM AND GOMORRAH

In narrating the separation of Abraham and Lot, the writer prepared us for the worst by telling us that the cities in the Jordan Valley, where Lot chose to make his home, were exceedingly wicked places. In *chs. 18-19*, we see something of the extent of the wickedness of these cities and the judgment which God brought upon them.

In a singular display of his regard for Abraham, the Lord appeared to him at his dwelling-place by the Oaks of Mamre and informed him of his intention to destroy the cities of the Plain because of their sin. Abraham was deeply concerned for the welfare of Lot and his family, and whatever other righteous people might be in the cities. After a period of bargaining he persuaded God to spare the cities if as few as ten righteous men could be found within their walls. Unfortunately, these cities were thoroughly filled with evil. When two angels of the Lord visited Sodom in the form of men, they were welcomed into the home of Lot. The residents of the city, ignoring the rules of oriental hospitality which provided for the safety of guests, surrounded Lot's home and demanded that the men be turned over to them, to engage in homosexual practices (hence the term "Sodomy") with them. When they pressed closer to the house, they were struck blind by the angels and spent the night groping about in the darkness. This incident seemed to seal the Lord's resolve to destroy Sodom and Gomorrah. In the morning "the Lord rained on Sodom and

Gomorrah brimstone and fire from the Lord out of heaven" (*19:24*). At God's warning, Lot and his family managed barely to escape the holocaust. Lot's wife, unable to keep her eyes from the flames that devoured the city she had loved, was destroyed but Lot and his two daughters fled to a cave near the tiny village of Zoar. Archaeologists have not as yet located the ruins of Sodom and Gomorrah, but there is evidence of a tremendous upheaval and conflagration in the plain south of the Dead Sea, where the cities are believed to have been situated.

The last scene in which Lot figures is one of drunken, incestuous squalor. His two daughters, reflecting the moral depravity which had characterized Sodom, managed to get their father drunk and to have sexual relations with him. The nations of Moab and Ammon were regarded to be descended from the children of this unnatural union, and, in later years, were frequently in conflict with the descendants of Abraham.

### ABRAHAM AND ABIMELECH

After the destruction of Sodom and Gomorrah, Abraham moved his dwelling from Hebron toward the Negeb. He settled for a time near Gerar, in the area that came to be known as Philistia. While there, Abraham repeated his faithless error of lying to the king, Abimelech, about his relationship to Sarah. Abimelech took less stern measures than had the Pharaoh, but we can see a certain wariness in his words as he later makes a covenant of peace with Abraham and his tribe (*21:22-4*).

### THE BIRTH OF ISAAC

In *ch. 21*, we have the account of the birth of Isaac. This long-awaited child of promise brought happiness to all in Abraham's family; to all, that is, except Hagar and Ishmael, who were again sent away from the camp at Sarah's insistence. But the Lord was with

them, protecting them in the wilderness until Ishmael reached maturity. In the meantime, Isaac grew to be a great source of delight to his mother and father. The Lord had indeed rewarded Abraham richly for his faith.

Then, without a word of warning, God commanded Abraham to take this beloved child and sacrifice him as a burnt offering. We have noted previously that Abraham's faith sometimes waved, that his trust in God was not always faultless. His unwavering obedience on this occasion, however, forever marks him off as one of the giants of faith. It is this incident that gives meaning to the phrase "Abrahamic faith." This story illustrates the point we made earlier, that the head of a family completely dominated all those who claimed to be a part of his household. There is a touch of sadness in these proceedings, but there is no indication that anyone doubted Abraham's right to perform this act, nor any hint that Isaac's "rights" were even taken into consideration. On the other hand, there is a certain elevation of human rights involved, for the story was probably regarded by the Israelites as a sure sign that God disapproved of human sacrifices. Whether this be true or not, the chief result of the incident was to make it clear that Abraham was a man of profound faith and to make it clear to Abraham that God would definitely stand behind his promises.

### ABRAHAM'S LAST DAYS

Abraham had proved to be a faithful servant of God, and the Lord had made clear his unshakable resolve to fulfill the promises he had made to him. The chief purposes of his life had been accomplished. All that remained was the discharge of a few family responsibilities.

The first of these was the securing of a family burial plot. On the occasion of the

34

death of Sarah, Abraham purchased the cave of Machpelah, and the field in which it was located, from Ephron the Hittite. Many of Abraham's descendants were later to be buried in this cave, including Isaac, Rebekah, Jacob, and Leah. Excavations in Palestine have uncovered a number of burial caves which are probably quite similar to the cave of Machpelah.

A second task was arranging for Isaac's marriage. Abraham was strongly set against Isaac's taking a wife from among the Canaanite women. It would be far better, he felt, for him to marry a woman from among the relatives who had remained in Aram, a woman who would already be somewhat familiar with the religion and culture of the clan she was entering. To obtain such a woman, Abraham sent his eldest and most trusted servant, probably the same Eliezer we mentioned earlier, and sent him to the Mesopotamian city of Nahor. There the servant found Rebekah the daughter of Bethuel and, with the approval of her father and her brother Laban, brought her back to the Negeb, the southern part of Palestine in which Abraham was then living, to become Isaac's wife. Throughout this story, there is a strong sense of God's control over the whole affair. God's providence is ever at work among his people. Nothing is left to simple chance.

In Abraham's last years, he married a second wife, Keturah. She was evidently a woman much younger than Abraham, for she bore him six sons. Then, at the age of 175, "Abraham breathed his last and died in a good old age, an old man and full of years, and was gathered to his people" (25:8).

## Isaac

Isaac is a transitional figure in the patriarchal narrative. That is, his major importance seems to be to serve as a bridge between Abraham and Jacob. The incidents for which we remember him are those in which others figure as the main characters. Even his lying to Abimelech king of Gerar about his wife (*ch. 26*), the one incident in which he is the principle actor, is overshadowed by the fact that Abraham had already been credited with the same deceitful action on two previous occasions. Apart from this apparent lack of confidence in God's protection, Isaac is regarded as a faithful worshipper of the true God and served well as a bearer of the promises made to Abraham and as a party to God's covenant with men.

## Jacob

### JACOB AND ESAU

Throughout Israel's history, one of the nations with which she was in continual conflict was Edom. The traditional ancestor of the Edomites was Esau, Jacob's twin brother. In *Genesis 25:19ff*, we are told that the conflict between these two nations could be traced all the way back to the struggling of the unborn twins in Rebekah's womb. When Rebekah inquired of the Lord concerning the violent activity within her body, she was informed that her sons would be the founders of two great nations, that their relationship with one another would be one of enmity and strife, and that, contrary to oriental custom, the elder would be subordinate to the younger. The account of the relation between Jacob and Esau is probably influenced by, or perhaps influenced, the general opinion of the Israelites toward Edom. The Edomites were darker-skinned and were viewed by Israel as a rather scrubby, uncouth group of people, with little real sense of value, in contrast to their picture of themselves as calm, refined men of culture. The mention of Jacob's grasping Esau's heel as they came forth from the womb is a humorous touch, indicating that, even as babies, it was evident that Jacob would get the better of his hapless brother.

The brief story of Esau's sale of his birthright in return for "a mess of pottage" is one of the best known in all Biblical literature, and illustrates Esau's contempt for those things that are of lasting value. The birthright consisted largely in the position of honor at the head of the family and in a double share of the inheritance. Normally, this should have fallen to Esau, since he was the elder son. But, momentarily overcome by hunger, he surrendered his claim to the birthright to Jacob, for the sake of a bowl of meaty soup.

Jacob's supplanting of Esau did not stop with the purchase of his birthright. It was customary for a father, when he felt that death was approaching, to call his children together and to pronounce the "patriarchal blessing" over them. This blessing, which was primarily a prediction about the future of the son, based on what the father knew of his character and what he desired for him, was believed to have a real determining effect on a man's life. Therefore, it was highly important to receive a favorable blessing. As Jacob and Esau developed into manhood, their dissimilar personalities caused some lines to be drawn in the family. Esau was an athletic, rough-and-tumble outdoorsman whose ruggedness appealed to his father. In contrast, Jacob's quiet, peaceful behavior made him the delight of his mother's eyes. Both parents were anxious for their favorite to get the best that was available. When Isaac made preparation to give his patriarchal blessing to Esau, Rebekah set about to secure for Jacob the blessings she knew Isaac intended for Esau.

Since Isaac was almost blind, the simplest plan was for Jacob to enter Isaac's tent, pretending he was Esau. Jacob was wary of this plan, since Esau was an extremely hairy man and he was "a smooth man." If his father should happen to touch him, his intentions would be unmasked and, instead of the blessing, he would receive Isaac's curse. Finally, however, he donned animal skins and went in to his father while Esau was in the field, hunting. Isaac sensed something strange about the situation, but was deceived into bestowing on Jacob the blessing intended for Esau. Scarcely had Isaac finished speaking than Esau returned from the field and came to receive the promised blessing. The violent reaction of Isaac and Esau at the craft of Jacob and Rebekah helps us to see the mysterious power attributed to the words of the blessing. Even though Jacob had obtained the blessing fraudulently, the words had been spoken and could not be recalled.[*]

Isaac tried to salvage what he could of a bad situation by uttering a blessing of sorts over Esau, but the intended blessing was forever lost. The only way Esau could get even was simple revenge. He resolved that, after Isaac's death and the following period of mourning, he would kill Jacob. When Rebekah became aware of this, she instructed Jacob to go to her relatives in Haran, where he was to stay until Esau's anger subsided. Such a trip would have the added advantage of enabling Jacob to obtain a wife from among the relatives who had remained in Aram. The undesirability of intermarriage with the Canaanites had been brought home to Isaac and Rebekah in a most forceful way. Esau had married not one, but two Hittite women, and their inability or unwillingness to adapt to the Hebrew way of life had "made life bitter for Isaac and Rebekah" (*Gen. 26:35*). Doubtless, this reflects what was going on all over Canaan as the infiltrating tribes began to mingle and intermarry with the native population.

---

[*]According to the Nuzi tablets, the courts would uphold a son's right to those things bestowed in such an oral blessing.

## "JACOB'S LADDER"

So, Jacob made the long journey from Beersheba, in the South of Palestine, to the ancestral home in Haran. On one of the days of his journey, he was forced by the approaching darkness to make camp at what appears to have been a deserted place. While he slept, "he dreamed that there was a ladder set up on the earth, and the top of it reached to heaven; and behold, the angels of God were ascending and descending on it!" (*Gen. 28:12*). In the course of the dream God revealed himself to Jacob as the God of Abraham and Isaac and renewed the promises of land and offspring. When Jacob awoke, he set up a stone pillar and poured oil over it, consecrating the spot as a holy place where God could be worshipped. The name he gave to the spot was Bethel, meaning "The house of God." In addition, he made a vow of faithfulness to the God who had revealed himself at this spot.

The trappings of Jacob's dream were in keeping with contemporary religious thought regarding the dwelling-place of God and the activity of the angels. The word translated "ladder" probably refers to something more like a ramp or stair-like pavement, reaching from earth to "the gate of heaven" (*28:17*), on which the angels of God traveled back and forth as they carried out God's divine commands. This ramp served as the link between the place of God's appearing and his actual heavenly dwelling. A similar conception is reflected in the Babylonian temple-towers, or *ziggurats* (see p. 22), in which the tiny chapel at the top of the structure, signifying God's dwelling-place, is joined by a ramp to the temple below, the place where he was actually believed to appear.

This story serves a double purpose in the patriarchal narratives. Not only does it record the renewal of the covenant between God and the descendants of Abraham, but it serves as an explanation of how Bethel came to be regarded as a holy place. When Jeroboam I set up the calf worship to rival the temple worship in Jerusalem, he chose Bethel as one of the two main sanctuaries (*I Kings 12:28–30*), doubtless because it had been regarded as a holy place and had probably served as a place of worship ever since the time of the patriarchs. After its destruction by the great reformer, Josiah (*II Kin. 23:15*), the sanctuary seems never to have regained its importance.

## JACOB'S MARRIAGE TO LABAN'S DAUGHTERS

When Jacob arrived in Haran, he went to the home of Laban, his mother's brother. After staying with him a short time, he made the well-known bargain to work seven years for the right to marry Laban's younger daughter, Rachel. After the seven year period, however, Laban deceived Jacob by sending the older, less attractive daughter, Leah, into the marriage bed under protection of the darkness. After a week, Laban also gave him Rachel for a wife, but only on the condition that he would serve him for another seven years.

## The Twelve Patriarchs

The next portion of the narrative is an interesting account of the efforts of the two sisters to win Jacob's favor by presenting him with children. From the beginning Jacob had loved Rachel more than Leah, but Rachel was unable to bear children. Leah, however, was favored by God and bore him four sons: Reuben, Simeon, Levi, and Judah. Rachel, driven to despair by her barrenness, gave Jacob her handmaid Bilhah. As was the case in the similar incident involving Sarah and Hagar (p. 32f), all children born to Bilhah were to be regarded as legally belonging to Rachel. Bilhah bore Jacob two sons, Dan and Naphtali, thus restor-

37

ing to Rachel a measure of her status in the family. But Leah was not so easily to be deprived of her position as the leading mother in the family. Since she had ceased bearing, she gave Jacob her handmaid, Zilpah, and through her gained two additional sons, Gad and Asher.

The story of the birth of Leah's "second family" of children reveals something of the strained relationships in Jacob's family. Rachel was still deeply troubled over having borne Jacob no children. In the patriarchal culture, a barren woman could not help but be painfully aware of her failure in her obligation as a wife. Rachel was prepared to try just about anything. On one occasion, Leah's oldest son, Reuben, came in from the field with a bunch of mandrakes for his mother. Mandrakes were plants used extensively in ancient folk medicine and valued because of their supposed ability to promote sexual desire. Leah's reply to Rachel's request for some of these mandrakes indicates that Jacob had neglected her, depriving her of the normal sexual rights of a wife. Despite the embarrassment it must have caused her, Leah literally hired Jacob away from Rachel for a night. Again the Lord blessed Leah, for she conceived and bore a son whom she named Issachar. This apparently restored her to partial favor with Jacob, for she subsequently bore him two more children, Zebulun and Dinah.

Finally, the narrative tells us, "God remembered Rachel" and "opened her womb." After years of frustration and anguish, she bore a son, Joseph. It was this son who was later to be responsible for the survival of the family during the time of severe famine. Later, Rachel bore a second son, Benjamin, the youngest of Jacob's twelve sons. These twelve sons are sometimes referred to as the Twelve Patriarchs and are regarded as the ancestors of the twelve tribes of Israel.

## JACOB AND LABAN

There is good reason to believe that Jacob never fully forgave Laban for having tricked him into marrying Leah and causing him to work an additional seven years. It is not improbable that their relationship in this period was rather uneasy. Finally, after twenty years of serving in his house, Jacob, asked Laban's permission to take his wife and children back to his homeland in Canaan. At first, this seems to be a strange request. They were Jacob's wives and children; why not just pack up and leave? But the request was not just a courteous formality. Under the law of this period, when a servant left his master, he had no legal claim on whatever wives and children he may have accumulated during the period of his servitude. It is true that Jacob's status was not exactly that of a servant, but, since he had entered Laban's house as a stranger, a man without full legal rights in the community, he was regarded as a dependent of Laban. Laban's view of the matter is expressed in *31:43:* "The daughters are my daughters, the children are my children, the flocks are my flocks, and all that you see is mine." Still, Jacob's status had always been higher than that of a slave and Laban's assertion was certainly open to objection. The remaining paragraphs of *ch. 30* and most of *ch. 31* contain the record of the attempts of these two cunning orientals to get the better of one another in a rather delicate situation in which their precise legal rights were not too clearly defined.

The period of Jacob's stay in Laban's home was a time of great prosperity. Laban had learned "by divination" (*30:27*) that the Lord had blessed his household because of Jacob's presence. We do not know what this process of divination consisted of, or whether Laban's information was actually from God or merely the chance product of some superstitious practice. In any case, he was unwilling to turn loose of the man who had brought him such good fortune, so he promised to pay him whatever wages he asked. Jacob's request was that he be given all those animals in the flocks whose coloring differed from that of the majority of the rest of the animals. The flocks of this area and period consisted of sheep which were usually white and goats which were usually dark brown or black. A small percentage of the animals would be striped, or spotted, or colored in some other fashion which varied from the dominant pattern. The suggested arrangement would assure Laban that Jacob would receive only a small percentage of the animals. Furthermore, he would be able to determine by a quick inspection whether Jacob had taken any animals that were not rightfully his. Laban agreed to this, but immediately cut these mottled animals out of his flocks and had them taken to an area several miles from where Jacob was working. Jacob, however, was not to be outdone. Since the animals usually bred at the time they came to the watering troughs, Jacob placed striped rods in the troughs, hoping to assure the production of a high percentage of mottled animals. This peculiar procedure was based on the ancient belief that objects seen by human and animal mothers at the time of intercourse or during the period of pregnancy could have a visible effect on their offspring. Despite the fact that the science of genetics has established rather conclusively that visual impressions have no real effect on unborn offspring, this belief has persisted on into modern times. The time is not long past when expectant mothers were carefully shielded from any sight that might mark their babies for life. Few circus sideshows are without some unnatural specimen whose mother is supposed to have been scared by some unusual sight or occurrence. Thus, we need not be surprised

when our narrator tells his story without a trace of skepticism. He had no doubts that such action would produce the desired results. What probably happened is that the sheep and goats produced, as they had always done, a fair amount of mottled offspring, and that, eventually, Jacob was able to accumulate a sizable flock. If anything more than natural processes and coincidence is involved, the credit must go to God and not to the striped rods.

Although Jacob had been abundantly blessed by God and had grown exceedingly rich, he was still not content to remain in Aram. Laban and his sons were grumbling about his good fortune. Laban had begun to look at him with a jaundiced eye. Finally, God appeared to him in a dream and told him to return to Canaan. So, while Laban was off shearing sheep, Jacob packed up all

Jacob in the land of Canaan.

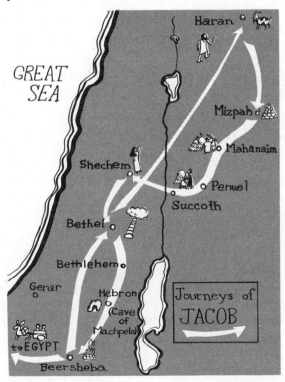

that he had and fled with his family toward Canaan. When Laban returned from the shearing and learned that Jacob had been gone three days, he immediately set out in pursuit of him. From a careful reading of this section, it seems Laban was less troubled about the loss of his daughters and his livestock than about the "household gods", or teraphim, which Rachel had stolen (*31: 19, 30, 33:35*). As we noted in the section on the Religion of the Patriarchs (p. 26ff), this seems to be evidence that there was some use of images in the worship of God before the time of Moses. Before the discovery of the Nuzi texts, it was unknown why Laban should have been so exercised about these images. These tablets have disclosed that the possessor of the family teraphim also held the legal rights to the family inheritance. Thus, Laban was concerned not only for his immediate loss, but feared that all his remaining property and cattle would eventually go to Jacob instead of his own sons. Rachel managed to conceal the idols from her father (*31:33–35*), but there is no indication Jacob ever laid claim to Laban's possessions.

When Laban saw he could no longer keep Jacob from leaving him, he surrendered to the instincts of a parent and father-in-law and proposed a covenant of peace between the two families. Jacob agreed to take no other wives than those he already had and both swore they would never approach one another again with an evil intent. The words of Laban by the pillar Mizpah have been repeated many times:

> The Lord watch between you and me, when we are absent one from the other.
> —*Genesis 31:49*

Early the next morning, we see Laban depart for his home in Haran. It is difficult not to sympathize with him now. As he rides into the approaching dawn, with his head bowed on his chest, we no longer see a cunning oriental chieftain who sought the advantage in every deal, but a tired old grandfather who has kissed his daughters and their children goodbye for the last time.

### PREPARATION FOR THE MEETING WITH ESAU

Twenty years had passed since Jacob had seen his brother Esau. Now that things had been ironed out with his father-in-law, he felt it was necessary to make an attempt at reconciliation with Esau. It is clear that Jacob felt considerable guilt about having cheated Esau. When his servants reported that Esau was coming to meet him with four hundred men, Jacob's conscience allowed him to interpret this in no other way than that Esau was on a mission of revenge. He decided that the best plan open to him was to divide his family and possessions into two groups. In this way, although the loss of one of the groups seemed certain, the other might possibly escape. Then, after a prayer that obviously came from a heart distraught with fear (*32:9–12*), Jacob began sending a series of elaborate presents to Esau, hoping that the accumulation of gifts would appease his anger before they actually confronted each other.

### JACOB'S STRUGGLE WITH THE HEAVENLY MAN

The story of Jacob's meeting with Esau is broken by the strange account of his all-night struggle with a heavenly assailant. On the day before the encounter with Esau, Jacob separated himself from his family. Suddenly, his solitude was interrupted by a mysterious representative of God. Elsewhere, it is suggested that Jacob was a man of extraordinary strength (*29:10*); this seems to be implied here also, as the apparently superhuman creature is unable to gain the advantage over Jacob in a wrestling match that lasted almost till dawn. Finally, Jacob's assailant put his thigh out of joint with what seems to have been a magical touch. By this time, Jacob sensed he was struggling with divine power and clutched at him in an effort to wrest from him a blessing. Instead of giving him a blessing the "man" asked Jacob the peculiar question, "what is your name?" To understand the significance of this we must remember that a man's name was held to be a real part of his personality, and not just a convenient device for identification purposes. In 25:26, we are told that Jacob's name was derived from his having grasped Esau's heel at birth, and that it had the general meaning of Supplanter or Cheater. Certainly much of what we know of Jacob to this time fits this name. Here, however, because he has "striven with God and men" and has refused to be subdued, his name is changed from Cheater to He Who Strives, from Jacob to Israel. Thus the people of God gained the name they were to wear throughout history.

### JACOB AND ESAU ARE RECONCILED

As the sun rose, Jacob limped out to meet his brother Esau, whom he saw approaching in the distance. The manner in which he staggered his family indicates clearly the status of the different segments. The two handmaids, Bilhah and Zilpah, and their children, were placed at the front of the procession, followed by Leah and her children and then by Rachel and Joseph. In this arrangement, if Esau began to attack, Rachel and Joseph would have the greatest chance of escape. As Jacob approached Esau, he bowed before him seven times, following the practice of vassal kings and princes before the Pharaoh or other great suzerain. His speech is that of a slave before his master.

Immediately we see that Jacob's fears have been unwarranted. Twenty years and a reasonable amount of prosperity have healed Esau's wounds. At the sight of Jacob, his only reaction is one of pure, spontaneous joy. Jacob's years of practicing deception have left him totally unprepared for this. He cannot believe Esau's innocence does not cloak some dark plot of revenge. His only desire is to put as much distance between Esau and himself as possible. Finally, he persuaded Esau to return to Seir, or Edom, implying that he would soon join him there. As soon as Esau returned to the south, Jacob moved eastward, coming to rest in Shechem, where he purchased a plot of ground and erected an altar to the God of his clan, *El-Elohe Israel*—God, the God of Israel.

### THE RAPE OF DINAH

The hostility between the Aramean semi-nomads and the natives of Canaan is reflected in the account of the rape of Dinah by Shechem, prince of the Hivite city near which Jacob was caused (*ch. 34*). To the ancient Israelite, and apparently to his ancestors, rape was regarded as the most serious of sexual offences. Shechem's crime is compounded when we remember that, according to the narrator's apparent chronology, Dinah can hardly have been more than a child.

Shechem appears less an ogre than a man overcome by his passions when he and his father, Hamor, approach Jacob and his sons with the request that Dinah be given to him in marriage. The brothers offer their consent, on the condition that all the males of the city submit to the rite of circumcision. In view of the rest of the story, it is quite possible that this was not offered in good faith, but was simply part of a plot for revenge. At any rate, Hamor convinced the citizens of Shechem that a marriage alliance would work to their economic advantage and all the males were circumcised. On the third day, the day on which the men would be most feverish and incapacitated by the operation, two of Dinah's full brothers, Simeon and Levi, "took their swords and came upon the city unawares, and killed all the males" (*34:25*). Afterward, the other sons of Jacob plundered the city. When Jacob learned of their action, he was disturbed because he feared the inhabitants of other Canaanite cities would band together and attack them. In the patriarchal blessing recorded in *49:5–7*, Simeon and Levi are censured for their tendency to violence, surely reflecting this incident.

### THE RETURN TO THE HOUSE OF GOD

From Shechem, Jacob journeyed back to Bethel, the place where the Lord had appeared to him in vision of the Heavenly Ladder. This action had the character of a religious pilgrimage and was accompanied by practices typical of such pilgrimages. Since its purpose was to erect an altar to the God who had caused Jacob to prosper, all matter pertaining to foreign religious cults was to be put away. This included any images they might have accumulated in their contacts with Canaanite culture and even such items as earrings, which were perhaps thought to have some magical powers. In addition, the pilgrims underwent a process of ritual purification which included a change of garments and, probably, some type of asceticism, or self-denial.

The remainder of *ch. 35* and *ch. 36* seem to be more of an odd-lot of traditions which the narrator had in his possession than an integral part of the saga of Jacob. From a literary standpoint, they form a rather uneven conclusion to the engaging narrative that has preceded them. Nevertheless, they contain some items of real interest to us and should be noted briefly.

When the pilgrimage was completed and the covenant between Jacob and his God had been renewed once again, Jacob set out for Ephrath, or Bethlehem. In the course of this journey, Rachel gave birth to Jacob's twelfth son, Benjamin. Unhappily, Rachel died in childbirth and Jacob lost the wife he had loved most truly. Not long afterward, his father Isaac, who, it would seem, had been in ill-health for years, also "died and was gathered to his people, old and full of days; and his sons Esau and Jacob buried him" (*Gen. 35:29*). *Ch. 36* is a collection of lists of Esau's family, the ancestors of Edom, and was doubtless of greater interest to the original readers of Genesis than it is to us.

## Joseph

In the opening pages of this book, we asserted that the basic event in the history and religion of Israel was the Exodus from Egypt. The primary purpose of the story of Joseph is to tell us how the ancestors of Israel came to be in Egypt in the first place.

### JOSEPH SOLD INTO EGYPT

Joseph is one of the best-loved characters in the entire Bible. His virtuous conduct in Egypt leads us to think of him as a man without fault, who did nothing to deserve the hatred of his brothers. The writer of *Genesis*, while obviously holding Joseph in high regard, looks at the situation somewhat more objectively. It is true that Joseph's brothers treated him more harshly than he actually deserved, but it is also true that the picture we have of Joseph as a teenager is one of insufferable arrogance. Joseph, you will remember, was the first son born to Rachel, Jacob's favorite wife. Because of this attachment, and because he was born when Jacob was an old man, Joseph became the favored son. As a token of his love for him, Jacob presented Joseph with a lovely coat. The revised versions describe this garment as "a long robe with sleeves" (*37:3*). It is something of a disappointment to learn that this is a correct translation of the original Hebrew text since, for most of us, a long-sleeved robe will never match the image conjured up by the famous "coat of many colors", of the King James Version. In any case, the coat was a special dress garment, as distinguished from the cloaklike wrap which was usually worn. Naturally, this obvious favortism did little to endear Joesph to his brothers. Unfortunately, Joseph showed little interest in regaining their affection. He gave bad reports to his father concerning their activities (37:2) and boasted of dreams he had which implied that he would one day have the rule over the whole family. Finally, his brothers grew so indignant at his attitude that they plotted to kill him, planning to tell their father he had been slain by a wild beast. At the urging of Reuben, however, they altered their plans and sold him to a caravan of merchants who took him to Egypt, where he became the slave of Potiphar, the captain of the guard in Pharaoh's army.

### JUDAH AND TAMAR

The story of Joseph is interrupted here by the insertion of the strange affair between Judah and Tamar (*ch. 38*). The reason for its inclusion is something of a mystery, and its occurrence at this point in the narrative is even more baffling, but it does provide us with a glimpse of several interesting features of life in Canaan during the patriarchal period. Judah's eldest son, Er, died, having left no children to inherit his property. In such cases, it was customary for the brother or nearest relative of the deceased to assume the sexual responsibilities toward his widow, with the understanding that children born of this union would be counted as the rightful heirs of the deceased (*Deut. 25:5–10*). This is called the law of Levirate marriage, from *levir*, meaning "brother." For some reason, Onan, the oldest surviving brother, did not want to fulfill his obligations in this matter and, although he did have sexual relations with Tamar, Er's widow, he practiced *coitus interruptus* and

"spilled the semen on the ground, lest he should give offspring to his brother" (*38: 10*). For this faithless act, God slew Onan. Judah was reluctant to give this remaining son, Shelah, to Tamar, fearing that perhaps she had been responsible for the death of his first two sons. He promised her that Shelah would become her husband when he reached the age of marriage, but it is clear he did not intend to keep his promise.

Unable to obtain children through the customary process, Tamar devised a bold plan by which Judah himself would father her child. When she learned he was going to Timnah to shear sheep, she disguised herself as a prostitute and sat by the roadside where Judah would pass. The word translated "harlot" in this story implies that she was posing as one who was temporarily engaged in prostitution as part of a religious vow. This practice was strictly forbidden in the later Mosaic law, but is known to have been common in Babylon and Canaan. Judah had nothing of real value to give her at that time, but he left her his staff and his signet and cord as a pledge, to be redeemed when he sent her a kid from his flock. The signet was probably a cylindrical engraved seal which, when rolled over wax or soft clay, left an impression which served as the official signature of its owner. The cord mentioned was used to hang the seal about the neck. These items had little value for anyone except the owner, so Judah felt sure he would be able to redeem them. But Tamar saw them as a means of proving that the child she would bear would be a legitimate heir to the family property and did not give Judah the opportunity to reclaim them. When Tamar was found to be pregnant, Judah self-righteously announced that she should be put to death by burning, the severest form of execution available. Dramatically, she produced his signet and cord and staff, calling on him to admit that his failure

43

**A signet and cord.**
**The engraved signet left its owner's personal mark when rolled in soft clay.**

in providing her with a husband had driven her to behave in this way and that he was the father of her child. Despite the fact she had posed as a prostitute, Tamar is clearly regarded as the heroine, because her motive was to preserve the name of her deceased husband. Tamar gave birth to twins, Perez and Zerah. Perez is named in the genealogy of Jesus (*Matt. 1:3*).

### JOSEPH'S EARLY DAYS IN EGYPT

When the narrator picks up the story of Joseph again, we find that his abilities have caused him to be promoted to the position of overseer of Potiphar's house. As Joseph has matured, the arrogance of his adolescence has left him and he has acquired the noble character and dedication to God we commonly associate with him. When he rejected the amorous advances of his master's wife, she had him thrown into prison, on the false charge that he had tried to seduce her.

But even in prison God was with him and he became a trusted assistant to the chief jailer. While he was in jail, he correctly interpreted the dreams of two of his fellow prisoners. Later, when the Pharaoh had a dream which troubled him, Joseph was called upon to offer an interpretation. Joseph informed Pharaoh that the dream was a portent of a seven year famine which was to fall upon the land. Before this famine, however, there was to be a seven-year period of abundant harvest and prosperity which would enable the Egyptians to prepare for the approaching famine. The Pharaoh was overwhelmed by Joseph's wisdom and favor with his God, and appointed him as his personal assistant in administering the affairs of Egypt. Thus, in the course of thirteen years, the youth who entered Egypt as a slave now sat at the right hand of the Pharaoh.

When the period of famine arrived, Joseph's skillful administration had left Egypt prepared for the emergency. As was customary in times such as these, people poured in from the North and East in order to get food. Among these were the sons of Jacob, Joseph's brethren. Joseph displayed no real desire for revenge against his brothers, but, when he saw they did not recognize him, he could not resist the opportunity to manipulate them a bit. First, he spoke roughly with them and accused them of being spies. Then, he kept Simeon as a hostage until they should return from Canaan with his full brother, Benjamin, who had remained at home with his father.

Jacob was extremely reluctant to allow Benjamin to go to Egypt, but finally relented at Judah's urging. When they appeared before Joseph a second time, he prepared a feast for them and inquired of the health of his father. Still, he concealed his identity from them and always spoke through an interpreter. As they prepared to return home with their grain, Joseph instructed his steward to secrete his silver cup in the grain sack belonging to Benjamin. Before the brothers had gone very far, Joseph had them apprehended and brought back to him. When Benjamin's sack was found to contain the cup, Joseph announced that Benjamin would have to remain in Egypt at his slave. The brothers were dismayed. Judah, who had convinced his father of the safety of the mission, offered himself in Benjamin's place, pleading with Joseph that the shock of losing Benjamin would probably kill their father.

It is not possible to say just what lay behind all of Joseph's actions concerning his brethren, but when they spoke of their love for their father and their concern for his welfare, the bond of brotherhood overcame the last vestige of resentment. With uncontrollable sobs that could be heard throughout the royal buildings, Jacob made himself known to his brethren, who stood before him in speechless bewilderment which bordered on terror. When Joseph sensed their discomfort, he called them close to him and assured them they had no cause to be distressed. There was no reason for their fear, he told them, "for God sent me before you to preserve life . . . to preserve for you a remnant on earth, and to keep alive for you many survivors" (45:5, 7). This statement is characteristic of the theological outlook of the patriarchal narratives and for much of the rest of the Old Testament. God will be faithful to his promises. Despite whatever reverses and near disasters his people may suffer, there will always be a remnant left through which his will may be brought to fulfillment. First, it seemed incredible that Abraham and Sarah should have a son of their own. Then, it appeared as if that promised child would be sacrificed on Mt. Moriah. Even after Jacob became the father of twelve sons, there was reason to fear his entire clan would be wiped out by an angry Esau. Now, ten of these brothers have committed a crime of envy against their brother, but this, too, becomes a channel of God's blessing. So pervading is this idea that Joseph is led to declare: "so it was not you who sent me here, but God; and he has made me a father to Pharaoh and lord of all his house and ruler over all the land of Egypt" (45:8). If Joseph had not been sold into Egypt, the people of God would have starved in the great famine. Through God's providence, however, they were to live in comfort in the land of Goshen in the delta area of the Nile, which was truly "the best of all the land of Egypt" (45:20).

In *ch. 47*, we read of Joseph's wise, though somewhat harsh by modern standards, administration of Egypt during the years of famine. In return for food from the Pharaoh's granaries, men gave their money, their cattle, and their land; finally, they sold themselves into state slavery, preferring even this to death by starvation.

## Last Days of the Patriarchs

The remainder of the book of *Genesis* deals mainly with the last days of Jacob, now called Israel. Before his death, Israel pronounced the patriarchal blessing on his male descendants. First, he called Joseph's two sons, Manasseh and Ephraim. These were not the only grandchildren (50:21), but they were definitely regarded by the Israelites as more important than any of their cousins. When the tribal structure developed in Israel, there was no single tribe of Joseph, but two half-tribes of Manasseh and Ephraim. Next, Jacob summoned his twelve sons and made prophetic statements concerning them. Several of the sons, notably Reuben, Simeon, and Levi, were censured because of their past sins:

> Reuben, you are my first-born,
>   my might, and the first fruits of
>     my strength.

45

pre-eminent in pride and pre-eminent
    in power.
Unstable as water, you shall not
    have pre-eminence
because you went up to your
    father's bed;
then you defiled it—you went
    up to my couch!
Simeon and Levi are brothers;
    weapons of violence are their swords.
Cursed be their anger, for it is fierce;
    and their wrath, for it is cruel!
I will divide them in Jacob
    and scatter them in Israel.
        *—Genesis 49:3-5, 7*

Judah and Joseph received the words of greatest blessing:

Judah, your brothers shall praise you;
    your hand shall be on the neck
        of your enemies;
    your father's sons shall bow down
        before you.
The scepter shall not depart from Judah,
    nor the ruler's staff from between his feet,
until he comes to whom it belongs;
    and to him shall be the obedience
        of the peoples.
        *—Genesis 49:8, 10*
Joseph is a fruitful bough,
    a fruitful bough by a spring;

his branches run over the wall.
The archers fiercely attacked him.
    shot at him, and harassed him sorely;
yet his bow remained unmoved,
    his arms were made agile
by the hand of the Mighty One of
    Jacob.
The blessings of your father
    are mighty beyond the blessings
        of the eternal mountains,
    the bounties of the everlasting hills;
may they be on the head of Joseph,
    and on the brow of him who was
        separate from his brothers.
        *—Genesis 49:22-24, 26*

Although Joseph emerges as the hero among the twelve sons, the men who would bring the greatest blessings to Israel and to all humanity were to come from the tribe of Judah. The two most famous of Judah's descendants were, of course, David and Jesus.

The history of the patriarchs closes with an account of the deaths of Israel and Joseph. Though they did not live to see the promises to Abraham brought to fulfillment, both symbolically partook in the blessings by instructing their descendants to embalm their bodies and carry them back to the Promised Land.

# PART TWO

## *Israel Becomes a Nation*

# 3

# The Exodus

*Moses leads the people of God
across the Sea to Sinai*

## HISTORICAL BACKGROUND

### The Period of the Sojourn in Egypt

The Bible provides us with precious little information concerning the period of the sojourn of Israel's ancestors in Egypt, the period extending from Joseph's sale into Egyptian slavery to the Exodus under Moses. In fact, we cannot be absolutely certain even as to the centuries covered by the sojourn. Unfortunately, at least from the historian's point of view, *Genesis* and *Exodus* make no attempt to identify the Pharaoh under whom Joseph served or the Pharaoh at the time of the Exodus. We can, however, on the basis of the findings of archaeology, make an educated guess as to the approximate dates of the sojourn, and reconstruct a picture of what was going on in the Near Eastern world during this period.

In about 1720 B.C. Egypt was engulfed by a tide of Western Semitic invaders who were called Hyksos, or "Rulers of Foreign Lands." These Hyksos were skilled warriors and, with the aid of the horse-drawn chariot which they introduced, were able to rout the native rulers in Egypt and to establish a strong government that stood for about a century and a half.

It seems quite probable that the story of Joseph is to be placed during the rule of the Hyksos. For one thing, the first Hyksos King, Salatis, moved the capital from Thebes, in upper Egypt, to Avaris, in the delta area not far from Goshen. The account of the migration of Joseph's family to the land of Goshen seems to indicate it was not far from the royal capital. When the Hyksos rule was overthrown in the sixteenth century, Avaris was destroyed and the capital was moved back to Thebes; therefore, the natural assumption is that Joseph was in power at some time during this 150 year period. Furthermore, the very fact that the Hyksos were themselves foreigners and Semites helps to explain how a foreigner and a Semite such as Joseph could have risen to such a position of eminence. Many other characteristics of this period serve to confirm details in the Joseph story, lending considerable weight to its historical authenticity. Joseph's title as "overseer over the house" of Potiphar (*Gen. 39:4*) is known to have been in current usage. Similarly, the titles "chief of the butlers" and "chief of the bakers", which were worn by Joseph's

Wall painting of an Egyptian supterintendent of public granaries.

fellow-prisoners (*Gen. 40:2*) are used in Egyptian writings to refer to officials in the royal palace. There is even some evidence for the release of prisoners on Pharaoh's birthday (*Gen. 40:20*). Joseph's position in the administration of Pharaoh corresponds exactly to the twin office of Minister of the Interior and Superintendent of Granaries. Even the gifts presented by Pharaoh at the time of his "inauguration" are entirely in keeping with this period. Egyptian archives tell of seven-year famines and of the influx of foreigners during such periods and of the distribution of food from the royal granaries. This correspondence between the Biblical record and Egyptian documents does not *prove* the Biblical account is true. It is not likely we shall ever possess the kind of "proof" some would seek. It does, however,

provide us with good evidence that there is nothing necessarily improbable about the story of Israel's descent into Egypt.

### THE EIGHTEENTH DYNASTY

During the first half of the sixteenth century B.C., the native leaders in Egypt began to revolt against the Hyksos government. By 1570, Egypt was once more ruled by Egyptians. In about 1550 B.C., the Hyksos were completely expelled from Egypt by Amosis, the first Pharaoh of the powerful Eighteenth Dynasty which ruled Egypt for almost 250 years. Utilizing chariotry and the superior weaponry developed by the Hyksos, the Egyptians began to extend their borders northward. Within a century, Egypt's holdings stretched from the Fourth Cataract of the Nile in the south to the Euphrates river in the North. This brought Egypt face to face with the two major powers in the North, the Kingdom of Mittani, which extended across Upper Mesopotamia, and the Hittite Kingdom, situated around the Halys River, about ninety miles from modern Ankara, Turkey.

### THE MITANNIAN KINGDOM

For a period of about 150 years, beginning around 1750 B.C., Northern Mesopotamia had been the scene of invasion and infiltration by large numbers of non-Semitic people. By 1500 B.C. they had established the kingdom of Mitanni and had control of all the land between Mesopotamia and Media. In the Bible, the people of Mitanni are called Horites (*Gen. 14:6; Deut. 2:12*, etc.), but in other sources they are usually called Hurrians. The ruling class was Indo-Iranian and worshipped the Vedic gods of India: Mithra, Indra, and Varuna.

Pharaoh Thutmosis III (*c. 1496–1435 B.C.*) conquered much of the Mitannian land west of the Euphrates, but instead of trying to push deeper into Mitannian territory, ne-

Pharaoh Akhenaton (1375-1356 B.C.),
worshiper of the sun-god Aton.

Nefertiti, the beautiful wife of
Pharaoh Akhenaton.

gotiated an alliance with the Mitannians
that benefited both sides and established a
balance of power for several decades.

### THE RISE OF THE HITTITES

The Hittite Kingdom had been in existence since the seventeenth century B.C.,
but, except for brief moments of power, had
never really played much of a role in world
politics. Near the end of the fifteenth century B.C., however, the Hittites began to
gain in strength and aggressiveness. By 1370
B.C., the Hittites had reduced Mitanni to the
status of a vassal state and had begun to
move into Egyptian-held Syrian lands.

### INTERNAL DISSENSION IN EGYPT

The Hittite encroachments on Egyptian
territory came at a time when Egypt was
preoccupied with domestic problems and
unable to launch any effective resistance
movement. The Pharaoh during this period was the frail Amenhotep, IV, whose
queen, incidentally, was the beautiful Nefertiti. The official god of Egypt was Amon,
but Amenhotep became a devoted convert to the cult of Aton, the sun-god who
was worshipped as the creator of all things
and the only true God. This was in sharp
contrast to the contemporary polytheism,
which had different gods for different
aspects of life. Amenhotep's zeal for Aton
was so great that he changed his name
to Akhen*aton* ("it pleases Aton") and built a
new capital city which he named Akhet*aton*
("the horizon of Aton"). Unfortunately for
Egypt, the young King's religious fervor
outdistanced his political prudence. The

51

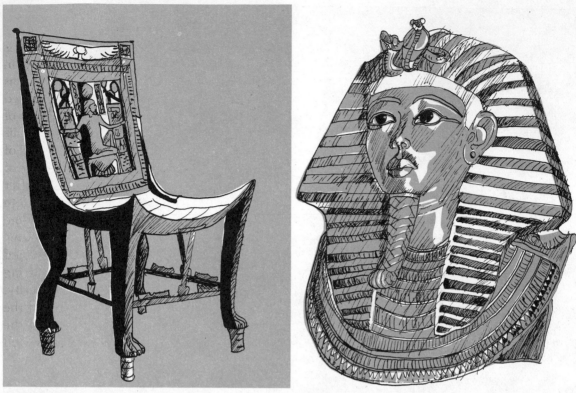

**Objects from the tomb of Pharaoh Tut-enkh-amon (King Tut):
a chair of cedar wood and gold and a golden mask that covered the mummy.**

new cult had little appeal for the unsophisticated masses and was openly opposed by the official priests and the conservative forces in the government. Letters that have been recovered from Tell el-Amarna (the site of the ruins of Akhetaton) reveal the damaging effect all this had on Egypt's political and military stability. It was probably the primary cause of the eventual downfall of the Eighteenth Dynasty. The heretic king was succeeded by a son-in-law, Tut-enkh-aton, the legendary King Tut whose tomb was discovered in A.D. 1922, still full of its precious furniture. Just as Amenhotep's changing his name to Akhenaton signified royal favor toward the cult of Aton, so the changing of Tut-enkh-*aton* to Tut-enkh-*amon* marks the official shift back to the old familiar Egyptian deity. Tut-

enkh-amon was followed by two insignificant figures within a period of two years. Complete collapse of Egyptian government seemed imminent. But, as has so often been the case in the course of the world's history, the slipping reins were grasped by the sure hands of a general in the royal army. This general was Horemheb, who took control of the government in 1340 B.C. After eradicating possible sources of internal strife such as the remaining supporters of the Aton heresy, Horemheb brought Egypt back into the ranks of world powers.

### THE NINETEENTH DYNASTY

Horemheb ruled until 1310 B.C., at which time he was succeeded by another general, Rameses, a descendant of the old Hyksos rulers. Rameses ruled less than two years

(1310–1309 B.C.), but he was able to secure the throne for his son Seti I, thus becoming the founder of the Nineteenth Dynasty. The primary task which lay before the Pharaohs of this dynasty was the recovery of territory which had been lost during the period of instability. The Hittites had overrun North Syria and invaders from the desert to the East had been harassing Palestine. The Amarna letters (those found at Tell el-Amarna) reflect the despair of local rulers at the failure of the Egyptian government to provide any aid against these invasions. Seti I, (1309–1290 B.C.) was able to regain control of Palestine and to consolidate his power in Phoeniciea and parts of Syria. He managed to avoid open war with the Hittites by means of a treaty he made with their king, Muwattali. But this merely postponed the inevitable. In the fifth year of the reign of Seti's son and successor, Rameses II (1290–1224 B.C.), Egyptian troops began the long trek into Syria. At Kadesh, they were ambushed by Hittite forces and suffered severe losses. As a result of Rameses' courage and military skill, the Egyptians managed a victory, but were forced to retire to Egypt to lick their wounds. A number of skirmishes took place in the next decade, but neither the Egyptians nor the Hittites were able to gain a real advantage in the conflict. Finally, when Hattusilis III (1275–1250 B.C.) acceded to the Hittite throne, a non-aggression pact was made between the two nations. Copies of this treaty, in both Egyptian and Babylonian, have been found in Thebes, the capital of Egypt, and in Khattushash, the Hittite capital.

It is worth noting that it was about this time that Assyria, which had been freed from Mitannian control, as a result of the Hittite conquests, began to push westward. Over the next six centuries this awakening nation was to become the dominant political force in all of Western Asia.

## The Date of the Exodus

If the chronology followed in this book is correct, our sketch of the salient points in the history of the Ancient Near East has brought us to the time when God performed the Mighty Act which stood at the heart of the religion of Israel—the deliverance of his people from Egyptian bondage. The book of *Exodus* picks up the story of the people of God at a point several hundred years after the descent of Joseph and his family into Egypt. Egypt had experienced revolution, religious dissension, and near chaos. Now, the stable nineteenth Dynasty had gained control and Egypt was once again enjoying a period of relative peace and prosperity. The attitude of the new regime toward the band of foreigners who had inhabited the land of Goshen for four centuries is well

The child Rameses II being guarded by the falcon-god.

53

An Egyptian wall painting of about 2,000 B.C.
depicting the process of brickmaking.

summed up in the phrase, "Now there arose a new king over Egypt, who did not know Joseph" (*Ex. 1:8*). No longer was there any recollection of the wise young man who had saved Egypt from economic disaster through his ability to interpret dreams and his administrative prudence. No longer were the ancestors of Israel treated as a privileged class. To the Pharaoh of the Nineteenth Dynasty, the motley group of squatters in the Delta land were simply a minority problem to be dealt with and exploited to the advantage of the government. Therefore, they were drafted into state slavery and put to work in government building projects. Thus, in the early years of the thirteenth century B.C., we find the people of God hard at work, making bricks for the building of the "store-cities" of Pithom and Raamses (*Ex. 1:11*).

In all fairness, it should be noted that not every Old Testament scholar accepts the theory that the events of *Exodus* are to be placed in the thirteenth century B.C. In the light of what we know of this period from ancient documents and other archaeological discoveries, however, it seems to us that this is by far the most satisfactory hypothesis. In the first place, this date fits nicely with the date we assigned to Joseph. We have already asserted that Joseph probably came to prominence under the Hyksos rule in the latter part of the eighteenth century, per-

haps around 1710 B.C. If this assertion is correct, then the 430 year period mentioned in *Ex. 12:40* would place the Exodus somewhere near 1280 B.C. This in itself is, of course, insufficient evidence for the theory we are adopting here, since the dates of Joseph are by no means beyond question. Fortunately, this does not constitute our strongest evidence. The Pharaohs of the Nineteenth Dynasty are known to have engaged in an extensive building program in the old Hyksos capital of Avaris, which Rameses II renamed Raamses ("house of Rameses") when he made it his capital. There is every reason to believe that the work project referred to in *Ex. 1:11* was part of this same program of construction. As was pointed out earlier, the land of Goshen, in which the Israelites were settled, was near Avaris. It was natural that the Pharaohs should recruit workers from the surrounding region. In support of this, Egyptian texts reveal that *Habiru* made up a substantial part of the working force on these royal projects. While no positive identification can be made between *Habiru* and Hebrew, we have already seen that Israel's ancestors almost certainly belonged to this unsettled class (p. 23f). There is also evidence that an enormous number of Semitic words passed into the Egyptian vocabulary during this period, in-

54

dicating extensive social intercourse between Egyptians and natives of Palestine.
Admittedly, none of these circumstances is
proof positive of a thirteenth century setting
for the events narrated in *Exodus,* but, when
taken together, and when viewed in the
light of the probable date of the conquest
(see p. 97f), the evidence seems to favor this
date, and indicates that Rameses II (1290–
1224 B.C.) was the Pharaoh of the Exodus.

## Moses

As we have emphasized repeatedly, the
Exodus from Egypt was regarded by Israel
as the most dramatic of God's acts on behalf
of his people. It was the central act in the
fulfillment of the promises he had made to
the patriarchs. It was the primary material
of faith. God's purpose in delivering Israel
from Egypt was to create for himself a people. It is true, of course, that they were already his people, in the sense that they were
descendants of Abraham, to whom the
promises had originally been given. It is perhaps true that at least a few of them clung
firmly to these promises through the centuries of the Egyptian sojourn. But they cannot really be called a people until they were
summoned to follow God by the man he appointed to be his representative. That man
was Moses. Moses was more than a courageous leader, able to convince a band of
slaves of the possibility of escape. He was

the interpreter of God's mighty acts, the
mediator between God and man who made
known the meaning of the wonderful things
that were being accomplished by the hand
of God. Therefore, it is important that we
know something about this man who stands
at the fountainhead of the religion of Israel.

Moses was born at a time when the Hebrews had become such a troublesome minority problem that the Pharaoh decided to
kill all newborn male children. There is no
way of knowing how many infants were
slain as a consequence of this cruel order.
But this is not of primary importance. What
is important is that at least one infant survived. A Hebrew woman named Jochabed
contrived to save her baby by playing on
the kindness of the daughter of the Pharaoh.
Placing her infant son in a little boat constructed of bulrushes and slime, she sent him
sailing near the place where Pharaoh's
daughter was accustomed to bathe. According to plan, the princess discovered the baby
and adopted him as her son. The name she
gave to him was Moses. The narrative tells
us that she named him this because of the
similarity between the name and the verb
"to draw out," alluding to her act of having
drawn him out of the water. Whatever her
reasons for giving him this name, it was well
known among Egyptians, having been a
part of the name of several Pharaohs—
namely, Thut*mosis* and Ra*meses*.

55

While Baby Moses floated down the river in his crude little boat, his sister Miriam stood at the water's edge and watched anxiously. As soon as she saw that Pharaoh's daughter would keep the child, she ran to her and asked if she would like a nursemaid from among the Hebrew women. Pharaoh's daughters agreed and the woman was brought to the palace. She was, of course, Moses' own mother, Jochabed. Thus, even though he was reared in the midst of Egypt's royal family, Moses learned the values of the people of God.

### THE FLIGHT TO MIDIAN

We can imagine that, as Moses grew to manhood, it was not always easy for him to know just where his loyalties lay. Probably, he loved the members of the royal family and many of the Egyptians at Pharaoh's court. At the same time, he was disturbed that his true kinsmen, the Hebrews, were being treated like animals by the taskmasters under whom they worked. One day Moses saw an Egyptian beating a Hebrew. In the heat of the moment, he struck the Egyptian and killed him. A rash act like this was certain to get Moses in trouble if the Pharaoh heard about it. When he found out that the Hebrews did not trust him and might report the killing to the Egyptian officers, Moses fled to the region of Midian, in the peninsula between the branches of the Red Sea. There he met and married Zipporah, the daughter of Reuel (or Jethro; See *Ex. 2: 16; 3:1*), who is described as a "priest of Midian."

### THE BURNING BUSH

One day, while tending Reuel's flocks, Moses saw a strange sight on Mt. Horeb, or Sinai (*3:1*).

> The angel of the Lord appeared to him in a flame of fire out of the midst of a bush; and he looked, and lo, the bush was burning, yet it was not consumed.          —*Exodus 3:2*

Moses "turned aside to see" this marvelous sight and recognized it as a symbol of God's presence. There on that desert mountain Moses entered into a dialogue with the Holy One, a dialogue that was forever to place its mark on the faith and history of the people of God. There Moses learned that God is not some uncaring being who watches the events of history in a bemused fashion. On the contrary, he is fully aware of oppression and suffering of his people and is willing to enter into the stream of human history in order to work out his redemptive purposes. To this end, he summoned Moses as the agent through whom he would make known his intentions and his demands. Moses' specific task would be to represent God before Pharaoh and to lead the chosen people from Egypt. Once free, he was to bring them to that very mountain, where the covenant between God and the people Israel would be formally sealed.

### THE NAME OF GOD

Somewhat overcome by the enormity of this commission, Moses asked a very practical question. When he confronted the Israelites with this message of deliverance, who should he say had sent him? What was the name of this God who spoke from the bush? In Old Testament times, a name was believed to reveal something of the fundamental character of its bearer. Moses felt it would be necessary to identify the source of his message by name. The answer God gave to Moses was a cryptic "I AM WHO I AM" or "I WILL BE WHAT I WILL BE."

The Hebrew phrase used here is subject to a number of possible translations and each of these is capable of a wide range of interpretations. Quite possibly, the phrase is intended to heighten the sense of the infinite capacity of him who bears the name. Then, in *3:15*, God reveals to Moses the name by which he is to be known. There he identifies himself as "The Lord the God of your fathers, the God of Abraham, the God of Isaac, and the God of Jacob." The Hebrew word translated "The Lord" in most English versions is composed of the four letters YHWH (or JHWH). This is the third person singular of *hayah,* the verb used in the phrase I AM WHO I AM. It is now fairly well established that these four letters constituted what the Israelites regarded as the proper name of God. The ancient Hebrew alphabet had no vowels, so it is impossible to be absolutely certain as to how this so-called Sacred Tetragrammaton (literally, "four letters") was pronounced. However, most Hebrew scholars believe that the original pronunciation was quite close to Yahweh, or Jahweh. In the later period of Israel's history, especially after the exile, an aura of almost magical holiness enshrouded the name, causing Jews to avoid using it in ordinary conversation. In its place they substituted the Hebrew word *Adhonai,* meaning "Lord" or "Master." When vowels were eventually added to the Hebrew text of the Bible in the sixth and seventh centuries A.D., the vowels of *Adhonai* were combined with the consonants of YHWH. The result was the familiar "Jehovah." This has been hallowed by centuries of use, but it is a pure invention and almost certainly bears little resemblance to the original form. In this book, we shall regularly use the form Yahweh to designate the God of Israel.

The overall significance of all this wordplay over the name of God was probably that the nature of God was not something that could be encapsuled in a single name but something that would be progressively revealed in the course of his participation in the historical processes. Moses' task would not be to describe the nature of the God he proclaimed so much as to help Israel perceive his presence in the historical crisis it was to experience.

## God vs. Pharaoh—the Plagues

Still, Moses was in doubt as to his ability to accomplish the great work for which God had called him. He feared the people would ridicule his claim that Yahweh, the God of the Fathers, had appeared to him. To calm his fears, God granted him several miraculous feats which would serve to convince the people. Even this could not overcome Moses' uneasiness about his qualifications. The man needed for this great task was a man who could weld the people together through the burning power of his eloquence. Moses thought of himself as "slow of speech and of tongue" (4:10). He would say the wrong thing, or stammer in reply to crucial questions. The narrative tells us that the Lord grew somewhat exasperated with Moses at this point, but agreed to allow Aaron, Moses' brother, to serve as his "mouth," declaring his words to the congregation. Thus supported, Moses and his family left their Midianite kinsmen and set out for Egypt. After he and Aaron proclaimed the message of God to the enslaved Israelites, attesting to its truth by the wonders God enabled them to perform, they were ready to confront the Pharaoh himself.

When they came face to face with this most powerful of the world's leaders, Moses and Aaron declared to him in the simplest terms the will of God: "Let my people go." The specific request they presented to Pharaoh was not for complete emancipation, but for permission to go into the wilderness to observe a religious festival. To the Pharaoh, this was pure foolishness. Such an action would mean at least a week's delay in the building program and might set a troublesome example for other slaves. Not only would he refuse this request, but he would inflict even greater burdens upon the slaves, to discourage anyone else who might be entertaining such ideas.

The specific task in which the Israelites were engaged was brickmaking. The bricks they made were not simply mud blocks, but contained straw to give them strength. Heretofore, the Egyptians had provided the necessary straw; now, as punishment for the bold request of Moses and Aaron, the Israelites were to be required to gather their own straw, but were still expected to produce the same number of bricks as before.

Naturally, this increased burden did little to enhance Moses' position of leadership among his people. The people were openly disgusted with Moses and he was in dismay at Yahweh's apparent failure to make good on his promises. But the Lord revealed to Moses that this was all part of his plan. He had chosen Pharaoh as an instrument to magnify his own power and majesty. He was allowing Pharaoh to assert his own authority to the fullest extent, in order to dramatize the complete superiority of the power of Yahweh. Nothing, not even the king of Egypt, could withstand the arm of the Lord.

Thus reassured, Moses and Aaron confronted Pharaoh a second time. As a sign that they had been sent by God, Aaron "cast down his rod before Pharaoh and his servants, and it became a serpent" (7:10). Somehow, the Egyptian magicians, the custodians of the power of the Egyptian gods, were able to duplicate the feat, causing their rods to become serpents also. We are told that Aaron's serpent devoured those of the court magicians, but Pharaoh was still not impressed. But this was far from the greatest of the "signs and wonders" Moses and Aaron would perform. It was, in fact, only a preliminary to the classic contest between God and Pharaoh which we commonly refer to as The Ten Plagues.

The account of the Plagues is a gripping dramatic story. With each plague, the Pharaoh moves closer to granting the request of the Israelites, but, at the last minute, goes back upon his word and refuses to allow them to leave. Everything builds toward the dramatic climax when Pharaoh is revealed as absolutely powerless before the God of Israel. The battle lines are clearly drawn. On one side stand God and his representatives, Moses and Aaron; on the other stand Pharaoh and his magicians. When Moses and Aaron initiate the first two plagues, the turning of water to blood and the plague of frogs, the magicians are able to duplicate them through their "secret arts." On the remaining plagues—gnats, flies, the disease of the cattle, boils, hail, locusts, darkness, and the death of the firstborn—the magicians are unable to perform similar wonders.

This matter of the Egyptian magician's being able to duplicate even the first few of the plagues has often posed a problem for Bible students. Part of the confusion arises from the fact that our understanding of a miracle is almost totally different from the understanding possessed by the early Israelite. We think of a miracle as an interruption or setting aside of Natural Law. The ancient Israelite had very little idea of anything called "Natural Law;" that is, he did not conceive of nature as a realm subject to a set of impersonal, static laws ordained by God. For him, all that happened in nature was an expression of God's providence. God was in complete control; therefore, nothing he did could really be designated as *un*natural or *super*natural. God's hand could be discerned in everything that took place. There were certain events, however, which had the special character of a "sign" or "wonder." In these happenings, the eye of faith could discern God's acting in an *extraordinary* fashion in order to give men some assurance of his presence and activity among them. The plagues, at least the first nine of them, are in this class of "signs and wonders" (7:3). They would not convince everyone who witnessed them; they did not convince the

Pharaoh, against whom they were primarily directed. Each of them, save the death of the firstborn, can be explained naturalistically. Scholars have shown that even the sequence of the plagues can be accounted for scientifically. Certain organisms in the Nile River have been known to turn its waters almost blood red at the season of flooding. On such occasions, the waters become fetid and unfit for consumption. It is not uncommon for the flooding to lead to a proliferation of frogs, gnats, and other insects, which could easily lead to various sorts of diseases in cattle and humans. Hailstorms are not unusual in the month following the flooding of the Nile, nor are hordes of locusts brought in on the wind. This same west wind has been known to fill the air with particles of dust to such an extent that the sky becomes dark with "a darkness to be felt" (*10:21*).

We cannot be sure what would have been our attitude had we witnessed these plagues. If a similar sequence of pestilence were to occur today, some would doubtless call it an act of God's judgment. Most would dismiss it as an unfortunate coincidence of catastrophe. It is difficult to know just where we would have stood had we been in Egypt in 1280 B.C. But we may be sure of one thing. To the oppressed slaves in the land of Goshen—the people of God—the plagues were a religious sign that left no doubt as to the supremacy of Yahweh over man and nature.

The last plague, the death of the firstborn of all Egyptian life, cannot be rationalized or glibly explained away as a "natural" occurrence. If the Biblical record of what happened is accurate, then none but God can have been behind it. It was this conviction that transformed a band of homeless state slaves into the covenant people of Yahweh. Before the plagues began, God revealed to Moses that part of his purpose in sending them was that "the Egyptians shall know that I am the Lord" (*7:5*). It is as if the events of the coming days are to be viewed as the showdown conflict between Yahweh and the god's of Egypt. An element of this is seen in the efforts of the Egyptian magicians to duplicate the feats performed by Moses and Aaron. The final crushing blow, the blow that shows the gods of Egypt to be utterly powerless, is struck in the Death of the Firstborn. At the midnight hour, when the gods of Egypt were believed to gain a mighty victory over the hostile forces of darkness, their complete helplessness to defend their subjects would become clear. The "great cry" that would go up throughout Egypt would be not only a sign of mourning for the firstborn, but a signal of the death of Egypt's gods.

## The Lord's Passover

The tenth plague, the death of the firstborn of Egypt, was the occasion for the establishment of the most sacred of all Israelite religious observances—Passover. Yahweh's desire was not merely to release a group of slaves with whom he had enjoyed some association. He sought to create a community which would, because of these mighty acts, worship him as its sovereign Lord. As a means to assure the perpetual memory of their deliverance from slavery, the Lord gave to Moses and Aaron instructions for the Passover celebration (*Ex. 12*).

Since the release from Egypt would be the beginning of a new life for the Israelites, it was fitting that the month in which it took place should be the first month in the Hebrew calendar. This month was known as Abib. It corresponds roughly to our March-April. On the tenth day of this month, the head of each Israelite household selected a male lamb a year old. Four nights later, in the early evening of the same night the Lord was to slay the sons of Egypt, each family killed its lamb and poured the blood into a

59

hollowed out place, or basin, at the threshold of the house. Then, with a leafy plant called hyssop, this blood was sprinkled on the doorposts and lintel (the crossbar at the top of the door) of the house, as a symbolic protection against the destroying hand of the Lord.

After they completed the sprinkling ceremony, each family retired into its own house to await the dreadful passing over of the Lord. That night they roasted the lamb and ate it. What a strange feast it was! Instead of the leisurely comfort we associate with a special meal such as Thanksgiving, the Passover meal was eaten in a hurry. Their robes, which would ordinarily be draped loosely about them, were arranged and tied in readiness for a journey. Each man wore his sandals, although it was customary to go barefoot inside the house. To complete the picture of readiness to go on a journey, they ate with a walking staff in one hand.

In later years the Passover was linked with the Feast of Unleavened bread, which began with the Passover meal on the fourteenth day of the month and continued through the evening of the twenty-first day. During this period, no bread could be eaten that contained any leaven. The immediate practical reason for this was the simple fact that in their haste to escape from Egyptians, the Israelites had no time to stop long enough for leavened bread to rise before cooking it. But it also had symbolic value. In both the Old and New Testaments, leaven is a symbol for corruption and sinfulness. The removal of all leaven from the house symbolized purifying of one's heart in readiness for the confrontation with God.

Because of its simple beauty, because of the deep significance of the act which it remembers, the Passover is still celebrated by the sons of Israel 3,200 years after its institution. It is one of the few religious or natural holidays that have not degenerated into a

vulgar display or gross commercialism. It had, and still has, some curious aspects. How curious the children in the households of the Israelites must have been to have seen their parents eating while dressed for a trip. And how curious they would be in generations to come, when they knew no journey was planned, no danger near. How strange it must be to modern Jewish children when for the first time they see their father wear a hat to the supper table, in place of the old sandals and staff. Moses was able to foresee all this. It was, in fact, part of the abiding worth of the Passover service. With this in mind, he told the elders of Israel:

> And when your children say to you, "What do you mean by this service?" you shall say, "It is the sacrifice of the Lord's passover, for he *passed over* the houses of the people of Israel in Egypt, when he slew the Egyptians but spared our houses."
> —*Exodus 12:26, 27*

And the people bowed their heads and worshiped the Lord.

## The Exodus

### THE DEFEAT OF PHARAOH

At midnight the Lord smote all the first-born in the land of Egypt, from the first-born of Pharaoh who sat on his throne to the first-born of the captive who was in the dungeon, and all the first-born of the cattle.
> —*Exodus 12:29*

This was too much for even the hard hearted Pharaoh. Egypt needed slaves, but it was clear she could not afford to keep these Israelites. The picture is a dramatic one. Pharaoh had gone to bed several hours earlier, perhaps satisfied that he had finally gotten through the worst of this irksome Israelite trouble. Then shortly after midnight, he is awakened with the news that his first-born son, the son he had groomed to take his place as ruler of all Egypt, was dead, slain by the God of the Israelites. Soon he learns that every household in Egypt has suffered a similar tragedy. The grieving father, the distraught monarch, the bewildered worshiper of defeated gods sends for Moses and Aaron. In marked contrast to his previous cyncial treatment of their requests, he begs them to leave Egypt as quickly as possible, then adds in a pathetic voice, "and bless me also!"

As dawn breaks the people of Israel, led by Moses and Aaron, begin the journey to Mt. Sinai. Now, they are a rather loosely organized group of refugees from state slavery. Soon they shall become the "sons of the covenant," the people of God.

### THE LONG WAY AROUND

The shortest route to the land of Canaan lay along the coast of the Mediterranean sea, through the area later settled by the Philistines. But there were Egyptian outposts all along this road and the Israelites were not ready for a pitched battle with trained soldiers. So, led by a pillar of cloud in the daytime and a pillar of fire at night, they set out toward the wilderness to the southeast.

After a short period of thinking about what the loss of the slave force would mean to the economy of Egypt, the Pharaoh decided to try to recapture them. It is somewhat baffling as to why a group of 600,000 men (*Ex. 12:37*) should be terrified by a few hundred charioteers, but the narrative tells us this was the case. Perhaps it was their lack of organization or their inexperience in fighting that gave rise to their fear.* In any case, when the Israelites saw they were pinned between water and the advancing Egyptian army, they turned their fear into an angry attack on Moses:

> Is it because there are no graves in Egypt that you have taken us away to die in the wilderness? What have you done to us, in bringing us out of Egypt? Is not this what we said to you in Egypt, 'Let us alone and let us serve the Egyptians'? For it would have been better for us to serve the Egyptians than to die in the wilderness. —*Exodus 14:11-12*

When Moses asked the Lord for his help, he was told that this was but another opportunity to convince the exiles of his power and "to get glory over Pharaoh and all his host." Then as Moses stood with his hand stretched out over the sea, Yahweh drove the waters back with a strong east wind and enabled the people to cross over on dry ground.

### RED SEA OR REED SEA?

You may have noticed that we have not yet given the name of this sea. But perhaps you did not notice, since the name is so familiar you probably supplied it yourself. Everyone knows it is the Red Sea. Everyone, that is, but the ancient Israelite who first wrote this story in the original Hebrew. The Hebrew text, from which our Old Testament is translated, has the words *yam suph*, which mean "Sea of Reeds." During the period of the Great Dispersion of the Jews, in the third century B.C., the Hebrew text was translated into Greek, for the benefit of Jews who could no longer read Hebrew. This translation is called the Septuagint. It was used widely in the time in which Jesus and the apostles lived. Often, New Testament quotations of Old Testament passages are from this translation. This translation was

---

*This difficulty has caused scholars to conclude that this number is either a mistake made in later copies of the original text or an intentional exaggeration by some later writer. They contend this conclusion is supported by the fact that 603,550 *fighting men* (*Num. 2:32*) would imply the total population was at least two or three million. It is questionable that either the land of Goshen or Canaan could support such a horde, or that two midwives (*Ex. 1:15–20*) could serve such a population adequately. We do not possess all the knowledge we should like to have about this matter and must therefore reserve final judgment.

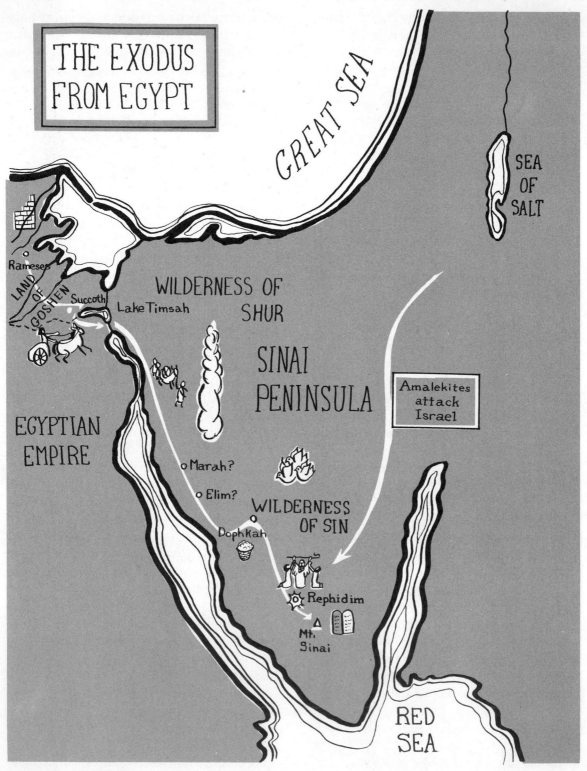

THE EXODUS FROM EGYPT

GREAT SEA

SEA OF SALT

Rameses

LAND OF GOSHEN

Succoth

Lake Timsah

WILDERNESS OF SHUR

SINAI PENINSULA

EGYPTIAN EMPIRE

Amalekites attack Israel

o Marah?

o Elim?

Dophkah

WILDERNESS OF SIN

Rephidim

Mt. Sinai

RED SEA

The route of the Exodus.

extremely valuable in its time, and is still a tool of real use to Biblical scholars. It does, however, contain a number of known mistakes. These are easy to find once we compare the Hebrew and Greek texts. One such mistake has to do with this sea through which the Israelites passed. When the Greek translator was working on this passage, he either misread the Hebrew text or decided that the writer had really meant the Red Sea. So, in his version, he wrote Red Sea instead of the correct Reed Sea. Although our English Bibles are translated from the original Hebrew, we have gotten so used to reading Red Sea in this story that it has usually been retained. In some of the latest translations, however, it is being correctly translated Reed Sea or Sea of Reeds.

Actually, it is something of a relief not to have to insist that the Sea in question was the Red Sea as we know it. As our map (p. 62) shows, even the northernmost portion of the Red Sea is far enough south that it would have taken several days to get there. In addition, geographical references in the story fit much better with a location to the north of the Red Sea. For example, Baal-zephon, the place where the Israelites camped before crossing the sea (*Ex. 14:1*), has been identified by archaeologists. It is located only a short distance to the east of Rameses, far north of the Red Sea. For a long while, scholars tried to overcome the geographical difficulty by claiming that the western arm of the Red Sea once reached much farther north than it now does, but this is no longer generally believed. Fortunately, the difficulty is resolved simply by reading what the Bible said in the first place. But this does not completely satisfy the map-maker. If it is not Red Sea, but Reed Sea, where shall we find our Reed Sea? Fortunately, we have a pretty good idea about this. It is now generally agreed that the Reed Sea is to be identified with a

swampy area on the eastern section of Lake Timsah, an extension of the present-day Gulf of Suez. This section of the lake fits the geographical requirements of the story. Also, it is filled with papyrus reeds and could justly be called *yam suph*. Incidentally, as a further mark against the traditional view, the Red sea does not contain such reeds.

### "A STRONG EAST WIND"

*Exodus 14:21* tells us that the Israelites were able to escape across this marshy lake because "the Lord drove the sea back by a strong east wind all night, and made the sea dry land, and the waters were divided." On several occasions, men have seen the waters of this region pushed back by such a wind. We do not mean to imply by this that this was a perfectly natural occurrence. We believe it was a miraculous act of God as surely as did the ancient Israelites. But the miracle was not merely in the drying up of the lake to allow Israel a passage. The case is quite similar to that of most of the ten plagues. It was not that a horde of locusts or an abundance of frogs or a cattle disease was in itself miraculous. Egyptians had seen all these things before, and would see them again. The miracle was that they came at a particular time and for a particular purpose. God's time and God's purpose. The same seems to hold true in the separation of the waters of the Reed Sea. The miracle was that God used the natural power of the wind to serve his divine purposes at that particular time. As was the case with the plagues, it would have been possible for a bystander to have interpreted the event as merely a remarkable piece of bad luck. But Israel knew that Yahweh was in the midst of his people.

### THE DEFEAT OF PHARAOH'S ARMY

When the Egyptian charioteers tried to follow the fleeing slaves, their horses and chariots bogged down in the swampy lake bottom. Before they could escape, the Lord allowed the winds to subside and all those who had ridden out were drowned. We should be careful to note that this does not mean the entire military force of the Egyptian army was lost in the Reed Sea. The loss was certainly an important one, but Egypt still had sufficient military strength to maintain her dominant position in world affairs.

Egyptian records make no mention of the escape of the Israelites. This may be because of the embarrassment involved in defeat at the hands of unarmed slaves. Again, it may be simply because the Egyptians did not think it was important enough to record. After all, slaves had escaped before, and battles had been lost before. In short, we just do not know how the Egyptians reacted to the events of the Exodus. But we can have few doubts about the response of the community of Israel itself. For these people —the people of God—the Exodus inspired the same awe and reverence as the Cross and the Empty Tomb do for Christians. The wondrous events connected with the Exodus showed Yahweh to be a God who had supreme control over man and nature. He was a God who could use the weak and downtrodden to defeat the powerful and haughty. He was a God who showed redemptive love and grace to a people unable to offer rich gifts in return. It is no wonder that throughout her history Israel looked to the Exodus as a source of comfort and inspiration. It is no wonder that she interpreted the rest of her history in terms of this event.

### TWO SONGS OF VICTORY

Israel's first awareness of the importance of these events is reflected in the two songs of victory contained in *Exodus 15*, the Song of Moses and the Song of Miriam. Moses' song is a balanced literary composition praising Yahweh and recounting the main features of his victory over Pharaoh. The last section (*verses 13–18*) describes the fear of the inhabitants of Canaan and expresses confidence that the Lord will "plant his people on the mountain."

The Song of Miriam, only two lines long, seems somehow to capture even better what must have been the spirit of the Israelites as they stood on the eastern shore of the Reed Sea, thinking about what the Lord had just done. Unable to restrain the joy that was bursting within them, Miriam and the other women snatched up timbrels, something like our tambourines, and began to dance. From earliest times, elemental religious emotions have been expressed in the ecstatic dance. In fact, it has been said that "primitive religion is not believed; it is danced." Belief, of course, played a profound role in Israel's religion, but the spontaneous action of the women on this occasion shows the naturalness of dancing as a religious expression. As we read through the Old Testament, we can see that the Israelite women frequently celebrated the victories of their armies in this manner (*Judg. 5:1ff; 11:34; I Sam. 18:6*).

In the midst of this noisy celebration, Miriam sang:

Sing to the Lord, for he has triumphed
　　gloriously;
The horse and his rider he has thrown
　　into the sea.　　—*Exodus 15:21*

Years before, a little girl had watched her infant brother float down the river in a straw boat. Now that same sister, grown to maturity, celebrated the victory for which the Lord had nurtured that same brother.

### The Journey to Sinai

The trip from the sea to Mt. Sinai (*15:22 —18-27*) was a difficult one. Existence in the Egyptian slave camp had been rough, but it had offered a good deal of security. There had been sufficient food and water, and the threat from hostile people had been negligible. Now, food and water were in short supply, and native tribes were understandably hostile at the instruction of such a motley horde of strangers. The Israelites were free from the Egyptians, but they were not free from the moral and physical struggles which trouble other men.

### BREAD FROM HEAVEN

Within three days of the triumph at the sea, the Israelites had "murmured" against Moses over the lack of good water (*15:22–25*), but this had been remedied and they had pressed on toward the south. Several weeks passed, and the food they had brought with them ran out. Now, they began to complain in earnest. The old life in Egypt looked good to them now. It had been over a month since they had worked in the brickyards and they had forgotten how cruel the taskmasters could be. All they could remember were the times when they "sat by the fleshpots and ate bread to the full." On an empty stomach, this seemed quite appealing. So, they accused Moses and Aaron of having brought them out into the wilderness to die of hunger.

Happily, Yahweh provided the solution. In the evening a cloud of quails descended on the camp. These were easily caught and gave the people enough meat to satisfy their desires. The next morning, when the dew disappeared, a fine, flake-like substance lay on the ground. This, of course, was manna. When the Israelites saw it they asked, in Hebrew, "*Man hu?*" or "What is this?" The name "manna" is derived from this question.

Manna is described as having looked like a flat white seed, with a taste something like that of a wafer made of honey. A number of efforts have been made to provide a naturalistic explanation of manna. None of them is entirely satisfactory. The substance that seems most nearly like the Biblical

manna is the honeydew excretion produced by insects as they feed on a certain kind of tamarisk tree or shrub. This substance is sweet and Arabs consider it a real delicacy. As in the Biblical account, it disappears shortly after the sun rises, not because of melting, but because it is carried away by ants. The Arabs refer to this substance as *man es-simma* (the manna of heaven). It is worth noting that, contrary to what we often think, manna was not the sole article in the diet of the Israelites. Numerous passages from the wilderness period mention other articles of food (See *Ex. 24:5; 34:3; Lev. 8: 2, 31; 10:12*).

### MASSAH AND MERIBAH

Eventually, the complaints of the people got under Moses' skin. At Rephidim, they were so discontented that Moses feared they were going to stone him. Moses was able to quiet them temporarily by bringing water from a rock, but his feelings are mirrored in the name he gave to the place. He called it Massah and Meribah, or Faithlessness and Faultfinding.

### THE FEUD WITH AMALEK

The Amalekites were descendants of Esau (*Gen. 36:12*) who lived in the region north of Kadesh. They were an old tribe (*Num. 24:20*) and probably resented the fact that a strange multitude was wandering through their country and drinking from their oases. Whatever the reason for their hostility, they attacked the Israelites while they were encamped at Rephidim. The military leader of the Israelites was Joshua. This is the first mention we have of this great warrior who was to succeed Moses as the leader of God's people. He is thrust into the narrative without any introduction, but we may assume he had enjoyed a close relationship with Moses and had established himself as a leader before this occasion.

This was the first battle in which the Israelites engaged and it set the pattern for future battles. Israel would fight, but it would be clear that the victory really belonged to Yahweh. As the battle began, Moses climbed to the top of a nearby hill and stood with "the rod of God," (*17:8*) extended toward the battle. As long as he held his arms up, this same rod that had devoured the magicians' serpents in the court of Pharaoh served to rally the power of the Lord to the side of the Israelites. When his weary arms drooped, the Amalekites prevailed. With the aid of Aaron and Hur, whom tradition has called the husband of Miriam, Moses managed to hold his arms upward until the sun set. "And Joshua mowed down Amalek and his people with the edge of the sword" (*17:13*).

This battle was the beginning of a long and bitter feud that was to last over five hundred years. Because of the unjustified attack on his people, Yahweh told Moses that he intended eventually to "utterly blot out the remembrance of Amalek from under heaven." According to the scriptures, the Lord had war with Amalek from generation to generation until, finally, in the reign of Hezekiah (*I Chron. 4:42, 43*), the last remnant of the Amalekite tribe seems to have been annihilated.

### JETHRO'S VISIT

You will remember that when Moses fled from Egypt after killing the taskmaster, he fled to this same area near Mt. Sinai where he met and married Zipporah, the daughter of Jethro. As the Israelites moved into this area, their fame traveled before them, and Jethro was anxious to visit once more with this son-in-law of his who had been enjoying such favor at the hands of the Lord. This visit gives us one of the few brief glimpses into Moses' family life that we have. Unfor-

tunately, all we can really say for sure is that things were not as pleasant as we might wish them for this great leader. In an earlier episode (*Ex. 4:24–26*) there is a hint of friction between Moses and Zipporah. Still, when Moses returned to Egypt, he took Zipporah and his two sons with him. In the meantime, for reasons unknown to us, he had sent her back to her father. There is no real indication they were reconciled on this occasion, since Zipporah's name is never again mentioned. At a later date, we are told of a problem that arose over Moses' wife, but this may well have been another woman (*Num. 12:1*). At any rate, Moses seems to have been a good deal more elated at the reunion with his father-in-law than with his family, although this may simply reflect the difference in status between the head of a family and women and children.

After the proper Oriental greetings, Moses and Jethro retired into Moses' tent to discuss the wondrous things the Lord had done for Israel. In *18:1*, Jethro is called "a priest of Midian," a designation whose meaning is rather uncertain. The distinct impression we get from this story, however, is that Jethro had not previously been a worshipper of Yahweh. When he heard of God's mighty act in delivering the Israelites out of the hand of Pharaoh, he confessed, "Now I know that Yahweh (the Lord) is greater than all gods" (*18:11*). As a token of his conversion, he offered a sacrifice to the God of Israel.

### THE BEGINNINGS OF BUREAUCRACY

The latter part of *chapter 19* gives us a glimpse at the loose governmental structure of the Israelite horde. Among the Bedouin tribes of the desert, it was, and still is, customary for the sheik of the tribe to sit in front of his tent for a short period each morning. During this period, various members of the tribe bring their disputes and grievances to him and he passes judgment on these matters. Moses was trying to fill this role for the Israelites. The trouble was that although this system was practical for the average desert tribe, it was completely impractical for a group the size of the Israelites. Moses was having to hold court all day every day, and the people who needed to see him were forced to stand around his tent for long and tiresome periods, waiting for their turn to come.

Doubtless, Moses was aware that this was not the well-oiled governmental machine one might desire, but his limited experience as a leader had not provided him with an alternative solution. Fortunately, his wise old father-in-law, a leader among his own people, immediately suggested a practical solution. Under the new arrangement, the Israelites were divided into groups and subgroups, with a judge appointed over each grouping. These judges handled the everyday complaints and disputes. The more difficult cases were still brought to Moses, but having these assistants freed him from the lesser matters that had been robbing his time and energy.

ARRIVAL AT SINAI

After three months of traveling, the refugees reached the wilderness around Mt. Sinai, the same mountain on which Moses had seen the burning bush. We cannot be absolutely certain about the exact location of Mt. Sinai, but ancient Jewish and Christian tradition identifies Sinai with a mountain called *Jebel Musa* (The Mountain of Moses) at the southern tip of the peninsula. This location squares with the Biblical data, and has been the site of pilgrimages for thousands of years. There is every good reason for believing that, for once, the traditional site is also the correct one.

The experiences in the wilderness had helped teach the Israelites that they were to trust Yahweh, regardless of the hardships their wanderings caused. As we shall see, their loyalty was by no means perfect. Still, the experience at the sea, the provision of food and water, and success in battle had made them aware that Yahweh looked on them with special favor and planned to use them in a unique way. Now the time had come to enter into covenant with their Deliverer and Protector.

# 4

# The Covenant

*The covenant between the
King of Heaven
and the children of Abraham*

THE ANCIENT WORLD was full of covenants. A covenant might be an agreement about an exchange of goods or services, or an agreement to keep peace between two parties, or an agreement about practically anything the parties want to agree on. Ordinarily we think of a covenant as an agreement between more or less equal parties. But the covenant Yahweh was to make with Israel was not to be a covenant between equals. If the experience in the wilderness had failed to convince the Israelites of Yahweh's superiority and their own helplessness, the scene at Sinai was designed to remove all doubt. Sinai's heights were wrapped in a thick dark cloud of God's power. Thunder, lightning, and the blast of trumpets declared his awesome presence. The wide gulf of holiness which separates men from God was emphasized by the instructions to the people to stay away from the base of the mountain, on pain of death.

No, Yahweh was not a smalltime nature god trying to persuade a group of ex-slaves that both parties could benefit from a well-worded covenant. He was Lord of Creation, Ruler of the Universe. To condescend to enter into a covenant relationship with these helpless refugees was an act of unimaginable grace. His willingness to make such a covenant should be enough to inspire faithfulness on the part of his subjects.

## The Form of the Covenant

Recent archaeological findings have shown us that this type of covenant was not something which would be an entirely new idea to the Israelites or to her neighbors who might hear of it. We now know that it was not uncommon for a suzerain—a sort of super-king who ruled over a number of lesser kings—to make a treaty or covenant with these vassal kings which was strikingly similar in form to that between Yahweh and Israel. The purpose of this type of covenant, which is called a suzerainty treaty, was to spell out the obligations of the vassal kings to the great suzerain. Mainly, this involved an agreement to come to war whenever the suzerain commanded, to pay certain taxes, and to avoid any kind of alliance with neighboring kingdoms. The suzerain himself was under no formal obligation, unlike the case in a treaty between equal powers. In practice, of course, it was to his own advantage to defend the territory of his vassals against attacks by foreign powers.

This kind of covenant was widely used in the ancient Near East at the time of the Exodus. There was no rigid standard form for international documents in those days, but the copies of suzerainty treaties that archaeologists have found almost always contain the following six items:

1. *Preamble.* In this section, the suzerain is introduced, usually with a long list of adjectives describing his majesty and power.

2. *Historical Prologue.* This part of the treaty rehearses those benevolent actions which the Great King has performed for the benefit of the vassal nation. This may seem unimportant to modern men, who want their legal documents to get right down to the business of spelling out who owes what to whom, but it was a vital part of the suzerainty treaty. The mention of these great deeds was expected to cause the vassals to feel obligation toward the suzerain. This would cause them to do whatever he asked of them. In other words, they promised to obey him in the future because he had helped them in the past.

3. *The Stipulations.* Here the suzerain laid down the specific obligations of the vassals. As we have already pointed out, these include such things as avoiding any alliance with any nation outside the suzerain's empire and being ready to go to war whenever the suzerain demanded. The number and details of these obligations varied from covenant to covenant.

4. *Provision for depositing in the temple and for periodic public reading.* Since the gods of both nations were called upon to witness the making of such a covenant, a copy was to be kept in the sanctuary of that god's temple. The reason for the periodic public reading is obvious; it was simply to remind the people of their obligation to their great Protector and Overlord.

5. *The Witnesses.* The deities of both nations were called upon to witness the covenant ceremony. In addition to the better known Near Eastern gods, heavenly witnesses often included the deities believed to inhabit springs, rivers, mountains, etc.

6. *Curses and Blessings.* In the last section, the suzerain sets forth the consequences which may be expected as a result of the keeping, or failure to keep, the stipulations of the covenant. As the title of the section implies, the formula was fairly simple. If the covenant was broken, the gods would curse the offenders. If it was kept, abundant blessings would flow down. Obviously, the suzerain's army would serve as the arm of divine wrath, but this is never mentioned in the treaties.*

If the reader is familiar with the form of the covenant between Yahweh and Israel, he will see how closely it resembles the form of the suzerainty treaty. Notice how naturally the Mosaic covenant can be divided into these same six sections.

1. *Preamble.* The heavenly suzerain is introduced as "Yahweh (the Lord) your God" (*Exodus 20:2*).

2. *Historical Prologue.* In the *Exodus* account of the covenant, the historical prologue is limited to the affirmation that Yahweh "brought you out of the land of Egypt, out of the house of bondage" (*Ex. 20:2*). In *Joshua 24*, however, which describes a renewal of this same covenant after the Israelites had settled in Canaan, the historical prologue is much more detailed. But the essence is here in *Ex. 20:2*. Israel was to serve Yahweh out of boundless gratitude for the marvelous deliverance from Egypt.

3. *The Stipulations.* The basic document of the Mosaic Covenant was, of course, the

---

*For a complete analysis of the suzerainty treaty, see G. E. Mendenhall, *Law and Covenant in Israel and the Ancient Near East* (Pittsburgh, Pennsylvania: The Biblical Colloquium, 1955).

Decalogue,* or Ten Commandments (*Ex. 20:3–17*). In addition, there were the more complicated rules contained in *Exodus 21–23*. These three chapters are often referred to as The Book of the Covenant.

4. *Provision for Depositing in the temple and for periodic public reading.* Since the tabernacle had not yet been built, there was no sanctuary in which to deposit the covenant. Once the tabernacle was built, however, the tables of stone on which the Ten Commandments were engraved were stored in the Ark of the Covenant (*Ex. 25:16, 21; Deut. 10:1–5*). Once Israel reached Canaan, there was to be a regular reading of the covenant, together with the curses and blessings, on the twin mountains of Ebal and Gerizim (*Deut. 27:1–13*).

5. *The Witnesses.* Naturally, we would not expect to find an appeal to other gods to act as witnesses of a covenant in which Yahweh was the chief actor. Even so, there is some parallel in the renewal ceremony in *Joshua 24.* After charging the people to re-affirm the Mosaic covenant, Joshua took a large stone and set it up as "a witness against us; for it has heard all the words of the Lord which he spoke to us" (*Joshua 24:27*).

6. *Curses and Blessings.* There is a hint of a curses and blessings formula in *Ex. 23:21–22*, but the full form which was used when the covenant was read to the people is found in *Deut. 27–28*. Here we have a full catalogue of the dire consequences for disobedience and the bountiful rewards for faithfulness to the covenant.

Perhaps you are wondering why we have gone to such lengths to point out the parallels between Yahweh's covenant with Israel and the Near Eastern suzerainty treaties. The reason is twofold. First, we have been able, hopefully, to see the covenant in much the same form as the Israelites saw it, and

* (Literally, "Ten Words.")

not just as four or five chapters in a sacred history book. Secondly, it helps us appreciate the wisdom of God. It would have been entirely possible for Yahweh to have invented a completely new form of covenant. But the Israelites were likely to be familiar with this particular kind. The nature of the covenant itself would cause them to understand more fully the nature of the Great King who offered it and their responsibility in responding to his gracious offer.

## The Stipulations of the Covenant

### TWO KINDS OF LAW

As we have said, the *stipulations* section of the Mosaic covenant contained two parts, the Decalogue (Ten Commandments) and the Book of the Covenant. These are not just two convenient groups of rules. They are different kinds of law. The Decalogue contains absolute laws. It does not go into detail to explain what will happen if one of them is broken. It simply says, "Don't break them!" These commandments summarized Israel's moral and religious obligations.

A new nation needs more than general principles, however noble they might be. It must have some kind of code that tells what will happen if the commandments are broken. It must be able to distinguish between stealing a yoke of oxen and stealing a loaf of bread, and to prescribe a punishment appropriate to the crime. The Book of the Covenant fulfills this need. Its laws are not in the form of direct commands. Their usual form is, "If a man does *this,* his punishment shall be *that.*" Actually, they are a more detailed elaboration and explanation of the general code contained in the commandments. We have something similar to this in all the state and local laws which define, explain, and make specific application of the general precepts of the Bill of Rights and the other amendments of our constitution.

### THE DECALOGUE

There is probably no document in the history of mankind that has had greater influence on moral and religious life than the Decalogue. The Book of the Covenant contained regulations for the common things of everyday life, but the Ten Commandments were "straight from God." The other laws were developed under divine guidance, but these ten "Words" were straight from the finger of God in a sense that other laws were not (*Ex. 31:18; 32:16; 34:1; Deut. 4:14; 5: 22; 10:1–4*). As we have said, the Decalogue served as a summary statement of the basic duties of the Israelites toward God and toward their fellowmen. Unless these minimum moral and spiritual requirements were heeded, there could be no religious community. Morality and religion could not be separated. We take this for granted, but many of Israel's neighbors saw no necessary connection between the two.

We have all quoted the Ten Commandments so often that we feel we have a fairly good understanding of them. Frequently, however, we have looked at them through Christian eyes and have made them mean things they never meant to the ancient Israelites. A brief exposition of each commandment will help us to get a more accurate idea of what Yahweh really expected of his covenant people.

1. *Thou shalt have no other gods before me.* The insistence on monotheism, the worship of one God, was one of the unique features of Israel's religion. This commandment makes it clear that Yahweh alone is Lord. There is no other power in the universe who rules the destinies of the earth; all power in other beings, heavenly or earthly, is derived from Yahweh. He does not rule with a female consort, as did many of the Near Eastern deities. He is not simply the Chairman of a Board of gods. It is true that he is sur-

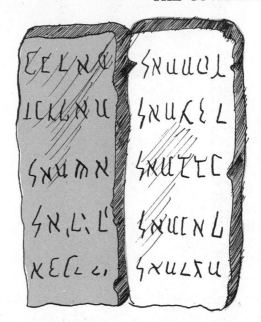

The tables of the Ten Commandments.

rounded by a heavenly host. (*Deut. 33:2; Psa. 29:9*), but worship of these is always forbidden (*Deut. 4:19; II Kin. 23:4; Jer. 8: 2*). By this commandment the Israelites were delivered from the confusion of polytheism (worship of many gods) which surrounded them and directed to Yahweh as the only proper focus of their allegiance. As a result they became the special people of Yahweh, with a new and unifying interpretation of life.

2. *Thou shalt not make unto thee any graven image.* This prohibition against images is perhaps even more in conflict with Israel's environment than monotheism. A chief characteristic of pagan religion was that men worshipped only those things that could be represented in some kind of physical form. The religion of Israel, however, tolerated no images of its God. It is true that the Israelites engaged in idolatry throughout much of their history, but archaeologists have never found a single figure of Yahweh. All this makes it clear that Yahweh is a spiritual being who resists any kind

71

**Hittite household gods. Israel's religion forbade worship of religious images such as these.**

of representation man can devise. He is the Lord of History and not a being whose personality can be reflected adequately in a power of nature, or captured in the figure of a beast or a bird.

3. *Thou shalt not take the name of the Lord thy God in vain.* This is one of the most commonly misunderstood of the commandments. The Hebrew term translated "in vain" in this commandment carries with it the idea of "without result." Since there is no evidence that profanity was a serious evil in this period—no Israelite would have dreamed of using the name of God as part of a slang expression—it is quite likely that the prohibition here is against speaking the name of Yahweh "without result"—without doing what one vows to do "in the name of Yahweh." This commandment was probably intended as a prohibition against breaking an oath.

4. *Remember the sabbath day, to keep it holy.* The Mosaic covenant supplied an aimless group of runaway slaves with a remarkably stable structure of life. The setting aside of the seventh day of the week, as a day when man's attention should be turned to God in a special way, was a part of that structure. By keeping the sabbath, Israel declared that Yahweh was not only the Lord of History, but the Lord of every man's days and hours.

5. *Honor thy father and thy mother.* Here there is a shift from the service of God to the service of mankind. This commandment provides for the preservation of the basic unit of society, the family. We usually think of "honoring" our parents in terms of being polite and obedient to them, as a token of respect and love. Certainly this was involved. In a situation in which all members of a family usually lived together, it was even more important than it is now. Family solidarity was essential for both physical and economic survival. It is also possible that the commandment was designed to prevent the common practice of abandoning aged parents.

6. *Thou shalt not kill.* The Hebrew verb in this commandment is best translated "murder." It does not refer to killing to avenge a murder, to capital punishment, or to killing in war. The concern here is with the protection of human life within the community of Israel and the prevention of the weakening of society that is brought about by murder.

7. *Thou shalt not commit adultery.* The interest of the seventh commandment is probably not on moral purity, except by implication. The verb used here always refers to sexual relations with the wife of another man, and not to fornication. This commandment may also be seen as an effort to preserve the family unity by treating the marriage relationship as sacred and inviolable.

72

8. *Thou shalt not steal.* This is just what it appears to be—a simple, straightforward prohibition of stealing. It attests to the necessity of private property rights for a unified society.

9. *Thou shalt not bear false witness against thy neighbor.* The primary concern of the ninth commandment is the preservation of the judicial system. The verb in this prohibition means "to answer." The meaning is that when a man appears at court, whether as plaintiff, defendant, or witness, he is obligated to speak the truth about any charge involving his fellowman. This does not rule out the traditional ideas about slander or other forms of character assassination which we have usually connected with this commandment, but the central concern is probably with the integrity of the judicial system rather than with these.

10. *Thou shalt not covet.* As we have seen, most of the commandments are fairly concrete and practical. They are concerned more with the actual act than with the motives behind it. In the tenth commandment, however, God's people were commanded not to covet anything that belonged to another. Covetousness, as used here, refers to desire in the bad sense of inordinate, ungoverned, selfish desire. When a man allows this emotion to develop in his heart, he is but a short step removed from breaking one of the other commandments. Yahweh must be the Lord of the heart as well as the hands.

### THE BOOK OF THE COVENANT

The second body of covenant stipulations are those contained in *20:18–23:33*, called the Book of the Covenant. As we noted in the section on types of law, the laws contained in the Book of the Covenant are quite specific in nature and are usually in the form, "if a man does *this,* he shall be punished by *that.*" In many respects, the regulations of the Book of the Covenant are quite similar to those found in the codes of Israel's contemporaries. Many of the legal provisions have their parallel in the famous Code of Hammurabi, which dates from about 1700 B.C. This does not mean that the Book of the Covenant is copied from the Hammurabic Code. It simply means that Israel's common law was largely of a piece with that of other peoples of the ancient Near East. By reading through this collection of laws, we are able to get a fair idea of the social structure in which the Israelites lived.

## The Religion of Israel

With the conclusion of the covenant ceremony at Mt. Sinai, it becomes proper to speak of the religion of Israel. We have already used this phrase, but it is not really accurate until the completion of the events at Sinai. Before the Exodus, Yahweh had played little part in the lives of the Hebrew slaves. Before Sinai, whatever religious ideas they may have had were without much form or content. Now, they were Yahweh's people, and Yahweh was their God. Now, they were to worship only him who had brought them forth out of Egypt. He alone had power over the universe. Not only did he control the forces of nature; he directed the course of history itself and used it to accomplish his holy purposes. Israel did him no favor in submitting to his sovereignty. They could not claim to have been selected because of their righteousness. In fact, it seems almost as if Yahweh chose them because of their perversity, for they continually revelled against him and his covenant. He did not choose the Israelites because they were a rising young nation whose power could be put to good use by an enterprising deity. They had no army, no program for world domination, not even any plans for escaping from Egypt. Yahweh chose a people unable to free themselves from the slavery of Egypt to serve as an in-

The tabernacle in the wilderness.

strument by which all mankind might be freed from the slavery of sin.

## A Dwelling-place for Yahweh

The second commandment makes it clear that Yahweh cannot be adequately represented in any graven image. Neither can he be contained in any building. Nevertheless, it was useful to have some kind of focal point for religious observances. A natural impulse would have been to build a temple on Mt. Sinai, but Israel was not going to stay at Sinai forever, so this would have been useless. The solution was a portable sanctuary, or tabernacle. When Moses ascended the mountain to receive the tables of the law, Yahweh said to him, "Let them make me a sanctuary, that I may dwell in their midst" (25:8). *Chapters 25–31* contain detailed instructions for the construction of this tabernacle, its various articles of furniture, and the garments that were to be worn by the priests who served at its sacrifices. These details are repeated in chapters 35–39 in the account of the carrying out of Yahweh's instructions.

Moses, of course, was the over-all superintendent of the work, but the actual supervision of the carpentry and artistic details were handled by two specially gifted artisans, Bezaleel and Aholiab (35:30–35). The primary materials used to construct the sacred tent were acacia wood, ram and lamb skins, and tentcloth made of goats' hair, all of which would have been readily available to the wilderness wanderers.

The Biblical description of the tabernacle is extremely complicated. For our purposes, the following broad-stroke description and the accompanying illustration will be sufficient. If the reader desires more detail, the Biblical text will satisfy his hunger. The tabernacle was situated toward one end of a rectangular courtyard which measured approximately 150 by 75 feet.* This courtyard consisted of a fence on which were hung fine linens and embroidered cloths. Within the courtyard, in front of the tabernacle, were the altar of burnt offerings and the laver. The altar was constructed of boards and overlaid with brass. It was here that sacrifices were offered to God.† The laver was a great brass bowl in which the priests washed their hands and feet before officiating at the altar or in the tabernacle.

The tabernacle itself was a rectangular tent consisting of a framework covered with linen, mohair tentcloth, and animal skins. There were two rooms inside the tabernacle, separated by a veil. The larger of these two rooms, which took up two-thirds of the space, was called the Holy Place. Inside this room stood three major articles of furniture, the altar of incense, the table of shewbread, and the golden lampstand. The altar of incense was constructed of acacia wood overlaid with gold. This stood in front of the veil that separated the two rooms. The table of shewbread stood along the north side of the tent. It held twelve loaves of bread, representing the twelve tribes, and various accessories such as dishes, flagons, and spoons. Across from it stood the golden lampstand with its accessories.

The small room in the tabernacle, a perfect cube, was called the Most Holy Place or the Holy of Holies. Except for the times when the tabernacle was moved from place to place, only the high priest was allowed within the Holy of Holies and he only once a year, on the Day of Atonement. Within this room stood the Ark of the Covenant. This seems to have been an oblong chest of acacia wood. The chest obtained the tables of the Law (*Ex. 25:16*), the rod of Aaron which budded (*Num. 17:10*), and a pot of

---

*The measurements are given in cubits. For convenience, we are figuring the cubit at eighteen inches.

†See pp. 81f for a description and explanation of the various types of offerings in Israel's sacrificial system.

**The throne of Yahweh, formed by two cherubim (winged sphinxes) atop the ark of the covenant.**

manna (*Ex. 16:33, 34*). On top of the ark was the "mercy-seat," Yahweh's symbolic throne. This throne consisted of a slab of pure gold, adorned by two cherubim. We should not confuse these cherubim with the modern idea of a tiny winged boy. The popular conception of a cherub is a product of Renaissance art, not Biblical scholarship. The cherubim of the Bible were winged sphinxes, or winged lions with human heads. In the art and religious symbolism of Syria and Palestine during the Biblical period, it is quite common to find kings or deities enthroned on these cherubim. This symbol of superhuman power was a fitting throne for a king or a god.

The depths of Israel's religion are profoundly symbolized by the tabernacle and its furnishings. On the altars, they offered their praise and thanksgiving to Yahweh for his gracious salvation and guidance. At the laver, they purified themselves from the contamination of the world. The golden lampstand which burned continually reminded them of God's continual presence and the table of shewbread called them to be thankful for the produce of the ground which he provided them. At the very heart of the tabernacle stood the Ark of the Covenant with the tables of the law, which stood at the heart of Israel's relationship with Yahweh. The throne of God was surrounded by an aura of mystery, but it rested upon the pot of manna, symbolizing God's providential concern for his people, and the rod of Aaron the High Priest, through whom men could approach the unapproachable. In the New Testament, the tabernacle is viewed as a copy of heavenly things and a foreshadow of things to come (See *Heb. 9*). Truly, the tabernacle was not just a tent, not even just a most elaborate tent, but the point at which human life was touched and moved by the divine.

## The Priestly Garments

Hardly less elaborate than the tabernacle were the garments of the high priest. The illustration gives an approximate idea as to how the high priest looked in full ceremonial dress. The most significant features of his dress were the ephod, the breastpiece of judgment, and the turban.

The ephod seems to have been the central feature of the outfit. It was a richly designed cloth that draped over the chest and back of the priest. The front and back pieces of the ephod were joined at the shoulder by shoulder-pieces. Each shoulder piece was set with a large onyx stone. Engraved on each stone were the names of six of the tribes of Israel. These stones were called "stones of remembrance." Whenever the high priest wore the ephod, he was symbolically reminding Yahweh of the covenant he had made with the sons of Israel.

The breastpiece of judgment was a thickly woven cloth pouch, about six or eight inches square, which hung on the outside of the ephod. On the front of this pouch were twelve stones, in four rows of three stones each, representing the twelve tribes. Inside were the mysterious Urim and Thummim. We speak of them as mysterious because no one knows just what they were or how they were used. Probably, they were two stones which the High Priest used in rendering judgment on problems brought before him. In answer to a question, he would "inquire of the Lord" by reaching into the pouch and drawing out one of the stones. The answer was governed by which of the stones was drawn out.

The turban interests us because of the gold plate which was fastened to its front.

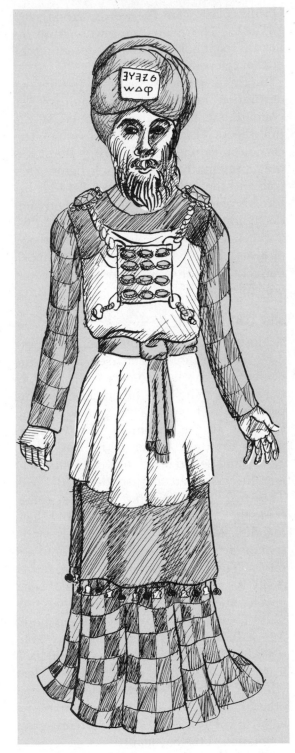

The High Priest of Israel, in his sacred garments. (See *Exodus 28*)

77

On this plate were the words *"Holiness to Yahweh."* The High Priest wore it on his head as a symbol of his role in presenting the gifts of the people to the Lord.

In these garments, with their fabulous decoration and rich symbolism, we see pointed out the vital importance of the priesthood. Through the priest came intercession and atonement. The High Priest was the representative of the people before Yahweh and the representative of Yahweh before his people. Only when we properly understand this role of the priesthood can we appreciate the significance of the priesthood of Jesus Christ, who was able to accomplish perfectly what this earthly priesthood could only foreshadow.

## The Golden Calf

Moses remained on the mountain many days while Yahweh rehearsed to him the contents of the law and gave the instructions concerning the tabernacle and the priesthood. Down below, camped around the foot of the mountain, the Israelites waited for their leader to return. Weeks passed and he did not return. They began to fear he was dead, or had deserted them. They needed something tangible, something they could see and feel, to hold them together. Moses had been Yahweh's representative, but now, it seemed, he would not return. The crowd convinced Aaron, rather easily it seems, to melt down some of their jewelry and to make a golden calf, to represent the God who had brought them out of Egypt. Probably it was a wooden figure laminated with gold, a process they would have learned in Egypt. It is not entirely clear whether the people viewed this as a god other than Yahweh, or were trying to create an image of Yahweh. Either alternative was a violation of the covenant.

When the calf was finished, Aaron ordered a special feast to the Lord, "and they rose up early on the morrow, and offered burnt offerings and brought peace offerings; and the people sat down to eat and drink, and rose up to play" (*32:6*). When Yahweh saw the orgiastic celebration being carried on in the name of religion, he told Moses of his intention to annihilate the entire lot of the faithless Israelites and to fulfill his promises to Abraham through Moses' descendants (*32:10*). Here Moses proved his selfless concern for his people and for Yahweh's ultimate purposes. This impulsive action of theirs was as much a rejection of Moses as it was of Yahweh. We could hardly have condemned him if he had agreed that annihilation would be the best thing for them, and good riddance, too. Instead, he pointed out that their destruction, though wholly deserved, would cause the Egyptian pagans to mock the Exodus as a trap laid by a de-

**An Egyptian goddess of love, in the form of a cow.**

ceitful and capricious god. The Lord heard Moses approvingly, and turned the discipline of the Israelites over to him. In the following scenes, we see the Avenger of Yahweh, storming down the mountainside, smashing the tables of the Decalgoue against the base of the mountain, snatching up the molten calf and throwing it into the fire, then mixing the ashes in the drinking water and making the Israelites drink it. He listened impatiently to Aaron's lame excuse. Then he ordained the punishment to be meted out to the idolatrous crew. When the sons of Levi answered his call, "Who is on Yahweh's side?" he ordered them to take their swords and go through the camp, executing every man they could. By nightfall 3,000 had fallen. A heavy price had been paid for Israel's idolatry. Even so, it was but a token of the suffering she would bear throughout her history for this same sin.

The next day, Moses again ascended the mountain of the Lord. Already, his anger had abated. Now, he asked the Lord to forgive them their sins, even at the cost of his own life. But the giving of a human life for the life of God's people was not the appointed role for Moses. That remained for another man and another day. Moses' task was to continue to lead Israel to the land promised to Abraham and to do what he could to make them faithful to the Lord of the covenant.

In the coming days, Moses spent most of his time in the Tent of Meeting, over which the pillars of fire and of cloud hung, and in which "Yahweh used to speak to Moses face to face, as a man speaks to his friend." We also notice that Joshua, the young warrior of Rephidim, was spending more and more time at Moses' side and at the tent, in preparation for the day when he would assume the leadership of God's people (33:11).

Soon Moses ascended Sinai once more. New tables of the covenant were prepared to replace those Moses had smashed, and new instructions were given for the "stiff-necked" Israelites, including a severe warning against participating in the idolatry of Canaan. During this period of forty days, Moses communed with God in a manner that even he had not previously enjoyed. We cannot understand all we would like to know about Yahweh's glorious appearance described in 33:17–22 and 34:5–9, but it was of such a nature that when Moses finally descended the mountain, "the skin of his face shown because he had been talking with God."

## The Response to Grace

This time, Moses returned to find a chastened people ready, for a time at least, to serve God with all their might. They were beginning to understand that Yahweh had chosen them not because of their moral or spiritual superiority. They were as idolatrous as any pagans when they forgot the stipulations of the covenant. Their role as a chosen people was purely an act of God's grace. Now, they yearned to respond to this grace in any way that would be acceptable. When Moses returned with the order to build the tabernacle, they gladly responded. "And they came, everyone whose heart stirred him, and every one whose spirit moved him, and brought the Lord's offering to be used for the tent of meeting" (35:21). According to 36:5–7, Moses had to tell them to stop their gifts, "for the stuff they had was sufficient to do all the work, and more."

Finally, the dwelling-place for Yahweh's continual presence was completed and consecrated. Aaron and his sons were ordained as priests, and the daily worship and sacrifice was begun.

The stormy book of *Exodus* closes on a secure and peaceful note. God's people have escaped the army of Egypt in a breathless chase through the sea. Through providence, they managed the trek to Sinai, where the covenant was entered. Doubt and division have been overcome and a house of the Lord erected. Now, the Israelites were truly the people of Yahweh, and Yahweh was their God. And in their midst, throughout all their journies, "The cloud of the Lord was upon the tabernacle by day, and fire was in it by night, in the sight of all the house of Israel" (40:38).

## The Priestly Legislation

To many modern readers, the most notable feature of the book of *Leviticus* is its consistent dullness. Probably no book in the Bible has caused more resolutions to "read the Bible straight through" to be broken. For the most part, it is really unimportant for Christians to try to remember what this formidable book actually contains. If we are to have a proper understanding of Judaism, however, we must know what the book meant to the Jews.

*Leviticus* receives its name from the fact that it deals primarily with the religious obligations of the priests, all of whom came from the tribe of Levi. Almost every chapter makes the claim that this collection or religious and civil regulations was delivered to Moses, presumably at Mt. Sinai. Many reputable scholars feel that the form in which we now have the book dates back to about the fourth century B.C., when the Jews had returned from Babylonian exile and were worshiping once more at the temple in Jerusalem. The theory is that the priests felt a great need for a detailed code book, to keep them from even the tiniest errors in carrying out their ceremonial duties. To fill this need, they collected all the old regulations that had come down from the time of the establishment of the tabernacle and compiled them into the book of *Leviticus*.

We cannot say exactly what happened, for the simple reason that we were not there.

*Leviticus* itself tells us nothing about when it was written or compiled. It merely tells us that its regulations were delivered to Moses. Whether or not the modern theory is correct, it does point out one important thing: the Levitical regulations do seem to have been much more important in the four centuries after the Babylonian exile then they ever were in Israel's earlier history. The rest of the Old Testament makes very little reference to the strict application of these rules. Presumably, the worship of Yahweh was carried on according to the rules, but Israel had other things to hold her attention as well. There was the rise to international power in the time of David and Solomon. After the split in the kingdom, the ten northern tribes abandoned the worship at the temple and set up shrines of their own. Certainly, the book of *Leviticus* played little part in their worship. In fact, except for brief periods of religious revival, correct worship does not seem to have been of great interest in either the northern or southern kingdoms.

The years of Babylonian exile changed all this. The exiles had time to reflect on the cause of their devastating humiliation. They concluded, rightly, that their condition was a punishment for their failure to honor the covenant. They also concluded, with somewhat less justification, that the main thing involved in the keeping of the covenant was scrupulous attention to the details of sacrifice and ritual. Jewish sources outside the Bible tell us that, on their return to Jerusalem, the Jews gave their full attention to the cultivation of the life described in *Leviticus*, under the direction of the Levitical priesthood.

To most of us, it will seem that paying strict attention to the Levitical regulations would be depressing and unable to inspire the joy we seek in worship. The sacrifices seem cruel. The sprinkling of blood and scattering of entrails are distasteful. The smell of burning hide and hair do not impress us as "a pleasing odor to the Lord." But to the Jews, however they may have felt about these things from an aesthetic standpoint—and certainly their culture caused them to feel differently about them than we do—the overriding factor was that they were keeping the covenant and were at peace with God. This was the source of their joy. They did not feel disgust at the endless round of sacrifices and observances, but were filled with a sense of exaltation at being brought by the mysterious rituals into the presence of God Most High.

### THE SACRIFICIAL SYSTEM

As we stated above, it is not too important for Christians to spend much time in memorizing the Levitical regulations. Still, it will not harm us to get an overall view of the book. The first nine chapters deal with the various kinds of offerings that made up the sacrificial system. These offerings were made simply as a gift of gratitude and thanksgiving for blessings that had been received, as an accompaniment of a request for some favor or blessing, and in atonement for certain sins. The Israelite sacrificial system contained five main sacrifices. The *burnt-offering* was a public ceremony, performed each morning and evening, with special offerings on the Sabbath and various other religious holidays. In this ceremony, the sacrificial animal, always an unblemished male, was completely burned. Nothing was left for the priests or the worshipper who provided the sacrifice. A second class of offerings was the *meal-offering*, or *cereal-offering*, which consisted of fine flour, or unleavened cakes or wafers. A portion of this was mixed with oil and frankincense and offered in the fire. The rest went to the priests for their own consumption. It frequently accompanied meat and drink-offerings. The

A priest making a wave offering. The sacrifice was raised heavenward, then lowered to signify God's returning it to the priests.

*peace-offering*, so called because it promoted a peaceful relationship with God, was ordinarily a private affair, except at the feast of Pentecost (*9:4; 23:19*). In this sacrifice, only the fat of the entrails, the kidneys, and a portion of the liver were burnt on the altar; the remainder was divided between the priests and the family of the offerer. The *sin-offering* was not designed, as its name might imply, to atone for every sort of sin. It was only for those sins which were committed unwittingly. In this ceremony, the fat of the entrails, the kidneys, and part of the liver were burnt, as in the peace-offering, but the remainder, instead of being eaten, was taken outside the camp and burnt on a wood fire near the place where the ashes from the altar were poured out. The *guilt-offering* was made to atone for a certain class of sins, such as failure to testify on some matter before the courts, accidentally touching some unclean thing, neglecting to pay the required religious taxes, or failure to return borrowed property. This method of offering seems to have been the same as in the sin-offering. In all of flesh offerings, the sacrifice might range in value from a bull to a pair of turtle-doves, depending on the economic status of the worshipper. The terms "heave-offering" and "wave-offering" refer to the priests' portion of the offering which was waved in the air, perhaps as a sign that it was being offered to God but that God "waves it back" to those who minister to him. There are variations on these main sacrifices, but this description contains the main feature.

### CLEAN AND UNCLEAN

A second major concern of the Levitical rules is cleanness and uncleanness. When a man touched or associated with certain animals, objects, or people, he was considered "unclean." Consequently, he was unfit to approach God in worship until certain provisions of cleansing were fulfilled. This idea is quite similar to the concept of *tabu* which is often found in primitive and ancient religions. *Leviticus* lists four main types of uncleanness: (1) uncleanness connected with functions of reproduction, especially menstruation; (2) uncleanness connected with food; (3) uncleanness connected with leprosy; and (4) uncleanness connected with death. "Cleanness" is simply the opposite of uncleanness. It does not imply any special dedication to God, but simply indicates that the individual or object in question has no defiling qualities. The clean person may freely approach God in worship. (See *chs. 11 and 12*).

Chapters *13* and *14* deal with leprosy, which seems to be a broad term covering various kinds of infectious skin diseases.

Chapter *15* contains various instructions for personal hygiene.

### THE DAY OF ATONEMENT

The high point of the book is found in *ch. 16*, which contains the description of the Day of Atonement. This was one of the most important days on the Hebrew religious calendar. It fell on the tenth day of the seventh month. On this day, special sacrifices and rituals were performed to atone for all unforgiven sins of ignorance and ommission which had been committed in that year, including those of the high priest himself. The high priest, clad in a simple white linen robe instead of the elaborate garments described earlier, entered the Holy of Holies. Except for the times when he prepared the ark for traveling, this was the only day of the year he entered this sacred room. There he sprinkled the mercy seat with the blood of the sin-offering. The other main act of the Day of Atonement was the scapegoat ritual. With his hands on the head of a goat, the high priest confessed the sins of the people, symbolically transferring these sins to the head of the goat. The scapegoat, bearing the sins of the people, was then led into the wilderness to wander in "a solitary land."

The final section of *Leviticus* (chs. *17–27*) is usually referred to as the Holiness Code. It receives its name from the fact that, although its rules cover a wide range of subjects of varying importance, all of them are designed to insure the holiness—moral and ceremonial purity—of the people of God. The code contains regulations dealing with various sexual relationships, proper weights and measures, forbidden religious practices, appointed feasts and festivals, slavery, vows, tithes, and a generous assortment of miscellaneous rules. The arrangement is sometimes a bit haphazard and there are few guides to tell us which were considered the most important. For example, *Leviticus*

19:18 instructed the people of the covenant to "love your neighbor as yourself." This may be seen as the high water mark of Old Testament religion. The very next verse, however, warns against letting different kinds of cattle breed together, against sowing a field with two kinds of seed, and against making a garment that contains both linen and woolen cloth. This failure to distinguish between more important and less important matters of the law was probably partially at fault in the rise of the legalism that had robbed Judaism of its spiritual power in the time of Jesus. We can see the result in Jesus' condemnation of the Pharisees who "tithe mint and dill and cummin, but neglect the weightier matters of the law, justice and mercy and faith." (*Matt. 23: 23*). From the Sermon on the Mount we learn that part of Jesus' mission was to put the law back in proper perspective, to show the Jews how far they had declined from the spirit of Sinai.

The book closes with the traditional curses and blessings section. If the statutes of the code are observed, peace and prosperity will follow naturally. If they are neglected, disaster will come swiftly. Even in the face of disobedience, however, Yahweh would not forget his covenant relationship to Israel. In spite of all their sins,

when they are in the land of their enemies, I will not spurn them, neither will I abhor them so as to destroy them utterly and break my covenant with them; for I am Yahweh their God; but I will for their sake remember the covenant with their forefathers, whom I brought forth out of the land of Egypt in the sight of the nations, that I might be their God: I am Yahweh. —*Leviticus 26:44, 45*

# 5

# Forty Years of Wandering

*The people of God prepare to enter the Promised Land*

Yahweh brought Israel out of Egypt to give them the land he had promised to Abraham long centuries before, the land of Canaan. After the covenant ceremonies at Sinai, we expect them to move northward for a few months and to settle in this promised land. Instead, we are told that forty years passed between the events of Sinai and the actual entry into Canaan. The book of *Numbers* contain what scant record we have of these forty years.

In *Exodus*, we saw a band of slaves become the people of God. In the opening chapters of *Numbers*, we see the people of God being transformed into an organized military force. The book gets its name from the two "numberings," or census reports, of all those fit for military service (chs. *1, 26*). This included all able-bodied men over twenty years of age, with the exception of the Levites, who were exempted from military service to attend to the religious affairs of the community. The total force was then broken down by tribes and assigned a camping area around the tabernacle.

When these arrangements were completed, Israel was ready to move out from Sinai. They had no schedule of their own, but they needed none. Yahweh was their Commander, and they followed where the cloud of his presence led them.

And whenever the cloud was taken up from over the tent, after that the people of Israel set out; and in the place where the cloud settled down, there the people of Israel encamped. . . . Whether it was two days, or a month, or a longer time, that the cloud continued over the tabernacle, abiding there, the people of Israel remained in camp and did not set out; but when it was taken up they set out.                    —*Numbers 9:17, 22*

### The Israelites Murmur (Again)

Few people are at their best when "living out of a suitcase." The Israelites were no exception. They were hardly out of sight of Sinai before they began to complain about their condition. They complained about the hardships of travel. They complained about the lack of meat. They complained about the insipid taste of the manna. Back in Egypt they had enjoyed such delicacies as leek and garlic and onions. The mere suggestion that they would have been better off in Egyptian slavery caused Yahweh's anger to "blaze hotly." He would give them meat;

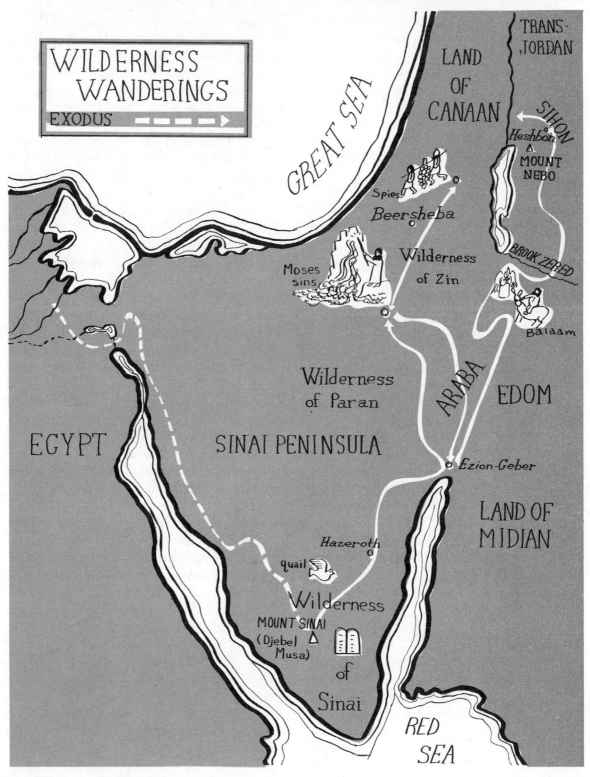

The Wilderness Wanderings.

so much meat that they would get sick of it; so much that it would be coming out of their nostrils (*11:20*). The meat came, in the form of another flock of quails from the sea. But with it came a deadly plague that struck the greedy complainers "while the meat was yet between their teeth." Fittingly, the name given to the site of the plague was Kibroth-hattaavah, which means "Glutton's Grave" (*11:34*).

Food was not the only cause of complaint. Just as much trouble was stirred up by jealousy. Most of this was aimed at Moses. He was not an accomplished speaker. There were others who felt they could do just as good a job if they were given half a chance. Perhaps they could do even better. The desire for power does strange things to men and women.

The first show of rebellion came from, of all people, Aaron and Miriam, Moses' own brother and sister. They were already disgruntled at Moses because of his new bride, a Cushite woman (*12:1*). A few months before, they had all been slaves, but they still did not want their brother to marry a Cushite. Even more galling to them was the fact that Moses got all the glory as leader. They were as capable as Moses. Why shouldn't they be recognized as equal in status? Yahweh made no attempt to defend his choice of Moses. Instead, he expressed surprise and anger that his choice had been questioned. As a dramatic demonstration of the punishment for rebellion, Miriam was struck with leprosy.

### SPYING OUT THE LAND

The second leadership crisis came over the report of the twelve spies. When Israel reached the wilderness of Paran, spies were sent into Canaan to get some idea about the land and the people. None of the Israelites had ever seen Canaan. Before any sort of attack could be made, it would be necessary to have some knowledge of the terrain and the approximate military strength of the inhabitants. The spies crossed the Negeb and penetrated as far North as Hebron and the Valley of Eschol. After about six weeks, they returned with their report.

All the spies were full of wonder at the richness of the land. In comparison with the barren wilderness, Canaan appeared to be a land flowing with milk and honey. They had brought back a single cluster of grapes that was so large it had to be carried on a pole between two men. But there was a dark side —and to all but Joshua and Caleb, it was the important side. The spies had seen the people of the land. To them, the comparison between the Canaanites and the Israelites was like a comparison between giants and grasshoppers. An attack on Canaan would be suicide. When the crowd heard this, their first impulse was to elect a leader to take them back to Egypt. Better to admit the whole affair was a ludicrous failure than to die in a senseless battle. Joshua and Caleb tried to convince the people that, with Yahweh's help, no one could defeat them, and were nearly stoned for their efforts.

Once again, Yahweh was tempted to destroy the whole unbelieving lot. As a result of Moses' intercession, however, he decided on an alternate plan. All those who had come out of Egypt as adults would be sentenced to wander in the wilderness until their deaths. In return for their repeated faithlessness, none of them except the faithful Joshua and Caleb would live to enter the promised land. They had used the safety of their children as an excuse for their lack of trust. Now, ironically, only the children would live long enough to share in Yahweh's victory.

Professing a loss of interest in entering Canaan was one thing. Being told they could never enter was quite another. The awful finality of the sentence caused them to grope about anxiously for a solution. If they displayed their willingness to go into battle right away, surely the Lord would reconsider. So, without the Ark of the Covenant, and consequently without Yahweh's presence and protection, they stormed into the hill country to meet the Amalekites. The result showed the futility of trying to force God into doing their will. Just as Moses had warned, the Amalekites as the Canaanites easily defeated them, throwing them back into the wilderness.

### KORAH'S REBELLION

It would seem that Miriam's punishment and the defeat in the hills would be enough to stop all thoughts of rebellion against Yahweh's representatives. Unfortunately, Israel seemed cursed by a poor memory. Before long, a full scale revolt was underway. The key leaders of this movement were Korah, Dothan, and Abiram. With a group of 250 well-known men of the congregation, they confronted Moses and Abiram and accused them of using their positions for personal glory and gain. For this act of disrespect for his chosen representatives, Yahweh wreaked wholesale vengeance on the Israelites. The families of Korah, Dothan, and Abiram were swallowed by an earthquake. The 250 were destroyed by fire. And of those who complained at the harshness of the punishment, thousands died by a plague.

With this event, the major internal crisis was past. Yahweh's mighty acts vindicated Moses' undisputed leadership, and Aaron's budding rod (ch. *17*) established him as the true priest of God. As a perpetual reminder to the rebels, Yahweh instructed Moses to place the rod in the Ark of the Covenant "that you may make an end of their murmurings against me lest they die" (*17:10*).

### WATER FROM THE ROCK

Throughout all these incidents, we are amazed at Moses' patience and selfless concern for his people. Again and again, he heard the charges laid against him by jealous rivals, but left vengeance to Yahweh. Again and again, he persuaded Yahweh not to extract the full measure of vengeance he had proposed. All this makes it sadder to read that the constant prodding by the people finally caused Moses to lose control momentarily and claim glory for himself. At Meribah, the people set up their cry for food and water, especially water. Yahweh instructed Moses to speak to a certain rock which would provide ample water. When Moses called the people together he could not resist chiding them a bit. "Hear now you rebels," he said, "shall *we* bring forth water for you out of this rock?" (*20:10*). Then, instead of speaking to it, he struck it with his rod, as he had done at Horeb. For his failure to give all the glory to Yahweh, Moses was told he would not lead Israel into Canaan. This may strike us as too harsh a punishment for a man who had served so well, but it may be that Moses' attitude was far more arrogant than the narrative indicates. It may be he had no one to plead his case as fervently as he had often done on Israel's behalf. Whatever the reason, it is saddening to see this noble servant of the Lord deprived of the goal for which his life had been spent.

## The March to Canaan

The murmurings, the rebellions, the punishments—all had served to make Israel aware of the awesome power of their God, and to strengthen their belief that, with his help, they could conquer Canaan after all. So, after most of the forty years have passed, we see them girding up their loins for the last big push into the land of milk and honey.

From their position at Kadesh, the natural route was the King's Highway, the main route from the rich copper mines at Eziongeber in the south to Syria in the north. They

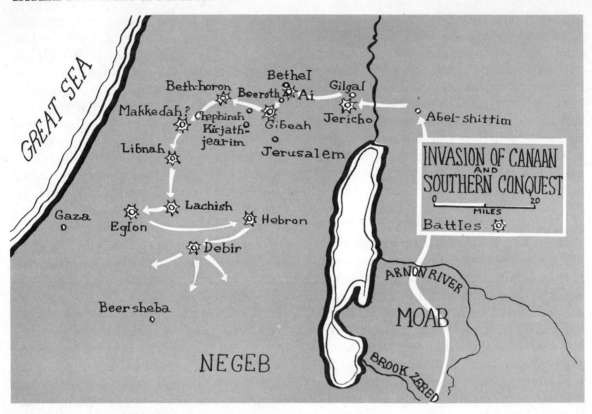

**The early campaigns in southern Canaan.**

could follow this northward until they found a suitable place to turn westward into Canaan. But first, it would be necessary to get permission from the kings who ruled the small nations through which the highway ran. Unfortunately, they immediately ran into difficulty. Despite the appeal to kinship —the Edomites were regarded as having descended from Jacob's brother Esau—and the promise to stay on the highway and to touch nothing which belonged to the Edomites, the Israelites were refused passage. They did not feel ready to force their way through, so they decided to follow a circuitous route which would take them along the western border of Edom to the Valley of Zered, from which point they would circle Moab on the eastern side.

When they came to the land of the Amor-ites, they sent messengers to King Sihon, asking for permission to pass through peaceably. Sihon not only refused, but sent his army out to attack Israel in the wilderness. The Israelites had avoided a fight whenever possible, but now they turned on Sihon's army and completely devastated it, taking possession of the whole Amorite Kingdom, including the capital city of Heshbon.

The next opponent was Og the King of Bashan. Og seems not to have given much trouble. In fact, we would probably never noticed him if it were not for the fact that he slept in a bed that was thirteen feet long and six feet wide—truly a kingsize bed (see *Deut. 3:11*).

An interesting sidelight on these kingdoms Israel was fighting is that archaeologists have shown that they all arose in about

1,300 B.C. Before this time, the inhabitants were nomads and did not live in cities. This gives additional support to the contention that the exodus and conquest are not to be dated earlier than the thirteenth century B.C.

## Balaam

The news of Israel's victories traveled fast. The sudden offensive had caught the nations of Transjordan completely by surprise. They surely knew something of the band which had wandered in the south for the last forty years, but they had been peaceful for the most part. The one attack they had launched, after the spies' report, had been handily repulsed. There was certainly nothing to fear from them. Then, almost without warning, Israel had defeated and occupied the lands of Sihon and Og. Who would be next?

Quite naturally, as a glance at the map will explain, Moab expected to be the next victim of the invaders. When the Israelites camped in the plain of Moab across the Jordan River from Jericho, the Moabites began to groan that "this horde will now lick up all that is round about us, as the ox licks up the grass of the field" (22:4). Balak, the king of Moab, was desperate. His army would be no match for them under ordinary circumstances. He could hope to drive them out only with a little supernatural aid. To this end, he hired a Mesopotamian diviner named Balaam to pronounce a curse on Israel, hoping that this would turn the trick. The result was one of the most interesting and funniest incidents in the entire Bible.

When Balak's messenger came to Balaam, they had great difficulty in persuading him to return with them. Finally, at the promise of a substantial reward, he "saddled his ass and went with the princes of Moab." As Balaam and his servants rode along, an angel of the Lord appeared in the road before them. According to the story, the angel was visible only to the ass, not to the rest of the company. Frightened, the animal skittishly headed off the road into a field. Balaam managed to get his ass back on the road, but the angel appeared again. This time, they were riding along a narrow path between the walls of two vineyards. When the ass saw the angel, she pushed up against one of the walls and mashed Balaam's foot, and he struck her a second time.

The third appearance of the angel was at another narrow place in the road. This time there was no place to go but forward. The ass was not about to get any closer to the angel, so she simply lay down in the path, with Balaam still on her back. By now, Balaam was furious. He struck her a third time with his staff. Then, the ass struck back, not with a stick, but with words. Calmly, as if speaking were the most natural thing in the world for an ass to do, she asked, "what have I done, that you have struck me these three times?" Balaam seems so angered by the ass' actions that he does not even question the fact that she is talking. "You are just lucky all I had was a stick," he said. "If I had a sword, I would have killed you." After a bit more of this type conversation, the Lord enabled Balaam to see the angel and the mystery began to unravel. Balaam fell on his face before the angel and declared he would go no further if Yahweh did not desire it. He was told to continue his mission, but to speak only that which the Lord directed him to speak. Under this condition, Balaam went to meet Balak.

The events of the next few days must have been as frustrating to Balak as the behavior of the ass had been to Balaam. Early the next morning, Balak led Balaam to a mountain from which he could see the Israelite camp. At Balaam's instruction, he had seven altars built and offered seven bulls and seven rams. Then, after a brief visit with the Lord, Balaam returned to Balak's side to pronounce the curse—but it wasn't a curse. Instead, he cried out:

How can I curse whom God has not cursed?
How can I denounce whom Yahweh has
   not denounced?     *—Numbers 23:8*

Balak was upset, but figured that Balaam might do better with a change of scenery. He led him to the top of Mt. Pisgah, built the altars, offered the sacrifices, and waited. But again, when Balaam spoke, he spoke a blessing instead of curse:

Behold, I received a command to bless:
   he has blessed, and I cannot revoke it.
He has not beheld misfortune in Jacob;
   nor has he seen trouble in Israel.
The Lord their God is with them,
   and the shout of a king is among them.
God brings them out of Egypt;
   they have as it were the horns of
     the wild ox.
For there is no enchantment against Jacob,
   no divination against Israel;
now it shall be said of Jacob and Israel,
"What hath God wrought!"
          *—Numbers 23:20-23*

Now Balak was furious. "If you can't say something bad," he demanded, "don't say anything at all." But Balaam was his last hope. He would give him one more try. Another mountain, more altars, more sacrifices. As Balaam looked out over the encampment of Israel from the top of Mt. Peor, he began once more to speak:

How fair are your tents, O Jacob,
   your encampments, O Israel!
Like valleys that stretch afar,
   like gardens beside a river,
like aloes that the Lord has planted,
   like cedar trees beside the waters.
Water shall flow from his buckets,
   and his seed shall be in many waters,
his king shall be higher than Agag,
   and his kingdom shall be exalted.
God brings him out of Egypt;
   he has as it were the horns of the wild ox,

he shall eat up the nations his adversaries,
   and shall break their bones in pieces,
   and pierce them through with his arrows.
He couched, he lay down like a lion,
   and like a lioness; who will rouse him up?
Blessed be every one who blesses you,
   and cursed be every one who curses you.
          *—Numbers 24:5-9*

At this, Balak pounded his fist into his hand in anger. The experiment had been a complete washout. For his failure to do his assigned task, Balaam was fired without pay. With a shrug of his shoulders he reminded Balak that he had come only on condition that he could speak the word of the Lord as it came to him. He had no real choice in the matter. But he did have a thing or two more to say about Israel. "And he took up his discourse and said:

I see him, but not now;
   I behold him, but not nigh:
a star shall come forth out of Jacob,
   and a scepter shall rise out of Israel;
it shall crush the forehead of Moab,
   and break down all the sons of Sheth.
Edom shall be dispossessed,
   Seir also, his enemies, shall be
     dispossessed,
   while Israel does valiantly.
By Jacob shall dominion be exercised,
   and the survivors of cities be destroyed.
          *—Numbers 24:17-19*

"Then Balaam rose and went back to his place; and Balak also went his way."

The die was cast. Nothing could stop Israel now. The next few weeks would be spent in physical and spiritual preparation. Then, the conquest of Canaan would begin.

## Final Preparations

First of all, Moses ordered a new census to be taken, to determine how many fighting men were available and to get some idea as to how the land and booty should be divided among the tribes. When the matter of dividing the land arose, three of the tribes with a lot of cattle—Reuben, Gad, and the half-tribe of Manasseh—asked permission to settle on the eastern side of the Jordan, in Gilead, where the land was better for raising cattle. They were granted this right, but only on the condition that they would first help the other tribes in the conquest of Canaan.

With these administrative details out of the way, all that remained was the transfer of power from Moses to Joshua. The book of *Deuteronomy* is written in the form of addresses by Moses to the congregation as they camped here in the plains of Moab. These addresses rehearse the trip from Egypt, with both its high and low points, and summon the people to faithful obedience to the Law. Then, Moses called Joshua and said to him in the sight of all Israel:

> Be strong and of good courage; for you shall go with this people into the land which the Lord has sworn to their fathers to give them; and you shall put them in possession of it. It is Yahweh who goes before you; he will be with you, he will not fail you or forsake you; do not fear or be dismayed.
>
> —*Deuteronomy 31:7, 8*

Moses could speak these words with full understanding. How often it had seemed that he and Yahweh stood alone against the world. Each time, Yahweh upheld him and brought victory out of defeat. Moses knew that Yahweh would also stand at the side of his successor. To assure Joshua of the truth of Moses' words, Yahweh spoke to him, saying "Be strong and of good courage; for you shall bring the children of Israel into the land which I swore to give them; I will be with you" (*Deut. 31:28*).

## The Death of Moses

Now, Yahweh's greatest servant was ready to depart from life. But first, he wanted to look at the land beyond the river. We can imagine the electric atmosphere that must have filled the camp of Israel as Moses walked from the tent of meeting to the top of Pisgah. He was old, but "his eye was not dim, nor his natural force abated." As he passed through the camp for the last time, men who had grown from childhood under his leadership must have stood silently, trying to realize what life would be like without Moses. Mothers, with tears in their eyes, must have told their children softly, "Look. I hope you will remember this day. We shall not see Moses again." Moses had not been everything they expected, or everything they wanted. But this was what had made him great. He was God's man, and they knew it. They had murmured, they had complained, they had rebelled. Now, as he passed from among them, they could only weep.

Moses climbed Mt. Nebo, to the peak called Pisgah, and looked out on the land to which he had brought his people. Then, he died quietly and was buried in an unknown tomb. "And there has not arisen a prophet since in Israel like Moses, whom the Lord knew face to face."

# 6

# The Conquest of Canaan

*Joshua leads the army
of the Lord
to victory over Canaan*

## The Official History of Israel

The book of *Joshua* is the first of a group of books which form a unified history of Israel from the time of its entry into Canaan to the time of the Babylonian exile. If we erased the titles from *Joshua, Judges, I-II Samuel,* and *I-II Kings* and treated them all as a single book, we would scarcely feel any break in continuity. The story flows along in a unified manner through all these books, and is governed by the same religious, or theological, outlook. The main points in this theology are contained in the book of *Deuteronomy*, in the form of speeches by Moses to the congregation. Thus we can look at *Deuteronomy* as a summary and interpretation of the Mosaic faith, and an introduction to the Official History of Israel. Before we take up the historical narrative, let us review the key aspects of the theology which serves as its underlying support.

In the first address, Moses traced the adventures of Israel from Mt. Sinai to the plain of Moab. The purpose of this, you will re-

member, was to arouse gratitude in the hearts of the people, to make them responsive to the demands of the covenant. Then, a summary of the covenant obligations is given, in the form of the Ten Commandments. Chapters *6–11* could be characterized as notes on the meaning of the commandments, especially the first two. Israel is repeatedly reminded that her loyalty is to Yahweh and Yahweh alone. She is not to try to confine him to any graven image, nor is she to take part in any of the idol-worship which will surround her in her new home. The land is being given only on condition that Israel remember these commandments. Failure to worship the One True God in the manner prescribed in the law will bring devastating punishment and loss of the land of promise. Yahweh gives and Yahweh can take away. These ideas are summarized in chapter *6*, in the so-called Great Commandment, often quoted in the New Testament, and the verses that follow.

Hear, O Israel: The Lord our God is one Lord; and you shall love the Lord your God with all your heart, and with all your soul, and with all your might . . . You shall fear the Lord your God; you shall serve him, and swear by his name. You shall not go after other gods, of the gods of the peoples who are round about you; for the Lord your God in the midst of you is a jealous God; lest the anger of the Lord your God be kindled against you, and he destroy you from off the face of the earth.

*—Deuteronomy 6:4, 5, 13-15*

Being a child of God has always been a serious business. It is not something one can do in his spare time as a hobby. Yahweh demands of his people nothing less than complete dedication, unwavering loyalty.

With the memory of Moses fresh in their minds and the faith he had delivered to them engraved on their hearts, Israel was ready to take the land the Lord had promised to Abraham. The story of that conquest is found in the book of *Joshua*.

## The Invasion of Canaan

It is perhaps a bit of an exaggeration to call Israel's actual entry into Canaan an invasion, if we think of an invasion in military terms. Unlike her march through Transjordan, Israel seems to have met no opposition as she crossed the Jordan into central Palestine. The setting up of the monument of twelve stones, the circumcision of all males, and the keeping of Passover were carried on in an unhurried manner. This, together with the fact that there is no mention of any battles in this area, has led scholars to believe that the region was settled by people who were quite friendly, perhaps related to the Israelites. Whatever the case, they camped peacefully at Gilgal to await marching orders from the Lord. These orders were not long in coming. An angelic being appeared to Joshua and announced himself as "Commander of the Army of Yahweh" (5:14). This was the signal to Joshua to mount the attack in God's Holy War.

## Holy War

The term "Holy War" seems almost self-contradictory to the sensitive modern mind. We do not ordinarily associate holiness and warfare. It disturbs us that the Old Testament tells of so much mayhem carried on in the name of the Lord. There is no easy answer to this difficulty. The most likely explanation seems to be that these battles are viewed as an all-out struggle between the forces of good and the forces of evil. There can be no compromise with evil. Just because things get bloody does not mean we can expect God to bow out of the picture. His aims are just and good; they justify the means he chooses to achieve them. This does not wholly satisfy us, but it seems to be the best answer we can get from the Bible. Our task is not to decide what God ought to be like, but to study the ways in which he has revealed himself to us.

Holy War, as described in the Old Testament, is not just another war, embroidered by a bit of ritual here and a religious flag there. It follows a distinct pattern that shares very little with ordinary warfare. Not every case was exactly the same, of course, but a typical example of Holy Warfare would include most of the characteristics given below.

Yahweh himself was the Supreme Commander in Holy War. He either gave the initial order to fight or was consulted regularly to make certain that the war was in keeping with his will. His presence among them was symbolized by the Ark of the Covenant, which went into battle with them. Frequently, the march into combat was begun by a blast of trumpets and a great shout. The number of those in the combat force was unimportant. Yahweh was the real warrior. Without him, a large army could not win. With him, a small army could not lose.

Two other features are also prominent. In many of the accounts, the reader will notice that the enemy troops break into confusion and panic. In their blind fear, they help to bring about their own destruction. This does not seem to be mere coincidence, but the

93

normal result of the presence of Yahweh at the head of the attack. The final peculiar characteristic of Holy Warfare is the disposal of the booty. Ordinarily, an ancient soldier got to keep whatever booty he could lay his hands on. Under the rules of Holy Warfare, however, the spoil was "devoted" (The Hebrew word is *herem;* see *Josh. 6: 18–19; 7:1, 15*) to Yahweh. In some cases, the soldiers were allowed to keep part of the booty, but the general rule was that the spoil belonged to Yahweh, since it was he who had won the battle.

It will be helpful to keep this general description of Holy War* in mind as we study the events recorded in *Joshua* and *Judges.*

### Jericho and Ai

The first target was to be nearby Jericho. But how could Israel capture Jericho? The inhabitants had heard of the invaders even before they crossed the Jordan. They knew that Israelite spies had visited Rahab while they were in the city. In fear, the people of Jericho had locked themselves within the city walls. In an open fight, the Israelites would win, but how could they get past the walls? Every Sunday school child, of course, knows the answer. Seven days later, the walls of the city lay in a heap, levelled not by siege engines, but by an ark, some marching, and a handful of trumpets (*ch. 6*). Every living thing in the city was killed, except for the harlot Rahab and her family. All of the treasure of the city was put into the treasury of the Lord. All, that is, but a lovely garment from Babylon, a bar of gold, and a few shekels of silver. These were kept back and hidden by a warrior named Achon. The price for these treasures was to be high.

From Jericho, they turned to Ai. Spies had told Joshua that Ai would be a pushover, so

he sent only two or three thousand into battle. The battle was a disaster. The men of Ai routed them from the start. "And the hearts of the people melted, and became as water" (*7:5*). They were completely unprepared for this. Joshua and the elders fell on their faces and piled dirt on their heads as a sign of their deep anguish and humiliation. Yahweh had deserted them. The Canaanites would hear of their defeat and would band together to annihilate them.

Then Yahweh spoke to Joshua. He told him that part of the devoted things had been held back, violating the rules of Holy Warfare. Until the offender was detected and punished, Yahweh would march no more with Israel. By process of elimination, Joshua finally ferreted out the culprit, Achan. Achan confessed and the devoted things were recovered. "And all Israel stoned him with stones; they burned them with fire, and stoned them with stones. And they raised over him a great heap of stones that remains to this day; then the Lord turned from his burning anger" (*Josh. 7:25, 26*).

With the sin purged from the camp, Joshua set out against Ai once more. This time, he stationed a force of about five thousand men on the west side of the city. The rest of the army encamped on the north side, as if to attack the city in the conventional manner from the front. The confident men of Ai stormed down the hillside to meet these Israelites who were so foolhardy as to attack them again. When they were a sufficient distance from the city the Israelites on the west side rose up, entered and burned the city, and surrounded the confused Aiites, killing all but the king, who was taken to Joshua for execution. The first phase of the conquest was completed.

### The Stratagem of Gibeon

Word of the great power of the foreign invaders spread through the land. The various

---

*For a full treatment of Holy War in Israel, see G. von Rad, *Studies in Deuteronomy* (London: SCM Ltd., 1948).

city-states formed coalitions to try to stop them. The people of Gibeon, however, were more realistic. They realized these Israelites had a secret weapon that made them invincible. So, instead of trying to fight them, they decided to try to trick them. The cunning Gibeonites, dressed in old and worn-out clothes and carrying dry and moldy provisions, wandered into the camp of Israel claiming to be wanderers from a far country. Israel had been forbidden to make any kind of covenant with any of the inhabitants of Canaan, but surely there could be nothing wrong with a treaty with people who had come so far to show their interest in Yahweh and their desire for peace with Israel. And thus they were taken in. Yahweh was not consulted, a treaty was made, and Israel swore to live at peace with the Gibeonites. Within three days, they learned the Gibeonites had tricked them, but the covenant had been made and there was nothing to do but keep it. So the deceivers became "hewers of wood and drawers of water for all the congregation" (*Josh. 9*).

## The Southern Coalition

The reaction of the kings of Southern Palestine to the action of the Gibeonites was immediate and intense. Gibeon was a powerful city. Her surrender left a dangerous gap in the defense of the south. She should be punished for her defection. To this end, the kings of Jerusalem, Hebron, Jarmuth, Lachish, and Eglon joined together "to smite Gibeon."

Because of the covenant, Israel was obligated to defend Gibeon. But this was all right. Now was as good a time as any to meet the kings of the south. In the battle which followed, it was clear that Israel did not fight alone. First, a rain of hailstones was credited with more victims than the swords of Israel. Then, to allow the Israelites time to complete their victory,

The sun stood still and the moon stayed,
until the nation took vengeance on
their enemies. —*Joshua 10:13*

In the heat of the battle, the five kings hid in a cave at Makkedah. Joshua sealed them in with stones until the battle ended, at which time he brought them out and executed them. Their bodies were displayed on trees until evening, and then were unceremoniously tossed back into the cave where they had been found.

The armies of the southern cities had been met in the field and overcome. Now there remained the actual conquest of the cities themselves. First, nearby Makkedah was destroyed. Then, in a geographically sensible progression, Joshua took Libnah, Lachish, Eglon, Hebron, and Debir. (Notice that Jerusalem was not conquered at this time.) Now, most of the southern and central portions of Palestine was in the hands of Israel. Next the battle would turn to the North.

## The Northern Conquest

The major power in northern Palestine was Hazor. When the king of this great city heard of Israel's triumphs in the south, he summoned all the leaders of the north to meet together at the waters of Merom, north of the Sea of Galilee. They were a formidable foe, "a great host, in number like the sand that is upon the seashore, with very many horses and chariots" (*11:5*). But Yahweh assured Joshua he had nothing to fear. On the next day, the armies of the north were completely routed. Their houses were hamstrung and their chariots burned with fire. As he had done in the south, Joshua then turned to the weakened cities themselves. Hazor, the mightiest of them all, was completely destroyed and burned to the ground. Then came the smaller, less powerful cities. In *11:13* we are told that "none of the cities that stood on mounds did Israel burn, except Hazor only." The phrase "stood

95

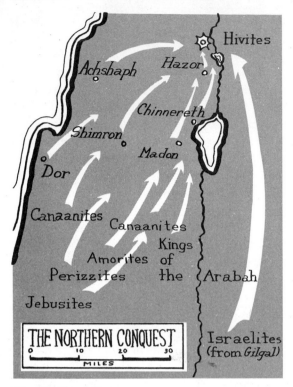

**The Northern Conquest.**

on mounds" indicates that the city was fortified and more difficult to attack than a city which sat on flatland. This verse probably means that Joshua was not able to devastate the other fortified cities as completely as he had Hazor. It was probably this same factor that kept him from capturing Jerusalem. For the time being, Israel would have to be content with the more vulnerable cities.

Taken as a whole, the conquest was an amazing success. With the exceptions of a few heavily fortified cities,

> Joshua took all that land, the hill country and all the Negeb and all the land of Goshen and the lowland and the Arabah and the hill country of Israel and its lowland from Mount Halak, that rises toward Seir, as far as Baalgad in the valley of Lebanon below Mount Hermon. And he took all their kings, and smote them, and put them to death. Joshua made war a long time with all those kings. There was not a city that made peace with

the people of Israel, except the Hivities, the inhabitants of Gibeon; they took all in battle ... So Joshua took the whole land, according to all that the Lord had spoken to Moses; and Joshua gave it for an inheritance to Israel according to their tribal allotments. And the land had rest from war.—*Joshua 11:16-19, 23*

## Archaeological Notes on the Conquest

Archaeology has shed a great deal of light on the condition of Palestine during the period of the conquest and has helped to confirm much of the Biblical account. There are still some problems, but the overall picture squares nicely with the findings of this science.

### JERICHO AND AI

The two most serious problems have to do with Jericho and Ai. For a number of years following the excavations by the archaeologist Garstang in the 1930's, Jericho was regarded as one of the best examples of archaeological proof of the Bible. Ruins of great walls were found at the ancient site of Jericho. The direction in which they had fallen indicated an earthquake, or some other act of God. This was viewed as clear proof that the walls of Jericho did indeed "come a-tumblin' down," just as the Bible says. Furthermore, the date of the catastrophe was placed in the fourteenth century, causing scholars to date the Exodus and Conquest much earlier than the date we have assigned to it. Subsequent excavations, however, have pushed the date of these ruins well back before 2000 B.C., long before the sons of Jacob entered Egypt. One still sees the older information in popular handbooks on Archeology and the Bible, but competent scholarship no longer accepts this view. Now, scholars agree that Jericho was not much of a city between 1500 and 1200 B.C. This leaves us with two alternatives regarding the Biblical story. We can contend that, since Jericho was the first Canaanite city to be captured, the memory of it was embellished to make it seem like a more remarkable event than it really was. Or, we can look forward to the time when archaeologists will find extensive ruins which date from the time of the conquest.

A similar problem confronts us in the case of Ai. According to the best archaeological information thus far available, Ai was a great city between 3300 and 2400 B.C. After that, there is no evidence that it was inhabited again until about 1000 B.C. In addition, the Hebrew meaning of Ai is "The Ruin." That is not the sort of name one ordinarily gives a great city. Several theories have been advanced to explain these difficulties. One suggests that the story was invented to explain the existence of the great ruin. The first attack at Ai was a disaster. Men seldom invent stories to boast of their defeats. A second theory is that the story of Ai is really the story of the defeat of Bethel. Since the Israelites did not leave Bethel in ruins, however, but settled in it quickly, the story of the battle was eventually transferred to the great ruins at nearby Ai. Neither of these explanations can be fully harmonized with the Biblical account. Again we have the alternative of choosing one of the theories or hoping that archaeology will turn up additional information.

We are accustomed to hearing our ministers speak to us of the wondrous ways in which archaeology has confirmed the Bible stories. As we have pointed out several times, not every claim made by popular handbooks is accurate, but, by and large, archaeology has done a great service in substantiating the Biblical narratives. We should be grateful for it. In view of this, when we run across cases like Jericho and Ai, in which the findings of archaeology cast doubt on the Biblical account, we must show the same kind spirit toward the archaeological scientist as we did when he was

"on our side." His task is not to prove that the Bible is true. In fact, he cannot do this. He can show that a city was destroyed at about the same time Israel invaded Canaan, pershaps even that Israel was the cause of its destruction. But he can never prove that Yahweh marched before Israel. And that, after all, is what makes these stories important. The task of the archaeologist is to find what he can, and to interpret these findings to the best of his ability. His interpretation may not be correct. Archaeology—and the same holds true for any responsible branch of scholarship—does not claim to have the final word. It merely does the best it can with the information it has at the moment.

### THE PLAN OF ATTACK

Happily, most of the data from thirteenth century Palestine fits quite nicely with the Biblical account of the Conquest. For a long time, the plan of the southern campaign, as set forth in *Joshua 10*, was viewed by critics of the Bible as a hopeless hodge-podge. According to the best maps then available, it seemed that Joshua could have hardly worked out a worse plan of attack. Subsequent research, however, has located all of the cities except Makkedah and has shown that the old maps were inaccurate. Now we can see that Joshua's strategy was exactly what the situation called for. Before any settling of the southern land could begin, it was necessary to defeat the fortified cities which protected the area. After defeating the coalition of the kings, Joshua directed his forces to this very task. The battle with the kings was near Makkedah; it was natural that the attack should turn to that city. After Makkedah came Libnah, and then Lachish. Lachish has a key role in the dating of the Conquest. In ancient times, records were often kept on bowls and dishes and scraps of broken pottery. A broken bowl found among the burnt debris of Lachish has been shown to be a record of tax payments made by Lachish to a pharaoh of Egypt. Specialists in Egyptian writing have dated this writing in or near the reign of Pharoah Merneptah, (1224–1216 B.C.), thus adding to the mounting evidence for a late thirteenth century B.C. date for the conquest.

The next city to fall was Eglon, situated at the bottom of the hill country south of Lachish. Excavations at Eglon also indicate it fell near the end of the thirteenth century B.C. With Eglon out of the way, Joshua moved into the hills and attacked Hebron, a relatively easy target. Then, he circled around to the southwest to take Debir. There is strong evidence that Debir also fell about the same time as Lachish and Eglon.

The most recent discovery pertaining to the conquest has shown that Hazor in Galilee was truly a large and powerful city which was destroyed in the thirteenth century. Thus, despite the problems with Jericho and Ai, scientific research has shown the book of *Joshua* to contain reliable historical information—by anyone's standards.

## The Division and Settling of the Land

It would be a mistake to conclude that, after Joshua's campaigns were over, the Israelites moved in without further resistance. One has only to look at the opening chapter of *Judges* to see that a great deal more fighting was still left to be done. Not all the Canaanites had been killed, not all the cities burned (See *Josh. 13*). Those that remained were still determined to keep those foreign intruders out. Joshua's sweeping campaign had broken the main lines of resistance. The long and tiresome task of "mopping up" would be left to the individual tribes.

After the great campaign was finished, Joshua assigned the tribes to the portion that was to be theirs. The Levites had no section of their own, but were distributed throughout the territory in special cities. In this way, they could minister to the whole nation and not just to a few who lived near the tabernacle. When this process was completed, the people set out for their new homes. The men of Reuben, Gad, and Manasseh went back to Transjordan, but not before setting up an altar at the Jordan as a witness to their kinship to the rest of Israel and to their belief that Yahweh is God (ch. 22).

Some years later—we are not told how many—"when the Lord had given rest to Israel from all their enemies round about and Joshua was old and well advanced in years," Joshua assembled the leaders of Israel together for a last charge and a renewal of the covenant.* Joshua rehearsed all that Yahweh had done for Israel and spoke of all that he could be counted on to do in the future. Then he gave to them the famous challenge of faith for which he is remembered:

> Now therefore fear the Lord, and serve him in sincerity and in faithfulness; put away the gods which your fathers served beyond the River, and in Egypt, and serve Yahweh. And if you be unwilling to serve Yahweh, choose this day whom you will serve, whether the gods your fathers served in the region beyond the River, or the gods of the Amorites in whose land you dwell; but as for me and my house, we will serve the Lord.
> —*Joshua 24:14-15*

And the people answered, "We will serve the Lord."

Then Joshua died, and his body was laid to rest in the land the Lord had given him. He was a great general, a magnificent leader. Most important, he was "the servant of the Lord." His influence for good was immense, for we are told that

> Israel served the Lord all the days of Joshua, and all the days of the elders who outlived Joshua and had known all the work which the Lord did for Israel.    —*Joshua 24:31*

---

*For discussion of covenant renewal, see p. 70.

# 7

# The Time of the Judges

*Life in a time when each man
did what was right
in his own eyes*

## The Land of Canaan

For four hundred years, the descendants of Abraham had lived with the promise of a land that was to be their own. Finally, the promise had been fulfilled and they were "at home" in the land of Canaan. Before we talk about the problems they faced in coming to terms with the kind of life and culture they found in Canaan, it will be helpful to get a clearer view of the land and its people at the time Israel invaded it.

## The Land and Its People

In the Old Testament, the term Canaan is used to designate the whole area of Palestine west of Syria and the Jordan River. In the Bible, the inhabitants of this area are known by two main terms, Canaanites and Amorites. At an earlier period these two names signified two distinguishable, if similar, groups of people. The Canaanites were the people who settled along the coastland that ran from Egypt to Ugarit in Syria. The Amorites had come into Palestine from the West

(the name Amorite means "Westerner") and had settled in the mountainous region of the interior of the land. This distinction had pretty well fallen out of use by the time of the conquest, and both terms are used to refer to the whole population. Both of these groups came from an ethnic stock known to anthropologists, because of the language they spoke, as Northwest Semitic. The Israelites themselves were of this same stock. You may remember that Abraham and his family were part of the Amorite infiltration (See p. 22). It is possible that some of the groups named among the inhabitants of Canaan—such as the Hittites, the Horites, the Jebusites, the Girgashites, and the Perizzites—were not of this Northwest Semitic stock, but in general we can safely conclude that the Israelites were closely akin to most of the people among whom they were settling. It is good to keep this in mind when we read the prohibitions against intermarriage with the Canaanites (*Ex. 34:11–16*). The prohibition was on religious, not racial, grounds. As we shall see, Canaanite religion was a much greater threat to Israel than any racial difference could ever be.

## The Political Situation

Throughout most of her long history, Canaan seldom enjoyed the status of an inde-

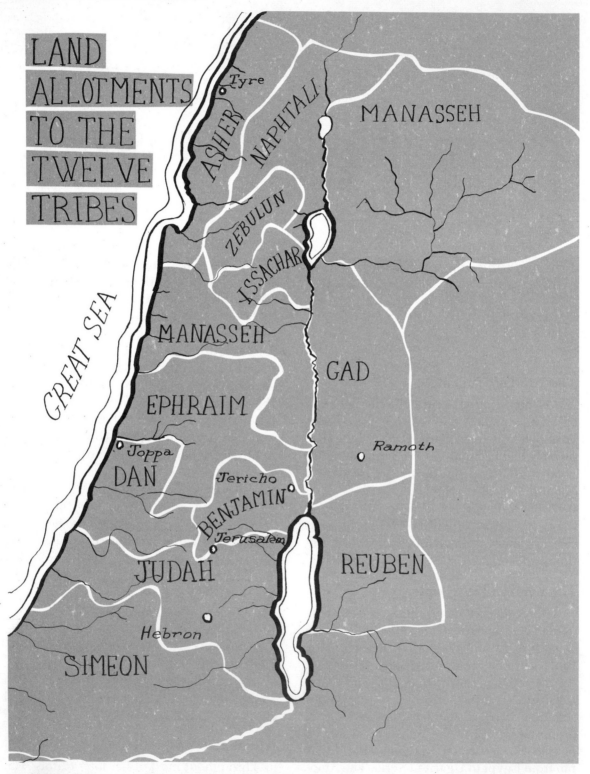

LAND ALLOTMENTS TO THE TWELVE TRIBES

GREAT SEA

Tyre

ASHER

NAPHTALI

MANASSEH

ZEBULUN

ISSACHAR

MANASSEH

GAD

EPHRAIM

Joppa

Ramoth

DAN

Jericho

BENJAMIN

Jerusalem

JUDAH

REUBEN

Hebron

SIMEON

**Canaan divided between the twelve tribes of Israel. Levites lived in special cities throughout the land.**

pendent political power. Much of the time, she was dominated by the Egyptian Pharaohs. The Pharaohs controlled the land through the kings of the various city-states which constituted the political units of Canaan. These kings,—"military mayors" might be a better term—were responsible for collecting and delivering the annual taxes and for keeping the people loyal to Egypt. Naturally, the Pharaohs didn't trust the Canaanites fully, so a check was placed on the kings in the form of imperial commissioners and garrisons of Egyptian soldiers situated in strategic points throughout the land. This arrangement had two unfortunate consequences for Canaan. In the first place, the high taxes exacted by the corrupt Egyptian government were a terrific economic strain, especially since virtually all of the money had to come from the pockets of the small number of rich landowners in each city-state. Secondly, Canaan's dependence on Egypt for military protection meant that when Egypt was weak, Canaan was extremely vulnerable to attack. This was exactly the situation in the latter part of the thirteenth century and partially explains why Joshua was able to move through the land with such comparative ease. Another factor in Israel's favor was that Canaan had been breaking into smaller political units for a century and a half before Israel invaded. In the early part of the fourteenth century B.C., there were far fewer city-states than are listed in *Joshua 10–12*. This made for a more even distribution of the population, but at the same time it lessened the strength of the individual city-states. It has been suggested that Egypt may have had a hand in breaking up the larger city-states, in an effort to keep possible centers of revolt from developing. Another plausible explanation is that the Canaanites had learned to make rock cisterns watertight by plastering the inside surface. This enabled them to store water and

thus to live in areas where springs and oases were scarce. Whatever the reason, the important point is that, at the time of the conquest, Canaan was politically rather disorganized and militarily vulnerable.

## The Social Structure

The economy of Canaan was based on agriculture. Part of the land was state-owned, but a good portion was under private ownership. This land was cultivated either by the owner and his family or, especially in the case of land belonging to the state and the state religion, by tenant farmers. The biggest landowner was usually the king. This meant that he was also the most important businessman, in addition to his function as the head of the military and religious organizations. The king had the power to levy and collect taxes, tolls, and fines, and to force his subjects into labor gangs to work on royally supported projects such as government buildings and temples.

Underneath the king on the social scale came the priests of the official religion, the professional warriors, the merchants, and the craftsmen. Next, but much lower down, were the tenant farmers, and at the bottom of the ladder were the slaves. Some of the slaves had been captured in war, but most had sold themselves into slavery either in payment of a debt or as an alternative to starvation, or had been sold by their parents while they were still children.

## Canaanite Culture

The Canaanites were a culturally advanced people. Their cities were strong and carefully built. Those who could afford them lived in fine sturdy houses. The king's dwelling was often an elaborate affair. Excavations at Megiddo have shown the royal palace to have been at least as large and extravagant as any built by later Israelite kings, even King Solomon. The excavations

Canaanite religious articles from
the tenth century, discovered at Megiddo:
an incense altar, bowls on stands, and pitchers.

at this palace, and others like it, have turned up numerous objects of art made of gold and other precious materials. Ivory seems to have been a favorite of Canaanite craftsmen, since large quantities of ivory inlay have been found in pieces of furniture and on wooden walls. From the writings of Amos, we learn that rich Israelites adopted this sign of luxury for themselves in later years (*Amos 6:4*). As was so often the case in ancient times, such sumptious living extended only to a privileged few. In the shadow of these great houses were the houses and lean-tos of the poor creatures who passed through life with but a scant mouthful between them and starvation. Despite the primary role of agriculture and the typically feudal pattern of manor house and serfs' hovels, Canaan was not a completely self-contained feudal society. Archaeolo-

gists have found documents, pottery, and other imports which show that the Canaanites had considerable contact with the outside world, not only with Egypt and Mesopotamia, but with the far-away (for that time) lands of the Aegean Sea. Canaan itself exported various textiles and did a large trade in the purple-dye industry. In fact, there is a strong possibility that the land received its name from the word *kinahhu*, which seems to have been the Canaanite word for red-purple dye. This theory is strengthened by the fact that Phoenecia, the northern section of Canaan, almost certainly gets its name from the Greek word for red-purple, *phoinix*.

Without question, the most significant achievement of Canaanite culture was the development of writing. Even before the year 2000 B.C., the Canaanites had developed a practical kind of writing. In the following centuries they used and refined the scripts and symbols of their neighbors. Finally, they developed an alphabet. The Phoenecian sailors passed this on to the Greeks and from there it went through the many revisions that have brought it to the form we use every day.

This was not a nation of savages. They were a literate people with a highly developed culture. This did not make the Israelites' task of remaining true to the laws they had received any easier. It would have been far simpler for them if they had moved into an empty land. Then, they could have unpacked their bags and organized things the way they wanted them. Instead, they had to come to terms with the culture as they found it. From the time of Israel to this day, this has been one of the most difficult challenges faced by the people of God.

## The Religion of Canaan

The most serious challenge to Israel's faith and life—the one she was never able to overcome for long—came from the religion of the Canaanites. For many years, about all we knew of Canaanite religion was what we could read in the Old Testament, and this was not enough to get a clear picture. Archaeology has been an immeasurable help here. In 1929, an expedition dug in the ruins of ancient Ugarit, on the coast of Northern Syria. These ruins yielded up a group of texts which give us a rather broad understanding of the religious situation in Canaan during the fourteenth century B.C. There is no good reason for doubting that Israel found substantially the same religious beliefs and practices when she came into Canaan. The modern name for the site of these excavations is Ras Shamra. For that reason, in this book, and in most books that deal with these matters, the documents are called the Ras Shamra texts.

The Ras Shamra texts give us the mythology on which Canaanite religion was based. This material enables us to identify the various deities, to see what the Canaanites thought about their place in the world order, and to understand religious practices suggested by the Bible or by other archaeological discoveries.

The general Canaanite word for any divine being was *el*. But this was also the proper name of the chief Canaanite god. El was thought of as a sky god who ruled over all the other gods when they assembled at their meeting place in the Northern mountains. The descriptions of El are vague. He bothered very little with mortals, and they returned the favor. He was thought to live far away at the underworld source of the two fountains that supply water to the springs, rivers, lakes, and oceans of the earth. It is notable that most ancient Near Eastern peoples associated elemental powers with fountains and "deeps."

El's consort, or wife, was Asherah. She was regarded as the mother goddess in charge of fertility. Asherah is mentioned in the Old Testament many times. In the King James Version, her name is translated "grove," but in the more accurate translations, her proper name is given. Asherah was usually represented by a tree or pole standing near an altar (*I Kin. 16:33; II Kin. 21: 3*). That the worship of Asherah was a threat to the worship of Yahweh is made clear by the frequent injunctions to pull up, or cut down, or burn these trees and poles (*Deut. 7:5; 12:3; 16:21;* etc.).

The most important of the Canaanite gods, and the one Bible students have heard the most about, was an offspring of El and Asherah—Baal. As was true with *el*, the term *baal* was originally a title meaning "lord" or "master." The proper name of this deity was Hadad, but by the time the Ras Shamra texts were written and certainly by the time Israel reached Canaan, he was known only as Baal. Baal was thought to live on a mountain top in the North, from which he controlled the storms and rains, and therefore the vegetation. He is often pictured as riding on the back of a bull.

There is some confusion about Baal's consort. Sometimes she is called Anath; at other times she is Astarte, or Ashtoreth. The latter is the form found most often in the Old Testament. She was credited with an odd combination of attributes. At one moment, she is seen as a bloody goddess riding about naked with a spear and shield. At another, she is the goddess of love and fertility. The manner in which these apparently opposite qualities are related will become clear when we look at her role in the agricultural myth.

One of the first things that strikes us as we read Canaanite religious mythology is that the gods were considerably less moral than most human beings. They completely disregarded the standards of conduct that ancient law codes, such as the code of Hammurabi, demanded of ordinary men. It is

Baal, the Lord of the Phoenicians and the Canaanites.

hard for us to understand this, because we commonly associate God with moral perfection. The highest compliment that can be paid a religious man is to say that he is a godly man, a man whose character is so pure that we think of it as almost godlike. In ancient Canaan, to have acted like the gods could have brought severe punishment. Why did this not disturb the ancient worshippers of these deities? Because they had never supposed there was any necessary connection between being good and being a god. The stories of the gods were not designed to give men a standard of righteous perfection. Their only purposes were to explain how the present order (or disorder) came into being, and what keeps it going.

There are two main myths we want to look at: the creation myth and the fertility, or agricultural, myth.

### THE CREATION MYTH

The details of the Canaanite creation myth are not yet clear, but it seems it followed along the same lines as other Near Eastern creation stories (see p. 12), in that it was a triumph of the hero-god (Baal) over the dark forces of chaos (Leviathan, or the Sea). With the defeat of chaos, order came into the world. Nature, man, and even the gods were subject to this order. There was some freedom, some variation, but the main lines were clearly marked out.

### THE FERTILITY MYTH

The aspect of this order which was most important to the Canaanites, and which they tried the hardest to control, was the agricultural cycle. But before we notice how they tried to influence it, let us first notice how they explained it.

In Palestine, the rainfall is pretty dependable. For six months of a normal year it will rain a good deal and for the other six months, very little. The rainy season starts in late October and continues through April. Spring planting is done in February, and the crop harvested in May or June. The rains also bring a variety of wild vegetation in April and May. By the time the harvest is ended, these are dead and things are quite barren once again. The dry season continues through October, when the rains come, and the cycle begins all over again.

The Canaanites saw this yearly process as the earthly result of what was going on in the realm of the gods. Baal was the Lord of Rain and Vegetation. Each spring, he is killed in the struggle with Mot, the god of death, or with his evil servants. Throughout the hot dry summer, Death is in control. But every fall, Baal's mourning wife Anath makes her way to the underworld home of Mot. In a ferocious battle, the warlike Anath overpowers Mot and frees Baal from the power of death. Reunited, they make love and the result is the vegetation that covers the ground in the spring. An extended period of drought indicated that Death was stronger than usual that year, and that Anath was having a harder time gaining victory over him.

The actual worship of the Canaanites was tied in closely with these myths, especially the fertility myth. Through his acts of worship, the Canaanite tried to influence the gods to favor him with their blessings of fertility and productivity. He was not concerned with being helped spiritually or morally. That was not the task of the gods. As we have already seen, they could hardly be expected to give much real assistance along these lines.

The details of Canaanite worship are not very clear, but we do have a good idea of the broad outlines. Sacrifice was a major feature. Animals and birds were, of course, the usual victims, but child sacrifice was occasionally heard of, presumably when the worshiper was in more desperate circum-stances. The other major aspect of Canaanite worship involved what anthropologists call "sympathetic magic." In practicing sympathetic magic, the worshiper performs an act which represents what happens in the heavens. In ceremonies used by American Indians to produce rain, the magic-maker will beat rocks together to represent thunder and lightning, or will pour a bowl of water on the ground to represent rain. Since the Canaanites were particularly interested in fertility and sex, their sympathetic magic frequently involved sexual intercourse. Sacred prostitutes, both male and female, were quite common. Anath herself was represented by an especially sacred prostitute, who was called "The Holy One." Intercourse with these prostitutes was believed to cause Baal and Anath to copulate, resulting in fertility and vegetation upon the earth. The Holy Prostitute was often pictured as a nude woman with lilies, a symbol of sex appeal, in one hand, and snakes, a symbol of fertility, in the other. Judging from the large number of these images which have been found in excavations in Palestine, it seems probable that most Canaanites kept at least one in their home as a kind of good luck charm. It is very hard for us to see how many people could associate this kind of thing with religion, but there is abundant evidence of the practice not only in Palestine, but throughout much of the ancient world.*

There were two main types of settings for this worship: "high places" and temples. The "high places" were country sanctuaries, scattered throughout the land. These usually consisted of an altar of burntoffering, accompanied by a wooden pillar, or a grove of trees, symbolizing the presence of the great goddess Asherah. A number of smaller altars, believed to be altars of in-

---

*For Israel's reaction to this practice, see *Deut. 23: 17–18.*

cense, have also been found at these sites. The temples were far more elaborate affairs and were located in the major cities. These were often substantial, even elaborate, buildings. As we might expect, some of the temple ruins that have been found indicate they were destroyed in the last twenty years of the thirteenth century, the period we have designated as the time of Israel's conquest of Canaan.

When we compare these beliefs and practices with those of Israel, the contrast is striking. Yahweh was not one god among several, having to struggle with them to maintain his position. He was the One True God, the only Being with power over the universe. He was not subject to the fixed order of the world, but was himself the Lord of Nature, Man, and the Universe. He had created the world, not in combat with a dragon, but as an act of his sovereign will. He ruled the world alone, without consort or offspring. He was not worshiped by debasing sexual practices whose end was to control his powers, but by acts of grateful response to his unmerited love and benevolence.

Despite these clear differences, the Israelites again and again turned to the groves and high places. Perhaps they reasoned that Yahweh was fine in matters of war and conquest, but Baal had had more experience when it came to agriculture. Perhaps they thought Yahweh would not mind so long as they gave him top billing. Whatever their reasons, worship of Baal and the other Canaanite deities was a violation of one of the fundamental laws of the covenant: "You shall have no other gods before me." There could be no compromise without disaster. This was a lesson that took Israel over five hundred years to learn. The history of the Israelites in the land of Canaan can accurately be called a history of compromise and disaster.

106

## The Ancient World in the Time of the Judges

This picture of Canaan will help us to understand a little better the problems Israel faced in adjusting to her new environment. But Canaan was only one piece in the jigsaw puzzle that was the Ancient Near East. If we are to get the whole picture, we must also notice what Canaan's neighbors were doing and how this affected the Israelites.

The period we are concerned with is the century and a half between Israel's arrival in Canaan and the rise of the monarchy under King Saul. This was the time when Israel was led by men called "judges." We shall have more to say about these judges in a little while, but first, let us see what was happening in the world about them.

This period saw Egypt slip from her post of world domination to a relatively minor position on the ladder of world powers. The Nineteenth Dynasty, which had held power during the time of the Exodus, was fast coming to an end. The last great ruler of this dynasty was Pharaoh Merneptah (1224–1216 B.C.). Merneptah made a few successful forays into Palestine. On one of these, he fought and defeated a group of Israelites. The Bible does not mention this incident, but fortunately, Merneptah thought enough of it to include it on a monument describing his victories. This monument has been a valuable aid in establishing an accurate Biblical chronology, since it is the first datable record of Israel's presence in Palestine. The greatest threat to Merneptah's empire came from the first waves of a group of invaders from the North and West called the Peoples of the Sea. Merneptah was able to keep them out of Egypt during his reign, but the supreme effort this required so weakened his nation that it was unable to maintain control over its holdings outside of Egypt. Because of this weakened condition, Egypt was powerless to stop the invading Israelites from overrunning much of Palestine.

A small handful of weak rulers finished out the century and this brought the Nineteenth Dynasty to an inglorious end. Shortly after 1200 B.C. the Egyptian throne was siezed by Set-nakht. He was not much of a ruler, but he was successful in passing the rule on to his son Rameses III and thus in establishing the Twentieth Dynasty. Rameses III brought one last flash of glory to Egypt. He re-established control of the strategic military post of Esdraelon in Palestine and enjoyed success in battle as far away as the Euphrates. The bubble of hope for a New Egypt was soon burst. The influx of the Peoples of the Sea was now in full swing. They were coming from everywhere, from the Aegean lands, from Libya, from Asia, by land and by sea, streaming down the coastland of Palestine and rushing like a torrent against the borders of Egypt. Like Merneptah before him, Rameses III was able to keep them out of Egypt, but he was unable to stop them from settling at will in lands which nominally belonged to Egypt. Egypt was once more at the point of collapse. Unrest and discontent culminated in Rameses' assassination in 1144 B.C. The dynasty somehow managed to hang on for another eighty years, but the eight kings which reigned in this period, all named Rameses, were equally unable to do anything more than hold on to Egypt proper. The Twentieth Dynasty was overthrown in 1065 B.C. and a new dynasty, the Twenty-first (sometimes called the Tanite), was set up. The Pharaohs of this dynasty were of a different family, but that was the only significant difference. They were as helpless as their predecessors. The situation was plain for all to see. Egypt's days as a world power were over.

Who was the great power in the Near East at this time? Actually, nobody. Assyria enjoyed a bit of conquest and prosperity for a brief period during the reign of Tiglath-Pileser I (1116–1078 B.C.), but her great time of power was still two centuries off. Babylon was fairly strong but she was certainly in no position to entertain thoughts of world conquest. The Arameans were gaining firm control of Syria and Upper Mesopotamia, but they were not yet a serious threat to anyone but Assyria.

Canaan itself was in a turmoil, with Israelites coming in from the east and occupying the mountainous areas and the Peoples of the Sea sweeping down and settling the western coastlands. The most important of these Peoples of Sea were those who settled in the southwest coastland of Palestine with the permission of Rameses III—really, he had little choice in the matter. Bible students know these people as the Philistines. It was from them that the land of Palestine got its name, indicating the extent of their influence over the area. By the end of the period of the judges, the Philistines were Israel's major enemy. This remained the situation until the time of David.

Now, finally, we are ready to look at the contents of the book of *Judges*.

## The Book of Judges

*Judges* is a collection of stories and fragments of stories that gives us a general picture of Israel's first century and a half in Canaan, from about 1220 to 1060 B.C. It is not as much concerned with history as it is with theology. The theological purpose of the writer is obvious. In *Deuteronomy*, Israel was warned against making any kind of alliance with the people of Canaan or with their gods. Any such violation of the covenant could be counted on to result in trouble. The writer of *Judges* viewed the stories he had collected as vivid proof of the truth of these warnings and was preserving them as an object lesson for future generations of Israelites to ponder. For this reason, he made no attempt to weave the stories into a strict chronological framework. If we are not aware of this, the result can be confusing. For example, the total number of years obtained from adding all the years the individual judges reigned is a little over four hundred, about two hundred fifty too many. The solution is simple. Obviously, several of the judges flourished at the same time. They were not leaders of the whole of Israel but of one tribe, or perhaps of several tribes that lived close together. To understand this, we need to look more closely at the kind of political organization Israel had at this time.

## The Amphictyony and the Judges

We sometimes get the idea that the Israelites settled thickly and evenly throughout the land, with only a picket fence to tell where one tribe's land ended and the next's began, and that they all met together for church each Saturday morning. But it was not like this at all. They were scattered all over the countryside, intermingled with the pagan Canaanites and separated from one another by valleys, ravines, rivers, mountains, and enemy-held territory. In addition to these natural barriers to communication, the nomadic Israelites were busy trying to adjust themselves to the settled life of a farmer. It is a cause for genuine wonder that they were able to maintain any sense of unity and identity as the covenant people of Yahweh.

The type of political organization which the twelve tribes formed was not uncommon in the ancient world. It was called an *amphictyony*. This is a difficult word—the most difficult in this book—but it is a good word and worth the trouble to learn. Actually, its meaning is simple. An amphictyony consisted of several tribes, or other groups of people, who were bound together by religious ties. Usually, there was some kind of central shrine or sanctuary to which all the

tribes could come to worship. The tribes were obligated to assist one another in battle and to protect the central sanctuary. Otherwise, they were relatively independent and could govern themselves however they saw fit. In other words, an amphictyony was a kind of religious federal government, a Twelve Tribe League.

In the light of all this, it would be natural to assume that each tribe appointed its own judge to rule over them. But this does not seem to be the case either. In the first place, the judges are not pictured as rulers so much as military leaders. In the second place, they were not appointed but were "raised up" by Yahweh in times of crisis. From the stories in *Judges,* a fairly consistent pattern emerges. A foreign power would intrude on a portion of Israel's territory and oppress the people. When the oppression became severe, a hero would arise who was especially gifted with wisdom, courage, military cunning, great physical strength, or some other gift, and would lead the revolt against the tyrants. His obvious abilities gave him the supreme command at least as long as the period of danger lasted. After that, it is difficult to know just what his status was. *Judges* usually tells us simply that he "judged Israel for X years," without further comment. In many cases, he probably slipped back into his old place in the society. If a new danger arose, he could be counted on to lead once again. If it did not, he would probably spend the rest of his life farming. A man was judge because he earned the position. He did not inherit it from his father, nor did he pass it on to his son.

The opening chapter of *Judges* reminds us once again that Joshua's conquest left a great deal still to be done by the individual tribes. Each tribe had to finish the task of driving out or coming to terms with the Canaanites who remained in its section. Unfortunately, they did a great deal more coming to terms than driving out. We can almost anticipate what will follow when we see the recurrent phrase, "but the Canaanites dwelt among them" (1:27, 28, 30, 32, etc.). In chapter 2, the theological presuppositions are set forth. The writer clearly intends for us to interpret his book in light of this chapter. His argument runs like this:

> There arose another generation . . . who did not know the Lord or the work which he had done for Israel. And the people of Israel did what was evil in the sight of the Lord and served the Baals. . . . So the anger of the Lord was kindled against Israel, and he gave them over to plunderers, who plundered them; and he sold them into the power of their enemies round about, so that they could no longer withstand their enemies. Whenever they marched out, the hand of the Lord was against them for evil, as the Lord had warned, and as the Lord had sworn to them; and they were in sore straits.
>
> Then the Lord raised up judges, who saved them out of the power of those who plundered them . . . Whenever the Lord raised up judges for them, the Lord was with the judge, and he saved them from the hand of their enemies all the days of the judge; for the Lord was moved to pity by their groaning because of those who afflicted and oppressed them. But whenever the judge died, they turned back and behaved worse than their fathers, going after other gods, serving them and bowing down to them; they did not drop any of their practices or their stubborn ways. So the anger of the Lord was kindled against Israel. . . .     —*Judges 2:10-20*

Each section of the book of *Judges* is designed to illustrate this sequence of faithfulness and idolatry, of reward and punishment.

The book is structured around six major invasions of Israelite tribes and the six judges who delivered the tribes from these invaders. Other judges are mentioned, but they are minor characters and we need not spend much time trying to remember them.

### OTHNIEL

The first threat came from the Mesopotamian nation ruled by Cushan-rishathaim. Israel suffered under this yoke for eight years before God raised up Othniel to deliver his people. Othniel was Caleb's younger brother;—bravery ran deep in this family. He had already proven his mettle as a warrior by capturing the city of Debir (1:11–15), and now, with Yahweh's aid, he defeated Cushan-rishathaim and brought Israel back to the service of Yahweh. (3:7–11).

### EHUD

The second of the enemy invaders were the Moabites. Ever since the Moabite king Balak had tried in vain to get Balaam to pronounce a curse on the Israelites, there had been bad blood between these nations. Israel had defeated Moab and the land had been given to the tribe of Reuben, but apparently, the Moabites recovered rather quickly and regained control of their land. We hear very little about the tribe of Reuben after this time. Once they got back on their feet, the Moabites decided it was unfair that Israel should get all the milk and honey. So, at the first opportunity, Eglon king of Moab enlisted the aid of a few neighbors and established a rule over Israel that was to last eighteen years. The area that Eglon controlled seems to have been the land immediately across the Jordan from Moab. This was inhabited by the tribes of Benjamin and Ephraim. This is supported by the fact that the only city which Eglon is said to have captured was the "city of palms" (3:13) a well-known nickname for Jericho, which was in Benjamin's territory. Also, the judge who defeated the Moabites, Ehud, was a member of the Benjaminite tribe (3:15).

A curiosity of Bible history is the fact that the tribe of Benjamin seems to have had an

**Two women, Deborah and Jael, execute the defeat of the Canaanites.**

unusually high number of left-handed warriors (See *Judg. 20:16*). Ehud belonged to this peculiar group, and when the Lord raised him up to deliver Israel, he put his skilled left hand to good use. When the time came to pay the annual tribute money to Eglon, Ehud was appointed to lead the delegation that delivered it. On the pretense that he had a secret message to deliver, Ehud managed to get a private audience with the king. When they were alone Ehud whipped a small sword out from under his garments and thurst it into Eglon's huge belly. Then, with the calm of a professional assassin, Ehud quietly locked the doors and left the palace. By the time the assassination was discovered, Ehud was on his way back to the hill country of Ephraim, where he marshalled a large fighting force. Excited by Ehud's cunning and inspired by his daring

leadership, this army of minutemen left their fields and completely devastated their Moabite oppressors. "And the land had rest for eighty years." (See *Judg. 3:12–30*)

### DEBORAH

The next threat to the Twelve Tribe League came from within Canaan itself. This was, incidentally, the only major difficulty with native forces. We have mentioned several times that Joshua was unable to wrest certain areas from Canaanite control. One of these was the plain of Esdraelon, which runs across the center of Canaan, and divided the tribes into two groups (see Map). In the latter part of the twelfth century, the Canaanites in the area consolidated their power and, under the leadership of Jabin and Sisera, were able to cause real discomfort to the Israelites living on both sides of the plain.

God's instrument of deliverance on this occasion was Deborah, the only woman who is known to have been a judge. We have said that the judges usually arose in the heat of a crisis. Deborah is something of an exception. She is described as a prophetess and was already recognized as one to whom people could turn for assistance in settling disputes. In other words, she was a judge in a much more conventional sense than the others seem to have been.

When Deborah saw the plight of her people she called for Barak, a local military leader, to gather his men for a showdown battle with Sisera, the commander of the Canaanite army. Barak was hesitant, but finally agreed, on condition that Deborah would accompany him on the expedition. She consented, but she told Barak that his dependence on a woman would mean that a woman was going to receive the glory for the victory. This prophecy was fulfilled when Barak routed the Canaanite army, but allowed Sisera to escape. Sisera ran away on foot until he came to the camp of Heber the Kenite, who was on friendly terms with Sisera's king, Jabin. The story is familiar. Jael, Heber's wife, welcomed him warmly, gave him a glass of milk, tucked him in bed, and drove a tent peg through his head.

The story of this battle has been preserved in the vital poetry of the Song of Deborah (*ch. 5*). Here we learn that tribes from all over Canaan took part in the battle, but that some had remained in their territory, or had come only with great reluctance (*5:14–18*). It also appears that a terrific rainstorm flooded the Wadi* Kishon, which would have caused the Canaanite chariots to bog down, giving an advantage to the Israelite footsoldiers (*5:4, 21*). Near the close of the poem, the singers complete the task of making sure that Barak gets less glory than Jael. Deborah and Barak are both credited with composing this poem (*5:1*), but we can probably assume that Deborah was primarily responsible for this section. The last stanza indicates, in a poignant way, that Israel had scored an upset victory.

> Out of the window she peered,
>     the mother of Sisera gazed
>         through the lattice:
> "Why is his chariot so long in coming?
>     Why tarry the hoofbeats of his chariots?"
> Her wisest ladies make answer,
>     nay, she gives answer to herself,
> "Are they not finding and dividing the spoil?—
>     A maiden or two for every man;
> spoil of dyed stuffs for Sisera,
>     spoil of dyed stuffs embroidered,
>     two pieces of dyed work embroidered for
>         my neck as spoil?"
> So perish all thine enemies, O Lord!
>     But thy friends be like the sun
>         as he rises in his might.
> —*Judges 5:28-31*

And the land had rest for forty years.

*A wadi is a valley or ravine. Except during the rainy season, it is usually dry.

### GIDEON

In many ways, the next period of oppression was the worst Israel had suffered. The invaders were the Midianites and they possessed a fearful secret weapon—the camel. As far as we know, this was the first use of the camel as an instrument of warfare. It may be that these Midianites were the first people to domesticate camels on a widespread scale. At any rate, they presented an awesome sight as they stormed across the Western desert to ravage the land of the Israelites.

The result was devastating. The Israelites were forced to leave their farms and hole up in mountain caves like animals. They would sneak down to plant a crop, only to have the raiders return at harvest time and destory whatever had come up. The people were near starvation. Herds died for lack of food. To make matters worse, larger groups of these nomads were beginning to move into the land, stripping it bare as they came, like a great horde of locusts. Finally, the situation became intolerable, and Israel turned to Yahweh. And Yahweh turned to Gideon.

Gideon is an interesting character. He was cautious, skeptical, and ruled by his reason, but once committed to a task, he executed it faithfully. When Yahweh first appeared to him in the form of an angel, Gideon was threshing wheat, not out in the field, but in the winepress within the vineyard, to keep the Midianites from seeing him. When the angel declared that Yahweh stood by the Israelites, Gideon was a bit cynical: "Pray, sir, if the Lord is with us, why then has all this befallen us? And where are all his wonderful deeds which our fathers recounted to us?" Gideon had heard a lot about this Yahweh, but he had not seen much first hand evidence. When the Lord told him that he, Gideon, would deliver Israel from the despised Midianites, this seemed the height of the ridiculous. He could not begin to do what Yahweh was suggesting. Finally, he demanded a sign that would prove that he was not dreaming, but that it was truly the Yahweh of Sinai who spoke to him. Yahweh did not rebuke Gideon for his doubts. After all, he had been reared by a father who had built an altar to Baal and Asherah on his farm. It was little wonder that he should have some peculiar religious ideas and some doubts about Yahweh. When Gideon saw the sign—a sacrifice he prepared was consumed by a fire from God—he was ready to do whatever Yahweh asked.

The first task was a dangerous one; Gideon was told to tear down the idolatrous altars his father had erected and to build an altar to Yahweh on the same spot. Gideon did as he was told, but he did it in fear. The townspeople had evidently become ardent devotees of Baal. He was taking his life in his hands to desecrate their high places. Probably, they were especially touchy about the matter at this particular time. It was bad enough to have the Midianites stealing and destroying most of the crops. If, in addition to this, Baal became offended and held back the vegetation, they would all surely starve.

Gideon's fears were justified. As soon as word spread that the altars had been torn down, angry citizens sought out Gideon, intending to kill him. They were talked out of it by Gideon's father, who seems to have been converted by his son's bold action. "If Baal is truly a god," he reasoned, "let him contend for himself." When Baal did not punish Gideon for his act, the people began to view the young man with more respect. When he summoned an army to overthrow the Midianites, the response was quite heartening. In fact, it seemed just a little too good to be true. Gideon still could not fully accept the fact that he was actually going to overthrow the Midianites with this volunteer army. Once again he asked the

Lord for a sign and received it—the famous sign of the fleece (6:36-40). Now, at last, Gideon was convinced.

Convincing Gideon was not enough. Yahweh saw that Gideon's skepticism was just one example of a widespread malady. What was needed was a sign dramatic enough to convince all of Israel that Yahweh was worthy of their trust and loyalty. As the occasion of this sign, he chose the battle with the Midianites, an event of which all Israel was certain to hear.

As we have said, the response to Gideon's summons was great. Too great. With this many people, the Israelites were sure to claim they had defeated the Midianites by the sheer force of numbers. Their number must be reduced until such a claim would be ridiculous. The first reduction was simple and straightforward. Gideon told everyone who was afraid to go home. Twelve thousand of twenty-two thousand left. But ten thousand was still a sizable fighting force. They could still claim they had won without Yahweh. The second and final test was purely arbitrary and had nothing to do with bravery. When the men went to drink, most of them bent over and drank directly from the pool. A little group of three hundred picked the water up with their hands and lapped it up like a dog. These three hundred were chosen as the army which would meet Midian.

The story of the encounter is one of the great adventure stories of the Bible. How the old storytellers must have enjoyed telling this one! Gideon and his men divided into three companies and surrounded the camp of the Midianite army. Each man had, of all things, a torch, a pitcher, and a trumpet. They lit the torches, but covered them with the pitchers to hide the light. Then, at a signal from Gideon, they blew the trumpets and broke the pitchers. The noise of breaking pottery and blasting trumpets and the sudden appearing of hundreds of torches all around their camp threw the Midianites into a panic. They figured they had been ambushed by an army of thousands. In their frantic efforts to escape, they began to attack one another. Additional Israelite forces flooded out of the nearby hills to drive them back to the desert from which they had come. By the time the night was over, Midian's power had been broken.

Several incidents connected with the "mopping up" of the routed Midianites indicate that Gideon was a no-nonsense type of military leader with a cold and clear standard of justice. After the trumpet and torch episode, he called on the Ephraimites to join the pursuit. They managed to capture and behead a pair of Midianite princes, but they felt cheated at not having been invited to the initial encounter. When they complained to Gideon, he told them to be happy with their two princes. He was too busy running a war to bother with this kind of childishness.

Gideon and his band of three hundred pursued the main Midianite force across the Jordan and through the land of Succoth. He asked the inhabitants of Succoth for food, but was refused. The people of Penuel gave him the same reception. Gideon was in too much of a hurry to do anything about their churlishness now, but he promised to get even with them when he returned. He was true to his word. After he captured the two Midianite kings, Zebah and Zalmunna, he started back to Canaan. On the way he found a youth from Succoth and got a list of the elders of the city. "And he took the elders of the city and he took thorns of the wilderness and briers and with them taught the men of Succoth" (8:16). The lesson he "taught" at Penuel was a bit more harsh, perhaps because he and his men had been hungrier when they were refused food by that city. There, he broke down the tower, which

was a key defense post in ancient cities, and slew the men of the city.

Gideon's eye-for-an-eye justice extended to his treatment of captives. The two kings had slain some of Gideon's own brethren. He told them that if they had taken them alive, he would spare their lives, but since they had slain them, they too must die. And die they did, by Gideon's own hand.

Gideon's close relationship with Yahweh, his prowess as a warrior, and his sureness in dealing with complaints and wrongs marked him in the eyes of the people as the kind of man they needed to rule over them. They urged him to be their king, to establish a dynasty that would make Israel strong. It was a tempting offer, but Gideon refused. The Twelve Tribe League was a theocracy, not a monarchy. Its ruler was Yahweh, not a human king. Gideon did,

**Gideon's three hundred men free Israel from the Midianites.**

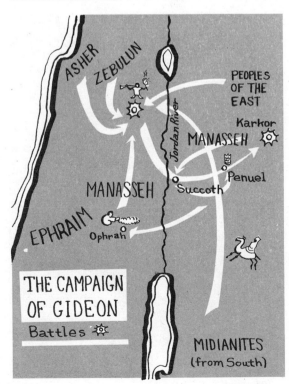

THE CAMPAIGN OF GIDEON
Battles ☼

113

however, accept one thing from the grateful tribesmen. He asked them to give him the earrings they had taken as part of their spoil, which they were happy to do. Then Gideon melted down the gold and fashioned an ephod from it. We can say very little about the nature of this ephod, apart from the fact that it was some type of religious image. Gideon's statement, "Yahweh will rule over you" (8:23) indicates that Gideon did not intend for this ephod to be used as an idol. Whatever his intentions were, they were corrupted "and all Israel played the harlot after it . . . and it became a snare to Gideon and to his family" (8:28).

The rest of Gideon's days were spent in peace and, apparently, prosperity. He had many wives, who bore him seventy sons, and a concubine, who bore him a son named Abimelech. The next major division of

**The adventures of Abimelech, the worthless son of Gideon.**

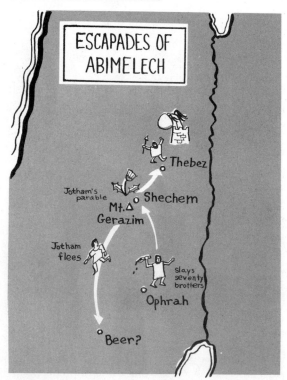

*Judges* deals with the career of this son. Abimelech was not a judge and his story involves none of the judges, but it does give a picture of the unrest that was characteristic of the time when the judges judged Israel.

### ABIMELECH

Gideon did not found a dynasty, but his sons seem to have formed a sort of unofficial ruling body. Abimelech was also Gideon's son, but since his mother was a non-Israelite concubine, he did not share in whatever measure power they had. This began to gnaw at Abimelech until he saw an opportunity to sieze some of this power for himself. Spurned by the Israelites, he turned to the men of Shechem, to whom he was related through his mother, and offered to become their king. They liked the idea of being ruled by one of their own and agreed to accept Abimelech's offer.

His first royal act shows what kind of man he was. He gathered a band of cutthroats and assassinated his seventy half-brothers. All, that is, but the youngest, Jotham, who managed to hide. When Jotham was told everything that had happened, he went to Shechem and stood atop Mt. Gerizim, which overlooks the city. From there he shouted the story which has come to be known as "Jotham's parable." In the parable Jotham compared Abimelech to a bramble among trees. Shechem had chosen the least fit of men to be their king. Jotham's words stuck in the minds of the Shechemites; gradually, they came to see the worthlessness of the man they had made their king. Guerilla bands formed in the hills to rob Abimelech's messengers and visitors. A revolutionary plot developed among the farmers, led by Gaal, a newcomer to Shechem.

The rebels had underestimated Abimelech's strength, and he was well on the way to putting down the uprising and vengefully exterminating those who had dared to chal-

This temple relief from Luxor shows an Egyptian officer leading feather-helmeted prisoners to the Pharoah.

lenge him. Then, as he attacked the nearby city of Thebez in order to reestablish his authority over the area, a woman dropped a millstone on his head from a window in the tower. Thus Abimelech's brief career as a king came to an end.

## JEPHTHAH

The next areas of Israel to feel foreign domination were the region around Gilead on the east side of Jordan and areas in Canaan belonging to Judah, Benjamin, and Ephraim. The Philistines had a small part in this oppression, indicating their growing power, but the real enemies were the Ammonites. For eighteen years they dealt misery to the tribes settled in Transjordan. They were encamped near Gilead, poised for another crippling campaign, when the Israelites decided it was time to try to throw off the Ammonite yoke.

The man who emerged as leader in this crisis was Jephthah. Like Abimelech, Jephthah was the child of an Israelite father and a prostitute mother. Perhaps this similarity between the two was the reason the writer placed the two stories together. Also like Abimelech, Jephthah was the leader of a band of tough guerilla fighters. Most of their talent had been spent in raiding activities, but they would be valuable in a revolution. When the tribesmen appealed to him for help, Jephthah agreed, but only on the condition that they accept him as their leader.

Jephthah delivered his people from the Ammonites, but he is remembered less for this than for his famous vow that cost the life of his only child, a beloved daughter. As he entered the contest with the Ammonites he realized the need for the aid of Yahweh. "If thou wilt give the Ammonites into my hand," he said, "then whoever comes forth from the doors of my house to meet me, when I return victorious from the Ammonites, shall be the Lord's, and I will offer

him up for a burnt offering." When his daughter danced out of the house to greet her victorious father, Jephthah was crushed by the consequences of his vow. Still, he made no attempt to go back on it. After a period of two months, in which she "bewailed her virginity," the girl "returned to her father, who did with her according to his vow which he had made" (*Judg. 11:39*). This incident and the *Judges* account of it show us that, although human sacrifice had no place in official Israelite worship, it could be practiced without stirring up undue notice or opposition.

An incident that took place in the aftermath of Jephthah's victory suggests that the unity the amphictyony brought was a fragile thing and could easily be shattered by tribal jealousy. The men of Ephraim complained that Jephthah had not let them share in the victory over the Ammonites. Apparently, Jephthah had given them the opportunity, but they had refused. Whatever the case, neither was inclined to have much sympathy for the other's claims. The result was a civil war which is said to have taken the lives of forty-two thousand Ephraimites (*12:6*). The story also contains the first notice of developing dialectical differences among the Israelite tribes. The Gileadites were able to identify escaping Ephraimites by their inability to pronounce *Shibboleth* correctly. The Ephraimite dialect contained no *sh* sound; consequently, they pronounced the word *Sibboleth*, and immediately betrayed their tribal membership. It is because of this incident, of course, that we use the term "shibboleth" to refer to a test phrase or a party cry.

### SAMSON AND THE PHILISTINES

In the early years of the period of the judges, the Philistines (Peoples of the Sea) were beginning to get a foothold along the coastlands of Palestine. By the eleventh century B.C. they had begun to harass the Israelites and, by the middle of the century, had virtually taken over Palestine. The story of Samson falls somewhere in this half century of growing Philistine power.

It is hard for a Bible student not to be prejudiced against the Philistines, because of the constant threat they posed for the people of God. When we look at them objectively, however, we see they were a vital people with a culture far in advance of the Israelites. The Philistine civilization was centered in five cities: Gaza, Ashkelon, Ashdod, Ekron, and Gath (see Map p. 128). There was no single king of all Philistia. Instead, each of these cities was controlled by a tyrant. An abundance of fine pottery found in the excavations of the Philistine cities indicates the high degree of cultural refinement that existed. From the large number of beer mugs that have been found,

**The feats of Samson.**

we can also conclude they were heavy drinkers (See *14:10; 16:25*). But Philistine power was not based on its lovely pottery or its conviviality. It was based on their knowledge of, and monopoly on, the iron industry. Presumably they had acquired this knowledge as they passed through the northern lands which had been under domination of the Hittites, who are thought to have been the first people to produce iron. Control of the iron industry meant military dominance by virtue of superior weapons. Military control gave them economic and commercial control as well. The Philistines recognized a good thing when they saw it and were determined to hold onto their monopoly. They refused to allow any iron production in subject lands, in order to prevent the development of weaponry comparable to theirs. This also meant they could charge high prices for selling and repairing iron farm tools (See *I Sam. 13:19–22*). The Philistines kept this monopoly, and with it the control of most of Palestine, until they were defeated by Saul and David. Then, Israel was able to exploit the iron industry to her own great advantage.

The first great hero in the long struggle with the Philistines was Samson. Samson is described as "A Nazirite to God from birth." The term Nazirite (from *nazar*, meaning consecrated, or devoted) ordinarily referred to a vow of special dedication to God, made for a limited period of time, and to the person making that vow. The conditions of the vow stipulated, among other things, that the Nazirite would not drink wine or cut his hair during the period of the vow (see *Num. 6:1–8; Judg. 13:5*). Samson's vow, announced before his birth by a heavenly messenger, was to last his entire lifetime. In return for his keeping of the vow, especially his refusal to cut his hair, Yahweh would give him phenomenal strength, which he was to use "to deliver

117

A Philistine beer jug. The large number of such jugs discovered by archaeologists gives an insight into Philistine social life.

Israel from the hands of the Philistines."

The story of Samson reads more like the adventures of a Palestinian Paul Bunyan than a moral or religious leader. One must search deeply to find any moral or spiritual lesson to be gained from reading about him. There is little doubt that part of the reason these stories were preserved in Israel was their superb entertainment value. A story-teller would have little trouble holding his audience when he told how Samson tore a lion apart with his bare hands, or how he destroyed the Philistine harvest by tying torches to the tails of foxes and letting them run through the grain fields. Imagine their delight when they heard how one Israelite had slain a thousand of the hated Philistines with nothing for a weapon but the jawbone of an ass. When he was trapped in Gaza, he simply pulled up the huge gates of the city and deposited them on a nearby hilltop—the original Hallowe'en prank. Nothing could stop Samson. Nothing but a woman. Women

were Samson's weakness and, eventually, his weakness caught up with him. His downfall was, of course, Delilah. When the Philistines learned of his love for Delilah, they persuaded her to try to find the secret of his great strength. Delilah was not immediately successful, for Samson, despite his many weaknesses, was not stupid. But after days of nagging and cajoling, he finally gave in and admitted to her that his strength lay in his hair. While he slept, she shaved his head. When the Philistines she had summoned attacked him, he was helpless to resist. The vengeful Philistines siezed him and gouged out his eyes, then took him down to Gaza, where he was put to work grinding grain in the prison mill.

This was a great triumph for the Philistines. With Samson out of the way, they could continue their harrassment of Israel. To celebrate, they staged a great festival and sacrifice to their god, Dagon. In the course of the celebration, Samson was brought out to "make sport." No matter what we have thought of Samson, the last scene is one of pathetic tragedy. Samson stands between the two supporting pillars of the temple of Dagon. As the crowd mocks and jeers, he seeths with anger and humiliation. He is aware of his own wasted life, of his failure to make his divinely-given powers a real blessing to Israel. In a last—and perhaps one of the few he ever uttered—prayer, Samson asked God for one last burst of strength. The prayer was granted. Samson braced himself between the two pillars and, with a mighty heave, brought the temple crashing down around him. "So the dead whom he slew at his death were more than those whom he had slain during his life."

## Miscellany

The remainder of the book is simply a miscellaneous collection of stories. They have nothing whatever to do with any

118

judges, but they do furnish us with windows through which we can get a few glimpses of life in this period.

As has been obvious throughout the book of *Judges,* the loosely-knit religious structure practically invited abuse. With the people scattered far from the central sanctuary, it was natural for them to "attend church" where the local people did. Even for those who did not worship the Baals, however, there was an increased likelihood of importing pagan ideas and practices into the worship of Yahweh. In the story of Micah (*ch. 17–18*), we have an example of how this could happen.

Both Micah and his mother were anxious to be pleasing to Yahweh (*17:2, 13*), yet neither saw anything amiss about making idols of silver, and they had no trouble in convincing a Levite to serve at the shrine in which these images were placed (*17:7–13*). Then, in *ch. 18,* the Levite is kidnapped, complete with images and regalia, by the men of the tribe of Dan, who wanted him to be their priest. The shrine they set up for him in the city of Dan was an active place of worship until the fall of the kingdom of Israel. It was one of the two centers of the calf worship instituted by King Jeroboam in 922 B.C. Probably, the writer's reason for including this story in his collection was to show how the northern shrine had originated.

The closing chapters record a series of related incidents which show the more barbaric side of life in Israel. A Levite and his concubine were traveling through the territory of Benjamin and found lodging in the city of Gibeah. Later in the evening, a group of carousers came beating on the door, demanding that the man be brought out to have homosexual relations with them. The host, following the same rules of Oriental hospitality that we observed in Lot (*Gen. 19:7–8*) refused to turn his guest over to them, but offered them his own virgin

daughter and the Levite's concubine. It is apparent that women's rights were not highly regarded in ancient Israel. The men took the concubine and assaulted her throughout the night. In the morning, when the Levite came out, she was lying dead, face down in the dust, with her hands stretched out toward the door. His sympathetic concern overwhelms us: "Get up, let us be going." But, if love for his concubine was not what we think it might have been, he was filled with indignation at the crime of the Benjaminites against a piece of his property. When he returned home to Bethlehem, he took his knife and divided the woman's body into twelve pieces. Then, he sent a piece to each of the twelve tribes. The gruesomeness of this act struck the Israelites in the same way it does us. But it also shocked them into horror at what the Benjaminites had done. The reaction was swift and violent. The men of Gibeah must be punished, lest the wrath of God consume them all. When the Benjaminites refused to surrender the guilty band, a bloody civil war broke out. The Benjaminites were badly outnumbered, but they were skilled warriors. With sword and slingshot (see *20:16*), they took a terrific toll of their attackers. Finally, however, superior numbers won out and Benjamin was defeated almost to the point of extermination.

When the victors met together at Bethel to rest, they began to feel the tragic effects of civil war. Benjamin had been guilty of great sin. There was no doubt of that. But now, one of the tribes which had come out of Egypt, a tribe of brethren, was facing extinction. When the tribes had met together at Mizpah to plan the attack against Benjamin, they had sworn not to give their daughters to become wives of Benjaminite men. This was beginning to sound too harsh. Not every Benjaminite man had been guilty. As is always the case, many were swept into the war with no real idea as to what it was about. The tribe had been sufficiently punished. Why should it suffer complete extinction? Since the vow had been made—and we have already noticed how seriously the Israelites took their vows—the only solution was to find wives from among some group which had not made this vow.

The men of Jabesh-Gilead had not been present at Mizpah. Since this was a violation of the amphictyonic covenant, they were subject to punishment. This was a perfect solution. The city was attacked and its inhabitants, with the exception of four hundred virgin women, killed. These virgins were given to the surviving Benjaminites to be their wives. This was a good start, but four hundred were not enough to go around. The course decided on this time once again illustrates the position of women and also shows how the Israelites managed to keep the letter of their vow while bending its spirit just a bit. The Benjaminites were given permission to kidnap girls when they came into the woods to dance at the annual feast of the Lord at Shiloh. Technically, this would not violate the vow, since they would not actually be "giving" their daughters to them. The morality is questionable, but no one seems to have complained too bitterly. The whole scene is reminiscent of the Rape of the Sabine Women in Roman history.

## The Story of Ruth

The story of Ruth, though probably written much later,* is set "in the days when the judges ruled" (*Ruth 1:1*) and illustrates several customs that are worth our consideration. It also shows us that not everything

Incidents in the last days of the Judges: the migration of the Danites, the theft of wives for the Benjaminites, and the story of Ruth.

that happened in the time of the judges was characterized by savage brutality.

The plot of this beautiful short story is well known. Ruth was a Moabite woman who had married an Israelite. When her husband died, she refused to leave the side of her Israelite mother-in-law, Naomi. Ruth's entreaty to Naomi is one of the classic gems of beauty in Biblical literature:

> Entreat me not to leave thee, or to return from following after thee: for whither thou goest, I will go; and where thou lodgest, I will lodge: thy people shall be my people, and thy God my God: Where thou diest, will I die, and there will I be buried: the Lord do so to me, and more also, if aught but death part thee and me. *—Ruth 1:16-17*

When the women returned to Bethlehem, Ruth "gleaned in the field of Boaz," a rela-

*The book of *Ruth* was included among what are called the "Writings" in the Hebrew Canon. This would mean that the story probably did not take its literary form until after the return from Babylonian exile, since the Writings were not officially accepted into the Hebrew canon until about 100 B.C.

tive of her late husband, and a wealthy and generous man. Naomi had told Boaz of her loyalty and he gave his servants instructions to treat her well and to make sure they left enough grain for her to get a good gleaning. In *Deuteronomy 24:19,* farmers were commanded to leave a little grain here and there in the field "for the sojourner, the fatherless, and the widow." Boaz went beyond the generous provisions of this rule. Since Ruth was a foreigner, he could have refused to allow her to glean at all. Instead, he told his men to take stalks from their own bundles to fill out her gathering.

When wise old Naomi saw that Boaz had taken favorable notice of Ruth, she decided that it was time to see if a marriage could be arranged. Actually, Ruth had a certain legal claim on Boaz. As we have already seen in the story of Judah and Tamar (See p. 43), when a woman's husband died before she bore him any children, his kinsmen were obligated to marry her. Since Boaz was related to her late husband, he would be one of those from whom the new husband would be chosen.

That evening, Ruth anointed herself and put on her best clothes. After Boaz lay down to sleep on his threshing floor, Ruth crept alongside him and lay down. When Boaz awoke about midnight, he was startled to find her there. Calmly, Ruth identified herself, and asked him to spread his skirt over her, a symbolic act indicating his intention to marry her. Boaz was older than Ruth and seems to have been somewhat shy, explaining, perhaps, why he had not married. But obviously, he was flattered by her action and would be delighted to have her for his wife. But first, there was a legal difficulty which had to be cleared up. There was a man in the village who was a closer relative to Ruth's husband than Boaz. He had prior rights to Ruth. If he refused to take her, Boaz would gladly make her his wife.

The scene between Boaz and the nearer kinsman gives a quaint picture of this ancient custom, and also of the high value placed upon keeping a plot of ground in the same family. Because there were no men left to farm the land that had belonged to her husband and sons, Naomi was prepared to sell it. The first option to buy it fell to the next of kin, this same relative. When Boaz told him of his opportunity, he was willing to take the land, but backed out when he learned that Ruth came with it. Then, as was the custom, the next of kin took off his sandal and gave it to Boaz, as a sign of his refusal to "do the part of the next of kin" for Ruth. The way was then clear for Boaz to announce to the assembled elders that he would take both the land and Ruth.

So, with the blessings of the people, Boaz took Ruth to be his wife. She bore him a son, Obed, who was the grandfather of David. Many scholars feel that the story was written and preserved in the canon for the specific purpose of showing that David's great-grandmother was a Gentile. We can imagine the effect this story must have had in the years after the exile. Ezra had emphasized that there could be no intermarriage with non-Israelite stock. Yet here was a story which clearly proclaimed that, if there was no place in Israel's religion for non-Jewish peoples, there was no place for King David, the epitome of all that was treasured by the Jews. In this story we see the tension between forces who equated purity of religion with purity of race and those who felt that God's grace could be extended to cover a larger section of humanity.

## Summary

This, then, was the time when the judges judged Israel. In general, it was a period of disorganization which sometimes approached chaos. Israel made no gains during the period. In fact, her hold on her territory was less secure in some places at the end of the period than it had been at the beginning. The lack of unity, the lack of a consistent system of justice, and the lack of ability to hold the people to the worship of Yahweh makes us wonder why God ever directed them to the amphictyonic form of government and how this form of government managed to hang on for almost two hundred years. Certainly a monarchy would have been much more efficient. In seeking the answer, we should consider the form of government we have in America. The slow, often clumsy, process of our constitutional government has caused many to advocate a system in which greater power is held by a smaller number. Such a system would have its obvious advantages, yet the American people have thus far felt that it was better to allow more people to have a hand in the governing process, on the theory that this will better safeguard the individual rights that are deemed expressive of the traditional ideals of America than would a monarchy.

In a similar way, the tribes of the amphictyony were jealous of their independence. They were not yet ready to be unified under a single ruler. Furthermore, this arrangement was felt to be most expressive of the ideals of the Mosaic covenant. Those who responded to God's grace were bound together by this grace and this response, and not by political authority. There was no king but Yahweh. Despite its weaknesses, the Twelve Tribe League might have survived even longer had it not been for the Philistine threat. When the Philistines began to extend their power over more and more of Palestine, it seemed to the Israelites that the only alternatives open to them were disappearance as a distinct people, or unity under a single king who could throw off the oppressive Philistine yoke. The latter won out, but not without a struggle. We are ready now to turn our attention to the rise of the monarchy in Israel.

# PART THREE

## *The Era of Kings and Prophets*

# 8

# The Rise of the Monarchy in Israel

*Under her first three kings, Israel becomes the mightiest power in the Near Eastern world*

ISRAEL had been in the land for two centuries. As the stormy book of *Judges* shows, these had been troubled years. Again and again, the tribal league was almost destroyed by foreign invaders, but each time the area under attack had somehow managed to throw off the oppressors. But these had all been sectional affairs. Not all of Israel's territory had ever been oppressed at the same time. While one section was suffering, another had time to recover from its past troubles and to flourish for awhile before its borders were invaded. This up-and-down situation did not make the amphictyony a very stable form of government, but it did enable it to stay in existence for longer than one might have expected.

The Philistine aggression posed a different kind of threat, not only to the amphictyonic government but to the continued existence of the Israelites as a distinct people. Previously, Israel's enemies had been content to rob them of their produce and money. They were not concerned to press their culture on them. Occasionally, these foreign kings were able to make an alliance of some kind with each other, but these were flimsy affairs. Each king was interested in his own nation and was unwilling to share much of the spoil with his neighbors. And so, he would attack only as much of Israel as he felt he could safely handle.

The ruling tyrants of the five Philistine city-states, however, managed to work together as a much more unified force. It was not Gaza or Ashkelon that was uppermost in their minds, but Philistia as a whole. This unity enabled them to extend their aggression over a much greater area than would have been possible for any one of them. Unlike Israel's other enemies, the Philistines were interested in more than spoil and tribute money. They were an ambitious people with a vital culture. Their aim was to gain full control of Palestine, to force their culture on the land. In other words, they wanted the whole of Palestine to become a Philistine nation and they wanted its inhabitants to adopt the Philistine culture and outlook. What is more, their well trained army with its superior iron weapons made it seem

125

probable they would achieve their goal.

The nature of this Philistine threat made it clear to the Israelites that the only hope for preserving their identity was to bind themselves together in a more unified arrangement than the Tribal League had provided. What could be more unifying than a king? The other nations had them and they seemed to do all right. Why not have a single king over all of Israel?

Israel got her monarchy, and her kings saved her from the Philistines. But she did not get it without a struggle, and her salvation did not come cheap. In this chapter, we shall deal with the rise of the monarchy in Israel, with the theological struggle that accompanied its rise, and with the histories of the three great monarchs of the United Kingdom of Israel: Saul, David, and Solomon. Fortunately, our sources for this period are quite good; better, in fact, than for any other period in Israel's history. *I–II Samuel*, and *I Kings 1–11* form a continuous historical narrative covering the period from the last judge to the death of Solomon and the division of Israel into two kingdoms. The reigns of David and Solomon are also dealt with in *I Chronicles* and *II Chronicles 1–9*. Much of the material in these books is based on official historical records made at the time these kings were reigning (see *I Chron. 29:29–30; I Kin. 11:41; II Chron. 24:27*). Thus, while many of the historical sections of the Old Testament were written down long after the events took place, these records come from actual eyewitnesses.

The material dealing with the transition from Tribal League to Monarchy (*I Sam. 1–12*) is of a different order, however, and this causes some special problems in interpretation. It describes situations for which we have no preliminary information and contains ideas that are difficult to harmonize. Let us turn now to a consideration of these somewhat troublesome chapters.

## The Transition from Judges to Kings

### ELI AND SONS, PRIESTS

The first four chapters of *I Samuel* tell of a time when the primary power in Israel was in the hands of Eli and his sons, Hophni and Phinehas, the priests who served at the tabernacle at Shiloh. It is possible that there was a judge somewhere in Israel. However, since the situation with the Philistines was so critical that the activity of a hero would surely have been recorded, it seems likely that there was not. In the absence of such a figure, the leadership of the tribes had fallen to the family of Eli. Perhaps the people were beginning to sense that their only hope lay in Yahweh. Since Yahweh's presence was symbolized by the Ark of the Covenant, and since Eli and his sons had charge of the Ark, it was only natural that they should look to them for guidance. Eli himself seems to have been a righteous man, but his sons were thoroughly worthless men. The Biblical writer characterizes them well when he says, "they had no regard for the Lord" (*2: 12*). By cynical and systematic graft, they took for themselves the sacrifices that worshipers had brought to the Lord (*2:12–17*). And to further profane their divine office, they had sexual relations with the women who helped with the tabernacle services.

Yahweh could not tolerate this kind of blasphemy. For almost two hundred years the people had repeatedly turned from the tabernacle at Shiloh to the high places of Baal and Asherah. Now, even those who served at Shiloh had shown their contempt for the way of holiness. Yahweh could no longer remain in their midst. And so, he withdrew from them—but they did not know he was gone.

The reckoning came at the disastrous battle near Aphek, in about 1050 B.C. The war was going badly for Israel. The elders realized, rightly, that their losses were a sign that Yahweh was not among them. They assumed, wrongly, that all they needed to reverse the situation was to bring the Ark of the Covenant into the battle. Word was sent to Shiloh and, soon, Hophni and Phinehas came into the camp with the Ark. The warriors greeted it with an earth-shaking shout and the Philistines were dismayed that "the gods have come into the camp." They had heard of the mighty acts of the Israelite god and were certain that his wrath was about to fall upon them. But they were professional soldiers; they would not surrender without a fight. Despite their fear, they shouted to each other, "Take courage, and acquit yourselves like men, O Philistines." With this spirit the Philistines fought, and Israel was defeated. The Israelites had thought of the Ark as a good luck charm or a magical talisman. If it were there, they could not lose. But they did. Thirty thousand Israelites, including Hophni and Phinehas, were slain and the sacred Ark was captured by the pagan Philistines. The victories Yahweh had brought them had failed to keep them faithful to the covenant. Perhaps defeat would shock them to their senses.

There are indications that the disaster had just this effect, if we may view the incidents preserved in the tradition as typical. The messenger who carried the news to Shiloh had ripped his clothes and covered his head with dirt. When he told Eli of the death of his sons and the loss of the Ark, the old man toppled over backward, broke his neck, and died. At the moment when the wife of Phinehas learned of his death, she went into labor and bore a son whom she named Ichabod, signifying that "The glory has departed from Israel" (*4:12–22*).

Although the Bible does not tell us in so many words, there is little doubt that the Philistines destroyed Shiloh at this time. It is not mentioned again as a religious center. Archaeological evidence indicates that it

was completely destroyed in the mid-eleventh century. And, almost five hundred years later, when Jeremiah was warning the people of Jerusalem not to think of the temple as a magical charm, he reminded them of what Yahweh had done long before when their ancestors had made this same mistake:

> Go now to my place that was in Shiloh, where I made my name dwell at first, and see what I did to it for the wickedness of my people Israel. And now, because you have done all these things . . . therefore I will do to the house which is called by my name, and in which you trust, and to the place which I gave to you and to your fathers, as I did to Shiloh. —*Jeremiah 7:12–14*

Israel was prostrate. The Philistines were forced to return the Ark, because of a plague that broke out among them (see *5–6*), but its presence at Kiriath-jearim did little for Israel's political fortunes. For one reason or another, the Philistines did not completely subjugate all of Israel, but virtually everything west of the Jordan from the southern Desert to much of Galilee was under their control. Israel was held in a stranglehold by a hand of iron (cf. *I Sam. 13:19–22*). Her government was gone. Her center of worship was gone. It would be reasonable to expect that her religion was also gone; but it was not. In fact, the worship of Yahweh began to enjoy a sort of revival. The chief figure in this revival was a man called Samuel.

### SAMUEL

Samuel had been destined before his birth to be a servant of Yahweh. His mother, Hannah, had made a vow to Yahweh that if he would end her barrenness and give her a son, she would "give him to the Lord all the days of his life." Her prayer was granted and Samuel was born. His name means "heard of God." As soon as he was weaned, his mother brought him to Shiloh and turned him over to Eli the priest. There he "ministered to the Lord" and "continued to grow both in stature and in favor with the Lord and with men." As a result of visions which he had, in a time when "the word of the Lord was rare" and "there was no frequent vision," Samuel came to be recognized throughout the whole of Israel as a prophet of the Lord. When the priestly family was killed and the sanctuary at Shiloh destroyed, the nation inevitably looked to Samuel for guidance.

His role was a multiple one. As a *judge,* he presided over legal cases that were brought before him and gave his advice wherever it was needed. His residence and main headquarters were at Ramah, but he also worked a circuit that included Bethel, Gilgal, and Mizpah (*7:15–17*). This enabled a larger number of people to get the benefit of his wisdom. As a *seer,* he could be consulted to find the answer to problems, such as the location of lost animals. As a *priest,* he offered sacrifices to Yahweh at sacred altars. As a *prophet,* he was the recognized representative of God, with the power to act in his behalf. The great prestige and authority that Samuel enjoyed in these different roles made him the most important figure in Israel since the time of Moses.

Samuel was the key figure in the transition from government by judges to rule by kings. Despite this fact, however, it is extremely difficult to know just how he felt about this transition. At one point, he seems to be pushing Saul into the kingship. At another, he is warning Israel of the dire con-

**Key events in the transition from Judges to Kings.**

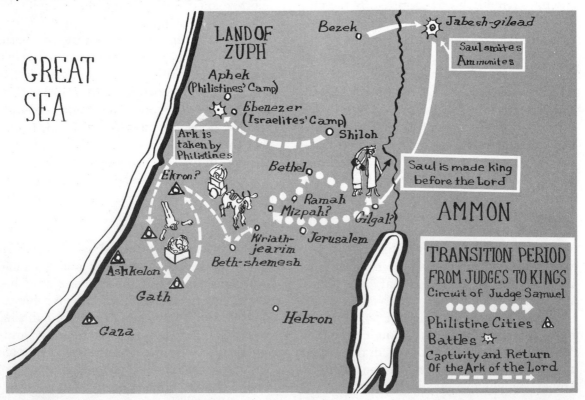

sequences that will follow if they do make Saul a king. If we were to sort out these sections and read them separately, we could hardly believe they are talking about the same man. If the reader would care to make such a comparison, the passages may be categorized as follows: *pro-monarchy* (*I Samuel 9:1–10:16; 11*) and *anti-monarchy* (*7: 3–8:22; 10:17–27; 12*).

In the *pro-monarchy* sections, Samuel first encounters the young man Saul when he comes to inquire about the location of his father's lost asses. Samuel was immediately impressed with the young man and, at Yahweh's instruction, anointed him as the future king of Israel who would deliver his people from the Philistines. Saul was skeptical, but Samuel told him of several signs he would experience on his way home that would confirm the truth of the prophet's words. The most significant of these was Saul's seizure by the spirit of prophecy. Israel was experiencing a new phenomenon in those days. Bands of "prophets" were going through the country stirring up religious fervor by their frenzied dancing and shouting, all to the accompaniment of musical instruments (*10: 5*). Samuel's role as a prophet was of a different order from these ecstatic individuals, but he did not frown on what they were doing. Apparently, he looked on their activity as a legitimate form of religious devotion. Samuel told Saul that he would meet such a band on his way home and that the spirit of the Lord would "come mightily" upon him and that he would "prophesy with them and be turned into another man." From what we know of Saul's personality as a king, we can imagine that this type of exhibition was the last thing he would ordinarily be expected to engage in. His neighbors felt the same way. When they saw Saul shouting and dancing about wildly in the midst of a band of prophets, they gasped in amazement, "What has come over the son of Kish? Is

Saul also among the prophets?" (*10:11*). In this passage, Samuel seems to be taking the initiative in setting up a king to rule over Israel. In the second pro-monarchy passage (*ch. 11*) Saul gains final acceptance as king, with the encouragement and blessing of Samuel. This came after the battle with the Ammonites. The Ammonites had not posed a major threat to Israel, but the battle did give Saul an opportunity to display his talents as a leader and warrior. The Ammonites had attacked the city of Jabesh-gilead and were about to subdue it when the men of the city offered to surrender. The Ammonite king agreed, but only on the cruel condition that the right eye of every man of the city be gouged out. If the Ammonites were allowed to get away with this cynical act, all the nations would know that the Israelites were powerless to protect their people; more such attacks and atrocities would occur. Israel would be brought even lower than she already was.

When word of this reached Saul, he had been out in the field plowing, a fact that shows us how far the kingship had to go before it reached the level attained in Solomon's time. Saul's reaction was swift and dramatic. In a symbolic act reminiscent of that we noted in *Judges 19*, he butchered a yoke of oxen and sent the pieces throughout the tribes with the warning that "whoever does not come out after Saul and Samuel, so shall it be done to his oxen!" Israel responded as one man. A great army was mustered and the Ammonites were so thoroughly defeated that "those who survived were scattered, so that no two of them were left together." For this act Saul received the lasting gratitude of the citizens of Jabesh-gilead (see *I Sam. 31:11–13*). More important for our purposes is the response of the Israelites to Saul's inspiring example. They were so captivated by their new hero that they threatened to execute all who had ever been skeptical of his fitness to rule. Then, at Samuel's bidding, they gathered at Gilgal to pledge their loyalty to Saul "before Yahweh." From these two passages, one could not guess that Samuel felt anything but joy at having found such a capable leader and pride at his part in having rallied the people to his support. But now, let us look at the *anti-monarchy* passages.

In the *anti-monarchy* passages, it is not Samuel who takes the initiative, but the people. The old method of waiting for a crisis to produce a leader was not adequate in the present political situation. They wanted a king who could be ready to meet a threat before it had a chance to develop into a crisis. On the basis of the pro-monarchy passages, we should expect to hear Samuel agree with them and to suggest a bright young man whom he had been thinking about as especially well qualified for the job. Instead, he seems to want to have nothing to do with the monarchy. He has even tried to set up his sons to succeed him in the judgeship. Israel had been willing to accept Samuel's leadership, for he was truly an exceptional man, but he was old and his sons were simply not of the same calibre. They demanded a king, "like all the nations" (8:4–5).

According to 8:6–9, this request was displeasing both to Yahweh and Samuel. It was seen as a rejection, not primarily of Samuel, but of Yahweh himself. At Yahweh's instruction, Samuel addressed the people, warning them of the severe price they would pay for chosing a king. He would draft their sons into the royal army and their daughters to be servants in the palace. He would take the best fields and vineyards and orchards to feed those who served him. Of what was left to the people he would demand a tenth in taxes. Their servants, their flocks and herds, and they themselves would be made royal slaves. "And," warned Samuel, "in that day you will cry out because of your king, whom

you have chosen for yourselves; but Yahweh will not answer you in that day" (8:18).

But the people were determined. They demanded a king, that they might be like the other nations, "and that our king may govern us and go out before us and fight our battles" (8:20). When Yahweh saw they could not be discouraged, he resigned himself to their will and instructed Samuel to "hearken to their voice and make them a king."

In the second anti-monarchy passage (10:17–27), Samuel rebuked the Israelites for their decision even as he drew lots to determine who should serve as their king. The lot fell, of course, to Saul the son of Kish, whom Samuel had already anointed.

The last of these passages is found in *I Samuel 12*. This contains Samuel's speech after Saul's thrilling victory over the Ammonites. To begin his speech, Samuel reminds the people that he has never used his office for personal advantage (as a king might be expected to do). Then, he recalls Israel's great victories, all won without the benefit of a king. "In the face of all this," says Samuel—we can almost hear the bitterness in his voice—"you have said, 'No, a king shall reign over us,' when Yahweh your God was your king." This speech makes it clear that Samuel felt quite deeply that Israel was taking a course that pointed toward estrangement from Yahweh and ultimate destruction. Nevertheless, he would do what he could to avoid calamity. He would advise the new king and the people, and would continue to serve as Yahweh's prophet.

> Far be it from me that I should sin against the Lord by ceasing to pray for you; and I will instruct you in the good and the right way. Only fear the Lord, and serve him faithfully with all your heart; for consider what great things he has done for you. But if you still do wickedly, you shall be swept away, both you and your king. —*I Samuel 12:23-25*

How are we to understand these two groups of passages? Was Samuel against or in favor of the monarchy? Which passages are presenting the true picture? Some scholars have argued that Samuel probably expressed himself both ways at different times and that those who favored the kingship saved one set of stories and those who opposed it saved another set. When the writer of *I–II Samuel* gathered his materials together, he found himself with two apparently contradictory traditions. Instead of deciding for one and throwing the other out, he fit them together the best way he could, trying to minimize the contradiction.

This view seems to complicate things unnecessarily. Obviously, Samuel did have mixed feelings about the matter. He felt strongly that Israel should stick with the Tribal Confederacy, cumbersome as it was. Still, as a practical man, he could see that Israel was determined to have a king and would achieve no kind of unity until she got one. In this circumstance, it was better to go ahead and try to find the best man available and to give him full support. Then, as the people began to place their confidence in Saul instead of in Yahweh, and Saul began to think a bit too highly of himself, Samuel's doubts rose to the top. Eventually, these feelings predominated and Samuel completely broke off relations with him.

It is possible the defenders and opponents of the monarchy emphasized those statements of Samuel that agreed with their point of view, but there is no good reason to believe the inspired writer had to pull any literary tricks to put his material together. The passages seem a bit inconsistent because Samuel, like all men, was a bit inconsistent. If we read them as a continuous narrative, instead of as two separate sources put together like a jigsaw puzzle, we have a rich picture of a godly man's effort to resolve the tension between the ideal and the possible.

## King Saul (About 1020–1000 B.C.)

### THE EARLY YEARS

When Saul left off plowing to rescue Jabesh-gilead from the Ammonites, he was never to return to the quiet pastoral life he had enjoyed. His reign began and ended in battle, and was characterized throughout by wars and rumors of wars. In the early years Saul was highly successful. He proved himself to be the kind of military hero Israel had sought and he was able to bring enough stability to the nation to insure the acceptance of monarchial government.

The greatest success in these early years was the defeat of the Philistines at Michmash. This battle arose out of a skirmish at Geba in which Jonathan, Saul's son, defeated the Philistine garrison stationed there. This angered the Philistine command. If this were allowed to go unpunished, Israelites in other areas might try the same thing. So, to crush any seeds of revolt, the Philistines brought out a tremendous force of horsemen and chariots, "and troops like the sand on the seashore in multitude." When they made their camp at Michmash, the Israelites lost all heart and scurried into holes and caves like frightened animals. Saul had his small fighting force together at Gilgal, but they "followed him trembling."

Apparently, Samuel had told Saul to wait at Gilgal for seven days, at which time he would join them and offer sacrifices to insure Yahweh's presence among them when they went into the battle. Saul waited, for he knew, at least in his cooler moments, that his and Israel's success depended on the arm of Yahweh. When Samuel did not come at the precise hour, Saul's army began to disintegrate. If the holy man was not coming, perhaps Yahweh had deserted them. When Saul saw what was happening, he impulsively ordered the sacrifices to be prepared and offered them himself, usurping the au-

131

thority which belonged to the priesthood. The smoke was still rising from the altar when Samuel arrived at the camp. When Samuel rebuked him, Saul tried to justify his action on the ground that he needed Yahweh's favor and, since Samuel had not come, it looked as if the only way he could get it was to offer the sacrifices himself. This makes sense, but Saul had broken a commandment which he obviously understood. For his lack of faith and his disobedient spirit, Samuel told him the kingship would not remain in his family. There would be no dynasty of Saul. Yahweh would raise up another to sit on the throne that could have been reserved for Jonathan. We can see here that Samuel's ambiguous feelings about Saul have become more concrete. The doubts he had were now confirmed. From here on, their relationship would only grow worse.

Despite Samuel's announcement of Yahweh's displeasure with Saul, the outnumbered Israelites turned what looked like certain defeat into a decisive victory. Again it was Jonathan who got things off to a good start. He and his armor-bearer walked into a Philistine outpost and, working as an efficient team, killed twenty of the soldiers who manned it. In our discussion of Holy War (See p. 93f*) we noted that numbers were an incidental factor in a war in which Yahweh fought and that the enemy camp was frequently thrown into a panic that could scarcely be explained by natural causes. Both these elements are present here. Jonathan sought a sign from the Lord to assure him of victory (14:9). When he received it, he showed no reluctance to walk into a battle where the odds were at least ten to one against him. Yahweh brought him the expected victory, and the enemy camp was filled with the expected terror. When Saul and the Israelites saw the confusion, they took heart and joined the attack. Hebrews who had deserted to the Philistine camp were moved by Yahweh's presence among them to rejoin Saul and Jonathan. Even the refugees who had hid in the hills of Ephraim streamed down to join in the rout of the fleeing Philistines.

This was a great day for Israel. The hated Philistines had been met and defeated in a major battle. The threat was by no means removed, but Israel had whipped the best Philistia had to offer. She was no longer confined to the hills where Philistine chariots could not come, but could move much more freely throughout her land.

And so it went in the early years of the reign of Saul, Israel's first king.

> He fought against all his enemies on every side, against Moab, against the Ammonites, against Edom, against the kings of Zobah, and against the Philistines; wherever he turned, he put them to the worse. . . . And when Saul saw any strong man, or any valiant man, he attached him to himself.
>
> —I Samuel 14:47, 52

In this last sentence, we see Samuel's words about the kingship beginning to come true. What good was a king if he was hamstrung by a volunteer army that had to be pulled out of holes in the mountains? It was essential for him to have a standing army he could count on at all times. Actually, however, this was about the only demand Saul made on the people, and there is no indication that these men were not perfectly willing to join him. Saul needed no large number of servants for his palace or girls for his harem. His "palace" at Gibeah, which archaeologists have excavated, was a plain stone fortress, built for strength and practical function rather than luxury. He had no harem; Solomon was the first to adopt this custom of oriental potentates on a large scale, although David had several wives and concubines. He had no cabinet of royal officers, no bureaucratic administrative structure, not even a system of taxation. Nevertheless, the entire nation—not just Saul's own tribe, but all the tribes—recognized him as a king, and began to think of themselves in more nationalistic terms. It was a crude monarchy, but it was a monarchy. The transition had been made.

Despite his early successes, Saul is one of the most tragic figures in the entire Bible. He was a skilled warrior and a capable leader, but his emotional instability poisoned the good he did and left the nation in as bad a shape at the end of his reign as it had been at the beginning. If Saul had lived today, he would probably have been committed to a mental hospital in the closing years of his life. From the beginning, there were contradictory facets in his character that suggest some imbalance. He was modest and shy to the point of hiding among the animals and baggage when the people were

**The Kingdom of Saul.**

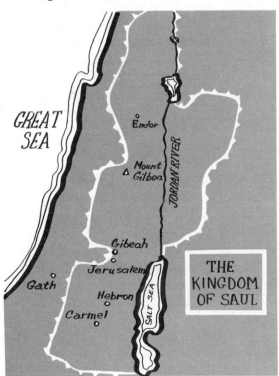

THE KINGDOM OF SAUL

seeking him to proclaim him king (*I Sam. 10:20–24*). Yet, when he was aroused, as in the case of the threat to Jabesh-gilead, the force of his anger was enough to transform the trembling Israelites into a fierce fighting machine. His anxiety over the sacrifices at Gilgal, his taking a priest into battle (*14:3*), and his sacred vows (*14:24*) make it clear that he recognized his and Israel's dependence on Yahweh. However, his impulsive seizing of religious authority and his refusal to carry out the command of Yahweh cost him the valued friendship of Samuel, the prophet of Yahweh. In his dealings with David, to which we shall turn shortly, we can see that, at least part of the time, he was a man bereft of his senses. The decisive break with Samuel, and the point at which Saul's fortunes began a downward spiral was the battle with the Amalekites.

### SAMUEL BREAKS WITH SAUL

The Amalekites, you may remember, were Israel's oldest enemies. The rivalry between the two nations dated back to the time of the Exodus, when Yahweh had said they would be in conflict until Amalek was utterly wiped out. They lived in the desert wilderness around Kadesh, south of Beersheba, the southernmost city of Palestine. Just as neighboring nations had done all through the time of the judges, Amalek began to raid settlements in the Negeb. At the command of Yahweh, Samuel told Saul to "go and smite Amalek, and utterly destroy all they have; do not spare them, but kill both man and woman, infant and suckling, ox and sheep, camel and ass" (*15:3*). This sounds a bit harsh, and we begin to wonder if it is not Samuel instead of Saul who is unbalanced. But we need to remember once again the rules of Holy Warfare. When Yahweh led his people against their enemies, all of the product of the war—the booty, the animals, the captives—fell under the princi-

133

ple of *herem*. That is, they were set apart for him, they belonged to him and him alone. No booty was to be taken for personal use. No captives were to be taken as slaves. Everything was to be destroyed or put in the priestly treasury. This was a religious command, and it could not be violated without serious consequences both to the offender and the nation.

Saul marched his army into the Negeb, as far as the city of Shur, east of Egypt, indicating the great freedom of movement his victory over the Philistines had given him. With apparent ease, he defeated Amalek. Following Samuel's command, he destroyed all the booty and animals and killed all the people. All, that is, but the very finest of the animals and the Amalekite king, Agag. These he decided to spare. By altering the command just a bit, he could bring even greater glory to Yahweh. With a light heart and a confident spirit, he started back for Gilgal. At Carmel, he set a monument, declaring to all who passed by what an heroic fellow he was. "How delighted Samuel will be," he thought, "when he learns how successful I have been." But Samuel was not delighted. On the contrary, he burned with the fury of the Lord. When he demanded to hear Saul's explanation for the presence of Agag and the sound of the animals, Saul said he had saved the king as a trophy of the victory God had brought them, and the animals were to be offered in a mammoth sacrifice at Gilgal. Samuel's reply is one of the classic statements in the Bible on the importance of placing the will of God before one's own opinions about how he may best be honored:

> Has the Lord as great delight in
> burnt offerings and sacrifices
> as in obeying the voice of the Lord?
> Behold, to obey is better than sacrifice,
> and to hearken than the fat of rams.
> For rebellion is as the sin of divination,

> and stubbornness is as iniquity
> and idolatry.
> Because you have rejected the word
> of the Lord,
> he has also rejected you from being king.
> —*I Samuel 15:22-23*

Saul was penitent, but Samuel would not budge. He refused even to go with him to Gilgal, where he might worship the Lord and ask forgiveness. As he turned to leave, Saul clutched at his garment in a gesture of desperation. The garment tore and Samuel said hotly, "Yahweh has torn the kingdom of Israel from you this day and has given it to a neighbor of yours, who is better than you." But Saul continued to beg Samuel to stay with him. Finally, the old man agreed to go with him to Gilgal to worship, but the command of the Lord still had to be fulfilled. So, after they worshipped, Samuel summoned the Amalekite king. Then, releasing the fury he had pent up against Saul, "Samuel hewed Agag in pieces before Yahweh in Gilgal."

Samuel had gone to Gilgal with Saul, but he would go no further. The rift was now permanent. Never again would Samuel convey the will of Yahweh to Saul. As he returned to his home, Samuel "grieved over Saul" and "Yahweh repented that he had made Saul king over Israel."

### SAUL AND DAVID

Samuel's announcement to Saul that the kingship would be denied his own son Jonathan and put in the hands of another upset the already precarious balance in the king's mind and started him hurtling down the path to the tragic and total disintegration of his personality. The picture of the last years of his life marks him as one of the most pathetic figures in the Bible.

*The Rise of David.* The young man who was to take the throne Saul coveted for his son was, of course, David. The scene in which David comes to our attention is a kind of ancient Cinderella story. Samuel had been instructed to go to Bethlehem to the home of Jesse, to anoint the man who would succeed Saul. Samuel had not been told which of the sons Yahweh had chosen, and as they were brought before him, he began to look for the strongest and most handsome. One by one, Jesse's sons were rejected. They were fine-looking young men, but, as each one came forward, Yahweh told Samuel that he was not the one. Samuel was a bit perplexed, but he recognized that "Yahweh sees not as man sees; man looks on the outward appearance, but Yahweh looks on the heart" (16:7). When all those present had been rejected, Samuel asked if Jesse had another son. There was another, but he was the youngest and had been left to tend the sheep. Surely Samuel would not be interested in him. Samuel insisted that he be brought. The young man was handsome, with a ruddy complexion and beautiful eyes. As he entered, Yahweh said to Samuel, "Arise, anoint him, for this is he." Samuel did as he was commanded, "and the Spirit of Yahweh came mightily upon David from that day forward." This coming of the Spirit of Yahweh was the same sort of thing that had happened to the judges and to Saul. Their leadership did not depend on the fact that their fathers had been leaders, but on the fact that Yahweh had given them a divine *charisma*, or blessing. They were *charismatic*, not hereditary rulers. David was to be the last of these charismatic leaders. When he died, the rule would go to his son and the dynastic state would be established.

The Biblical writer dramatically anticipates the conflict between Saul and David by the manner in which he speaks of the going and coming of the Spirit of Yahweh. In the verse immediately following the announcement of the Spirit's descent on David, he declares that "the Spirit of Yah-weh departed from Saul" (16:13–14). First, Samuel, the priest and prophet of Yahweh, had cut himself off from Saul. Now, Yahweh himself had departed from his side. Saul was left to bear the weight of the kingship of Israel alone. Unfortunately, he was not a large enough man.

The Bible is unclear as to how Saul first met David. In *I Samuel 16:14–23*, David is said to have been invited by Saul to play the lyre for him, to soothe his tormented soul. In the story of David's victory over the giant Goliath, however, Saul seems to have no idea as to who the young hero is (see *17:55–58*). When Saul invited David to serve with him at this time, it seems clear that this was his first trip to the royal court. One possible explanation is that Saul's condition while David played for him kept him from recognizing him. But this is pretty far-fetched. In *16:21*, it is stated that "Saul loved him greatly, and he became his armor-bearer." This would mean that David was with him when he was in a normal mental state. A more likely explanation is that the writer had two stories in his possession and worked them into the narrative in the wrong order. If they can be harmonized, David probably slew Goliath first, then came to the court, then played for Saul in his periods of torment. This theory does not remove all of the difficulties in reconciling the two traditions, but it does provide an explanation that is not improbable.

However they may have met, the warm friendship soon began to deteriorate. Saul had placed David in command over his army. Whenever Saul sent him, he was victorious. This should have pleased Saul; instead, he grew envious of the enthusiastic reception David was receiving at the capital. Whenever the young warrior returned from battle, the women would dance and sing in the streets and all the people would shout:

Saul has slain his thousands
And David his ten thousands.
—I Samuel 18:7

This irritated Saul. He had given the youth his chance, and now the people were making David sound ten times as great as Saul. "He already has the people," thought Saul; "next he will want the throne."

From that day to the day of Saul's death, David's life was in constant danger. Several times, Saul threw his spear at David as he played for him. When he learned that his daughter Michal had fallen in love with David, he set the bride-price at one hundred foreskins taken from Philistines killed by David in battle. Surely, he thought, David cannot fight in hand to hand combat with a hundred Philistines and not be killed. David killed two hundred. When Saul saw this, he knew that Yahweh was with David and he grew even more afraid and envious of him. "So Saul was David's enemy continually."

The more David fought, the more successful he was. The more the people cheered him, the more determined became Saul to kill him. Through the efforts of Jonathan and Michal, David managed to foil a plot to kill him in his sleep and escaped to Samuel at his home in Ramah (ch. 19). After a brief period in Ramah, David returned to Gibeah and consulted with Jonathan about Saul's current attitude. Jonathan, who loved David dearly (See 18:1–4), could not believe his father would actually try to kill David, but agreed to test him the next day at dinner. When he saw that David's fears were justified and that Saul resented his friendship with David, he reluctantly agreed that David should flee. But first, they pledged their devotion to each other, vowing that Saul's bitterness would not be allowed to poison their relationship.

As he fled, David came to Nob, the town about a mile northeast of Jerusalem in which the tabernacle* had been set up and in which the priests now lived. David was hungry and persuaded the high priest Ahimelech to give him the loaves from the table of the Shewbread. This was against the regulations of the tabernacle service, but, as Jesus explained to the Pharisees centuries later (Matthew 12:1–8), the life of his people was dearer to God than any legal stipulation. In such an emergency, no sin was involved. As David left, Ahimelech gave him the marvelous sword that had belonged to Goliath. We are not told how it got there, but apparently it had been kept as a kind of trophy celebrating this great victory of Yahweh and David over the Philistine hero. As we shall see directly, this kindness on the part of Ahimelech was to provoke an act of vengeance that showed the depths to which Saul had been carried by his sick and twisted mind.

From Nob, David fled to the Philistine city of Gath, where he was refused entry by its king, Achish. Then he went to the cave of Adullam, probably near the city of Adullam in Judah. When word got out that he was there, a motley congregation of debtors, malcontents, and miscellaneous ruffians began to form around him. Soon, he had an "army" of about four hundred men. When Saul heard of this, he began to imagine that the whole country was about to revolt against him. As he grumbled about how his disloyal servants failed to tell him about anything that was going on, Doeg the Edomite stepped forth. Doeg had been on an errand to Nob when David had passed through, and he told the king about Ahimelech's giving David the bread and the sword. When Ahimelech was summoned and questioned, he protested to Saul that he

---

*There is no way of knowing if this was the original tabernacle. Because over two centuries had passed since the erection of the first tabernacle in the wilderness, and because the sanctuary at Shiloh was overrun in 1050 B.C., it is probable that this was a new structure.

136

had no reason to fear David, who had served him better than any other of his subjects. But Saul was in no rational frame of mind. Now, it seemed, even the priesthood had joined the rebellion. He ordered his servants to slay the priests, but they refused. Apparently, they were beginning to realize that their master was no longer in control of his emotions. They would not strike the priests of God on the order of a madman. Doeg the Edomite had no such reservations. Without hesitation, he slew the priests and, presumably with a force he commanded, destroyed the city of Nob. Only one priest, Abiathar, escaped Doeg's massacre, and he fled to the protection of David. One by one, Saul was managing to drive his loyal supporters into the camp of the man he feared.

*Saul Pursues David.* David's position was extremely precarious. He could not return to the capital, and he found no real haven anywhere else. He rid various Israelite cities of Philistine raiders, but they always seemed quite willing to betray him to Saul at the first opportunity. Probably, the inhabitants of these cities could see very little real difference between occupation by the Philistines and occupation by David's renegades. Finally, Saul had David trapped in the wilderness of Maon, in the desert to the south of Jeshimon. Just as Saul's men were closing in for the kill, a messenger came with word that the Philistines were raiding the land. It was harvest time, and a successful series of raids could be disastrous to Israel's economy. Saul had no choice but to abandon the chase for David and attend to this more urgent matter.

**The Conflict between Saul and David.**

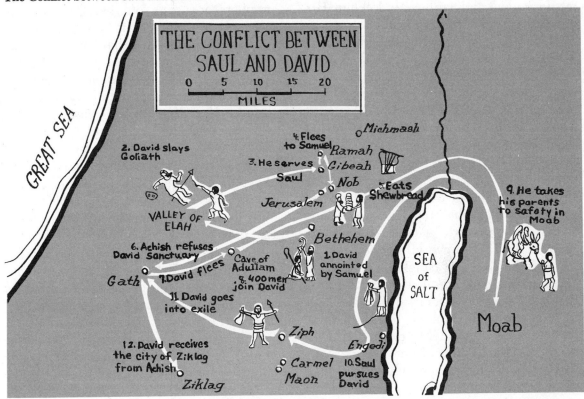

137

One of the remarkable things about this whole series of incidents is that David made no attempt to fight back. To him, Saul was Yahweh's Anointed, and was not to be opposed, despite his obvious incompetence. On two occasions, he had a clear chance to kill Saul, but refused to harm him in any way. The first time (*ch. 24*), he cut off part of his robe while Saul was relieving himself in a cave where David and his men had been hiding. The second time (*ch. 26*), he crept into Saul's camp at night and stole the spear and water bottle that stood at the king's head. Both times, he showed himself at a distance and held up his trophies as proof that he had no intention of killing the king. Both times, Saul was temporarily overcome with shame at his senseless behavior, but it was not long until he was at it again.

David finally realized that it was useless to try to reason with Saul. He was crazed with jealousy. Eventually, David's luck would run out and Saul would kill him. His best hope, for the time being at least, was to try to settle in the land of the Philistines. Saul would not come after him there. For awhile, he found refuge in Gath. King Achish had turned him away before, but now he was sure that David had been rejected by his countrymen. Besides, his rough warriors, who had grown to six hundred, could be a valuable addition to Philistine military strength. Before long, Achish gave David control of Ziklag, one of the country towns in the province surrounding Gath. During the sixteen months he spent in Philistia, David did everything he could to prove to the people of Israel that he was not a traitor. He made frequent raids on tribes that had been troublesome to the Israelites. At least part of the time, he distributed the booty among the Israelite towns that had been friendly to him. After making sure there were no survivors to tell what he had done, David would report to Achish that he had been raiding Israelite towns. This pleased Achish, since he thought these raids were making David so hated by the Israelites that he could not return to them even if he wanted to.

Meanwhile, the Philistine storm cloud was growing darker. The tyrants were preparing their forces for an all-out assault on Saul's kingdom. Perhaps they saw that his instability gave them a good chance of winning back the territory he had taken from them. They began the march up-country to the plain of Esdraelon. If they could gain control of this piece of territory, they could cut off the tribes of Galilee from the southern tribes. Also, the level terrain here enabled them to maneuver their chariots, giving them a decided military advantage.

When Saul saw what was happening, he grew terrified. He tried every method he knew of finding out what would be the outcome. None of the usual means—dreams, prophets, or casting lots—had provided any answers. In desperation, he visited a medium at Endor. Earlier, Saul had issued an order that all mediums and wizards should be driven out of the land. In order to get the woman to practice her occult art, he had to disguise himself in strange garments. She welcomed him and agreed to try to make contact with whatever spirit he wished. The old prophet Samuel had died shortly before. If she could contact his spirit, surely Samuel could be of some help. We simply do not know exactly what happened in that house that night, or how to explain what the Bible says, but, whatever it was, Saul was told that he would die in battle on the following day.

The scene as Saul and his two companions leave the witch's house is a pathetic one. There is no way to avoid the encounter with the Philistines. If only Yahweh would fight at his side as he had done in the old days. If only the priests would be there with the ark or the ephod. If only David were there to command the Israelite troops. But the Spirit of Yahweh had departed from Saul. What was left of the priesthood had been driven into David's camp, and David had been driven to the land of the Philistines. Imagine the mental torture Saul inflicted on himself as he realized that the unfolding tragedy was a product of his own twisted heart.

On the next day, "the Philistines fought against Israel; and the men of Israel fled before the Philistines, and fell slain on Mount Gilboa" (31:1). Saul's sons were slain and Saul himself was mortally wounded. To avoid any further humiliation at the hands of the Philistines, he asked his armor-bearer to kill him. When the man refused Saul fell on his own sword. So ended the life of Israel's first monarch.

With their leader dead, the Israelites were undone. The Philistines easily routed them and took control of their cities. As a gruesome proclamation of their victory, they took the bodies of Saul and his sons and tied them to the wall of Bethshan. There they would have hung until they rotted, had it not been for the touching bravery of the citizens of Jabesh-Gilead. Saul's first victory had saved them from the Ammonites, and they had not forgotten him. He had kept them from the humiliation of having their eyes gouged out. They would see that his body was not desecrated by pagans. So, in the night, they risked their lives to cut the bodies from the wall. Then, they took them to Jabesh, burned them, and buried the bones and ashes under a tamarisk tree.

### DAVID'S LAMENT

Several of the Philistine tyrants had not trusted David and feared, correctly, that he would betray them once they got into battle. They insisted, against the wishes of Achish, that he remain in Philistia. Therefore, he did not immediately learn of the death of Saul and Jonathan. The message

was brought to him by an Amalekite warrior who claimed that he had found Saul dying and had, at the king's request, applied the *coup de grace* with his sword. David's first reaction was one of indignation over the fact that a common soldier would strike the Lord's Anointed and then show no apparent remorse. In anger, he ordered the soldier executed. David's act may not have been fully rational, but it shows the deep feeling he had about the significance of Saul's divine appointment. As we follow his career, we shall see that he viewed his own role as a divinely designated servant of Yahweh with similar seriousness.

After his initial burst of shock and anger, David began to think in terms of the loss to Israel and his own personal loss. The result of his sorrow and meditation is the moving memorial lament in which he pays tribute to Saul as a hero of Israel, and to Jonathan as a beloved friend:

> Saul and Jonathan, beloved and lovely!
>> In life and in death they were not divided;
> they were swifter than eagles,
>> they were stronger than lions.
>
> Ye daughters of Israel, weep over Saul,
>> who clothed you daintily in scarlet,
>> who put ornaments of gold upon
>> your apparel,
>
> How are the mighty fallen,
>> in the midst of the battle!
>
> Jonathan lies slain upon thy high places.
>> I am distressed for you, my
>> brother Jonathan;
> very pleasant have you been to me;
>> your love to me was wonderful,
>> passing the love of women
>
> How are the mighty fallen
>> and the weapons of war perished!
>> —II Samuel 1:23-27

David's touching tribute was apparently circulated widely in Israel. The writer of

*I-II Samuel* took his copy from the Book of Jashar, a lost book also referred to in *Joshua 10:13*. We can appreciate these words all the more when we recognize that they came from a man who had refused to allow the most flagrant kinds of injustice to diminish his loyalty to his king.

## King David (About 1000–960 B.C.)

With the death of Saul at the hands of the Philistines, Israel was on the point of collapse. This was about 1000 B.C. Forty years later, when David turned the kingdom over to his son Solomon, Israel was the major power in the Near East. It is no exaggeration to say that virtually every stage in this fantastic transition bore the personal stamp of David. We usually think of David as a gallant warrior or a remarkable religious poet. He was both of these and this endeared him to the hearts of the people. But, the remarkable success of his rule was due less to these qualities than to his sheer political genius. This will become apparent as we follow the steps that took him from political exile to the throne of a united Israel.

### THE STRUGGLE WITH ISHBOSHETH

It is important to remember that the disaster at Gilboa had once again made Israel a Philistine land. There was no question of David's simply stepping in, announcing that he was Yahweh's Anointed, and taking over the reigns of the United Kingdom. The best he was able to do for the time being was to get himself proclaimed King of the tribe of Judah (*II Sam. 2:4*). He almost surely did this with the full knowledge and consent of the Philistines who controlled the territory. As far as they were concerned, having David as king of Judah was as good as having a Philistine. The arrangement was also pleasing to the people of Judah, since David had made himself popular with them by sharing the booty from his raids with them.

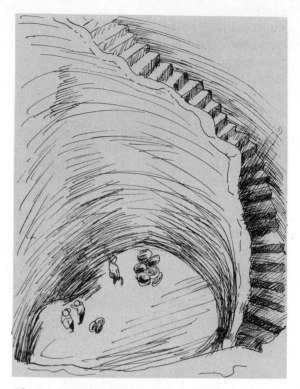

**The Pool of Gideon, site of the first conflict. between the supporters of David and Ishbosheth.**

The Philistines were not David's only concern. A rival capital was being set up in Mahanaim, in Transjordan, out of reach of the Philistines. The titular head of this government was Ishbosheth\*, the youngest of Saul's legitimate† sons and the only one who had not been killed at Gilboa (See *I Sam. 31:2*), but the real power belonged to Abner, who had been the commander of Saul's armies. Neither of these two small "kingdoms" had much chance of restoring the glory to Israel by itself. The only hope of either was to bring the other under its control. So, for two years, they contended with

---

\*In *I Chronicles 8:33* this man is called Eshbaal. Scholars generally agree that this was his original name. It was probably changed to Ishbosheth by the writer of *I-II Samuel* to clear Saul of any suspicion of worshipping and naming his son after the Canaanite god, Baal.

†Saul also had two sons by his concubine Rizpah (*II Sam. 21:8*).

each other for the top position. From the first conflict at the pool of Gibeon (2:12ff), it became increasingly clear that David would eventually triumph. After a time, Abner began to abandon the fiction that Ishbosheth, and not he, was the actual ruler of the northern and Transjordanic tribes. His taking Saul's concubine for himself (*II Sam. 3:6–11*) was an open announcement that he no longer considered Ishbosheth his superior. When Ishbosheth rebuked him for his action, Abner was infuriated: "Am I a dog's head of Judah? This day I keep showing loyalty to the house of Saul your father, to his brothers, and to his friends, and have not given you into the hand of David; and yet you charge me today with a fault concerning a woman." Ishbosheth had proven to be a hopeless weakling. Abner saw that it was useless to try to preserve the line of Saul any longer. This incident gave him the excuse to do what he had probably been thinking about for some time—"to transfer the kingdom from the house of Saul, and set up the throne of David over Israel and over Judah, from Dan to Beer-sheba." Abner sent a messenger to Hebron to ask David to make a covenant with him. David agreed, but only on condition that his wife Michal, who had married again after David had fled to Philistia, be returned to him. David's reasons for demanding Michal's return were probably more political than romantic. Those who had supported Ishbosheth because they felt the kingship ought to stay in Saul's family would be pacified if Saul's daughter were married to the king.

After delivering Michal to Saul, Abner made the rounds of the various tribes and convinced them they should throw their support to David. When he finished this mission, he came to Hebron and was graciously received by David. As he started back to Transjordan, however, he was arrested and slain by the commander of David's armies, Joab. In the first encounter between the armies of David and Ishbosheth, Abner had killed Joab's younger brother. Joab claimed that vengeance for his brother's death was his sole motive in slaying Abner, but it is not unlikely that he had given some thought to the possibility that Abner might one day be a rival for his own position as high commander, or even for the throne of his beloved master.

We might have expected David to show some signs of relief that his most powerful opponent was out of the way. But this would have given the cynical a chance to say that David had betrayed Abner and ordered his death. David removed all suspicion from himself by placing a curse on Joab, by weeping and lamenting as he followed Abner's bier to the grave, and by fasting until the sun went down. There is no reason to doubt David's sincerity; nevertheless, his behavior did not hurt him politically. "All the people took notice of it, and it pleased them: as everything that the king did pleased the people" (3:36).

With Abner dead, Ishbosheth was powerless. His supporters were dismayed, partly because they genuinely wanted the crown to remain in Saul's family and partly because they feared David would punish them for their opposition to him. In an effort to assure David of their support, and perhaps to win a position of favor for themselves, two of Ishbosheth's officers crept into his house at noon and killed him in his bed. Then they cut off his head and traveled all night to present their grisly trophy to David. Obviously, they had not heard the story of David's execution of the messenger who brought word to him of Saul's death. When he heard they had assassinated Ishbosheth in his sleep, he not only ordered them killed, but had their hands and feet cut off and their bodies hung in a public place, as a sign of the shameful act they had committed.

141

Now, nothing stood between David and the undisputed rule over all of Israel. David realized it, and the people realized it.

> So all the elders of Israel came to the king at Hebron; and King David made a covenant with them at Hebron before the Lord, and they anointed David king over Israel.
>
> —II Samuel 5:3

### THE CONSOLIDATION OF POWER

The covenant at Hebron was a good start, but David was shrewd enough to recognize that it would take more than an oath of loyalty to produce a unified Israel. The steps that he took to consolidate Israel and to strengthen his own position clearly demonstrate his political brilliance.

His first move was to find a new capital. Hebron was too far south and too closely associated with the tribe of Judah to be fully acceptable to the northern tribes. Similarly, a capital in the north would be offensive to Judah. David's solution was perfect: he would set up his throne in Jerusalem. The Israelites had never been able to conquer Jerusalem. The mountainous terrain on which it sat and its almost impregnable defenses had enabled it to withstand whatever attacks might have been made on it. From the time of the conquest, it had remained a Canaanite thorn in Israel's side. It made no efforts to oppress the Israelites, as far as we know, but it kept Israel from gaining effective control of the land and it kept both the northern and southern tribes from gaining a decisive military advantage over the others. By gaining control of this strategic city, David made possible a truly united Israel. By naming it the City of David, he announced to all his role in creating that unity.

Once David established himself in his new capital, he began taking on the customary trappings of an oriental monarch. First he built himself a house of cedar sent to him by Hiram king of Tyre. Then he began adding wives and concubines to his harem. Truly, Israel was becoming "like the nations" and her king was becoming like their kings. By the time the Philistines realized what David was doing, he was already firmly entrenched at Jerusalem. If they could not drive him out quickly, he was sure to make good his bid for independence. Twice they approached the city from the valley of Rephaim to the southwest and twice David drove them back. After the second encounter, he "smote them from Geba to Gezer" and drove them back to their original territory. From that time forward, Israel was never again seriously troubled by the Philistines.*

The taking of Jerusalem and the final defeat of the Philistines were no small feats, but the most far-reaching of David's actions was yet to come. From the time she had become a "nation" at Sinai, Israel's political life had been inseparable from her religious life. Her constitution and by-laws were given to her by God. The wars by which she had won her land were religious wars, carried out according to divine regulations, with the priests of Yahweh in attendance. Once settled in the land, what government she had revolved around the central sanctuary. When she had been oppressed by foreign nations, the reason was always declared to be her lack of fidelity to the Mosaic covenant. Saul had abetted his own downfall by alienating Samuel and slaughtering the priests of Nob. With this kind of national background, it would be utter folly to try to create a strong kingdom without giving a major role to religion.

A man of less imagination might have set up the ark of the covenant at Shiloh or Shechem and led a great pilgrimage to the ancient shrine. This would have its merits, but

---

*Other conflicts are mentioned (*II Sam.* 8:1; 21:18 —22), but they are treated so casually that we may be almost certain they were not of major proportion.

as soon as the pilgrimage was over, religion and politics would again be divorced from one another. David had a much better idea. He would wed the religious forces to the political by bringing the ark to Jerusalem, thus making the political capital the religious capital as well. David himself led the delegation to bring the ark from its resting place in Baale-Judah. On the return trip, Uzzah was struck dead when he touched the ark (6:6–7). David took this as a bad omen and left the ark in the house near where the incident had occurred. At the end of three months, however, he decided that he would go ahead and carry out his original plan. The ceremony which symbolized Yahweh's entry into the city must have been impressive. Led by David, the people sang and danced and played on various musical instruments. When the ark was placed within

the tent David had prepared for it, the King offered burnt-offerings and peace-offerings and blessed the people in the name of Yahweh. Then he distributed cakes of bread and raisins and a portion of the meat of the peace offering, and the people joined in a solemn communion with Yahweh, with Yahweh's Anointed, and with one another.

David did not rest content with the fact that his capital now stood in the stream of sacred memories that flowed down from Mt. Sinai. He would bring even greater glory to the worship of Yahweh. He lived in a fine house built of the "cedars of Lebanon." It did not seem fitting that the Lord of Hosts should dwell in a tent. He would build a temple for Yahweh. He was kept from doing this, however, by a word from Yahweh, spoken through the leading prophet at the court, Nathan. Yahweh told David that he

**Ancient musical instruments.**

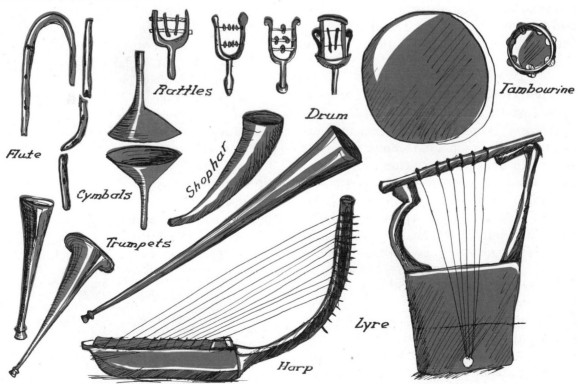

need not be concerned about building him a house. His glory had dwelt in a tent for years and he had never found cause to complain. A house for Yahweh would come in its own good time. There was no reason for David to trouble himself about it. More important was the house Yahweh intended to build for David. When he died, the kingdom would not be thrown into the turmoil that accompanied the death of Saul. One of David's sons would take the rule and Yahweh would bless him as he had blessed David.

> And your house and your kingdom shall be made sure for ever before me; your throne shall be established for ever.
>
> —*II Samuel 7:16*

The people of Israel never forgot this promise. When the line of Davidic kings was eventually broken and Israel herself crushed, they did not suppose that Yahweh had gone back on his word. Instead, they began to look for a new king who would one day arise and restore Israel to the glory she had known in the time of David. This king for which they longed was called Messiah.

### DAVID BUILDS AN EMPIRE

David's hold on Israel was secure. Now he could turn his attention to the expansion of his territory. On the eastern frontier, he reduced Moab, Edom, and Ammon to vassal states. His most notable victories, however, came against the Aramean (Syrian) states of Damascus and Zobah. Hadadezer, the king of Zobah, was an especially troublesome foe, but David finally managed to bring him to his knees and to extend his rule over this considerable territory to the north. At the height of this period of conquest, David was master of virtually everything from southern Syria in the north to the Gulf of Aqabah in the south, and from the Mediterranean Sea to the desert on the east. Two apparent exceptions were the city-states of

Phoenecia and Philistia. The friendly relations with Hiram, king of Tyre, indicate that some kind of treaty existed with Phoenicia. As for the Philistines, while they may not have been actually subject to David, he certainly had them under control.

With an empire to run, David needed an imperial cabinet (See *II Sam. 8:15–18; 20:23–26*). Joab was commanding officer of the Israelite troops and Benaiah was put in charge of the foreign troops employed by David. Abiathar,* the sole survivor of the massacre at Nob, and Zadok, whose origins are unknown, were installed as co-priests at the tabernacle. Civil appointments included an officer in charge of slave labor forces, and two offices identified as "recorder" and "secretary." These latter titles sound rather unimpressive, but there is good reason to believe they were quite important positions. The recorder was probably David's personal representative to the people, functioning somewhat in the manner that a press secretary functions for our president. The "secretary" seems to have held a position roughly equivalent to our secretary of state. These offices are known to have existed in the Egyptian bureaucracy, leading us to suspect that David may have stolen a glance or two at the Egyptian court as he set up his own royal government. This suspicion is strengthened by the fact that the secretary's name is Egyptian. Possibly, David had sent to Egypt to secure an experienced man to fill this post. Doubtless, David also appointed many subordinate officials to care for internal administrative affairs and to oversee the government of subject nations.

---

*In *II Sam. 8:17*, this priest's name is given as Ahimelech. In *20:25*, he is called Abiathar. The latter is almost certainly correct. Abiathar had fled to David from Nob and had served with him since that time. In other passages (e.g., *15:24–28*) he is called Abiathar. Apparently, the text has been scrambled somewhat in transmission. Probably, *8:17* should read "And Abiathar the son of Ahimelech the son of Ahitub and Zadok were priests."

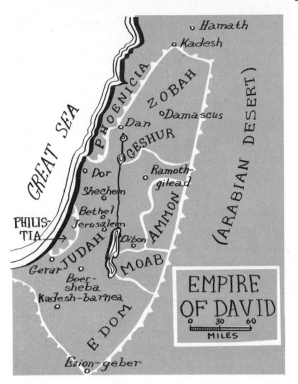

The empire of David.

Unfortunately, neither the Bible nor archaeology give us any knowledge of these.

### THE COURT HISTORY—II SAMUEL 9:1–20:26

So far, we have been mainly concerned with David's rise to power, with the enlargement of his territory, and with the development of monarchical government. In the main, we have dealt with politics, wars, and statecraft. In *II Samuel 9–20*, sometimes called the Court History of David, we have a candid and intimate picture of life at court in the middle years of David's reign. There is a striking contrast between these chapters and non-Biblical chronicles of the lives of kings. In the latter, usually composed by a court appointee, the king is always seen in a good light. His faults are minimized or ignored and his virtues and victories magnified out of true proportion. In the Court History, the most unlovely of David's actions

are dealt with as fully as his noblest virtues.

This section begins by telling of David's kindness to Mephibosheth, the son of Jonathan (*II Sam. 9*). Mephibosheth had been five years old when his father was slain at Gilboa. As his panic-stricken nurse fled to escape the attacking Philistines, Mephibosheth fell from her arms and became lame in both feet. When David learned that the child, now grown to a man, was still alive, he invited him to live at the royal residence and to eat at the king's table for the rest of his life. A servant of Saul's named Ziba was put in charge of all of Mephibosheth's land and possessions.

*David and Bathsheba (II Sam. 11–12).* As David grew older, he left more and more of the fighting in the hands of his commander, Joab. One spring, "the time when kings go forth to battle," Joab went out against the Ammonites, but David remained in Jerusalem. Late one afternoon, David was walking along the roof of his palace when he saw a beautiful woman bathing nearby. The woman, of course, was Bathsheba, the wife of Uriah the Hittite, one of David's faithful soldiers. David's passions overpowered his reason and he had his servants bring Bathsheba to him. They slept together, and in time she reported that she was pregnant. Since Uriah had been off at war, it would be obvious that he was not the father. If word got around that the king was taking the wives of those who fought in his name, his image would suffer serious damage. The solution seemed simple enough. He summoned Uriah from the battle lines, pretending that he wanted first hand information about the war. His real purpose, of course, was to get Uriah to sleep with his wife, so that he would think he was the father of the child she was expecting. But Uriah was a man of unusual character. His fellows in battle were deprived of the comforts of their homes and the love of their wives. He would

145

not use his assignment as a messenger to the king for his personal advantage. David tried everything, including getting him drunk, but Uriah would not succumb. In desperation, David sent him back to the front lines, carrying a letter to Joab which called for his own death. Joab was to put Uriah into the hottest part of the battle, then draw back from him to leave him an exposed target. The cruel stratagem worked and Uriah was slain. The ugliness of David's sin is magnified by the manner in which he received the news of Uriah's death. A messenger from Joab gave David an account of the battle, adding the post script, "and your servant Uriah the Hittite is dead also." Instead of expressing any remorse or guilt, David simply said, "Tell Joab not to let this matter trouble him, for the sword devours now one and now the other." Then David sent for Bathsheba and she became his wife.

David had managed to protect his reputation, but his sin did not go unnoticed. The leading prophet of the day, Nathan, told him a parable of a rich man who had stolen his poor neighbor's pet lamb. David was fired with anger at the injustice of the rich man's cynical act. When Nathan said, "Thou art the man," David was finally struck by the enormity of what he had done. We can feel the desolation of his soul as he confesses simply, "I have sinned against the Lord."* Nathan told him he would not die, but the expected child would. David fasted and prayed for days, but the child died. "Then David comforted his wife, Bathsheba and went in to her and lay with her; and she bore a son, and he called his name Solomon."

As a footnote to this story, the scene shifts back to the battlefront in Ammon (12:26–31). Perhaps Joab had been somewhat sickened by his part in the death of Uriah, though he was not a man with a particu-

larly sensitive conscience. This whole affair would not have happened had David been with his armies as in the past. Whatever his reasons, Joab felt strongly that David should be at the front lines. To pressure him into coming, he sent word that he was about to capture the Ammonite city of Rabbah. If David did not join him with additional troops, he would take the city for his own personal possession. In ancient times, it was not uncommon for the commander of the army to lead a revolt against his king. Joab probably never seriously considered actual revolt, but the threat was enough to get quick action from David. Within a short time he arrived with fresh troops and captured the city. Two items in this brief account are worth noting. The first is that, instead of following the usual procedure of making a vassalage treaty with a conquered king, David apparently crowned himself king of the city (12:30). The second has to do with a matter of translation. In 12:31, the King James Version states that David made the Ammonites "pass through the brickkiln." The phrase should be translated "toil at the brickkiln." David was not quite so cruel as the King James Version suggests, although slave labor was not a fate to be coveted.

*The Rebellion of Absalom* (II Sam. 13–18). The possession of great power is seldom an unmixed blessing. It leads men to identify their personal whims and desires with what is right, without reference to any kind of higher moral law. Thus, when David wanted Bathsheba, he took her, without regard for her husband or for God's law. But power corrupts not only those who possess it; it also corrupts those who desire it. The exercise of power, even when used judiciously and righteously, is sure to stir up resentment. And resentment, when it is fullgrown, brings forth rebellion. David's reign was threatened by two such rebellions. The first was led by his own son Absalom.

---

*It was probably near this time that David composed *Psalm 51*, the so-called Penitential Psalm.

146

Absalom and his sister Tamar were David's children by an Aramean princess of Geshur (3:3). When Ammon, their half-brother, raped Tamar, Absalom slew him and was forced into exile. For three years he remained in Geshur, probably among his mother's relatives. David, after some artful maneuvering on the part of Joab, finally allowed him to return to the capital, but refused to see him. Absalom was anxious to see his father. Joab had gotten him back into the city; Joab would have to get him an appointment with the king. Joab tried to stay out of the matter by ignoring Absalom's request to talk to him. In desperation, Absalom set fire to Joab's barley field. This got Joab's attention and Joab got the interview for Absalom.

The reunion seems warm and sincere, but soon after, Absalom began plotting to seize the throne. Absalom had all the qualities needed to endear himself to the people. He is described as the most handsome man in all Israel—"from the sole of his foot to the crown of his head there was no blemish in him" (14:25). His hair was long and beautiful and he had four attractive children. When he traveled about the city, he made certain that no one missed his coming or going. Men could not see his chariot and horses, and the fifty men who ran before him (15:1), without recognizing that this was an extraordinary young man.

Taken by themselves, Absalom's natural gifts and his flashiness might have caused the people to be resentful. But Absalom had inherited from his father a genius for endearing himself to the people. His most effective device was to stand at the gate of the city, where men gathered to talk and to bring their claims for justice. Because he was the king's son, men sought him out to register their complaints. He showed great personal interest in each man and lamented that the king made no provisions for righting the wrongs they had suffered, or even for hearing their complaints. "If I were king," he assured them, "you could come directly to me, and I would personally see to it that you received justice." If anyone tried to pay honor to him by bowing before him, he would lift him up and kiss him as a sign of equality. He could not help it that he was the king's son, but that made him no better than anyone else. All he wanted was what was good for the people. Few politicians have ever failed with this line, if they could convince the people of their sincerity. Absalom was most convincing. So, he "stole the hearts of the men of Israel."

For four* years, Absalom continued this conspiracy against his father. When he felt his support was strong enough, he left the capital and began gathering his forces at Hebron. Absalom's conspiracy was not just a movement of the common people. The fact that Ahithophel, David's chief counselor, joined the rebels, is an indication that he had secured the support of people at all levels in the government.

When David learned the state of affairs—we are not told whether he had any prior suspicions—he decided that the only course open to him was flight. He could not be sure of the loyalty of anyone, and if he tried to defend Jerusalem against an attack, many would be unnecessarily killed. The picture of King David's being driven from his beloved city by a conspiracy led by his own son is one of the most poignant in the Bible. The people come out with him to the edge of the city and stand crying aloud as the heartsick king, his feet bare and his head covered, leads his company across the brook Kidron and up the slope of Mt. Olivet, on the way to the wilderness of Jordan.

We noted that Ahithophel, David's counselor, had joined with Absalom. This was a

---

*Not forty, as in the King James Version; see 15:7.

serious loss, but David still retained some capable and influential men in his ranks. He had sent the loyal priests, Abiathar and Zadok, back into the city to serve as his informants. As he traveled eastward he was greeted by Hushai, a longtime friend from the Archite people who lived west of Bethel (See *Joshua 16:2*). David instructed Hushai to pretend to join Absalom and to pass along any information he received to Abiathar and Zadok. Hushai reached Jerusalem at about the same time Absalom did and greeted him with an enthusiastic, "Long live the king!" The rebel leader was skeptical of his father's old friend, but Hushai proved himself to be a politician equal to Absalom. It was obvious, he said, that Yahweh and all the people of Israel had chosen Absalom. He was not one to try to fight a combination like this. As he had served Saul, so he would serve Absalom (*16:15–19*).

The value of Hushai to David's cause became immediately apparent. Ahithophel, whose counsel was regarded "as if one consulted the oracle of God" (*16:23*), correctly assumed that David and his men were in no condition to withstand a well-organized attack. He wanted to set out immediately with a force of 12,000 men and ambush the king. His men would be so weary and discouraged that David could be killed with a minimum of bloodshed. With David dead, a politician like Absalom would have little trouble in restoring peace and in winning the loyalty of his father's supporters. This made sense to Absalom and his advisers—indeed, it probably would have worked quite well. But, thought Absalom, it would not hurt to get Hushai's advice. He knew David well and would be able to detect any flaw in the plan. Hushai saw no flaw; therefore, he had to think of an alternative, and quickly. His nimble mind did not fail him. Hushai cautioned Absalom to remember that his father was an expert in war and that he was sur-

rounded by valiant and skilled warriors. Instead of being discouraged, they would be enraged, "like a bear robbed of her cubs." Besides, David was much too clever to spend the night with his troops. Any attack would not only fail to get David, but would be sure to result in losses by the attackers. Word would spread that Absalom had been defeated, the people would rally once more around David, and the revolt would be crushed. No, a surprise attack at night was definitely out of the question. A much better plan would be to gather an overwhelmingly large army and to meet David in open conflict. This way, David's skill would be more than offset by the sheer force of numbers. It is amusing to notice the flight of Hushai's rhetoric:

> we shall light upon him as the dew falls on the ground; and of him and all the men with him not one will be left. If he withdraws into a city, then all Israel will bring ropes to that city, and we shall drag it into the valley, until not even a pebble is to be found there.
> —*II Samuel 17:12, 13*

Hushai's persuasive presentation convinced Absalom and he decided against the counsel of Ahithophel. While the humiliated counselor went to his house and hanged himself (*17:23*), Absalom began to gather the army that would drag cities into the valley and kings into the grave.

David set up his battle headquarters in the city of Mahanaim, the same city which had been Ishbosheth's capital. From there he dispatched his army in three divisions to meet the warriors of Absalom. David had his serious shortcomings, but we sense the largeness of his spirit as he instructs his commanders, "Deal gently for my sake with the young man Absalom."

The battle took place in the forest of Ephraim and raged fiercely all day. The forest was a treacherous place. Thousands who escaped the sword were killed or injured as they fell into pits in the rocky terrain which had been covered with undergrowth (18: 8). Apparently, Absalom had not been able to raise quite the overpowering force he had hoped for. As the day wore on, it became increasingly clear that his men had been defeated. Absalom's own undoing came in a most unheroic way. While he was riding through the forest on a mule, he met a group of David's servants. As he fled, his mule ran under an oak tree and Absalom's head, and perhaps his long hair, became stuck in the tree and "he was left hanging between heaven and earth, while the mule that was under him went on" (18:9).

When a soldier reported to Joab that he had seen Absalom hanging in a tree, the vengeful old warrior was beside himself. Why had the soldier not killed him? Joab would have given him a handsome reward. The man replied that he would not have touched him for any amount of money; David had specifically commanded that no harm was to come to him. Besides, if he had killed him, Joab would not have rewarded him; he would not even have said a word in his defense when the king inquired about it (18:13). The soldier had come to understand Joab's character pretty well. Joab saw there was no point in arguing with him. He would kill Absalom himself. But, just a moment. Is it not strange that Joab should be so angry at Absalom? After all, Joab had been Absalom's main supporter during the years of his Syrian exile. Also, Joab and David had had their differences (II Sam. 3:26–29; 12: 26–28). It is actually rather surprising that Joab was not the general of Absalom's army. Probably, the clue to the mystery is found in 17:25. This verse tells us that Absalom had set Amasa over his army "instead of Joab." This suggests the possibility that Joab may have been favorable to Absalom throughout the growth of the conspiracy, but that he had been bypassed when Absalom chose his officers. Joab's treacherous execution of Abner proved that he was a man who could hold a grudge. It is not at all unlikely that his demonic determination to slay Absalom stemmed from his indignation at the treatment he had received from the young rebel. When he found Absalom, he thrust three darts into his heart and then let his armor-bearers strike him until he died.

Joab dispatched a Cushite man, probably a slave, to run to David with news of the victory. Ahimaaz, the son of the priest Zadok, also begged permission to go. The Cushite got a head start but set out over the hilly territory. Ahimaaz, who probably knew the land better, ran the easier route across the plain and arrived at the city first. When Ahimaaz told David of the victory, the King's first question was, "Is it well with the young man Absalom?" Ahimaaz honestly did not know, so they had to wait for the Cushite. When he was asked, he admitted that the young man was dead. David's reaction contained nothing of the gloat of victory. At that moment he was not a victor. He was not a king who had held his throne against a treacherous usurper. He was a father who had lost a son. The words of his lament are a classic gem of pathos:

> O my son Absalom, my son, my son, Absalom!
> Would I had died instead of you, O Absalom,
> my son, my son!          —II Samuel 18:33

The people were touched by David's sorrow over his son, but those who had supported him against Absalom were also a bit confused. They had been victorious, but his mourning made them feel like criminals. Joab, who was not a tender man, warned him that he would alienate those who had risked their lives for him if he did not go to the gate of the city as an expression of his gratitude to them. Joab was aware that the victory over Absalom had not healed the division in the kingdom. His suspicion was borne out in the conflict that arose out of David's return to Jerusalem.

*King David's Return.* David was in an awkward position. Absalom was dead, it was true, but Absalom had not driven out David by himself. He had had the support of a large segment of the people. If they truly did not want him for their king, there was little point in his returning to Jerusalem. The people of Israel—notice that a clear distinction was already arising between Israel and Judah—were also in a quandary. They had supported Absalom, but he had lost. If they could not have Absalom, David was far better than no king at all (*19:9–10*). Before long, word began to reach David that the men of Israel were on the verge of asking him to return to Jerusalem. The king obviously desired to return, but he still resented the men of Israel for having joined the rebellion. Judah, for the most part, had remained loyal to him. They should also take the lead in getting him back.

David communicated his feelings to Abiathar and Zadok, who were still in Jerusalem. They told the elders, the elders spread the word to the people, and "as one man" they sent word to Mahanaim, asking the king to return. So David started back "and Judah came to Gilgal to meet the king and bring the king over the Jordan" (*19:15*).

*Sheba's Rebellion.* When the men of Israel saw that Judah had gotten the jump on them, they were openly upset (*19:41–43*). This would very likely mean that, once he got things back under control, David would show greater favor to Judah than to Israel. He might even launch a war of vengeance against the northern tribes. Feeling ran high over the matter, but it is doubtful anything serious would have come of it had it not been for a worthless opportunist named Sheba. Sheba capitalized on the fears of the men of Israel and convinced them that the best thing they could do would be to unite around him and prepare themselves to meet any threat offered by David.

The kingdom could not stand another civil war. Sheba had to be destroyed. The expedition was to have been led by Amasa. Because Joab had killed Absalom, in direct defiance of David's order, the king had appointed Amasa to serve as commander of his armies in Joab's place. As we have already seen, Joab was not a man to be put down easily. He had been the most valuable man in David's administration and he knew it. He was not going to lose his rank simply because David had disagreed with his way of handling things. Amasa's commandership was short. On their first meeting in the field, Joab grasped him by the beard, as if to kiss him, and stabbed him with a concealed sword. Standing by the body, he called to the men of Judah, "whoever favors Joab, and whoever is for David, let him follow Joab." And off he went after Sheba, once more at the head of David's army. Joab trapped Sheba in the ancient city of Abel and, by threatening to destroy the city if they refused, persuaded the citizens to execute Sheba and toss his head over the wall.

The efficient and decisive quashing of this rebellion made it clear that it was futile to try to oppose King David. So the land once again knew peace.

### MISCELLANY

The remainder of *II Samuel* is a miscellaneous collection of incidents, poetry, and lists that provide a few glimpses into the closing years of David's long reign. The two main incidents are David's surrender of Saul's descendants to the Gibeonites (*ch. 21*) and the numbering of the kingdom (*ch. 24*). In the first of these, the Gibeonites reminded David of the ancient covenant Joshua had made with them, promising that Israel would never attack them. Saul had ignored this covenant and had made war on

Gibeon. When David asked how he might repay them for this injustice, they requested that seven of Saul's male descendants be turned over to them for hanging. David granted the request, and the Gibeonites were pacified. Some have interpreted David's willingness to surrender these men as an indication of his desire to rid the kingdom of any who might threaten the succession of one of his own sons to the throne after his death. This is a possible, though not a necessary, inference. The reader may draw his own conclusions.

The account of the census in *ch. 24* is thoroughly puzzling. We are told in *v. 1* that God directed David to take the census. In *v. 10*, however, David is smitten with remorse for having "sinned greatly" in carrying out the command, and, in *v. 15*, the people are stricken with a pestilence as a punishment for David's sin. We are not told why it is that David should feel remorse at having carried out a divine command, or why there should be anything sinful about a census. Complicating the matter even further is the fact that, in the account of the incident in *I Chronicles 21*, Satan, not Yahweh, is said to have incited David to take the census. It is possible that David perverted God's command in some way that is not obvious to us. It is also possible, and *v. 1* seems to support this, that God told David to do this thing in order to have an excuse to punish Israel. This does not fit well with our conception of God, and it still leaves us with the question of what is so sinful about a census. We shall probably do well simply to admit the difficulty and be happy that a proper understanding of the passage is not vital to our salvation.

A list of David's mighty men (*ch. 23*) and two pieces of poetry round out this miscellaneous collection and the book of *I-II Samuel*. The first of the poems is the Song of Deliverance (*ch. 22*), which is also pre-

served in *Psalm 18*. The second purports to be David's last words. The fact that they are inserted here, long before the Biblical narrative comes to the end of David's life, makes it clear that these closing chapters are just what we have called them—a miscellaneous collection of odds and ends which the author of *I-II Samuel* inserted at the end of his book.

### THE STRUGGLE FOR THE THRONE

David was growing old and feeble. It was evident he would not live much longer. Since all of Saul's descendants except the crippled Mephibosheth were dead, it was generally accepted that one of David's sons would succeed him to the throne, but which one? Apparently, only two were in real contention: Adonijah and Solomon. David favored Solomon (*I Kings 1:17*), but Adonijah was not a rival to be lightly dismissed. Taking a lesson from Absalom, he arranged for a chariot and horses and appointed fifty men to run before him in the streets. More important, he had gotten the support of some key men in David's administration, including Abiathar the high priest and Joab. No one had ever lost yet who had the support of Joab.

When he felt the time was right, Adonijah held a great celebration at a spot with the intriguing name of The Serpent's Stone. Here he offered sacrifices and proclaimed himself king. All of the important men in the kingdom were invited. All, that is, but Solomon and his chief supporters, Nathan the prophet, Zadok the priest, and Benaiah the commander of the foreign mercenary troops. It seemed that Adonijah had made good on his bid for the throne. But Solomon was far from out of the picture. The chief engineers of his campaign were his mother, Bathsheba, and the prophet Nathan. It is an interesting twist of fate that Nathan should be in league with Bathsheba, since it was he

151

who had delivered the withering attack on David for his adulterous affair with her, but many years had passed, and time does strange things.

In a carefully staged audience with King David (See *I Kin. 1:15–31*), Nathan and Bathsheba reminded him of his promise to name Solomon as his successor and reported to him what Adonijah had done at the Serpent's Stone. With a revival of the energy that had characterized his earlier years, David moved into action. At his instructions, Solomon was placed on his father's royal mule and led to Gihon, a spring in the nearby Brook Kidron. There, Zadok and Nathan anointed him and proclaimed him king. Adonijah may have had the support of the officials, but Solomon was clearly a favorite of the common people (*I Kings 1:39–40*). Their celebration was so raucous that the noise of their shouting was heard by Adonijah and his guests. While they were trying to figure out what all the commotion was about, a runner came with the news that Solomon was sitting on the royal throne, and that David had given his blessing to the whole affair. "Then all the guests of Adonijah trembled, and rose, and each went his own way." Adonijah's tenure as king had been rather short. He feared greatly for his life, but Solomon assured him he was in no danger if he behaved himself properly. We shall have an opportunity shortly to assess the sincerity of Solomon's pardon.

### DAVID'S LAST DAYS

We do not know just how long David lived after Solomon began to reign. Because of his age and poor health (*I Kin. 1:1–4*), it was probably not long. But these last days were not days of idleness. David did not simply retire to his bedroom and wait for death. Instead, he channeled all his remaining energies into preparing for the temple which Solomon was to build and overhaul-

ing the administrative machinery of the tabernacle (and temple) services. The source of our knowledge of David's activity in this period is *I Chronicles 22–29*.

The reorganization of the religious bureaucracy did not signify any change in religious belief. It was simply a step made necessary by changing conditions. In the days when the tabernacle traveled from place to place, the sons of Gershon, Kohath, and Merari were responsible for moving the sacred tent and its furnishings (*Num. 3:21–37*). Now that the ark was permanently settled in Jerusalem, they were assigned to other duties about the sanctuary (*I Chr. 23*). The priests and Levites were divided into twenty-four divisions, or "courses." Each of these divisions served at the temple for approximately two weeks of the year (*ch. 24*). The innovation which probably brought David the greatest personal satisfaction was the appointment of men to provide music for the divine services (*ch. 25*). Under the leadership of Asaph (*25:2*), these men were trained to "prophesy" with lyres, with harps, and with cymbals "in thanksgiving and praise to Yahweh." Since David himself was a musician and a composer of some of the most magnificent religious poetry of all time, it is not surprising that he would take a special interest in this aspect of the worship. In addition to these strictly religious offices, David also appointed divisions of men to oversee both the religious and the royal treasuries, to act as gatekeepers at the sanctuary and at other locations in the city, and to serve in numerous other capacities throughout the kingdom (See *I Chr. 26–29*).

Doubtless, David had thought about these changes for a long time and was happy to have the chance to put them into effect. The project dearest to his heart since the early days of his reign, however, was a temple for Yahweh. The privilege of building this temple was to be Solomon's, but David did all he could to make sure it would be done correctly. His words to the people reveal his tender concern both for his son and for the work to be done: "Solomon, my son, whom alone God has chosen, is young and inexperienced, and the work is great; for the palace will not be for man but for the Lord God. So I have provided for the house of my God, so far as I was able" (*I Chr. 29:1, 2*). He presented Solomon with a set of plans he had made for the building of the temple. He also turned over to him great, quantities of gold, silver, and precious stones he had collected, and he called on the people to donate even more to the tabernacle treasury. Then, reluctant to turn the work over to another, but realizing he must, David fervently imployed Yahweh to "grant to Solomon my son that with a whole heart he may keep thy commandments, thy testimonies, and thy statutes, performing all, and that he may build the palace for which I have made provision" (*I Chr. 29:19*).

Then David slept with his fathers, and was buried in the city of David.

## King Solomon (960–922 B.C.)

"So Solomon sat upon the throne of David his father; and his kingdom was firmly established" (*I Kin. 2:12*).

But Solomon was not satisfied with the firmness of his establishment. He did not rest until those who had opposed him for the throne were dead or in exile. In each case, Solomon looked for some pretext to justify his action. In each case, the excuse fails to satisfy fully. The first to suffer Solomon's wrath was Adonijah. Solomon had promised to spare him if he caused no further trouble, but it seems clear that Solomon's interpretation of "trouble" was not very liberal. When Adonijah asked Bathsheba to help him obtain Abishag the Shunnamite, who had been David's nurse (*1:1–4*), to become his wife,

Solomon ordered him killed. Solomon's excuse was that, by asking for a woman who had belonged to David, Adonijah was still claiming royal privileges. This interpretation of Adonijah's action is possible, but highly unlikely. In the first place, Abishag was a beautiful young woman. This was enough reason to prompt Adonijah's request. In the second place, if he had been seeking to usurp royal authority, Bathsheba would have been about the last person he would have asked to help him. Solomon's action almost surely should be seen as part of a systematic purge of all whom he thought might be a threat to his position.

Because he was a priest of God and because he had given many years of faithful service to David, Solomon spared Abiathar's life, but he removed him from the priesthood and banished him to his estate in Anathoth. Joab was not so fortunate. Before David had died, he had charged Solomon to kill Joab at the first opportunity. David recognized that Joab had been the strong man in his administration, but he deeply resented Joab's treachery in killing Abner and Amasa (*2:5*), not to mention his slaying of Absalom. In addition to his personal feelings for the man there was also the matter of blood guilt. In his role as commander of David's army, Joab acted as the king's personal representative. Thus, when he shed innocent blood, the king was also thought to share in the guilt. This matter of blood guilt was taken quite seriously. If the house of David was to be freed from the curse Joab had brought upon it, Joab would have to be killed. Doubtless, Joab was aware of his precarious situation. As soon as he learned of Adonijah's death, he ran to the tabernacle and caught hold of the horns which projected from the corners of the altar of burnt-offerings. This was a traditional place of sanctuary (see *I Kin. 1:50*), but Solomon was unmoved by tradition. His instructions to Benaiah were terse and to the point: "Go, strike him down." Benaiah tried to get Joab to come away from the altar, but when he refused, Benaiah struck him down where he stood. Now, Benaiah was commander of the royal army.

"So the kingdom was established in the hand of Solomon" (*I Kin. 2:46*). This time Solomon seems to have agreed with the inspired writer's assessment of the situation, for we hear of no further purges.

### THE WISDOM OF SOLOMON

Despite his early flashes of bloodthirstiness, Solomon is portrayed by the writer of *I-II Kings* as essentially a pious man who loved Yahweh and walked in the steps of David his father (*3:3*). It was true that he offered sacrifices at the "high places" (*3: 3–4*), but the writer minimizes the offence of this by pointing out that "no house had yet been built for the name of Yahweh" (*3: 2*). The crown of Solomon's piety was his humble request that Yahweh grant him "an understanding mind" to equip him for the awesome task of governing the people of God. Yahweh granted Solomon's request and the king became known far and wide for his great wisdom. He was put to the test by prostitutes (*3:16–28*) and queens (*10: 1*). Each time he astounded the people with his answers. He is also said to have composed three thousand proverbs (*4:32*), many of which are contained in the book of *Proverbs*. But Solomon's brilliance was not limited to the field of riddles and wise sayings. During his reign (c. 960–922 B.C.) Israel soared to the greatest heights she was ever to know. It is true that his reign coincided with a time of weakness in Egypt and Assyria, but this Golden Age was not just the product of historical accident. It was the creation of a military, political, and commercial genius. As we turn our attention to highlights of this genius' reign, it will be-

come increasingly clear that Jesus was paying the lilies of the field quite a compliment when he compared them to Solomon in all his glory (*Mt. 6:28–29*).

### THE GLORY OF SOLOMON

We have called Solomon a military genius, even though his reign was one of unparalleled peace in Israel. His genius consisted in setting up and maintaining the kind of military establishment that effectively discouraged any would-be conquerors. His chief defense measure consisted in fortifying cities which guarded the major routes into the land (*9:15–19*) and in equipping them with a striking force of chariots and horsemen. Archaeologists have excavated one of these military bases at Megiddo, just south of the plain of Esdraelon, and have found stables for about 450 horses. Assuming that other fortified cities were similarly equipped, this supports the Biblical claim that Solomon had 4,000 stalls for horses and chariots, 1,400 chariots, and 12,000 horsemen (*I Kin. 10:26; II Chr. 9: 21*). Despite the fact that the Canaanites and Philistines had used their chariots to good effect against Israel, no Israelite leader had ever made extensive use of them. Solomon wisely recognized that a highly mobile force was necessary for effective control of Israel's borders and trade routes, and for keeping check on possible internal disturbances. These troops enabled Solomon to keep a firm hold on the lands he had inherited from his father, with the exception of Edom (*11:14–22*) and Syria (*11:23–25*). When Joab had defeated Edom in David's name, he had slain all of the royal house except a young lad, Hadad, who had been spirited away to Egypt by some of his father's servants. At some time in Solomon's reign—the Bible does not tell us just when— he returned to Edom and began "doing mischief" against Solomon. The extent of his mischief is unknown, but it is probable that he was more of a pest than a real threat.

The Syrian uprising was more serious. The villain here was Rezon, a former servant at the court of the King of Zobah who gathered a band of outlaws and seized control of the city of Damascus. Damacus was the key city of Syria and its loss was no small thing. Judging from the fact that the Bible tells us nothing of Solomon's actions against Rezon, it is probable that the matter resolved into something of a stalemate. Rezon was powerful enough to make a good fight to maintain his hold on Syria, but not strong enough to be a real threat to Israel. Although the loss of Damascus was regrettable, it was not worth an all-out campaign, especially since the kingdom was prospering so well elsewhere. Apart from these two relatively mi-

nor uprisings, Solomon seems to have had little difficulty in holding on to his territory.

In addition to his impressive military strength, Solomon used careful diplomacy to avoid conflicts with rival nations. One of his favorite diplomatic devices was the "marriage alliance," in which an agreement of peace was sealed by a marriage between members of the royal families. Of Solomon's fabled seven hundred wives, many are sure to have been acquired in such an arrangement. The outstanding prize of his harem, at least from a political point of view, was the daughter of Pharaoh. It is a tribute to Solomon that he was able to make sure an alliance, for the Pharaohs did not give their daughters to minor kings. The record makes it clear she was held in higher esteem than his other wives (*I Kin. 3:1; 7:8; 11:1*).

A "ship of Tarshish," used to transport precious cargo.

155

The most successful of Solomon's political measures, however, was the treaty with Hiram king of Tyre (5:1–2). Hiram had made Tyre the mistress of a great colonial empire, reaching as far west as Cyprus and Sicily, and possibly as far as Spain. His relations with David had been peaceful (II Sam. 5:11) and he was careful to maintain these desirable ties with Solomon. In exchange for grain and oil from Israel, Hiram supplied Solomon with cedar and cypress for his building programs (I Kin. 5:7–12), and personally supervised much of the work (7:13–14). The two kings also cooperated in a shipping venture which opened up, via the Red Sea and Indian Ocean, extensive trade with the lands to the south (9:26–28; 10:11, 12, 22). The home port of this sea trade was Ezion-geber, at the northern tip of the Gulf of Aqabah, the eastern arm of the Red Sea (See map). The location of Ezion-geber was in doubt until the late 1930's, when it was discovered and thoroughly excavated by an American archaeologist, Nelson Glueck. The ruins indicate that the city was built all at one time; in other words, Solomon did not pick out a convenient city to serve as his seaport; he built one. The plan and style of the buildings were similar to structures found at the fortified cities we have already mentioned. Ships sailing under the flag of Israel, though manned by experienced Philistine sailors (9:26–28), made long voyages to points as far away as Ophir*, bringing back gold, silver, ivory, almug wood, precious stones, and, presumably as a curiosity, apes and baboons.† In I Kings 10:22 Solomon's fleet is called by the romantic name,

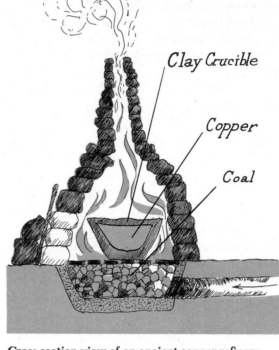

Cross-section view of an ancient copper refinery. The air tunnel at bottom right was situated to take advantage of prevailing winds.

"ships of Tarshish." The word *tarshish* meant "refinery," and a ship of Tarshish was one built along the lines of those used by the Phoenicians to transport copper and other metals from their refineries in such distant places as Sardinia. The term came to refer to any large commercial vessel that sailed great distances. But Solomon's ships were ships of Tarshish in the narrow, as well as the broad, sense of the term. Ruins of a large and well-engineered smelting plant that supplied metal for Solomon's building projects can still be seen today by visitors to the ancient site of Ezion-geber. This is the largest refinery that has been discovered in the Near East. It is situated in an area that is constantly whipped by the winds which blow across the desert from the north. The layout of the refinery indicates that these

---

*The location of Ophir is much disputed. The prevailing opinion among scholars favors a location in Africa, near Somaliland. Others have contended for sites in India and Arabia. For a fuller discussion of the matter, see Wm. F. Albright, *Journal of Biblical Literature*, LXXI (1952), p. 248.

†The Hebrew word translated "peacock" in I Kings 10:22 actually means "baboon."

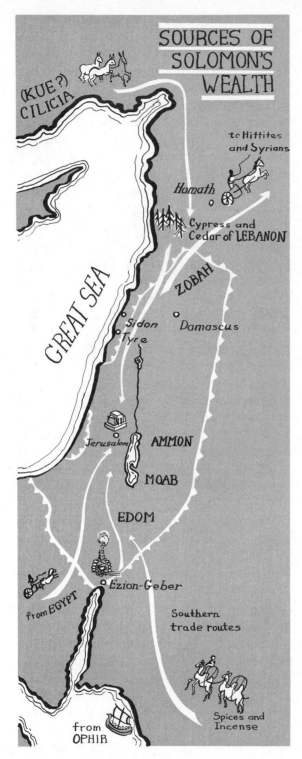

**Sources of Solomon's wealth: Horses, lumber, copper, gold, spices and incense.**

winds were used as a forced draft to drive the smelting fires.

Solomon's commercial activity was not limited to sea trade and his exchanges with Phoenicia. He controlled the major caravan routes of the northern Near East and was able not only to trade with these caravans, but to collect sizable taxes in return for the use of the routes. It is quite probable that the famous visit of the Queen of Sheba (*ch. 10*) is to be understood as an effort at reaching an agreement about trade routes in the south. The kingdom of Sheba, whose inhabitants were called Sabeans, was situated in Southern Arabia and had control of the valuable spice and incense (myrrh and frankincense) trade of the region. Through his expanded sea trade in the south, Solomon was in a position to become a real competitor. The Bible does not tell us that this was the occasion of the visit, but we can be sure that the great queen did not ride a camel all the way to Jerusalem just to ask Solomon a few brain-twisters. No specific agreement is mentioned, but we are told that "King Solomon gave to the Queen of Sheba all that she desired" and that the coffers of Israel were filled by taxes from the merchants and traders of Arabia (*10:13–15*). Presumably, they were able to work out their problems in a mutually advantageous manner.

Solomon also distinguished himself as something of a horse trader. In *I Kings 10: 28–29* tells us that he purchased chariots from Egypt and horses from Kue, or Cilicia,* and sold them to the nations in the north. Since Egyptian chariots and Cilician

---

*The Hebrew text of these verses is uncertain, and Kue is translated "linen yarn" in several English versions, including the King James version. Since one does not ordinarily associate horses and chariots with linen yarn, and since Kue, or Cilicia, produced the finest horses in the ancient world, we may be fairly certain that the Revised Standard Version of *10:28* is approximately accurate : "and Solomon's import of horses was from Egypt and Kue, and the king's traders received them from Kue at a price."

horses were the finest to be obtained, and since Solomon's control of the territory between his northern buyers and southern suppliers gave him a monopoly on the trade, Solomon was undoubtedly able to command at least a fair price for his merchandise.

### A HOUSE FOR YAHWEH

As Solomon grew richer, he turned to the task that was to absorb much of his attention and much of the nation's wealth—the creation of a New Jerusalem. Jerusalem was the city of David. By the time he finished with it, it would be the city of Solomon.

Solomon's building projects included the royal palace, which took thirteen years to complete (*I Kings 7:1*), the House of the Forest of Lebanon, a huge building constructed mainly of the fine cedars obtained from Hiram of Tyre (*7:2–5; 10:16, 17, 21*); the Hall of Pillars (*7:6*), the Hall of Judgment (*7:17*); and a house for the daughter of Pharaoh (*7:8*).

The crown of all of Solomon's achievements was, of course, the great temple, the House of the Lord. Because we have heard of Solomon's temple all our lives, we are apt to think of it as a very large building. Actually, it was smaller than many modern church buildings,* but it was still a most impressive building. If we study the sketch on p. 160 briefly, it is possible to get a general notion of how the temple looked without wading through all the details of the Biblical description.

The temple proper contained three rooms. The first was a vestibule or foyer, much like one finds in modern buildings. From this room, one passed through two large double doors which were themselves divided into folding leaves, into the largest room, the Holy Place. The floor was cypress

---

*Figuring the cubit at eighteen inches, the temple measured 90 x 30 x 45 feet (*6:2*). The House of the Forest of Lebanon was much larger (*7:2*).

and the walls were lined with ornately carved cedar boards, inlaid with gold. This room, like the Holy Place in the temple, contained the table of shewbread, golden lampstands, a small incense altar, and the various accessories that went with them.

The third room, a perfect cube, was the Holy of Holies, the throne room of Yahweh. Like the Holy Place, it also had a floor of cypress and walls of carved cedar wainscoting. In all probability, this room had no windows and was filled with "thick darkness" (See *6:16; 8:12*). In the center of the room stood two huge cherubim, or winged sphinxes, fifteen feet high. These cherubim were made of olivewood and overlaid with gold. As we noted in discussing the smaller cherubim which originally adorned the "mercy-seat" in the tabernacle (see p. 76), these served as the throne of Yahweh's glory. Their wings were extended and, between the two of them, stretched from wall to wall. The only other article in the room was the little ark of the covenant which rested on the floor beneath the outstretched wings of the cherubim (*I Kin. 8:6*).

This main structure of the temple was enclosed on the sides and rear by a three-story system of rooms. These were entered through side doors and served as storage rooms, mainly for the temple treasure.

On the outside of the temple, on either side of the main entrance, stood two large bronze pillars, which were given the names Jachin and Boaz (*7:21*). They supported nothing; if they had a significance other than decoration, we do not know what it was. In the inner court of the temple stood a large bronze altar, twenty feet square and fifteen feet high, which was the altar of burnt-offerings (*II Chr. 4:1*). It was probably mounted by a flight of stairs on the east side (See *Ezekiel 43:17*). Other items in this inner court before the temple were the "Molten Sea" and ten ornate wagons carrying lavers. The Molten Sea was a huge basin or tank fifteen feet in diameter and seven and a half feet deep, with a capacity of about 10,000 gallons of water. It sat on top of twelve bronze bulls arranged in groups of three. The smaller lavers which sat on the wagons had a capacity of about 200 gallons each and were arranged in rows of five on either side of the inner court of the temple. The Sea and the lavers were used by the priests to wash in after performing their sacrificial duties.

In the ancient Near East, the temple, or "house," of a god was not usually regarded as the literal dwelling-place of a god. Instead, it was viewed as a kind of scale model of the deity's world. A god's presence in the temple symbolized his presence in the world. Most Canaanite temples had a small room corresponding to the Holy of Holies in the temple of Solomon.* This room contained a statue of the god of the temple. The worshipers did not equate this statue with the god, but they did regard the statue as proof of the god's presence in his temple. That is, they did not think he was confined within the idol itself, but the idol assured them he was there.

The reader has probably already noted certain similarities between these Near Eastern temples and the temple of Solomon. In David's Song of Deliverance, Yahweh's descent to the earth is described in these vivid words:

> He bowed the heavens, and came down;
>> thick darkness was under his feet.
> He rode on a cherub, and flew;
>> he was seen upon the wings of the wind.
>> —*II Samuel* 22:10-11

As we have seen, this same symbolism is present in the Holy of Holies. At the point where Yahweh "tabernacled"* among his people, the unlighted Holy of Holies, "thick darkness was under his feet" and "he rode on a cherub." It was forbidden to make an image of Yahweh, but the cherubim symbolized his presence much as the idols symbolized the presence of the deity of pagan temples. Let us emphasize once again that similarities between aspects of the religion of Israel and pagan religions do not mean that Israel copied her religion from her neighbors. We do not believe that to be the case. It simply means that God revealed himself and his will to his people in terms that were familiar to them. Just as the covenant at Sinai had its counterpart in the Hittite suzerainty treaties (p. 68ff), so the temple of Solomon had certain features in common with the temples of Canaan. This not only enabled the Israelites to understand the significance of their temple more clearly; it also helped them present their religion to their pagan neighbors in terms they could understand.

We have said that Israel's neighbors did not regard their temples as the actual dwelling-places of their gods for whom they were built. While this was no doubt true of the leaders and the more sophisticated worshipers, some of the common people probably failed to make such distinctions. For them, the god's existence was confined to his temple and his statue was equated with the god himself. Solomon wanted to make certain that this sort of thing did not happen in Israel. In his speech at the dedication of the temple, he made it clear that the temple

---

*For a discussion of the significance and types of Near Eastern temples, see G. Ernest Wright, "The Temple in Palestine-Syria," *The Biblical Archaeologist Reader* (Garden City, New York: Doubleday Anchor Books, 1961), pp. 169–184.

*In the Hebrew text of the Bible, the word most often used to designate God's presence among his people was a word used by nomads, meaning "to tent" or "to tabernacle." This implied a temporary, or at least a non-permanent, settling. When the Bible speaks of "inhabiting" or "dwelling" in a more permanent sense, an entirely different Hebrew verb is used. For a full discussion of this matter, see Frank M. Cross, Jr., "The Priestly Tabernacle," *The Biblical Archaeologist Reader*, pp. 225–7.

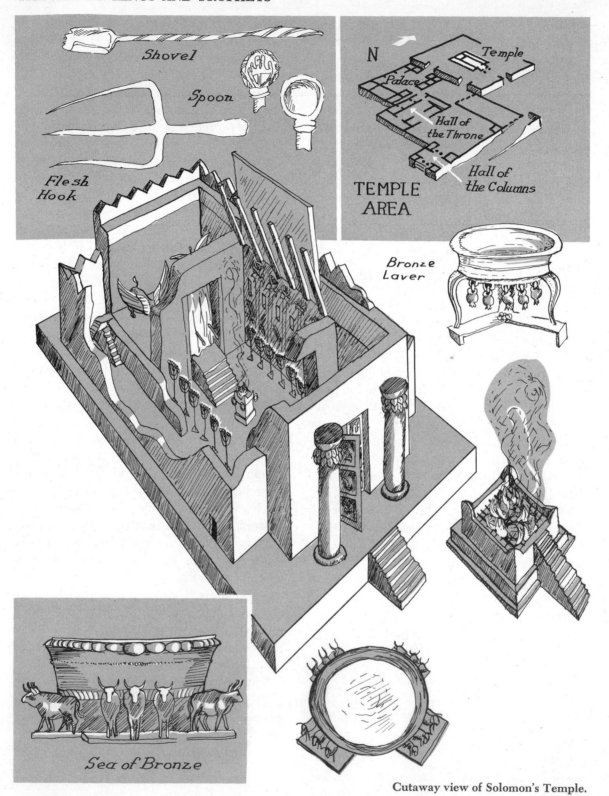

Shovel

Spoon

Flesh
Hook

N

Temple

Palace

Hall of
the Throne

Hall of
the Columns

TEMPLE
AREA

Bronze
Laver

Sea of Bronze

Cutaway view of Solomon's Temple.

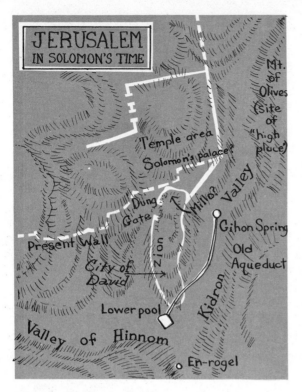

Topographical map showing
Jerusalem as it appeared
during the reign of King
Solomon.

was not to be regarded as the place where man had "captured" God. Note his words carefully:

> But will God indeed dwell on the earth? Behold, heaven and the highest heaven cannot contain thee; how much less this house which I have built! Yet have regard to the prayer of thy servant and to his supplication, O Lord my God, hearkening to the cry and to the prayer which thy servant prays before thee this day; that thy eyes may be open night and day toward this house, the place of which thou has said, "My name shall be there," that thou mayest hearken to the prayer which thy servant offers toward this place. And hearken thou to the supplication of thy servant and of thy people Israel, when they pray toward this place; yea, hear thou in heaven thy dwelling place; and when thou hearest, forgive. —I Kings 8:27-30

Here we see that the temple is holy not because Yahweh is confined to it, or even because his cherubic throne is found there, but because he has allowed it to be called by his name. The temple that bears his name is proof that Yahweh indeed tents or tabernacles, "among his people."

Seven years were required to complete the temple. The dedication ceremony took place in the seventh month of the year, which was probably 950 B.C. A number of scholars have viewed the fact that the temple was dedicated in the seventh month as more than a coincidence. The seventh month was the time of the Canaanite New Year. In some Near Eastern societies, the New Year was the occasion of a major religious festival, in which the drama of creation was acted out in an effort to keep nature on the right track for another year. The king always took a leading role in these dramas, usually as the king of the gods. By winning the mock battle over the characters representing chaos, the king assured the land of another year of rain and fertility.

At the dedication of the temple, Solomon led the procession which brought the Ark of the Covenant from Zion, the section of the city where David had made his headquarters, to its new resting place in the great temple (I Kin. 8:1–5). Scholars who believe there is a connection between the pagan festivals and the dedication of the temple view this procession as symbolic of Yahweh's triumph over the forces of chaos, not only in the creation of the world, but in the creation of the covenant people Israel through the events of the Exodus. This is an attractive theory, and, if true, it injects new significance into the Biblical account. It would be another example of the use of familiar religious practice to call attention to the mighty acts of Yahweh. It is, however, only a theory. The Biblical narrative leaves room for this interpretation, but it does not tell us that

161

this is what really happened. It may well be that the dedication ceremony was held in the seventh month because that was when the temple was finished. The procession from Zion to the temple may have signified nothing more than the transfer of the Ark to its new quarters. And Solomon may have led the procession because—well, who else would have led it? Nevertheless, the theory is worth our consideration.

### CULTURE IN THE GOLDEN AGE

This Golden Age of Israel was not limited to commerce and architecture. It was also a time when cultural activities flourished. The center of this activity was, of course, the court of Solomon. As we have already mentioned, the king himself was a great hand at composing proverbs (*I Kin. 4:29–34*). In later years, we know Israel took great interest in so-called "Wisdom Literature" (See pp. 341 ff). It is probable that the ancestors of this movement were to be found in small groups which clustered together at the court of this wisest of Israel's king.

Since Solomon was also a musician, said to have written 1,005 songs (*4:32*), and since David had created an official order of temple musicians in the early days of Solomon's reign, we can be almost certain that Israel's music reached a high point in its development in this period. Many scholars feel that it was probably during this time of peace and prosperity that scribes began to work many of the oral and written traditions that had been handed down from Moses and others into the form they now have in our Bibles. In addition to collecting these ancient traditions, there was the serious business of keeping historical records of what was going on at the time. Court historians preserved what they saw in such books as the "Book of the Acts of Solomon" (*11: 41*). None of these records have been preserved in their original form, but it seems

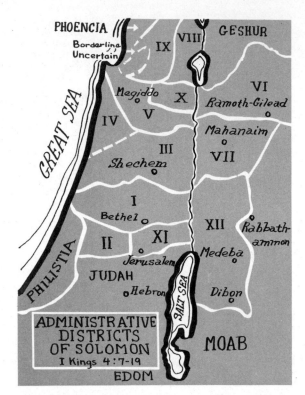

Major administrative divisions of Solomon's kingdom.

clear that the Biblical writers used them in composing the inspired record.

### AN EVALUATION OF SOLOMON'S REIGN

*Rumblings of Discontent.* This was the high point in Israel's history, at least as far as peace and material prosperity were concerned. The commercial wizardry of the king had brought more jobs and higher pay for many throughout the populace. Farmers benefitted from the sale of wheat and oil. Carpenters and other laborers found jobs on the royal building projects. Thousands were paid to serve as full-time soldiers. Others sailed the seas, worked in the refineries, or handled Solomon's horse trading for him. More money was circulating in Israel than had ever been seen before.

Still, there were rumblings of discontent. Solomon had made the nation rich, but he had spent an incredibly large amount on himself and his projects. The expense just of feeding seven hundred wives, three hundred concubines, and the servants employed by Solomon is staggering. In *I Kings 4:22* we are told that "Solomon's provision *for one day* was thirty measures of fine flour, and sixty measures of meal, ten fat oxen, and twenty pasture-fed cattle, a hundred sheep, besides harts, gazelles, roebucks, and fatted fowl." Solomon divided the nation into twelve provinces and gave the governor of each of them the responsibility to furnish these provisions for one month of the year. Even in a good year, this could be quite a strain on the people, and was bound to stir up resentment. One only has to read the descriptions of the temple, then notice that most of the other buildings in the royal complex were larger and more expensive, to realize that Solomon spent money on the same grand style that he did everything else.

Extravagance was not the only complaint that could be laid at Solomon's feet. The escape from Egyptian bondage had given Israel a heady taste of freedom. Her love for it never abated. When the tribal independence Israel had cherished so long, and had clung to even in the days of David, was eliminated and replaced by a provincial system designed to centralize the government, bitterness was sure to result. And we can well imagine the indignation when Solomon, in order to raise money, sold twenty towns of Galilee to Hiram of Tyre, as if they were twenty horses or cows (*9:10–14*). Even more galling was Solomon's use of Israelite slave labor to cut timber and stone from the mountains of Lebanon to be used in the royal building projects (*I Kin. 5:13–18*). Israel's whole life had revolved around her escape from state slavery. To be put back into it by a king of her own making was the supreme irony. How Samuel's words of warning must have burned Israel's ears!

*Solomon's Apostasy.* Even before Israel entered into the land of Canaan, Yahweh commanded his people not to marry the daughters of the Canaanites. As we have pointed out, this prohibition was based on religious, not racial, grounds. The Canaanites and Israelites were of the same general ethnic stock, but their religions were poles apart. Israel had never kept this commandment very well. Solomon ignored it completely. Of his seven hundred wives and three hundred concubines, many, perhaps most, were foreign (*I Kin. 11:1*). In the early days of his reign, he was preoccupied with building the temple and apparently remained reasonably faithful to Yahweh. But the result of his disobedience was inevitable; "for when Solomon was old his wives turned away his heart after other gods; and his heart was not wholly to Yahweh his God as was the heart of David" (*11:4*).

When Yahweh saw Solomon's disobedience, he resolved that Solomon's empire would not be left intact for his descendants. Through the prophet Ahijah he informed Jeroboam, one of the commanders of the slave labor forces, that he would rule over the ten tribes in the North. Solomon's descendants would be left with only Judah and Benjamin. When Solomon learned of the words of Ahijah, he tried to have Jeroboam arrested and killed, but Jeroboam fled to Egypt and took refuge with Shishak, the Pharaoh of Egypt. He remained there until Solomon died. But he did not forget the words of the prophet.

*The Status of the Monarchy.* Solomon raised the monarchy to the highest stage of its development. In other days, the tabernacle had stood at the center of the nation. The tabernacle had been replaced by a more magnificent temple, but the temple had become a royal chapel. In other days the priest of God had renounced the king and left him stripped of religious support. When Solomon was displeased with the actions of Abiathar, he banished him from the capital and replaced him with a man more favorable to the official policy. In other days the everyday actions of the people were governed by the covenant of Sinai. Under Solomon, the supreme and pervasive law was the law of the state, and Solomon was the state.

*The Theology of the Kingship.* How did David and Solomon manage to accomplish this remarkable transformation of Israel from a tribal confederacy to a dynastic state? Obviously, fortunate political circumstances and sheer genius in military and commercial ventures played enormous roles. It would be a mistake, however, to overlook the importance of the fact that, at every point, they undergirded their position with divine sanctions and developed a theology that changed the monarchy from a suspect to a hallowed institution.

David took the first, and perhaps the most important, step when he brought the Ark of the Covenant to Jerusalem. No longer were there two focal points of Israel's loyalty. Instead of being a threat to the covenant, as symbolized by the Ark, David showed himself to be its protector. In return, he received the promise of God that his throne would endure forever. In the light of the New Testament, we see that this promise was fulfilled in the Heavenly King who reigns in the New Jerusalem. But Israel had no New Testament. She interpreted the promise literally: Jerusalem and the House of David would never be brought low. Yahweh had promised and his promise could not fail. As we shall see again and again, the prophets of God were never able to convince the people that any other interpretation was possible.

Solomon's reign reinforced this optimistic outlook. Israel might not like everything Solomon did, but he was so overwhelmingly successful that it was hard to doubt that Yahweh was with him. With the Ark secure

in the temple and Solomon reigning as the greatest power in the Near East, it seemed certain that God would dwell in Jerusalem forever. Surely the Lord approved of the monarchy. Solomon did nothing to destroy this image. When the Ark was transferred to the temple, he marched at the head of the procession. All Israel could see that Yahweh and Solomon walked together. Judging from his role in this procession and at the dedication of the Temple, it is quite possible that Solomon had a definite place in other cultic activities at the temple. If this is true, it certainly would enhance his image in the eyes of the people.

These acts of David and Solomon provided the raw materials for the development of a theology of the kingship. The substance of this theology is set forth in Nathan's oracle in *II Samuel 7:4–17* and in the so-called "Royal Psalms" (*Ps. 2, 18, 21, 45, 89, 101, 110, 132, 144*). These passages assert that God has chosen David and his house to reign forever.* The Davidic kings are not just ordinary earthly rulers; they are anointed "sons" of God. That is, he has chosen them for their task and they bear a special religious relationship to him.† Because of this covenant relationship, the king would prevail over his enemies, and Zion, or Jerusalem, would forever reign as queen of the nations.‡

In the eyes of many, this new theology took the place of, or at least revised, the older covenant theology, which made no provision for a king. But some were never fully convinced. The notion persisted that the kings were usurping the authority and glory that properly belonged only to Yahweh. Both the king and his subjects frequently made the mistake of automatically

---

*(*II Sam. 7:14–16; Ps. 89:3–4, 19–37; 132:11–14*)
†(*II Sam. 7:14; Ps. 2:2, 7; 18:50; 20:6; 89:27*).
‡(*Ps. 2:1–12; 18:31–45; 21:7–12; 72:8–11; 132:17–18; 144:10–11*).

identifying the policies of the king with the will of God. As long as the monarchy existed, prophets would arise to decry this error and to warn the kings and people of the inevitable consequences of their rejection of the kingship of Yahweh. This tension between the old traditions of the Twelve Tribe League and the new traditions of the dynastic monarchy will occupy much of our attention in the following chapters as we study the fortunes of the kingdoms of Israel and Judah.

# 9

# The Divided Kingdom

*An era of kings and prophets: two centuries of struggle between men of God and the gods of men*

IN 922 B.C., the empire of David and Solomon divided into two kingdoms. The northern portion retained the name Israel. The southern portion took the name of its largest tribe, Judah. After a troubled existence of exactly two hundred years, the ten tribes of the northern kingdoms were carried into Assyrian captivity (722/21 B.C.) and passed forever from the pages of history. The southern kingdom survived almost a century and a half longer, but finally succumbed to the mighty armies of Nebuchadnezzar and went into Babylonian captivity in 586 B.C. These were centuries of decline and despair. There were brief periods of peace and prosperity, but neither of the two kingdoms ever approached the glory that had been Solomon's.

This period of Israel's history is one of the least well-known to most Bible students. There are good reasons for this. In the first place, the books of *I-II Kings* and *I-II Chronicles*, our major sources for the period, are not written in what one would call a captivating style. King Ahasuerus of Persia had his servants read the royal chronicles aloud to him in order to put him to sleep (*Esther 6:1*). Most of us who have read *Kings* and *Chronicles* can appreciate his request. The narrative skips back and forth from Israel to Judah so often, and the names of the kings are so many and so similar, that one must keep his eye sharp and his mind nimble to know which kingdom is under discussion.

The rather monotonous quality of these books results from the fact that the writers were less interested in giving us an exciting record of events than in issuing a verdict on the worth of each of the kings of Israel and Judah. The criterion for their verdict was not material prosperity or military success, but faithfulness to the covenant with Yahweh. Earlier, we said that the section of the Bible from *Joshua* through *I-II Kings* could be read as a continuous historical narrative, with the book of *Deuteronomy* serving as an introduction. This Deuteronomic introduction sets forth the major theological ideas which control the thinking of the writers of this whole section. The speeches of Moses in *Deuteronomy* emphasize the covenant of Sinai and warn of the dangers of turning from Yahweh to the Gods of Canaan. They also urge that the worship of Yahweh be confined to the central sanctuary; that is, to the place where the Ark of the Covenant is

166

located (See *Deut. 12:13–14; 16:5–6*). The writers of *Kings* and *Chronicles* judge their subjects by their faithfulness to this Deuteronomic standard. In a typical record of a king's reign, we are told when he took office, where and how long he reigned before he "slept with his fathers," and, if we are fortunate, a few key facts about his administration. But these are not the primary interests of the writers. Again and again they tell us that, if we are interested in learning more about what actually took place in a king's reign, we should consult the Book of Chronicles of the Kings of Israel (or Judah).* Their real purpose lies in telling us just how well these kings measured up to the Deuteronomic standard. This is done according to a regular formula. When the king is a king of Judah, he is measured by comparison to "David his father," the exemplar of a faithful king (See *I Kin. 15:3, 11* etc.). When a king of Israel is under discussion, he is, in virtually every case, censured for the fact that "he did what was evil in the sight of Yahweh, and walked in the way of Jeroboam and in his sin, which he made Israel to sin" (*I Kin. 15:34*).

Why were the inspired writers so concerned to render such a judgment on each of the kings of these two nations? The answer seems fairly evident. Yahweh had promised Abraham that his children would inherit the land of Canaan. When these books were written, Abraham's descendants had been driven from the land by pagan invaders. Had God lied? Had he been unable to keep his promise to Abraham? Not at all, said our historians. Yahweh would have upheld his people forever if they had not persistently forsaken the covenant. Because of their repeated infidelity, exemplified by their kings,

it was necessary to punish them, in the hope of bringing a blessing even greater than the gift of the land. However things might appear, Yahweh had not failed his people.

Unfortunately, at least for the purpose of writing a history, we do not possess the royal chronicles used by the Biblical writers in composing their books. Still, our sources do allow us to get a reasonably accurate picture of the period. Despite the fact that the Biblical writers were a bit stingy with details, they have provided us with a dependable historical framework. To flesh out this skeleton, we have the works of the prophets. Most of them (*Isaiah* and *Jeremiah* are notable exceptions) contain little or no straight historical narrative, but through their poetic oracles, they often give us informative glimpses both of the social situation in Israel and of larger historical movements in the Near Eastern world. In addition to these Biblical sources, archaeologists have discovered numerous inscriptions and documents left by kings of surrounding nations that mention their dealings with the kings of Israel and Judah. Thus, our sources are actually quite good. When we fit them all together, we can obtain a rather complete and, hopefully, clear picture of the period of the kings.

It is our intention in this chapter and the next to provide the reader with such a picture. In order to avoid the confusion often encountered in reading *Kings* and *Chronicles*, we shall not skip back and forth between Israel and Judah quite so often as the Bible does, but will trace the fortunes of each of the kingdoms through the reigns of several kings at a time. We shall also deal with the various prophets in connection with the kings in whose reigns they prophesied, instead of discussing them as a group after we have finished Israel's history. They were the key representatives of Yahweh during the Divided Kingdom. If we are going to

---

*See, for example, I Kings 15:1–8. The Books of Chronicles mentioned in these passages were the official royal histories and are not to be confused with the Biblical books of *Chronicles*.

understand their messages, it is vital to place them in the proper historical context. Before beginning a new section, the reader should study the chronological chart placed near the beginning of each major section in order to get a clear overview of the whole period.

## The Division of the Empire

### REHOBOAM IS REJECTED

As we noted in chapter 7, not everyone in Israel viewed Solomon's reign as one of undimmed glory. There was good reason for complaint, and we may be sure that complaint was heard. Apparently, the northern tribes were particularly resentful of Solomon's harsh measures. It is not unlikely that the Israelite slaves who cut timber in the forests of Lebanon were drawn from these northern tribes, for the simple reason that they were closer to Lebanon than the southern tribes. Then there was the matter of the twenty towns of Galilee that were sold to Hiram of Tyre. Solomon had been powerful enough to discourage any thought of revolt, but when his son Rehoboam came to the throne, the dam of feeling burst and the pent-up resentment surged across the land.

The particular incident which marked the division of the kingdoms was Rehoboam's meeting with the elders of North Israel at Shechem. The very fact that such a meeting took place is a sign that the empire had not destroyed all traces of independence. The tribes of the north still thought of themselves as separate from the southern tribe of Judah. Rehoboam had already been crowned king at Jerusalem, but it was still necessary for him to go to Shechem to receive the allegiance of the northern tribes.

Rehoboam's behavior at Shechem is that of a young man still too immature to lead a great nation. The men of Israel did not hesitate to let him know how things had to be before they would accept him: "Your father made our yoke heavy. Now therefore lighten the hard service of your father and his heavy yoke upon us, and we will serve you" (*I Kin. 12:4*). The young king requested three days to consider their demand.

Rehoboam could have given in to their demands without any real loss to himself. It was unnecessary to launch any further building programs that would drain the nation of men and money. The expenses of maintaining the royal court could surely be cut down drastically. Rehoboam had it within his power to grant their demands, to present himself as a benevolent ruler who wanted the best for his people, and to win a loyalty and affection that his father had not enjoyed. The older and wiser heads about him urged him to do just that. But the young men, who had lived off the earnings of other men, counselled him differently. Solomon had not held his empire by granting the demands of weaklings. If Rehoboam gave in now, there would be no end to the liberties they would seek. If he would be a great king, he would have to be even sterner and harsher than his father.

When the elders assembled on the third day, Rehoboam gave his reply to their proposal: "My father made your yoke heavy, but I will add to your yoke; my father chastised you with whips, but I will chastise you with scorpions" (*12:14*). When the men of Israel heard this, they replied in the words the rebel Sheba had shouted when he led his revolt against David (*II Sam. 20:1*):

What portion have we in David?
　We have no inheritance in the son of Jesse.
To your tents, O Israel!
　Look now to your own house, David.
　　　　　　　*—I Kings 12:16*

So Israel departed to their tents.

In desperation, Rehoboam sent Adoram, a slavemaster, to whip the rebels into line. When Adoram not only failed, but was stoned to death for his trouble, Rehoboam

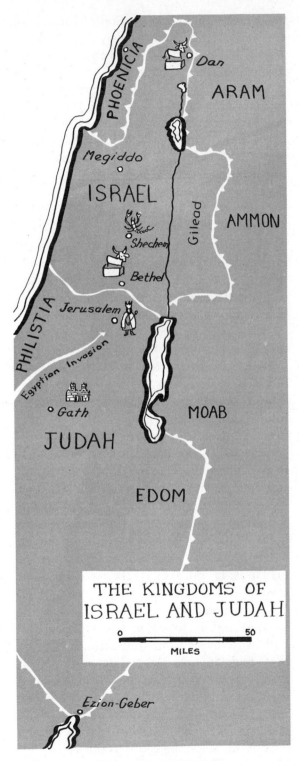

THE KINGDOMS OF
ISRAEL AND JUDAH

0 _____ 50
MILES

The territory of the northern and southern
kingdoms at the time of their division in 922 B.C.

rushed to Jerusalem and mustered a large fighting force to crush the rebellion. It seems probable he could have executed such a campaign successfully, but Shemaiah, a prophet of Yahweh stopped him and told him that the thing was from the Lord. This time, Rehoboam was in more of a disposition to listen to a wiser man, and he told his soldiers to return to their homes. "So Israel has been in rebellion against the house of David to this day" (*12:19*).

### JEROBOAM MAKES THE SCHISM PERMANENT

Israel did not wait long to find a king. Apparently, it was generally known that the prophet Ahijah had named Jeroboam to be king over the northern tribes. When the men of Israel learned that he had returned from Egypt, they summoned him to Shechem and made him king over all Israel.

Jeroboam feared that, after the heat of the rebellion had passed, the northerners would drift back into Rehoboam's camp. Immediately, he took steps to prevent this. First, he established his capital in Shechem. But this was nothing compared to his other move. Since David had brought the Ark to Jerusalem, the men of Israel had gone up at least once a year to offer sacrifice. This practice had been strengthened by the building of the magnificent temple. Jeroboam realized that if people made the yearly trip to Jerusalem, they would be impressed by the beauty of the temple and the other great buildings Solomon had built. Jeroboam's modest capital would suffer by comparison. If Rehoboam caught them at the right psychological moment, it would not be too difficult to unite them once again. Jeroboam was unwilling to let this happen. The best way to see that it did not, he reasoned, was to set up a rival religious cult that would keep the people going to Jerusalem in the first place. So, he instituted the cult of the golden calves, or bulls. He had two of the bulls

169

made and sat one up in Dan and Bethel, both of which were already hallowed religious shrines. He established a priesthood and appointed the fifteenth day of the eighth month as a special feast day.

Throughout the books of *Kings* and *Chronicles,* this action of Jeroboam is condemned as the act by which "he made Israel to sin." In the eyes of the Biblical writers, it ranks as the most grievous sin committed in Israel's long history. Most of us have assumed that Jeroboam's sin consisted in idolatry pure and simple. This may be correct. Certainly, in later years, the bull cult was little more than this. There is good reason to believe, however, that Jeroboam's action was not a direct rejection of Yahweh. When Jeroboam presented the bulls to the people, he said, "Behold your gods, O Israel, *who brought you up out of the land of Egypt*" (*12:28*). It is almost inconceivable that he would try to persuade them that some god other than Yahweh had delivered them from Egyptian bondage. This tradition was so deeply ingrained that we can hardly imagine their accepting another one. It is quite possible, as a number of scholars have suggested, that Jeroboam intended for the bulls to serve in roughly the same function as the cherubim of the tabernacle and temple; that is, as the throne of the invisible God. This idea is strengthened by the fact that the Canaanites often pictured Baal as riding on the back of a bull. Never, however, did they or other Semitic peoples picture their high gods in the form of animals. In other words, instead of instituting a practice that would be sure to alienate a large number of his followers, Jeroboam may well have been trying to win as many people as possible by combining several familiar features of Canaanite religion with the worship of Yahweh. This is just a theory, of course, but we believe it is worthy of serious consideration. It makes Jeroboam's acts more intelligible and still

leaves us with an explanation of the severe condemnation of Jeroboam by the prophets. As we shall see, one of the primary interests of the prophets was to outlaw worship at any place other than the central sanctuary in Jerusalem (See p. 202f). Even if Jeroboam's cult had been an exact replica of the Jerusalem worship, they probably would have opposed it. Mixed as it was with elements of Canaanite worship, it became the target of their full fury.

### RESULTS OF THE SPLIT

The split between the northern and southern tribes marked the collapse of the Israelite empire. Neither Jeroboam nor Rehoboam was able to maintain control over the kingdoms which bordered on their territory. The most serious loss was that of the Aramean provinces northeast of Israel. Damascus had been independent since the latter years of Solomon's reign. Now, with Jeroboam powerless to stop them, the other Aramean states followed Damascus' lead. Within a short time, Aram became Israel's most dangerous enemy. When the kingdom divided, Rehoboam apparently lost control of the troops stationed in Northern Israel. It is likely that, without either the guarantee of a salary or the threat of punishment, they simply went home. Whatever the case, Rehoboam had no better luck than Jeroboam in holding on to his lands. It appears that the two kingdoms east of Judah, Ammon and Moab, gained their independence at this time. The Bible says nothing of a rebellion, but we know that both were free a short time later. Probably, they took advantage of the instability of these early years of the schism and achieved their freedom with little or no opposition. There is no evidence to indicate that Judah lost control of the Edomite lands to the southwest. Since the route to the vital shipping and refining center of Ezion-geber ran through this territory, the Biblical writers almost certainly would have mentioned the loss of this land had it occurred. To the southwest, the Philistines had regained control of much of their territory, although Rehoboam had not only kept his hold on Gath, but had made it one of his key defense posts (See *II Chron. 11:8*). The Philistines were not a serious threat to Judah, but they did manage to be troublesome from time to time (See *I Kin. 15:27; 16:15*).

The loss of surrounding territory meant the loss of tribute money. As we have noted, Judah probably still controlled the mining center of Ezion-geber, but she could not maintain the trade monopolies that had made Solomon rich. Thus, within an amazingly short time and without a major war, the chief power in the Near Eastern world was reduced to two rather insignificant and economically depressed rival states, scrapping with one another to hold on to what little they had left (*I Kin. 14:30*).

## The Fortunes of Israel and Judah: 922–876 B.C.

### THE INVASION OF SHISHAK

The vulnerable condition of both Israel and Judah was dramatized by the devastating invasion by Shishak in 918 (*I Kin. 14:*

| JUDAH | Related History | ISRAEL |
|---|---|---|
| **Rehoboam** *8* (*17*)* ..922–915 | | **Jeroboam** *22* ........922–901 |
| | 918: Shishak (Egypt) attacks Judah, Philistia, Edom. | |
| **Abijah (Abijam)** *3*...915–913 | | |
| **Asa** *41* ............913–873 | | |
| | | **Nadab** *2* ..........901–900 |
| | | **Baasha** *24* .........900–877 |
| | | **Elah** *2* ............877–876 |
| | | **Zimri** *7 days* ...........876 |
| | | **Omri** *8* (*12*) .......876–869 |
| **Jehoshaphat** *25* .....873–849 | | |
| | 870: Assyria stirring under Asshur-nasir-apli. Campaign in Northern Syria. | **Ahab** *20* (*22*) ......869–850 |
| | | PROPHETS: **Elijah** |
| | | **Micaiah** |
| | 853: Battle of Qarqar | |
| | | **Ahaziah** *2* .........850–849 |
| **Jehoram** *8* .........849–842 | | **Joram** *8* (*12*) .......849–842 |
| **Ahaziah** *1* .............842 | | PROPHETS: **Elijah** |
| | | **Elisha** |

### CHRONOLOGICAL CHART: 922-842 B.C.

*Italic figures following names indicate length of reign. Figures in parentheses indicate that the Bible gives a different figure, or is inconsistent in the figures it gives. Because of conflicting Biblical testimony and incomplete historical records, it is not always possible to arrive at the exact date or length of the reigns of the kings of Israel and Judah; therefore, many of the dates given in this chart are approximate. Few can be regarded as absolutely settled. They are, however, based on careful historical investigation and may be trusted to be reasonably accurate.

A wall painting in the temple of Karnack telling of Shishak's triumphant Palestinian campaign.

25–28). Shishak had led a successful rebellion against the Twenty-first Egyptian Dynasty and had established the Twenty-second. Shishak was an ambitious man. When he took the throne of Egypt in 935 B.C., he set his sights on the treasures of Solomon. He gave political asylum to Jeroboam when he fled to Egypt to escape death at the hands of Solomon. This gesture was motivated less by benevolent generosity than by a desire to encourage enemy weakness and dissension in Israel. As soon as he saw that Israel and Judah were ready to be plucked, he swept through Palestine on a campaign of pillage and destruction that included the whole of Israel and Judah. The Bible tells only of the plundering of the treasures of Jerusalem (*I Kin. 14:26–8; II Chron. 12:1–12*), but Shishak was thought-

172

ful enough to provide us with a detailed record of his exploits. In the magnificent ruins of the temple of Karnak, outside Luxor in Upper Egypt, Shishak left an inscription which lists over 150 towns of Palestine which he conquered. Archaeological evidence of widespread destruction in this period confirms Shishak's claim. The internal weakness of the Egyptian state made it impossible for Shishak to follow up this campaign with the reestablishment of the Egyptian empire. It did, however, so weaken both Israel and Judah that neither was able to force the other into a union with itself. The division of the kingdom was permanent.

### A TIME OF UNREST

Despite the fact that conquest was virtually impossible, the two kingdoms fought along the frontier as long as Jeroboam lived

The magnificent ruins of the temple of Karnack, outside Luxor in Upper Egypt.

(*I Kin. 15:1*). The most important of the skirmishes occurred during the short reign of Rehoboam's son and successor, Abijah (915–913 B.C.). This battle, described in *II Chronicles 13*, had several of the earmarks of Holy War (see p. 93f). When Abijah assembled his troops in the hill country of Ephraim, he chided Jeroboam and the northern tribesmen for their religious apostasy, warning them they stood no chance against the faithful army of Judah. At the head of the southern troops marched the priests with their battle trumpets (*II Chron. 13:12*). Israel had twice as many men and managed to ambush the troops of Judah, but when the battle shout was raised, Israel's army was thrown into confusion and soundly defeated. Abijah followed up the victory by establishing control over Bethel and other nearby cities, but this was only a temporary extension of Judah's territory.

### ASA, KING OF JUDAH (913–873 B.C.)

Abijah's reign was properous, but short. He was succeeded by his son Asa, who was one of the finest of Judah's kings. He is best known, perhaps, for his zeal as a religious reformer. Rehoboam had made no attempt to be faithful to the holy covenant. Abijah's condemnation of Israel's apostasy (*II Chron. 12:14*) indicates he was a worshiper of Yahweh, but "his heart was not wholly true to Yahweh his God" and he had allowed the high places and altars of pagan gods to stand. When Asa came to power, "he took away the foreign altars and the high places, and broke down the pillars and hewed down the Asherim" (*II Chron. 14:3*). He expelled the male prostitutes who were associated with some of the temples. His zeal was so complete that he removed his own mother from her position as queen mother because she had made an image for Asherah. Asa was not content simply to destroy the evil. When his purge was complete, he "commanded

Judah to seek Yahweh, the God of their fathers, and to keep the law and the commandments." At the encouragement of the prophet Azariah, he gathered the people to Jerusalem for a thrilling covenant-renewal ceremony (*II Chron. 15:1–15*).

Early in his long reign, Asa thoroughly routed the troops commanded by Zerah the Ethiopian (*II Chron. 14:9–15*). After this battle, the southern kingdom had peace for twenty-five years. At that time, Baasha king of Israel mounted a campaign designed to give him a stranglehold on the southern kingdom. He moved into the territory of Benjamin, which belonged to Judah, and gained control of the city of Ramah. Control of Ramah meant control of the major route into Jerusalem. It also gave Baasha a superb base of operations for an attack against the capital of the Southern kingdom.

Asa had to act before Baasha finished the work of fortifying Ramah. In desperation, he sent a large treasure to Ben-hadad king of Aram (Syria), asking him to attack Israel from the north, forcing Baasha to abandon his southern activities. Ben-hadad had previously formed an alliance with Baasha (*II Chron. 16:3*), but he was not a man of unimpeachable integrity. He readily sent his armies against his former allies. Baasha pulled out of Ramah as expected and Judah got out of trouble without lifting a sword. When Baasha's troops withdrew, the men of Judah took the building materials from Ramah and used them to fortify Geba and Mizpah, two cities of Benjamin north of Ramah. This strengthened Judah's northern frontier and prevented a recurrence of the Israelite threat.

In the aftermath of this crisis, we find the only blemish on Asa's record. The prophet Hanani rebuked Asa for his lack of trust in Yahweh. From the beginning, alliances with foreign nations had never brought God's people anything but trouble. Had Yahweh

173

ever failed his people when they were faithful to the covenant? Had it ever mattered before who had the largest army or the strategic fortress? Asa was basically a good man. It was hard for him to listen to criticism that called his loyalty to Yahweh into question. So, he cast Hanani into prison. In addition, he "inflicted cruelties upon some of the people" (*II Chron. 16:10*). We are not told who they were or what they had done, but, presumably, they had shared Hanani's viewpoint. This incident seems to have embittered Asa. We are told that when he contracted the foot disease that eventually killed him, "he did not seek Yahweh, but sought help from physicians" (*II Chr. 16: 12*). We cannot help but be disappointed by these last actions of Asa, but we must not let them obscure the long years of faithful service that he gave.

### THE THRONE SUCCESSION IN ISRAEL

Northern Israel began her existence as a rebel state consciously trying to distinguish herself from her southern sister. Without loyalty to the house of David, and without a priesthood established by tradition, Israel had no conservative bulwarks to hold her on a steady course. Consequently, her history was much stormier—and much shorter—than that of Judah. The contrast between the stability of the nations may be seen in the fact that Asa's reign overlapped the reign of six kings of Israel. In Judah, the king was always a descendant of David. In Israel, the king was the man who was powerful enough to sieze and hold the throne. Jeroboam was succeeded by his son Nadab (901–900). This effort to found a dynasty failed quickly when Nadab was assassinated while laying siege to the Philistine city of Gibbethon. The assassin was Baasha, one of his soldiers. If a soldier of Judah had assassinated a son of David, he would almost certainly have been executed. In Israel, the as-

sassin became the king. According to *I Kings 16:1–2*, it seems Baasha had received the blessing of the prophet Jehu.* Whatever religious favor he might have enjoyed, however, was lost when he proved himself to be just another king who "walked in the way of Jeroboam." Jehu announced to him that his lineage would suffer the same fate as that which he had meted out to the house of Jeroboam—nothing less than total destruction. "Anyone belonging to Baasha who dies in the city the dogs shall eat; and anyone of his who dies in the field the birds of the air shall eat" (*I Kin. 16:4*).

Baasha reigned for twenty-four years and died a natural death, but the words of the prophet did not die in the air. His son Elah had reigned less than two years when he was slain by Zimri, the commander of half his chariots. Zimri reigned just long enough to fulfill the words of the prophet. When word reached the Israelite army, once again encamped at Philistine Gibbethon, that Zimri had killed the king and all his house, the troops proclaimed their commander Omri as counter-king and marched on Tirzah, the Israelite capital. Zimri saw the situation was hopeless. To avoid public humiliation, he ran to the royal house, set fire to it, and died in its flames. He had ruled seven days. Now Omri was king in Israel.

## Israel and Judah from Omri to Jehu: 876–842 B.C.

The reign of Omri marked the beginning of a new era in Israel. Omri himself ruled only seven years (876–969), but in that brief period he regained much that Israel had lost, not only in territory, but in prosperity and stability as well. He established a strong dynasty that lasted until Jehu's purge in 842. Also, for the first time since the schism in 922, Israel and Judah enjoyed harmonious

---

*Not to be confused with the king of the same name. See pp. 190ff.

Ben-hadad's monument to Baal-Melqart, official god of the Phoenician kingdom of Tyre.

relations with one another during most of the reign of the Omride Dynasty.

### THE WORLD SITUATION IN 876 B.C.

Israel needed a strong king. Almost half a century had passed since the death of Solomon, and Israel had long since ceased to be a terror to her neighbors. Now it was their turn to terrorize her. The immediate threat came from the kingdom of Damascus in Aram (Syria), ruled by the crafty opportunist Ben-hadad I (880–842). A year before, in 877, Ben-hadad had accepted Asa's bribe to attack Israel and had probably extended his holdings into the northern portions of Galilee and Transjordan. Archaeologists have discovered a small monument that Ben-hadad dedicated to Baal-Melqart, the official god of the Phoenician kingdom of Tyre. This suggests that, if he did not control Tyre,

he was at least on friendly terms with this northern neighbor.

Naturally, Israel was more concerned about Ben-hadad than anyone else. But Ben-hadad was not the only—nor, in the long run, the most serious—threat to her existence. Assyria, which had lain almost dormant since the twelfth century, was once again stirring to life, partly as the result of the threat of Aramean conquest. The Assyrian king was Asshur-nasir-pal II (883–859 B.C.), a ruthless man bent on conquest. By the time Omri came to power, he had extended his territory westward to the Euphrates River. In about 820, he pushed beyond the river across northern Syria and Phoenicia to the Mediterranean. For some reason, Asshur-nasir-pal II was content with booty and tribute and did not follow up his victories by establishing control over these lands. Nevertheless, he had served notice on them—and on any others who might be interested—that Assyria was a power to be reckoned with.

Judah was in less immediate danger. Israel served as a buffer zone between her and the aggressors to the north and northeast. The only major nation with direct access to Judah was Egypt, and Egypt, unable to capitalize on the exploits of Shishak, was too weak to pose a serious threat. Judah would enjoy peace and a reasonable amount of prosperity throughout most of this period.

### JUDAH UNDER THE HOUSE OF JEHOSHAPHAT: 873–843

*Jehoshaphat (873–849).* Jehoshaphat, the son and successor of Asa, ruled over Judah for twenty-five years. Like his father, he was a good king. He was a worshipper of Yahweh who did "what was right in the sight of the Lord." His faithfulness to Yahweh is seen in the fact that, although he had close political and family ties with the Baal-worshipping Ahab and Jezebel, "he did not seek the

Baals, but sought the God of his father, and walked in his commandments, and not according to the ways of Israel" (*II Chron. 17:3–4*). In his zeal for the Lord, Jehoshaphat sent royal officers, priests, and Levites throughout the kingdom to instruct the people in the law of Moses (*II Chron. 17:7–9*). He also carried out a sweeping reform of the judicial system that aimed at eliminating injustice by closer control of the judges and by providing a system of appellate courts to try disputed cases (*II Chr. 19*).

As we have already mentioned, Jehoshaphat's reign was a time of prosperity and, for the most part, peace. He apparently kept the nations to the south and west of Judah—Philistia, Arabia, and Edom—in a vassalage relationship (*II Chr. 17:10ff*). His most notable effort at peace and security was the establishment of an alliance with the king-

dom of Israel. This alliance was secured by the marriage of his son, Jehoram, to Athaliah, daughter of Ahab and Jezebel (*II Chr. 18:1; II Kin. 8:18*). This unfortunate introduction of Omride blood into the royal family of Judah was to cause its ruthless extermination during the revolution of Jehu in 842. Shortly after the union was made, Jehosaphat joined with Ahab against the Syrian army of Ben-hadad, in the battle at Ramoth-gilead, that cost the life of the northern king (see pp. 184ff). Later, he accompanied Ahab's son Jehoram on an expedition against the Moabites (*II Kin. 3*). There is some confusion in the scriptures about a joint shipping project between Jehoshaphat and Ahaziah king of Israel. It is impossible to determine whether Jehoshaphat ever accepted Ahaziah as a full partner or not. Actually, the question is academic,

**Assyrian relief of Asshur-nasir-pal hunting lions.**

since it is clear that the venture came to nothing when the ships were wrecked (See *I Kin. 22:48–49; II Chr. 35–37*).

*Jehoram* (849–842). Jehoshaphat was succeeded by his son Jehoram. Jehoram's first act after taking the throne was to murder all his brothers and any others at the court who might prove a threat to his reign. It is shocking that the son of Jehoshaphat should perform such a cruel deed, but we do not have to seek far for a probable explanation. Jehoram had a good father, but his wife, Athaliah, was the daughter of Jezebel. Athaliah's influence on Jehoram is summed up in the statement, "he walked in the way of the kings of Israel, as the house of Ahab had done" (*II Kin. 8:18*). Not only did he neglect the worship of Yahweh, but he made "high places" in the hills and led the people into idolatry. For this sin, he received a letter of condemnation from the fiery prophet of the north, Elijah (*II Chr. 21:12–15*).

Jehoram's reign was a time of weakness in Judah. The territories of Edom and Libnah revolted successfully and an alliance of the Philistines and Arabians overran Judah and carried off virtually everything and everybody that belonged to Jehoram except his youngest son Jehoahaz (also called Ahaziah). When Jehoram died of a horrible disease of the bowels, "he departed with no one's regret" (*II Chr. 21:20*). The people built no funeral fire to honor him, and he was not buried in the traditional tombs of the kings.

*Ahaziah* (842). Jehoram's son Ahaziah suffered from the same malady that had beset his father: Athaliah. Apparently, the queen mother had escaped the Philistine invaders who had carried off most of the royal family, for the Chronicler tells us she was Jehoram's "counselor in doing wickedly" (*II Chr. 22:3*). Ahaziah reigned just long enough to join his uncle Jehoram, king of Israel, in an expedition against Ben-hadad

of Syria. They succeeded in capturing Ramoth-gilead, but Jehoram was wounded and had to retire to Jezreel to recover. While Ahaziah was visiting his recuperating uncle, Jehu stormed down from Ramoth-gilead to begin his violent purge of the house of Ahab (see pp. 190ff). Both Israel and Judah lost their kings on the same day.

### ISRAEL UNDER THE DYNASTY OF OMRI: 876–842

We have passed over the history of Judah in this period rather quickly. The reason for this is simple: not much was happening in Judah. At least, not by comparison with Israel. This was one of the most exciting periods in all Israel's history, a time when the forces of good and the forces of evil were pitted against one another in a struggle to the death. In studying this period, we come across some of the most fascinating characters in all Biblical history.

*The Reign of Omri* (876–869). The Bible tells us very little about the reign of Omri. In fact, it is summarized in six verses. But this is a reflection of the purpose of the writer and not of the importance of Omri. The Biblical writer dismisses Omri quickly because, to him, he was just one more king of Israel who "walked in the way of Jeroboam." The historian must give him more space, for he was truly a remarkable man. Fortunately, archaeologists have provided us with enough reliable information to fill in the Biblical outline considerably.

As we have already seen, Omri was proclaimed king by the army after Zimri assassinated King Elah and the members of the Royal family. Zimri was no problem for Omri, but an ambitious leader named Tibni had considerable popular support, and it took Omri about four years to gain undisputed control of the kingdom (*I Kin. 16:15–23*). After a few years at Tirzah, Omri moved the capital to the hill of Samaria, northwest of Shechem. The hill was an impressive site. An archaeologist has commented: "It would be difficult to find in all Palestine, a situation of equal strength, fertility, and beauty combined. In all these particulars it has greatly the advantage over Jerusalem." Its strength lay in the fact that it was surrounded on all sides by a valley and was thus quite difficult to attack. It is a tribute to Omri's judgment that he chose it for his capital. Excavations have shown that he and Ahab added magnificent fortifications to its naturally strong defenses. Omri further strengthened Israel by reestablishing the treaty with Tyre which had been so beneficial to King Solomon. This treaty was sealed by the marriage between his son Ahab and Jezebel, the daughter of Ethbaal king of Tyre. We shall hear more of this famous couple later. Omri may also have had a hand in establishing friendly relations with Judah, although no formal alliance was made until the time of Ahab.

The Bible tells us nothing of any conquests by Omri, but the famous monument of King Mesha of Moab, discovered in 1808 and known popularly as the Moabite Stone, tells us that Omri had Moab a subject nation. Omri may have been neglected by the Biblical writers, but his contemporaries could not dismiss him so lightly. His stature as a world leader is reflected in the fact that foreign inscriptions written long after his death refer to Samaria and the kingdom of Israel as the "House of Omri."

*Ahab and Jezebel.* Ahab (869–850) was, for the most part, a strong and efficient king, a suitable successor to his capable father. He was an able administrator who continued Omri's policy of allying Israel with neighboring states. The league with Tyre was secure, since Ahab was the son-in-law of the king of Tyre. Ahab sealed an alliance with Judah by the marriage of his daughter Athaliah to Jehoram, the son of Jehoshaphat king

of Judah. There was no effort to unite the two nations under one ruler, but they sought to coexist peacefully and to cooperate in activities that would benefit both nations. Neither of the cooperative ventures mentioned in the Bible—the attempt to revive the sea trade out of Ezion-geber and the war against Syria in 850—were unqualified successes. The ships were wrecked before they got out of port and Ahab lost his life in the battle. Still, it was no small accomplishment for these two kings to heal the rift their ancestors had made.

The nation that received the largest share of Ahab's attention was Syria, still ruled by Ben-hadad I. The chronology is uncertain, but it was probably sometime in the last decade of Ahab's reign that Ben-hadad encamped around Samaria and demanded that Ahab surrender an enormous tribute, including his prettiest wives and children (*I Kin. 20*). Ahab complied with this demand, but when the Syrian proposed to send his servants into the city to loot it at will, he refused. This was too much. Supported by the elders of the city, Ahab sent word to Ben-hadad that he could not loot the city without a fight. The exchange between the two kings is amusing. Ben-hadad said: "The gods do so to me, and more also, if the dust of Samaria shall suffice for handfuls for all the people who follow me." Ahab's calm reply was: "Let not him that girds on his armor boast himself as he that puts it off" (*I Kin. 20:10–11*). Ahab was outnumbered, but Yahweh—who surely must have been an unexpected ally—gave him the victory. The Syrians were driven back, but Ben-hadad escaped. An unnamed prophet of Yahweh, one of a band who did not worship at the shrines of Baal or the Golden Bulls, told Ahab that Ben-hadad would return in the spring. Sure enough, the mighty Syrian force swooped down from the North once more. This time, instead of going into the hill country around Samaria, they camped at Aphek, in the plains to the northwest. Ben-hadad's advisers had convinced him that the god of Israel was a god of the hills and would be powerless in a battle in open country.

When Ahab marched out to meet his foes, the contrast was striking. The Biblical historian tells us " the people of Israel encamped before them like two little flocks of goats, but the Syrians filled the country" ( *I Kin. 20:27*). As we have seen again and again, numbers were of no significance in a Holy War. The small band of Israelites routed the Syrians and captured Ben-hadad. But, instead of killing the Syrian, as the rules of Holy War prescribed, Ahab made a covenant with him and let him go. This raised the ire of one of the prophets—whether he was the same man who had previously counseled Ahab we cannot say. In an object lesson with some interesting side effects (See *I Kin. 20: 35ff*), he announced to the king that his failure to kill Ben-hadad, a man "devoted to [Yahweh for] destruction," would cost him his own life. "And the king of Israel went to his house resentful and sullen."

Despite the prophet's condemnation, Ahab maintained his covenant with Ben-hadad, at least for a time. Although the Bible makes no mention of the event, Assyrian recods tell us that Ben-hadad and "Ahab the Israelite" joined with the king of Hamath to lead a coalition force against Shalmaneser III of Assyria. The battle, regarded as quite important by secular historians, took place in 853 at Qarqar, on the Orontes river in Syria. Shalmaneser III claimed a great victory, but he apparently made no attempt to follow it up with permanent conquest, indicating that he suffered great

**Reconstruction of stables at Megiddo, believed to have been built by Omri.**

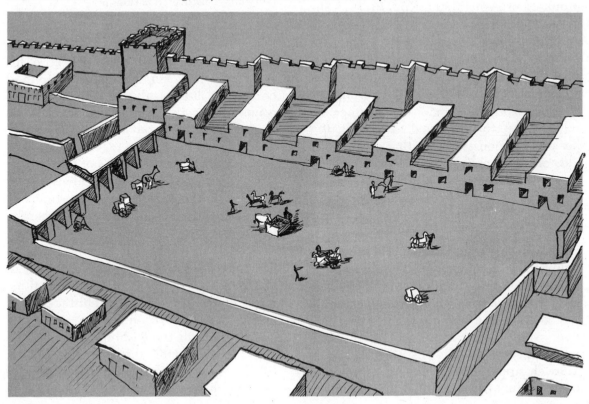

losses himself. Ahab is said to have furnished ten thousand infantrymen and two thousand chariots for this battle. Since no other king provided so many chariots, we may safely assume that Ahab was far more than a junior partner at this outing.

For all his talent and strength, in foreign affairs, Ahab was weak and wishy-washy in the face of his powerful wife, Jezebel. Jezebel is undoubtedly one of the most remarkable women who ever lived. Her personality was so powerful that her name has come to be a symbol for the kind of woman she was. Jezebel's father, Ethbaal, was not only king of Tyre, but priest of the Phoenician god Baal-Melqart as well. When Jezebel came to Samaria, she came not simply as princess, but as missionary. She was determined to root out all traces of the worship of Yahweh and to replace it with the worship of Baal. She almost succeeded. She is said to have fed at her table 450 prophets of Baal and 400 prophets of Asherah (*I Kin. 18:19*). She persecuted the prophets of God (*I Kin. 18: 4, 13*) and proved herself almost a match for the fiery Elijah. It would be difficult to judge Jezebel too harshly solely on the basis of her actions in behalf of Baalism. After all, she was supporting the religion of her father, the religion she truly believed to be best. But her other actions show us that the popular idea of her as a supremely wicked and unscrupulous woman has not been erroneous.

### TROUBLERS OF ISRAEL:
### ELIJAH, MICAIH, AND ELISHA

Ahab apparently made some minor attempt to be a worshipper of Yahweh. The names he gave his children—Athaliah, Ahaziah, and Jehoram—were derivatives of the sacred name YHWH, not the sort of names one would expect a confirmed Baalworshipper to give his offspring. In return, Yahweh apparently made an attempt to convince him this was the proper course to

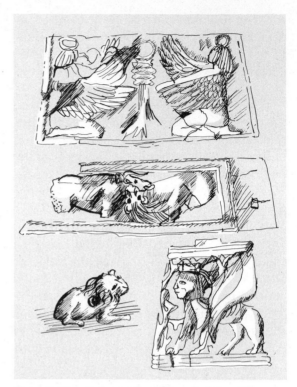

**Ivory inlays discovered in ruins of Ahab's palace in Jezreel.**

follow. When he went to battle against Benhadad, Yahweh marched at the head of his army and sent one of his prophets to counsel him. Ahab did not always respond to this counsel perfectly, but, left to himself, he might have turned out to be a reasonably faithful king.

Unfortunately, Ahab was not left to himself. His wife Jezebel was a zealous enemy of Yahweh who seized every opportunity to oppose Yahwistic religion. Consequently, much of the story of Ahab and Jezebel, and their sons who ruled after them, is the story of a pitched battle between the house of Omri and the prophets of God. The three major figures in this long and bitter conflict were Elijah, Micaiah, and Elisha.

*Elijah.* Elijah the Tishbite is one of the most colorful of all the characters in the Bible. He was capable of performing acts of great kindness and tenderness (*I Kin. 17:8–*

180

24), but he was also capable—and seemed to enjoy it more—of acting as the avenging sword of the Lord. Elijah came from Gilead, east of the Jordan. He lived a rugged life in sharp contrast to that of the prosperous and cultured people of Samaria. Imagine how out of place he must have appeared in his haircloth garments and leather girdle (*II Kin. 1:8*) as he stood outside Ahab's fabulous "ivory house" (*I Kin. 22:39*).*

When Elijah first confronted Ahab, he condemned the king for the altars he had built for Jezebel's gods and announced to him that the land would not see rain again until he, Elijah, commanded it. Then, "with the keys of heaven hanging from his girdle, he went away and hid." For a long time, he camped around the Brook Cherith, east of the Jordan. The brook furnished his water and ravens brought him food twice a day (*17:2–7*). When the brook dried up, Elijah traveled all the way to the Phoenician city of Zarepheth, where he roomed with a widow and her son (*2:8–24*).

A drought in Palestine can be devastating. Elijah's drought caused a great famine in Israel. Ahab had searched high and low all over Palestine for the prophet to demand that he turn the water back on. Things got so desperate that the king himself and one of his servants (who was, incidentally, a faithful worshipper of Yahweh) set out to seek little pools of water that might be used to keep some of the animals alive. At the same time, Elijah set out for Samaria to find Ahab. On the way, he ran into Obadiah, the king's servant,† and instructed him to tell Ahab he

wanted to see him. Obadiah's reaction attests to the aura of mystery that had grown up around Elijah. In his searchings for the prophet, Ahab had made foreign kings swear they were not hiding him somewhere. Obadiah was reluctant to deliver Elijah's message to the king for fear that "the Spirit of the Lord will carry you whither I know not; and so, when I come and tell Ahab and he cannot find you, he will kill me" (*18:12*). Obadiah had proved himself to be a faithful servant of Yahweh by saving a hundred prophets from the wrath of Jezebel. He was unwilling to risk his life again. Finally, though, Elijah assured him he would not disappear, and Obadiah delivered the message.

When Elijah appeared before Ahab, the king's hatred bristled through his first words: "Is it you, you troubler of Israel?" But Elijah was not a man to be intimidated by words—or kings. He fired back at Ahab, "I have not troubled Israel, but you have, and your father's house." Then, he told Ahab to send the 850 prophets of Baal and Asherah who ate at Jezebel's table to the top of Mt. Carmel. There all Israel could decide whether to follow Baal or Yahweh.

The prophets came, and so did all Israel. When they quietened down, Elijah addressed the multitude: "How long will you go limping with two different opinions? If Yahweh is God, follow him; but if Baal, then follow him" (*18:21*). This was the challenge to the people; now to test the gods.

Two bulls were selected from sacrifice. An old altar that had once been used to worship Yahweh was repaired and the prophets of Baal built a new altar. One bull was put on each altar. The test was this: Jezebel's prophets were to call on Baal and Elijah was to call on Yahweh. The god who answered by sending down fire to consume the sacrifice was to be regarded as the One True God. The prophets of Baal tried first. From

---

*This undoubtedly means that Ahab's house was richly inlaid with ivory, not that it was made of solid ivory. Archaeologists have discovered numerous fragments of decorative ivory around the foundations of a large building in the ruins of Samaria. No positive identification can be made, but it is possible that this was Ahab's royal palace.

†Not to be confused with the prophet Obadiah. No less than thirteen Biblical characters bear this common Israelite name.

morning till noon they limped around the altar crying out, "O Baal, answer us!" But there was no voice, and no one answered. If the prophets of Baal did not enjoy the situation, Elijah certainly did. Ordinarily a man of little humor, about noon he began to mock them sarcastically: "Cry aloud, for he is a god; either he is musing, or he has gone aside, or he is on a journey, or perhaps he is asleep and must be awakened." This drove the false prophets into an even greater frenzy. They began to cut themselves with swords and lances, causing their blood to gush out over their bodies—"but there was no voice; no one answered; no one heeded." Now it was Elijah's turn.

It would have been sufficiently impressive if Elijah had simply called on Yahweh to burn his sacrifice and Yahweh had done it. But Elijah, like most of the prophets, was something of a showman. To heighten the effect, he directed his helpers to drench his altar and sacrifice with four large jars of water. They did this three times, until the water filled a trench Elijah had dug around the altar. Then, in a calm fashion, Elijah asked Yahweh to consume the offering with fire, as proof that he was the God of power.

> The fire of Yahweh fell, and consumed the burnt offering, and the wood, and the stones, and the dust, and licked up the water that was in the trench.      —I Kin. 18:38

When the people saw this, they were overwhelmed. They fell on their faces and repeated the confession, "Yahweh, he is God; Yahweh, he is God." Then, at Elijah's command, they seized the prophets of Baal and killed them by the brook Kishon.

When the carnage was complete, Elijah went to the top of Mt. Carmel and sat down with his head between his knees. Eight times he sent a servant to go to a high point and look toward the Mediterranean Sea for the sign of clouds that would bring rain to

the parched land. On the eighth trip, the servant reported that he had seen "a little cloud like a man's hand rising out of the sea." This was the sign Elijah was waiting for. The last scene of this chapter is unforgettable. The sky becomes black as night; the heavy rains begin to fall; their force is increased by the winds from the sea; Ahab drives his chariot furiously to avoid being trapped in a flood; and in front of the horses, his long hair and beard soaked by the rain and his haircloth garment girded tightly about his waist, runs Elijah, the triumphant prophet of God.

Ahab reported to Jezebel the events of the day. Instead of being dismayed at the failure of her god, she became all the more determined to exterminate the prophets of Yahweh. Elijah was forced to flee to Mt. Horeb (Sinai), "the mount of God" (19:1-8). While he was here, Elijah reached the lowest point of his career. A few days before, he had been glorious in victory. Now, he was convinced that all this was in vain, that he was the only faithful servant of Yahweh who remained alive, and that it was only a matter of time until he would be killed, too.

But Yahweh had not been defeated. There on Mt. Horeb, perhaps not far from the spot where God had appeared to Moses, he passed by the cave of his servant Elijah. There was a strong wind that split the rocks, an earthquake, and a fire, but Yahweh was not in these. In the past, Yahweh had been associated with phenomena of nature such as these. To appear in them now, however, would confuse things, since Baal was believed to appear in the storm. This incident removed all doubt as to who was really the victor on Mt. Carmel. It also marked a step in the disentangling of Israelite religious symbolism from the symbolism of paganism. Here on Horeb, Yahweh spoke to Elijah in "a still small voice" (19:12). From this time forward the word of the Lord delivered

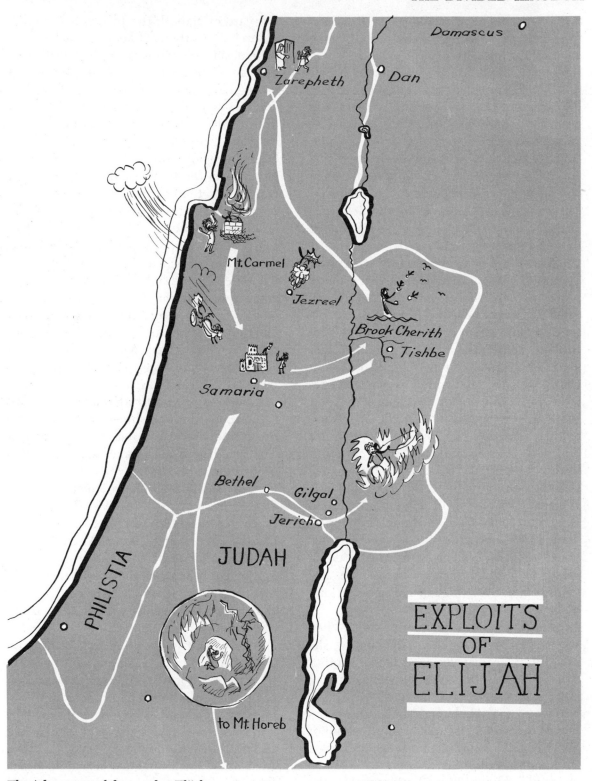

Damascus

Zarepheth

Dan

Mt. Carmel

Jezreel

Brook Cherith

Tishbe

Samaria

Bethel

Gilgal

Jericho

PHILISTIA

JUDAH

EXPLOITS
OF
ELIJAH

to Mt. Horeb

**The Adventures of the prophet Elijah.**

through the prophets would begin to replace the outbursts of nature as the sign of God's communication with men.

The still small voice of God told Elijah that he was not the only faithful man left (*19:18*) and that Jezebel had not won the war. The contest on Carmel was just a start. The climax came in the purge of Jehu, whom Elijah was to anoint. Yahweh also told Elijah that Elisha, a farmer, would become the chief prophet in Israel in place of Elijah.

Elijah found Elisha out in the field and anointed him as his successor (*19:19ff*), but the old prophet was not ready to retire just yet. King Ahab had not been fully converted by the events of Mt. Carmel. Like many powerful men, Ahab never learned to be satisfied with what he had. The example of this shortcoming which is best remembered by Bible students is the affair of Naboth's vineyard. Ahab had built a "second home" in nearby Jezreel. He wanted to plant a vegetable garden on a spot near this house, but the land was owned by one Naboth. Ahab made a generous offer for the land, but Naboth refused. The land had been in his family for generations. It was a sacred possession; he did not really feel free to sell it as if it were an ox or a jar of wine. Ahab had no legal right to the land, and knew it. But, petulant as a four-year-old, he "went into his house vexed and sullen . . . and he lay down on his bed, and turned away his face, and would eat no food" (*21:4*). This was the king of Israel.

Jezebel was not a woman to sulk. When she came in and found Ahab pouting, she asked him, "Aren't you the king?" In other words, he was the supreme power in the land; if he wanted the vineyard, why didn't he just take it? Ahab might be bound by Israelite reverence for family inheritances not to take what he wanted, but Jezebel suffered from no such disability. "Let your heart be cheerful," she told him, "I will give you the vineyard of Naboth the Jezreelite" (*21:7*).

Jezebel's methods of keeping her promise were despicable. She bribed two of the sorriest men in town to accuse Naboth of having cursed God and the king. This they did, and a gullible mob took Naboth out of the city and stoned him. As soon as word of his death came to Jezebel she told Ahab that he could go down and claim his vineyard. As he stood in the midst of the vineyard that Naboth had tended lovingly, Ahab was surprised by the abrupt appearance of Elijah. "Have you found me, O my enemy?" Ahab asked Elijah. Elijah replied, "I have found you, because you have sold yourself to do what is evil in the sight of Yahweh" Then he announced to him that his entire household would be wiped out, that "in the place where dogs licked up the blood of Naboth shall dogs lick your own blood," and that "the dogs shall eat Jezebel within the bounds of Jezreel" (*21:19, 21–23*).

Ahab's penitent attitude moved the Lord to postpone the punishment until after his death, but that was not to be so far away. The prophet in attendance on the day it occurred was Micaiah.

*Four Hundred to One: Micaiah (I Kin. 22).* In the year 850, three years after the battle of Qarqar, Jehoshaphat king of Judah made a state visit to Israel. While he was there, Ahab asked him if he realized how long it had been since they had had a really first-class war with Syria. Across the river, Ramoth-gilead was just waiting to be taken out of Ben-hadad's hands.

Jehoshaphat was willing but, being a religious man, he asked if they might not ask the prophets for a word from the Lord on the matter. Ahab was happy to comply. In fact, the speed with which he gathered four hundred prophets together suggests he had anticipated Jehoshaphat's request. When Ahab asked the prophets if he should attack Ramoth-gilead, they replied unanimously,

"Go up; for Yahweh will give it into the hand of the king." Jehoshaphat was suspicious of their unanimity. When four hundred preachers can agree, something must be wrong! He asked, "Is there not another prophet of Yahweh of whom we may inquire?" There was another, but Ahab had deliberately left him off the program. His name was Micaiah, and Ahab admitted, "I hate him, for he never prophesies good concerning me, but evil." Obviously, most of Micaiah's statements had been true, or Ahab would have had no reason to fear what he had to say. His complaint was not that Micaiah could not be trusted, but that he could. Ahab did not want his prophets to tell him the truth. He wanted them to echo the royal decrees and to give religious approval to national policy.

At Jehoshaphat's urging, Ahab sent for Micaiah. The messenger must have been a friend of Micaiah's for he urged him to go along with the other prophets, regardless of what he thought. Ahab had already made up his mind. The only thing that could come from disagreeing was trouble for Micaiah. Micaiah's reply shows us what kind of man he was: "As the Lord lives, what the Lord says to me, that will I speak."

Micaiah was brought into the presence of the two kings. Their thrones had been set up at the threshing-floor, a large clear space at the gate of Samaria. Before them, the four hundred prophets were working themselves into an ecstasy and repeating their optimistic advice. Their leader, a prophet named Zedekiah, had made a pair of iron horns and, mimicking the action of a bull, said to the kings, "Thus says Yahweh, 'With these you shall push the Syrians until they are destroyed.'" When Micaiah saw what was going on, he said to Ahab, "Go up and triumph; for Yahweh will give it into the hand of the king." With all this going for him, how could he lose? Ahab saw that Micaiah was

mocking him and ordered him to tell the truth. Micaiah minced no words: "I saw all Israel scattered upon the mountains, as sheep that have no shepherd; and Yahweh said, 'These have no master; let each return to his home in peace.'" This clearly signified Israel's defeat and Ahab's death. The king was no doubt shaken by this news, but, for the present, he was more upset that Micaiah had once more delivered a message of bad news.

Still, Micaiah could be wrong. What about the other prophets? They had all predicted victory. The odds were four hundred to one in favor of going to war. Micaiah had an answer for this, too. He told of a vision of the heavenly court, at which Yahweh and his heavenly host discussed how they might lure Ahab to his death. After some discussion, a spirit stepped forth and volunteered "to be a lying spirit in the mouth of the prophets." Zedekiah heard this, and did not appreciate its implications. He struck Micaiah and asked sarcastically, "How did the Spirit of Yahweh go from me to speak to you?" Micaiah did not argue or strike back; he simply told Zedekiah to wait and see.

Ahab was enraged. He ordered that Micaiah be thrown into prison and given nothing but bread and water until he returned in victory. Even this could not daunt Micaiah. He replied, "If you return in peace, Yahweh has not spoken by me." Then, as he was being led away to prison, he cried out to the crowd, "Hear, all you peoples."

Soon after, the kings set out for Ramoth-gilead, but not without misgivings. Ahab told Jehoshaphat to wear his royal robes, but he disguised himself as a common soldier. His disguise was no help. A certain man drew his bow at a venture—perhaps he had aimed all his other arrows and missed and figured that one random shot could not hurt—and struck the king of Israel "between the scale armor and the breastplate." By evening, the battle was over and the men of Israel, as sheep without a shepherd, had turned for home.

Not long afterward, a grisly sight was seen at the pool of Samaria. A bloody chariot was being washed. Dogs were lapping up the blood and harlots were washing in its redness. . . . So Ahab slept with his fathers, and Ahaziah his son reigned in his stead.

What happened to Micaiah? No one knows. He may have been killed by friends of Ahab, or he may have been left to rot in prison. Archaeologists have learned a great deal about ancient Samaria, but they have not found a trace of Micaiah. But men of faith will never destroy the memory of the prophet of Yahweh who stood against the crowd and spoke with inspiring courage: "As the Lord lives what the Lord says to me, that will I speak."

*Elisha and the last of the Omrides.* Elijah and Micaiah both proclaimed Yahweh's displeasure with the House of Omri. Elisha presided over its dissolution. We noted earlier that Elijah anointed Elisha* to be his successor after coming down from Mt. Horeb. From then on, Elisha traveled with the old prophet, learning what was involved in being the chief prophet in Israel. He saw Elijah call down fire from heaven on the servants of King Ahaziah, Ahab's son and successor, and he saw him tell the king face to face that he would die because of his unfaithfulness (*II Kin. 1*).

The actual transfer of the prophetic authority from Elijah to Elisha is told in *II Kin. 2*. The writer tells of Elijah's last journey through the land of Israel. As he passed through Gilgal, Bethel, and Jericho, groups of prophets came out to pay their last respects. There is no evidence Elijah ever belonged to one of these prophetic guilds who

---

*Bible students frequently confuse these two prophets because of the similarity of their names. A simple but effective way to remember which came first is to place them in alphabetical order. Just as "j" precedes "s," so Elijah preceded Elisha.

186

**The wondrous deeds of Elisha.**

went by the name, "sons of the prophets," but he apparently had considerable contact with them. Their goals had been the same, and they would miss him when he was gone.

The journey to the Jordan and across was also a testing of Elisha. Several times, Elijah told him to remain at a certain place, but the young man steadfastly refused to leave his master. When the waters of the Jordan miraculously parted to allow them to cross, Elisha asked Elijah for a double portion of his spirit. Elijah did not answer with an unqualified yes. He told his young companion that his request would be granted if he saw Elijah when he departed from him. The meaning seems to be that he would receive this his spiritual blessing if he were fit to receive it.

And as they still went on and talked, behold, a chariot of fire and horses of fire separated the two of them. And Elijah went up by a whirlwind into heaven. And Elisha saw it and he cried, "My father, my father! the chariots of Israel and its horsemen!"* And he saw him no more. —II Kings 2:11-12

Now Elisha was prophet in Israel. When he recrossed the Jordan, he was met by the sons of the prophets, who were rightfully skeptical of the story he had to tell. At their insistence, he allowed them to search the countryside for Elijah, but they found nothing. Now they were willing to accept Elisha's authority.

Elisha was a worthy prophet, but he had the misfortune to be the successor of one of the great heroes of Israelites faith. His life was much more settled and routine than Elijah's. His exploits were less daring, his wonders less spectacular. Nevertheless, he was a remarkable individual. As compared with the New Testament, the Old Testament contains very few accounts of miracles. Elisha performed a large share of those. His miracles include the "sweetening" of a spring of foul water (2:19–22); the production of a large amount of olive oil, which was used to pay a widow's debts (4:1–7); the gift of a child to a family that had befriended him, and the restoration of the child to life after it had died (4:8–37); purifying a poisonous pot of stew (4:38–41); multiplying bread and grain to feed a hundred men (4:42–44); and causing an axe-head to float (6:1–7). The most famous of Elisha's wonders was his curing Naaman of leprosy (ch. 5). The fact that Naaman was a foreigner and a leader of the armies of Syria, Israel's chief enemy, makes the story doubly interesting. Naaman had learned of the prophet from a little Israelite girl who had been carried off in a Syrian raid into the northern kingdom. King Ben-hadad was

anxious for his chief commander to be healed of this disease which would eventually disable him. So, he sent Naaman to Joram, king of Israel, and asked him to have Naaman cured. Joram, of course, had no idea about how to cure leprosy. His immediate reaction was that Ben-hadad was trying to pick a fight with him. Before he had time to do much moaning, however, Elisha sent word to him to send the commander to him. Relieved, Joram told Naaman how to find Elisha's house.

Elisha's reception of Naaman is amusing. The king of Israel may have been flustered by his presence, but Elisha was determined not to be overwhelmed. And overwhelmed he was not. When the great general pulled up outside his house, flanked by horses and chariots and attendants, Elisha did not even go to the door. He sent a messenger to tell Naaman to go and dip seven times in the river Jordan. Then he would be cured and could go on back to Syria. Naaman was not used to being put off so lightly, and he did not like it. What foolish instructions Elisha had given him! The Jordan was a dirty little river that would be more likely to *cause* rather than cure disease. The two rivers on which Damascus sat, Abana and Pharpar, were cleaner than Jordan. If this was all Elisha had to offer, he had made a long trip for nothing. His servants, showing a good deal of insight, pointed out to him that his real objection to what Elisha had told him was that it was nothing great or unusual. In fact, it was almost childishly simple, but since they had come so far, they could lose nothing by trying it. Naaman listened, and did what Elisha said. When he had dipped himself in the river seven times, "his flesh was restored like the flesh of a little child, and he was clean."

After his cure, Naaman was a different man. Full of gratitude, he confessed that there was no god except Yahweh, the God of

---

*This phrase referred to Elijah, not to the chariots and horsemen. It was an epithet to show the greatness of Elijah. Later, it is used of Elisha, when no horses or chariots were around (II Kin. 13:14).

Israel (5:15). Still, he did not think of Yahweh as god over all the earth. Yahweh alone had power, but his power was effective only in Israel. This was a typical nationalistic conception of deity. So, Naaman asked, and received, permission to load down two of his mules with dirt from around the prophet's house. He would take part of Israel back to Syria, and on this Israelite dirt he would offer sacrifice and worship the God of Israel. Naaman asked one more thing of Elisha. When he returned home, he would still be required, because of his official position, to perform certain formal acts of worship to Rimmon, the national god of Syria. Would Elisha please ask Yahweh to pardon him in this matter? This would seem to be contrary to the Mosaic covenant, but Elisha told him, "Go in peace," indicating that his request would be granted.

Naaman offered Elisha a generous present, but the prophet refused to take a cent. His servant, Gehazi, was not so scrupulous. Naaman was both willing and able to make some payment. Being a prophet's servant was not particularly lucrative. Why shouldn't he, Gehazi, take advantage of this opportunity to get a little something for himself? Gehazi got what he sought—and more. Naaman gladly gave him two talents of silver and two festal garments. And Elisha, when he found out what his greedy servant had done, gave him leprosy.

The miracle stories connected with Elisha make interesting reading, but for the purpose of writing history, they are not the most important part of his work. Elijah had announced the downfall of the house of Omri. Elisha made it a reality. The last of the Omride kings was Joram, also called Jehoram (849–842).* Elijah's work had had

---

*The various texts of the Bible are not in agreement as to what relation Joram bore to Ahab. The most likely answer is that he was a second son of Ahab's who took the throne after the death of his older brother Ahaziah. Several English translations have adopted this reading.

some effect on him and he put away the Baals, but he still worshiped at the shrines of the bull cult (3:1–3). Shortly after Joram came to the throne, he was faced with rebellion in Moab (II Kin. 3). Moab had been subject to Israel since the days of Omri (p. 178), but Mesha, king of Moab, felt that he was strong enough to throw off the heavy Israelite yoke. Apparently, Joram thought Mesha was strong enough, too, for he asked Jehoshaphat king of Judah to join him. The king of Edom also joined forces with them (3:9). As he had done before the battle at Ramoth-gilead (I Kin. 22), Jehoshaphat insisted that a prophet of Yahweh be consulted before they went into battle. And so they went to the home of Elisha. At first, because of Joram's idolatrous background, Elisha refused to give them any counsel. Finally, for Jehoshaphat's sake, he called a musician to play for him and began to prophesy. Elisha's prophecy is particularly interesting for the fact that only part of it came true. He predicted that water would be provided for their thirsty animals, that they would spoil the land of the Moabites, and that the Moabites would be given into their hands. The next day, the water came, as Elisha had said. The Bible does not tell us its source. It simply says it came from the direction of Edom (3:20). For some reason (possibly because a large quantity of the red sandstone of Edom had eroded into it) the water was red. The Moabites mistook the redness for blood and decided that the three kings had gotten into a fight and had slain each other. When they went to the Israelite camp to gather the spoil, they were surprised and suffered heavy casualties in the battle that followed. Then the Israelites did a strange thing. They threw stones all over the farmland, stopped up the springs, and cut down the good trees in Moab. At this point in the narrative, it seems that the Moabites have been defeated. Then, however,

The stele of Mesha king of Moab, better known as the Moabite Stone. The stone tells of Mesha's breaking free of the yoke of Israel.

we are told that, as the Israelites pressed the battle against the city of Kirhareseth, Mesha took his oldest son, the crown prince, and offered him as a sacrifice to the Moabite god Chemosh who was believed to favor human sacrifice. We should expect to read that this offended Yahweh and that he helped Israel to defeat the Moabites as a punishment for Mesha's sin. Instead, we are told that "there came great wrath upon Israel; and they withdrew from [Mesha] and turned to their own land." No explanation is given for this "wrath." Perhaps the most likely is that Mesha's act made the Moabites feel that Chemosh would be with them and gave them extra courage. At any rate, they were not given into the hands of Israel. The Moabite Stone, which we mentioned earlier (p. 178), confirms the Biblical account. On it, Mesha boasted that Moab had been subject to Israel since the days of Omri, but that he,

Mesha, had broken free in the days of Omri's "son."*

Elisha's next involvement in military matters came in a war with Syria. He entered the picture by serving as a sort of supernatural spy for Joram. Several times, he provided the king with tactical information and counsel that saved his life (6:8–10). Ben-hadad I, the king of Syria, was rather upset about the fact that Joram kept outguessing him. His first thought was that someone in his own camp was leaking information to the enemy. Eventually one of his servants told him the truth: "Elisha, the prophet who is in Israel, tells the king of Israel the words that you speak in your bedchamber." Ben-hadad figured that he would stand a much better chance if Elisha were out of the way, so he ordered his men to go to Dothan and capture him. Elisha was not afraid of them, for, as he confided to his servant, he was protected by the invisible army of Yahweh. When the men came for him, he struck them blind and led them to Samaria. There, instead of killing them, he directed Joram to entertain them royally and to send them back to Ben-hadad.

Ben-hadad's failure to capture Elisha did not hold him back long. Shortly afterward, he brought his whole army into Israel and camped around the hill of Samaria. This cut off the city from outside supply lines and caused a famine so severe that "an ass's head was sold for eighty shekels of silver, and the fourth part of a kab of dove's dung for five shekels of silver" (6:25). The situation grew so desperate that mothers were killing and eating their own children (6:28–31). King Joram was completely overwhelmed by the crisis. As men sometimes do when they can find no other answer, he blamed God. He remembered that Elijah had caused a drought.

*In the Bible, the word "son" sometimes means "grandson." Unless Mesha had his history confused, he probably meant "grandson" too, since we know that his rebellion did not come during the reign of Omri's son Ahab (3:4–5).

Somehow, he thought, Elisha must have persuaded Yahweh to afflict Samaria with this siege and famine. Joram sent for Elisha, with every intention of killing him, but the prophet assured him that by the same time the following day, the crisis would be over and Samaria would have plenty to eat.

In the twilight of that day, Yahweh caused the Syrian army to hear the sound of troops and chariots. They immediately concluded that Joram had hired foreign soldiers to attack them. In a panic, they fled back to the north without stopping to gather up the supplies they had brought with them. Since it was dark, the Israelites were unaware of what had happened. The empty Syrian camp was discovered by four lepers who were deserters from Samaria. For several hours, the four men who had lived as beggars feasted on the Syrian stores and carried silver, gold, and clothing to secret hiding places. Finally, guilt and the fear of being found out combined to convince them they should report their discovery to the men of the city. At first, the Samaritans were skeptical, fearing that the Syrians had set up a trap for them. But a scouting party was sent out, the lepers' word was confirmed, and the city went out to plunder the Syrian camp.

The siege of Samaria was followed by a period of peace between Israel and Syria. Taking advantage of the truce, Elisha journeyed to Damascus. Ben-hadad had long recognized that Elisha had powers beyond the reach of ordinary men. At the time, he was suffering from a rather severe illness and was anxious to find out if he would recover. So, he sent Elisha an enormous gift (8:9) and asked him to tell him if the illness would prove fatal. The messenger who came to Elisha was Hazael, who was probably a military leader. Elisha told Hazael that Ben-hadad would die. We do not know just what happened then. Perhaps Hazael's facial expression betrayed some ambitious design. In

any case, Elisha began to stare at Hazael intensely until Hazael grew ashamed and Elisha began to weep. When Hazael asked him why he wept, Elisha explained that he could forsee the evil Hazael would do as ruler of Syria. If Hazael had not had ambitions before this, he had them now. The next morning, he soaked a cloth in water and spread it over Ben-hadad's face until he suffocated. And Hazael became king in his stead.

### JEHU'S PURGE (842 B.C.)

The year 842 B.C. was a memorable year in the ancient Near East. It began with Hazael's assassination of Ben-hadad and his accession to the throne of Syria. But this was only a beginning of the violence that was to mark that year. Shortly afterward, Israel and Syria were once more at war in Ramoth-gilead. In the course of the conflict, Joram was wounded and was forced to retire to the royal residence at Jezreel to recuperate. While he was there, his nephew Ahaziah, king of Judah, decided to pay his uncle a friendly visit.

When Elisha learned that the kings were together, he realized it was time to take action that would bring to fulfillment Elijah's curse on the House of Omri. There was no time to lose. Hastily, he sent one of the sons of the prophets to Ramoth-gilead, where the army was still encamped. On Elisha's orders, the young man sought out Jehu, the commander of Joram's armies, anointed him king over Israel, and instructed him to "strike down the house of Ahab" and "avenge on Jezebel the blood . . . of the prophets."

Jehu paused only long enough to receive the acclamation of the soldiers. Then, he was off to Jezreel. When the watchman in the tower of Jezreel saw him coming, he thought he was bringing some news from the battlefront. A rider was sent out to learn if the peace had been won. Jehu evaded the question and continued to race toward the

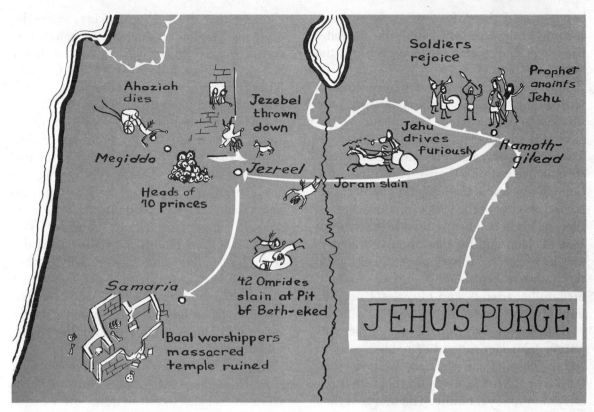

**Jehu's Purge of the house of Ahab.**

city. As his company drew closer, the watchman decided it must be Jehu, since no one else drove a chariot like he did (9:20). If Jehu himself was bringing word from the front lines, it must be important. Joram decided he and Ahaziah should go out personally to meet him. Joram asked expectantly, "Is it peace, Jehu?" Jehu's answer was no comfort: "What peace can there be, so long as the harlotries and the sorceries of your mother Jezebel are so many?" Immediately, Joram recognized what was happening and shouted to Ahaziah to turn his chariot and run. But it was too late. The arrows of Jehu's bowmen found their royal targets. Joram was shot through the heart and died instantly. As a touch of poetic justice, his bloody corpse was thrown into the vineyard of Naboth. Ahaziah managed to ride as far as Megiddo before he died.

Jehu's next victim was Jezebel (9:30–37). Even in the face of certain death, Jezebel demonstrated an amazing strength of character, even if it was a bad character. Instead of going into a frenzy of panic, she painted her eyes and fixed her hair while waiting for Jehu to arrive. As he entered the gates of her home, she leaned out the window and taunted him: "Is it peace, you Zimri,* murderer of your master?" Without replying to her sarcasm, Jehu ordered the eunuchs who served her to throw her out of the window. They did as he said and the horses trampled on her broken body. Then Jehu, demonstrating that his assignment had not made him squeamish, stepped over her body and went to lunch (9:34). When they came out to bury her, all they found left were her skull,

---

*See p. 174.

her feet, and the palms of her hands. According to the words of Elijah the Tishbite, the dogs had eaten Jezebel within the bounds of Jezreel.

Many butchers would have been satisfied with killing two kings and a queen. But Jehu was just getting started. The speed and efficiency with which he had dispatched his first victims shocked the nation into easy compliance with his demands. With a minimum of objection, the leaders of Samaria executed seventy of the king's sons and stacked their heads in two heaps outside the gates of Jezreel. Jehu and his men then slew everyone in Jezreel who had any close ties with the house of Ahab—"all his great men, and his familiar friends, and his priests, until he left him none remaining" (10:11).

As he traveled to Samaria to complete his purge, Jehu met a band of noblemen from Judah, kinsmen of Ahaziah, who were on their way to visit Jezebel and their other relatives in the royal family. The fact that they were from Judah did not deter Jehu a moment. They were related to the Omrides and should be killed. All forty-two of them were slain at the pit of Beth-eked (10:12–14).

The next incident (10:15–17) leads us to believe there was considerable popular support for Jehu's rebellion. We have already seen several signs of this. The readiness with which the soldiers proclaimed Jehu king, the ease with which he got men to turn against the royal family—these indicate there had been a good deal of resentment against the policies of the royal family of Israel. Some, doubtless, disapproved of the luxury in which Ahab and Jezebel had lived. Others, still faithful to Yahweh, or even to the bull cult, disliked the introduction of the Phoenician Baals. If the story of the crime against Naboth circulated widely, we can be sure that it stirred up harsh feelings. And, finally, there were some in the land who were just died-in-the-wool conservatives, who

thought that the only good days were the old ones. Jehonadab the son of Rechab was one of these. The Rechabites were a group who refused to adjust to life in Canaan. They felt that obedience to the Mosaic covenant was tied up with the nomadic life of the wilderness wanderings. So, they refused to live in anything more substantial or permanent than tents. They also refused to farm or grow vineyards, taking their living entirely from their flocks. Over two hundred years later, they were still faithful to this extremely simple form of life (See Jer. 35). With an outlook like this, it is not surprising that Jehonadab and, presumably, other Rechabites, were eager to join Jehu's revolt against the dynasty of Omri. With Jehonadab at his side, Jehu rode to Samaria, where he purged Ahab's friends and relatives as he had done in Jezreel.

The house of Ahab had paid dearly for its sins. Now those who had followed them were to feel the wrath of Jehu. In a bit of efficient strategy, Jehu announced that he was a devout worshiper of Baal and would offer a sacrifice greater than any that had been seen in Israel. Devotion to Baal, simple curiosity, and a desire to please this destructive new leader brought a great crowd of Baal-worshipers. The temple was filled from one end to the other. When they were all inside, he placed a guard of eighty men outside the temple. At Jehu's command, they entered the temple and slew the worshipers where they knelt. They then spoiled the house of Baal so thoroughly that it came to be used as a latrine (10:18–27). At last, Jehu's bloody purge was ended.

## A Time of Weakness in Israel and Judah: 842–798 B.C.

### THE WORLD SITUATION

*Political Results of Jehu's Purge.* Jehu's rebellion rid Israel of the Baals, but it left

| JUDAH | Related History | ISRAEL |
|---|---|---|
| Athaliah 7 . . . . . . . . .842–836<br>Jehoash 40 . . . . . . . .836–797<br>(Joash) | | Jehu 28 . . . . . . . . . . .842–814 |
| | 805: Adad-nirari III rising in<br>Assyria. Attacks Syria.<br>802: Syria weak. | Jehoahaz 16 (17) . . .814–798<br>PROPHET: Elisha |

CHRONOLOGICAL CHART: 842–798 B.C.

her in a precarious and vulnerable political situation. As we have seen, much of Israel's strength under the Omrides stemmed from her alliances with her neighbors. Jehu's purge had shattered these alliances. Phoenicia was alienated by the death of Jezebel and her children and Judah by the murder of her king and forty-two of her princes. Israel was alone against the world. For the next forty years her enemies would strike her almost at will.

*Assyria.* The first blow came from Assyria in 841. The Bible does not mention this attack, but Assyrian records give us a fairly clear picture of what happened. When Shalmaneser III saw that his enemies to the southwest were divided and weak, he set out to reap an easy harvest. He inflicted great damage on Damascus but was unable to wrest it from Hazael. Then he moved southward and forced Phoenicia and Israel to pay tribute. The Black Obelisk, a pillar decorated with scenes depicting the greatness of Shalmaneser III, shows Jehu and thirteen servants bringing precious gifts to the Assyrian king.

Assyria was not Israel's main concern for long. After a less extensive campaign in 837, the Assyrians stayed at home until the last years of the century. Much of this time was occupied settling internal disputes and maintaining control of her immediate area.

*Syria.* Assyria's weakness meant that Hazael had free run of Palestine. And Hazael was not one to pass up his opportunities. In Jehu's time, he cut away vast portions of Israel's holdings, including everything east of the Jordan (*10:32–33*). Then he took control of the Philistine city of Gath. This was a key post in Israel's defenses, and Hazael apparently intended to use it as a base for operations against Judah. There is little doubt he would have succeeded, had not Jehoash king of Judah paid him an enormous tribute to return home (*12:17–18*). Once more, Judah had escaped serious harm.

Hazael struck at the northern kingdom all through his long reign (842–806). By the time he died, the army of Israel had been reduced to fifty horsemen, ten chariots, and ten thousand infantrymen, "for the king of Syria had destroyed them and made them like the dust at threshing" (*13:7*).

### INTERNAL AFFAIRS IN JUDAH: ATHALIAH (842–836) AND JEHOASH (836–797)

The government of Judah was left in even greater chaos than Israel as a result of Jehu's rebellion. At least Israel had Jehu to take over. In Judah, the contest for the throne was wide open. When the smoke cleared, who should be sitting upon it but Athaliah the daughter of Ahab and Jezebel! Athaliah had been the wife of King Jehoram and the mother of King Ahaziah. When she saw that

193

her son was dead, she quickly had all his family—her own grandchildren and possibly some of her children—slaughtered. The only member of the royal family to escape was Ahaziah's infant son Jehoash, or Joash. His aunt, a sister to Ahaziah and wife of Jehoida the high priest, hid him within the grounds of the temple for six years.

Athaliah managed to reign for almost seven years (842–836), but she enjoyed little popular support. She was a foreigner; she was a Baal-worshiper; she was not in the lineage of David; and she had reached the throne in a most un-Davidic way. When Jehoida brought little Jehoash forward and proclaimed him the rightful king, he was immediately and enthusiastically accepted (*II Kin. 11:4–14*). When Athaliah heard the

noise of the cheering crowd, she knew something was wrong. The people were not accustomed to cheer during her reign. One glance told her what was happening. With a cry of "Treason! treason!" she fled through the horses' entrance to the palace. There the palace guards caught her and killed her.

Jehoida took great care to make it clear that this was not just another palace revolt, but a restoration of the divinely sanctioned Davidic kingship and the covenant with Yahweh. Jehoash was brought forth on a sabbath (*11:9*). The soldiers who guarded him were given spears and shields that had belonged to David and had been hanging in the temple (*11:10*). After the people proclaimed him king, Jehoida called on them to renew the covenant with Yahweh, and to

**Scene from the Black Obelisk of Shalmaneser III.**
**Jehu king of Israel (kneeling) is offering gifts to the Assyrian ruler.**

make a covenant with Jehoash. Jehoida's actions reminded the people of their forgotten obligations to Yahweh and filled them with a new religious fervor. They wrecked the temple of Baal and slew its priest. Then, in a joyous procession, they carried the boy king from the temple to the royal palace.

> So all the people of the land rejoiced; and the city was quiet after Athaliah had been slain with the sword at the king's house.
> —II Kings 11:20

A son of David was once again king in Jerusalem.

Since Jehoash was only seven years old when he began to reign, his uncle Jehoida naturally had a great influence on him. As long as Jehoida lived, Jehoash walked in the paths of righteousness. The most notable act of his reign, the repair of the temple (*II Kin. 12:4–16; II Chr. 24:4–14*), was probably

**Israel in the time of Jehu.**

begun at Jehoida's instigation. But when Jehoida died—at what point in Jehoash's long reign this occurred we do not know—Jehoash forgot his upbringing. Some of the young men at court persuaded him to worship the Asherim and other pagan idols. When Jehoida's son Zechariah reprimanded him, the king commanded that the young man be stoned. As Zechariah lay dying, he cried out, "May Yahweh see and avenge" (*II Chr. 24:22*).

Later that year, a small raiding party from Syria came into Judah and inflicted heavy damage. In the fighting, Jehoash was severely wounded. Several of his own servants, who had grown disgusted with his actions since Jehoida's death, formed a conspiracy and killed him in his bed. And Amaziah his son reigned in his stead.

### ISRAEL UNDER JEHU (842–814) AND JEHOAHAZ (814–798)

We have already said most of what can be said about Israel in the last half of the ninth century. The history of the northern kingdom in this period consists of little more than the record of repeated defeats. After Shalmaneser's raid in 841, the main antagonist was Syria. Hazael pillaged Israel regularly until he died in 806. His son Ben-hadad II (how ironic that he should bear the name of the man his father had murdered) took up where Hazael had left off. But Ben-hadad II was not able to enjoy his sport as long as his father had. He had ruled only a year or two when "Yahweh gave Israel a savior, so that they escaped from the hand of the Syrians" (*13:5*). There has been considerable speculation as to the identity of this savior. Jehoahaz seems clearly ruled out (*13:4, 7*). Some have suggested that the writer was looking ahead to the time of Joash or Jeroboam II, the kings of Israel who followed Jehoahaz. The text, however, indicates that the "savior" did his work dur-

195

| JUDAH | Related History | ISRAEL |
|---|---|---|
| Amaziah 29 .........797–769 | | Joash (Jehoash) 16..798–782<br>PROPHET: Elisha |
| Uzziah<br>(Azariah) 36 (52) .769–734 | | Jeroboam II 35 (41) .783–748<br>PROPHETS: Amos<br>Hosea<br>Jonah |

## CHRONOLOGICAL CHART: 798-748

ing the reign of Joahaz (814–798). If this is true, Adad-nirari III of Assyria is the most likely candidate for the role. By 805, the year after Ben-hadad II came to power, Adad-nirari was ruling Assyria with a firm hand. Assyria was ready to make another bid for world domination. She did not quite make it this time, but the first campaigns were smashing successes. In 802, Damascus was decisively defeated and Ben-hadad II was forced to pay an enormous tribute to Adad-nirari. Assyrian records tell us that Israel also had to pay tribute, but this was greatly to be preferred to the crippling Syrian raids. When compared with Hazael and Ben-hadad II, Adad-nirari could truly be called a "savior."

## A Period of Recovery: 798–749

### THE WORLD SITUATION

The Assyrian threat was short-lived. Internal strife—Assyrian's perennial problem—forced Adad-nirari III and his successors to concentrate their attention at home. Then, too, they were faced with a definite threat from the neighboring kingdom of Urartu (Ararat), which was threatening to become the major power in the East. Assyria's weakness took some pressure off Ben-hadad II in Damascus, but he was having troubles of his own with the sister Syrian kingdom of Ha-

math and was unable to do much damage to Israel or Judah. In other words, for the first time in over half a century, Judah and Israel were being left alone. Fortunately, both nations had rulers who took full advantage of the situation, raising their kingdoms to levels of prosperity and power unknown since the days of King Solomon.

### THE EARLY YEARS OF RECOVERY:
### JOASH OF ISRAEL (798–82)
### AND AMAZIAH OF JUDAH (797–769)

Joash* and Amaziah came to their thrones at a time when both nations had reached a low point in their history. Israel had almost nothing left of her once-great army (13:7). Judah was in a severe economic depression as a result of the wars with Syria. Joash came to power first and started Israel on the road to recovery almost immediately. The writer of *Kings* paints a somewhat inconsistent picture of Joash. In his characteristic summary appraisal of Joash's reign, he lumps him in with all the other kings of Israel who "did evil in the sight of Yahweh" and "walked in the way of Jeroboam" (13:11). Immedi-

---

*For the first year of Joash's reign (798), the kings of Israel and Judah had the same name. This is confusing. To complicate matters even further, both are called by both forms of their name, Jehoash and Joash. In this book, the southern king—the king who began to rule at age seven and who repaired the temple—is called Jehoash. The king of Israel is called Joash.

ately following this judgment, however, is a passage in which the king shows great respect and warm affection for the prophet Elisha (*13:14*). This may be another indication that not everyone considered worship at the shrines of the bulls to be wholly inconsistent with the worship of Yahweh (p. 170).

Elisha told Joash that Yahweh would give him victory over the weakened Syrians. Then he gave him a handful of arrows and told him to strike them against the ground. Joash struck three times and stopped. Elisha felt that if Joash had really had his heart in the matter, he would have struck the ground at least half a dozen times. Because of this lack of enthusiasm, Elisha told him that instead of defeating Syria permanently, he would gain only three victories.

According to the word of the prophet, who did not live to see his oracle fulfilled, Joash fought and defeated Syria three times. In the course of these battles, he regained all the territory his father and grandfather had lost to Hazael and Ben-hadad II. Israel was once again more than just an easy target for raiding parties. Under Jeroboam II (783–734), she would become a real world power.

In Judah, Amaziah decided he would try his hand at regaining lost territory. The goal was Edom, which had been lost under Jehoram. Amaziah gathered a large fighting force, including a sizable number of mercenary soldiers from the northern kingdom. As they prepared to march, a prophet warned Amaziah not to take the Israelites with him. Yahweh could give him the victory without the help of these idolaters. At this point, Amaziah was still moderately faithful to Yahweh. He heeded the words of the prophet, paid the soldiers the agreed price, and sent them home. But this was not the end of the matter. The mercenaries were enraged at being sent home as if they were just so much extra baggage. They expressed their anger by leaving a trail of plunder and death along their route back to Israel (*II Chr. 52:13*).

Amaziah was victorious in Edom (*II Chr. 25:11*). But his victory led to his undoing. First of all, he brought back some of the idols that the Edomites worshiped and set them up in Jerusalem. A prophet rebuked him for this, but the rebuke had little effect (*II Chr. 25:14–16*). The second result of Amaziah's victory was that it filled him with more confidence than the facts warranted. Boldly, he sent a message to Joash king of Israel that was, in effect, a challenge to do battle. It may be that he wanted revenge against Israel for the damage the mercenary soldiers had done. Whatever his reasons, his ambitions were more powerful than his army. Joash tried to discourage him with a bit of light ridicule (*II Chr. 25:17–19*), but Amaziah was determined. The battle was

**Israel and Judah under Kings Jeroboam II and Uzziah**

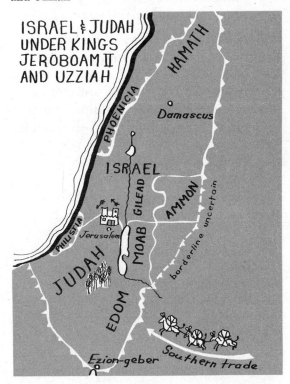

ISRAEL & JUDAH UNDER KINGS JEROBOAM II AND UZZIAH

197

fought at Beth-shemesh, on Judah's northern boundary. Judah was defeated and the Israelite army pushed on into Jerusalem, stripping the temple and the palace of their treasures and taking hostages back to Samaria (25:21–24).

From the time he had set up the gods of Edom in Jerusalem, the conservative men of Judah had been conspiring against Amaziah. This defeat at the hands of Israel doubtless increased the opposition. Those who had tolerated his religious practices would be sure to disapprove of his incompetent political leadership. In spite of the feeling against him, Amaziah managed to reign for twenty-nine years. Eventually, however, the conspiracy broke into the open and he fled the capital to save his life. His enemies found him at Lachish and killed him there. His sixteen year old son Uzziah (Azariah) was made king in his stead.

THE GOLDEN AGE REVISITED:
JEROBOAM II OF ISRAEL (783–748)
AND UZZIAH OF JUDAH (769–734)

*Jeroboam II.* The writer of *I–II Kings* tells the story of Jeroboam II in seven verses (*II Kin. 14:23–29*). As is the case throughout his writing, the truly significant fact about Jeroboam's reign is that "he did not depart from all the sins of Jeroboam" the man for whom he was named. Still, the remarkable success of his reign cannot be hidden entirely. We are told that Jeroboam II "restored the border of Israel from the entrance of Hamath as far as the sea of Arabah" (*14:25*), and that "he recovered Damascus" (*14:28*). Domination of the Syrian states of Hamath and Damascus meant that Jeroboam was undoubtedly able to regain the Israelite territory in Transjordan that had been under Syrian control. The Sea of Arabah is another name for the Dead Sea; thus, Israel's territory north of the Dead Sea was virtually the same as it had been in the days

of Solomon. The revenue that poured into Samaria from these vassal states brought a period of prosperity to Israel unlike any since the division of the kingdom. In *II Kings 14:25* we are told that the prophet who presided over this dramatic resurgence was Jonah the son of Amittai, the central character of the book that bears his name (See *Jonah 1:1*).

*Uzziah.* When Uzziah came to the throne of Judah, he was only sixteen and his nation was running a poor second to her northern sister. But Uzziah was an exceptional young man, and Judah did not long remain in the shadows. First of all, Uzziah wisely capitalized on the gains his father had made. Joash had subdued Edom, opening up the route to the Red Sea. *II Chronicles 26:2* tells us that Uzziah built Eloth and restored it to Judah. Archaeologists have shown that Eloth was another name for Ezion-geber, Solomon's famous commercial center on the Red Sea (see p. 156). Excavations indicate that Uzziah reopened the port and refining industry there, undoubtedly providing Judah with much-needed income. One of the prize discoveries from the ruins of Ezion-geber is a copper seal bearing the inscription "belonging to Jotham." Of course, we cannot be sure, but it is possible that this very seal once belonged to Uzziah's son Jotham, who served as acting king during the last sixteen years of his father's reign, when the latter was suffering from leprosy.

The rebuilding of Ezion-geber was just a start. Uzziah restored and maintained control of the major trade routes. He revitalized the agricultural industry in Judah and the southern wilderness, "for he loved the soil" (*II Chr. 26:10*). He carried on successful campaigns against Judah's old enemies, Philistia, Arabia, and Ammon (*II Chr. 26:8*). He strengthened Jerusalem's fortifications (*26:9*) and built his army into a fighting machine that could "make war with mighty

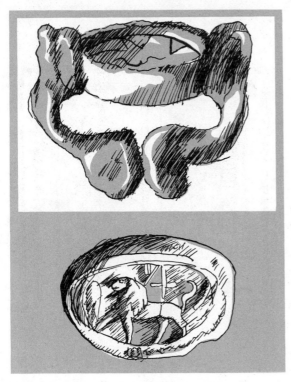

Top: the personal seal of Jotham found at
Ezion-geber. Bottom: the imprint left by
pressing the seal into soft clay.

power, to help the king against the enemy"
(*26:13*). *II Chronicles 26:15* speaks of siege
engines "to be on the towers and the corners,
to shoot arrows and great stones." The exact
nature of these "engines" is unknown, and
there is disagreement over whether they actually propelled arrows and stones or merely
protected the warriors who did. Whatever
the case, it was obviously an ingenious con-
traption that gave Uzziah's army a real advantage in defending Jerusalem.

Uzziah's fame spread far, until he was recognized as one of the great rulers in the Near
East. Unhappily, his pride also grew. His
military and commercial successes apparently caused him to feel he could make his
own rules in religious matters. So, he entered the temple and began to burn incense
on the altar. By doing this, Uzziah set himself above the priests of God. And they were
quick to point out his error. Had Uzziah accepted their rebuke humbly, he may have
escaped punishment, for he had been a
faithful ruler (*II Chr. 26:4–5*). But the king
was not used to being corrected, and he became angry with them. As a result, the Lord
caused leprosy to break out in his forehead.
Uzziah lived a number of years after this incident, but because of his disease, he had to
withdraw from public life. Although his son
Jotham took over as acting king, we may be
sure that Uzziah played an important
behind-the-scenes role in the direction of
the affairs of the kingdom.

By the middle of the eighth century B.C.
Israel and Judah were at the high water
mark of their existence as separate nations.
And both nations felt that God had brought
them there. Jeroboam II had been counseled by the prophet Jonah and was viewed
as a "savior" raised up by Yahweh (*II Kin.
14:27*). Uzziah, especially in the early years
of his reign, "did what was right in the eyes
of Yahweh." The prophet Zechariah* had
instructed him. There was a great deal of optimism among the people of both nations.
They were rich and growing richer, and
Yahweh could be counted on to raise them
to even greater heights. Or could he? A conflicting, and for that reason a most disturbing, viewpoint was advanced by two great
classical prophets of the northern kingdom:
Amos and Hosea. Before we listen to their
message, let us reflect on the changes that
were taking place in the field of prophecy.

## An Introduction to Prophecy

We sometimes get the idea—especially if
we do not study the Old Testament much—
that about all the prophets did was make
predictions about the birth of Jesus. Actu-

---

*Not to be confused with the author of the book of
*Zechariah,* who lived after the Babylonian exile (see p.
325).

ally, the overwhelming bulk of what the prophets had to say was directed to problems current in their own time. To think of a prophet simply as one who foretold the future is to miss the point of what Old Testament prophecy is all about. The prophets were human beings whom God used to communicate his will to mankind. Their messages and their ways of presenting them were geared to the times and varied from prophet to prophet. In addition to individual variation, the whole phenomenon of prophecy underwent considerable change in the course of Israel's history.

The first great prophetic movement flourished in the eleventh century B.C., at the close of the period of the judges. These prophets, of whom Samuel was the most important, served as all-around religious leaders. They were seers or diviners who gave people answers to such problems as the whereabouts of lost animals ( *I Sam. 9:6,9* ). They also presided over sacrifices and other religious functions. Frequently they delivered their oracles while performing an ecstatic dance ( *I Sam. 10:5–6, 10–13* ). Groups of these prophets often traveled together in guilds. Samuel was apparently the head of such a band ( *I Sam. 19:18–24* ).

With the rise of the monarchy, the prophet developed into a sort of counselor and critic-at-large of the national policies. As we have seen, Samuel had a great deal to say, on both sides of the question, about Israel's desire for a king. When Israel got her king, the prophets gave him advice, informed him of Yahweh's will in certain situations, and often rebuked him openly for his misbehavior. There were, of course, "prophets" who were no more than hangers-on at the court, but these do not represent the mainstream of the prophetic tradition. The true prophets were harsh in their criticism of these hirelings (See *I Kin. 22:19–25; Jeremiah 23:9–33; Micah 3:5,11* ).

Tombstone from the second century B.C., claiming to mark the remains of King Uzziah.

By the middle of the eighth century B.C., a type of prophet had arisen who was far different from the prophet of Samuel's time. The priestly functions had long since been surrendered to the regular officiants at the temple. The ecstatic behavior that had characterized the earlier prophets was replaced by a more sober attitude. These prophets were not trained for their calling in the prophetic guilds. They were men in varying secular occupations who were called by the Lord to become his special messengers. Perhaps most significant of all, these messengers of Yahweh began to create a prophetic literature that eventually became Holy Scripture.

We remember most of the pre-eighth-century prophets for their dramatic actions: Samuel rebuking Saul and hewing Agag in pieces; Nathan pointing an accusing finger at David and saying, "Thou art the man;" Elijah confronting Ahab in Naboth's vineyard or slaying the defeated prophets of Baal on Mt. Carmel; Elisha inciting Jehu to overthrow the house of Omri. But we remember the classical prophets—those ranging from Amos to Malachi—for what they said and how they said it.

The average Bible student is confused by the prophetic books. Since they are grouped together at the end of the Old Testament, it is easy to conclude that the prophets lived long after the period of the kings was over. If we look at the opening verses of most of these books, we can see that this is not the case. Unfortunately, many people who read these opening verses still fail to see how important it is to place the prophets in their historical context. Consequently, they read them as if it made no difference when they lived. To make this mistake is to deny oneself of the richness of the prophetic literature. The prophets were right in the thick of things. They were engaged in the all-important task of declaring to men the relevance of God's will to their particular historical situation. Their sermons reflect their times. If we want to understand their sermons, we must know something about their times. In the following chapters we shall treat the prophets in connection with the kings in whose reign they preached.

Establishing the proper historical context is only the first step in understanding the message of the prophets. Next we must become familiar with the composition of a typical prophetic book. Most of us have sat down and tried to read *Amos* or *Hosea* straight through. Our good intentions and firm resolutions carry us through a chapter or two. But eventually, we have to admit that it is pretty hard to find a logical sequence in these books, that just about the time we think we know what the prophet is driving at, he shifts to a new subject that seems entirely unconnected to the preceding section. We should not let this disturb us. In *Hosea 1:1*, for example, we are told that the book contains oracles spoken by the prophet during the reigns of four different kings of Judah. What we have in the book of *Hosea* is a collection of excerpts from some of his best sermons, preached over a number of years. How strange it would be if they fit together to form a perfectly ordered document!

It is impossible to say exactly how the prophetic books reached their present form, but the typical process was probably something like this:

1. The inspired prophets delivered their oracles at different times and on varying subjects.
2. The best of these were collected (and perhaps polished a bit) either by the prophet himself or his followers.
3. Eventually, the selected oracles were strung together, often in a sort of helter-skelter fashion, to form the books as we now have them.*

### THE FUNCTION OF THE PROPHETS

There was great diversity among the prophets of God. Some were geniuses. Some were not. Some were rugged backwoodsmen. Some were trusted friends of the royal court. Some were poetic, providing us with sublime religious literature. Others were blunt, delivering the message of Yahweh in its barest form. But all of them were men of insight. They were so in tune with the mind of God that they were able to interpret it to the men of their day. In this role as interpreter of the mind of God, the prophets fulfilled three main functions: 1) King-makers and king-breakers; 2) agents of Holy Warfare; and 3) guardians of the Mosaic faith.

---

*This, of course, did not include the chapters and verses. These were not added until the fifteenth century A.D.

Let us take a closer look at these functions.

*King-makers and king-breakers.* The prophets were political men. They took a special interest in keeping the kings in line. Throughout the period of the monarchy, we find prophets openly rebuking kings, announcing the downfall of dynasties, and guiding other men to the throne. Usually the reason for the prophets' rebuke was a rejection by the king of the sovereignty of Yahweh. A king might show his rejection of Yahweh by worshiping other gods, by making alliances with foreign nations, thereby declaring that he did not have enough trust in Yahweh's power to protect his people, or by other actions that violated the covenant laws regarding human rights.

Samuel was especially busy at this task, anointing Saul, announcing his downfall, and anointing David to reign in his place. Nathan was not exactly a king-breaker when he rebuked David for his sin with Bathsheba, but he was certainly one of the chief engineers in bringing Solomon to the throne (see p. 152). Ahijah announced that the northern tribes would be torn from Solomon's house and given to Jeroboam. Elijah condemned Ahab for his apostasy and declared that the land would be stained with the blood of the house of Omri. Elisha was responsible for the actual "breaking" of the Omride dynasty and for the setting up of the dynasty of Jehu. Isaiah rebuked Ahaz for his alliance with Syria. Jeremiah was in constant difficulty for his sermons against the policies of the various kings who ruled during his ministry. Amos, Hosea, and others spoke fearlessly against injustices that had been allowed or encouraged by the crown. This practice of repudiating the king did not make the life of a prophet a comfortable one. Very few of them enjoyed much favor at court. And yet, it would be difficult to overestimate the tremendous amount of political influence they wielded.

*Agents of Holy Warfare.* The prophets were frequently right in the middle of a nation's preparation for war. They told the king when to fight, when not to fight, and what to do with the spoil. Samuel directed Saul to attack the Amalekites and rebuked him when he broke the rules of Holy Warfare by sparing Agag. When Rehoboam wanted to force the northern tribes back into his kingdom, the prophet Shemaiah told him that "Yahweh has not appointed warfare." Elisha gained a victory for Joram without benefit of the Israelite army (*II Kin. 6:15–19; 7:5–7*), summoned Jehu to a Holy War against the family of Ahab and the worshipers of Baal, and promised Joash three victories over Syria. The record is sketchy, but we can assume that Jonah had his part in battles of reconquest in the time of Jeroboam II. When we turn to the prophetic books themselves, we shall see that many of their oracles have to do with war and rumors of war.

*Guardians of the Mosaic Faith.* When they were not busy making or breaking kings, or declaring Holy War, the prophets spent much of their time urging hearers to return to the worship of Yahweh and the Mosaic covenant. The major problem, of course, was Baal-worship and the other forms of idolatry that plagued Israel and Judah. A large portion of the prophetic writings deal with the sin of idolatry and its consequences. There is reason to believe, however, that outright idolatry was not the only religious problem the prophets were concerned with. There was a tradition in Israel that the only truly acceptable worship was that conducted at the central sanctuary in Jerusalem. This idea is set forth most clearly in *Deuteronomy.* In a number of passages (see, for example, *Deut. 12:13–14, 17, 21; 16:5–6, 16; 18:6–8*), the people are told not to offer sacrifices or observe the chief religious festivals "at every place that you see, but at the place which Yahweh will choose." The place that Yahweh chose, of course, was Jerusalem. When Jeroboam set up a rival cult in North Israel, he violated this command. We have suggested the possibility that Jeroboam intended to perpetuate the worship of Yahweh, although in a corrupted form. (see p. 170). If this theory is true, Jeroboam's sin lay not so much in leading the people to forsake the worship of Yahweh, as in leading them to forsake the worship of Yahweh *in Jerusalem*. To those who were strict adherents of the views set forth in *Deuteronomy*, the last state was almost as bad as the first.

The writer of *I-II Kings* obviously shared this position. Frequently, in summarizing the reign of a good king, he says, "but the high places were not taken away" (*I Kin. 15:14; II Kin. 12:3; 14:4; 15:4*). We can be almost positive that these "high places" were not centers of idolatry. For one thing, the writer usually makes this observation immediately after stating that the king in question had rid the land of idolatry. For another, he sometimes adds that the king "was wholly true to Yahweh all his days" (See *I Kin. 15:4*). He would not say this about a king who allowed idolatry to exist openly. The most reasonable conclusion is that these "high places" were centers of worship used by Yahwists who could not conveniently come to Jerusalem.* The writer of *I-II Kings* did not believe that worship of Yahweh at these high places was as bad as worshiping Baal, but he certainly did not approve of them. It is not unlikely that the prophets shared his view.

In addition to these theological problems, the prophets were greatly concerned about violation of the moral aspects of the covenant. Four centuries of close contact with pagans and the change in social structure that the monarchy had brought had left its mark on Israelite society. The rich no longer felt any responsibility toward the poor, and the poor were unable to protect themselves against exploitation and outright robbery. The prescriptions of the covenant designed to insure honest and considerate business practices were abandoned in favor of a get-all-you-can-by-any-means approach. Sexual immorality was rampant. Religious prostitution was practiced widely and may even have crept into the worship of Yahweh (see *Amos 2:7–8*). In short, the covenant people had forgotten the covenant law. They remembered Yahweh's promises to them, but not their promises to him. Again and again the prophets worked the theme of the Exodus into their oracles, reminding their hearers of God's mighty acts in their behalf and urging them to renew their obedience to the stipulations of the covenant before the already strained patience and mercy of Yahweh was exhausted.

### TYPES OF PROPHETIC ORACLES

The oracles of the prophets covered a wide range of subjects, but most of them can be sorted into one of three different categories: 1) oracles of Yahweh, the Divine Warrior; 2) oracles of Yahweh, the Divine Judge; and 3) oracles of Divine Kingship.

*Oracles of Yahweh the Divine Warrior.* The prophets frequently spoke of war. The war might be imminent, it might be at some time in the more distant future, or it might be a war that the Lord would wage in a final grand triumph over the forces of evil, to usher in the "Day of the Lord." Some of these oracles summon Israel to war. Others announce the destruction she will suffer for breaking the covenant. Still others are directed against the godless nations that oppress Israel and Judah. When the prophets

---

*Deuteronomy 12:21* seems to provide a loophole that would permit these to exist. In the contest on Mt. Carmel, Elijah offered his sacrifice on an altar that had been used to worship Yahweh (*I Kin. 18:30*).

are speaking of a great destruction or a great victory, they frequently support their statements by recalling the mighty acts God has performed in the past.

*Oracles of Yahweh the Divine Judge.* The model for this type of oracle is found in *Micah 6:1–8.* Here the Divine Judge, who sits in the midst of his heavenly council (see *I Kin. 22:19–23; Ps. 82:1*), carries on a legal controversy with his people. He is the plaintiff, the people are the defendants, and the charge is covenant-breaking. Through his prophet, Yahweh contrasts his faithfulness with the unfaithfulness of his people, and a "verdict" is reached. The verdict may be an admonition to do better or an announcement that punishment must be meted out. Other examples of this type oracle do not always contain these elements so clearly, but oracles of judgment against covenant-breaking are found throughout the prophetic literature.

*Oracles of Divine Kingship.* This class includes all oracles that make use of royal language. Some describe the greatness of Yahweh in terms of kingship instead of the customary language of warfare. *Isaiah 6: 1–8* is a striking example of this. Others speak of the various things expected of a king (See *Jer. 21:22*). This class also includes the type of oracles in which the prophets speak of a king who shall one day arise to redeem Israel from her troubles.

If the reader will keep these three broad categories in mind, they should serve to give him a clearer idea as to what the prophet is trying to do in any given oracle. It requires diligent study to understand the prophets, but the rewards are rich.

### THE PROPHETS AS PREACHERS

As a general rule, the prophets were superb preachers. Filled with the spirit of God and certain of the truth of their message, their words burned their way into the hearts of their listeners. When words were insufficient, they found other ways to drive their message home. Hosea named his children "Not Pitied" and "Illegitimate," to point out how Yahweh felt about Israel (*Hosea 1*). The sophisticated Isaiah wandered about naked for three years. When the curious asked him why, he told them, "This is how Egypt and Ethiopia will look when Assyria leads them into captivity" (*Isa. 20*). Jeremiah wore an ox-yoke on his neck (*Jer. 27, 28*) and Ezekiel cooked his food on cow dung (*Ezek. 4:9–17*)—all to dramatize their message. Their language moves back and forth between weal and woe. Oracles of judgment on the present are offset by expressions of hope for the future.

The prophets possessed a keen sense of social responsibility and displayed a passion for equality and injustice, repeatedly emphasizing the point that man does not stand alone before God but is always viewed in his relation to his fellowman as well. Western man is greatly indebted to the Old Testament prophets for a historical interpretation of man. Their work contains the basis for the view that God is sovereign over history and is working out his purposes in accord with an overall plan, sometimes hard to detect, but always in the hands of the Lord.

Now let us turn to the writings of Amos, the first of the great literary prophets.

## Amos

Amos was a native of the tiny village of Tekoa, on the edge of the wilderness of Judah, about twelve miles south of Jerusalem. He was not a member of the professional class of prophets.* He was a herdsman and a dresser of sycamore trees.† This

---

*See *Amos 7:14.* "Sons of the prophets" is a technical term applied to the prophetic guilds.

†The sycamores of the Near East bear a figlike fruit which must be opened to allow the insects that infest it to escape, and pinched to cause it to ripen into an edible state. This was Amos' job.

type of life was austere and simple, but Amos had evidently come in contact with the commercial centers of Palestine, because he displays considerable knowledge of the habits and attitudes of the people to whom he preached. His oracles are not those of a primitive rustic. They are literary masterpieces, full of vivid figures and allusions.

Amos was a resident of Judah, but his message was directed primarily at the northern kingdom. When Yahweh told him to "Go, prophesy to my people Israel" (7:15), the time was around 750 B.C. Israel was enjoying the prosperous reign of Jeroboam II. Samaria had become a great commercial center. On the surface, things looked wonderful—like a whitewashed tomb. But Amos could see the corruption within, and he had something to say about it.

In what was probably his first group of oracles (chs. 1–2), Amos spoke of Yahweh's wrath against Israel's neighbors and of the punishment they would receive for their iniquity. How delighted the Israelites must have been to have heard this new preacher predict the downfall of their enemies in such vivid language! How smug they must have felt as he announced that Yahweh would devour Judah with fire (2:4–5)! Then, when he had their attention, Amos began to lash out at Israel. Their smugness was unjustified. It was true that Yahweh had brought them out of Egypt (2:10; 3:1). It was true that he had chosen them to bear a special relationship to him—"you only have I known* of all the families of the earth." But, de-

---

*The Hebrew word for "know" is sometimes used for sexual intercourse, indicating the most intimate of personal relationships. Israel had been this close to Yahweh.

**An emaciated desert herdsman brings a gift of oxen to the king of Egypt.**

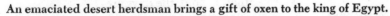

clared Amos, this did not give them license to behave as they pleased. On the contrary, it made them all the more liable for their actions. In short, election brings *responsibility,* not *privilege.* Instead of saying, "Because you are my chosen people I will wink at your sins and continue to bring you prosperity," Yahweh was saying, "Because you are my chosen people and have sinned, *therefore* I will punish you" (*3:1–2*). Israel knew God's will. There was no excuse for her behavior.

Amos condemned the exploitation of the poor by the strong and the rich:

> They sell the righteous for silver
>     and the needy for a pair of shoes.
> They . . . trample the head of the
>         poor into the dust of the earth,
>     and turn aside the way of the afflicted.
>                     —*Amos 2:6-7*

He condemned their gross sensuality and their indifference to the needs of others:

> A man and his father go in to the
>         same maiden,
>     so that my holy name is profaned;
> they lay themselves down beside every altar
>     upon garments taken in pledge;
> and in the house of their God they drink
>     the wine of those who have been fined.
>                     —*Amos 2:7-8*

> Woe to those who lie upon beds of ivory,
>     and stretch themselves upon their couches,
> and eat lambs from the flock,
>     and calves from the midst of the stall;
> who sing idle songs to the sound of the harp,
>     and like David invent for themselves
>         instruments of music;
> who drink wine in bowls,
>     and anoint themselves with the finest oils,
>     but are not grieved over the ruin of Joseph!
>                     —*Amos 6:4-6*

How far removed was all this from the warm neighborly love and concern for the poor that the law enjoined, and that had been practiced in the days of Israel's youth. Alas, the covenant had been forgotten.

Amos lampooned their injustice and dishonesty in business practices:

> When will the new moon be over
>     that we may sell grain?
> And the sabbath,
>     that we may offer wheat for sale,
> that we may make the ephah small
>         and the shakel great,
>     and deal deceitfully with false balances?
>                     —*Amos 8:5*

He saw that the merchants were encouraged in their unjust practices by their wives. To them he said:

> Hear this word, you *cows of Bashan,*
>     who are in the mountain of Samaria,
> who oppress the poor, who crush the needy,
>     who say to their husbands,
>     "Bring, that we may drink!"
> Yahweh God has sworn by his holiness
>     that, behold, the days are
>         coming upon you,
> when they shall take you away with hooks,
>     even the last of you with fish-hooks.
> And you shall go out through the breaches,
>     every one straight before her;
>     and you shall be cast forth into
>         Harmon,
>             says Yahweh.
>                     —*Amos 4:1-3*

### "PREPARE TO MEET THY GOD"

Next, Amos attacked the religion of Israel. The people had not neglected religion. On the contrary, they had "perfected" it. Apparently, they were worshiping according to strict rules and took great satisfaction in the scrupulous observance of these rules. But Amos was not impressed. With more than a touch of irony, Amos invites them to

> Come to Bethel, and transgress;
>     to Gilgal, and multiply transgression;
> bring your sacrifices every morning,
>     your tithes every three days;

offer a sacrifice of thanksgiving of
that which is leavened,
and proclaim freewill offerings,
publish them;
for so you love to do, O people of Israel!
—*Amos 4:4-5*

Then, speaking for Yahweh, Amos delivered this verdict on their hypocritical religion:

I hate, I despise your feasts,
and I take no delight in your solemn
assemblies.
Even though you offer me your burnt
offerings and cereal offerings,
I will not accept them,
and the peace offerings of your fatted beasts
I will not look upon.
Take away from the the noise of your songs;
to the melody of your harps I will not
listen.
But let justice roll down like waters,
and righteousness like an everflowing
stream.           —*Amos 5:21-24*

Yahweh could not be bought off with ill-gotten gain. He would not accept ritual as a substitute for right living.

After enumerating Israel's sins, Amos lamented over the failure of past chastisement to bring any repentance:

I gave you cleanness of teeth in
all your cities,
and lack of bread in all
your places . . .
I withheld the rain from you when there
were yet three months to the harvest;
I would send rain upon one city, and send no
rain upon another city . . .
I smote you with blight and mildew:
I laid waste your gardens and your
vineyards . . .
I sent among you a pestilence after the
manner of Egypt;
I slew your young men with the sword . . .
Yet you did not return unto me,
says Yahweh.     —*Amos 4:6-11*

Because of this failure to respond, Amos gave Israel the solemn warning, "Prepare to meet thy God" (*4:12*). When we see these words scrawled on a large rock by the side of the highway, we usually smile and try to imagine briefly the kind of person who may have put them there. When Amos spoke them, he was utterly serious. He wanted Israel to know that no nation could escape the judgment of him

who forms the mountains, and creates the
wind,
and declares to man what is his thought;
who makes the morning darkness,
and treads on the heights of the earth—
Yahweh, the God of hosts, is his name!
—*Amos 4:13*

### VISIONS OF JUDGMENT

Chapters 7–9 consist mainly of visions of Yahweh's judgment upon Israel. First, there is a vision of a plague of locusts about to ravage a field (*7:1–3*). In the second, a fire is about to sweep across the land (*7:4–6*). In both of these visions, Yahweh was persuaded to hold back destruction a bit longer (perhaps to give the people time to repent). In the remaining visions, this note of hope is gone. The key vision in this series is the vision of the plumbline (*7:7–9*), signifying that Yahweh had measured Israel for destruction, that it was merely a matter of time until the house of Jeroboam would fall by the sword and the religious sanctuaries would be left desolate. This sermon got Amos into trouble. Amaziah, the priest at the temple in Bethel, sent word to King Jeroboam II that Amos was starting a conspiracy against him. Presumably at the king's direction, Amaziah told Amos to go back to Judah. People in the north didn't want southern preachers coming in and telling them what to do. Amaziah's language indicates he thought Amos was one of the professional prophets who earned their "bread" by traveling about the country delivering oracles (7:12–13). Amos was not intimidated by the king's chaplain. He rejected the charge that he was a professional prophet. His job was herding sheep and pinching figs. He was prophesying because Yahweh had spoken to him. And when Yahweh speaks, "who can but prophesy" (see 3:8). Amos then issued the warning that "Israel shall surely go into exile away from its land" (7:17). For good measure, he revealed another vision he had seen. This time it was a basket of summer fruit. For the moment it was beautiful and appealing. In a short time, however, the ripeness would become rottenness and the basket would be cast out. The lesson was obvious: "The end has come upon my people Israel . . . the dead bodies shall be many; in every place they shall be cast out in silence" (8:2–3).

Amos is the first Biblical writer to speak of the Day of the Lord, but the manner in which he introduces it shows that it was a well-known theme in Israelite theology. Before Amos, it had apparently been thought of as a day of glory and victory for Israel, a day when Yahweh would permanently elevate his people above the nations. Amos turns it into a day of defeat and terror.

> Woe to you who desire the day of the Lord!
>     Why would you have the day of the Lord?
> It is darkness, and not light;
>         as if a man fled from a lion,
>         and a bear met him;
>     or went into the house and leaned
>         with his hand against the wall,
>         and a serpent bit him.
> Is not the day of the Lord darkness,
>         and not light,
>     and gloom with no brightness in it?
>                     —Amos 5:18-20

> "And on that day," says Yahweh God,
>     "I will make the sun go down at noon,
>     and darken the earth in broad daylight.
>     I will turn your feasts into mourning,

> and all your songs into lamentation;
>     I will bring sackcloth upon all loins,
>         and baldness on every head;
>     I will make it like the mourning for an
>         only son,
>     and the end of it like a bitter day."
>                     —Amos 8:9-10

### WORDS OF HOPE

The sermons of the prophets were geared to the needs of their times. In later years, when the people of God were sick with despair, Isaiah and Jeremiah and Ezekiel would remind them of Yahweh's enduring promises. In the middle of the eighth century B.C., Israel needed nothing to bolster her spirits. In the midst of her wickedness, she imagined that Yahweh would never cease to bless her, regardless of what she did. She needed a prophet like Amos. Few prophets spoke with such unrelenting condemnation as did Amos. But even Amos held out a glimmer of hope here and there. As a nation Israel was doomed, but a hasty repentance might move Yahweh to preserve a remnant.

> Seek good, and not evil,
>     that you may live;
> and so Yahweh, the God of hosts,
>         will be with you,
>     as you have said.
> Hate evil, and love good,
>     and establish justice in the gate;
> It may be that Yahweh, the God of hosts,
>     will be gracious to the remnant of Joseph.
>                     —Amos 5:14-15

Yahweh does not punish men to delight in their misery. Rather, he chastises them much as a father chastises disobedient children. To the small remnant who understand this and who respond to his correction by faithful obedience, he gives the promise of a glorious redemption:

> "Behold, the days are coming," says Yahweh,
>     "when the plowman shall overtake the
>         reaper

and the treader of grapes him who sows
the seed;
the mountains shall drip sweet wine,
and all the hills shall flow with it.
I will restore the fortunes of my people
Israel,
and they shall rebuild the ruined
cities and inhabit them;
they shall plant vineyards and drink their
wine,
and they shall make gardens and eat their
fruit.
I will plant them upon their land,
and they shall never again be plucked up
out of the land which I have given them,"
says Yahweh your God.
        —Amos 9:13-15

Jeroboam II is dead; the cows of Bashan are no more; the prophet Amos no longer preaches at Bethel. But his words ever summon us from the hypocrisy and superficiality of so much of life and religion and demand of us that we "let justice roll down like waters, and righteousness like an ever-flowing stream."

## The Beginning of the End: 748–732 B.C.

The sound of Amos' voice had scarcely died at Bethel before his words began to be fulfilled. Doubtless, many had scoffed at his oracles of doom. Some knew their history well enough to realize they could not ride this crest of prosperity forever. But even they could not believe that anything so disastrous as Amos pictured could ever really come to pass. There might be troubled times; Israel had had them before. There might even be periods of real oppression. But Israel would survive. She always had. What better argument than that? Israel, however, had never known a threat like that posed by the Assyrians in the middle of the eighth century B.C. Neither had anyone else.

As we have already seen, Assyria had been a significant world power for centuries. She was an ambitious, aggressive nation and had long looked at Syria and Palestine with a greedy eye. Possession of these lands would provide her with greater natural re-

| JUDAH | Related History | ISRAEL |
|---|---|---|
| Jotham { (co-regent) 16 . . . . . . 749–734 (king) . . . . . . . . 734 | | Zechariah 6 mo. . . . . . . . . 748 Shallum 1 mo. . . . . . . . . . 748 Menahem 10 . . . . . . . 748–738 PROPHET: Hosea |
| | 745: Tiglath-pileser III becomes king of Assyria 743: Tiglath-pileser meets coalition in central Syria. | |
| Ahaz 20 (16) . . . . . . . 734–715 | | Pekahiah 2 . . . . . . . . 738–736 Pekah 4 (20) . . . . . 736–732/1 |
| | 733: Tiglath-pileser conquers most of Israel. 732: Tiglath-pileser conquers Damascus. | Hoshea 9 . . . . . . 732/1–723/2 |

### CHRONOLOGICAL CHART: 748–732 B.C.

sources and tribute money. More important, it would give her access to the sea and furnish her a base for campaigns against Egypt. Several times, she almost succeeded in gaining permanent control of these lands. Each time, however, her dreams of empire were spoiled by troubles on the home front that forced her to withdraw her armies and to rest content with booty and tribute money. The last of these thwarted attempts had come in 802 B.C., when Adad-Nirari III devastated Damascus and pushed all the way to the Mediterranean, only to be called home to quell internal rumblings and to meet the growing threat posed by the kingdom of Urartu (Ararat), which bordered Assyria on the north. These two problems had occupied Assyria for the whole first half of the eighth century, allowing Israel to regain her political and economic footing. In fact, at the time of Jeroboam II's death in 748, Assyria had lost her northern provinces to Urartu and was in the throes of a serious civil war. There was no special reason to believe that conditions were going to get any better soon. Then, in 745, the rebel leader Pul (or Pulu) seized the throne, taking the name Tiglath-pileser III. The picture changed dramatically. Somehow, Tiglath-pileser III managed to mold the rival factions into a united Assyria. Then, with the nation solidly behind him, he inaugurated the most amazing program of conquest and rule the world had ever seen. In brief, Tiglath-pileser's aim was to break down nationalistic barriers and to bring the entire civilized world under direct and absolute Assyrian control. He proved to be remarkably successful.

First, he turned his attentions to the west. In 743, a campaign into Syria met opposition from a coalition force headed by—according to Assyrian records—"Azriau from Iuda." Although the Bible does not mention such a campaign, there is good reason to be-

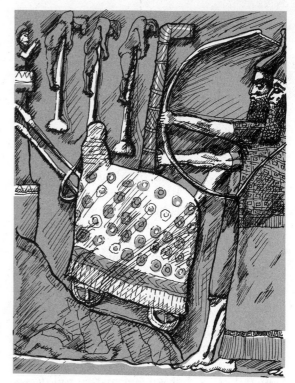

Siege engine used by the armies of Tiglath-pileser III.

lieve this was an Assyrian version of the name, "Azariah (Uzziah) of Judah." Because of his leprosy, Uzziah had surrendered the throne to his son Jotham in about 749, but he would still have been able to command an army (Naaman, the leper whom Elisha healed, had been the commander of Syria's armies). Uzziah, an astute man, had probably seen that, unless Tiglath-pileser were stopped immediately, it would simply be a matter of time until he devoured the whole Near Eastern world. So (if the theory is correct), he marched his troops to Syria, enlisted the support of other kings, and tried to stop him. The coalition army was no match for the well-trained and discipline-hardened Assyrian troops. Tiglath-pileser's juggernaut was irresistible. He marched on to the sea, taking tribute from all who stood in his path, and gaining control of the fine Phoenician seaports.

The next logical western opponent, or victim, was Israel. Before we observe Israel's behavior in the face of the Assyrian threat, let us notice how she had fared since the death of Jeroboam II.

### A BASKET OF SUMMER FRUIT

Amos had been right when he announced that the security of Jeroboam II's reign was an illusion. Things held together as long as Jeroboam lived, but in the year of his death (748 B.C.), the basket of summer fruit (*Amos 8:1–3*) was overturned and Israel's rottenness became tragically apparent. Within less than a year, three kings sat on Israel's throne (*II Kin. 15:8–28*). The first was Zechariah, Jeroboam's son. He was assassinated after six months, thus bringing the dynasty of Jehu to an inglorious end. His assassin, Shallum, held power for only a month before he was cut down by Menahem, a cruel warrior (*II Kin. 15:16*) who became king in his stead. Menahem was a bit more successful than his predecessors had been. He was still reigning when Tiglath-pileser made his first western tour. Apparently, however, his grip on the throne was shaky. He struck a bargain with the Assyrian: in return for help in holding on to his crown, Menahem paid an enormous tribute (*II Kin. 15:19*). In other words, the king sold out. It is doubtful that this action did much to endear Menahem to his people, especially since he raised the tribute by levying a tax on the prosperous landowners. Nevertheless, he held power for ten years and managed to die a natural death. His son Pekahiah was not so fortunate. After two brief years on the throne, he was assassinated by the captain of his army, Pekah.

### THE SYRO-ISRAELITE COALITION

Whatever his motives may have been, Menahem had been wise enough to see that it was useless to resist Tiglath-pileser and had decided to make the best of a bad bargain. Pekah was not so prudent. Soon after seizing power he joined with Rezin king of Damascus in a coalition designed to beat back the Assyrian invaders. Their first conflict, however, was not with Assyria, but with Judah.

Judah had remained relatively unscathed by the Assyrian forays into the West. While Israel was torn by intrigue and anarchy, Judah was plodding along her less interesting, but far more successful, way. Jotham, like his father Uzziah, had been an able ruler. In addition to continued commercial success, he had subjugated the Ammonites and had continued to fortify Judah's defenses. It is not absolutely clear just why Pekah and Rezin attacked Judah. Probably, Jotham refused to risk his nation's wealth and security by joining with the anti-Assyrian forces. If this was the case, we can understand their opposition. It simply would not do to have such a strong potential enemy camped on the back doorstep.

Before the attack was launched, Jotham died and was succeeded by his son Ahaz. Ahaz was neither as capable nor as faithful as his father and grandfather, and troubled times fell on Judah. Sensing the weakness of the new king, the Edomites made a successful bid for independence. In the process, they recovered the seaport and industrial center of Eloth (Ezion-geber), thus robbing Judah of a vital source of income. Then, the Syro-Israelite army struck. Their plan was to seize control of the government and place their own man, identified only as the son of Tabeel, on the throne in place of Ahaz (*Isaiah 7:6*). They were unable to capture Jerusalem, but they did inflict heavy damage on the nation and took a large number of prisoners (*II Chr. 28:15*). As if things were not bad enough, the Edomites invaded Judah and carried off captives. The Philistines also got into the act by raiding and seizing cities in the Shephelah and the Negeb, Judah's territory to the south.

Naturally, Ahaz was frantic (*Isa. 7:1–2*). It seemed to him that his only hope lay in persuading Tiglath-pileser to come to his rescue. At this point the first, and one of the greatest, of the classical prophets of the southern kingdom appeared on the scene. His name was Isaiah. We shall have more attention to Isaiah later. For the moment, let it suffice to say that he urged Ahaz not to make any sort of agreement with the Assyrian. Yahweh was going to use Assyria to defeat Israel and Damascus anyway. There was no point in getting tied up with Tiglath-pileser unnecessarily. But Ahaz could not wait for Yahweh. Despite Isaiah's protests, he appealed to Tiglath-pileser for help and accompanied his appeal with a large gift taken from the temple treasury (*II Kin. 16: 7–8*). We may be sure that Tiglath-pileser was delighted to receive the gift. It is always pleasant to be rewarded handsomely for something one was going to do anyway. He had no intention of allowing Pekah and Rezin to build up any real strength against him. And so, in 734 B.C., Tiglath-pileser headed westward once again.

The brilliant Assyrian did not begin with a frontal attack on the Aramean-Israelite forces. Instead, he prepared for the eventual showdown by cutting off possible sources of support. First, he marched to the sea and dropped down along the Palestinian coastland to conquer the Philistines. Then he moved on into Egypt and left troops there to prevent any build-up of resistance. Now that he had them isolated, he was ready to deal with Pekah and Rezin. In 733, the Assyrian troops devastated Galilee and Transjordan. Excavations indicate that the Galilean strongholds of Hazor and Megiddo were destroyed at this time, although the latter seems to have been rebuilt immediately, probably as an Assyrian government center.

**Tiglath-pileser III, brilliant king of Assyria.**

Tiglath-pileser was spared the trouble of punishing Pekah by a group of Israelite conspirators who assassinated him and raised Hoshea to the throne. This was done with the full knowledge and approval of Tiglath-pileser. In fact, in Assyrian records of the affair, he took credit for placing Hoshea on the throne. With the rebellious Pekah out of the way, Tiglath-pileser allowed Samaria to stand a bit longer. Hoshea could not cause him much trouble. And besides, he still had an appointment with Rezin. In 732, Tiglath-pileser attacked Damascus and easily defeated it. Then, he executed Rezin and, as he had done in Israel (*II Kin. 15:29*), deported a large number of captives (*16:9*).

Israel, or what was left of her, had ten years to live. By now, it must have been obvious to all that the end was near. Before we trace the course of this tragic last decade, let us turn to the writings of the prophet who had spent the previous decade trying to explain to bewildered Israel what was happening to her.

## Hosea

Hosea was a contemporary of Amos, but he prophesied for a much longer time (compare *Amos 1:1* with *Hosea 1:1*). His task was a bit more difficult. Amos merely announced judgment. Hosea had to interpret its meaning. Like Amos, he made it clear that the impending judgment was inescapable. But Hosea went further than Amos. He insisted that the judgment was an act of love, not of hatred. It was necessary for Yahweh to punish Israel, but he was not doing it just to hurt her. He was doing it to win her back. It was as if Yahweh were a loving husband and Israel were his unfaithful bride. He could not tolerate her repeated infidelity nor allow it to go unpunished, but he stood ready always to receive her back into his bosom. Not many men could have conveyed this message with any real conviction. But Hosea was perfectly suited for the task, for he had a bride like Israel.

### HOSEA AND GOMER

The heart of Hosea's message is contained in *chs. 1–3*, which contain the story of Hosea's own troubled marriage. The story is not quite as clear as we might like it to be. We cannot be absolutely certain that the woman of *ch. 3* is the same as Gomer of *ch. 1*. It is our feeling that they are one and the same woman. Fortunately, we do not have to solve this minor puzzle to appreciate what Hosea had to say. For the sake of simplicity—and probability—let us assume that the woman of *ch. 3* is Gomer and reconstruct Hosea's experiences with her.

Hosea married Gomer, a prostitute, at the command of Yahweh. It is surprising that a man of God should be asked to do such a thing, but this is simply another of the shocking acts the prophets used to dramatize their message. Hosea, of course, represents Yahweh and Gomer represents Israel. The names given to their children (*1:4–9*) revealed Yahweh's displeasure with his people. The first was named Jezreel, recalling the place where Jehu had purged the house of Ahab. Soon the dynasty of Jehu would also fall. This child was probably born while Jeroboam II was still reigning, since the dynasty lasted only six months after his death, ending with the assassination of his son and successor, Zechariah. The second child was given the sorrowful name, Not Pitied (*Lo-ruhama*). Again and again Yahweh had pitied Israel and had withheld the destruction she deserved. Now his patience was at an end. No longer would he show compassion to his people Israel. The name given to the third child—Not My People (*Lo-ammi*)—symbolized the complete estrangement between Yahweh and Israel. Now he was formally disowning her for her repeated infidelity. It is interesting to notice that *1:3* says, "she conceived and bore *him* a son." In *1:6* and *1:8*, we are told only that "she *bore* a son (or daughter)." It is possible that these were children of Gomer's lovers. This would make the name of the third child even more meaningful—"Not My People" is just another way of saying "Illegitimate."

Even if Hosea was the father of the three children, Gomer did not long remain faithful to him, but committed adultery with numerous lovers. According to the Law, Hosea had every right to divorce her, for she had broken the marriage covenant. Instead, because of his deep love for her, he extended grace and mercy to her. Even as she sought out fresh lovers, he continued to care for her needs, to guard her from harm. Finally, her sin became so flagrant that he could no longer tolerate it. He still loved her, but before he could accept her back into the marriage relationship, she would have to submit to an extended period of purification. Then, her harlotry left behind her, she and her longsuffering lover would be reunited. The parallels to Yahweh's experience with Israel are obvious. Israel had gone too far. She would have to be purified by chastisement before Yahweh could accept her back into the covenant bond. With this general framework in mind, let us notice how Hosea expanded on these themes of infidelity, punishment, and restoration.

### THE BROKEN COVENANT

Both Amos and Hosea were deeply concerned over Israel's complete lack of regard for the stipulations of the Mosaic covenant. Amos was appalled at the callous dishonesty and inhumanity he found in Israel. He was disgusted at the attempts to cover up this moral rottenness with a show of religious devotion. Doubtless, the social injustice in Israel was as disturbing to Hosea as it was to Amos, but his prophecies deal primarily with Israel's idolatry and her entangling alliances with pagan political powers. Both of these practices were clearly incompatible with the Mosiac covenant. Over the long period of his ministry, Hosea dealt with these two themes repeatedly.

The references to the Exodus from Egypt (*1:15; 11:1; 12:9, 13; 13:4*) recall the days of Yahweh's courtship and marriage of his bride Israel. The Exodus was the "brideprice," the gift that demonstrated Yahweh's love for this poor enslaved virgin. It was the basis of their marriage covenant. In the days of this idyllic "honeymoon," there was so much happiness, so much hope for the future. Yahweh and Israel *knew* each other intimately.

These early days of happiness had long since passed away. Israel had not been a chaste companion. Again and again she had broken the vows of the holy bond. Again and again the loving husband had forgiven

her and received her back into his bosom. But now there was no alternative. Her sin was so great that she must be put away. The bulk of the specific charges against Israel are contained in *chs. 4–14*. It is interesting to notice that these charges are set in the context of a lawsuit (see p. 204), almost as if Yahweh has brought Israel into a divorce court to dissolve their marriage formally. In *4:1* the prophet announces that "Yahweh has a controversy with the inhabitants of the land" (see also *4:4; 12:2*), and the trial is underway.

The fundamental charge is that "there is no knowledge of God in the land" (*4:1*). As we have seen, lack of "knowledge" did not mean simply that Israel was theologically ignorant. It meant that she no longer enjoyed a close personal relationship with him, that she had turned from following the fundamental tenets of the covenant. Amos had already pointed out the effects of this "lack of knowledge" on Israel's moral life. Hosea describes what it had done to their political and religious life.

*Israel's political sins.* The first of Israel's great political sins was the institution of the monarchy. As guardians of the Mosaic traditions, the prophets almost unanimously viewed the monarchy in an unfavorable light. In their eyes, the kings had usurped the position that rightfully belonged to Yahweh. Still, it was difficult to view it as altogether an invention of sin. Yahweh had given it at least formal approval by instructing Samuel to anoint Saul. And, the Ark of the Covenant might still be in Philistia if King David had not brought it back to Jerusalem as part of his great religious revival. The great temple itself probably never would have been built if Israel had continued to be ruled by judges. One could not say that the monarchy had never done anything to benefit religion. As a matter of fact, some reasonably faithful men had sat on the throne of Judah. But in Northern Israel—there was the problem! Every doubt about the monarchy had been realized in the northern kingdom. Practically all Israel's ills could be traced to her kings. This was proof that the monarchy was an undesirable institution. Yahweh may have given it grudging approval originally, but now it was clear that it deserved to be destroyed. Hosea's opposition to the monarchy may be seen in the following oracles. In the first, he declares the institution as it existed in Israel to be without any claim to divine sanction.

> They made kings, but not through me.
> They set up princes, but without my
> knowledge.        —*Hosea 8:4a*

In other oracles, he admits that Yahweh had granted Israel permission to have a king. Israel had felt that her national salvation depended on having a king, "like the nations." History had shown, however, that the major long-range effect of the monarchy was to deprive Israel of the continued protection of Yahweh.

> I will destroy you, O Israel;
> who can help you?
> Where now is your king, to save you;
> where are all your princes, to defend you—
> those of whom you said,
> "Give me a king and princes"?
> I have given you kings in my anger,
> and I have taken them away in my wrath.
> —*Hosea 13:9-11*

> I will love them no more;
> all their princes are rebels.
> —*Hosea 9:15b*

She had gotten a king and lost her God—hardly an even trade! Now she would lose even her king. As we have seen, the position of the kings who succeeded Jeroboam II was as unstable as "a chip on the face of the water" (*10:7*). In an oracle probably written during the year of anarchy that followed Jeroboam's death, Hosea describes the smoldering political situation.

> By their wickedness they make the king glad,
> and their princes by their treachery.
> They are all adulterers;
> they are like a heated oven,
> whose baker ceases to stir the fire,
> from the kneading of the dough
> until it is leavened.
> On the day of our king the princes
> became sick with the heat of wine;
> he stretched out his hand with mockers.
> For like an oven their hearts burn with
> intrigue;
> all night their anger smolders;
> in the morning it blazes like a flaming fire.
> All of them are hot as an oven,
> and they devour their rulers.
> All their kings have fallen;
> and none of them calls upon me.
> —*Hosea 7:3-7*

**Egyptian carving depicting representatives of weak nations begging an Egyptian royal servant for military aid.**

Even Menahem, who reigned all of ten years, had to rely on Assyrian help to do it (*II Kin. 15:9*). When the Assyrians turned on his successors, they ran to Aram and Egypt for help. What a pathetic sight this was. When Israel had trusted in Yahweh, she had been invincible. Now, trusting in her kings, she was like a frightened chicken, running blindly here and there in search of temporary safety. Hosea mocked the folly of her efforts to find help apart from Yahweh. Notice the metaphors he uses to describe Israel and her foolishness.

> When Ephraim* saw his sickness,
>     and Judah his wound,
> then Ephraim went to Assyria,
>     and sent to the great king.
> But he is not able to cure you
>     or heal your wound.     *—Hosea 5:13*

> Your love is like a morning cloud,
>     like the dew that goes early away.
>                                 *—Hosea 6:4*

> Ephraim is like a dove,
>     silly and without sense,
>     calling to Egypt, going to Assyria.
>                                 *—Hosea 7:11*

> For they have gone up to Assyria,
>     a wild ass wandering alone;
> Ephraim has hired lovers.  *—Hosea 8:9*

> Ephraim herds the wind,
>     and pursues the east wind all day long
> they multiply falsehood and violence;
>     they make a bargain with Assyria,
>     and oil is carried to Egypt. *—Hosea 12:1*

This desperate foreign policy was making Israel the laughingstock of the nations. Her neighbors were accepting her gifts and pledging their help. But, when the chips were down, they would desert her and laugh at her plight. Such a policy could lead only to ruin.

---

*Ephraim is another name for Israel. Samaria, Israel's capital, was located in the territory that had originally belonged to the tribe of Ephraim.

216

> Ephraim mixes himself with the peoples;
>     Ephraim is a cake not turned.
> Aliens devour his strength,
>     and he knows it not;
> gray hairs are sprinkled upon him,
>     and he knows it not.     *—Hosea 7:8-9*

> Israel is swallowed up;
>     already they are among the nations
>     as a useless vessel.
> Though they hire allies among the nations
>     I will soon gather them up.
> And they shall cease for a little while
>     from anointing king and princes.
>                                 *—Hosea 8:8, 10*

*Israel's religious sins.* Israel's political sickness could perhaps be traced to the monarchy, but her most serious problem was religious. From the making the golden calf at Sinai, Israel had repeatedly "gone after her lovers." But always before, she had come to her sense and returned to Yahweh. Now, she was completely reprobate. If one lover betrayed her, she turned to another, and another. She had completely given herself to other gods.

> My people inquire of a thing of wood,
>     and their staff gives them oracles.
> For a spirit of harlotry has led them astray,
>     and they have left their God to play the
>         harlot.
> They sacrifice on the tops of the mountains,
>     and make offerings upon the hills,
> under oak, poplar, and terebinth,
>     because their shade is good.
>                                 *—Hosea 4:12-13a*

The pagan religions Israel had taken up were designed to promote fertility. Sexual relations played a prominent part in these fertility religions. Some of the temples even had religious prostitutes. As one might expect, social and religious encouragement of extra-marital sexual relations had a tendency to lower the sexual morality of the nation. The situation had grown so bad that it was useless to try to correct it.

An Assyrian relief of a wild ass hunt.

Your daughters play the harlot
  and your brides commit adultery.
I will not punish your daughters
    when they play the harlot,
  nor your brides when they commit
    adultery;
for the men themselves go aside with harlots,
  and sacrifice with cult prostitutes,
and a people without understanding
    shall come to ruin.   —Hosea 4:13b-14

But morality had not been the only victim. Good common sense seemed also to have disappeared. Hosea was amazed at Israel's folly in worshiping idols. His contempt for idolatry in general and for the calf-worship in particular is seen in these two passages.

And now they sin more and more,
  and make for themselves molten images,
idols skilfully made of their silver,
  all of them the work of craftsmen.
Sacrifice to these, they say.

Men kiss calves! . . .         —Hosea 13:2
I have spurned your calf, O Samaria.
  My anger burns against them.
How long will it be
  till they are pure in Israel?
A workman made it;
  it is not God.
The calf of Samaria
  shall be broken to pieces.    —Hosea 8:5

As if it were not enough to forsake Yahweh for other gods, Israel added to his grief by crediting these pieces of silver and wood with providing the blessings that Yahweh himself had given.

For she said, "I will go after my lovers,
  who give me my bread and my water,
    my wool and my flax, my oil, and my drink.
And she did not know
  that it was I who gave her
  the grain, the wine, and the oil,
and who lavished upon her silver
  and gold which they used for Baal.
                    —Hosea 2:5, 8

The priests and the professional prophets —those who might have been able to save Israel—had contributed to her degeneration. As we noted in *Amos*, the priests were employees of the king. They discharged their duties with an eye for his favor and for personal gain. The professional prophets apparently were of the same stripe. Small wonder that Amos denied being one of them! Hosea indicts them with bearing a large share of the guilt for Israel's wholesale abandonment of true religion.

Yet let no one contend,
  and let none accuse,
    for with you is my contention, O priest.
You shall stumble by day,
  the prophet also shall stumble with you
    by night;
  and I will destroy your mother. . . .
They feed on the sin of my people;
  they are greedy for their iniquity.
And it shall be like people, like priest;

217

> I will punish them for their ways,
> and requite them for their deeds.
> —*Hosea 4:4-5, 8-9*

Clearly, Yahweh should have abandoned his faithless wife. No one—not even Israel herself—could have blamed him. But he loved her and he desperately longed for her to love him.

> I desire steadfast love and not sacrifice,
> the knowledge of God, rather than
> burnt offerings.　　　*—Hosea 6:6*

In these two lines, Hosea captured the essence of what God desires from men. Jesus quoted them at least twice during his public ministry (*Matthew 9:13; 12:7*). Neither Hosea nor Jesus meant that God was not interested in formal acts of worship. There is much in the Bible to show that he is. Yet, no amount of formal worship can replace sincere devotion and intimate, obedient acquaintance with the will of God.

### THE RENEWAL OF THE COVENANT BOND

Yahweh still loved Israel deeply, but their marriage was hopelessly on the rocks. What could be done? Obviously it would be pointless to plead with her. Neither would it do any good to woo her back with the promise of great blessings. She would claim Baal had given them to her.

> Like a stubborn heifer,
> Israel is stubborn;
> can Yahweh now feed them
> like a lamb in a broad pasture?
> *—Hosea 5:16*

Israel had gone too far for a gentle approach to succeed. She had sown the wind; now she must reap the whirlwind (*8:7*). But the whirlwind might bring her redemption.

Israel's only hope lay in renewing the covenant bond. The only way this could be done was by a return to the conditions of the original covenant. That is, the whole courtship, marriage, and honeymoon would have to be reenacted. Israel would have to undergo experiences corresponding to those of the Exodus and Wilderness wanderings. This meant, first of all, that Israel would have to go into bondage. That day was not far off. For part of Israel, it had already come. The Assyrian hordes would soon devour Israel as locusts devour a pasture.

> Set the trumpet to your lips,
> for a vulture is over the house of Yahweh,
> because they have broken my covenant,
> and transgressed my law.　*—Hosea 8:1*

> They shall not remain in the land of Yahweh;
> but Ephraim shall return to Egypt,
> and they shall eat unclean food in Assyria.
> For behold, they are going to Assyria;
> Egypt shall gather them,
> Memphis shall bury them.
> Nettles shall possess their precious
> things of silver;
> thorns shall be in their tents.
> *—Hosea 9:3, 6*

> They shall return to the land of Egypt,
> and Assyria shall be their king,
> because they have refused to return to me.
> The sword shall rage against their cities,
> consume the bars of their gates,
> and devour them in their fortresses.
> My people are bent on turning away
> from me;
> so they are appointed to the yoke,
> and none shall remove it.
> *—Hosea 11:5-7*

This period of captivity would be drab and discouraging. "For the children of Israel shall dwell many days without king or prince, without sacrifice or pillar, without ephod or teraphim" (*3:4*).

> And I will put an end to all her mirth,
> her feasts, her new moons, her sabbaths,
> and all her appointed feasts.
> *—Hosea 2:11*

Still, it would take Israel away from the temptations of culture. There would be no opportunity to deck herself with jewelry and run after Baal (*2:13*). Now, her sinfulness would be exposed for all to see.

> I will take away my wool and my flax,
>     which were to cover her nakedness.
> Now I will uncover her lewdness
>     in the sight of her lovers,
>     and no one shall rescue her out of my hand.
> >                             —*Hosea 2:9b-10*

Once she had been a faithful bride, then a fertile mother bearing faithful sons to Yahweh. Now, all her glory would "fly away like a bird"—

> no birth, no pregnancy, no conception! . . .
> Give them a miscarrying womb
>     and dry breasts . . .
> Even though they bring forth,
>     I will slay their beloved children.
> >                     —*Hosea 9:11b, 14b, 16b*

It was a terrible punishment—certainly no worse than Israel deserved, but still terrible. But Yahweh did not punish his beloved for sadistic pleasure. His only desire was that a period suffering might bring Israel to her senses. If it did, he would once again lead her from captivity and restore her to his bosom. In the following oracle describing Israel's restoration, notice the metaphors recalling the Exodus experience.

> Therefore, behold, I will allure her,
>     and bring her into the wilderness,
>     and speak tenderly to her.
> And there I will give her her vineyards,
>     and make the valley of Achor* a door of hope.
> And there she shall answer as in the days of her youth,
>     as at the time when she came out of the land of Egypt.
> >                             —*Hosea 2:14-15*

---

*The valley of Achor was a dry desert valley southwest of Jericho. Israel passed through this valley on her way into Canaan. In this verse and in *Isaiah 65:10*, the transformation from drabness to glory at the time of Israel's restoration is symbolized by the picture of this desert valley's becoming a fertile pasture land.

In that day Israel would renounce the Baals, the past would be forgiven and forgotten, and a new life under a renewed covenant would be begun.

> And I will betroth you to me in righteousness
>     and in justice, in steadfast love, and in mercy.
> I will betroth you to me in faithfulness; and
> you shall know Yahweh.
> And in that day, says Yahweh,
>     I will answer the heavens
>     and they shall answer the earth;
> and the earth shall answer the grain,
>         the wine, and the oil,
>     and they shall answer Jezreel;
>     and I will sow him for myself in the land.
> And I will have pity on Not pitied,
>     and I will say to Not my people,
>         "You are my people";
>     and he shall say, "Thou art my God."
> >                         —*Hosea 2:19-23*

Hosea was the first of the prophets to give expression to the twin themes of a new exodus and a new covenant. These became the dominant themes of the prophetic tradition, reaching their culmination in the new covenant of Jesus Christ.

Hosea's words were directed to the kingdom of northern Israel in the eighth century B.C. They spoke of specific historical events in Israel's past and immediate future. Still, there are few passages in the Old Testament that reveal the depths of God's love and mercy better than these oracles. Because of that, they are not bound to the eighth century. Their words, both of judgment and grace, speak to all men of faith in every age. Hosea himself furnishes us with a fitting conclusion to our discussion of his work:

> Whoever is wise, let him understand these things;
>     whoever is discerning, let him know them;
> for the ways of Yahweh are right,
>     and the upright walk in them,
>     but transgressors stumble in them.
> >                             —*Hosea 14:9*

219

| JUDAH | Related History | ISRAEL |
|---|---|---|
| **Ahaz** 20 (*16*) .......734–715<br>PROPHETS: *Isaiah*<br>*Micah* | 729: Tiglath-pileser crowned king of Asia.<br>727: Shalmaneser V becomes Assyrian emperor.<br>722: Sargon II succeeds Shalmaneser V. | **Hoshea** 9 ......732/1–723/2<br><br>721: Fall of Samaria |

CHRONOLOGICAL CHART: 922–842 B.C.

## The Fall of Samaria

Tiglath-pileser's highly successful western campaign was only one of a stirring succession. By the time of his death in 727 B.C., he had broken the power of Urartu. He had terrorized the Medes in Northern Iran. And, in 729 B.C., he had reached the summit of his attainments when, in Babylon, he was crowned ruler of all Asia. Before Tiglath-pileser, conquerors had usually been content to exact a tribute from the kings they defeated. This system eliminated a number of administrative problems, but it had a serious flaw in that it did nothing to break down nationalistic spirit. Naturally, no nation enjoyed paying tribute. From the moment the conquering armies left their borders, the defeated peoples would begin planning for the day when they could safely refuse to pay.

Tiglath-pileser was well aware of this weakness in the traditional system and devised a dramatic remedy for it. Instead of leaving the defeated peoples in their homeland, he deported them to Assyria, mixed them in with other captives, and then re-settled them in various parts of his empire. No national group was left intact. No sizable group of subjects remained in their native homelands. Thus, Tiglath-pileser deliber-

ately created an "homogenized" population, devoid of common religious, political, or national bonds, and placed them under Assyrian rulers. The practical wisdom of this policy is illustrated by what happened when Tiglath-pileser failed to deport Hoshea and the people of Samaria in 733.

Hoshea was a perfectly obedient vassal as long as Tiglath-pileser lived, but when the great suzerain died and his son Shalmaneser V came to power, Hoshea decided it was time for Israel to declare her independence. He apparently made some kind of alliance with So, the ruler of a minor Egyptian state in the delta region of the Nile (*II Kin. 17: 4*). Then, he witheld the annual tribute payment, the customary sign of rebellion.

Hoshea made a fatal error in assuming that Shalmaneser would not be as tough an overlord as his father. By the time he realized his mistake, Shalmaneser was already making preparations to invade Israel again. In 724, Hoshea traveled to the Assyrian court to try to patch things up. Shalmaneser was not interested in making any bargains with the treacherous pest. He clapped him into prison and set out for Samaria.

Samaria's natural defenses enabled her to hold out for two years, even without the Egyptian aid which never materialized. Shalmaneser died in 722, but the siege was continued by his successor, Sargon II (722–705). Samaria finally fell in 721 B.C. Its inhabitants—27,290 of them, according to Assyrian records—were carried away to Assyria, shuffled in with other captives, and resettled in Upper Mesopotamia and in "the cities of the Medes" (*II Kin. 17:6*). In place of the departed Israelites, captives from at least five other national groups were brought into Samaria. The Samaritans of the New Testament were descended from this mixed stock. They became worshipers of Yahweh when Sargon II sent a priest back from captivity to "teach them the law of the god of the land" (*II Kin. 17:27*). At the same time, however, they clung to many of the religious practices of their native countries. As a result, their religion was a strange mixture of Yahwism and a wide assortment of pagan beliefs and practices, including human sacrifice (See *II Kin. 17:27–41*). Undoubtedly, much of the anti-Samaritan prejudice on the part of Jews in New Testament times (*John 4:9*) was unjustified, but it is not too difficult to understand why orthodox Jews with a sense of history would consider Samaritans to be less than full-fledged brethren.

Thus, the kingdom of Israel passed forever from the pages of history. The writer of *Kings* has furnished a fitting epitaph:

> The people of Israel walked in all the sins which Jeroboam did; they did not depart from them, until Yahweh removed Israel out of his sight, as he had spoken by all his servants the prophets. So Israel was exiled from their own land to Assyria until this day.
>
> —*II Kings 17:22-23*

# 10

# Judah Under Assyrian Rule

*The effect of Assyrian domination on Judah's culture and religion*

THE KINGDOM of Judah managed to outlive her fallen sister by almost a century and a half. As long as she was alive, Israel captured most of the attention. Her rulers were more wicked, her sins more dramatic, her prophets more colorful. Because she was exposed to both Aram and Assyria, she was involved in more exciting wars. During most of these two centuries, Judah was plodding along her conservative way. The presence of the temple and a succession of reasonably good rulers kept her from the excesses of idolatry and immorality that prevailed in Israel. The socio-economic situation was far more stable in Judah. There was less difference between the very rich and the very poor, less inhuman exploitation of the kind that drew the attacks of Amos and, consequently, less ill feeling between classes.

The period of Assyrian conquest changed much of this. Suddenly, Judah was thrust into the main stream of world events. Ahaz's alliance with Tiglath-pileser saved the nation from destruction, but the subsequent

influx of Assyrian religion and culture loosed the same kinds of forces that had destroyed Israel. Moral and religious conditions were probably never as bad in Judah as they had been in Israel, but they were bad enough to receive the severe denunciation of the great prophets of the southern kingdom.

Judah did not accept Assyrian rule passively, at least not for long. King Hezekiah, supported by strong nationalistic sentiment and traditionally conservative religious elements, spent virtually all his long (715–687) reign struggling to throw off the galling Assyrian yoke. Manasseh, Hezehiah's son and Judah's most notoriously evil ruler (687–642), abandoned his father's dream of liberty and knuckled under the Assyrian rule once more. By the last quarter of the seventh century, Assyria had lost her grip on her empire and King Josiah (640/39–609/8) was left free by default.

Some of the greatest figures of world history lived during Judah's last 150 years: Tiglath-pileser III, Sargon II, Sennacherib, Nebuchadnezzar. From the point of view of the secular historian, Hezekiah and Josiah were less important; nevertheless, they left their mark. But the men from this period who, in the final analysis, have probably had the greatest influence on Judaeo-Christian civilization were not kings or generals. They

| JUDAH | Related History | ISRAEL |
|---|---|---|
| | | Pekah 4 (*20*) .....736–732/1 |
| **Ahaz** 20 (*16*) .......734–715 | | |
| 734: Alliance with Tiglath-pileser III. Assyrian gods imported. | | 733: Tiglath-pileser takes most of Israel |
| PROPHETS: *Isaiah* and *Micah* | 732: Damascus falls to Assyria. | **Hoshea** 9 ......732/1–723/2 |
| | 727: Shalmaneser V becomes Assyrian king | |
| | 722: Sargon II succeeds Shalmaneser V. | 721: Fall of Samaria |
| | 720: Sargon defeated in Babylon, puts down revolts in Hamath and Egypt. | |
| | 717: Sargon razes Carchemish. | |

**CHRONOLOGICAL CHART: THE REIGN OF AHAZ (732–715 B.C.)**

were the prophets of God: Isaiah, Micah, Jeremiah, and their colleagues. These men not only had an effect on numerous historical events; they provided an interpretation of the whole sweep of history, declaring that Yahweh was Lord of History and was using events and nations to work out his eternal purposes. In doing this, they reshaped the thinking of their people and gave them a vision of hope that sustained them through the dark years of Babylonian exile and enabled them to begin their national life anew in the expectation of a Messiah who would bring God's plan to fulfillment.

### THE SITUATION IN 734

To get a complete and unified picture of Judah under Assyrian rule, let us back up to the beginning of the reign of Ahaz. When Ahaz came to power in 734 B.C., Judah was having trouble on all sides. Edom and Philistia were inflicting heavy damage to the south and east (*II Chr. 28:17–18*). Even more serious was the Syro-Israelite coalition led by Rezin of Damascus and Pekah of Israel that was threatening to wreak total havoc with Judah. Ahaz could not stand to see his kingdom picked apart by his neighbors. In desperation, he began to think about appealing to Tiglath-pileser III for help. From a purely human viewpoint this may have seemed like the only alternative, but there was one man who disagreed, for he had a viewpoint that was not purely human. His name was Isaiah.

## The Prophet Isaiah

The career of the prophet Isaiah spanned the reigns of Ahaz and Hezekiah.[*] Unlike the great prophets of the northern kingdom, Isaiah enjoyed a favored place at the royal court. As a result, he was constantly embroiled in political controversy. He not only

---

[*]He also prophesied during the co-regency of Uzziah and Jotham (*Isa. 1:1*). Since his call to the prophetic ministry came in the same year Uzziah died, and since Jotham also died later that year, it is doubtful he did much of significance during their reigns.

**Assyrian lion-eagle creature similar to Isaiah's description of the seraphim.**

explained what was happening and foretold what was going to happen; he took a leading role in trying to make them happen.

### THE CALL TO BE A PROPHET

We do not know exactly when Isaiah began his prophetic ministry, but in 734, "the year that King Uzziah died" (*6:1*), he received a vision that marked his emergence as chief prophet in Judah. The vision occurred in the temple of Solomon. We are not told why Isaiah was in the temple. Ordinary worshippers were not allowed inside the temple itself. It has been suggested that Isaiah was a priest as well as a prophet. This may be true or it may simply be that Yahweh directed him to go to the temple. His reasons for being there are insignificant. What he saw there was unforgettable. He saw Yahweh sitting on a throne, "high and lifted up." His glory filled the temple like a

royal train. Above him were seraphim—fabulous creatures with heads of eagles, bodies of lions, and six wings. One of these otherworldly creatures called out (surely in a voice that matched its awesome appearance):

> Holy, holy, holy is Yahweh of hosts;
> the whole earth is full of his glory.
> —*Isaiah 6:3*

The unearthly voice shook the foundations and caused the temple to fill with smoke. The sights and sounds and odors and tremblings of this awesome experience completely overwhelmed Isaiah. In agony of spirit he cried:

> Woe is me! For I am lost; for I am a man of unclean lips, and I dwell in the midst of a people of unclean lips; for my eyes have seen the king, Yahweh of hosts! —*Isaiah 6:5*

Though his eyes had seen the Lord of Hosts, Isaiah made no attempt to describe Yahweh's appearance. He did not, because he could not. For Yahweh is the Holy One. In Isaiah's time, the word "holy" did not have quite the same meaning it does for us. We usually think of it as referring to moral purity. To Isaiah the word signified the radical otherness, the complete incomprehensibleness of God. Admittedly, "radical otherness" and "complete incomprehensibleness" are clumsy terms, but "holy" is a word that defies easy definition. To call God Holy is to confess that all symbols collapse, all words fail in any attempt to describe the indescribable.

As Isaiah lamented his "unclean lips," a seraph took a red-hot coal from the altar and touched it to his lips as a sign that his sins had been forgiven and his lips purified for the task that lay ahead. Until this moment, all the speaking had been done by the seraphim and the prophet. Now, Yahweh addressed his heavenly council, symbolized by the seraphim: "Whom shall I send, and who will go for us?" Isaiah, recognizing that the question was intended for him, answered simply, "Here am I! Send me." Many of the sermons that have been preached about Isaiah's inaugural vision have ended with this brave expression of the prophet's willingness to answer any call Yahweh might give. But the real nub of the passage is the part that informs the whole of Isaiah's ministry contained in *vv. 9–13*. Notice carefully Yahweh's commission to Isaiah:

> Go, and say to this people:
>    "Hear and hear, but do not understand;
>    see and see, but do not perceive."
> Make the heart of this people fat,
>    and their ears heavy,
>    and shut their eyes;
> lest they see with their eyes,
>    and hear with their ears,
> and understand with their hearts,
>    and turn and be healed.
>
> —*Isaiah 6:9-10*

How are we to understand this strange commission? Did Yahweh actually intend for Isaiah to work to make sure the people did not repent? Very likely, the sense of the passage is to be found by understanding these words to describe the *result* rather than the *purpose* of Isaiah's ministry. By declaring the word of God to rebellious Judah, he would drive them away. They would find the truth so hateful that, instead of repenting, they would accelerate on their headlong rush to destruction. His experiences with Ahaz at the time of the Syro-Israelite crisis provided dramatic confirmation of these words

## The Syro-Israelite Crisis

### "TAKE HEED, BE QUIET, DO NOT FEAR"

Isaiah's first confrontation with Ahaz took place "at the end of the conduit of the Upper Pool" (7:3). The exact location of this pool

is unknown. But it was somewhere near the Spring of Gihon, outside the eastern wall of the city. This spring was Jerusalem's primary source of water. Its waters were carried into a reservoir in the city (the Lower Pool) by means of an aqueduct. Part of the aqueduct was underground, but much of it was quite accessible. It would be a simple matter for an invader to cut off the water supply and just sit back and wait until the city was forced to surrender. When Isaiah appeared, Ahaz was probably trying to figure out some way to protect his water supply in case the city was attacked.

Isaiah was accompanied by his young son, Shearjashub. The boy's name meant "a remnant shall return." The names of Hosea's children foreshadowed the fate of Israel. Isaiah's little boy was a living symbol of the destruction that was to befall Judah. We can

The Spring of Gihon—a main
source of Jerusalem's water supply.

imagine that as he listened to Isaiah, Ahaz must have cast several anxious glances at the boy, puzzling over the significance of his ominous name.

In these troubled times Ahaz would surely have welcomed any council that made sense to him. Unfortunately, Isaiah's message did not fall into that category. Isaiah told Ahaz just to be calm and quit worrying about "these two smoldering stumps of fire-brands," Rezin and Pekah. If Ahaz would "take heed, be quiet, and fear not" Yahweh would destroy them before they could carry out their plan. (*Isaiah 1:4–9*) Yahweh was still Lord of History. Ahaz needed to place his trust in Yahweh, not in Tiglath-pileser.

### THE SIGN OF EMMANUEL

As we shall see, Ahaz' dedication to Yahweh left much to be desired. Probably, he gave Isaiah little reason to be optimistic, but Isaiah did not give up. A short time later, he confronted Ahaz again* and offered to furnish any sign the king could name, as proof that what he had said was true. Ahaz piously claimed that he did not wish to put Yahweh to the test (*7:15*), but Isaiah brushed this aside as just so much hypocrisy. In anger he declared that Yahweh would provide a sign whether Ahaz wanted it or not. The sign Isaiah promised was the famous sign of Emmanuel (*7:14–17*). A young woman would bear a son and call his name Emmanuel meaning "God is with us." Before that child was old enough to know the difference between good and evil, the kingdoms of Pekah and Rezin would be overrun and left desolate. Then Judah would suffer a similar fate. The Assyrians would descend upon the land like insects. The king of Assyria, whom Yahweh was using like a razor, would "sweep away the beard of Judah." (*7:18–25*)

---

*The text does not tell us where this meeting took place, but Isaiah's address to the House of David indicates that it was probably at the royal court.

The sign of Emmanuel is probably the most familiar of all Old Testament prophecies, for the reason that Matthew applied it to the conception and birth of Jesus. We do not wish to question the validity of this application in any way. For the present, however, let us confine ourselves to the task of understanding the significance of the prophecy for the time in which it was originally spoken. Since Isaiah definitely associated the birth and early years of the child with the Assyrian conquest in Palestine and Syria (*7:15–17*), it appears certain that he was referring to some child born about 733 B.C. Before we attempt to establish the identity of this child, a word about the manner of his birth is in order.

In the King James Version of the Bible, translated in A.D. 1611, the Hebrew word *almah* in *Isaiah 7:14* is translated "virgin." In the Revised Standard Version, published in 1952, it is translated "young woman." This change has caused a great deal of furor. Some have accused the translators of the Revised Standard Version of trying to undermine the doctrine of the virgin birth of Jesus. Actually, the word *almah* indicates *only* that a young woman has reached the age of sexual maturity—nothing more. She may or may not be a virgin; she may or may not be married. There is nothing in this passage to cause us to suppose that the young woman in question was a virgin. In fact, as we shall see, there is good reason to believe she was Isaiah's own wife who was already the mother of one child!

Part of the confusion can be eliminated by a better understanding of the term, "sign."* A sign was a visible confirmation or reminder of the prophetic message. It might be miraculous, but it did not have to be. Hosea's children, Jezreel, Not pitied, and Not my people, were signs. Isaiah's little

---

*See the discussion of signs on pp. 58f.

boy, "a remnant shall return," was a sign. There is no indication of anything supernatural about these children. Now, still another child would be born to remind Ahaz and the people of Judah that God was at work among them, even in the destructive activity of the Assyrians. The child himself was to be the sign; the details of his conception and birth were incidental. If there was anything supernatural involved, it was that Isaiah predicted the birth of a son before the mother became pregnant.* Thus, we cannot fault the translators of the Revised Standard Version for their use of "young woman" in this passage. On the contrary, we should be grateful to them. They have made us more aware of what the passage meant in Isaiah's time and they have saved us from the embarrassment of trying to explain *two* virgin births. Incidentally, the Revised Standard Version retains "virgin" in *Matthew 1:23* where both the Greek word *parthenos* and the unmistakable sense of the passage demand it.

Isaiah never specifically identifies either the young woman or the Emanuel child. Since the child was to be a sign to Ahaz, we may safely assume that the young woman was known to the king.† Many scholars believe that she was probably one of the women of his harem and that the child belonged to the House of David. We favor the view that identifies the young woman with Isaiah's own wife and Emmanuel with their son, Maher-shalal-hashbaz. Isaiah went out of his way to call attention to the birth of this child. Before his wife conceived, he took a large tablet and wrote on it before reliable witnesses "belonging to Maher-shalal-

hashbaz" (*8:1–2*). This tongue-twisting name—which, incidentally, is the longest in the Bible—had an ominous meaning: "the spoil speeds, the prey hastes." When the child was born, Isaiah removed whatever doubts there may have been about the significance of this cryptic name:

> Before the child knows how to cry "my father" or "my mother" the wealth of Damascus (Syria) and the spoil of Samaria (Israel) will be carried away before the king of Assyria. —*Isaiah 8:4*

The substance of this prediction is identical to the one made about the Emmanuel child in *7:16.* Unless we suppose there were two sign-children, it seems reasonable to conclude that Emmanuel and Maher-shalal-hashbaz were one and the same child. The chief difficulty with this theory, of course, lies in the obvious fact that Emmanuel and Maher-shalal-hashbaz are decidedly different names. And yet, both names signified the same thing: God was actively present in the affairs of history and would use the king of Assyria to defeat the Syro-Israelite coalition.

This slight difficulty is more than offset by the fact that the story of the birth of Maher-shalal-hashbaz (*8:1–4*) is found in exactly the place we should expect to find an account of the birth of Emmanuel. Immediately proceeding is the announcement that the child is to be born and the description of what may be expected after his birth (*7:10–25*). Immediately following are two oracles that clearly assume that Emmanuel has already been born and warn the nations to be ready for eminent destruction (*8:5–8, 9–10*). If Maher-shalal-hashbaz is Emmanuel, the position of the birth story is perfectly logical; if he is not, we are faced with the puzzling task of trying to figure out why Isaiah (or his followers) would insert an account of the birth of the second unheralded child at this point and completely neglect to mention the birth of Emmanuel elsewhere

---

*Actually, the Hebrew text of this passage may be translated "a young woman *is with child* and will bear." (See RSV footnote), but we feel the usual "shall conceive" is probably correct.

†In the Hebrew text of this verse, Isaiah refers to the mother as *the* young woman, indicating that he had a specific woman in his mind.

in his writings. A final item in support of this theory is found in *8:18* in the context of a passage in which Isaiah seems to be summing up his testimony to Ahaz (see *v. 16*). The prophet says, "I and the children whom Yahweh has given me are signs and portents in Israel." It is obvious from the preceding verses that Isaiah considered the Emmanuel child to be the most important "sign" that had been given. If this child had not been included among "the children whom Yahweh has given me," Isaiah almost surely would have made some mention of that fact. Admittedly, these arguments do not add up to absolute proof that Maher-shalal-hashbaz was the Emmanuel child, but we feel the evidence is sufficiently strong to make this the most reasonable explanation of these passages.

### AHAZ SUBMITS

In spite of the "signs and portents" Isaiah offered Ahaz, the king simply did not have enough faith to keep calm and place his trust in Yahweh, so he stripped the temple and the palace of their treasures and sent them to Tiglath-pileser begging him to attack Rezin and Pekah. The language of Ahaz's request–"I am your servant and your son" (*II Kin. 16:7*)–makes it clear that this was not a mere hiring of soldiers or even an alliance between peers. It was a formal submission to Assyrian rule in return for protection. (*II Kin. 16:7*). Tiglath-pileser leveled Damascus and took most of Israel. This relieved the immediate pressure from Judah's neck, but in its place she donned the yoke that she would wear for over a century.

In surrendering Judah's independence, Ahaz also surrendered the divine council of the prophet Isaiah. We can imagine that the king must have tried to defend his actions by pointing out the damage that Pekah and Rezin had already inflicted on Judah (*II Chron. 28:5–8*). In times like these, religious faith had to take a back seat to the harsh realities of war and politics. Perhaps Isaiah began to distrust the validity of what he had been saying. In any case, Yahweh warned him "not to walk in the way of his people" (*8:11*). Their view of things was completely out of focus. They feared Syria and Israel, when the real danger was Yahweh. They sought aid from Assyria, when Yahweh was their only hope. Now, because of their stubborn refusal to listen to his prophets, Yahweh would become "a rock of stumbling to both houses of Israel" (*8:14*).

Thus reassured that he had spoken the truth, Isaiah decided to leave Ahaz to his own devices. There is good reason to suppose that he turned much of his attention to a community of prophets that had grown up around him. All of the material in chapter 8 is introduced by such statements as "Then Yahweh said to me" (See *vv. 1, 5, 11*), suggesting that Isaiah may have been recounting his experiences and oracles to a group of his disciples who were then to "bind up the testimony" for the benefit of future generations (*8:16*). When he had finished telling of his fruitless talks with Ahaz, he announced his "retirement" from the court. Isaiah would trouble Ahaz no more. If the king wanted to consult "the wizards who chirp and mutter" (*8:19*), that was his business. If he wanted guidance from Yahweh, he could reflect on the signs Isaiah had already given.

### THE MESSIANIC KING

If Isaiah was disappointed with Ahaz's response to his message, he did not for a moment think that Yahweh's eternal purpose for his people had been frustrated. Since the glorious days of David and Solomon, the people of God had treasured a vision of a king who would sit upon the throne of David in Jerusalem and exercise a strong but benevolent rule over all the nations. This hope had been nurtured in the regular temple worship by the singing of such hymns as *Psalm 72*. Imagine the thrill of expectation the men of Israel must have felt as they chanted the words of this song!

> Give the king thy justice, O God,
> and thy righteousness to the royal son!
> May he judge thy people with righteousness,
> and thy poor with justice!
> Let the mountains bear prosperity for the
> people,
> and the hills, in righteousness!
> May he defend the cause of the poor of
> the people,
> give deliverance to the needy,
> and crush the oppressor!
> May he live while the sun endures,
> and as long as the moon, throughout all
> generations!
> May he be like rain that falls on the mown
> grass,
> like showers that water the earth!
> In his days may righteousness flourish,
> and peace abound, till the moon be no
> more!
>
> May he have dominion from sea to sea,
> and from the River to the ends of the earth!
> May his foes bow down before him,
> and his enemies lick the dust!
>
> May the kings of Tarshish and of the isles
> render him tribute,
> may the kings of Sheba and Seba bring gifts!
> May all kings fall down before him,
> all nations serve him! . . .
> May his name endure for ever,
> his fame continue as long as the sun!
> May men bless themselves by him,
> all nations call him blessed!
>
> —*Psalm 72:1-11, 17*

Even David and Solomon had not measured up to this ideal, and Ahaz must have seemed about as far from it as a king could get. But Isaiah did not abandon the hope despite the disappointing performance of past and present kings. Instead, he looked forward to "the latter time" (*9:1*) when the dross and deadly alloys that were crippling the nation

would be purged and a scion of David would begin his long-awaited reign. It is impossible to say just when Isaiah expected this "latter time" to begin, but it seems clear that the king he described was a messianic figure. He, too, could rightfully be called Emmanuel, for he would show, in the fullest possible measure, what it meant for God to be with man. Hear Isaiah's words concerning this Anointed One, this Messiah, this Christ* who was to come:

> There shall come forth a shoot from the
> stump of Jesse,
> and a branch shall grow of out his roots
> And the Spirit of Yahweh shall rest upon him,
> the spirit of wisdom and understanding,
> the spirit of counsel and might,
> the spirit of knowledge and the fear of
> Yahweh.
> And his delight shall be in the fear of
> Yahweh.
> He shall not judge by what his eyes see,
> or decide by what his ears hear;
> but with righteousness he shall judge
> the poor,
> and decide with equity for the meek
> of the earth;
> and he shall smite the earth with the rod
> of his mouth,
> and with the breath of his lips he shall
> slay the wicked.
> Righteousness shall be the girdle of his waist,
> and faithfulness the girdle of his loins.
>
> . . . . . . . . . . . . .
>
> In that day the root of Jesse shall stand as an ensign to the peoples; him shall the nations seek, and his dwellings shall be glorious.
>
> In that day Yahweh will extend his hand yet a second time to recover the remnant which is left of his people, from Assyria, from Egypt, from Pathros ,from Ethiopia, from Elam, from Shinar, from Hamath, and from the coastlands of the sea.
>
> —*Isaiah 11:1-5, 10-11*

---

*\*Messiah* is the Hebrew word for Anointed One; *Christ* is the Greek equivalent.

For to us a child is born,
    to us a son is given;
and the government will be upon his
        shoulder,
    and his name will be called
Wonderful Counselor, Mighty God,
    Everlasting Father, Prince of Peace.
Of the increase of his government and
        of peace
    there will be no end,
upon the throne of David, and over his
        kingdom,
    to establish it, and to uphold it
with justice and with righteousness
    from this time forth and for evermore.
The zeal of Yahweh of hosts will do this.
                                —*Isaiah 9:6-7*

## The Effects of Assyrian Domination

### RELIGIOUS APOSTASY

The disastrous effect of Ahaz' submission to Assyrian rule began to be seen almost immediately. Ordinarily, when one nation conquered another, the defeated nation was expected to pay homage to the god(s) of the victor. Given the typical pagan outlook toward gods, this was not particularly offensive. The defeated people were seldom forced to give up their own gods; they simply added the new god to their list of deities deserving of respect. Besides, the outcome of the battle had proven that this new god had real power. If he could prove useful to them, they would be happy to pay him a reasonable amount of homage. This practice of accepting whatever one liked about various religions is called *syncretism*. The covenant with Yahweh, of course, specifically repudiated this kind of thinking. One did not worship Yahweh as one among many, even as the greatest among many. When one entered the covenant with Yahweh, all other gods were to be renounced forever. This was the first commandment of the Decalogue. If it were violated, one could begin to look for

trouble. Failure to keep this basic commandment had been the root of most of Northern Israel's problems. Judah had flirted with the Baals and the Asherim, but she had remained relatively chaste. Ahaz led her to her first major apostasy.

Even before the submission to Assyria, Ahaz had not made even the slightest pretense of loyalty to Yahweh. The Chronicler tells us (*II Chr. 28:2–4*) that he made molten images for the Baals, burned incense in the valley of Hinnom (Gehenna), and burned his own sons as an offering, presumably to the Ammonite god Moloch. After Rezin defeated him, he began to worship the gods of Damascus (*II Chr. 28:22–23*). With this kind of background, it is easy to see why Ahaz readily imported aspects of Assyrian religion into Jerusalem. It was customary for vassal kings to appear before their masters regularly, to pay tribute and to renew the oath of allegiance. Ahaz paid his first official visit of this sort while Tiglath-pileser was still in Damascus after his successful conquest there. While he was on this mission, Ahaz had occasion to see an altar that fascinated him. The scriptures are not explicit, but the altar was probably one used by Tiglath-pileser in his worship of Ashur. If this was the case, Ahaz would have been expected to do exactly what he did. At any rate, he made a scale model of the altar, "exact in all its details," and sent it back to Jerusalem with instructions to Urijah the priest to duplicate it. When Ahaz returned to Jerusalem, the worship in the temple was modified so that Yahweh was forced to share his sacred dwelling with the gods of this foreign altar. The Molten Sea and the lavers were remodeled to suit the new pattern of worship, and the great bronze altar was moved from its hallowed location to give a more prominent place to the new altar. The king's private entrance to the temple was sealed off. He would not be needing it now that he was worshiping another god. It does not take much imagination to visualize the reaction of those elements that still clung loyally to the Mosaic faith!

### SOCIAL CONDITIONS

The breakdown of loyalty to the First Commandment had its effects on the rest of the covenant's stipulations. The injustice and oppression that had been so characteristic of Israel began to infect her more righteous southern sister; and all the while, the professional religionists gave their sanctimonious approval to the deadly shift in Judah's affairs. As long as the people were keeping the feast days and making their regular sacrifices, they seem to have reasoned, it was permissible to overlook minor faults like robbing the poor or offering children as sacrifices to Moloch. As one might expect, this

Round-topped Assyrian altar
from the time of Sargon II.

decay of religion and morals—the two are never really separate in the Bible—received the full attention of the inspired prophets.

### ISAIAH'S "HATEFUL MESSAGE"

Yahweh had commanded Isaiah to preach a hateful message. His withering attack on Judah's religious and social conditions, found in *chs. 1–5*, clearly demonstrate that he was an obedient servant.

*"Let us argue to the verdict."* The familiar idea of the lawsuit between Yahweh and his people appears regularly in these chapters. In the opening oracle, the witnesses are summoned: "Hear, O heaven, and give ear, O earth," (*1:2*). This is followed by a series of indictments against Judah for her increasing infidelity to the covenant. The true sense of the famous words of *1:18*—"Come now, let us reason together"—would be better expressed by "let us argue to a verdict." Yahweh is not inviting his people to sit down around a conference table and talk things over. He is accusing them before heaven and earth of having broken the covenant and denouncing the sentence that is bound to fall on them. This idea is expressed even more clearly in *3:13*:

> Yahweh has taken his place to content,
> he stands to judge his people.

*In the vineyard of the Lord.* The well-known Song of the Vineyard (*5:1–7*) has some of the characteristics of a lawsuit oracle. The prophet sings of his tireless and loving efforts to care for his vineyard and laments that it has yielded nothing but wild grapes. He calls on the men of Judah to witness that he has not been at fault. Then, it being clear that the fault lies with the vineyard, he renders his verdict.

> And now I will tell you
>     what I will do to my vineyard.
> I will remove its hedge,
>     and it shall be devoured;

231

I will break down its wall,
   and it shall be trampled down.
I will make it a waste;
   it shall not be pruned or hoed,
   and briers and thorns shall grow up;
I will also command the clouds
   that they rain no rain upon it.
                —*Isaiah 5:5-6*

The application is obvious:

For the vineyard of Yahweh of hosts
   is the house of Israel
and the men of Judah
   are his pleasant planting.
                —*Isaiah 5:7*

Isaiah drives his point home even more emphatically with a powerful bit of word play. Pronounce the Hebrew words in parenthesis and try to imagine the way these words must have rung in his hearers' ears:

He looked for justice (*mishpat*),
   but behold, bloodshed (*mispach*);
for righteousness (*zedaqah*),
   but behold a cry (*ze'akah*).
                —*Isaiah 5:7b*

In these oracles of denunciation, Isaiah calls attention to the wild grapes that were spoiling Yahweh's vineyard. The sins he lists are ominously similar to those that destroyed the social fabric of the northern kingdom, and Isaiah's attacks are scarcely less caustic than those of Amos. The judicial system had been corrupted by men who auctioned off justice to the highest bidder.

Every one loves a bribe
   and runs after gifts.
They do not defend the fatherless,
   and the widow's cause does not come to
     them.

. . . . . . . . . . . . .

(They) acquit the guilty for a bribe,
   and deprive the innocent of his right!
             —*Isaiah 1:23; 5:23*

The breakdown of legal restraints led naturally to the exploitation of the poor by the favored classes. Even the elders and princes

of Judah, who should have been the moral leaders, had succumbed to the temptation to get rich at the expense of the helpless (*3:14–15*). Judah's moral standards had been turned upside down (*5:20*). The hero was no longer the man who saved the orphan or widow from abuse, but the man who could hold his liquor best (*5:22*). It would not be fair to call the prophets women-haters, but both Amos and Isaiah recognized that ambitious wives can drive their husbands deeper and deeper into sin. Amos described the women of Samaria as "cows of Bashan" and spoke of the day when they would be led away with hooks in their noses (*Amos 4:1–3*). Isaiah was a bit more flattering in his description of the women of Judah, but the vivid picture of the future that he painted for them makes Amos' oracles seem tame by comparison:

Because the daughters of Zion are haughty
   and walk with outstretched necks,
     glancing wantonly with their eyes,
mincing along as they go,
   tinkling with their feet;
Yahweh will smite with a scab
   the heads of the daughters of Zion,
   and Yahweh will lay bare their secret
     parts.

. . . . . . . . . . . . .

Instead of perfume there will be rottenness;
   and instead of a girdle, a rope;
and instead of well-set hair, baldness;
and instead of a rich robe, a girding
    of sackcloth;
instead of beauty, shame.
           —*Isaiah 3:16-17, 24*

*The Day of Yahweh.* Throughout the long history of God's people, from ancient Israel to the present, men have tried to cover up their social and moral failures by emphasizing the importance of external details. At best, this results in a sterile legalism. At worst, it becomes sickening hypocrisy. It was perhaps true that Judah would never be able to match Israel for sheer vileness. Still, the contrast between her moral life and her unctuous display of piety were enough to cause Isaiah to liken her to the ancient sisters in wickedness, Sodom and Gomorrah.

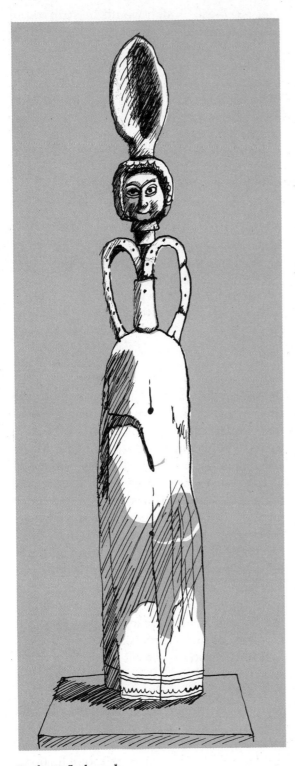

Perfume flask made out of an ivory tusk.

Hear the word of Yahweh;
  you rulers of Sodom!
Give ear to the teaching of our God,
  you people of Gommorrah!
What to me is the multitude of your
    sacrifices?
  says Yahweh;
I have had enough of burnt offerings of rams
  and the fat of fed beasts;
I do not delight in the blood of bulls,
  or of lambs, or of he-goats.

. . . . . . . . . . . . . . .

Bring no more vain offerings;
  incense is an abomination to me.
New moon and sabbath and the calling of
    assemblies—
  I cannot endure iniquity and solemn
    assembly.
Your new moons and your appointed feasts
  my soul hates;
they have become a burden to me,
  I am weary of bearing them.
When you spread forth your hands,
  I will hide my eyes from you;
even though you make many prayers,
  I will not listen;
  your hands are full of blood.
Wash yourselves; make yourselves clean;
  remove the evil of your doings
  from before my eyes;
cease to do evil,
  learn to do good;
seek justice,
  correct oppression;
defend the fatherless,
  plead for the widow.
                    —Isaiah 1:10-11, 13-17

The similarity between these early oracles of Isaiah and the oracles of Amos continues as Isaiah picks up the theme of the Day of Yahweh. As we have said before (see p. 208), the Day of Yahweh was apparently regarded by the pre-literary prophets as the day when Yahweh would bring great glory to Israel. With one startling oracle, Amos transformed it into a day when Yahweh would unleash the full force of his wrath upon his people (*Amos 5:18–20*). Amos' view of the matter came to be generally accepted. Isaiah speaks of the coming day as if it were widely recognized to be a day of judgment, not a day of triumph. On that day, "All that is lifted up and high"—the cedars of Lebanon, fortified cities, ships of Tarshish, human inventiveness—the insignificance of all these things would be made manifest.

> And the haughtiness of man shall be
>    humbled,
>   and the pride of men shall be brought
>      low;
>   and Yahweh alone will be exalted in that
>      day.
> And the idols shall utterly pass away
> And men shall enter the caves of the rocks
>    and the holes of the ground,
> from before the terror of Yahweh,
>    and from the glory of his majesty,
>    when he rises to terrify the earth.
> —*Isaiah 2:17-19*

*"His hand is stretched out still."* The Day of Yahweh lay beyond the immediate horizon. Still, Yahweh had his plans for Judah. Isaiah reminded his hearers that when Northern Israel persisted in her wickedness, Yahweh

> . . . stretched out his hand against them and
>    smote them,
>   and the mountains quaked;
> and their corpses were as refuse in the
>    midst of the streets.     —*Isaiah 5:25*

Then, in a voice that must have echoed with tones of doom, Isaiah solemnly warned:

> For all this his anger is not turned away
>    and his hand is stretched out still.
> —*Isaiah 5:25*

First there would come the kind of internal chaos that had marked the last days of Is-

rael (*3:1–12*). Judah would be stripped of responsible military and political leadership. Boys would try to fill roles that demanded men. Social conditions would disintegrate even further. And finally, when the nation lay weak and helpless, Yahweh's hand that was stretched out still would

> . . . raise a signal for a nation afar off,
>    and whistle for it from the ends of the
>      earth;
> and lo, swiftly, speedily it comes!

. . . . . . . . . . . . . . . . .

> their arrows are sharp,
>    all their bows bent,
> their horses' hoofs seem like flint,
>    and their wheels like the whirlwind.
> Their roaring is like a lion,
>    like young lions they roar;
> they growl and seize their prey,
>    they carry it off, and none can rescue.
> —*Isaiah 5:26, 28-29*

### MICAH

Isaiah was not alone in his attacks on the sins of the nation. Down in Moresheth, near the old Philistine city of Gath (*1:14–15*), there lived a prophet named Micah. Moresheth was not far from the little village of Tekoa, where Amos had lived a few years before. Perhaps Micah's passion for social justice and religious genuineness was a reflection of some influence the work of the fiery prophet of the northern kingdom may have had on him. But whether or not there was any direct influence, Amos would have had no cause to be ashamed of Micah. He holds an honorable place in the prophetic tradition of social criticism.

Isaiah began his assault on the moral and spiritual tradition of Judah with the language of a lawsuit: "Come let us argue to a verdict." As we stated earlier (p. 204), the best example of the use of a lawsuit imagery by the prophets is found in *Micah 6:1–8*. The prophet calls the courtroom to order with these words: "Arise, plead your case to the mountains and let the hills hear your voice" (*6:1*). Then, in order to underline what is to follow, the plaintiff (Yahweh) recalls the mighty acts he has performed on behalf of his people (*vv. 3–5*). What is the proper response to these acts of grace? Is it increased burnt-offerings, gifts of "rivers of oil." child sacrifice—"the fruit of my body for the sin of my soul"? No! Yahweh takes no delight in these things.

> He has showed you, O man, what is good;
>     and what does Yahweh require of you
> but to do justice, and to love kindness,
>     and to walk humbly with your God?
>                         —*Micah 6:8*

As the accusations against the defendant are presented, it becomes painfully evident how far short of this ideal Judah had fallen.

As a dweller in a small rural community, Micah was convinced, with a good deal of justification, that most of the sickness in Israel and Judah had spread from the sin-infested cities:

> What is the transgression of Jacob?
>     Is it not Samaria?
> And what is the sin of the house of Judah?
>     Is it not Jerusalem?     —*Micah 1:5*

When he began his ministry, Samaria had not yet fallen, and many of his most biting oracles are directed against the northern kingdom. But the sins of the North were the sins of the South, for the toxic pus of Samaria's incurable wound had oozed to the gates of Jerusalem, infecting Judah with the same loathsome disease (*1:9*). Its sores were visible everywhere. Greedy and callous land-grabbers were uprooting weak and defenseless· farmers, and tossing them off fields their families had tilled for generations (*2:1–2*). The leaders of the nation—the ones to whom the oppressed should have been able to look for redress—were just as bad. They bought and sold justice as if it were a cheap trinket (*3:1, 11*). Instead of acting as shepherds to protect their help-less flocks from harm, they were like fiendish cannibals

> who eat the flesh of my people,
>     and flay their skin from off them,
> and break their bones in pieces,
>     and chop them up like meat in a kettle,
>     like flesh in a cauldron.     —*Micah 3:3*

In Micah's eyes, the godly man had perished from the earth, and those that were left were out to cut their neighbors' throats (*7:2–3*). His pessimistic lament over the moral state of the population reaches a climax in these cynical words:

> The best of them is like a brier,
>     the most upright of them a thorn
>         hedge. . . .
> Put no trust in a neighbor,
>     have no confidence in a friend;
> guard the doors of your mouth
>     from her who lies in your bosom.
>                         —*Micah 7:4, 5*

Micah was no more popular in his day than Amos had· been in his (see *Amos 7: 10–13*). When the people urged him not to preach these disturbing words (*2:6*), he sarcastically observed that the only kind of preacher they would accept would be one who preached in favor of drunkenness (*2: 11*) and who could be persuaded to go easy on the local sins by the presence of a few extra shekels in the collection plate (*3:5*). Micah simply was not that kind of man. The will and word of Yahweh filled his heart. He had no choice but to proclaim it:

> But as for me, I am filled with power,
>     with the Spirit of Yahweh,
>     and with justice and might,
> to declare to Jacob his transgression
>     and to Israel his sin.     —*Micah 3:8*

Proclaiming the full will of Yahweh meant destroying the false illusion that no harm could come to Jerusalem. If the leaders of the nation continued to "build Zion with blood and Jerusalem with wrong" (*3:10*),

**Ancient wooden model of a man plowing with oxen.**

warned Micah, Jerusalem would be destroyed and the hill of the temple grown over with trees.

> Therefore because of you
>> Zion shall be plowed as a field;
> Jerusalem shall become a heap of ruins,
>> and the mountain of the house a wooded
>> height.                    —*Micah 3:12*

Somehow, Micah managed to burn these words into the heart of the men of Judah. Although we usually think of Isaiah as being far more important than Micah, the prophet Jeremiah quoted these same words a century later and gave Micah the credit for having inspired the sweeping reforms carried out by King Hezekiah, the son and successor of Ahaz (*Jer. 26:18–19*).

### ZION SHALL BE REDEEMED

Yahweh's case against his people had been presented. Judah was found guilty without excuse, and the sentence was an-

nounced. As always, however, the prophets held out a ray of hope. The hand of Yahweh was held out, not just to punish, but to heal. The chastisement Jerusalem would suffer at the hands of foreign nations would cleanse her of contaminating dross and alloys (*1: 25*) and would restore her to her place as queen of the nations. From this exalted position, she would proclaim the word of Yahweh to all people.

> It shall come to pass in the latter days
>> that the mountain of the house of Yahweh
> shall be established as the highest of the
>> mountains,
>> and shall be raised up above the hills;
> and peoples shall flow to it,
>> and many nations shall come, and say:
> "Come, let us go up to the mountain of
>> Yahweh,
>> to the house of the God of Jacob;
> that he may teach us his ways
>> and we may walk in his paths."

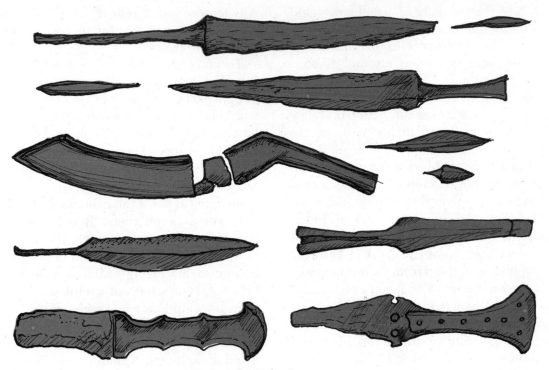

**Swords, arrowheads, spears, and daggers found in Palestine.**

For out of Zion shall go forth the law,
    and the word of Yahweh from Jerusalem.
He shall judge between many peoples,
    and shall decide for strong nations afar off;
and they shall beat their swords into
      plowshares,
    and their spears into pruning hooks;
nation shall not lift up sword against nation,
    neither shall they learn war any more;
but they shall sit every man under his vine
    and under his fig tree,
    and none shall make them afraid;
    for the mouth of Yahweh of hosts has
      spoken.

          *—Micah 4:1-4 (Isaiah 2:2-4)*

It would be difficult to overestimate the significance of these words of assurance, following as they do on the heels of unrelenting prophecies of doom. In the days when the judges had ruled Israel, the memory of the Sinaitic Covenant was still fresh in the national consciousness. Israel understood that if she violated the stipulations of the covenant, she could expect the wrath of Yahweh to fall upon her. She knew that her security depended on her fidelity. The theological developments that occurred in the time of David and Solomon (see page 164) had the unfortunate effect of destroying much of this sense of mutual obligation. Israel was so dazzled by the promises of an everlasting Davidic dynasty and an eternal Jerusalem that, in time, she forgot that these promises had conditions attached to them. If this blind optimism had never been challenged, the repeated defeats Judah suffered at the hands of Assyria and Babylonia, culminating in the complete destruction of Jerusalem in 586 B.C., might well have meant the end of the religion of Yahweh. "Why," they surely would have asked, "should the people continue to worship a god whose promises were obviously worthless?" The prophets furnished an answer to this question before it could be asked. In the process,

237

they gave the theology of Israel a new and profoundly important dimension.

Isaiah, the chief figure in this theological redevelopment, made no attempt to soft-peddle the promises Yahweh had made to David. They were in no sense an embarrassment to him. His strong conviction that they were true is reflected in his assurance to Ahaz that he need have no fear of Pekah and Rezin. The problem was not that Yahweh was unable to keep his promises concerning Jerusalem and the house of David; it was that Ahaz and the men of Judah would not give him a chance. If they would only place their complete trust in Yahweh, he would deliver them from their oppressors as he had in the days of Israel's childhood, but since they would not trust him, and since they had no regard for their part of the covenant, he would "stretch out his hand" against his people, cutting off the house of David and turning Jerusalem into a heap of ruins, but—and this is the key—this would not mean that he had turned his back on his promises. On the contrary this punishment was to serve as a refiner's fire that would yield a remnant worthy to receive these glorious promises.

To make this line of reasoning convincing, Isaiah emphatically reaffirmed what the people of God had always believed, but would be in danger of mistrusting when calamity came: that Yahweh is Sovereign Lord of History. They had believed it and had concluded that Yahweh would never allow them to be destroyed. Isaiah reaffirmed it and cited as proof the eminent destruction that would befall them. It was Yahweh's lordship over men and events that enabled him to use Assyria as "the rod of his anger" to punish his erring children (10:5–19). When Assyria's term of useful service was over, he would cast her aside and raise up another nation to help him carry out his eternal purpose. This eternal purpose consisted of nothing less than the fulfillment of his promises to his covenant people. Thus, Isaiah and his colleagues provided hope in the face of tragedy, hope that enabled the people of God to survive the agony of exile.

| JUDAH | Related History |
|---|---|
| **Hezekiah** 29 . . . . . . . . . . . . . . . . . . . .715–687<br>PROPHETS: *Isaiah* and *Micah* | 714: Sargon conquers Urartu<br>711: Fall of Ashdod<br>705: Sennacherib becomes king of Assyria. |
| 705: Hezekiah leads build-up of revolutionary forces.<br>701: Sennacherib puts down rebellion. | 701–700: Sennacherib puts down Babylonian revolt.<br>694–689: Babylon and Elam revolt again.<br>689: Sennacherib destroys Babylon, is free to come west again. |
| 689: Hezekiah ready to revolt again.<br>688: Sennacherib's second attack on Judah*; troops decimated by plague. Jerusalem is saved. | 681: Sennacherib is slain by his sons. Esarhaddon becomes king of Assyria. |

## CHRONOLOGICAL CHART: THE PERIOD OF HEZEKIAH (715–687 B.C.)

*Neither the scriptures or Assyrian records make it absolutely clear that Sennacherib made two campaigns against Hezekiah. On the basis of our present information, however, this seems to be the most reasonable hypothesis. The problems involved in reconstructing the situation and the reasons for adopting this hypothesis are discussed briefly on page 246.

Jerusalem would be destroyed for the sins of its rulers, who were themselves of the House of David, but "in the latter days" a prince of David's lineage would come forth from Bethlehem, a ruler "whose origin is from of old, from ancient days" (*Micah 5:2*). This Messiah would gather up the purified remnant of Israel and establish the eternal kingdom of God.

## The Fight for Freedom: Hezekiah

If it was puzzling that Uzziah and Jotham could have a grandson and son like Ahaz, it is downright amazing that Ahaz could have a son like Hezekiah. Ahaz was a confirmed syncretist, worshiping any god that came along and going to extreme length in his worship, sacrificing and burning incense (and children) "on the high places and on the hills and under every green tree" (*II Chr. 28:4*). Hezekiah, in sharp contrast, was thoroughly devoted to Yahweh, "so that there was none like him among all the kings of Judah after him nor among those who were before him" (*II Kin. 18:5*). Ahaz was content to be an Assyrian vassal as long as he was able to maintain his own position and live in peace. Hezekiah found it impossible to wear the Assyrian yoke and spent the whole of his reign trying to cast it off. Judah was no match for the mighty Assyrians but under Hezekiah (and Isaiah), she gave them a run for their money.

### THE WORLD SITUATION

When Hezekiah came to the throne, Sargon II, the son of Tiglath-pileser III and a brother of Shalmaneser IV, was ruler of Assyria. When Tiglath-pileser died, a number of nations he had dominated revolted. It took the better part of the reigns of both Shalmaneser and Sargon to whip these rulers back into line. Apparently, there was some strong feeling between Sargon and his brother, and it may be that there were some

Head of Sargon II of Assyria from Khorsabad.

internal problems which made it even more difficult to attend to the troublesome business of reconquest.

Sargon became king during the seige of Samaria in 722. When Samaria finally fell in 721, Sargon marched immediately to put down the rebellion in Babylonia. The offender there was Merodach-baladan (see *II Kin. 20:12; Isa. 39:1*), the ruler of the small kingdom of Bit-Yakin, who was encouraged and supported by the king of Elam (Old Persia). Whether because his troops were worn down from the long seige at Samaria or simply because he was outmanned, Sargon was soundly drubbed by the rebels and had to be content to let the reconquest of Babylon wait for a better day.

He was more successful the next year (720) against a coalition at Qarqar on the Orontes in northern Syria. The leader of this coalition was the Egyptian general Sib'e, who was joined by the Syrian states of

239

Hamath and Damascus. Sargon defeated the Syrians. Sib'e "like a shepherd whose flock has been stolen, fled alone and disappeared." Sargon chased him as far as the Egyptian border city of Raphia, which he then destroyed. After this decisive show of force by Sargon, the West remained docile for a few years. The next threat came from King Midas, the ruler of the Muski nation in Phrygia. He was taking control of southeast Asia Minor and was pushing as far east as Syria. In 717 he stirred up a rebellion in Carchemish, which Sargon put down rather ruthlessly. By 712, Sargon had pushed as far as Cilicia and had Midas back where he belonged. In the meantime, in 714, Sargon rid Assyria of a longtime threat by destroying Mussair, the capital city of Urartu. He was so proud of this piece of work that he wrote a letter addressed to his chief god, Ashur, describing his victory. As Judah and her neighbors watched Sargon chase about the world in a frantic, though largely successful, effort to hold his empire together, they began to discuss the feasibility of revolt. It seems entirely possible that Sargon was not too deeply concerned about Palestine. After all, he had stayed pretty free of the area since the siege of Samaria. The revolt was certainly worth risking.

Lending full encouragement to this line of thinking was Egypt. This is somewhat surprising since Egypt had been powerless for generations. In the last half century, both the Twenty-third and Twenty-fourth Dynasties had claimed power, but neither had the might to back up its claims. It was pitifully laughable to see Israel going to divided and impotent Egypt for help against the crushingly efficient Tiglath-pileser. Shortly after that, however, the tide began to turn in Egypt. About 715, Pi-ankhi, a strong Cushite (Ethiopian) king, began to push into Upper Egypt. With little difficulty he gained control of the whole of Egypt and established the vigorous Twenty-fifth Dynasty. He was not yet ready to lend actual military support, but he was fully ready to fan the fires of revolt among the smaller nations of Palestine, to promise anything they asked of him, and then to sit back and see what personal gain he might make off subsequent events. Pi-ankhi may have been an Ethiopian, but he had the mentality of a true Egyptian king!

### CONDITIONS IN JUDAH

We may be sure that the thought of gaining independence from Assyria was a welcome one in Judah. The concrete burden imposed by the payment of tribute was a major source of resentment, of course. But Judah's resentment was far from being merely a dollars-and-cents affair. From their earliest days in Canaan, the Israelite people had cherished their independence. They had not liked it even when their own kings had encroached too far on tribal and individual liberties. Certainly they would be hostile to any foreign power that tried to order their lives. In addition to these feelings of independence and natural patriotism, there was the religious factor. Some, of course, went along with Ahaz' policy. But a large segment of the people must have been apalled at the idea that Yahweh's sacred dwelling had been remodeled to suit a new tenant. These would also have viewed the breakdown in Judah's social and moral life with increasing alarm. These were the very sins that had brought the Northern Kingdom low. Judah could not afford to pursue this course any longer.

Of course, even a successful revolt against the Assyrians would not immediately heal all Judah's problems. On the other hand, extensive reforms were impossible until a measure of self-government was regained. As soon as Ahaz died and Hezekiah showed himself to be sympathetic to these forces,

240

the leaven of rebellion began to permeate Southern Palestine.

### THE REBELLION OF ASHDOD (713–711)

The first Palestinian rebellion against Sargon II was led by the Philistine city of Ashdod, although Ashdod clearly had a promise of support from the Ethiopian king of Egypt (*Isa. 20*). In 713, Azuri king of Ashdod withheld the annual tribute, the usual sign of rebellion. To make his intentions absolutely clear, he "sent messages full of hostility" to Sargon. Sargon made quick work of the upstart, replacing him with his younger brother, Ahimiti. The rebellion had widespread popular support, however, and the people replaced Ahimiti with a Greek, Yamani, whose only credential was his willingness to continue the revolt. For two years he tried to enlist the aid of neighboring kingdoms. Sargon's records specifically mention that Yamani made overtures to Judah. The promise of Egyptian aid and the obvious determination of the Ashdodites must have tempted Hezekiah to join the rebels. Fortunately for Judah, the prophet Isaiah saw the hollowness of the Egyptian promises and went to dramatic length to warn Hezekiah against having any part in the rebellion. For the better part of three years, he walked around naked and barefoot, declaring that Egypt and Ethiopia and those who trusted in them would be similarly stripped and humiliated by the Assyrians (*Isa. 20*). Sargon moved against Ashdod in 711 and easily defeated whatever coalition Yamani had been able to form. Apparently Hezekiah had heeded Isaiah's insistent warnings, because Judah suffered no serious damage at the time. The Egyptian king escaped the humiliation Isaiah had envisioned by relying on the traditional practice of reneging on his promise. Not only did he keep his troops at home; when Yamani fled to his territory for refuge, the

Ethiopian ruler obligingly chained him up and delivered him to Assyria. Sargon attributed the Ethiopian's action less to deceit than to what he modestly described as "the awe-inspiring glamour of my kingship," but the result was the same.

By this decisive stroke Sargon eliminated further rebellion in Palestine for the remainder of his life. In 709, he defeated Merodach-baladan and recaptured Babylon. This was the last of his great campaigns. He spent the last four years of his life on minor expeditions of annexation and containment. He was killed in battle on one of these campaigns in 705. His son, Sennacherib, ruled in his stead.

### REFORM IN JUDAH

As early as the first year of his reign, Hezekiah began to weed out the pagan practices that had crept into Judah's religion. Things had gotten so bad during the reign of Ahaz that the temple seems to have fallen into disuse. Hezekiah dispatched crews of Levites to re-open it and attend to needed repairs. He removed the cultic objects that had been used in pagan worship and threw them into the valley of the Brook Kidron. Hezekiah also ordered the high places and the shrines of Baal and Asherah cut down. The thoroughness of his reform is demonstrated by his destruction of the bronze serpent Moses had made during the plague of the fiery serpent (*Num. 21:6–9*). In its time, the object had served a legitimate and useful function. Over the centuries, however, it had been transformed from a reminder of Yahweh's wrath and mercy into an object of worship not unlike the pillars of Baal.

When the purification was completed, temple services were resumed. There were not enough properly sanctified priests to perform all the required duties, but their roles were filled by Levites—"for the Levites were more upright at heart than the priests in sanctifying themselves" (*2 Chr. 29:34*). How thrilling this renewal service must have been! Musicians were stationed all around the temple. At the moment the burnt-offering was placed on the altar, the trumpet sounded and the people began to sing the Psalms of David and Asaph, "accompanied by the instruments of David, king of Israel." They sang until the burnt-offering was consumed, then, the king and the princes and the priests and the Levites bowed down and worshipped the Lord (*II Chr. 29:25–31*).

Hezekiah was not content simply to get the temple services back in working order. He had a vision of Israelites returning from all over Palestine to form a reunited Israel under the spiritual lordship of Yahweh and the temporal oversight of the kings of the House of David. To bring this about he sent messengers throughout the length and breadth of Palestine calling on those Israelites who had not been carried to Assyria to come to Jerusalem to keep the Passover. Hezekiah's motives seemed perfectly noble and sincere:

> O, people of Israel, return to Yahweh, the god of Abraham, Isaac and Israel, that he may turn again to the remnant of you who have escaped from the hands of the kings of Assyria . . . for if you return to Yahweh, your brethren and your children will find compassion with their captors and return to this land, for Yahweh, your god, is gracious and merciful and will not turn away his face from you if you return to him.
>
> —*II Chronicles 30:6, 9*

The response was less than enthusiastic. A few humble souls from the northern tribes made the journey to Jerusalem, but the men of Ephraim, the province where Samaria was located, laughed the messengers to scorn (*2 Chr. 30:11; but see v. 18*). Loyalty to Yahweh had lost all meaning to these

men. Despite the disappointing size of the crowd, the Passover celebration was a great success; so great, in fact, that the whole assembly decided to keep it an additional week (*30:13–27*).

> So there was great joy in Jerusalem for since the time of Solomon the son of David, king of Israel, there had been nothing like this in Jerusalem.  *II Chr. 30:26*

The Bible speaks only of the cultic aspects of Hezekiah's reform. We can be sure, however, that he took steps to eliminate the moral offenses that had accompanied the religious apostasy. We have already observed that Jeremiah gave Micah most of the credit for Hezekiah's actions (*Jer. 26:16–19*). We have only to recall a few of Micah's attacks on the social sins of his day to be convinced that Hezekiah must have given some attention to these matters. Isaiah, of course, also had a great deal to say about injustice and oppression. The close relationship he enjoyed with the king must have reinforced the moral demands that he and Micah made. This is not meant to imply that Hezekiah would not have attended to these matters on his own; he was a righteous man and undoubtedly understood that religion and moral behavior were inseparable. Surely, he did everything he could to bring every aspect of Judah's society under the lordship of Yahweh.

### REBELLION AND DEFEAT: 705–701

*Preparations for war.* Hezekiah's reform measures must have been an affront to Sargon, but, probably because he had worse things to worry about, he never made any major attempt to stop Hezekiah. At the same time Hezekiah made no open declaration of rebellion as long as Sargon reigned. In the ancient world, the death of a strong king was frequently a signal for revolt. If a number of subject nations rebelled at once, the new ruler had his work cut out for him.

Sargon II spent most of his reign trying to recover what had been lost at the death of his father Tiglath-pileser III. When he was killed in 705 and succeeded by his son Sennacherib (705–681), rebellion began to break out again over much of the empire. In 703, Merodach-baladan returned from exile in Elam and gained control of Babylon once more. He immediately began to foment rebellion against Sennacherib. By 701, most of Palestine was in revolt. In the north, Tyre led the Phoenician coalition. Ashdod still remembered the high cost of revolting against Assyria and refused to join, but two other Philistine city-states—Ekron and Ashkelon—pledged their full strength. In Egypt, Shabako the Ethiopian had firmly established the Twenty-fifth Dynasty and stood ready to help. Rounding out the major western forces was Judah. Hezekiah had almost died a year or two earlier, but Yahweh had granted him fifteen additional years to live (*2 Kin. 20:1–11*). Doubtless, this promise bolstered his confidence in the rebellion!

The coalition forces seemed to have been usually well knit. The Bible tells us that Merodach-baladan had sent an envoy to visit Hezekiah during his illness. It is probably safe to assume they discussed some matters other than Hezekiah's remarkable recovery. Sennacherib's records tell us of an interesting bit of cooperation between Ekron and Judah. Padi, the king of Ekron, was loyal to Sennacherib and wanted to keep his nation out of the rebellion. Instead of going along with their king, the men of Ekron clapped Padi in irons like a common criminal and turned him over to Hezekiah for safe keeping.

Obviously, Hezekiah was right in the thick of the revolt. He had no illusions that Sennacherib would be an easy foe and he made extensive preparations for the inevitable conflict (*2 Chr. 32:1–8*). He repaired the city walls and strengthened existing for-

tifications. He had a large supply of weapons made and organized the citizenry into military groups. These measures all show admirable prudence. His management of the water supply showed genuine imagination. First of all, he gathered a large group of people together and sent them throughout the countryside stopping up springs and brooks. This would work a hardship on Sennacherib's army (*2 Chr. 32:2–3*). Then he set about to make sure Jerusalem would have enough water to enable her to withstand a long seige. Earlier we mentioned Ahaz's concern about the vulnerability of Jerusalem's water supply (page 225). Hezekiah eliminated this weakness in the city's defenses with a remarkable piece of engineering (*II Kin. 20:20; 2 Chr. 32:30; Isa. 22:9–11*). First he built a new reservoir on the west side of the "City of David" section of Jerusalem. This is the famous Pool of Siloam where Jesus directed the man born blind to wash (*John 9:7*). It is a deep, rectangular pool built between two walls (*Isa. 22:9–11*) and may still be seen today. When the pool was ready, Hezekiah's workmen, starting from both ends, cut a long winding tunnel that connected the spring to the pool —almost 600 yards through solid rock! An inscription discovered near the Siloam end of the tunnel by a group of boys in 1880 tells of the completion of the project*. When only four or five feet of rock remained to be cut through, the workers were able to call back and forth to each other. Imagine the excitement they felt as they hewed away at the last few feet "ax against ax." The spot where the workmen met can still be identified by the pick ax marks slanting in differ-

---

*Despite the fact that it contains only six lines, the Siloam inscription is perhaps the most important inscription that has been discovered in Palestine because its date can be fixed with certainty within five or six years. It is an invaluable tool in determining the age of other Hebrew writings. The inscription has been cut from the wall and is kept in the Museum of the Ancient Orient in Istanbul.

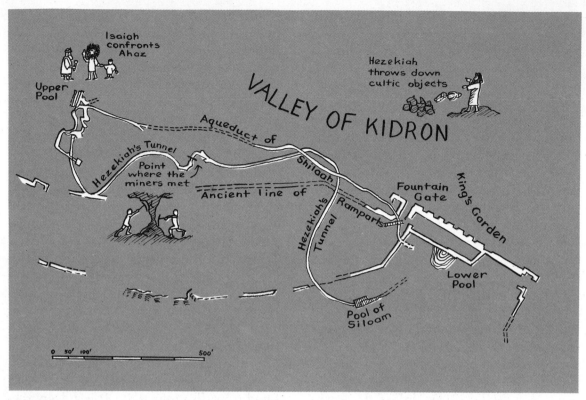

**The water works of Jerusalem in the time of Hezekiah.**

ent directions. When the tunnel was completed, Hezekiah sealed off the old aqueduct and covered the Spring of Gihon so that an attacker would not readily see it.

### "A COVENANT WITH DEATH"

In a series of brilliant oracles, Isaiah bitterly attacked Hezekiah's actions, especially the alliance with Egypt. Instead of being an "alliance for independence" it was "a covenant with death" (28:15). There was no *human* power or strategy that could save Jerusalem. Even if Pharaoh Shabako furnished the promised support, the allies would be crushed "when the overwhelming scourge passes through" (28:18). Judah's only hope was to lean on Yahweh "in quietness and in trust" (30:15). They had refused to do this; now they would suffer the full consequences.

"Woe to the rebellious children,"
  says Yahweh,
 "who carry out a plan, but not mine;
and who make a league, but not of my spirit,
  that the may add sin to sin;
who set out to go down to Egypt,
  without asking for my counsel,
to take refuge in the protection of Pharaoh,
  and to seek shelter in the shadow of
    Egypt!
Therefore shall the protection of Pharaoh
    turn to your shame,
  and the shelter in the shadow of Egypt
    to your humiliation.     —*Isaiah 30:1-3*

The Egyptians are men, and not God;
  and their horses are flesh, and not spirit.
When Yahweh stretches out his hand,
  the helper will stumble, and he who is
    helped will fall,
  and they will all perish together.
                              —*Isaiah 31:3*

244

Then your covenant with death will be
    annulled,
  and your agreement with Sheol will not
    stand;
when the overwhelming scourge passes
    through
  you will be beaten down by it.
As often as it passes through it will take you;
  for morning by morning it will pass
    through,
  by day and by night;
and it will be sheer terror to understand
  the message.
For the bed is too short to stretch oneself
  on it,
  and the covering too narrow to wrap
    oneself in it.          —*Isaiah 28:18-20*

For thus said Yahweh God, the Holy One
    of Israel,
  "In returning and rest you shall be saved;
  in quietness and in trust shall be your
    strength."
And you would not, but you said,

"No! We will speed upon horses,"
  therefore you shall speed away;
and, "We will ride upon swift steeds,"
  therefore your pursuers shall be swift.
A thousand shall flee at the threat of one,
  at the threat of five you shall flee,
till you are left
  like a flagstaff on the top of a mountain,
  like a signal on a hill. —*Isaiah 30:15-17*

These biting words had little effect. Hezekiah was a righteous man but the blazing
fires of revolution blinded him to the truth
of the prophet's words. The leaders of the
nation grew tired of hearing his variations
on the same theme and ordered him to stay
out of their way. Isaiah once again instructed his desciples to write his testimony
in a book, as a witness to future generations.
If they would not hear him, he would let the
king of Assyria become their instructor (*28:
11–13*). If he could not stop this catastrophe, he could at least leave a monument that

**The Siloam inscription in a tunnel south of Jerusalem.**

would warn of the futility of trusting men rather than God (30:8–14).

### SENNACHERIB'S FIRST WESTERN CAMPAIGN (701)*

Sennacherib won the next round in the seesaw battle with Merodach-baladan over control of Babylon. In 702 Merodach-baladan's allies, the Elamites and the Chaldeans, were defeated and Babylon surrendered. Sennacherib put a new king on the throne, but once again Merodach-baladan escaped to begin work on a new plot. For the time being, however, Sennacherib was free to come west to put down the tempest that was brewing there. The Assyrian quickly shattered whatever dream of independence the westerners may have had. The Phoenicians gave up with scarcely a struggle. With characteristic modesy, Sennacherib tells us that the king of Sidon, overwhelmed by "the terror inspiring glamour of my Lordship . . . fled far overseas and perished." When the Phoenicians gave up so easily the kings of Ashdod, Ammon, Moab, Edom, and other western nations, immediately brought tribute and gifts as a sign of their submission. Whether all of

---

*It is a difficult matter to reconstruct the events of this period with a satisfying degree of certainty. At best, the combination of the narrative portions of *Kings* and *Chronicles,* the oracles of Isaiah, and the records of Sennacherib yield a certain amount of confusion. In brief, the problem is this: *Kings* and *Chronicles* treat Sennacherib's adventures in the West as if they are all part of one campaign. These episodes make better sense, however, and harmonize more readily with *Isaiah* and the Assyrian records if we posit two western campaigns, the second falling sometime around 688 B.C. Unfortunately, Sennacherib's records break off in 689 B.C. leaving us without a direct confirmation of this hypothesis. Nevertheless, we feel the existing evidence warrants the tentative acceptance of the two-campaign period and this section is written on the assumption that a second campaign did occur. John Bright has made the classic presentation of this hypothesis. His argument is summarized in detail in a *History of Israel,* pp. 282-7. The chronological chart on page 238 provides a quick over view of the period reconstructed on the basis of Bright's theory.

these had originally been a part of the coalition force we cannot say. From Phoenicia, Sennacherib moved southward to deal with the Philistines. Eglon had, like others before her, relied on Egyptian aid; but this time, Shabako made good on an Egyptian promise. Even Sennacherib seemed surprised; in his chronicles he wrote, "they actually came to their assistance." The Egyptian army was apparently quite large but Sennacherib defeated it at Eltekeh.

Now only Judah was left. Sennacherib's records of his campaign against Judah are quite detailed. He tells us that he conquered forty-six strong cities and numerous small villages, mounting "well-stamped earth-ramps" to pound the walls with battering rams. He claims to have deported over two hundred thousand people plus innumerable horses and cattle. Hezekiah was trapped in Jerusalem "like a bird in a cage." Before Sennacherib had a chance to begin the assault on Jerusalem in earnest, Hezekiah realized the hopelessness of his situation and dispatched a message of complete surrender: "I have done wrong; withdraw from me; whatever you impose on me, I will bear" (*II Kin. 18:14*). Sennacherib imposed a great deal. In addition to the gold and silver mentioned in the Bible, Sennacherib recites a long list of gifts Hezekiah sent to the Assyrian capital, including several of Hezekiah's own daughters.

When Hezekiah sent his message of surrender, Sennacherib was busy attacking Lachish. Lachish was a strongly fortified city and was larger even than Jerusalem. Sennacherib obviously thought of his victory there as the most significant of the campaign against Judah. He speaks of Jerusalem simply as the royal residence but he had his royal artist carve a stone relief depicting his victory over Lachish. Lachish has been thoroughly excavated and has yielded a good deal of important information. Probably the most fascinating discovery is a network of pits on one of the slopes of the city. These pits contain scores of human skeletons and assorted bones, many of which had been burned and tossed into the pits in various stages of decomposition. On top of the human bones was a layer of animal bones, mostly from pigs, and a generous selection of broken pottery. The most likely explanation of this strange mixture seems to be that these pits were used as garbage dumps to hold the debris left from Sennacherib's assault. The pigs had probably served as food for Sennacherib's soldiers since faithful Jews would not have touched them. Three skulls found in this garbage heap give us an idea of the state of medical knowledge in Palestine at the end of the eighth century B.C. These skulls bear the marks left by the circular saw (a trepan) used in an operation to relieve pressure on the brain by removing a part of the bone. The saw marks on two of the skulls are quite distinct, indicating that the patient died on the operating table. On the third skull, however, the bone had begun to grow. Whether this patient died of after effects of the operation or of some other cause (perhaps in battle), we cannot say. But at least the operation was not an immediate failure.

### SENNACHERIB'S SECOND WESTERN CAMPAIGN (c. 688)

After the punitive expedition to Palestine in 701, Sennacherib returned to the East to resume the contest with Babylon. In 700 he put down a minor disturbance and left his son in charge of the city. There was relative peace for six years. Then, Elam managed to stir up another major rebellion. Sennacherib was tired of the constant meddling of the Elamites and decided to attack them as the first step in dealing with the Babylonian situation. To reach the coastal cities of Elam where most of the trouble was coming from,

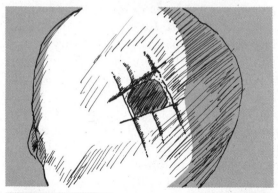
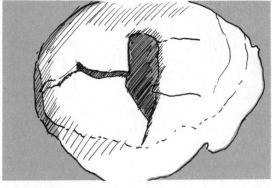

Skulls from pits on the slopes of Lachish showing evidence for early operations for concussion.

Sennacherib bought ships and floated his armies down the Euphrates River to the Persian Gulf. He took the coastal cities as planned (694/3), but the Elamites were far from defeated.

The struggle with Elam and Babylon continued for five years with both sides getting their share of victories. Finally, in 689, the Elamites were forced by internal strife to return home, leaving Babylon exposed and weak. Sennacherib unleashed his full fury on the troublesome city. According to his records, he completely demolished the walls and buildings of Babylon and redirected the Euphrates River to flow over the rubble.

Sennacherib's records break off after 689, although we know from other sources that he lived until 681. According to the reconstruction that we are following, he set out on a second western campaign in 688. We

247

believe the incidents described in *II Kings 18:17–19; 37* and *Isaiah 36–37* belong to this second campaign. If this theory is correct, Sennacherib again directed the major assault at the fortress cities of Lachish and Libnah. While he was at Lachish he sent a company of men to Jerusalem to demand Hezekiah's surrender. The spokesman for this band was Sennecherib's chief cup-bearer, called the Rabshakeh. From the outset the Rabshakeh's attitude was a scornful one, designed to cause the people of Jerusalem to lose confidence in Hezekiah. He took a position "by the conduit of the upper pool," near the spring of Gihon and close to the city walls. Then, addressing the chief member of Hezekiah's cabinet but speaking loudly enough for the people on the wall to hear, he began to ridicule Hezekiah's rebellion. What was the basis for Hezekiah's confidence? Did he think that words would defeat the Assyrian army? Was he so foolish as to be depending on Egypt, "that broken reed of a staff which would pierce the hand of any man that leans on it?" Hezekiah might claim to be trusting in Yahweh, but how did he expect help from him, when he had torn down the high places where men had worshipped him? Rabshakeh then began to scoff at Hezekiah's army. Sennacherib would give Hezekiah two thousand horses free of charge if Hezekiah could muster enough soldiers to mount them. Then, in a claim sure to unsettle the rebels, the Rabshakeh declared that Yahweh himself had given Sennacherib the command to attack Judah.

Hezekiah's aides were horrified at the Assyrian's words and by the effect that they might have on the people of the city. They urged the Rabshakeh to speak in Aramaic, the language of international diplomacy. They could understand it, but the people could not. The Rabshakeh made it clear he was not speaking Hebrew by accident. He wanted the men of Jerusalem to know that if they followed Hezekiah, they were doomed "to eat their own dung and to drink their own urine" (*II Kin. 18:27*). He raised his voice and addressed the people on the wall directly. "Do not let Hezekiah deceive you," he warned. If they would surrender peaceably, they could live in prosperity either in Judah or in a land just as good. It was useless to depend on Yahweh. The gods of other nations had never been able to protect their lands from the Assyrian armies. The Rabshakeh's arguments were persuasive, and there must have been considerable tension in the air as the men of the city weighed his words but they remained loyal to Hezekiah. Following the king's instructions, they "were silent and answered him (the Rabshakeh) not a word."

When his officers told him what the Rabshakeh had said, Hezekiah was completely distraught. He knew that much of what the Rabshakeh said was true. Even with Egyptian help, his armies would stand no chance against Sennacherib's in an open fight. In desperation, Hezekiah sent to Isaiah to see if he might possibly have some word of hope. In the past, Isaiah had pointed out the folly of resisting the Assyrians. This time, surprisingly, he counseled Hezekiah to stand firm. The king of Assyria had been a useful servant for Yahweh but he had gone too far and must now be brought low. Isaiah's understanding of historical processes comes through most clearly in a passage foretelling the downfall of the proud Assyrians. Yahweh is in control of the world and of its history. He uses nations against nations as a man uses a rod to beat his children. Of course, the pagan nations are not aware that they are being used by Yahweh and would scoff loudly at the notion. When their term of useful service is over, however, and their arrogant boasting becomes unbearable, Yahweh will raise up another nation to be a fire to "devour his thorns and briers."

> Ah, Assyria, the rod of my anger,
>> the staff of my fury!
> Against a godless nation I send him,
>> and against the people of my wrath I
>> command him,
> to take spoil and seize plunder,
>> and to tread them down like the mire
>> of the streets.
> But he does not so intend,
>> and his mind does not so think;
> but it is in his mind to destroy,
>> and to cut off nations not a few.

. . . . . . . . . . . . .

> When Yahweh has finished all his work on Mount Zion and on Jerusalem he will punish the arrogant boasting of the king of Assyria and his haughty pride. For he says:
> "By the strength of my hand I have done it,
>> and by my wisdom, for I have
>> understanding;
> I have removed the boundaries of peoples,
>> and have plundered their treasures;
>> like a bull I have brought down those who
>> sat on thrones.
> My hand has found like a nest
>> the wealth of the peoples;
> and as men gather eggs that have been
>> forsaken
>> so I have gathered all the earth;
> and there was none that moved a wing,
>> or opened the mouth, or chirped."

> Shall the ax vaunt itself over him who hews
>> with it,
>> or the saw magnify itself against him who
>> wields it?
> As if a rod should wield him who lifts it,
>> or as if a staff should lift him who is not
>> wood!
> Therefore Yahweh, the Lord of hosts,
>> will send wasting sickness among his
>> stout warriors,
> and under his glory a burning will be
>> kindled,
>> like the burning of fire.

> The light of Israel will become a fire,
>> and his Holy One a flame;
> and it will burn and devour
>> his thorns and briers in one day.
>> —*Isaiah 10:5-7, 12-17*

By the time the Rabshakeh carried the news of Hezekiah's refusal to surrender to Sennacherib, word had come that Tirhakah king of Egypt was on his way with support for Hezekiah. Sennacherib did not want to meet both of them at once, so he quickly sent messengers back to Jerusalem, hoping to bluff Hezekiah into a quick surrender. Hezekiah's calm actions are a testimony to his trust in Yahweh. Instead of going into a panic, he took Sennacherib's message and "spread it before the Lord" (*II Kin. 19:14*). In fervent prayer the righteous king begged Yahweh to deliver Jerusalem from Sennacherib's hands.

The old prophet Isaiah delivered Yahweh's answer to Hezekiah's prayer. The Assyrians had blaspehemed Yahweh and scoffed at Jerusalem. Now it would be Jerusalem's turn:

> She despises you, she scorns you—
>> the virgin daughter of Zion;
> she wags her head behind you—
>> the daughter of Jerusalem.
> Whom have you mocked and reviled?
>> Against whom have you raised your voice
> and haughtily lifted your eyes?
>> Against the Holy One of Israel!

. . . . . . . . . . . .

> Have you not heard
>> that I determined it long ago?
> I planned from days of old
>> what now I bring to pass,
> that you should make fortified cities
>> crash into heaps of ruins,
> while their inhabitants, shorn of strength,
>> are dismayed and confounded,
> and have become like plants of the field
>> and like tender grass,
> like grass on the housetops,
>> blighted before it is grown.

249

I know your sitting down
   and your going out and coming in,
   and your raging against me.
Because you have raged against me
   and your arrogance has come to my ears,
I will put my hook in your nose
   and my bit in your mouth,
and I will turn you back on the way
   by which you came.
            *—Isaiah 37:22-23, 26-29*
            *‖II Kings 19:21-23; 25-28*

Then, Isaiah boldly announced that Sennacherib

> shall not come into this city, or shoot an arrow there, or come before it with a shield, or cast up a siege-mound against it. By the way that he came, by the same he shall return, and he shall not come into this city, says Yahweh. For I will defend this city to save it, for my own sake and for the sake of my servant David.
>
>             *—Isaiah 37:33-35*
>             *‖II Kings 19:32-34*

That same night, the "virgin daughter of Zion" was saved from her Assyrian attacker by a wave of death that swept through the enemy camp.

> For the Angel of Death spread his wings on
>    the blast,
> And breathed in the face of the foe as he
>    passed.
> And the eyes of the sleepers waxed deadly
>    and chill,
> And their hearts but once heaved, and
>    forever grew still.
>
> . . . . . . . . . . . . . . . .
>
> And the widows of Ashur are loud in their
>    wail,
> And the idols are broke in the temple of Baal;
> And the might of the Gentile, unsmote by
>    the Sword,
> Hath melted like snow in the glance of the
>    Lord!
>
>       —From Lord Byron,
>       *The Destruction of Sennacherib*

Sennacherib returned home without ever striking a blow against Jerusalem. Probably he would have returned in a year or two for another try, but Hezekiah died in about 687 B.C. and his son Manasseh meekly submitted to the Assyrian yoke once again. The period of rebellion was over, at least for a long time. In 681, Sennacherib was slain by two of his sons while worshiping one of his gods (II Kin. 19:37)* After a bitter struggle, his son Esarhaddon, became king of Assyria in his stead.

The deliverance of Jerusalem was a stunning victory for Yahweh and his prophets. Hezekiah had trusted Yahweh's promise and Jerusalem had been saved, just as Isaiah had said. Nevertheless, in spite of all that Isaiah and Micah had said, it had the unfortunate effect of reinforcing the old belief that Jerusalem could never be destroyed. Years later, as we shall see, Jeremiah would find it impossible to get anyone to believe otherwise.

## The Reign of Manasseh

Hezekiah's death left Judah with a king who was only 12 years old (*II Kin. 21:1*). The boy king, Manasseh, was simply not equipped for the task of leading a rebellion against the world's most powerful ruler. Judah's bravest hour was over. Her darkest was about to begin.

### THE GREAT APOSTASY

Manasseh must have been a student of history, for he revived practically every pagan religious practice that Judah had ever known (*Kin. 21:2–9*). He rebuilt the high places Hezekiah had torn down. He reinstituted the cult of the Canaanite god Baal. He not only made an image of Asherah, but set it up in the temple of Yahweh. In the courts of the temple he built altars on which the sun, moon, and various stars could be wor-

---

*An Assyrian text indicates that Sennacherib was bludgeoned to death with an idol.

shipped. (This was probably done at the insistence of the Assyrians, who also worshipped the astral dieties.) He encouraged sorcery and supported those who claimed to be able to communicate with the dead. Then, like his grandfather Ahaz, he gave his own son as a burnt offering to the Ammonite god Moloch. *II Kings 21:16* tells us that Manasseh shed much innocent blood. It is not unlikely that part of this blood belonged to the devout worshippers of Yahweh who protested the king's religious policy. Tradition has it that one of the victims was the old prophet Isaiah, who, because of his opposition, was "placed in the trunk of a carob tree and sawed asunder."

At some point in Manasseh's long (687–642) reign, the king of Assyria had him put in chains and brought before him in Babylon (*I Chr. 33:11*). Presumably, the Assyrian suspected his vassal of some sort of disloyal action. From a political standpoint the incident was trivial. Assyrian records do not mention it and Manasseh was evidently allowed to return to Jerusalem after a short detention. From a religious standpoint, the result was dramatic according to *II Chronicles 33:12–17*. Here we are told that, in his distress, Manasseh has called on Yahweh to save him. When the king of Assyria subsequently released him, he "knew that Yahweh was god" and set about to repair the damage he had done. The heathen altars were torn down and Judah was urged to return to the worship of Yahweh. The people still sacrificed at the high places, but only to Yahweh.

It is surprising that the author of *Kings* does not mention this dramatic conversion. It may be that it occurred so late in Manasseh's reign that he considered the reform to be a case of too little too late. Whatever his reasons, it is clear that if he knew of Manasseh's conversion, he was not very impressed by it. He regarded Manasseh as the great se-ducer of Judah whose evil deeds had caused Yahweh to bring on Jerusalem and Judah "such evil that the ears of everyone who hears of it will tingle" (*21:9, 12*). Repeatedly he lays the blame for the eventual destruction of Jerusalem at Manasseh's feet. (*23:26–27; 24:3–4; cf. Jer. 15:4*). Because of this apparent divergence of opinion between *Kings* and *Chronicles*, it is difficult to know just what to make of Manasseh's change of heart. Probably we should conclude that, however thorough and sincere his actions may have been after the trip to Babylon, his wickedness beforehand had the more lasting effect.

### WORLD AFFAIRS IN MANASSEH'S REIGN

*The Zenith of Assyria's Empire.* Despite the fact that his submission to Assyria betrayed the same lack of faith in Yahweh his grandfather Ahaz had shown, it is easy to understand why Manasseh made little, if any, attempt to launch a serious rebellion during his reign. Sennerachib's son and successor, Esarhaddon (681–669) was an extremely capable ruler. As we have said, there was a fierce struggle for the Assyrian throne after two of his elder brothers murdered their father. According to Esarhaddon's records, Sennacherib had named him as his successor before his death, despite the fact that he was his youngest son. It is possible that Esarhaddon invented this story simply to enhance his position, but, in view of his subsequent achievements, it may be that Sennacherib was wise enough to realize that his youngest son was actually the best suited for the difficult task of managing the world. Once he became king, Esarhaddon moved quickly to secure his hold on his empire. First, he rebuilt Babylon which his father had destroyed in 689. Like any good emperor, he went on the usual tribute-raising campaigns and forced his vassals, including Manasseh, to provide men and ma-

An Assyrian relief of Asshurbanapal's forces pursuing Arabs.

terials for building projects in Nineveh. But the project that received most of his attention was the subjection of Egypt. Since the rise of the Twenty-fifth Dynasty under Piankhi, Egypt had been an irritating sore on Assyria's western flank. Even when she was too weak to be a serious military threat, she was busily trying to stir her neighbors to rebellion. Now, under Tirhakah, she was becoming a more serious threat. The first strike occurred in 673, when Tirhakah managed to keep the Assyrians from advancing beyond the border. In 671, however, Esarhaddon captured the Egyptian city of Memphis and placed the territory under Assyrian political control. Unfortunately for the Assyrians, Tirhakah managed to escape and was soon back at work fanning the fires of rebellion. By 669, he was once more firmly entrenched in Memphis.

Esarhaddon died before his armies reached Egypt's borders, but his son Asshurbanapal (669-p. 663) continued the march. Asshurbanapal's records inform us that twenty-two vassal kings, including Manasseh of Judah, joined him in the attack on Egypt. As he neared Memphis, Tirhakah sent his troops out to meet him on open territory. The Egyptian force was large and well-trained, but the "glamour of his kingship" (and the finest army in the world) enabled Asshurbanapal to gain a decisive victory. Tirhakah fled to Nubia, Memphis was captured, and the rebellion was apparently over. Since Tirhakah had been the mainspring of the revolt Asshurbanapal figured it was safe to allow the other Egyptian leaders to maintain their positions. Within a short time, however, they had gotten in touch with Tirhakah and were spending a great

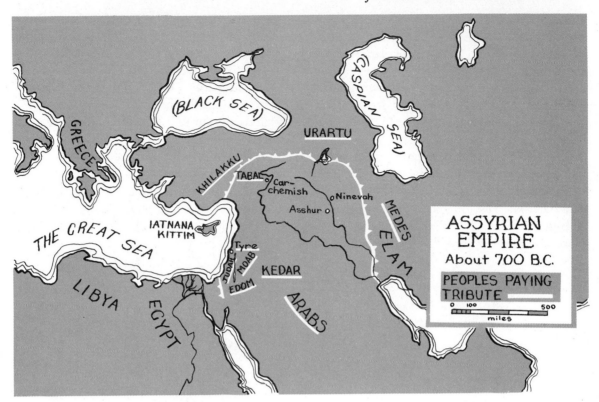

**The Assyrian Empire in the time of Isaiah.**

deal of their time in what Asshurbanapal described as "rebellious doings." As soon as the Assyrian commanders of the occupation troops got wind of what was going on, the rebels were placed in irons and sent to Nineveh to face Asshurbanapal. The Assyrian king executed all of them except Necho, who had been king of Memphis and Sais. For some reason—probably, he was able to convince Asshurbanapal that his part in the the rebellion had been unwilling and insignificant—Necho was spared and allowed to continue his rule in Sais. Down in Thebes, Tirhakah's successor, Urdamane, gathered an army and attacked the Assyrian garrison at Memphis. In retaliation the Assyrians marched on Thebes in 663 and completely destroyed it.* Urdamane fled to Nubia, marking the end of the Twenty-fifth Egyptian Dynasty.

With this extension of his holdings to Thebes in southern Egypt, Asshurbanapal was master of the largest empire the world had ever seen. It was, in fact, so large that it could not be effectively controlled. It soon became apparent that the rod of Yahweh's anger was beginning to strengthen.

*Signs of Weakness.* Asshurbanapal lived to regret his merciful treatment of Necho king of Sais. Necho remained submissive as long as he lived, but his son Psammetichus (663–609) was more troublesome. By about 655, he had managed to gain control of most of Egypt and announced his independence of Assyrian rule. Probably Asshurbanapal could have defeated him without too much

---

*The fall of Thebes is mentioned in *Nahum 3:8* (in the King James Version, Thebes is called by a variant name, No Amon), indicating that it was a well-known event in the Near Eastern world.

253

difficulty, but he was busy with more pressing problems on the homefront. To the north of Assyria several groups of Indo-Aryan peoples, including the Medes, were posing a much more serious threat. Asshurbanapal held them off successfully, but it was clear that not all the results were in from that quarter.

In Babylon, Asshurbanapal's own brother led a widespread revolt in 652. This was most serious and it was not until 648 that Asshurbanapal was able to regain control of Babylon. Meanwhile Palestine and Syria were threatening rebellion (this may have been the time of Manasseh's trip to Babylon.) To complicate matters even further, Arab tribes were streaming out of the Syrian desert to plunder the lands of eastern Palestine and Syria. Once again Asshurbanapal proved himself master of the situation. The vicious measures he took against the Arab tribes served to discourage any further thoughts of rebellion in Palestine and Syria. With the exception of the loss of Egypt, the Empire was still impact, but the events of the last decade had made it clear that Assyria could not control her far-flung holdings much longer.

# 11

# Judah's Last Days

*After a brief period of glorious independence, the nation of Judah is destroyed*

THE YEARS of Manasseh's long and evil reign were the darkest Judah had ever known. Assyria had controlled the land with an iron hand. Morals and religion had reached a new low. To many, it must have seemed that Judah was on the verge of becoming just one more pagan state. But suddenly, the picture changed dramatically. The Assyrian dragon was crippled and slain. Judah, ruled by a boy, enlarged her territory and experienced sweeping religious reforms. Unfortunately, these years of independence and reform were only a last flash of brilliance before Judah's flame was completely extinguished. Soon, she was once more a vassal, first of Egypt, then of Babylon. Finally, in 586 B.C., Babylonian troops overran Jerusalem and the nation of Judah ceased to exist.

Like those before it, this period had its great kings and generals: Josiah, Necho, Nebuchadnezzar. But once again, the voices that were heard most clearly above the din of battle and the cries of despair, and the voices that continued to be heard after Jerusalem and her temple lay in ruins, were those of the prophets of God: Nahum, Zephaniah, Habakkuk, and the greatest of them all, Jeremiah. In a time of crushing defeat, these men of God spoke the words that made it possible for a tiny scrap of a ruined people to look forward in faith to the day when God's kingdom would once again be established in Zion.

## The Fall of Assyria

After quelling the revolts of the 640's Asshurbanapal enjoyed peace throughout the rest of his reign. But it was an uneasy peace. The Medes to the northeast and the Babylonians to the south were coiling to strike the blows that would bring Assyria crashing to the ground. Asshurbanapal died in about 633 B.C. (the dating for this period is uncertain) and was succeeded by his son Asshur-etil-ilani, who held power only about three or four years. When he died in about 629 B.C., his brother Sin-shar-ishkun (c. 629–612) came to the throne. This unfortunate man had the dubious distinction of presiding over the complete collapse of the world's greatest empire. In 626, the Babylonian prince Nabopolassar won independence for his nation by defeating the Assyrian army near Babylon. Sin-shar-ishkun tried repeat-

| JUDAH | Related History |
|---|---|
| **Manasseh 45** .....................687–642 | |
| | 663: Psammetichus I becomes Pharaoh of Egypt. |
| **Amon 2** .........................642–640 | Revival of Egyptian culture. |
| **Josiah 31** ...................640/39–609/8 | 628: Death of Asshurbanapal, king of Assyria. |
| Religious revival. | Succeeded by Assur-etil-ilini, then by Sin-shar-ishkun. Chaos in Assyria. |
| 622: Book of the Law found in Temple. Covenant renewed. | Babylon: Nabopolassar gaining power. |
| | 612: Destruction of Nineveh. |
| 609: Josiah is killed in battle with Egyptians. | 609: Necho II becomes Pharaoh of Egypt. |
| PROPHETS: *Zephaniah* | |
| *Nahum* | |
| *Jeremiah* | |

**CHRONOLOGICAL CHART: 687–609 B.C.**

edly to recapture the city, with no success. The Medes saved their major strikes till later, but their various minor campaigns and skirmishes kept the Assyrians under constant and serious pressure. It was obvious that Assyria could not hold out much longer. Not many found this a cause for grief. Assyria had been a harsh mistress; she would deserve all she got. In Egypt, however, Pharaoh Psammetichus viewed the proceedings with mixed feelings. For years, Egypt had been one of Assyria's most troublesome foes. She had played a leading role in just about every anti-Assyrian rebellion that had flared in the West. Still, Psammetichus was reluctant to see the Assyrian kingdom destroyed. His reasons, of course, were selfish ones. If Assyria fell, both the Medes and the Babylonians would have a clear path to Egypt. As long as she could be kept standing, even in a weakened condition, she would be a troublesome obstacle to western campaigns by either of these two rising powers.

In 616, Egyptian troops joined the Assyrians to stop Nabopolassar's march up the Euphrates. At this point the Medes closed in for the kill. In 614, the Median leader Cyaxares overran the old Assyrian capital of Asshur. Shortly afterward, the Medes and the Babylonians made a formal anti-Assyrian treaty. Then, in 612, they attacked Nineveh itself. Three months later, the city lay in utter ruin. The Assyrian king Sin-shar-ishkun was killed in the battle. A new leader, Asshur-uballit II, tried to hold what was left of the Assyrian forces together, in the vain hope that they could drive the foreign invaders out. For two years he operated out of Haran, west of Nineveh. In 610, the Medo-Babylonian forces attacked Haran and Asshur-uballit was forced to retreat across the Euphrates. An abortive attempt to retake Haran in 609 was the last tragic scene in the drama of the Assyrian empire. The rod of Yahweh's anger had been shattered and ground to dust.

## Good King Josiah

The king in Judah during this period of the decline and fall of Assyria was Josiah (640–609). After Manasseh died in 842, his son Amon had ruled for two years. Amon abandoned all efforts at reform, reviving the practices that had characterized most of Manasseh's reign (*II Kin. 21:19–26*). After two years of this, members of his staff assassinated him, presumably with the intention of finding a ruler more to their liking. This plot was met by a counter-plot engineered by the "people of the land" (probably a group of influential landowners). This group killed those who had slain the king and raised Amon's eight year old son, Josiah, to the throne. These men almost certainly assumed the actual leadership of the nation while Josiah was still a child. Judging from the direction his reign took after he was old enough to manage the kingdom by himself, his advisers were probably righteous, god-fearing men.

As Josiah grew to maturity, the Assyrian grip on Judah began to weaken. The course followed by Josiah and his advisers was a remarkable exercise in restraint. They must have been tempted by Assyria's weakness to form a coalition with their neighbors and to declare themselves in open rebellion. But they did not yield to this temptation. Instead, they simply waited until Assyria's power was broken by the Medes and Babylonians and gained full independence without ever lifting a sword. As we have already seen, a vassal nation was usually expected to worship the gods of the ruling power. We know the Assyrians required this of their subjects. Thus, even though the writers of *Kings* and *Chronicles* had very little interest in purely political matters, we can trace the progress of the independence movement by noticing what was going on in the religious realm. In the eighth year of Josiah's reign, the young king "began to seek the God of David his father" (*II Chr. 34:3*). This "eighth year" was probably 633 B.C., the same year in which Asshurbanapal is believed to had died. Very likely, Josiah (or his counselors) thought that the period of uncertainty that usually accompanied the death of a great king would be a good time to take the first cautious step toward independence. Josiah did not openly renounce the Assyrian gods. He simply "began to seek" after Yahweh. The next major step occurred in the twelfth year of his reign, 629 B.C., when Josiah "began to purge Judah and Jerusalem" of foreign cults and other idolatrous practices (*II Chr. 34:3–7*). Once again, this was probably a time of crisis in Assyria, for it seems that Asshurbanapal's son and successor, Asshur-etil-ilani, was killed in that year. After that, Judah was pretty much free to do as she chose, since Sin-shar-ishkun, the new Assyrian king, was far too busy with the neighboring Medes and Babylonians to risk any sort of campaign to the West. By the time the reform movement reached its climax in 622, Judah no longer made any pretense of loyalty to Assyria. In fact, Josiah's efforts to carry the reform movement into what had been the Assyrian-held territory of Northern Israel (*II Chr. 34:6–7*) indicate that he had probably taken advantage of Assyria's weakness to reclaim this territory for Judah.

As we have mentioned, the Biblical writers tell us little about Josiah's long (640–609) reign apart from his dramatic and sweeping reform. They do, however, give us extensive information about this (*II Kin. 22:3—23:25; II Chr. 34:3—35:19*). Let us look more closely at this remarkable episode in the religious life of God's people.

## The Great Reform

The accounts of Josiah's reform found in *Kings* and *Chronicles* are somewhat difficult to reconcile. In the *Kings* account, we get the impression that it was the finding of the "book of the law" in the temple that touched off the reform. First, the book is found, then Josiah calls the people together, renews the covenant, cleanses the land of idolatry, and keeps the passover (*II Kin. 22:8ff*). The

Chronicler, on the other hand, tells us that the purge of idolatry had already occurred *before* the book was found (*II Chr. 34:3ff*). A likely explanation is that Josiah had made some attempt to suppress idolatry before the finding of the law book, but did not order the extensive measures described in *II Kin. 23:4–20* until after the discovery. A combination of these accounts helps us to see two things: 1) the reform did not occur all at once but was a long process, and 2) the finding of the "book of the law" dramatically fanned the fires of reform. We need not be too concerned about the precise sequence of events. It will be sufficient for our purposes to notice the main features of the reform and to gain some understanding of the forces behind it.

### THE BOOK OF THE LAW

As we have already seen, the first step in the reform movement occurred in the eighth year of Josiah's reign (probably 633) when the young king began to worship Yahweh. We do not know if he tried to encourage his subjects to do the same, but it showed where his sympathies lay. Then, in his twelfth year (probably 628), he launched the first attack against idolatry. But the decisive year of the reform was Josiah's eighteenth year (622 B.C.), for this was the year that the book of the law was found.

In the years of Manasseh's evil reign, little attention had been given to the temple of Yahweh. As part of his reform program, Josiah had ordered the rehabilitation of the temple and had asked the people to make donations for this purpose. One day, the young king sent his secretary to ask the high priest to count the money and turn it over to the workmen in charge of repairing the temple. The priest, excited at the prospect of seeing the temple in operation once again, had been poking about the various rooms and had found the "book of the laws"

(*II Kin. 22:8ff; II Chr. 34:14ff*). Surprisingly, he does not seem to have been particularly overwhelmed by his discovery. And, when the secretary took the book back to the king, he first gave him the message that the money had been turned over to the workmen and then, almost as an afterthought, added, "Hilkiah the priest has given me a book." When Josiah read the book for himself, he was thunderstruck. He had been a worshiper of Yahweh for ten years, but now, for the first time, he was discovering what this really involved. As he read the stipulations of the law and the curses that were to fall on those who disobeyed them, he was overcome by guilt and despair; in the characteristic oriental expression of extreme agitation, he began to tear his clothing. Fearing that the full force of Yahweh's wrath might fall at any moment, Josiah sent the high priest and several members of his cabinet to ask the prophetess Huldah for a word from the Lord. Huldah confirmed Josiah's fears that the curses contained in the book of the law would fall on the heads of the people of Judah as a result of their persistent disobedience, but she reassuringly told him that, because of his sincerity and his penitence, the land would be spared for the duration of his reign.

Josiah immediately set about to bring his people back into a covenant relationship with the One True God, Yahweh of Hosts. He summoned the leaders of the nation to Jerusalem and there, before the great assembly, he read the words of the forgotten book. At the conclusion of the reading, the young king

> made a covenant before Yahweh, to walk after Yahweh and to keep his commandments and his testimonies and his statutes, with all his heart and all his soul, to perform the words of this covenant that are written in this book; and all the people joined in the covenant. —*II Kings 23:3*

**A fertility image found in Palestine. Similar statuettes were common at the time of Josiah's purge.**

### THE CLEANSING OF THE LAND

The first step toward restoring the broken bond was cleansing the land of the various idolatrous cults and practices that had crept in and seduced the nation. This purge began with an all-out assault on Yahweh's old enemies, Baal and Asherah. The priests brought out the vessels used in their worship and burned them (*II Kin. 23:4*). They burned the pillar representing Asherah and scattered its ashes on the graves of paupers (*v. 6*). Then, they tore down the houses used by religious prostitutes who were part of the religion of Baal and Asherah and who had practiced their trade in Yahweh's own temple (*v. 7*). At the same time, they destroyed the articles of worship and banished the priests connected with the worship of "the sun, the moon, and the constellations, and all the host of the heavens" (*v. 5; cf. 11*).

The Assyrians are known to have worshiped these heavenly bodies; it is highly probable that their cults had been introduced into Jerusalem at the insistence—or at least the strong recommendation—of the Assyrian rulers. What a thrill it must have been for the freedom-loving men of Judah to see the reminders of the hated Assyrian oppression thrown into the fire! The priests also cleared the temple area and the royal palace of other altars and idols that Ahaz, Manasseh, and other kings of Judah had erected at various times (*v. 12*). From the vicinity of the temple, the priests branched out to centers of idolatry scattered around the city. In the valley of Hinnom southwest of the city, they destroyed the fireplace (Topheth) where children had been burned as a sacrifice to Moloch (*v. 10*). And east of the city, they wrecked the altars that Solomon had set up to enable his foreign wives to worship their native gods (*v. 13*). Finally, the zealous priests roamed all over Palestine ridding the land of its abominations (*II Chr. 34:6*). The climax came in the destruction of the shrine at Bethel, the place where Jeroboam had first set up the golden bulls. Here, Josiah not only had the shrine torn down, but ordered his men to dig up graves and scatter the bones over the altars as an act of supreme desecration (*vv. 15, 16*). The writer of *Kings* includes an intriguing tidbit in the account of this defilement. There was a monument not far from the shrine that made Josiah curious. When he asked about it, his men told him it marked the tomb of a man of God who had come from Judah and who had stood in that place and foretold the destruction of the shrine. When Josiah heard this, he instructed the workers not to disturb either this grave or that belonging to "the prophet who came out of Samaria" (*v. 17, 18*). Almost a century and a half before, Amos, a "man of God who came from Judah," had stood on that very spot, warning that "the sanctuaries of Israel shall be laid waste" (*Amos 7:9*) and had stirred up strong opposition to his message (*7:10ff*). God alone knows the name of these two brave prophets whose bones were allowed to rest in peace, but we cannot help but wonder if one of them may not have been the rugged herdsman from Tekoa.

### THE HIGH PLACES

Josiah also abolished the "high places" that were scattered throughout Judah. These were not shrines to pagan gods. They were altars at which men worshiped Yahweh, the One True God. Nevertheless, they were thought to be sinful—although not in the same category with outright idolatry— since many believed the only legitimate worship was that carried on at the temple in Jerusalem.* But, mainly because of the inconvenience of traveling to Jerusalem, the high places had persisted. Even the great reformers like Asa and Joash had been unable (or unwilling) to suppress them (*I Kin. 15:13, 14; II Kin. 12:2, 3*). Hezekiah had enjoyed some success in closing them down (*II Kin. 18:4*), but whatever gains he had made had been lost by Josiah's time. Somehow, Josiah showed that he meant business. He defiled the high places and made it clear he did not want them reopened.

In a chapter that tells of religious prostitution, human sacrifice, and horses and chariots of the sun god (*v. 11*), the closing down of a few "unlicensed" Yahwistic shrines may seem insignificant. But it was not insignificant. On the contrary, it provides us with some highly pertinent information about the "book of the law" and about the nature of the reform. Most scholars, including several fathers of the early church, believe that this "book of the law" was part or all of the book we call *Deuteron-*

*See pp. 202-3.

*omy*. More than any other book we possess, *Deuteronomy* contains what the book found in the temple must have contained in order to elicit the response it did. Josiah's conviction that the wrath of Yahweh was about to fall upon the nation could easily have been caused by reading the curses against covenant-breaking contained in *Deuteronomy 27* and *28*. The renewal of the covenant, the purge of idolatry, and the keeping of the passover (*II Kin. 23:23ff; II Chr. 35:1ff*) would also naturally follow a reading of *Deuteronomy*. But it was the abolition of the high places that was most clearly Deuteronomic. Of the various collections of laws contained in the Pentateuch (the first five books of the Bible), only *Deuteronomy* makes the point that worship was to be centralized at one shrine. Notice the following statements from this book:

> Take heed that you do not offer your burnt offerings at every place that you see; but at the place which Yahweh will choose in one of your tribes.    —*Deuteronomy 12:13-14*

> You shall eat (your sacrifices) before Yahweh your God in the place which Yahweh your God will choose.
> —*Deuteronomy 12:18*

> You may not offer the passover sacrifice within any of your towns which Yahweh your God gives you, but at the place which Yahweh your God will choose.
> —*Deuteronomy 16:5-6*

In all probability, it was these same words that moved the young king to prohibit worship at any place except *the* place, the temple in Jerusalem. Even his treatment of the priests of these shrines is in accord with the teachings of *Deuteronomy*. In *Deuteronomy 18:6–8*, the law states that a Levite is free to come to the central shrine, to minister to Yahweh and to share in the offerings that are made there. When the high places of Judah were closed down, it seems clear that although the priests—all of them surely Levites—chose to remain among their people, Josiah had given them the option of joining those who ministered at the temple in Jerusalem (*II Kin. 23:8–9*).

To many modern readers, it may seem that these high places could have been allowed to stand without causing much serious damage. After all, they were devoted to the same God that was worshiped in Jerusalem. Apparently, this had been the predominant attitude throughout most of Judah's history and, as we have seen, other reformers allowed the altars to stand. But Josiah was taking no chances. The book of the law promised destruction if its precepts were not kept, and blessing if they were. Its precepts called for the destruction of the high places; and so, they were destroyed. There was no question of tolerance or expediency, for this was one reform that went by the book.

But the book of the law, important as it was, cannot be given full credit for the reforms that occurred during Josiah's reign. On the contrary, the reform movement had been underway for several years before the book was found. In fact, if Josiah had not ordered the repair of the temple, the book might never have been found. Neither was Josiah solely responsible for originating the reform. We do not say this to detract from his image. He was a godly and courageous man. But he was not alone in feeling that Judah was badly in need of a drastic overhaul of her religious system. Others had seen this need just as clearly and had called on the nation to cleanse itself. Among these were the prophets Zephaniah and Jeremiah.

## Zephaniah

The voice of prophecy had been stilled throughout the long reign of Manasseh. Half a century had passed since Isaiah had delivered his memorable oracles of judgment and hope. With the reign of Josiah, there was a fresh outburst of vital prophetic activity. The first of this new wave of Yahweh's spokesmen was a man named Zephaniah. If the Hezekiah mentioned in *Zephaniah 1:1* is King Hezekiah—and there is no good reason for believing otherwise—Zephaniah was of noble birth and was a relative of the young King Josiah. Judging from his intimate knowledge of Jerusalem (*1:10–11*), it is probably safe to assume that he was a resident of the city. The opening verse of the collection tells us only that he prophesied during Josiah's reign, but the tenor of his prophecies indicates they were delivered before the famous reforms. The fact that he foresees the downfall of Assyria (*2:13*) suggests that the decline that followed the death of Asshurbanapal in 633 had already begun. We cannot be far off if we conclude that Zephaniah's ministry fell somewhere in the decade between 632–622 B.C.

Like any good prophet, Zephaniah heartily denounced the sins of his day. The social sins of violence and injustice receive some notice (*1:9; 3:3–4*), but Zephaniah is primarily concerned over the bankrupt state of Judah's religion. The people have gone after every sort of foreign god, even imagining that it was possible to worship Yahweh and Milcom (another name for Moloch, who received human sacrifices) at the same time (*1:4–6*). The sins of Judah and Jerusalem are summed up in these words:

> Woe to her that is rebellious and defiled,
>  the oppressing city!
> She listens to no voice,
>  she accepts no correction.
> She does not trust in Yahweh
>  she does not draw near to her God.
> Her officials within her
>  are roaring lions;
> her judges are evening wolves
>  that leave nothing till the morning.
> —*Zephaniah 3:1-2*

The long years of idolatry and prophetic darkness had deadened the sense of living in the presence of Yahweh. The prophet's task was made doubly difficult because the people had become convinced that Yahweh would not, because he could not, act either to help or harm them: "Yahweh will not do good, nor will he do ill" (*1:12*).

### THE DAY OF YAHWEH

In order to pierce this shield of depraved skepticism, Zephaniah revived the concept that Amos and Isaiah had used so effectively: the Day of Yahweh. A great day was near, he warned, when Yahweh would take vengeance on those who had dared to suppose his commands could be ignored. On that day, the haughty spirit would be broken (*3:11*), complacency would be turned to terror, and Yahweh's wrath would devour his enemies.

> The great day of Yahweh is near,
> near and hastening fast;
> the sound of the day of Yahweh is bitter,
> the mighty man cries aloud there.
> A day of wrath is that day,
> a day of distress and anguish,
> a day of ruin and devastation,
> a day of darkness and gloom,
> a day of clouds and thick darkness,
> a day of trumpet blast and battle cry
> against the fortified cities
> and against the lofty battlements.
> I will bring distress on men,
> so that they shall walk like the blind,
> because they have sinned against Yahweh;
> their blood shall be poured out like dust,
> and their flesh like dung.
> Neither their silver nor their gold
> shall be able to deliver them
> on the day of the wrath of Yahweh.
> —*Zephaniah 1:14-18*

But once again, a ray of hope shines through the blackness of the prophet's gloomy message. For not all will be destroyed. O lowly and humble remnant would be spared. Their hearts would be cleansed, their speech purified (*3:9*), and they would delight in the glories of a new Jerusalem.

> For I will leave in the midst of you
> a people humble and lowly.
> They shall seek refuge in the name of
> Yahweh,
> those who are left in Israel;
> they shall do no wrong
> and utter no lies,
> nor shall there be found in their mouth
> a deceitful tongue.
> For they shall pasture and lie down,
> and none shall make them afraid.
>
> . . . . . . . . . . . . . . . .
>
> At that time I will bring you home,
> at the time when I gather you together;
> yea, I will make you renowned and praised
> among all the peoples of the earth,
> when I restore your fortunes
> before your eyes.
> —*Zephaniah 3:12-13, 20*

## Jeremiah

It might have been possible to overlook the preaching of Zephaniah. Judging from the small number of oracles that comprise his book, his ministry was probably rather limited. But no one could ignore his colleague Jeremiah. Even in the company of the prophets, Jeremiah towers as a giant. Centuries later, when men witnessed the marvelous ministry of Jesus, some wondered if he might not be Jeremiah come back to life (*Matthew 16:14*).

We know more about the career of Jeremiah than of any other prophet. In fact, with the exception of Jesus and David, there is no Biblical character—not even Moses or Paul—about whom we have more actual biographical information. Jeremiah's ministry lasted almost half a century, from the thirteenth year of Josiah's reign (c. 628) until well after the fall of Jerusalem in 586.

This was a time of extreme tragedy in Judah, and Jeremiah was truly a man of sorrows, acquainted with grief. He was a bachelor, rejecting the joys and comforts of a family in order to devote full time to his prophetic calling. He was an intense patriot who was branded a traitor. He was in love with Jerusalem, but had the unhappy task of overseeing her destruction. He could be vindictive toward his hearers, but when they and his beloved city got what he knew they deserved, his broken heart overflowed with lamentation. He was plagued with inner torment over his own feelings of inadequacy and doubts about the real meaning of what was going on in the world. He was frustrated at his inability to turn his countrymen from a suicidal course of action. These doubts and frustrations would have been sufficient to break many a strong man, but, to make matters worse, he spent most of his later ministry under the constant threat of death or imprisonment.

Jeremiah arrested the attention of his hearers with vivid parables and symbolic acts, and—most of the time—drove his points home in unmistakably clear language. Unfortunately, this clarity did not extend to the composition of his book. We would expect a book that contains so much biographical information to be reasonably well-ordered, following some discernible scheme, preferably chronological or topical. Instead, the book of *Jeremiah* defies logical analysis. It seems to be a collection of oracles, parables, sermons, and personal experiences that were strung together with only the slightest regard for what came before or after. Despite this, however, it is a marvelous document that tells the story of one of the greatest of men. To read it straight through will almost inevitably lead to confusion. We shall try, insofar as is possible, to deal with the various incidents and oracles in the proper historical sequence.

### THE CALL TO BE A PROPHET

When Jeremiah received his call to be a prophet in 628 B.C., he was still "a youth" (*1:6*). Judging from the length of his ministry, it is quite possible that he was only a teenager when God commissioned him to be his messenger. Yahweh did not ask the boy if he would be interested in a job as a prophet. He told him he had been predestined for that work even before he was conceived.

> Before I formed you in the womb
>    I knew you,
> and before you were born I consecrated you;
> I appointed you a prophet to the nations.
> —*Jeremiah 1:5*

What an awesome experience it must have been to receive a commission from Yahweh! It frightened even the greatest men of God. Moses protested that he was "slow of speech." Isaiah hesitated because of his unclean lips. Now, understandably, Jeremiah wondered how he, a mere youth, could possibly be "a prophet to the nations." But, Yahweh would not be put off. The effectiveness of Jeremiah's ministry would not depend upon his age, but upon the source of his message, and Yahweh would be that source (*1:7–8*). Then, the prophet tells us, "Yahweh put forth his hand and touched my mouth; and Yahweh said to me:

> Behold, I have put my words in your mouth.
> See, I have set you this day over nations
>    and over kingdoms,
> to pluck up and to break down,
> to destroy and to overthrow,
> to build and to plant.    —*Jeremiah 1:9-10*

How these words must have sounded to a boy who did not want to be a prophet in the first place!

### THE EARLY MINISTRY

For the most part, the material contained in the first six chapters probably comes from

Jeremiah's early ministry—that is, from his call in 628 until the reforms of 622.

*The Northern Peril.* Soon after Jeremiah's call, he saw a vision of a pot boiling in the north, tilted over so that its steaming, noxious contents were about to spill out over Judah (*1:13–19*). This threat of invaders "from the north country" is a recurrent theme in these chapters (*4:5–8; 6:22–24; see also 4:16; 5:15–17*). What nation Jeremiah had in mind at this point is a bit difficult to determine. Most of the older commentaries identify this northern peril with the "Scythian hordes." The basis for this identification was a statement by the Greek historian Herodotus to the effect that the Scythians were exercising a twenty-eight year rule over Asia at this time and would have posed the greatest threat to Judah. In recent years, this traditional view has been called into serious question. In the first place, archaeology has not yet yielded a shred of evidence to support Hezekiah's claim. In the second place, almost any serious threat to Judah would have to come from the north. Even the Babylonian army —which eventually overran Judah—came from the north, because the eastern desert would not support troops, making a direct march impossible. Perhaps Jeremiah knew the northern peril would be Babylon; perhaps not. It is not important. For Jeremiah, as for Isaiah before him, the real foe was Yahweh. Whether it be Scythian or Median or Babylonian, the northern foe was but another rod of Yahweh's anger, for Yahweh was still the Lord of History.

After showing his young messenger this vision, Yahweh commanded him to begin to speak to the doomed nation. Their hard-hearted sinfulness would be discouraging, but Jeremiah was not to grow faint in the face of it. However harsh their reception of his message might be, however they might oppose him, Yahweh would enable him to stand firm. In the midst of a people whose decayed foundations were about to be smashed and ground into the dust, Jeremiah would stand as

> a fortified city, an iron pillar, and bronze walls, against the whole land, against the kings of Judah, its princes, its priests, and the people of the land. They will fight against you; but they shall not prevail against you, for I am with you, says Yahweh, to deliver you. —*Jeremiah 1:18-19*

Thus strengthened and encouraged, Jeremiah began his public ministry.

*The Unfaithful Bride.* In oracles strikingly like those of Hosea, Jeremiah compares Israel to an unfaithful wife. He recalls the honeymoon days in the wilderness, when Israel followed Yahweh as an adoring bride follows her new husband (*2:2*). She had been "holy to Yahweh" (*2:3*), giving her love only to him. But these days of chaste bliss were no more. Long ago, Yahweh's bride had burst the marriage bond (*2:20*). Now, she was a shameless harlot, giving herself under every tree to any lover who might beckon (*2:20; 3:1–5, 13*). Now, she wandered about like a beast in heat, insatiable in her lust, ever seeking new lovers to satisfy her depraved cravings (*2:23–25*). So reprobate was Judah that even those with a reputation for wickedness had to come to her for lessons (*2:33*). What a pathetic sight this was. Yahweh had planted a people of pure seed, the seed of Abraham, but they had become a wild vine (*2:21*). He had created a people, but they said to a tree, "You are my father" and to a stone, "You gave me birth" (*2:27*). As if Baal and Asherah would or could provide for her needs! Judah had forsaken "the fountain of living water" in the vain hope that she could slake her thirst at the broken, empty cisterns of idolatry (*2:13*). It seemed that God's bride could not learn the lesson of history. Yahweh lamented:

The fortified city of Lachish that stood in the Judean lowlands during Jeremiah's time.

In vain have I smitten your children,
    they took no correction.
                —*Jeremiah 2:30*

Not even the awful fate that had befallen her sister Israel a century earlier could turn Judah from her course. In fact, "faithless Israel [had] shown herself less guilty than false Judah" (*3:11*).

The oracles that form the bulk of *chs. 3–6* give us a touching insight into the Husband/Father's attitude toward his bride/children. He is justifiably hurt, even enraged, at the infidelity of his people. He knows they must be severely punished. But at the same time, he is incurably merciful. Again and again, he says words to this effect: "You have deserved punishment for a long time and now you are going to get it. My mind is made up! You can do *nothing* to avert the catastrophe. Still, if you would show some small sign of genuine repentance —well, perhaps there might be a chance."

The northern kingdom is cited as an example of wickedness—but a remnant is urged to admit its guilt and return to the throne of Yahweh in Jerusalem (*3:12–4:2*). Judah's fate is sealed and the northern peril is coming like the whirlwind—but a genuine repentance, a circumcision of the heart, might somehow stay Yahweh's wrath (*4:3–4, 11–14*). The horsemen and archers are pictured as if they were already in the city—but word goes out that if one truly righteous man can be found, the city will be spared for his sake (*5:1*).

"*An appalling and horrible thing.*" It seemed to Jeremiah that no such righteous man could be found. If he were not a lusty stallion neighing for his neighbor's wife (*5:8*), he would be a fowler, trapping and selling men like a flock of birds (*5:26–27*). If he were not a judge perverting justice for his selfish ends, he would be a false prophet or a priest who sought only to please the peo-

265

ple (5:30). Jeremiah's feelings are summed up in these words:

> An appalling and horrible thing
> has happened in the land.
> —*Jeremiah 5:30*

We do not know the relationship between Jeremiah and King Josiah during these years. We do not even know for sure if Jeremiah took a direct role in Josiah's reforms. But we do know that Jeremiah had a good opinion of Josiah (22:15–16), and it is hard to imagine that Josiah could regard Jeremiah as anything other than an ally. In all likelihood, these two courageous young men were zealous co-workers in the heroic attempt to save a fallen nation.

## The Reform: An Appraisal

Between them, Josiah (and his backers), Jeremiah, Zephaniah, and the book of the law brought off a truly remarkable reform. And yet, it could hardly be called an unqualified success, as Jeremiah was to learn so painfully. There can be no criticism of the purge of idolatry, the renewal of the covenant, or the keeping of the passover. These were impressive accomplishments and greatly improved the existing situation. But there were other, decidedly less salutary effects.

The shutting down of the country shrines firmly established Jerusalem as the only legitimate place of worship, as the book of the law prescribed. At the same time, however, it cut off the only opportunity to worship Yahweh that was open to many who lived in remote areas. The worship at these outlying "high places" was not all it should have been, to be sure, but even this imperfect setup had kept alive some sense of obligation to Yahweh. When it was destroyed, religion probably ceased to exist for many of these people. Even though the priests who had officiated at these shrines remained among the people they had served (*II Kin.*

23:9), we can hardly expect them to have encouraged the people to get to Jerusalem as often as possible. Men seldom give their all-out support to movements that have put them out of work.

Another measure that proved to be a mixed blessing was the elevation of the written code to a place of prime importance. Obviously, the people needed authoritative guidance. This the lawbook provided. It specifically told them what needed to be done and set forth the consequences of obedience and disobedience. But its strength was also its weakness. Yahweh had promised to preserve his people from harm as long as they were obedient (*Deut. 28:1ff*). Tragically, they failed to see the vital distinction between formal compliance with external requirements and genuine obedience. They freely submitted to physical circumcision, but their hearts remained uncircumcised. Nevertheless, they fully expected Yahweh to keep his part of the bargain. They had thrown out the idols and shut down the high places. Now, Yahweh had no choice but to provide the peace and prosperity he had promised.

Jeremiah spent most of his life struggling vainly against this false sense of security. When he warned of imminent disaster, the men of Judah smugly pointed to the promises of the lawbook. If he challenged their concept of obedience, they laughed at him —or tried to kill him. They were keeping the letter of the law; someone else could worry about the spirit. Obviously, Judah's religion was a brittle structure.

When Judah *was* defeated and Jerusalem *did* fall and its inhabitants *were* carried into captivity, Jeremiah and the prophets who came after him had to do a massive job of theological reinterpretation to keep it from splintering beyond repair. But even their heroic effort was not wholly successful. They managed to provide their exiled countrymen with a new hope, but they were unable to stem the mounting tide of legalism. The exiles realized their plight was due to their failure to keep the Law. This was a definite improvement. But their conception of what was involved in keeping the law was little better than it had ever been. They mistakenly assumed that Yahweh would be pleased by stricter observance of the sabbath, greater attention to the details of sacrifice, and the multiplication of regulations covering every facet of life. In the early days after the return from exile, the Jews probably had the inner devotion to Yahweh that alone gave these practices any value. Soon, however, the spirit once again gave way to the letter, and a brand of legalism arose that outstripped anything Jeremiah ever saw. Jesus spent much of his ministry attacking the self-righteous scribes and Pharisees who gave a tithe of the plants in their garden while completely ignoring "the weightier matters of the law—justice, mercy, and faith" (*Matt. 23:23*).

## Josiah's Last Years

Little is known of Josiah's reign in the decade after the great reform. The lamentation that accompanied his death (*II Chron. 35:24–25*) indicates he maintained his popularity to the end. These must have been wonderful days for the glory-starved people of Judah. Something of "the good old days" of David had been regained. A man of God was on the throne. Judah was not only independent, but had enlarged her territory to include most of the old northern kingdom. And best of all, the book of the law seemed to guarantee that these conditions would prevail as long as its rules were kept.

The woes of Assyria reinforced this optimistic mood. The old enemy was receiving her just deserts. She had ruled the world, but it was becoming increasingly evident that little Judah would outlive her. Judah's satisfaction (glee is perhaps a better word) at Assyria's plight is reflected in the oracles of Nahum.

### NAHUM

Of all the prophets, Nahum had the most satisfying task. Others had been persecuted for their preaching. Nahum's message must have been received with sheer delight. Others had told their countrymen that Assyria would punish them for their wickedness. Nahum attacked haughty Assyria and foretold her obliteration. Then, for good measure, he commended Judah's return to righteousness and assured her of Yahweh's continuing favor. What more could a prophet desire than to be able to deliver a message like this?

Nahum began to prophesy shortly before the fall of Nineveh in 612 B.C. By this time, it was clear that the wicked Assyrian capital was about to be repaid in kind for the suffering she had inflicted on her neighbors.

Woe to the bloody city,
    all full of lies and booty—
        no end to the plunder!
The crack of whip, and rumble of wheel,
    galloping horse and bounding chariot!
Horsemen charging,
    flashing sword and glittering spear,
hosts of slain,
    heaps of corpses,
dead bodies without end—
    they stumble over the bodies!
And all for the countless harlotries of the
        harlot,
    graceful and of deadly charms,
who betrays nations with her harlotries,
    and people with her charms.
                            —*Nahum 3:1-4*

In the opening chapter, the prophet declares that it is Yahweh who will bring destruction on the city:

Yahweh has given commandment about
        you:
"No more shall your name be perpetuated."
                            —*Nahum 1:14*

Then, in vivid and exciting language, he describes the tumult and confusion that will overwhelm the city when the armies of "the shatterer" (*2:1*) pour through its gates.

> The shield of his mighty men is red,
>     his soldiers are clothed in scarlet.
> The chariots flash like flame
>     when mustered in array;
>     the chargers prance.
> The chariots rage in the streets,
>     they rush to and fro through the squares;
> they gleam like torches,
>     they dart like lightning.
> The officers are summoned,
>     they stumble as they go,
> they hasten to the wall,
>     the mantelet is set up.
> The river gates are opened,
>     the palace is in dismay;
>
> . . . . . . . . .
>
> Nineveh is like a pool
>     whose waters run away.
> "Halt! Halt!" they cry;
>     but none turns back.
>
> . . . . . . . . .
>
> Desolate! Desolation and ruin!
>     Hearts faint and knees tremble,
> anguish is on all loins,
>     all faces grow pale!
>
> —*Nahum 2:3–6, 8, 10*

There will be no escape for the bloody whore (*3:1–4*). All the nations will view her slave (*3:5–6*) and none shall mourn or bind her wounds.

> There is no assuaging your hurt,
>     your wound is grievous
> All who hear the news of you
>     clap their hands over you,
> For upon whom has not come
>     your unceasing evil?
>
> —*Nahum 3:19*

Nahum almost embarrasses us by the fervor of his intense nationalism and his frank joy at Assyria's misery, but we cannot doubt that his reaction to Assyria's plight was typical of most of his countrymen.

268

### THE END OF INDEPENDENCE

The Medo-Babylonian alliance leveled Nineveh in 612 B.C. and the exultant cries of Nahum echoed throughout Judah. With Assyria broken, it seemed certain Judah could look forward to a long period of continued independence and growth. Then, in an ironic turn of fate, these cries of joy become cries of lamentation.

After the defeat of Assyria, the Medes pulled back to strengthen their position in the East and North. For the time being, they were content to leave the West to Babylon. Babylon, of course, was anxious to seize the West, but she was not unchallenged. Egypt had regained much of her lost vigor and her new Pharaoh, Necho II (609–593) was not about to surrender the West without a fight. In assessing Egypt's strength as compared

Bust of Psammetichus II, son of Necho II and father of Hophra, all pharaohs of the Saite Dynasty.

| JUDAH | *Related History* |
|---|---|
| **Jehoahaz (Shallum)** *3 mos.* . . . . . . . . . .609/8<br>Deposed by Necho II | |
| **Jehoiakim** *11* . . . . . . . . . . . . . . . .609/8–597<br>Placed on throne by Necho.<br>Became vassal of Nebuchadnezzar | |
| | 605: Nebuchadnezzar defeats Necho at Carchemish. Establishes successful dynasty in Babylon. |
| 601: Revolt against Babylon.<br>PROPHETS: *Jeremiah*<br>            *Habakkuk* | |
| **Jehoiachin** *3 mos.* . . . . . . . . . . . . . . . . .597<br>Taken to Babylon in first deportation. | Egypt: Psammetichus and Apries make token efforts to help Judah against Babylon. |
| **Zedekiah** *11* . . . . . . . . . . . . . . . . . . . .597–587<br>587: Fall of Jerusalem.<br>Second deportation to Babylon. | |

**CHRONOLOGICAL CHART: 609–587 B.C.**

to Babylon's, Necho prudently recognized he would stand little chance in a one-to-one conflict. On the other hand, if Babylon were kept occupied in the East, Egypt would be free to expand her holdings—and her military strength. With this in mind, Necho decided to back Asshur-uballit in his efforts to regain his kingdom. It seems incredible that Egypt should be an ally of Assyria, but ambition makes strange bedfellows. The decisive move came in 609. When Nineveh fell in 612, the Assyrian government had set up a makeshift capital in Haran. In 610, this rump government had been driven back across the Euphrates. A year later, Asshur-uballit and what was left of his army decided to make one last attempt to retake Haran. It was at this point that Necho II threw in his support.

When Necho marched through Judah on his way to Carchemish, where the battle against the Babylonians was to be joined, Josiah unexpectedly decided to stop him. Just why Josiah did this is hard to say. There is no good reason to suppose he had any special feelings for Babylon.

Still, experience had taught him that Judah could only lose in the event that either Egypt or Assyria should come out on top. When Josiah marched out against him, Necho was more annoyed than frightened. He tried to persuade Josiah to stop pestering him and go back home where he belonged (*II Chr. 35:21*), but the years of peace had made Josiah overconfident. And so, the two armies met at Megiddo. The battle was brief and, for Judah, disastrous. An Egyptian arrow brought down the finest king Judah had known, and with him her dreams of glory. The body of the beloved ruler was returned to Jerusalem for burial amidst great lamentation. Then, the "people

269

of the land" tried to pick up the pieces by raising Jehoahaz, Josiah's son, to the throne.*

Meanwhile, Necho II continued on his way to Carchemish. But he, too, was backing a lost cause. Assyria had been dead for three years. Finally, the Babylonian general Nebuchadnezzar buried her. In the process, he sent Necho reeling back to Egypt. Necho failed to stop Babylon but, as a consolation prize, his march through Palestine and Syria had given him control of most of the West.

Since the "people of the land" had made Jehoahaz king, they probably felt confident he would continue his father's policies. The writer of *Kings* thought Jehoahaz was more like his evil grandfathers than his father (*II Kin. 23:32*), but Necho apparently judged the resemblance to Josiah strong enough to be dangerous. He deposed Jehoahaz and put him in prison in Syria. In his place he installed a second son of Josiah, Jehoiakim, who had apparently communicated his willingness to be a puppet-king. The land was placed under tribute, which, instead of being taken from the royal treasury, was raised by levying a head tax on the "people of the land" (*II Kin. 23:33–35*). What a galling burden this must have been to these lovers of freedom! The taste of independence had been just enough to whet Judah's appetite, but now the cup was empty.

## Jehoiakim and Jeremiah

The years of Jehoiakim's reign were a dark time for Judah. The king was a selfish and petty young man, far more interested in his royal "image" than in the physical or spiritual welfare of his people. While his nation faced possible destruction at the hands either of Egypt or Babylon, Jehoiakim pressed men into slave gangs to build a more spacious royal palace (*Jer. 22:13–14,*

18*). At a time when the nation's only hope lay in seeking righteousness and justice, this son of David was setting an example of dishonesty, violence, and oppression (*Jer. 22: 17*). It comes as no surprise that the nation followed the example of its king. The results of Josiah's faithful labor began to be overturned. Pagan practices began to drift back in (*Jer. 7:16–18; 11:9–13*). If a prophet of God dared lift his voice in protest, he was risking the wrath of the king, which might well mean death (*Jer. 26:20–23*). Even if he managed to make himself heard, it was virtually impossible to get anyone seriously disturbed about the condition of things, for the priests and many of the professional prophets were assuring the people that Yahweh would protect them as long as they kept the covenant (*Jer. 7:4; 14:13–16; 23: 9–40*). Indeed, Yahweh had so promised, but his conception of covenant-keeping was poles apart from theirs. They boasted of the presence of the temple and the new-found lawbook, and of their elaborate sacrifices. Yahweh did not scorn these, but they were odious to him without love and justice, without knowledge of God.

Jeremiah denounced these false prophets and priests as "the burden of Yahweh" (*Jer. 23:33–40*), and declared that the wrath of God would burst upon their heads like fire for their part in leading the people to destruction with pious-sounding lies.

Thus says Yahweh concerning the prophets who prophesy in my name although I did not send them, and who say, "Sword and famine shall not come on this land": By sword and famine those prophets shall be consumed. And the people to whom they prophesy shall be cast out in the streets of Jerusalem, victims of famine and sword, with none to bury them—them, their wives, their sons, and their daughters. For I will pour out their wickedness upon them.

—*Jeremiah 14:15–16*

---

*In *Jeremiah 22:10–12*, Jehoahaz is called Shallum.

Severe as he was in his condemnation of Judah's religious leaders, Jeremiah saved his fiercest attacks for King Jehoiakim. The memory of Josiah was still fresh in Jeremiah's mind. There was a real king! He had proved his mettle not by the size or ornateness of his palace, but by his dedication to the welfare of his people. And now, his half-baked son was playing at the game of being king, heedless of anything but his own selfish desires. When Josiah had died, the streets of Jerusalem were filled with lamentation. Jehoiakim's death would bring no more grief than the death of an ass. Notice the bitterness in Jeremiah's words:

Woe to him who builds his house by
   unrighteousness,
   and his upper rooms by injustice;
who makes his neighbor serve him for
      nothing,
   and does not give him his wages;
who says, "I will build myself a great house
   with spacious upper rooms,"
and cuts out windows for it,
   paneling it with cedar,
   and painting it with vermilion.
Do you think you are a king
   because you compete in cedar?
Did not your father eat and drink
   and do justice and righteousness?
   Then it was well with him.
He judged the cause of the poor and needy;
   then it was well.
Is not this to know me?
   says Yahweh.
But you have eyes and heart
   only for your dishonest gain,
for shedding innocent blood,
   and for practicing oppression and
      violence."
Therefore thus says Yahweh concerning
Jehoiakim the son of Josiah, king of Judah:
"They shall not lament for him, saying,
   'Ah my brother!' or 'Ah sister!'
They shall not lament for him, saying,
   'Ah Lord!' or 'Ah his majesty!'
With the burial of an ass he shall be buried,

dragged and cast forth beyond the gates
   of Jerusalem." —*Jeremiah 22:13-19*

Kings are not accustomed to this sort of frank appraisal. We may be certain Jehoiakim made a note of it for future reference.

### PREACHING AND PERSECUTION

Jeremiah did not restrict his outbursts to prophets, priests, and kings. He often addressed the general population, urging them to disregard the assurances of their leaders and to submit to Yahweh in true obedience. Three of his best-known sermons are the Temple Sermon, the Potter's House Sermon, and Clay Pot Sermon.

*The Temple Sermon.* The account of Jeremiah's sermon at the gate of the temple is recorded both in *ch. 7* and *ch. 26*. It is possible that these refer to two different sermons, but it seems more likely that they are two accounts of the same event, *ch. 7* giving more attention to the actual content of the sermon and *ch. 26* describing the reaction of Jeremiah's audience.

Early in the reign of Jehoiakim (*26:1*), Yahweh directed Jeremiah to stand at the gate of the court of the temple and address all who entered. Apparently, it was one of the great religious holidays for people from all the cities of Judah were expected to be present (*26:2*). Jeremiah began his sermon by warning the people against putting false trust in the promises the priests and prophets were making. Nothing, not even their pilgrimages to the temple, could replace genuine obedience. They were deceiving no one but themselves if they thought Yahweh would wink at their injustice and immorality as long as he did not have to share his temple with foreign gods (*7:4–10*). The sanctuary of Yahweh was a place where men might come to offer formal worship to him whom they served in every moment, not a magic charm to ward off enemies. For proof, let them go to Shiloh, the first place

271

in Canaan where Yahweh had made his name to dwell (7:12; 26:6). Had the people remained true, the sanctuary might still be standing, but because of their wickedness of priest and people, Shiloh had been reduced to ashes (I Sam. 1:4). Now, even as people from all over the nation crowded into the temple, Yahweh was but a hair away from bringing the same sort of destruction on Jerusalem (7:13–15). It would do no good to increase the offerings and prayers. The immorality and idolatry and hypocrisy that were becoming so characteristic of Judah turned the sweet savor of incense into an acrid stench, and the sound of prayers into a contemptible cacophony.

This sermon very nearly brought Jeremiah's career to an untimely end (26:7ff). As soon as he finished speaking, the priests and prophets and people crowded around him in anger and began to rough him up, threatening to kill him for his "blasphemies" against the temple and the holy city (7:7–9). News of the commotion reached the princes of the city and they hurriedly came to the temple. The priests registered their charges with the princes and again demanded the death sentence. Jeremiah's courage and composure before this angry crowd is stunning. He made no attempt to water down his message. He had indeed prophesied against the city. He had done so at the command of Yahweh and he would not take a word of it back. Killing him would not change a thing, except that it would bring even more innocent blood on the city (20:10–15).

Surprisingly, the princes of the city paid more attention to Jeremiah than to the priests. Probably, a number of them had been supporters of Josiah and had also had serious reservations about the way things were going in Jehoiakim's reign. They pointed out that perhaps Jeremiah's message *was* from God. Perhaps they should

heed his warnings. After all, when Micah had declared that Jerusalem would be "plowed as a field," Hezekiah had not killed him. He had begged, and received, Yahweh's forgiveness. Perhaps they would do well to do the same (7:10–19).

With the support of these princes, especially one Ahikam ben Shaphan (26:24), Jeremiah escaped the wrath of the crowd. But the crowd still got its victim, with the compliments of King Jehoiakim. Another prophet, Uriah, began to prophesy against the city, using words quite similar to those of Jeremiah. This was too much for Jehoiakim to take. If this sort of thing were allowed to continue, there was no telling what might happen. And so, Jehoiakim sent his men to arrest Uriah. The poor prophet heard of the scheme in time to flee to Egypt, but this merely delayed his fate. Jehoiakim sent a search party to Egypt, brought Uriah back, executed him, and threw his body into the paupers' graveyard. Jeremiah had important friends to protect him for the time being, but this would serve as a warning to any lesser lights who might be toying with the idea of criticizing the current administration.

*Preaching about Pots.* Like most of the great prophets, Jeremiah had a profound talent for illustrating his sermons. He was able to take everyday items and events and draw memorable lessons from them. On one occasion he went to a potter's house and watched the potter at his wheel. The vessel he was making did not turn out as he planned, so he shaped the clay into another vessel. Jeremiah likened the potter's handling of his clay to Yahweh's handling of nations. If a nation began to assume an undesirable shape, Yahweh could destroy it or reshape it to suit his purposes. And at present, because of Judah's moral and spiritual deformation, Yahweh was shaping evil against her (18:1–12).

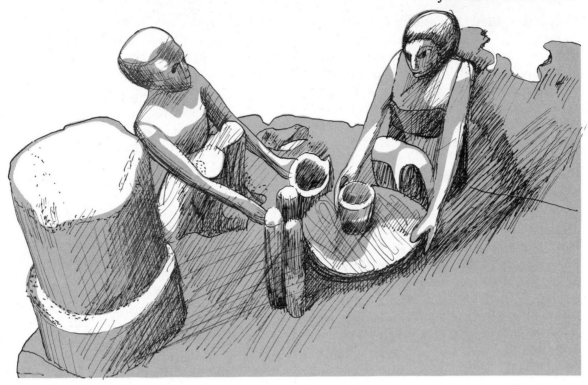

**Ancient model of a potter's shop.**

On another occasion, he bought a clay pot and took it out to the valley of Hinnom, the site of the city dump. There, in the presence of the elders and senior priests of the city, he broke the pot in pieces. The time was not far away, he declared, when Jerusalem would be like that clay pot—shattered beyond mending, fit for nothing but the garbage heap (*19:1–15*).

Neither of these two sermons was especially popular. After the first, the religious leaders plotted to "smite him with the tongue" in an effort to destroy his reputation and thus discredit his attacks against them. After the Broken Pot sermon, a priest named Pashhur decided to take more direct action. Pashhur beat Jeremiah and put him in stocks outside one of the gates of the temple. The next day, when Pashhur came to release him, Jeremiah picked up right where he had left off. Pashhur had been misnamed, he de-

clared. His name should have been Terror (*20:3*), for his false words and actions would result in terror for the people of Judah. As punishment, Pashhur would be among those carried off to Babylonian captivity.

*"Without Honor in His Own Country."* These incidents were just the beginning of the misery Jeremiah would suffer during his long and sorrowful ministry. For most of the rest of his life, he was mocked, rejected, and hated by those for whom he was giving his life. He was a laughingstock throughout the city (*20:7*). His enemies slandered him and set traps to destroy his ministry (*20:10*). Even in Anathoth, the town where he had grown up, he was despised (*11:21–23*). Part of the resentment at Anathoth may have been stirred up by a group of unemployed priests who lived there. Anathoth was the town to which Solomon had ex-

273

pelled the priest Abiathar for supporting Adonijah's cause after David's death. This had left Zadok and his descendants in charge of the priesthood. It had left Abiathar and his descendants with a bad taste in their mouths. Very likely, the priests of Anathoth had staffed some of the country high places. If this is true, Josiah's reforms, which Jeremiah had supported, put them out of work. Since they could not very well take out their resentment on the king, they took it out on their fellow-townsman, who they thought had betrayed them. The feeling against Jeremiah was so intense that even his own brethren, while pretending to be on friendly terms with him, had joined the plot to take his life (*12:6*). We do not know how far these plots went or how much, if any, physical discomfort Jeremiah suffered. But rejection by those whom he loved filled him with deep agony of the soul.

*"Yahweh, thou hast deceived me."* It would be inspiring if we could report that Jeremiah met all these persecutions and rebuffs with a greatness of soul that never allowed him to waver or become bitter. But this was not the case, and precisely because it was not, Jeremiah becomes an even more moving figure, for we can see that he was not a plaster saint, but a man of emotions and doubts and weaknesses like our own. He did not always believe that "all things work together for good to them that love the Lord." He did not think it was fair for the wicked to prosper while the righteous suffered, and he could not help feeling at times that God had let him down.

Some of the time he voiced his complaints rather cautiously:

> Righteous art thou, O Yahweh,
>     when I complain to thee;
>     yet I would plead my case before thee.
> Why does the way of the wicked prosper?
> Why do all who are treacherous thrive?
> > *—Jeremiah 12:1*

At other times, he grew more belligerent and demanded that Yahweh make his own lot easier and punish those who were opposing him.

> Let those be put to shame who persecute me,
>     but let me not be put to shame;
> let them be dismayed,
>     but let me not be dismayed;
> bring upon them the day of evil;
>     destroy them with double destruction!
>
> . . . . . . . . . . . . . . . .
>
> Therefore deliver up their children to
>     famine;
>     give them over to the power of the sword,
> let their wives become childless and
>     widowed.
>     May their men meet death by pestilence,
>     their youths be slain by the sword in
>     battle.
> May a cry be heard from their houses,
>     when thou bringest the marauder
>     suddenly upon them!
>
> . . . . . . . . . . . . . . . .
>
> For they have dug a pit to take me . . .
> Forgive not their iniquity,
>     nor blot out their sin from thy sight.
> Let them be overthrown before thee;
>     deal with them in the time of thine anger.
> > *—Jeremiah 17:18; 18:21-23*

Without question, this is not the sort of thing we should expect of a man of God, but which of us would not think such thoughts if we were in the same situation?

Jeremiah suffered a great deal for God and for country; so much, in fact, that on more than one occasion he expressed sorrow not only that he was a prophet, but that he had ever been born.

> Cursed be the day
>     on which I was born!
> The day when my mother bore me,
>     let it not be blessed!
> Cursed be the man
>     who brought the news to my father,
> "A son is born to you,"
>     making him very glad.

Let that man be like the cities
   which Yahweh overthrew without pity;
let him hear a cry in the morning
   and an alarm at noon,
because he did not kill me in the womb;
   so my mother would have been my grave,
   and her womb forever great.
Why did I come forth from the womb
   to see toil and sorrow,
   and spend my days in shame?
           *—Jeremiah 20:14-18*

What shocking language from a man chosen before his birth to be God's messenger! But even this was not the worst. Not only did he confess his inability to fathom God's will. Not only did he complain about his own lot. He finally became so depressed and disgruntled that he actually charged Yahweh with having tricked him into being a prophet simply in order to torment him.

Why is my pain unceasing,
   my wound invurable,
   refusing to be healed?
Wilt thou be to me like a deceitful brook,
   like waters that fail?

. . . . . . . . . . . . . . . .

Yahweh, thou hast deceived me,
   and I was deceived;
thou art stronger than I,
   and thou hast prevailed.
          *—Jeremiah 15:18; 20:7*

This was not the cry of an agnostic. This was not the accusation of a backslider attacking God to cover up his own shortcomings. This was a charge levelled by Jeremiah, perhaps the greatest of God's prophets. His experience was a supreme example of the sometimes overlooked truth that the religious life is not always the serene life, that the fully consecrated man is not always free from doubt. Those who have suffered outer conflict and inner torment in their quest for religious certainty may gain strength from the outpourings of Jeremiah's soul.

Yahweh did not deceive Jeremiah, for he never promised his prophets a life of peace and comfort. But he did prevail over him. From the beginning, Jeremiah had sought to avoid the awful task of being Yahweh's spokesman, but the plans of heaven could not be thwarted. There is no reason to believe that Jeremiah ever came to enjoy his work, but he did finally come to accept it as his inescapable burden. At the end of the same oracle in which he charges Yahweh with deceit, Jeremiah grudgingly acknowledges the futility of struggling against the word and will of the Lord.

If I say, "I will not mention him,
   or speak any more in his name,"
there is in my heart as it were a burning fire
   shut up in my bones,
and I am weary with holding it in,
   and I cannot.      *—Jeremiah 20:9*

### JEREMIAH'S SCROLL

In 605 B.C., the fourth year of King Jehoiakim, Yahweh directed Jeremiah to collect the oracles he had spoken since the beginning of his ministry and write them on a scroll. It is easy to forget a sermon, especially when part of the audience is poking fun at the preacher. Perhaps the men of Judah would pay more attention if they could see a written copy of all Jeremiah had said. Dutifully, Jeremiah dictated his oracles to his companion and secretary, Baruch. Now they were ready for publication.

Since there were no printing presses to make copies to slip under doors or hand out in the streets, publication of the document consisted in reading it in a public place. The natural place to catch the people who would be most likely to listen was the temple. Jeremiah had lost his license to preach at the temple. His enemies had not been able to kill him, but they had exerted enough pressure to have him debarred from the temple grounds (*36:5*). But this was no great problem. Baruch would be a worthy

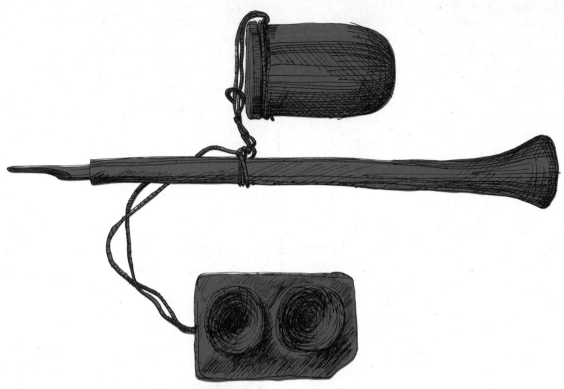

**Ancient writing equipment such as Jeremiah's scribe, Baruch, might have used.**

substitute. Jeremiah did not send Baruch to the temple as soon as the ink was dry on the scroll. He realized that the same people who had banned him from the temple would probably also ban Baruch as soon as they found out he was representing the prophet. So, it was necessary to wait for just the right occasion before attempting the first reading. They waited patiently for about a year. Finally, toward the end of 604 B.C., at the time of a fast that brought men to the temple from all over Judah, Baruch read the scroll in the hearing of the assembled crowds (*36:9–10*).

Among the listeners was a prince named Micaiah.* When he heard the doom-laden words, he reported them to the council of princes. Naturally, they were interested in hearing for themselves and sent for Baruch to come to their chambers. Probably, many of these princes had supported Josiah's reforms and had been responsible for persuading Jehoiakim not to kill Jeremiah. When they heard Baruch read the oracles, they were afraid and decided that the king must also hear them. Baruch, however, was not the man who should read them to Jehoiakim. In fact, since they remembered how the king had reacted to Jeremiah's preaching earlier, the princes advised both Baruch and his master to go into hiding for awhile (*36:16–19*).

Jehoiakim did not frighten easily. He agreed to have the scroll read to him, but his only reaction was one of utter contempt. As his servant unrolled and read an eight or ten-inch section, Jehoiakim would cut it off

---

*Not to be confused with the prophet Micaiah (*II Kings 22*).

with his penknife and throw it into the fire,* over the protests of several of the leading princes (*36:23–25*). When the scroll was consumed, the king ordered the arrest of Jeremiah and Baruch, "but Yahweh hid them" (*36:26*).

This was a setback for Jeremiah, but he was far from finished. Almost immediately, he dictated another scroll, including everything the first had contained, and adding a few oracles against Jehoiakim. It is quite likely that this second scroll is a major source of our present book of Jeremiah.

In both the first and second scrolls, Jeremiah had revived the theme of the northern peril and had clearly identified it with Babylon (*25:8–9, 13; 36:29*). The first scroll had been written with the faint hope that repentance might prevent the catastrophe. By the time of the second, it was clear there would be no escape for Judah. The preaching of the prophets had been rejected. Now, no word of warning, no prayer of intercession would be of any help (See *7:16; 11:14; 14:11; 15:1*). Now the deadly contents of the pot boiling in the north were about to spill over Judah, leaving behind a scene of desolation like that described in one of Jeremiah's earlier visions:

> I looked on the earth, and lo, it was waste
>     and void;
>   and to the heavens, and they had no light.
> I looked on the mountains, and lo, they were
>     quaking,
>   and all the hills moved to and fro.
> I looked and lo, there was no man,
>   and all the birds of the air had fled.
> I looked, and lo, the fruitful land was a
>     desert,
>   and all its cities were laid in ruins
> before Yahweh, before his fierce anger.
> —*Jeremiah 4:23-26*

---

*Scrolls were made either of papyrus or leather. Jeremiah's scroll was obviously papyrus, since one does not throw leather into a fire in a closed room in the wintertime (see *36:22*).

This stark description contains a bit of poetic exaggeration, to be sure, but the ruin that befell Judah in the next two decades was so severe that the people of God may well have concluded that the heavens truly had no light.

## The Coming of the Babylonians

By the end of 605 B.C., Babylon had gained clear access to Syria and Palestine. Early in that year, Nebuchadnezzar defeated Pharaoh Necho's forces first at Carchemish (See *Jer. 46*) and then at Hamath in Syria. He might have crushed the Egyptians completely had it not been for the death of his father, Nabopolassar king of Babylon. Nebuchadnezzar returned to Babylon in August, 605, in order to make certain no usurper tried to seize the throne. As soon as he was satisfied his grip was sure, he set out for the West once again. By late 604, about the time Baruch was reading the scroll at the temple, the Babylonian army had come down the Mediterranean coastal plain and was wreaking havoc with the cities of Philistia (*Jer. 47:5–7*).

To those who possessed anything like a realistic outlook, it was clear that Judah was next on Nebuchadnezzar's list. Some, like the people who had been duped by the false priests and prophets, blithely expected Yahweh to protect Jerusalem as he had always done before. Others, like Jeremiah, knew that Judah was at last going to receive what she had deserved for so long. Still others recognized there was little hope for escape from the Babylonian juggernaut, and yet, they could not understand how a righteous God could allow this sort of fate to befall his people imperfect as they were. The most outspoken of these was Habakkuk.

### HABAKKUK

Habakkuk took seriously the belief that Yahweh was Lord of History. But he also took seriously what he could see with his own eyes, and he was having trouble reconciling these two things. The first chapter of *Habakkuk* is cast in the form of an harangue between the prophet and Yahweh. In his opening oracle (*1:1–4*), Habakkuk complains of the unpunished injustice and immorality that is found in Judah. If Yahweh is righteous and in control of history, why does he allow such behavior to go unpunished? Yahweh's answer (*1:5–11*) is that it will not go unpunished much longer. It would just be a matter of time before the "dread and terrible" Babylonian army would become a new rod of his anger to punish Judah. This did not fully satisfy Habakkuk. By Yahweh's own admission, the Babylonians were a worthless lot, with no reverence for anything but their own might (*1:9–11*). Granted that Judah deserved chastisement for her sins, why did a righteous God have to depend on faithless scoundrels like the Babylonians to carry out his discipline? How could this possibly be defended? What sort of righteousness was it that, in order to punish one evil, raised up an even greater evil?

> Thou who art of purer eyes than to
>     behold evil,
>     and canst not look on wrong,
> why dost thou look on faithless men,
>     and art silent when the wicked
>         swallows up
>     the man more righteous than he?
>
> . . . . . . . . . . . . . . .
>
> Is [Babylon] then to keep on emptying his
>     net,
>     and mercilessly slaying nations for ever?
>                 —*Habakkuk 1:13, 17*

Habakkuk's questions go right to the heart of a fundamental problem of Biblical religion. The Bible clearly affirms that God is in control of historical processes, that he rewards the righteous and punishes the evil. And yet, at almost any given point in history, one can find abundant evidence that seems to refute these claims. The righteous *do* suffer, the evil *do* flourish, and, as often as not, history stumbles along as if it were completely without direction. It would be comforting if Yahweh had answered Habakkuk's questions with a detailed explanation of the relationship between his divine will and actual historical events. But he did not. Instead, he told Habakkuk that he would have to be content with delayed answers, half-answers, and, sometimes, no answers. One day, God's plan would be revealed and his purposes vindicated (*2: 2–3*). But until that day, "the righteous shall live by his faith" (*2:4*). In other words, despite the ambiguity of the historical situation, the righteous man can find meaning and power for living by trusting that somehow, in spite of all the apparent evidence to the contrary, God will be true to his promises. With Habakkuk, he can take his place on the watchtower of history (*2:1*) and look into the future with full confidence that in the fulness of time, Yahweh, the Sovereign Lord of History, will bring order out of chaos.

We do not ordinarily pay a great deal of attention to Habakkuk. His book is so short that we tend to think it must also be rather less important than most of the others. But we owe Habakkuk a debt, for he had the courage to face squarely a problem that has troubled religious men for ages. In the dark years of the Babylonian exile, Habakkuk's words must have been pondered again and again as righteous men tried to understand what had happened to them. And as they pondered them, these righteous men must have received strength from Habakkuk's simple, yet somehow grand, expression of trusting submission:

> Yahweh is in his holy temple;
>     let all the earth keep silence before him.
>                 —*Habakkuk 2:20*

When Nebuchadnezzar carried away ten-thousand of Judah's finest men and women, scenes like this one in an Assyrian wall carving must have been common.

### JUDAH BECOMES A VASSAL OF BABYLON

In 603 B.C. Jehoiakim decided it would be the better part of wisdom to switch his loyalty from Pharaoh Necho to Nebuchadnezzar (*II Kin. 24:1*). This maneuver postponed disaster temporarily, but it apparently used up Jehoiakim's supply of prudence. Late in 601, Nebuchadnezzar and Necho met once again, near the Egyptian border. Nebuchadnezzar got the best of the contest, but his army suffered severe losses and he was forced to return home to recover. With both Egypt and Babylon licking their wounds, Jehoiakim thought the time was ripe for rebellion and refused to pay the annual tribute. Nebuchadnezzar was not quite ready for another trip west, but he could not afford to let puny little Judah go unchastised, lest other vassal states begin to get ideas. So, as a temporary mea-

sure, he sent a number of small bands against Judah, from his own army and from his vassals around Judah, to keep Jehoiakim too busy to think about exporting his rebellion.

This holding action continued for about three years. Then, late in 598 B.C., Nebuchadnezzar decided it was time to lead another campaign to the West. Before he reached Judah, Jehoiakim died and was replaced by his eighteen year-old son, Jehoiachin (*II Kin. 24:6, 8*). Jehoiachin had barely taken the throne when the Babylonian armies reached Jerusalem. After a brief siege, the young king surrendered and threw himself on the mercy of the Babylonian ruler (*II Kin. 24:10–12*). For all practical purposes, this was the blow that marked the end for Judah and Jerusalem. This time Nebuchadnezzar was not content

279

merely to take home the treasures of the palace and the temple. This time he took home treasures that were far more necessary to the life of the nation: her king and the royal family, her princes, her judges, her soldiers, her craftsmen, her smiths. In short, he stripped Judah of ten thousand of her finest men, leaving her in the hands of the poor, the unskilled, and the ignorant. To shepherd these leftover sheep, the Babylonians appointed Zedekiah as king.

## A Time of Tragedy

With its leadership gone, Judah was a crippled nation. The new king, Zedekiah, was not really wicked in the sense that some of his predecessors had been. In fact, he allowed the prophets to appear in public and sought Jeremiah's advice on several occasions. But he was a weak, vascillating man whose policies and opinions were easily swayed (See *Jer. 38:5*). Good advisers might have rescued him, but, unfortunately, the new "nobility" that had come to power in the wake of the first deportation was also ill-suited for the task of political and moral leadership. For the most part, they were untrained men with little understanding of politics and little appreciation of religion. Judah was in a desperate state. No one knew this any better than Jeremiah.

### TWO BASKETS OF FIGS

As Jeremiah fretted about the state of the kingdom, Yahweh showed him a vision of two baskets of figs. The figs in one basket were ripe and beautiful. These were the exiles in Babylon. The other basket contained figs stunted by nature or so spoiled and rotten they were repulsive and totally unfit for consumption. This basket represented the scraggly crew the Babylonians had left in Judah. The point of the vision was clear. There was no hope for saving the diseased and decaying kingdom of Judah.

Yahweh would treat Zedekiah and his remnant like so much rotten fruit. They would be cast off the land, to be regarded by the other kingdoms of the earth as "a horror, . . . , a reproach, a byword, a taunt, and a curse" (*24:9*). But the freshly-plucked captives in Babylon Yahweh would cherish:

> I will set my eyes upon them for good, and I will bring them back to this land. I will bring them up, and not tear them down; I will plant them, and not uproot them. I will give them a heart to know that I am Yahweh; and they shall be my people and I will be their God, for they shall return to me with their whole heart. —*Jeremiah 24:6-7*

Soon after seeing this vision, Jeremiah wrote a letter to the exiles (*ch. 29*). He did not gloat over the fact that he had been right all along and that they were getting what they deserved. Instead, he urged them to adjust as quickly as possible to life in Babylon. Rather than sit around mourning their fate until they dried up and disappeared, they should build houses and plant gardens and do everything possible to maintain a vigorous community life. And above all, they should pay no attention to the false prophets who had already begun to prophesy that Yahweh would shortly overthrow Babylon and return them to Judah. With few exceptions, they would be in Babylon the rest of their lives (*29:10*). Instead of pinning their hopes on the defeat of Babylon, they would do well to pray for its welfare, since they now depended on Babylon for protection (*29:7*). Yahweh had not forgotten them. Their days were not over. They still had "a future and a hope" (*29:11*), but Yahweh would execute his plans in his own good time. The prophets currently at work among them were speaking lies in the name of Yahweh, and for this they would be destroyed.

> I am the one who knows, and I am witness, says Yahweh. —*Jeremiah 29:23*

## RUMBLINGS OF REVOLUTION

Nebuchadnezzar had made an impressive show of strength, but not all his recent victims were convinced he was unbeatable. The new Egyptian Pharaoh, Psammetichus II (594–588), felt that a well-organized coalition might be able to field an army that would be a match for the Babylonians. With his encouragement, the Phoenician states of Tyre and Sidon joined with Moab, Ammon, and Edom in an anti-Babylonian alliance. Envoys were sent to persuade Zedekiah to commit Judah to the cause (*Jer. 27:3*). Zedekiah was under considerable pressure to join. There was, of course, the threat of reprisal by the other coalition members if he refused. Then, within Judah itself, the professional prophets were busily earning their bread by assuring the people they would never have to serve the king of Babylon (*27:9*).

*The Yoke of the King of Babylon.* Impressive as it looked on paper, this coalition could not hope to handle Nebuchadnezzar's army when actual conflict came. Judah's only hope lay in keeping the good will of the Babylonian king. Jeremiah realized this and went to considerable length to convince his countrymen. In one of the symbolic acts characteristic of the prophets, he made a wooden yoke-bar and strapped in to his own neck. Then, he appeared before Zedekiah and the envoys of the coalition forces. He warned them that Yahweh was supporting Nebuchadnezzar and that it was useless to oppose him, despite what the false prophets were saying. If they went through with their plans, they would be driven off their lands. If they submitted to the yoke of the king of Babylon without further incident, they would be allowed to remain in their homeland in peace (*27:1–15*). After delivering his message to Zedekiah and the representatives of the heads of neighboring states, Jeremiah turned to the priests and the people, also urging them to reject the empty promises of the false prophets (*27: 16–22*).

Naturally, Jeremiah's preaching was a threat to the professional prophets. The people might not like what he was saying, but they might start listening to him simply because he had been right before. If they did, there was a good chance the popular prophets would lose their influence (and their income). Jeremiah had to be stopped. Simply ignoring or ridiculing him would not be sufficient; a direct attack was required. The man chosen for the task was Hananiah, a prophet from Gibeon. He confronted Jeremiah in the temple. There, in front of the priests and a large crowd, he announced that Yahweh had told him that within two years he would break the yoke of the king of Babylon and bring Jehoiachin* and the exiles back to Judah (*28:1–4*).

In an admirable show of restraint, Jeremiah applauded Hananiah's words—with qualification. He would be delighted, he said, if Hananiah's words would come true. One thing, however, should be kept in mind. Throughout Israel's history, the true prophets of Yahweh had always prophesied "war, famine, and pestilence." So far, those who had promised peace and comfort had been proven wrong. If Hananiah's words came true, then he was surely a prophet of Yahweh, but the burden of proof lay with him, not Jeremiah.

Hananiah recognized that Jeremiah had made his point well. In an effort to regain the advantage, he took the yoke-bars from Jeremiah's neck and broke them, declaring that Yahweh would break the Babylonian yoke with the same ease (*29:10–11*). Jeremiah apparently made no attempt to reply

---

*Jeremiah calls him Jeconiah, a variant form of the same name. In *22:24ff,* he calls him by an abbreviated form, Coniah.

at that moment (29:11), but a few weeks later he confronted Hananiah again. A false prophet could break bars of wood, Jeremiah told him, but the yoke Judah would wear would be an "iron yoke of servitude" that could not be broken (28:14). Then Jeremiah announced that, for his part in causing the people to trust in a lie, Hananiah, would die before the year was out. "In that same year, in the seventh month, the prophet Hananiah died" (28:17).

## THE REVOLT OF 588

Jeremiah's preaching and the death of Hananiah must have had their effect on Zedekiah, for he did not join the rebellion. As a result, the anti-Babylonian movement lost its steam and things rocked along for several years without much external change. But the figbasket continued to ferment. When Pharaoh Apries (called Hophra in *Jeremiah 44:30*, etc.) took the throne of Egypt in 588, talk of rebellion began to buzz once more. By this time, Zedekiah's prudence had worn thin. We do not know how he achieved the position, but he was apparently one of the key revolutionary leaders.

Nebuchadnezzar could not afford to allow this movement to spread any further. Apries' army was fairly large and skillful and the smaller nations had been free of war long enough to build up respectable forces. Together, they could pose a real threat to continued Babylonian control of the West. Soon, Nebuchadnezzar set out for Palestine. He took the expedition seriously enough to seek all the help he could get. The prophet Ezekiel, who had been carried to Babylonian in the first deportation, tells us that the Babylonian king consulted various signs and omens to see which nation he should attack first (*Ezek. 21:18–23*). The lot fell to Judah and, late in 588, Nebuchadnezzar's army laid siege to Jerusalem.

When Zedekiah saw the awesome might of Nebuchadnezzar hammering at his walls, he realized Jerusalem was in grave danger. He sent word to Jeremiah, asking for a word from Yahweh (*Jer. 21*). Zedekiah was hoping Yahweh would turn Nebuchadnezzar back with one of his mighty acts, but Jeremiah held out no such hope. Instead, he told the king that Yahweh would be fighting on the side of the Babylonians and that the city would be destroyed (21:3–7). Zedekiah did not give up. In a pathetic effort to secure Yahweh's favor—a sort of political deathbed repentance—Zedekiah urged the people to release their slaves as a sign of their desire to obey the covenant (*Jer. 34:8–10*). The law called for the release of slaves after six years of servitude (*Deut. 15:12–18*), but the slaveholders of Judah had apparently ignored this stipulation. By this time, they were willing to grasp at any straw. If releasing their slaves would save their own skins, they would gladly release them. They did so and, shortly afterward, the Babylonians lifted the siege. But the withdrawal of the Babylonians had not been a mighty act of Yahweh and the repentance of the slaveholders had not been genuine. Nebuchadnezzar had withdrawn after receiving word that the Egyptian army was marching toward Jerusalem (37:5). Nebuchadnezzar's forces were divided between Jerusalem and two other fortified cities of Judah, Lachish and Azekah (34:7), and he was not anxious to take on the Egyptians with only one-third of his army. As for the slaveholders, as soon as the Babylonians were out of sight, they backed down on their proclamation of liberty and reclaimed their old slaves. This bit of hypocrisy thoroughly disgusted Yahweh. Through Jeremiah, he declared that he would reward their faithless action with his own proclamation of liberty. Now that they had given final proof of their utter reprobateness, he would set free on them sword, pestilence, and famine. The king of

Babylon was gone, but he would return, and the next time there would be no respite. Jerusalem would be burned, and all the cities of Judah would be left "a desolation without inhabitant" (34:15–22).

### THE FIELD IN ANATHOTH

After the Babylonians withdrew Jeremiah set out for his home town of Anathoth. As he left the gate of the city, a guard seized him and accused him of deserting to the Babylonians. Jeremiah vigorously denied the charge but with no success. The princes before whom the guard took him also refused to believe him. After all, for years he had urged Zedekiah to surrender to the Babylonians. That was hardly the advice of a patriot! To make matters worse, his true reason for going to Anathoth sounded utterly fantastic—he was going to check on a plot of land he had just bought (37:11–12). No one who had listened to Jeremiah's preaching would have concluded that 588 B.C. was a banner year for investing in real estate in Judah. Surely Jeremiah must be lying. The princes beat him and cast him into prison (37:15).

But Jeremiah was not lying. As he explained to King Zedekiah later (32:1ff) he *had* bought a plot of ground in Judah; in fact, he had bought it at the very time the Babylonians were attacking Judah (32:25). And, despite the way it must have seemed, the purchase had not been a case of incredibly poor business judgement. On the contrary, it was an act of faith in Yahweh's promise to restore his people to their land after a period in exile. He had made the purchase in the presence of witnesses (32:12) and had sealed the deeds in an earthen vessel, to insure preservation for many years.

> For thus says Yahweh of hosts, the God of Israel: Houses and fields and vineyards shall again be bought in this land.
>
> —*Jeremiah 32:15*

### JEREMIAH IN PRISON

Jeremiah remained in prison many days. During this time, the Babylonians did not come back to Jerusalem, but they were still at their western headquarters at Riblah, on the Orontes River in Syria. Obviously, they were waiting for just the right moment to strike. When the suspense grew too great for King Zedekiah to bear, he had Jeremiah brought to his house secretly (37:16ff). He asked the prophet if there was any word from Yahweh. Jeremiah could doubtless have gained his freedom if he had assured Zedekiah that he had nothing to fear from Babylon. Instead, he told the king that he did indeed have a word from Yahweh: "You shall be delivered into the hands of the king of Babylon." Then, before the king could get angry, Jeremiah asked what crime he had committed by telling the truth. Where were those prophets who had promised Nebuchadnezzar would never attack Judah? This did not make Zedekiah happy, but he was honest enough to realize that Jeremiah had been right so far. He did not feel he could release him, but he did transfer him from his miserable dungeon cell to the "court of the guards," where he had considerable freedom and an adequate supply of food (37:18–21).

From Zedekiah's point of view, this bit of kindness proved to be a mistake. Jeremiah took advantage of his semi-freedom to resume his declarations of doom. Repeatedly, he pictured the horror that was to descend on Jerusalem and warned his hearers that their only chance for survival lay in surrendering to the Babylonians (38:1–4). This was too much for the princes of Judah to take. Before long, Jeremiah would have the whole city ready to surrender. They went to Zedekiah and demanded that Jeremiah be killed. Zedekiah's reply shows that he had lost effective control of the nation: "He is in

The seal of Gedeliah, whom Nebuchadnezzar appointed governor of those left in Judah after the fall of Jerusalem.

your hand; for the king can do nothing against you" (38:5). So, the princes lowered Jeremiah into an empty cistern, and he sank into the mire (38:6).

Jeremiah would have remained half-buried in the muck and slime until he starved to death if it had not been for Ebed-melech, a negro servant in the palace. When Ebed-melech learned of Jeremiah's fate, he rushed to the king, imploring him to act on the prophet's behalf. Zedekiah had not acted to save Jeremiah from the princes, but in his heart he knew the prophet was not a traitor and did not deserve to die. He sent several men with Ebed-melech and ordered them to free Jeremiah from the pit. Ebed-melech took a pile of rags from the palace and lowered them to Jeremiah by a rope. He put these under his arms for padding and fastened the rope around him in a loop. Then the servants slowly lifted him out and took him back to the court of the guards.

After a few days, Zedekiah again sent for Jeremiah to ask his counsel. Jeremiah was reluctant to say anything, fearing the king would kill him if he spoke the truth. When

Zedekiah promised he would not harm him, Jeremiah again urged him to surrender without a fight, lest the beloved city be destroyed by fire. Zedekiah was dismayed to hear that there was still no hope, but he was true to his promise not to harm Jeremiah. He sent him back to the court of the guard, with strict instruction to say nothing of the subject of their conversation. Jeremiah remained in the court of the guard until the day Jerusalem was taken (38:28).

### THE FALL OF JERUSALEM

Late in 588, the Babylonian army struck again. Jerusalem held out bravely for several months, but finally, on the ninth day of Tammuz (July), 587 B.C., the Babylonians made a breach in the wall and entered the city. Zedekiah tried to escape under cover of darkness, but was overtaken in the plains of Jericho. His captors bound him and carried him to Nebuchadnezzar's headquarters at Riblah. There, the Babylonian king cruelly underscored his victory by forcing Zedekiah to watch the execution of his young sons. Zedekiah himself was then blinded and carried to Babylon in chains (39:4-6).

Meanwhile, Nebuzaradan, the chief Babylonian military officer, was wrapping things up in Jerusalem. To make sure the city would not again be a threat, its walls were broken down and the dwellings were burned (39:8). Then, most of the inhabitants were carried to Babylon. A few paupers, who could be no help in Babylon and no threat in Judah, were allowed to remain in the land, under the supervision of Gedeliah, a man of Judah whom Nebuchadnezzar appointed as governor of the land (40:5). As for Jeremiah, the Babylonians apparently felt the princes of Judah had been right in branding him a traitor. Nebuchadnezzar himself gave orders that he was not to be harmed and that he should be allowed to decide for himself whether he would remain in Judah or go to Babylon with the exiles. When he chose to stay in Judah, he was given a present and an allowance for his expenses and was assigned to live with Governor Gedeliah (39:14; 40:5).

### GEDELIAH

Part of Jeremiah's decision to remain in Judah may have been based on his high regard for Gedeliah. Gedeliah's father was Ahikam ben Shaphan, the man who had saved Jeremiah's life when Jehoiakim wanted to kill him (Jer. 26:24). Since Nebuchadnezzar appointed him governor, it is obvious that Gedeliah had not been an outspoken leader of the anti-Babylonian forces. Probably, Gedeliah and Jeremiah had worked hand in hand during the years of Zedekiah's rule.

Gedeliah proved to be an able ruler, taking seriously both his responsibility to his people and his loyalty to Nebuchadnezzar. Soon, a considerable group of refugees formed around him. He assured them peace and security if they would submit to the moderate requirements of the Babylonian rule. Before long, he had them busily at work harvesting grapes and other summer fruit (40:7–12). For some reason, Baalis king of the Ammonites viewed Gedeliah's stable government as a threat to his own plans and plotted with Ishmael, a Jewish soldier, to have him assassinated. News of the plot reached Gedeliah through Johanan, a loyal soldier, but the trusting governor refused to believe such a thing of Ishmael. Unfortunately, his trust was misplaced. Later in the year, Ishmael and ten companions successfully executed their plot, slaying Gedeliah and fleeing to Ammon and the protection of Baalis (Jer. 41).

### THE FLIGHT TO EGYPT

Johanan and the other loyal soldiers feared they would be punished by the Babylonians for Gedeliah's death and decided to run for Egypt (41:17). Jeremiah urged them to stay in Judah, promising that Yahweh would cause them to prosper (42:7–12). If they went to Egypt, Yahweh would punish their faithlessness "by the sword, by famine, and by pestilence." They would become "an execration . . . and a taunt" and would never be allowed to return to Judah (42:13–22). Once again, Jeremiah's preaching went unheeded. Johanan and his cohorts rounded up all those they could find, including Jeremiah and Baruch, and marched them off to Tahpanhes in Egypt.

Jeremiah continued his ministry in Egypt. The old prophet was over sixty now. He deserved a congregation that would recognize the truth of his former oracles and listen to him in fear, humility, and love. He deserved such a congregation, but he did not get it. The exiles in Egypt had even less spiritual understanding than their ancestors. Previously, about the worst Israel had done was to ascribe the good gifts of Yahweh to the heathen gods. Now, they had the gall to claim that all their troubles had arisen as a result of worshiping Yahweh!

This must have been heart-breaking but Jeremiah did not waver. He preached with the same vigor as always, warning of the doom to befall those men and nations who refused to hear the word of the Lord (Jer. 46:51). Most of the details of these last years are lost. Presumably, Jeremiah and Baruch collected and arranged most or all of the materials that form the book of Jeremiah. Like Isaiah and the other prophets, Jeremiah was "binding up the testimony" as a witness to future generations of the futility of resisting the will of Yahweh.

## Hope Beyond Tragedy: The New Covenant

The fall of Jerusalem was the severest spiritual crisis the people of God had ever

Stele of a goddess from Beth-shan,
probably representing Baal's consort, Ashtoreth,
the "queen of heaven" worshipped by
the exiles in Egypt. (See Jeremiah 44:18-19.)

prophets who had gone before him, held forth a vision of hope beyond tragedy. The heart of this vision of hope was a New House of Israel and the cornerstone of this New House would be a New Covenant, a New Testament between God and man. Like the covenant of Sinai, this covenant of which Jeremiah spoke would be a gift of God's grace, to which men would respond in grateful trust. But the demands of the new covenant would not be written upon tables of stone. It would be written upon the hearts of men. The reforms of Josiah had shown that even the most careful observance of external rules could fail to produce the knowledge of God the Mosaic covenant was designed to produce. This new covenant could not be met by formal compliance with external rules. It would demand a response that welled out of the depths of one's being.

Jeremiah described the New Covenant in language similar to that used by Hosea, comparing the exile in Babylon to Israel's early wanderings in the wilderness. Only through pride-destroying, purifying discipline could Israel become fit to be Yahweh's virgin bride (*Jer. 31:1–6, 21–22; Cf. Hosea 1:14–23*). When she had undergone the chastisement, she would be forgiven of her past sins and invited to join in the new covenant that heralded the dawn of a new age (*31:34*). The promise of a new age and a new covenant probably meant very little to most people in Jeremiah's time. But in the years after the fall of Jerusalem, it began to loom much larger in the collective mind of the remnant of Israel. Six hundred years later, the writer of *Hebrews* recalled Jeremiah's words and asserted that the new age had begun, that the promised covenant had become a reality (*Heb. 8:8–12; 10:16–17*). He also made the claim that the mediator of this new covenant was the Son of God himself, who is called the Christ.

faced in their long history. The land God had promised to Abraham hundreds of years before had been taken from them. The Holy City of King David lay in ruins. Yahweh's own temple was but a heap of rubble. How could they continue to believe in and worship a God who would allow this to happen? It would not have been surprising if the religion of Yahweh had entered the graveyard of great religions at this point. Indeed, we can hardly imagine any other consequence had it not been for the great heroes of faith like Jeremiah.

Jeremiah was unrelenting in his insistence that violation of the Mosaic covenant would result in disaster. And yet, even as he warned of the awful consequences of covenant-breaking, he, like the great

# PART FOUR

## *The Exile and Beyond*

# 12

# The People of God
# in Exile

*In Babylonian exile,
the people of God await
a new Age*

IN MANY WAYS, the period of the exile was one of the most important in the history of God's people. After the havoc the Babylonians had caused, the chances that Judah could ever recover must have seemed terribly small. Her cities and towns lay in ruin. Her leadership was gone, killed in battle or taken captive to Babylon. Of those the Babylonians had left, most were looking for the first good opportunity to leave the country. The one thing that might have served as a rallying point for the tiny remnant and their exiled compatriots—the temple of Solomon—was a heap of ash and rubble. The nation of Judah had ceased to exist. But, of course, that was not the end of the story. The exile was a refining and tempering fire. When the faith of Israel passed through it, it emerged stronger and more secure. It was this faith—reexamined, disciplined, renewed—that gave the remnant of God's people the will to survive. It is this post-exilic form of the religion of God's people that we usually call Judaism.

As important as the time of the exile was, we have very little concrete information about it. The historical books of the Bible break off shortly after the fall of Jerusalem and when *Ezra* and *Nehemiah* take up the narrative again, the Jews are in the process of returning to Jerusalem. All that we know of the years between the destruction of Jerusalem in 587 B.C. and the return of the first captives in 539 B.C. comes from occasional statements in the prophetic books and from incidental references in non-Biblical materials discovered by archaeologists. It is possible, however, to gain a general picture of what was going on and to notice the chief ways in which the exiles responded to their situation. By doing this, we can have a much better understanding of the later development of Judaism.

## The Dispersion

The fall of Judah marked the beginning of what has come to be known as the Dispersion, or Diaspora. These terms refer to the widespread settlement of Jews outside Pal-

A reconstruction of Babylon's Ishtar Gate, named after the fertility goddess known in
Israel as Ashtoreth. The royal procession is shown on its way to the palace, which
had the Hanging Gardens on its roof.

estine. It would still be some years before the Dispersion would attract much attention as cultural phenomenon, but, in one way or another, the children of Abraham were being separated from their brethren. Many were probably absorbed by neighboring peoples. Others, like the group that took Jeremiah with them, sought refuge in Egypt. And of course, there were those who had been taken to Babylon. But before we turn our attention to those who had left the homeland, let us look briefly at those who remained. If they were not technically part of the Dispersion, they were certainly far from representing the mainstream of Jewish life.

### THE REMNANT IN JUDAH

As we have seen, Judah was a wreck. The land was not completely deserted, but those who remained served only to underline the scope of the disaster. The population was reduced to about one-twentieth of what it had been in the days of King Hezekiah, and the influx of Samaritans from the north and Idumeans from the south threatened to engulf the remainder. After the tragic experiment in self-government that cost Gedaliah his life, formal political organization in Judah probably all but disappeared. The people just scratched out a living as best they could, always on the verge of starvation. The abject misery of their condition mirrored in the little book of *Lamentations*.

*Lamentations* is a collection of five poems dealing with the calamity that had befallen Jerusalem. In the English translation there is nothing special about these poems except their content. In the Hebrew text, however, the first four poems are in acrostic form; that is, each stanza begins with the succeeding letter of the Hebrew alphabet. In chapters *1*, *2*, and *4*, only the first word of the stanza bears the appropriate letter, but in chapter *3*, the letter appears in the first

word of each of the three lines. Chapter *5* is not in acrostic form, but, like the others, it does have twenty-two stanzas, the number of letters in the Hebrew alphabet. This rather artificial arrangement helps us to make an educated guess as to the purpose of these poems. From *Jeremiah 41:5* we learn that people still came to offer sacrifice at the charred spot where the temple had stood. It appears likely some kind of regular worship was carried on there, probably by second-rate priests who had not even been good enough to be deported. It may be they chanted these very poems, as an act of mourning over the desolation of the land. If this was the case, we may assume that the acrostic form of the poems was designed to make them easy to memorize.

Traditionally, Jeremiah has been regarded as the author of *Lamentations* and his name appears in the title in most translations. There is nothing in the book itself, however, to support this viewpoint. In the Hebrew Bible, no effort is made to connect the poems with Jeremiah. In fact, their place in the collection is with the so-called "writings"* found at the end of the Hebrew Bible, and not after *Jeremiah*, as in the English versions. Also, the style and tone of the poems are not what one would expect of Jeremiah. He was a free and hard-hitting preacher, not the sort who would arrange his oracles in a pedantic acrostic form. This is not to say Jeremiah could not have been the author of these laments. He may have been. But the text itself nowhere indicates that he was, and the evidence seems to favor another author. Probably, they are the work of some unknown poet or group of poets who remained in Judah throughout most of the exile.

These five laments are part of an anguished effort to make sense out of what

---

*See footnote, p. 120

had happened to Judah. They brim with sorrow and desolation. They reflect the despairing conviction that Yahweh had deserted his people. The tone of dejection is set from the opening lines:

> How lonely sits the city
>     that was full of people!
> How like a widow has she become,
>     she that was great among the nations!
> She that was a princess among the cities
>     has become a vassal.
>
> . . . . . . . . . .
>
> Is it nothing to you, all you who pass by?
>     Look and see
> if there is any sorrow like my sorrow
>     which was brought upon me,
> which Yahweh inflicted
>     on the day of his fierce anger.
>                 —*Lamentations 1:1, 12*

Then, the poet describes the awful scenes he sees about him. The destruction of the city and the temple (*2:5–10*) are mute testimony to the fact that

> Yahweh has done what he purposed,
>     has carried out his threat;
> as he ordained long ago,
>     he has demolished without pity;
> he has made the enemy rejoice over you,
>     and exalted the might of your foes.
>                         —*Lamentations 2:17*

But more was destroyed than city walls, and buildings, and altars. With a bitter, sometimes almost distasteful realism, the poet tells of the terrible toll the catastrophe had taken in terms of human life—strong men decaying in body and spirit, children fainting and dying of starvation, mothers becoming cannibals, men of God being slaughtered on the temple grounds.

> The chastisement of the daughter of my
>     people has been greater
>     than the punishment of Sodom.
>
> . . . . . . . . . .
>
> Her princes were purer than snow,
>     whiter than milk;

> their bodies were more ruddy than coral,
>     the beauty of their form was like sapphire.
> Now their visage is blacker than soot,
>     they are not recognized in the streets;
> their skin has shriveled upon their bones,
>     it has become as dry as wood.
>
> . . . . . . . . . .
>
> Infants and babies faint in the
>     streets of the city.
> They cry to their mothers,
>     "Where is bread and wine?"
> as they faint like wounded men
>     in the streets of the city,
> as their life is poured out
>     on their mothers' bosom.
>
> . . . . . . . . . .
>
> The hands of compassionate women
>     have boiled their own children;
> they became their food
>     in the destruction of the daughter
>         of my people.
>
> . . . . . . . . . .
>
> Should women eat their offspring;
>     the children of their tender care?
> Or should priest and prophet
>     be slain in the sanctuary of Yahweh?
>     —*Lamentations 4:6-8; 2:11, 12; 4:10; 2:20*

The faith of the poet obviously runs deep. Even the ghastly sights that confront him at every turn do not completely erase all trace of trust in God. The third lament expresses a quiet determination to wait patiently for Yahweh's deliverance.

> The steadfast love of Yahweh
>     never ceases,
>     his mercies never come to an end;
> they are new every morning;
>     great is thy faithfulness.
> "Yahweh is my portion," says my soul,
> "therefore I will hope in him."
> Yahweh is good to those who wait for him,
>     to the soul that seeks him.
> It is good that one should wait quietly
>     for the salvation of Yahweh.
>                         —*Lamentations 3:22-26*

But such hope is difficult to maintain forever. This the poet also realized. In the clos-

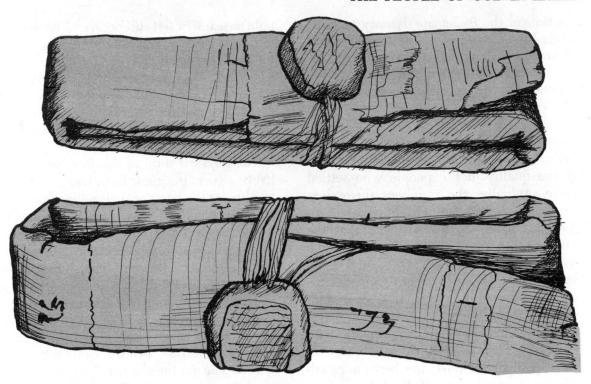

**Sealed papyri from the Jewish colony at Elephantine.**

ing lament, after a summary picture that is in some ways more heart-rending than those that have gone before, he lifts a desperate plea for restoration and renewal of the nation. We can almost see the drawn faces and hear the sorrow-strained voices of the worshipers gathered around the ash heap that had been Jerusalem.

> Thou, O Yahweh, dost reign forever,
>   thy throne endures to all
>     generations.
> Why dost thou forget us for ever,
>   why dost thou so long forsake us?
> Restore us to thyself, O Yahweh, that we may
>     be restored!
>   Renew our days as of old!
> Or hast thou utterly rejected us?
>   Art thou exceedingly angry with us?
>                     —*Lamentations 5:19-22*

For those who left in Judah, even the expressions of hope seemed hopeless.

## EXILES IN EGYPT

For centuries, whenever famine or hardship struck the ancient Near East, large numbers of refugees turned to Egypt for succor. Even when she was weak politically, Egypt always had the Nile to assure at least a minimal existence. When the Babylonians ravaged Judah, large numbers of refugees once again headed for Egypt. We have already noticed the group that forced Jeremiah to accompany it to Tahpanhes, in lower Egypt. This took place relatively soon after the fall of Jerusalem. As conditions in Judah grew worse, other waves of refugees must have made the trip to the south. Most of these also seem to have settled in lower Egypt (*Jeremiah 44:1*). A century later, there was a large colony at Elephantine, located on the first cataract of the Nile, the site of Modern Aswan. These early colonies expanded and spread to other cities until, in

293

the time of the Ptolemaic dynasty (305–30 B.C.), Egypt was one of the major centers of Judaism (along with Babylon and Palestine). But that time was not yet. For now, the center of the Jewish world was Babylon.

## BY THE WATERS OF BABYLON

Babylon became the center of Judaism not simply because of numbers, but because of the quality of the people who settled there. Actually, the numbers themselves were not overwhelmingly impressive. In *Jeremiah 52:28–30*, we are told that the total of those carried to Babylon in the three major deportations of 597, 587, and 582 B.C. was only 4,600. Probably, this number includes only adult males, but even with women and children added, the total is still relatively small. But, as has already been pointed out, these 4,600 were skimmed off the top. They included the best educated, the most capable political and religious leaders, the finest soldiers, the most skillful of the artisans. If God's people were to make a comeback, the major thrust would have to come from this group. Fortunately, their situation in Babylon made such a comeback possible.

*Life in Captivity.* Life in Babylonian captivity was not as severe as one might suppose. The exiles were under general supervision, but within this framework of supervision, they enjoyed considerable freedom. Unlike the Assyrians, the Babylonians made no attempt to destroy the sense of national solidarity among their captives. Jehoiachin, who had been brought to Babylon in the first deportation in 597 B.C., was regarded as the legitimate king of the Jews. In fact, toward the end of his life, he lived at the Babylonian court and was treated with considerable honor and generosity. Several passages in *Ezekiel* and *Jeremiah* seem to indicate that the exiles themselves lived in communities of their own with a consider-

able measure of self-direction and were permitted to carry on normal activities of farming and business (*Jer. 29:5; Ezek. 3:15; 8:1; 14:1; 33:30*). Many of the exiles grew so content in their new situation that they (or their children) refused to return to Judah when the opportunity was offered them.

The physical state of the Jews was relatively secure, but their faith was in serious trouble. At the heart of their religion lay the almost unshakable conviction that Yahweh would never allow serious harm to befall Jerusalem, or the royal house of David, or the temple. But now he had. What were they to think, in light of this calamity?

The obvious conclusion was that their faith had been wrong. But what did that mean? Were they wrong in believing that Yahweh was an all-powerful God? If he was, why had he not been able to keep his promises? Was he really the Lord of History? If he was, why had things taken such an unexpected course? Were they really his chosen people? If they were, why had they been swept off their homeland, and what did the future hold for them? If Yahweh was the One True and Powerful God, if he was the Lord of History, if they were indeed his elect, if his promises did have any validity, how were they to reinterpret these notions in a way that could have any meaning for them? This was the crisis of faith the exiles faced. Their responses to this crisis forever altered the face of Judaism.

## HEARING THE VOICE OF THE PROPHETS

Not everyone had been surprised by what had happened to Judah. For hundreds of years, the prophets of God had warned of the disastrous consequences that were bound to accompany the disregard of the covenant. Practically all the exiles in Babylon must have known of Jeremiah and his continual development of this theme. And so, when they began to reflect seriously on their fate and on what Jeremiah and the other prophets had said, it was possible to conclude that what had happened to them was not a sign that Yahweh had no power, or that he had deserted them. On the contrary, it was a sign that he *was* still in control of things. Through his prophets, he had warned that his righteous wrath would fall on those who broke the covenant. Judah had broken the covenant, and Yahweh's wrath had fallen. They had deserved the punishment they were receiving. It must have been difficult for the stubborn exiles to admit the hated prophets had been right after all, but it was this grudging realization that enabled them to hold on to their faith and to survive the trauma of the exile, for even the most bitter of the prophets always included a note of hope somewhere among their oracles of doom. When they had spoken of the destruction of the nation, they had pictured a remnant that would be spared. When they had described the dark days of exile and oppression, they had promised a restoration of glorious proportions. When they had bewailed the continual disregard of the covenant by the people of God, they had spoken of a day when God and men would be joined together in a new and everlasting covenant.

All this gave the exiles a basis on which to build a new community and a hope on which to build a dream. As one might expect, there were varying convictions about the shape of the future. Three "programs" for the future were especially important in shaping the development of Judaism: 1) the conservative legalism of the priestly circles, 2) the utopian situation pictured by the prophet Ezekiel, and 3) the glorious triumph of Yahweh's purpose so beautifully described in the Captivity Oracles (*chs. 40–66*) of *Isaiah*. We shall now turn our attention to each of these.

## The Priestly Tradition

From the time of the establishment of the monarchy, the people of Israel and Judah seem to have paid little attention to the details of the law. In *Kings* and *Chronicles*, we read very little about sabbaths or feast days or rules of sacrifices. When the Book of the Law was found in Josiah's time, its contents had obviously been long forgotten. Those who found it did not even know what it was (see p. 258). The Passover had not been kept since the days of the judges (*II Kings 23:22*). The temple itself had been closed for a number of years. Josiah did much to correct this situation, but after his death, there were again long periods of time when the law was almost wholly ignored. When the exiles became convinced that Yahweh was punishing them for their disregard of the covenant law, a large segment of them decided that the best way to placate his wrath would be to keep the law with greater strictness than it had ever been kept before.

It is safe to assume that the leaders of this conservative movement were the priests and Levites. The task of preserving and teaching the law had been their responsibility before the exile. It was only natural that they should continue this function in Babylon. Never had their task been so easy. Back in Palestine, the people had been too concerned with their business and pleasure to spend much time worrying about either learning or keeping the law. They knew that Yahweh had promised to protect them —and that was all the religion many of them felt they needed. But now, they recognized that Yahweh's promises depended on their obedience to the law. If they were to be delivered, they would have to give much greater attention to the law than ever before. And so, under the guidance of the priests, they began to emphasize those de-

295

tails of the law that seem to have received little attention during the monarchy: circumcision, the rigorous keeping of the sabbath regulations, tithing, and the complex laws dealing with ritual cleanness and uncleanness (see p. 82). Such attention to detail was not bad in itself, but, like any legalistic approach, it was easily perverted. In Jesus' time, the Pharisees were far more concerned about all the minute regulations of the law than about the great principles that supported them. Neither God nor man is served by such a religion. But we must not charge the exiles with the sins of the Pharisees. These broken people were seeking for the heart of their religion. Their attention to what we might dismiss as rather unimportant details was an expression of their deep desire to render complete obedience to the will of Yahweh.

In their desire to restore the kind of community of obedience that had existed (at least to some extent) in Moses' time, the exiles paid special attention to the written records and oral traditions that had been handed down from the past. Much of the Old Testament probably reached its final form in this period. Before the exile, we hear almost nothing about any sacred books in Israel or Judah. Within a few years after the return to Jerusalem, attempts were being made to collect and label those writings that were to be regarded as scripture. Obviously, the exile had generated much of this interest.

The literary work of the exile included both original composition and editing of earlier materials. Some historical sections, such as the last chapters of *II Kings*, cannot have been written before the exile, for the simple reason that they describe the fall of Jerusalem and the deportation to Babylon, as well as the flight of refugees to Egypt. But *I–II Kings* cover a long period, and much of the material they contain was

available either in oral form or in the official records of the various kings. So, the writing of *I–II Kings* consisted of gathering the available materials and working them into the form they have in our Bibles. Earlier (see p. 92) we noted that *Joshua* through *II Kings* could be read as one continuous history, dealing with the experiences of God's people from the time they entered Canaan until the beginning of the exile. It is not unlikely that the material found in *Joshua, Judges,* and *I–II Samuel* also received its final shaping at this time. Most Biblical scholars believe that the priestly circles engaged in this important literary activity also produced a final edition of the first five books of the Bible. According to this viewpoint, their work included arranging the available materials in an orderly fashion, and making sure that the various collections of laws and regulations received adequate emphasis.

The oracles of the prophets, once despised, but now confirmed by the events of history, were also cherished as a source of divine guidance. We do not know in just what form the exiles possessed these poems. Probably, some were in collections that were already quite close to the form in which we know them, while others were much more loosely arranged—or scarcely arranged at all—and required considerable editing to bring them to their final form. Some of the most important work of the prophets, of course, was yet to occur. The first great prophet of the exile was Ezekiel, whose ministry we shall now consider.

## Ezekiel

The first great religious leader to arise from among the exiles was the prophet Ezekiel. Ezekiel was one of the strangest and most exciting figures in all of religious history. By almost any standard, he possessed an abnormal personality. This is not to say that he was mentally disturbed, although some have rendered this verdict. But there can be little question that his unusual sensitivity to a variety of moods and influences enabled him to have and to give expression to experiences of the presence of God that lie beyond the powers of the vast majority of men.

As is the case with most of the prophets, the Bible tells us little of Ezekiel's background. We know he was a married man (*ch. 24*). From the opening verses, we gather that he was a priest and the son of a priest. This means that he was a member of the Zadokite family, which gained control of the priesthood during the reforms of Josiah. The date of his first vision is given as the fifth year of the exile of King Jehoiachin, or 593 B.C. (*1:2*). This was five years before the fall of Jerusalem, which means that Ezekiel had come to Babylon in the first deportation in 597 B.C., along with King Jehoiachin and the rest of Judah's elite. He had apparently settled with a group of exiles on the banks of the river Chebar,* near the town of Tel-abib (*1:1; 3:14–15*). His ministry, insofar as we have record of it, lasted twenty years (see *1:2* and *40:1*) and falls into three natural divisions. For the five years following his first vision in 592 B.C., he spoke repeatedly of the doom that was to befall Jerusalem (*chs. 1–24*). When word came that Nebuchadnezzar was besieging Jerusalem, he abruptly altered his approach and began, like a true prophet, to deliver oracles against "the nations" (*chs. 25–32*). Finally, when he learned that Jerusalem had actually fallen, he began to speak words of hope and to envision an idealized future based on the priestly traditions and cen-

---

*Chebar was actually a canal that carried water from the Euphrates through the city of Nippur, which was situated southeast of Babylon, and then flowed back into the Euphrates.

tered around a new and glorious temple (*chs. 33–48*).

### EZEKIEL'S CALL

In the year 593 B.C., as he sat among the exiles on the banks of the river Chebar, Ezekiel received his call to the prophetic ministry. In several ways, his inaugural vision reminds us of that of Isaiah (*Isa. 6*), except that it is more spectacular. In the midst of a great storm cloud, Ezekiel saw a vision of "the likeness of the glory of Yahweh." As the cloud flashed with fire and lightning, Ezekiel saw four remarkable creatures. Each had the body of a human and glistened like burnished bronze. Each had four wings and four faces. The faces were those of a man, a lion, an ox, and an eagle, symbolizing all the dominions of animal life. By the side of each was a marvelous "wheel within a wheel" that enabled the chariot to roam the universe without ever pausing to change directions. Over these creatures and these wheels, on a sapphire throne that sat on a platform of crystal, was the likeness of the glory of Yahweh. This "likeness" resembled a human form, but had the appearance of gleaming, fiery bronze.

This picture may appear grotesque at first, but a little reflection will reveal it as a profound symbolization of a God who has dominion over all living creatures and who cannot be confined within the limits of one nation or one people. When the vision assaulted Ezekiel's sense, he was completely overwhelmed and fell upon his face in awe and reverence—and perhaps a bit of terror.

Then, a voice ordered him to stand upon his feet. Calling him by the name "Son of man," which occurs repeatedly in Ezekiel's visions and serves to underline the already obvious distinction between man and God, the voice gave Ezekiel his commission. He was not to be an evangelist, to tell the Babylonians of the mighty acts of Yahweh. His

Ezekiel's vision
—the four creatures and the "likeness
of the glory of Yahweh."

mission was to the rebellious exiles. Remember, at this point, Jerusalem had not yet fallen and many of the exiles doubtless looked forward confidently to the day when they would return to Judah and Jehoiachin would once more reign as their rightful king. Ezekiel's mission was to be to them.

Like Isaiah before him, the purpose of his ministry was not to convert the house of Israel, but to leave it without excuse. He was like a watchman on a wall (*ch. 33*). His task was to warn of impending danger and of the folly of rebellion. If they did not choose to heed his warning, he could not be blamed for the catastrophe that was sure to follow. This did not mean Ezekiel would have a relatively carefree, pleasant ministry. The rebels of Israel were a hard-headed lot. But Yahweh would make Ezekiel's forehead harder than flint (*3:7ff*). When he had preached to them, promised Yahweh, "they will know that there has been a prophet among them" (*2:5*).

For a full week, Ezekiel sat speechless among his companions.* Then, the word of the Lord came to him again, telling him that his ministry was about to begin.

### SIGNS OF SIEGE AND EXILE

As we have already noted, a characteristic mark of the prophets was their profound gift for illustrating their sermons. Even in this elite company, however, Ezekiel stands out. No other prophet—not even Jeremiah—went to such great lengths to get his points across.

*A Model of Destruction (4:1-3).* To teach the confident exiles that Yahweh would not protect Jerusalem from Nebuchadnezzar, Ezekiel built a tiny model of a city under

---

*The meaning of *3:24-27* is puzzling, but it may indicate that the public appearances of Ezekiel were often preceded by periods in which he lay in a trance, dumb and motionless, for some time. Other scriptures support this view (*24:27; 33:22*).

siege. He drew a picture of a city on a brick, and let this represent Jerusalem. Then, much like a small boy might do, he piled dirt up around it to represent siege-mounds (see p. 243) and built little models of the enemy camps, and placed pieces of wood or metal around it in various places, to represent battering rams. We can imagine that it was an impressive piece of miniature craftsmanship, of the same type one frequently sees in museums of history. But Ezekiel was not primarily concerned to announce that the Babylonians would besiege Jerusalem. The exiles would not have been surprised at this, but they were confident Yahweh would allow no serious harm to come to the city. To symbolize Yahweh's attitude, Ezekiel erected an iron plate between himself and his model. This signified that Yahweh had cut himself off from Zion, that he would not resist the Babylonian juggernaut.

*The Years of Exile (4:4–17).* When Ezekiel finished the model of the siege of Jerusalem, Yahweh commanded him to lie down beside it for 430 days, almost a year and a quarter. He lay on his left side for 390 days, and on his right side for 40 days, to symbolize the number of years the people of the northern and southern kingdoms, respectively, would be in exile.* To dramatize the poor conditions of the exile, Ezekiel's daily nourishment during this period consisted of a single cup of water and a small loaf of bread. At first, Yahweh instructed him to use human dung for fuel, but this ran counter to Ezekiel's priestly upbringing, and he was granted permission to use cow dung instead.

*The Symbol of the Razor (5:1–17).* In another striking portrayal of what Yahweh would do with his rebellious people, Ezekiel took a sharp sword and used it to shave

---

*These numbers are a bit puzzling, since neither agrees with the historical data.

his head and face. A third of his hair he cast into a fire built in the midst of the model of Jerusalem. Another third was scattered on the ground around the model and beaten with a sword. The remainder was tossed into the wind and struck at with the sword. These acts symbolized the fate of the people of Judah—some would be consumed by pestilence and famine, others would die by the sword, and still others would be scattered to the four winds. Jerusalem was about to feel the consuming wrath of Yahweh.

*An Exile's Baggage (12:1–16).* Shortly after Ezekiel completed the ordeal of the signs of the siege and exile, Yahweh transported Ezekiel in a vision to Jerusalem. There, he beheld the idolatry and other abominations that were going on right in the temple. What Ezekiel saw must have been quite a shock to his priestly sensibilities. Some kind of offensive image had been set up at the entrance to the inner court of the temple. Inside, the walls of the holy place were covered with pictures of various creatures the people had begun to worship. Ezekiel saw women worshiping Tammuz, the Babylonian goddess of agriculture, and men bowing down to the sun. The House of the Lord could not long bear the weight of such abominations.

This sickening vision prompted Ezekiel to perform two more symbolic acts. First, he packed his baggage and crawled through a hole in a wall, as a sign that the people would soon be going into exile. Then, he trembled and shook as he ate his meals, to symbolize the fear and dismay that would overwhelm Judah when the Babylonians attacked Jerusalem (*ch. 12*).

### JUDGMENT ON A HARLOT

In true prophetic fashion, Ezekiel devoted considerable energy—and some of the most vivid language in the Bible—to point-

299

ing out that his hearers fully deserved everything they were about to receive. Time and again they had listened to false prophets and rejected the messengers of Yahweh (*ch. 13*). Never had they been faithful to Yahweh for any appreciable length of time. Israel and Judah had been like two prostitutes—a familiar comparison in prophetic literature—seeking lovers in every corner of the world. In fact, they were worse than prostitutes, for prostitutes receive payment for their favors. Israel and Judah were so depraved they had paid their lovers to come to them (*chs. 16, 23*).

But now, the reckoning would be made. The King of Babylon was standing "at the parting of the ways" waiting for his advisers to tell him to advance on Jerusalem. In his hand he held a gleaming sword, "sharpened for slaughter" (*ch. 21*). In the past, Yahweh had agreed to spare a city for the sake of a few righteous men. Now, even if the three paragons of righteousness, Noah, David, and Job, dwelt in Jerusalem, their righteousness would suffice only to save themselves.

*Sin and Responsibility.* In *ch. 18*, Ezekiel added a new dimension to prophetic preaching. Ordinarily, the prophets addressed the people as a whole. Here, Ezekiel applies what he is saying directly to the individual Israelite. Apparently, the people had been explaining their condition in terms of a popular proverb: "The fathers have eaten sour grapes and the children's teeth are set on edge" (*18:2*). The implication was that the people of the present generation were undeserving of the calamity that was upon them. Their fathers had been the wicked ones, but they, the innocent children, were having to bear the brunt of the suffering. Since this was the case, there was little reason for them to be concerned about righteousness—things were already too far gone for anything to help.

Ezekiel vigorously attacked this line of reasoning. He was willing to admit that Judah's current troubles had been brought on by generations of sinful ancestors, but this did not leave the present generation blameless or free of responsibility. They, too, had engaged in all the sins Ezekiel had decried. As fully as their fathers, they deserved their punishment. If they wished to escape from the wrath of Yahweh, they should renounce the ways of their fathers and walk in the statutes and ordinances of the Lord. Yahweh would not punish men indiscriminately, for he finds no pleasure in punishment (*18:23, 32*). Each man would be held responsible for his own life, not the life of his father—"the soul that sinneth, it shall die" (*18:20*).

There are problems with Ezekiel's interpretation of the justice of God. It is a plain and undeniable fact that the innocent do suffer, often as a result of the sins of their parents, while the wicked prosper. The book of *Job* was composed in an attempt to deal with this matter in a systematic way. But Ezekiel's observations about the guilt of his audience were undoubtedly correct and his primary purpose in bringing up this subject was not to treat the problem of suffering in an abstract manner, but to point out this guilt and to move his listeners to repent and place their dependence on Yahweh.

### THE BEGINNING OF THE SIEGE

Nebuchadnezzar began his two-year siege of Jerusalem in 589 B.C. The news of this event was the occasion of Ezekiel's most moving symbolic act. As we stated earlier, Ezekiel was a married man. We are told nothing of his wife except that she was "the delight of his eyes." On the evening of the day the exiles received the news of the beginning of the siege, Ezekiel's beloved wife died. Following the instructions of Yahweh, the prophet exhibited none of the custom-

A lion from the wall of the processional street in Nebuchadnezzar's city. This fierce symbol of power was made of white and yellow fired brick on a blue background.

ary signs of mourning. He did not assume the disheveled and distraught look common to mourners in the Near East. He did not tear his clothing or cover his face with ashes. He made no cries of mourning to express his grief. Instead, he dressed and acted just as he would dress and act on any other day (24:1–2; 15–18).

The exiles had no doubt come to expect the unusual from Ezekiel. In fact, there is no evidence that his previous activities, strange as they were, had stirred up much more than moderate curiosity. But, to a people given to excesses of emotion in mourning their dead, Ezekiel's behavior was inexplainable. When they pressed him for the meaning of his actions, he told them their reaction to the fall of Jerusalem was to be like his response to his wife's sudden death. When the inevitable word came that the

Holy Temple had fallen and that the sons and daughters they had left behind had died by the sword, they would be so stunned that they could give no thought to the customary rituals of mourning.

### ORACLES AGAINST THE NATIONS

For three years Ezekiel busied himself with composing oracles against the nations that had multiplied Judah's sorrow. The bulk of these are directed at Tyre and Egypt. Tyre probably came in for Ezekiel's wrath because of her current importance in international politics and her apparent willingness to take advantage of Judah's misfortunes (see ch. 26).

The oracles against Egypt are delivered against a backdrop of the familiar prophetic theme of the Day of the Lord (see 30:1–3). Egypt was a favorite target of angry proph-

301

ets, mainly because she had played a principal role in much of the political difficulties that had plagued the people of God throughout their history. Time and again, Egypt had persuaded Judah to revolt against her overlords, purely as a device to further her own ends. Time and again she had bolstered Judah's hopes by promising military aid against an aggressor, but had failed to appear when the fighting began. In chapter 17, Ezekiel had described the latest of these incidents in allegorical form. The great eagle (the king of Babylon) had made a treaty with the lowly vine (Zedekiah king of Judah), promising protection as long as "its branches turned toward him" (17:6). But then, the vine had turned its branches toward another great eagle (Pharaoh Hophra), hoping to escape from the dominion of the first. Ezekiel had condemned Zedekiah's overtures to Pharaoh Hophra as a breach of a legitimate treaty and as an affront to the name of Yahweh, in whose name Zedekiah had taken the oath of the treaty (17:16–21). For all she had done to make life miserable for Judah, Egypt would be repaid in the Day of the Lord.

### PROPHECIES OF RESTORATION AND RENEWAL

Jerusalem fell in 587 B.C., but word of its fall did not reach the exiles for about six months after it fell. This would seem to be an unusually long time for the arrival of the news, but that is of no consequence. What is important is the change the news made in Ezekiel's ministry. When the fugitive messenger arrived at the exile settlement with the terse announcement, "The city has fallen," Ezekiel was already prepared for the new phase of his work. On the evening before, "the hand of Yahweh" had been upon him, awakening him to the task that lay ahead.

Now that Jerusalem was fallen, there was no longer any need to convince the exiles

that Yahweh would render judgment for their sins. The judgment had been pronounced and executed. Judah's pride and confidence in her election had been shattered. Now the task was to convince them that the situation, as bad as it was, was not irredeemable. Finally, Ezekiel would be permitted to turn from words and signs of doom to oracles of restoration and renewal.

It would not be difficult to gain an audience for these new words of hope. The people would flock to hear him as they would to "one who sings love songs with a beautiful voice and plays well on an instrument" (33:32). At first, simply because the notion of active obedience had fallen into disuse, they would not stop to consider that anything was actually demanded of them. Eventually, however, Ezekiel's message would soak through and the exiles would realize that they must act as well as hear. Yahweh promised Ezekiel:

> When this comes—and come it will!—then they shall know that a prophet has been among them.          —Ezekiel 33:33

*The Shepherd and His Flock.* The first oracle of hope was built around the image, so common in both the Old and New Testament, of a shepherd and his flock. It opens with a ringing attack on Israel's past shepherds, those kings who had lived off the bounty of the flock, while paying no attention to its welfare. No longer would the sheep be forced to suffer under shepherds like these, for Yahweh himself would be their Good Shepherd.

> For thus says Yahweh God: Behold, I, I myself will search for my sheep, and will seek them out. As a shepherd seeks out his flock when some of his sheep have been scattered abroad, so will I seek out my sheep; and I will rescue them from all places where they have been scattered on a day of clouds and thick darkness . . . I will feed them with good

pasture, and upon the mountain heights of Israel shall be their pasture; there they shall lie down in good grazing land, and on fat pasture they shall feed on the mountains of Israel. I myself will be the shepherd of my sheep, and I will make them lie down, says Yahweh God. I will seek the lost, and I will bring back the strayed, and I will bind up the crippled, and I will strengthen the weak, and the fat and the strong I will watch over; I will feed them in justice.

—*Ezekiel 34:11-12, 14-16*

When the scattered sheep had been rescued and tenderly nursed back to soundness, Yahweh would set over them a shepherd of the house of David, to care for them in an age of idyllic peace (*34:20–25*).

*The Valley of Dry Bones.* Of all Ezekiel's remarkable visions, none has captured the imagination of Bible students like the vision of the valley of dry bones (*37:1–14*). In this vision, the Spirit of Yahweh set Ezekiel down in the midst of a valley covered with a miscellaneous collection of dry, sun-bleached human bones. When Yahweh asked the question, "Can these bones live?" Ezekiel had no answer. Such an idea was inconceivable. Still, at Yahweh's command, Ezekiel prophesied to the dry bones, calling them to "hear the word of the Lord." Suddenly there was a rattling sound, and all over the valley, "thigh bones connected to the hip bones" and other bones found their appointed sockets until human skeletons were formed. Sinew and flesh and skin began to cover the bones. Then, when this was completed, Ezekiel prophesied to the wind (or spirit), commanding it to enter these human forms and to give them the breath of life; "and breath came into them, and they lived, and stood upon their feet, an exceedingly great host" (*37:10*).

The meaning of the vision is clear. The bones represent a slain and scattered Israel, a fallen people whose restoration seemed

incredible. By the power of the Spirit of Yahweh, however, Israel would rise from her grave \* to be restored to her own land and to resume her role in God's salvation history.

*God's Motive for Restoring Israel.* Judah and Israel had fallen because they had trusted blindly in Yahweh's covenant promises, with no regard for keeping their part of the bargain. Now that Yahweh was promising to restore them to their own land, he wanted it clearly understood that it was not because they deserved to be restored. They had sinned repeatedly and had no cause for anything but shame. Rather, it was because their pagan neighbors had belittled his power by saying, "These are the people of Yahweh, and yet they had to go out of his land" (*36:20*). It was to vindicate his holy name before their eyes that Yahweh was about to act (*36:21–23, 32*). Nevertheless, the restoration of Israel would be much more than a mechanical act of vindication. The restored Israel would be of a different order than that which had gone before. It would be a holy nation, cleansed from its iniquities, and filled with a new spirit and a new heart.

For I will take you from the nations, and gather you from all the countries, and bring you into your own land. I will sprinkle clean water upon you, and you shall be clean from all your uncleannesses, and from all your idols I will cleanse you. A new heart I will give you, and a new spirit I will put within you; and I will take out of your flesh the heart of stone and give you a heart of flesh. And I will put my spirit within you, and cause you to walk in my statutes and be careful to observe my ordinances. You shall dwell in the

---

\*The reference to rising from the grave (*37:12-13*) probably should not be understood as an early reference to individual resurrection. Here, the image is of the restoration of the nation of Israel, not of the resuscitation of people who were actually physically dead.

land which I gave to your fathers; and you shall be my people, and I will be your God.
—*Ezekiel 36:24-28*

*The Great Battle with Gog.* The ultimate vindication of Yahweh is also the theme of chs. 38–39. Here Ezekiel depicts, in highly imaginative language, a climatic battle between Yahweh and Gog, of the land of Magog. Gog is not to be identified with any concrete historical figure, but is a symbol for all the evil forces that continually struggle against God. It is quite likely that the symbol was already current in the Near East and that Ezekiel capitalized on its familiarity to make his message more effective—a perfectly legitimate thing to do. The use of Gog as a symbol of evil occurs several times in the Old Testament Apocrypha, the collection of books found in Catholic Bibles, but omitted from most Protestant versions. It also appears in *Revelation 20:8*. In that passage, Magog no longer appears as Gog's homeland, but as his ally in the battle of Armageddon. In our passage, Ezekiel foresees the attack on Israel by Gog and his allies, and assures his hearers that it will be followed by Yahweh's ultimate and devastating victory over the attackers, culminating in the restoration of the scattered house of Israel to its Jerusalem.

### THE VISION OF THE TEMPLE

Ezekiel's last recorded vision occurred at the beginning of the year 573 B.C. (*40:1*). The Spirit of the Lord transported him to the top of a high mountain and set him down before a building complex consisting of a temple and its grounds. Guided by a bronze figure with a measuring rod in his hand, Ezekiel toured the structure, describing what he saw in great detail.

When the tour of the temple was complete, Ezekiel saw another vision of the glory of the Lord similar to the one he had seen twenty years earlier on the banks of the river Chebar (*43:1ff*). The first vision had been a call for Ezekiel to proclaim to the exiles that the glory of Yahweh was about to depart from Jerusalem. This vision signified that Yahweh would one day return to his holy temple (*40:5*).

There are several aspects of the vision of the new temple that must have pleased this prophet who was also a priest. The Levites, who had held an exalted place in the worship of Yahweh since the days of Moses and the tabernacle, were demoted to the performance of menial tasks, as a punishment for their having officiated at the high places and idolatrous altars back in Judah. In the new order, the family of Zadok would have charge of the temple service (*ch. 44:9ff*). The new order would also feature a return to the theocratic pattern of government, where God was supreme and the temporal ruler exercised his power in a framework of strict subordination to the religious law (*chs. 45–6*).

This section reaches its climax in *ch. 47*, with the vision of the sacred stream issuing forth from below the threshold of the temple. In both the Old and the New Testaments, the power and glory of God is frequently symbolized by water. Here, the picture is one in which the temple of Yahweh stands at the heart and pinnacle of the land, and from it there flows forth a stream full of life and strength, a stream so fresh and pure that it can cause the Dead Sea to abound with swarms of fish like those found in the Mediterranean.

This was Ezekiel's vision of the New Israel. The land would be divided among the tribes, as it had been in the days of Joshua. All life would be regulated by the laws of holiness and would revolve around the worship of the new temple, the throne and footstool of God. And, in keeping with her new status, Jerusalem would receive a new name: "Yahweh-is-there."

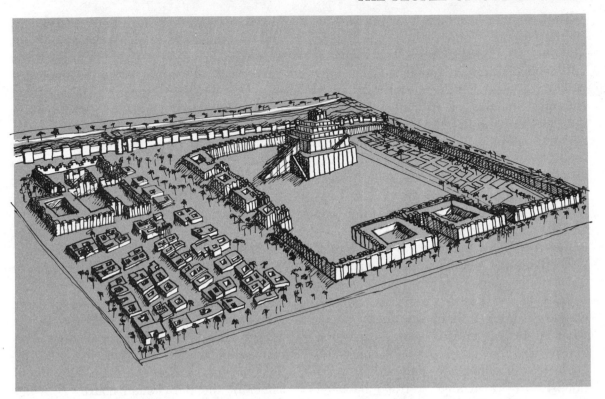

Nebuchadnezzar's building projects included the Tower of Babel (upper right), the temple of Marduk (upper left), and a wall along the Euphrates (background). From a reconstruction.

## The Last Days of Babylon

When we think of the New Babylonian Empire (625–539 B.C.), we automatically think of Nebuchadnezzar. This is as it should be, for this great empire was, far more than most, a one-man show. It had been brought into existence by Nebuchadnezzar and his father, Nabopolassar. It reached its peak under Nebuchadnezzar (605–562 B.C.). And when he died, his empire began to disintegrate. We have already traced Nebuchadnezzar's career down to his conquest of Jerusalem. Unfortunately, our sources for the remaining twenty-five years of his reign are quite sketchy, since only a fraction of his royal annals have been preserved. We know that during this time his

efforts to develop Babylon made it one of the wonders of the ancient world. He dug canals, lined a portion of the Euphrates with brick, surrounded Babylon with a moat, erected a strong fortress, built new temples to Babylon's gods, and constructed the famous "hanging gardens" to please his wife Amyitis, a Median princess who had grown lonely for the fruits and flowers of her homeland. But we can speak with confidence only of the most important developments in the political and military realms.

### NEBUCHADNEZZAR'S LATER YEARS

When Nebuchadnezzar defeated the Assyrians in 612 B.C., he was aided by Cyaxares king of Media. Twenty years later, Media loomed as Babylon's most serious rival in the quest for world domination. The defeat of Assyria had not automatically placed all of her holdings under Nebuchadnezzar's control. Assyria had been growing weaker by the year and some of her vassals were unwilling to submit to the yoke of Babylon until Nebuchadnezzar convinced them they had no real choice in the matter. The rather tiresome business of forcing them back into line kept the Babylonian army tied up in Mesopotamia, Syria, and Palestine for some years. Meanwhile, Cyaxares was building an enormous empire, with its capital in Ecbatana. By 585 B.C., he had extended his holdings into Asia-Minor and was putting heavy pressure on Lydia.

Because of his marriage to the Median king's daughter, Nebuchadnezzar enjoyed a distinct advantage over other Near Eastern nations, in that he was in little immediate danger of attack. Still, he was uneasy about what might happen if Cyaxares' expansion efforts were allowed to continue unchecked. So, he used his influence—and perhaps a little pressure—to arrange a truce between Media and Lydia and to set the eastern limit of the Median Empire at the Halys River. Then he set about to expand his own frontiers in that direction, and eventually succeeded in gaining control of a small section of Cilicia. Later in 585 B.C., Nebuchadnezzar laid siege to Tyre, but the stubborn little nation managed to hold him off and did not finally submit to Babylon until 572 B.C., thirteen years later.

In the years that followed, Nebuchadnezzar conducted several more campaigns in the West. We know very little about these, but it is probably safe to assume that Egypt figured in them somewhere, either as participant or agitator. In 582, Nebuchadnezzar's forces combed Judah a third time, taking an additional 745 men captive to Babylon (*Jeremiah 52:30*). The only other western campaign of note occurred in 568 B.C. In 570, the troublesome Pharaoh Hophra had been the victim of a military coup that cost him his life and put Amasis on the Egyptian throne. While the situation was still unsettled, Nebuchadnezzar sent his armies against Egypt. The only information we have about this campaign is a small and most incomplete fragment that does not even tell us how the battle turned out. Since Egypt and Babylon enjoyed friendly relations after this time, it is usually thought that the purpose of the mission was to keep Amasis from following Hophra's example of stirring up rebellion against Babylon, and not an outright attempt at conquest.

## THE DECLINE OF POWER (562–539 B.C.)

Nebuchadnezzar died in 562 B.C. Almost immediately, Babylon started into a tailspin. Amel-Marduk, Nebuchadnezzar's son, succeeded his father to the throne. In the Bible he is called Evil–Merodach and is remembered as the king who released Jehoiachin from prison and made him a pensioner of the Babylonian court (*II Kings 25:27–30*). Other than this, we know nothing of his brief reign. In 560 B.C., after some sort of struggle, Amel-Marduk was replaced by his brother-in-law, Nergilassar, also called Nergal-shar-usur. In the Bible, he appears as a Babylonian officer called Nergal-sharezer (*Jer. 39:3, 13*). Nergilassar kept the empire intact, but he died within four years. According to custom, the throne passed to his young son, Labashi-Marduk, but he was little more than a cipher. Before the year was out, he had been shoved aside and replaced by Nabonidus, a prince of Haran, in the northern part of the empire.

Nabonidus was a strange character, with little appreciation for public relations. The chief god of Babylon was Marduk, but Nabonidus chose to honor Sin, the moon god worshiped in his native Haran. Naturally, this offended the powerful priests of Marduk and stirred up a good deal of resentment against Nabonidus. Archaeologists have discovered fragments of a long poem

| THE JEWS | BABYLON | MEDIA |
|---|---|---|
| | Nebuchadnezzar ....605-562 | Cyaxares ...........625-585 |
| 597: First deportation to Babylon | | |
| 587: Fall of Jerusalem, second deportation | | |
| 582: Third deportation | | Astyages ..........585-550 |
| | Amel-Marduk (*Evil-merodach*) ..562-560 | |
| PROPHETS: | Nergilassar .........560-556 | |
| *Ezekiel* .........593-573 | Nabonidus ..........556-539 | 550: Cyrus the Persian defeats Astyages, establishes Persian Empire. |
| *Captivity Oracles* (*Isa. 40-66*) come to prominence ...ca. 540 | | |

**CHRONOLOGICAL CHART: THE PERIOD OF THE EXILE (597-540 B.C.)**

composed by the priests of Babylon that is openly and severely critical of Nabonidus and his policies.

Actually, Nabonidus did not really seem to care much about what the priests or people of Babylon thought of him. For eight years of his reign (c. 552–545 B.C.) he made his headquarters at the oasis city of Tema in northwest Arabia, leaving his son Belshar-usur (Belshazzar) in charge of things in Babylon. During this period, he did not even bother to arrange for the New Year's Day celebration. New Year's Day was the chief holiday in Babylon and this was a serious social and political blunder, roughly equivalent to a modern president's cancelling Christmas.

Despite his somewhat cavalier attitude toward Babylon and its traditions, Nabonidus managed to hold onto his throne for sixteen years, but the people of Babylon resented him so bitterly that when the Persian army forced him to flee in 539 B.C., they were hailed as liberators rather than conquerors.

CYRUS THE PERSIAN

While Nabonidus was raising the ire of the people of his empire, one of the most important developments in the history of the world was taking place in Media. That was the rise of Cyrus the Persian. Cyrus was a vassal ruler in southern Iran. In 553 B.C., he engineered a revolt against Astyages, who had succeeded his father Cyaxares to the Median throne in 585 B.C. Within three years, Cyrus had stormed Ecbatana, driven Astyages from the capital, and placed himself atop the vast Median empire. Then, he initiated the program of conquest that eventually placed him atop the world.

A generation earlier, Nebuchadnezzar had realized that Media posed the most serious threat to Babylon and had moved to check Cyaxares' advances into Asia-Minor (p. 308). When Nabonidus saw that the hungry Median giant was again on the prowl, he quickly formed a military alliance with Lydia and Egypt. But a determined giant is hard to stop. By 546, Cyrus had marched

307

A Median attendant leads two
noble mounts in this fragment from an
Assyrian wall carving.

deep into Asia-Minor, scooping most of
northern Babylon and Lydia into his net.
With characteristic prudence, Egypt decided to back down on her obligations and
left Babylon to fend for herself.

Babylon's unstable condition under Nabonidus made her an easy prey, but Cyrus
was in no hurry. For the present, he con-
tented himself with solidifying his own position and enlarging his holdings in the East.
It was during this period between Cyrus'
rise to power and his conquest of Babylon
that the Captivity Oracles of *Isaiah 40–66*
came into prominence.

## The Captivity Oracles: Isaiah 40–66

In many respects, *Isaiah 40–66* is the pinnacle of Biblical literature. The oracles contained in these chapters bring the classical
prophetic tradition to a thrilling climax.
They possess a lyrical beauty surpassing
anything in the Bible and establishing their
composer as a superb literary artist, ranking
among the truly great poets of all time. But
their significance is far more than literary.
It is perhaps no exaggeration to say that
these oracles did more to shape the faith of
Judaism and Christianity than any portion
of the Old Testament.

We call these oracles the Captivity Oracles to distinguish them from the material
found in *Isaiah 1–39*. A close examination of
the book of *Isaiah* will reveal a sharp difference between these two sections. The first
part, with the exception of chs. *34–35*, per-
tains almost entirely to the latter half of the
eighth century B.C., the time when the
prophet Isaiah actually lived. The material
in *34–35* and *40–66* presupposes the circumstances of the period of the Babylonian empire. In *1–39*, Jerusalem and the temple are

still standing, and Isaiah is having little success in convincing the people that Yahweh would ever allow harm to come to his holy city. The opening verse of the Captivity Oracles is a song of comfort to a fallen Jerusalem whose "warfare is ended" and who "has received from Yahweh's hand double for all her sins" (*40:1*). Elsewhere the prophet specifically speaks of Jerusalem as having drunk the cup of Yahweh's wrath to the dregs and urges her to free herself from the yoke of captivity and put on her beautiful garments once again (*52:1–2*). Clearly, Jerusalem, the temple, and the cities of Judah are in ruins (*44:26; 49:19*), and the prophet speaks of going forth from Babylon to rebuild them (*44:26–8; 48:20*).

When Isaiah was prophesying, Assyria was the great world power threatening the future of the nation. In the Captivity Oracles, there is no mention of Assyria as a present threat. Babylon is the "mistress of kingdoms" (*47:5*), but even she is near the end of her time, for Cyrus has already appeared on the scene and has begun "to subdue nations before him and ungird the loins of kings" (*45:1*). The prophet calls Cyrus by name, and expresses his confidence that when the Persian king has taken Babylon, as he soon will, he will rebuild fallen Jerusalem (*44:26–8; cf. 47:1, 5–7; 48:14*). The natural conclusion to all this is that these two sections of the book of *Isaiah* were written for two entirely different historical situations, separated in time by more than 150 years. For practical purposes, they may be studied as two separate books. It is for this reason that we did not deal with chapters *40–66* in our discussion of the ministry of *Isaiah*, but have saved them until the time in which they had the greatest significance for the people of God.

## YAHWEH IS LORD OF HISTORY

The predominant feature of the Captivity Oracles is their exultant confidence in the absolute sovereignty of Yahweh in history. As we have seen, the exile had put Israel's faith to a severe test at precisely this point. In light of what had happened to them, the exiles had great difficulty in believing Yahweh had any real control over what went on in the world. If he did, why had he brought calamity on his chosen people, and why was he allowing them to languish in captivity without any sure sign of his presence? Right from the opening verses, the prophet seeks to assure his audience that the world has not slipped out of God's pocket, that Yahweh has not deserted his people, and that a glorious restoration is assured.

Comfort, comfort my people, says your God.
Speak tenderly to Jerusalem,
   and cry to her
that her warfare is ended,
   that her iniquity is pardoned,
that she has received from Yahweh's hand
   double for all her sins.

. . . . . . . . . . . . . . .

Behold, Yahweh GOD comes with might,
   and his arm rules for him;
behold, his reward is with him,
   and his recompense before him.
He will feed his flock like a shepherd,
   he will gather the lambs in his arms,
he will carry them in his bosom,
   and gently lead those that are with young.
     —*Isaiah 40:1-2, 10-11*

This sounded good, but could Yahweh really do it? Was it possible he had met his match—and more—in the gods of Babylon? To dispel any doubts the captives might have about Yahweh's ability to make good on his promises, the prophet launches into a magnificent affirmation of Yahweh's unchallenged sovereignty over the universe.

Who has measured the waters in the hollow
   of his hand
   and marked off the heavens with a span,

enclosed the dust of the earth in a measure
  and weighed the mountains in scales
  and the hills in a balance?

. . . . . . . . . . . . . . . . . .

Have you not known? Have you not heard?
  Has it not been told you from
    the beginning?
  Have you not understood from the founda-
    tions of the earth?
It is he who sits above the circle of the earth,
  and its inhabitants are like grasshoppers;
who stretches out the heavens like a curtain,
  and spreads them like a tent to dwell in;
who brings princes to nought,
  and makes the rulers of the earth
    as nothing.

. . . . . . . . . . . . . . . . . .

To whom then will you compare me,
  that I should be like him?
    says the Holy One.
Lift up your eyes on high and see:
  who created these?
He who brings out their host by number,
  calling them all by name;
by the greatness of his might,
  and because he is strong in power
    not one is missing.

. . . . . . . . . . . . . . . . . .

Have you not known? Have you not heard?
Yahweh is the everlasting God,
  the Creator of the ends of the earth.
He does not faint or grow weary,
  his understanding is unsearchable.
                    —Isaiah 40:12, 21-23, 25-26, 28

Indeed, what did the Babylonians have to compare with the God who had created all things and who directed the destinies of nations? Their gods were made of wood and stone and metal. With biting satire, the prophet describes those who worship idols. First, a man plants a tree. When it has grown, he cuts it down and uses half of it for firewood, to warm himself and cook his food. Then he takes the other half and fashions it into an idol. And finally, he falls down before this product of his own hands and says, "Deliver me, for thou art my god" (44:9-20).

Marduk, king of all the Babylonian gods, hailed by his worshippers as giver of life. He is the Merodach-Baladan of Isaiah 39:1.

These gods were worth no more than the materials of which they were formed. Yahweh alone is God. He is the first and the last, and beside him there is no other God (44:6; 45:22; 46:9). His word alone is worthy of trust—"the grass withers, the flower fades, but the word of our God will stand forever" (40:8). He alone "has announced from of old the things to come." If the gods of Babylon wish to prove their power, let them declare what the future will bring (44:7). Let them try to stop the advances of Cyrus, or even predict what his next step will be. They cannot, for they have neither sense nor power. Only Yahweh can say exactly what Cyrus will do, for it is Yahweh who has raised him up and who guides his activity. Yahweh has anointed

310

the Persian prince for a vital role in his plans for history; specifically, the freeing of the exiles and the rebuilding of Jerusalem.

> I am Yahweh, who made all things,
>> who stretched out the heavens alone,
>> who spread out the earth—Who
>>> was with me?
> who frustrates the omens of liars,
>> and makes fools of diviners,
> who turns wise men back,
>> and makes their knowledge foolish;
> who says of Cyrus, "He is my shepherd,
>> and he shall fulfill all my purpose";
> saying of Jerusalem, "She shall be built,"
>> and of the temple, "Your foundation
>>> shall be laid."
>
> . . . . . . . . . . . . . . . . . .
>
> I have aroused him in righteousness,
>> and I will make straight all his ways;
> he shall build my city
>> and set my exiles free,
> not for price or reward,
>> says Yahweh of hosts.
>> —*Isaiah 44:24-25, 28; 45:13*

No, Yahweh had not lost control of history. His purposes might sometimes be difficult to discern, but they would not go unfulfilled. Admittedly, it was not easy to maintain courage or to put full trust in God's promises in times of hardship and heartbreak. But, promised the prophet,

> they who wait for Yahweh shall renew their
>> strength,
> they shall mount up with wings like eagles,
> they shall run and not be weary,
>> they shall walk and not faint.—*Isaiah 40:31*

### A NEW EXODUS

We have often noted that the key event in the life of God's people was the exodus. Whenever a leader or a prophet wished to recall the mighty acts Yahweh had performed on Israel's behalf, he always began with the exodus from Egypt. This had marked the birth of the nation of Israel. As the relationship between God and his people deteriorated, it became increasingly evident that more than occasional periods of reform were needed to get Israel back on the right track. Nowhere was this more graphically illustrated than in the book of *Hosea*. Hosea's wife Gomer was repeatedly unfaithful to him. At first, he mercifully accepted her back into his home after each affair. Finally, however, he told her there could be no further relationship between them until she had submitted to a period of chastening that would, hopefully, help her to see the folly of her wanton behavior. Hosea, of course, represents Yahweh and his wife represents unfaithful Israel. The language Hosea uses to describe the period of chastening is full of the imagery of the exodus tradition (*Hosea 2:14–20*). The implication is clear: before Israel can be fully reconciled to Yahweh, she will have to undergo an experience analagous to the original exodus.

The Captivity Oracles announce that the time for that experience has come. The redemption that was being promised was not just a happy historical accident that would bring joy to a handful of homesick exiles. It was to signal the birth of a New Israel, a chastened Israel, an Israel prepared to assume her place in a "new thing" (*42:9; 43:19*) Yahweh was creating.

These oracles abound with glorious descriptions of this New Exodus. The theme appears early in the opening oracle:

> A voice cries:
> In the wilderness prepare the way of
>> Yahweh,
> make straight in the desert a highway for our
>> God.            —*Isaiah 40:3*

In flights of lyric fancy, the prophet pictures the beginning of the New Exodus as an oc-

---

*Notice that this passage was later applied to John the Baptist. (*Matthew 3:3*) Notice also that the familiar "a voice crying in the wilderness, 'prepare the way of the Lord'" should actually be read "a voice crying, '*In the wilderness* prepare the way of the Lord.'"

casion so stirring that all of nature will give out with expressions of joy. Even the desert wilderness through which Yahweh will lead the exiles will be transformed to a blooming garden paradise as sterility and death are overcome by the God of Life.

> For you shall go out in joy,
>     and be led forth in peace;
> the mountains and the hills before you
>     shall break forth into singing,
>     and all the trees of the field shall clap their
>         hands.
>
> . . . . . . . . . . . . . . . . . .
>
> The wilderness and the dry land shall be
>     glad,
>     the desert shall rejoice and blossom;
> like the crocus it shall blossom abundantly,
>     and rejoice with joy and singing.
> The glory of Lebanon shall be given to it,
>     the majesty of Carmel and Sharon.
> They shall see the glory of Yahweh,
>     the majesty of our God.
>                 —Isaiah 55:12; 35:1-2

*Creation, Exodus, and Redemption: Isaiah 51:9–11.* The climax in the development of the New Exodus theme is *Isaiah 51:9–11.* In this passage, the matchless poet-theologian relates the New Exodus and the return to Zion not only to the events of the original exodus, but to creation itself. Yahweh's dominion over history did not begin with the exodus. It began with time itself. From the creation to the end of time, the entire span of history is shot through with the activity and purposes of God.

Since this passage provides us with such rich insight into the theology of the Captivity Oracles, let us look at it in some detail.

> Awake, awake, put on strength,
>     O arm of Yahweh;
> awake, as in days of old,
>     the generations of long ago.
> Was it not thou that didst cut Rahab in
>     pieces,

> that didst pierce the dragon?
> Was it not thou that didst dry up the sea,
>     the waters of the great deep;
> that didst make the depths of the sea a way
>     for the redeemed to pass over?
> And the ransomed of Yahweh shall return,
>     and come with singing to Zion;
> everlasting joy shall be upon their heads;
>     they shall obtain joy and gladness,
>     and sorrow and sighing shall flee away.
>                 —Isaiah 51:9-11

In the midst of a chapter treating the theme of the new salvation, this passage breaks in as an unrestrained outburst designed to stir Yahweh to immediate action by recalling his mighty acts of earlier days. Then, the prophet continues with an extremely skillful blend of mythology and history. In Near Eastern mythology the process of creation is described in terms of a cosmic battle between the great god (whose name varies according to the people who told the story) and the forces of chaos, usually represented by the sea and various sea-monsters. Rahab (*v. 9*) was the name of one of these monsters. Another was Tannin, which appears in most English translations as "the dragon." The prophet is not suggesting here that "once upon a time" Yahweh actually slew a dragon. He is simply using commonly understood poetic images to call attention to Yahweh's concrete historical acts.

The central event in Israel's history was the exodus. Yahweh's greatest victory was the defeat of Israel's opposition at the Sea of Reeds, when he made "a way for the redeemed to pass over." What better way to dramatize the magnitude of this event than to weave it into the fabric of Yahweh's primordial victory over his cosmic enemies, to unite creation of the world with creation of Israel, and then to unite these with the creation of the new salvation Yahweh was to bring to his people! By embellishing the historical acts of Yahweh with the classical imagery of Semitic methology in a way that gives force to the historical and to point to the hoped-for future, the prophet shows himself to be a first-rate literary artist.*

The closing lines (*v. 11*) are exactly what one would expect, in the light of the other passages we have noted. The elect of Yahweh, chastized but not abandoned, are *ransomed*—redeemed by an act of free choice—and return to the Holy City under the leadership of their king who leads them as a warrior returning from conquest.

In this brief oracle, the prophet forcefully affirms Yahweh's lordship over Creation and History. The beauty and profundity with which he intermingles the language of mythology, history, and expectation is a superlative witness to the poetic and spiritual grandeur of the Captivity Oracles.

### THE SERVANT OF YAHWEH

One of the most important and striking features of the Captivity Oracles is their profound development of the concept of service. Reference to Israel as the servant of Yahweh appears in a wide range of passages.† These imply that God has chosen Israel to fill a certain role in his plans, but they do not elaborate much on the exact nature of that role. The heart of what the prophet has to say on this subject is found in four passages sometimes referred to as the Servant Songs: *42:1–4; 49:1–6; 50:4–10;* and *52:13–53:12.* These passages describe the character and mission of a mysterious figure who fulfills the purposes of Yahweh through a life of unselfish, suffering service.

*The Mission of the Suffering Servant.* God is able to use all sorts of men to carry out his will. He had appointed proud Assyria to be the rod of his anger to punish his unfaithful children (*Isa. 10:5ff*). He had

---

*For other examples of the use of mythological imagery by Biblical writers, see *Job 3:8; 7:12; 9:13; 26:12; 41:1; Psalms 74:14; 89:11; Isaiah 27:1.*

†See *41:8-10; 42:18-19; 43:1, 10; 44:1-3, 21; 45:3-5; 48:12; 48:20.*

sent for Nebuchadnezzar king of Babylon to carry Judah into exile (*Jer. 25:8*). And now, he had anointed Cyrus the Persian to free the captives and to send them back to Jerusalem (*Isa. 45:1, 13*). These had served God with great armies and weapons of destruction. In performing their errands, they had burned cities, erased nations, and shattered lives. The mission of the Suffering Servant would be of an entirely different order, characterized by mercy and an unflagging zeal for justice.

> Behold my servant, whom I uphold,
>     my chosen, in whom my soul delights;
> I have put my spirit upon him,
>     he will bring forth justice to the nations.
> He will not cry or lift up his voice,
>     or make it heard in the street;
> a bruised reed he will not break,
>     and a dimly burning wick he will not
>         quench;
>     he will faithfully bring forth justice.
> He will not fail or be discouraged
>     till he has established justice in the earth;
>     and the coastlands wait for his law.
>                                —*Isaiah 42:1-4*

The path this servant would tread would not be easy. Times would come when he would feel he had failed. But he would never yield his faith in Yahweh, who had chosen him before his birth, who had guided his steps, who would give him strength equal to his task, who would make him "a light to the nations."

> Listen to me, O coastlands,
>     and hearken, you peoples from afar.
> Yahweh called me from the womb,
>     from the body of my mother he named my
>         name.
> He made my mouth like a sharp sword,
>     in the shadow of his hand he hid me;
> he made me a polished arrow,
>     in his quiver he hid me away.
> And he said to me, "You are my servant,
>     Israel, in whom I will be glorified."
> But I said, "I have labored in vain,

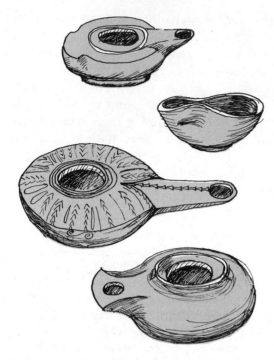

Lamps of ancient Palestine.
From top to bottom: Persian period,
Israelite style of the Second Century,
Hellenistic period, and Roman period.

    I have spent my strength for nothing and
        vanity;
    yet surely my right is with Yahweh,
        and my recompense with my God."
    And now Yahweh says,
        who formed me from the womb to be his
            servant,
    to bring Jacob back to him,
        and that Israel might be gathered to him,
    for I am honored in the eyes of Yahweh,
        and my God has become my strength—
    he says:
        "It is too light a thing that you should be
            my servant
        to raise up the tribes of Jacob
        and to restore the preserved of Israel;
    I will give you as a light to the nations.
        that my salvation may reach to the end of
            the earth.        —*Isaiah 49:1-6*

With this kind of faith in his calling, and
in the God who had called him, the servant

could bear the taunts and persecutions of
his enemies patiently, confident that the
Lord would ultimately vindicate him and
put his proud adversaries to shame.

    I gave my back to the smiters,
        and my cheeks to those who pulled out the
            beard;
    I hid not my face
        from shame and spitting.
    For Yahweh God helps me;
        therefore I have not been confounded;
    therefore I have set my face like a flint,
        and I know that I shall not be put to
            shame;
        he who vindicates me is near.
    Who will contend with me?
        Let us stand up together.
    Who is my adversary?
        Let him come near to me.
    Behold, Yahweh God helps me;
        who will declare me guilty?
    Behold, all of them will wear out like a
            garment;
        the moth will eat them up.
                                —*Isaiah 50:6-9*

The best known of the Servant Songs
(*52:13–53:12*) begins by announcing the
vindication and exaltation of the servant.
His enemies have beaten him so cruelly that
he is scarred almost beyond recognition.
And yet, Yahweh shall elevate him above
them all.

    Behold, my servant shall prosper,
        he shall be exalted and lifted up,
        and shall be very high.
    As many were astonished at him—
        his appearance was so marred, beyond
            human semblance,
        and his form beyond that of the sons
            of men—
    so shall he startle many nations;
        kings shall shut their mouths because
            of him;
    for that which has not been told them they
            shall see,
        and that which they have not heard they
            shall understand.     —*Isaiah 52:13-15*

In the lines that follow this announcement of triumph, we are given, in a sort of prophetic flashback, a description of the career of the Servant of Yahweh that is also a commentary on the meaning of suffering.

When the servant first appeared on the scene of history, not even the most perceptive of observers could have guessed he had been chosen for a task of any importance.

> Who has believed what we have heard?
> And to whom has the arm of Yahweh been
>     revealed?
> For he grew up before him like a young
>     plant,
>     and like a root out of dry ground;
> he had no form or comeliness that we should
>     look at him,
>     and no beauty that we should desire him.
> He was despised and rejected by men;
>     a man of sorrows, and acquainted with
>     grief;
> and as one from whom men hide their faces
>     he was despised, and we esteemed him not.
>                                    —Isaiah 53:1-3

Then, speaking for those who had despised the servant, the prophet expresses the anguished guilt that accompanies the recognition that this abhorrent creature had been chosen by God to bear the sins and sorrows of all the nations.

> Surely he has borne our griefs
>     and carried our sorrows;
> yet we esteemed him stricken,
>     smitten by God, and afflicted.
> But he was wounded for our transgressions,
>     he was bruised for our iniquities;
> upon him was the chastisement that made us
>     whole,
>     and with his stripes we are healed.
> All we like sheep have gone astray;
>     we have turned every one to his own way;
> and Yahweh has laid on him
>     the iniquity of us all.     —Isaiah 53:4-6

The "man of sorrows" meekly accepted all the afflictions that were pressed upon him, even death at the hands of unrighteous men.

And when he died, few paused to give a second thought; certainly, none considered the possibility of a resurrection.

> He was oppressed, and he was afflicted,
>     yet he opened not his mouth;
> like a lamb that is led to the slaughter,
>     and like a sheep that before its shearers is
>     dumb,
>     so he opened not his mouth.
> By oppression and judgment he was taken
>     away;
>     and as for his generation, who considered
> that he was cut off out of the land of the
>     living,
>     stricken for the transgression of my
>     people?
> And they made his grave with the wicked
>     and with a rich man in his death;
> although he had done no violence,
>     and there was no deceit in his mouth.
>                                    —Isaiah 53:7-9

But the final scene in the drama of the Servant was not the martyrdom of a sacrificial lamb. He had been chosen for victory, not defeat. By making himself an offering for sin, he would cause many to recognize their guilt and turn to perform the will of Yahweh. For himself, he would survive the grave and be granted prosperity, offspring, and length of days, as a reward for his great work of redemption and reconciliation.

> Yet it was the will of Yahweh to bruise him;
>     he has put him to grief;
> when he makes himself an offering for sin,
>     he shall see his offspring, he shall prolong
>     his days;
> the will of Yahweh shall prosper in his hand;
>     he shall see the fruit of the travail of his
>     soul and be satisfied;
> by his knowledge shall the righteous one,
>     my servant,
>     make many to be accounted righteous;
>     and he shall bear their iniquities.
> Therefore I will divide him a portion with
>     the great,
>     and he shall divide the spoil with the
>     strong;

because he poured out his soul to death,
and was numbered with the transgressors;
yet he bore the sin of many,
and made intercession for the
transgressors. —*Isaiah 53:10-12*

*The Identity of the Suffering Servant.*
The prophet's portrait of this gentle figure
who surrenders his life on behalf of others is
most appealing, but who is he? Is he someone already alive in the time of the prophet,
or someone expected to arise during the
time of exile, or someone to come in the
distant future? Scholars have suggested all
of these possibilities at one time or another.
Moses, Cyrus, and the prophet himself have
all been identified as the servant. And, of
course, Christians have viewed these poems
as a description of the life of Jesus. But what
did these oracles mean to the prophet who
spoke them and the people who heard him?
This must always be the first question in interpreting any passage of scripture. Within
the Captivity Oracles themselves, who is
the leading candidate for identification with
the Servant of Yahweh?

Outside the four key passages we have
noted, the servant is explicitly identified
with Israel (see *41:8; 43:10; 44:1–2, 21;
28:20;* also, *42:18, 25*). This clear identification occurs once within the Servant Songs
themselves (*49:3*). This would seem to settle the matter. Yet, only two verses later
(*49:5–6*), the mission of the servant is said
to be the restoration of Israel. How can Israel be both the servant and the object of
the servant's mission? And how can rebellious Israel be portrayed as a gentle, longsuffering lamb of God who meekly bears the
sins of the world?

Despite these problems, the evidence
seems to favor the conclusion that the
prophet thought of Israel as the Servant of
Yahweh. This statement, however, requires
some qualification. The Israel personified in
these passages is not any concrete manifes-

tation of Israel in history. Rather, it is an
idealized portrait of Israel as she played her
vital role in Yahweh's plans for history. It is
the prophet's way of saying that this lowli-
est of peoples will become a light to the nations (*51:16; 42:5–9*), the human agent by
which Yahweh will bring the dawning of a
new day. It is possible for him to speak of
the servant as an individual because of the
strong sense of community that existed
among the Israelites. The prophets often
addressed their audiences as "Jacob" or
"Ephraim," so the fact that the servant is
always spoken of in the singular should not
be particularly troublesome. In a sense,
however, the prophet is also calling individual Israelites to give a faithful response to
the call to servanthood. What is expected of
the community is likewise expected of each
individual in the community. In other
words, the Servant of Yahweh is both the
ideal Israel and the ideal Israelite.

This interpretation of these passages has
the advantage of accounting for the specific
identification of Israel and the servant. It
offers an explanation for the mission of the
servant to Israel in terms of the individual
Israelite's responsibility to the whole community. And it does not violate the interpretation Christians have placed on the passages. During the years when (their) Messianic hopes were highest, the Jews made
no particular point of identifying the suffering servant with the Messiah. But when
Christians reflected on the life of him whom
they accepted as Messiah, it seemed clear to
them that here was the ideal Israelite, one
who embodied the fullness of Israel, one
through whom God's mission to Israel and
to the world was being fulfilled. So, when
the evangelist Philip found the treasurer of
Ethiopia reading from *Isaiah 53*, it was entirely natural and proper that "beginning
with this scripture, he told him the good
news of Jesus" (*Acts 8:35*).

# 13

# The Return to Jerusalem

*Out of the struggles of
the community of returned exiles,
Judaism is born*

THE CAPTIVITY ORACLES had given the people of God a vision of a new day that was about to break upon their horizon. Soon, they were sure, a great deliverer would free them from the grip of Babylon and send them home to Jerusalem. They would restore the Holy City and make her the queen of the universe, and men from all nations would come to pay homage to her and her God. When Cyrus the Persian overthrew Babylon and granted the exiles permission to return to Jerusalem, it seemed the glorious day was dawning. But the hope was never quite fulfilled. The desert they crossed did not bloom, the hills and the trees neither sang nor clapped, and the structure they raised from the ashes were scarcely a jewelled city. The drab existence they met in Judah seemed a far cry from the glorious restoration the prophets had promised.

For awhile, every crisis in world affairs raised their hope that Yahweh was about to intervene. But these hopes failed to materialize, and the burden of their disappointment grew heavier. They stumbled under its weight and, at times, it seemed certain they would fall and be devoured by their enemies. The heroes who brought them through this crisis were Nehemiah and Ezra. These two courageous and strong-willed men brought order to the political and religious life of the community. They gave it strength to endure internal stress and external pressure, and they infused it with a character that can still be seen in modern Judaism.

### THE WORK OF THE CHRONICLER

Our chief sources of information for this period are *Ezra* and *Nehemiah*. Although they contain material taken from the personal memoirs of Nehemiah and Ezra, scholars are agreed that the finished products are the work of the same individual who wrote *I-II Chronicles*.* A comparison of the last verses of *II Chronicles* (*36:22–23*) with the opening verses of *Ezra* (*1:1–3*) will reveal they are virtually identical. The logical inference is that this was the writer's way of showing that he was picking up in *Ezra* right where he had left off in *II Chronicles*. Since we do not know the

---

*Many also feel that *Ezra-Nehemiah* were originally a single work, but this is relatively unimportant for our purposes.

name of this ancient writer, he is usually called the Chronicler, for obvious reasons.

Many people think of *I-II Chronicles* as simply a parallel version of *I-II Kings*. There is a good deal of truth in the assumption, but it is far from being the whole story. As we have seen, *I-II Kings* was an integral part of the great historical narrative that traces the fortunes of Israel from the time of the death of Moses to the fall of Jerusalem (See p. 92). The final edition of this history, which included the account of the fall of Jerusalem, was almost surely completed during the early years of the exile. On the basis of genealogical lists,* style, and vocabulary, we may be reasonably certain that the Chronicler did his work at least a century and a half later, around 300 B.C.

This ancient historian used the best sources available to him in compiling his works. He specifically names over twenty sources he used in putting *I-II Chronicles* together. It is likely that he used a good many more than this, since much of his writing sounds as if it could have been copied from official public documents.† It is also quite probable that he had access to a copy of the Pentateuch and the historical books from *Joshua* through *II Kings*.

There is probably no such thing as a completely "objective" history book, for the simple reason that no historian can record all the facts. He must choose some and omit others. If we notice carefully which facts he chooses and which he omits, we can usually discover why he decided to write his book. The intentions of the Chronicler are

particularly easy to discern. Quite obviously, he was deeply and primarily concerned with the formal religious life of the restoration community.

As we shall see in this chapter, one of the great difficulties connected with the restoration period was the maintenance of the temple services at Jerusalem. To keep the services running properly, two things were necessary. The first was seeing that the priests and Levites were in Jerusalem at their appointed time of service and that they fulfilled their proper function. Since the various offices in the temple service were assigned by families, proper genealogical records were essential. Secondly, the proper support of the Levites had to be insured if the temple service was to be maintained. Since the payment of tithes, firstfruits, etc., was dependent upon each family's receiving and being settled in its proper share of the land, it was even more necessary to provide trustworthy genealogies. *I Chronicles 1–8* contain the efforts of the author to meet this need, and *ch.* 9 notes that the people were able to settle in their rightful inheritance.

After providing this much-needed information, the Chronicler turns to the task of writing history. His major concern is with two divine institutions—the temple service and the Davidic dynasty. He scarcely mentions the northern kingdom, and then only where it affected the fortunes of Judah. The events mentioned in connection with David are those that relate to the worship in Jerusalem and preparations for building the temple. In dealing with the life of Solomon, he emphasizes the building and dedication of the temple instead of the splendor of his kingdom and the personal events of his life. Similarly, he gives prominence to the formal worship of the temple and the functions of the Levites whenever possible. The kings whose reigns he stresses are those who op-

---

*In *I Chron. 3:19-24*, the writer lists six generations of descendants of Zerubbabel, who was active in Jerusalem about 520 B.C. This would require a date of at least 350 B.C.

†A fascinating possibility in connection with this is suggested in a passage from the Apocrypha. In *II Maccabees 2:13-15*, reference is made to a library Nehemiah was collecting which would include just such documents as those mentioned by the Chronicler.

posed the idolatry that constantly seduced the Israelites. Then, in *Ezra-Nehemiah,* he describes the rebuilding of Jerusalem and the temple, and the reestablishment of the Law as the basis for individual and community conduct.

All this is precisely what we should expect of a true child of post-exilic Israel. Now let us look more closely at the period which produced him.

## Cyrus the Persian

Every Jew in Babylon must have followed the career of Cyrus the Persian with rapt interest. The Captivity Oracles had announced that Cyrus would overthrow Babylon and restore the exiles to Palestine. As Cyrus' territory and power grew, it became clear that war with Babylon was inevitable. Cyrus could have taken Babylon almost any time after his defeat of Lydia in 546 B.C. But, by waiting for the precise moment, he managed to conquer the once-great empire in one swift campaign.

In October, 539, the Persian army met and easily defeated the Babylonian troops at Opis, on the Tigris river near the Babylonian border. This was the only battle in the conquest of Babylon. The people were more than ready for a change. In the past few months Nabonidus had been making a frantic attempt to atone for his past blunders and to rally the people behind him. He had revived the neglected New Year's Festival and had celebrated it "according to the complete ritual." In an effort to secure divine favor, he had gathered a large collection of idols from all over the empire. But it was a case of too little, too late. When word of the battle at Opis reached Babylon, the people made it clear they preferred to surrender rather than support Nabonidus. On October 10, 539, the Persian troops, led by Gobryas, occupied Babylon without a fight. When Cyrus himself entered the city

a few weeks later, he was greeted as a deliverer, not a conqueror. The people of Babylon were so relieved to be rid of Nabonidus, who had fled when the Persians entered the city, that they spread green twigs in Cyrus' path and welcomed him with "jubilation and rejoicing."

### A RULE OF BENEVOLENCE

Cyrus' treatment of Babylon is an excellent example of the benevolence and wisdom that characterized his rule. Most ancient conquerors, as soon as the battle was over, turned their armies loose to plunder houses, attack women, and burn temples. Cyrus' soldiers strolled through the streets without their weapons, under strict orders not to terrorize or offend the inhabitants in any way. This dramatic policy was only a start. Among other things, Cyrus abolished the degrading system of state slavery, by which ordinary citizens were forced to work on government projects. He initiated a program of urban renewal to provide better housing for the poor and to carry out the building programs the great Nebuchadnezzar had left unfinished. According to a narrative poem celebrating his triumphs, Cyrus himself "took up hoe, spade, and earth basket" and led the people in the completion of the wall of Babylon.

Cyrus' customary policy regarding the religious practices of his subjects was equally enlightened. Instead of destroying their cults and forcing them to worship his god, he urged the people to continue in their traditional practices, and even rebuilt shrines and temples all over the empire. In Babylon, he personally took part in the worship of Marduk and claimed that god had enabled him to defeat Nabonidus—a claim the worshipers of Marduk could accept quite easily.

The administrative machinery of the vast empire also reflected the wisdom of this po-

A cunieform cylinder which praises the Babylonian god Marduk for enabling Cyrus to defeat Nabonidus.

litical genius. Naturally, the chief officials of the various provinces of the empire were Medes and Persians who answered directly to Cyrus, but the responsibility for the bulk of the day-to-day affairs of the province was placed in the hands of local leaders. In short, all that Cyrus required of the nations he conquered was loyalty to the empire. As long as they paid their annual tribute and made no effort to revolt, he allowed them to retain their local customs and institutions and to live much as they had before his coming. When we understand that this was his standard procedure in dealing with captive peoples, we are in a better position to appreciate his action in behalf of the Jewish exiles.

### THE EDICT OF RESTORATION

In 538 B.C., only one year after the conquest of Babylon, Cyrus issued an edict providing for the return of the exiles to Jerusalem and the rebuilding of the temple of Yahweh. The Bible contains two accounts of Cyrus' decision, one in Aramaic, the official language of the Persian empire (*Ezra 6:3–5*), and one in Hebrew (*Ezra 1:2–4*).

The two accounts differ somewhat and this once puzzled Bible students. Recent study of ancient royal decrees, however, has cleared up the difficulty.

We are not dealing with conflicting versions of the same document, but with two documents relating to the same event. The Hebrew document (*1:2–4*) is a copy of the proclamation Cyrus issued to Judean exiles throughout the empire. The second document (*6:3–5*) bears the title, "A record" (*v. 2*), which is a translation of the Aramaic word, *dikrona*. A *dikrona* was a written record of an oral decision. When Cyrus decided to finance the rebuilding of the temple out of the royal treasury, his secretary took a copy of the decision to those officials who would be involved in handling whatever arrangements needed to be made. When they were finished with it, the document was filed in the archives at Ecbatana, where Cyrus was staying in 538. It was not intended for the general public, and, if it had not been necessary to dig it out during the reign of Darius (see p. 328), we probably would never have heard of it.

These two documents assured the lowly remnant of Israel of the official support of the mightiest empire the world had ever seen. Thus armed, she who was to be "a light to the nations" began trimming her wick in preparation for the long trek home.

## THE FIRST RETURN

Soon after Cyrus issued the edict of restoration, the first group of exiles was ready to return to Judah. We do not know how many brave souls made the trip at this first opportunity. In *Ezra 2*, the Chronicler speaks of 50,000 who returned from Babylon, but this figure seems to include several different waves of returnees (*2:2*). It is rather doubtful that the first group had anywhere near this many people in it. And, it is easy to understand why. The trip to Jerusalem would be long and hard. By this time, many of the Jews had come to feel quite at home in Babylon. No one under forty-five could remember another home. Why should they trade a comfortable existence in this great world center for the hardship that was bound to meet them back in Judah? Some, no doubt, longed to go back, but wanted someone else to make the first trip. Still, a sizable number had caught the vision of a New Exodus and a New Israel, and they were ready to go.

As these hardy pioneers prepared to leave, their more timid brethren gathered round to bid them godspeed and to present them with gifts for themselves and offerings for the temple. At the same time, the royal treasurer of Babylon, following the order of Cyrus, brought out over five thousand gold and silver vessels that Nebuchadnezzar had taken from the original temple (*Ezra 1:7–11*). Surely, some present on that day must have thought of another band that had left a land of bondage for a land of promise, laden down with silver and gold that would be used to build a dwelling-place for the Lord. To be sure, not everything was the same. But, then, this was to be a New Exodus.

The leader of the first migration was a Judean prince named Sheshbazzar (*Ezra 1:8, 11*, etc.). The role of Sheshbazzar is something of a puzzle, for the reason that the Chronicler seems to have confused his career with that of Zerubbabel, who was the first really important figure in the restoration community. In his description of the rebuilding of the temple, the Chronicler names both Sheshbazzar and Zerubbabel as the initiator of the project. Consequently, some have supposed they were one and the same person. This seems rather unlikely, however. It was common for Jews in exile to have both a Hebrew and a Babylonian name (see *Daniel 1:6–7*). But Sheshbazzar and Zerubbabel are both Babylonian names, and it is unlikely that a Jew would have worn both of them.

If, as some language experts have suggested, the name Sheshbazzar is a variant form of "Shenazzar," then Sheshbazzar was probably the son of Jehoiachin, also called Jeconiah (*I Chron. 3:18*). The Babylonians had regarded Jehoiachin as the legitimate king of Judah, and it was appropriate that one of his sons, a prince of the house of David, should be chosen to lead the returning exiles. If Sheshbazzar was Jehoiachin's son, he was also Zerubbabel's uncle (*I Chron. 3:18*). It is not unreasonable to conclude that the two of them worked quite closely together, with Sheshbazzar acting as the titular head and his nephew Zerubbabel assuming most of the actual duties of leadership. If this was the case, it is easy to see why the Chronicler, who wrote about two hundred years later, may have had some difficulty in keeping their careers perfectly straight in his mind.

We know almost nothing of the political status of the restoration community. The

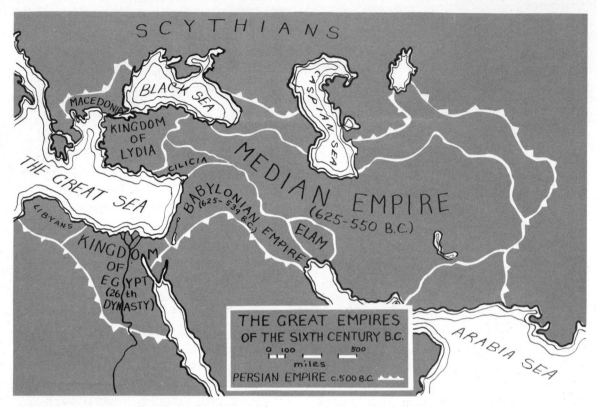

**The great empires of the Sixth Century B.C.**

fact that Sheshbazzar and Zerubbabel are called "governor" is not much help. This was a vague term that could have meant anything from the head of a province to a local ruler with little real authority. There is, however, every reason to believe that Cyrus gave Sheshbazzar the authority to set up the community as he saw fit, as long as he posed no threat to the general welfare of the empire.

### The Early Years: 538–515 B.C.

At last, the restoration community was a reality. In a sense, the prophecies had been fulfilled. Cyrus had liberated the captives and sent them home under the leadership of a Davidic prince. Apart from these facts, however, there was little correspondence between the vision of the prophets and things as they actually were. Far from being

an event that signalled a revolution in nature and history, the return of the Jewish exiles went virtually unnoticed by most of the world. The nations did not beat a path to Jerusalem to acknowledge the sovereignty of Yahweh. There were times when it seemed extremely doubtful that the worship of Yahweh would ever be reestablished in Judah on a firm basis. Years of drought and famine, and harassment by hostile neighbors added to the already heavy burden of disillusionment. Again and again, the whole venture teetered on the brink of failure. The prophet Zechariah spoke truly when he called these early years "the day of small things" (*Zech. 4:10*).

### THE WORLD SITUATION: 538–515

In the decade that followed his conquest of Babylon, Cyrus concentrated on expanding his holdings in the East. In 529, in an expedition against the Massegetae people, who lived beyond the Jaxartes River, he was either killed in battle or mortally wounded. Fortunately for the stability of the empire, Cyrus had taken the precaution to name his son Cambyses as the one who was to succeed him in the event of his death. This, plus the fact that he had served well as the governor of Babylon, enabled Cambyses to assure control of the empire with a minimum of disturbance.

Cambyses' contribution to the Persian empire was the annexation of Egypt, the only major power of the Near East that Cyrus had not found time to conquer. Both sides made careful preparation for the conflict. Cambyses arranged to have Arabian chieftains supply his troops with water as they crossed the desert and Pharaoh Amasis hired Greek soldiers to bolster Egyptian defenses. Amasis died in 525, leaving his son Psammetichus III to face the advancing Persians. Psammetichus had no chance. The hired Greeks defected and threw in with Cambyses. When the battle was joined, the defenders were overpowered and Egypt became a Persian province.

For several years, Cambyses used Egypt as a base for further African campaigns. He managed to add the kingdom of Libya to his holdings but was unsuccessful in an attempt to take Ethiopia. Then, in 522, word came that a usurper had seized the throne, claiming to be Bardiya, the brother of Cambyses whom Cyrus had left in control of the Eastern provinces. Cambyses knew the usurper was an imposter, for he had killed Bardiya before leaving for Egypt, to avoid just this sort of thing. Still, the news broke his spirit. In March, 521, as his troops marched homeward, Cambyses committed suicide rather than face the prospect of a full-scale rebellion.

One of Cambyses' officers, Darius, was re-lated to the royal family. At Cambyses' death, he stepped forward and proclaimed himself king. The army accepted him and he set out for Media. There he and six friends gained entrance to Gaumata's fortress and assassinated the pretender. This gave Darius undisputed title to the crown, but it also set off a series of revolts that rocked the empire from one end to the other. Several opportunists followed Gaumata's example of claiming kinship to the royal family. In Persia itself, another imposter posed as the true Bardiya. Babylon revolted twice in two years. In both cases, the leader claimed to be the son of Nabonidus and called himself Nebuchadnezzar. For two years, Darius, a handful of loyal generals, and a small army of Medes and Persians struggled to put down these and other nationalistic uprisings. It was an enormous task, but by the end of 519 B.C., the empire was quiet and Darius was its undisputed master.

### CONDITIONS IN JUDAH

Life in the new Israel was a hard and disappointing affair. The normal difficulties of any pioneer community were compounded by drought, locusts, and the crop failures that accompanied them. In addition to these natural woes, the Jewish settlement suffered continual harassment at the hands of her northern neighbors, the Samaritans.

The Samaritans resented the fact that the Jewish pioneers had moved in on territory that had formerly been administered as a sub-division of Samaria, but there were deeper reasons for their hostility. Samaria was a nation of half-breeds. After the Assyrian conquest of the old northern kingdom, of which Samaria was the capital city, many of the people were carried into captivity and large numbers of foreigners were settled in the land to mix with those who were left (see p. 221). The Samaritans were

323

the product of this mixture. Somehow, the religion of Yahweh had managed to survive in Samaria and the people considered themselves faithful worshipers of the God of Israel. But the orthodox Jews of the restoration community regarded them as heathen foreigners.

The first tension between the two groups arose over the rebuilding of the temple. Sheshbazzar probably died within a year or two after returning to Jerusalem, for he drops out of the picture completely, leaving the community in the hands of Zerubbabel and Jeshua the high priest. Their first recorded act was to bring the people together "to raise up the house of Yahweh." When the Samaritans learned of the project, they approached Zerubbabel and Jeshua to ask permission to share in the work. Zerubbabel and Jeshua, together with the other leaders of the community, answered them flatly: "You have nothing to do with us in building a house to our god; we alone will build to Yahweh, the God of Israel" (*Ezra 4:3*).

The reaction of the Samaritans to this curt refusal was predictable: if they could have no part in building the temple, they would do what they could to see that it did not get built. They mocked and threatened. They hired professional agitators to frustrate the project in any way they could. And apparently,* they wrote letters to the king to the

_____

*Ezra 4:6-23* is a record of correspondence between the Samaritans and the king of Persia in which the Samaritans convince the king to call a halt to the rebuilding of Jerusalem. Despite their position in the narrative, however, these verses do not refer to the trouble over the temple. The Persian king in this correspondence is Artaxerxes (*4:7ff*), who did not come to the throne until 465 B.C. By this time, the temple had already been standing for fifty years, having been completed in 515, the sixth year of Darius I (*Ez. 6:15*). The letters described here never mention the temple. Their concern is with the rebuilding of the city itself, especially the wall (*4:12, 16, 21*). These verses are out of place in this context. The most natural place for them would be just before *Nehemiah 1*. This dislocation is probably due to an error either on the part of the Chronicler himself or of some later scribe.

effect that the temple would represent a threat to the empire, since it would serve as a focus for nationalistic activity.

The campaign of discouragement accomplished its purpose, at least temporarily. Sometime before the death of Cyrus, the Jews ceased work on the temple (*Ez. 4:24*). They had finished only the foundation and the altar of burnt-offering (*Ez. 3:3, 6; 5:16*). For a good part of twenty years, these abandoned beginnings stood as an eloquent symbol of the despair that filled the hearts of the struggling little community. In 520 B.C., when the rebellions against Darius were at their peak, interest in the temple project was revived by two prophets, Haggai and Zechariah. Apparently, they viewed the explosive situation as a sign the New Age was about to begin and felt it was imperative that the temple be completed, since it would be the focal point of Yahweh's new activity.

### HAGGAI

The book of Haggai consists of four prophecies, all delivered within a four month span in 520, "the second year of Darius the King" (*1:1*). Haggai began his ministry in the sixth month (about August-September) of 520. We can imagine that the abandonment of the temple project had caused great sorrow. But now, the general feeling was one of indifference. The people had built "paneled houses" for themselves, but were saying that there was no hurry about building a house for Yahweh. Haggai's first oracle (*1:1–15*) was addressed to Zerubbabel and Jeshua, rebuking them for the spiritual laziness that had allowed the temple to lie unfinished for such a long time. He announced that the drought and crop failure that had made their lives so miserable were Yahweh's punishment for this laziness (*1:6ff*). Haggai's words were so effective that twenty-four days later the work of rebuilding the temple was resumed.

As the people worked, it became more and more evident that the new temple was going to be definitely second-rate in comparison with the glorious structure Solomon had built. Haggai's second oracle (*2:1–9*), delivered about a month after the work had begun, was designed to encourage those who had grown despondent over this realization. He assured them that a greater glory than that of the past temple was to come to the house of Israel. In this oracle he announced that Yahweh would soon "shake the heavens and the earth and . . . all nations" (*2:6–7*). It is difficult to know exactly what Haggai meant by these words, but they may be a reference to the explosive conditions that were currently prevalent in the empire.

Two months after the second message, Haggai spoke to the people for a third time. In this oracle (*2:10–19*), he tells the people their past indifference had kept them from accomplishing the things they had set out to do. Beginning from the day they had resumed the work on the temple, however, Yahweh had resolved to give them good harvests and to bless their future endeavors.

The last of Haggai's recorded oracles (*2: 20–23*) was delivered later the same day. In this oracle, the prophet again envisions the overthrow of the kingdoms of the world, and announces to Zerubbabel that he has been chosen for a place of special authority in the new age. Haggai refers to Zerubbabel as both the servant and the signet ring, or official representative, of Yahweh. When we place this oracle alongside several found in *Zechariah*, it is difficult to avoid the conclusion that these two prophets regarded Zerubbabel as some kind of Davidic Messiah.

### ZECHARIAH

Haggai's co-worker in this ministry of encouragement was the prophet Zechariah. Although Zechariah may have worked with Haggai right from the start (see *Ezra 5:1*), we have no record of any public statements until "the eighth month, in the second year of Darius," just after Haggai had delivered his second oracle (*Hag. 2:1*). He preached at least two years after Haggai ceased to prophesy (*Zech. 7:1*) and possibly even longer. Many of Zechariah's oracles are cast in what is called an *apocalyptic* form. We shall have more to say about apocalyptic literature later (see p. 362). For now, it will be sufficient to define it as literature that describes, in highly figurative language, the climax of history in which God overcomes all the forces of evil and ushers in a glorious reign of peace. The best Biblical examples of apocalyptic literature are *Daniel* and *Revelation*. In Catholic Bibles, the book of *Revelation* is called *The Apocalypse*.

In reading apocalyptic literature, it is unnecessary to try to attach a meaning to every strange symbol the writer may use. It is the overall meaning that is important. If we do not become frightened or confused by such things as red horses (*1:8;6:2*), flying scrolls (*5:1*), and bronze mountains (*6:1*), the meaning of Zechariah's oracles is fairly easy to discern. The day of small things was finally over. Yahweh had roused himself (*2:13*) and was about to bring his plans for Jerusalem to consummation. The Jews who were still in Babylon were urged to hurry to Zion, for Yahweh would soon come to dwell again in the midst of the city (*2:6–12*), and all the nations would flock there to seek his favor (*8:22*).

Yahweh would rule in the New Jerusalem through his special earthly representatives, Zerubbabel and Jeshua the priest. Haggai had singled Zerubbabel out for a special role in the new establishment. Zechariah repeatedly speaks of him in language that is clearly messianic. Especially important is his calling Zerubbabel "the Branch." Generations before, Isaiah had spoken of a great leader

325

who was to come, calling him "a shoot from the stump of Jesse, a *branch* . . . out of his roots." Jesse, of course, was the father of David, and this was Isaiah's way of saying that the expected Messiah would be a descendant of David. By calling Zerubbabel, who was of the house of David, the Branch, Zechariah was explictly identifying him as a messianic figure.

The role of Zerubbabel and Jeshua in the New Jerusalem is pictured in these verses:

> Behold the man whose name is the Branch: for he shall grow up in his place, and he shall build the temple of Yahweh. It is he who shall build the temple of Yahweh, and shall bear royal honor, and shall sit and rule upon his throne. And there shall be a priest by his throne, and peaceful understanding shall be between them both.
>
> —*Zechariah 6:12-13*

Zerubbabel's primary task was to build the temple. By the power of the Spirit of Yahweh, he would see it through to completion (*5:6–10*) and would then assume his place of honor on the royal throne.

The language of Zechariah's oracles were strange and unfamiliar. But the content was in perfect harmony with the prophets who had gone before him, for they, too, had looked for the day when Yahweh would raise up a son of David to rule over a faithful remnant of Israel in a Jerusalem that would never perish.

### THE COMPLETION OF THE TEMPLE

Before long, word spread that the Jews were working on the temple again. And, although we have no direct evidence, it is likely that the statements of Haggai and Zechariah about the new kingdom of Israel also fell on ears that were not exactly delighted by the news. At any rate, Tattenai, the governor of the Persian province that included Syria and Palestine, and several subordinate governors soon appeared on the

scene to demand to know who had given the Jews permission to rebuild the temple and to get the names of the major leaders (*Ez. 5:3–5*). The elders of the Jews seem not to have given them the names of Zerubbabel and Jeshua, probably because they feared the governors would imprison the two leaders. They did, however, inform them that the project had been authorized by Cyrus (*5:6–16*).

Tattenai and his associates sent a letter to Darius, explaining the situation and asking for a check of the records to see if Cyrus had ever issued such an edict (*5:17*). A search was made in the archives at Babylon, with no success. Finally, someone thought to check the archives building at Ecbatana, in Media, where Cyrus had been living at the time the edict was supposed to have been made. There they found the record we discussed earlier, which not only authorized the project but declared that it should be financed out of the royal treasury (*6:1–5*). If Darius had heard any of the nationalistic rumblings from Judah, he was not seriously disturbed by them. As soon as he saw the memorandum of Cyrus' decree, he ordered Tattenai and the governors to keep away from Jerusalem and to see to it that the Jews got a quick and generous supply of anything they needed, including animals for burnt-offerings (*6:6–12*).

With all obstacles removed, work on the temple progressed rapidly under Zerubbabel's direction. It was finished "in the sixth year of Darius the king," or 515 B.C. At the joyous dedication ceremony, hundreds of animals were sacrificed as burnt-offerings and the complex machinery of the temple services was set in motion (*6:16–18*). Shortly afterward, the Passover was kept. At last, the New Israel was a reality. Unfortunately, the reality did not measure up to the vision. To an outsider, it was hard to see any change in Jerusalem, except that the Jews had themselves a new building. Yahweh may have begun his glorious reign, but most of the world was paying homage to Darius. Zerubbabel, the Davidic prince who was to wield the scepter of Yahweh in the new kingdom, disappears from the historical narrative. He may have been removed by Persian power, or he may have died, or he may have ruled quietly for a number of years. The only thing we know for sure is that he was not the world-renowned leader the prophets seem to have expected. And when his rule was ended, no scion of David rose to take his place. The dream of a Davidic kingdom passed away and the high priest became both spiritual and temporal leader.

This disparity between hope and reality must have brought great disappointment to the restoration community. But the experiment had not been a total failure. The house of Israel had been reestablished. It had met and passed a severe crisis. And it would stand until another son of David, who was also called Messiah, arose to announce that the Kingdom of God was among men.

## From Zerubbabel to Ezra and Nehemiah

The Chronicler moves from the completion of the temple in 515 B.C. to the reconstruction under Nehemiah and Ezra in the middle of the fifth century B.C. with scarcely a nod to the sixty or more years that passed between. Our knowledge of the reconstruction community in these years is limited to secular historical sources, a few scraps of Biblical narrative, three minor prophetic works, two of which may not even come from this period, and educated guesses based on conditions at the time when the narrative resumes. These were desperate years for the people of God. The Persian Empire seemed invincible. The prosperity and security that were expected to follow the completion of the temple do not seem to have materialized. The religious fervor inspired by Haggai and Zechariah gradually died down. By the time Nehemiah and Ezra arrived in Jerusalem, Israel was once again dangerously close to losing her identity as a separate people, holy unto the Lord.

### THE PERSIAN EMPIRE, 515–450 B.C.

As we have seen, Darius gained full control of the Persian Empire by 519. By the end of the sixth century B.C., he had enlarged the borders of the empire until it sprawled all the way from India to the west coast of Africa, and from Arabia to Southern Russia (see p. 324). Even more astonishing than the sheer immensity of Darius' empire was the efficiency and brilliance with which he administered it. Cyrus the Great had divided the empire into provinces. Darius gave sharper form to these provinces by arranging them into twenty great regions called *satrapies*. Over each of these satrapies, he placed a governor, who was usually a Persian or Median. The official title given to these governors was *Khshatrapavan*, which is usually translated simply as "satrap." The satraps were charged with maintaining the safety of the roads in their region and with collecting and remitting the taxes from the various cities within the province. They had wide power within their own realm, but were under definite checks set by the Great King. Foremost among these checks was the lack of any real army. All major divisions of the Persian army were commanded by royal officers directly responsible to the king. In addition, a network of royal secretaries and other emissaries traveled about the empire to serve as "eyes" for the king.

Tight military and political control was not Darius' only achievement. He built roads all over the empire. He carried out sweeping legal and judicial reforms. He in-

The apadana, or audience hall, at Persepolis, built by Darius and Xerxes.

stituted coinage and postage systems that lasted for centuries. And to crown his efforts, he built the city of Persepolis which he made the capital of the empire. The ruins of its magnificent buildings still stand as a tribute to this noble and enlightened ruler.

When Darius died in 486 B.C., he was succeeded by his son Xerxes, who is called Ahasuerus in the Bible. Xerxes was given the throne in preference to two older half-brothers because his mother was the daughter of Cyrus the Great. Unfortunately, Xerxes was not quite as successful at running an empire as his father and grandfather had been, although he does not deserve all the blame for the things that went wrong during his reign. In Egypt, he inherited a rebellion that had broken out in Darius' last year. When he had put this down successfully, he appointed his brother Achaemenes as satrap and, according to

the ancient historian Herodotus, "brought Egypt under a much heavier yoke than it had been before." This increased harshness was characteristic of Xerxes. In 484, he responded to a hostile situation in Babylon by destroying the great city and stripping the province of many of the privileges it had formerly enjoyed.

Xerxes spent the bulk of his reign in an attempt to bring Greece under Persian control. Darius had led a campaign against Greece in 490, but had been defeated at Marathon and forced to withdraw. In 480, after three years of careful preparation, Xerxes fought his way through Macedonia. From there, he backed the Greek forces to Corinth and prepared to deliver the crushing blow. At that point, however, the Greeks lured him into a naval battle under conditions that gave them a decided edge. The Persian fleet suffered disastrous losses. With his major source of troops and supplies cut off, Xerxes was forced to retire from Greece, leaving it under the control of an occupation army that was too small for its assignment. In 479, the Greeks cut this army to ribbons. There was a good deal of sparring for several years, but by the end of Xerxes' reign (465) Europe was completely free of the Persian yoke.

During the latter years of his reign, Xerxes occupied himself with the pleasures and intrigues of his court. The story of Esther reflects the situation of these years. In 465, Xerxes was assassinated in a court plot that brought his younger son Artaxerxes to the throne.

Artaxerxes had to deal with several routine minor rebellions and a major uprising in Egypt, but his reign (465–425) was, on the whole, rather peaceful. Persia was no longer invincible, but Artaxerxes was prudent enough not to attempt anything that might weaken her further. He is said to have been handsome, good-natured, and generous. It was during his reign that the Jewish religion was established by law in Jerusalem, under the leadership of Nehemiah and Ezra. With this brief sketch of the world situation as background, let us notice what was happening in Judah itself.

### LIFE IN JUDAH

Trying to depict life in Judah during this period is something like trying to do a jigsaw puzzle with only three or four pieces. Our information is so scarce that, at best, we get only glimpses of the total picture. The three key pieces of our puzzle are the

**Relief of King Darius, carved on the treasury wall at Persepolis. In front of the king are two incense burners and a Median noble; behind him are the Crown Prince Xerxes and the royal cupbearer.**

books of the prophets Joel, Obadiah, and Malachi. Between them, they reflect a period of plague and famine, harassment from neighbors, and laxity in religion and morals.

*Joel.* The occasion of the prophetic activity of Joel was a severe locust plague. We do not know just when this occurred, since locust plagues were fairly common in the Near East. Scholars have never been able to agree on a date for the book and we may be mistaken in placing Joel's ministry at this time. However, the references to Israel's being scattered among the nations (*Joel 3:2*) and to the sale of Jews into slavery (*3:4–6*) made a post-exilic date seem probable. Still, almost any time from 500–350 B.C. would be an acceptable date.

Joel describes the devastating plague of locusts in four stages:

> What the cutting locust left,
>   the swarming locust has eaten.
> What the swarming locust left,
>   the hopping locust has eaten,
> and what the hopping locust left,
>   the destroying locust has eaten.
>                           —*Joel 1:4*

This may refer to four kinds of locusts or to four stages of development in the common locust. Joel also paints a vivid picture of the awesome character of a full-fledged locust plague.

> Fire devours before them,
>   and behind them a flame burns.
> The land is like the garden of Eden before
>     them,
>   but after them a desolate wilderness,
>   and nothing escapes them.
>
> Their appearance is like the appearance
>     of horses,
>   and like war horses they run.
> As with the rumbling of chariots,
>   they leap on the tops of the mountains.
> like the crackling of a flame of fire
>   devouring the stubble,

like a powerful army drawn up for battle.

> Before them peoples are in anguish,
>   all faces grow pale.
> Like warriors they charge,
>   like soldiers they scale the wall.
> They march each on his way,
>   they do not swerve from the paths.
> They do not jostle one another,
>   each marches in his path;
> they burst through the weapons
>   and are not halted.
> They leap upon the city,
>   they run upon the wall;
> they climb up into the houses,
>   they enter through the windows
>     like a thief.            —*Joel 2:3-9*

Joel felt the plague might be a sign that the long-awaited Day of Yahweh was about to break in on history (*1:15; 2:1, 11*). He called the people to fast and repent with all the customary signs of mourning (*2:12ff*). Then, in describing the Day that was to come, Joel said:

> And it shall come to pass afterward,
>   that I will pour out my spirit on all flesh;
> your sons and your daughters shall prophesy,
>   your old men shall dream dreams,
>   and your young men shall see visions.
> Even upon the menservants and
>     maidservants
>   in those days, I will pour out my spirit.
>
> . . . . . . . . . . . . . . . .
>
> And it shall come to pass that all who call upon the name of Yahweh shall be delivered; for in Mount Zion and in Jerusalem there shall be those who escape, as Yahweh has said, and among the survivors shall be those whom Yahweh calls.
>
>                        —*Joel 2:28, 29, 32*

The Day of Yahweh was a favorite theme of the prophets. The language they used to describe it was colorful and highly imaginative. To the dismay of many, nothing ever happened that quite fit these vivid descriptions. But on the first Pentecost after the resurrection of Jesus, an event signifying God's victory over sin and death, some strange things did happen. As the disciples of Jesus gathered to pray, they heard a sound like a mighty wind. Suddenly, little tips of fire appeared over their heads and they began to speak about "the mighty works of God," each one speaking in a different language, so that all the foreigners gathered in Jerusalem for Pentecost could understand them. Some were amazed. Others dismissed the disciples as drunken babblers. But the apostle Peter said that what was happening that day was fulfilling "that which was spoken by the prophet Joel" (*Acts 2:1–21*).

*Obadiah.* The prophecies of Obadiah, which make up the shortest book in the Old Testament, announce the approaching doom of Edom. The Edomites, as we have seen, were regarded as descended from Esau and thus related to the Jews. Nevertheless, their relationship to each other had been one of longstanding enmity. Throughout the Old Testament, there are frequent denunciations of Edom. The Edomites lived in the rocky range south of the Dead Sea and had built almost impregnable fortresses in the canyons and gorges of these mountains. From these rocky heights, they had regularly swooped down to harass Judah, either on their own, or in league with other attackers. They had earned the hatred Judah felt for them. With considerable satisfaction, Obadiah announces Yahweh's decision concerning Edom:

> Behold, I will make you small among the
>     nations,
>     you shall be utterly despised.
> The pride of your heart has deceived you,
>     you who live in the clefts of the rock,
>     whose dwelling is high,
> who say in your heart,
>     "Who will bring me down to the ground?"
>                                 —*Obadiah 2:3*

Of all Edom's hostile actions against Judah, none seems to have been remembered with more bitterness than her behavior at the time Nebuchadnezzar destroyed Jerusalem. Notice the vividness with which Obadiah describes this incident:

> You should not have gloated over the day
>     of your brother
>   in the day of his misfortune;
> you should not have rejoiced over the people
>     of Judah
>   in the day of their ruin;
> you should not have boasted
>   in the day of distress.
> You should not have entered the gate of my
>     people
>   in the day of his calamity;
> you should not have gloated over his disaster
>   in the day of his calamity;
> you should not have looted his goods
>   in the day of his calamity.
> You should not have stood at the parting of
>     the ways
>   to cut off his fugitives;
> you should not have delivered up his
>     survivors
>   in the day of distress.    —*Obadiah 12-14*

Edom's day of gloating is about over. Soon, cries the prophet,

> As you have done, it shall be done to you,
>   your deeds shall return on your own head.
>                                 —*Obadiah 15*

Like Nahum's gleeful announcement of the fall of Nineveh, Obadiah's message is a bit troubling because of its apparent lack of compassion. But we can scarcely doubt that it was an accurate expression of the feelings of the frustrated Jewish colony.

*Malachi.* The prophecies of *Malachi* are more important as a source of information about this period than either *Joel* or *Obadiah*. For one thing, the evidence that Malachi actually lived during this period is much stronger than in the cases of Joel and Obadiah. And for another, the scope of Malachi's prophecies is much wider than that of the other two.

Like Joel and Obadiah, Malachi does not follow the prophetic custom of naming the king in whose reign he prophesied, but he does give us several clues that indicate his ministry occurred around 460 B.C. The exiles had returned from Babylon and were living under a governor (1:8). The temple had been completed and enough time had lapsed for the people to grow weary and lax in observing the various rituals and sacrifices. This calls for a date well after 515 B.C. The denunciation of mixed marriages (2:10–12) and failure to pay tithes suggests a date close to the time of Nehemiah and Ezra, since these were two chief targets of their reform efforts. For these reasons, most scholars conclude that Malachi was probably active between 465 and 450 B.C.

The book of *Malachi* is divided into six sections, each beginning with a statement that leads to a question that leads, in turn, to an elaboration of the issue thus raised.* Through his spokesman Malachi, Yahweh asks, "If I am a father, where is my honor?" Laymen, priests, and Levites were guilty of dishonoring the father: the laymen because they brought blind, lame, and sick animals to offer as sacrifices; the priests because they let the laymen get away with this kind of behavior; and the Levites because they had not properly taught the people about the nature of their covenant responsibilities (1:6–2:9).

Another section (2:10–16) begins, "Have we not all one father?" This is rhetorical, but the question that follows demanded an answer: "Why then are we faithless to one another, profaning the covenant of our fathers? The chief example of covenant-breaking the prophet wished to score was the breakdown of the sanctity of the mar-

riage bond. Israelite men were divorcing their Jewish wives to marry heathen women. To make matters worse, they were then adopting the religion of their new wives. Concerning this practice the prophet warned: "Take heed to yourselves, and let none be faithless to the wife of his youth. 'For I hate divorce,' says Yahweh the God of Israel" (2:15–16).

The other major sin to receive Malachi's attention was the withholding of tithes and offerings. He introduces his discussion of this matter with the startling question, "Will man rob God?" Of course, no one would admit to stealing from God. And yet, by failing to pay their tithes and by offering Yahweh the scabby leavings of their flocks and herds, that is exactly what they were doing. If they would make their obligation to Yahweh their first concern, he would "open the windows of heaven . . . and pour down an overflowing blessing" (3:6–12).

In true prophetic fashion, Malachi climaxed his message with a declaration about the Day of Yahweh. The momentous day was not far off when Yahweh would come to purge and refine the dross from his people (3:1–3). This much was part of the standard language about the Day of Yahweh, but Malachi added a new dimension to the expectation. Before the day would come, he said, Elijah the prophet would come to prepare the way. This is the first known reference to Elijah as the forerunner of the Day of Yahweh, but it soon became an accepted part of Jewish Messianic thought. The idea seemed perfectly natural. After all, Elijah had not died, but had been taken to heaven in a chariot of fire (II Kings 2:11). Yahweh must have preserved him from death in order to use him to herald the coming of the messianic age. The Jews came to believe in Elijah's return so strongly that, in later years, they prepared a special place for him at the Passover meal, fully ex-

*The six sections are 1:2-5; 1:6-2:9; 2:10-16; 2:17-3:5; 3:6-12; 3:13-4:3.

pecting him to show up at any time. Like so many other hopes the Jews held, the hope of the actual physical return of the colorful eighth century prophet was never realized. But when Jesus, whom Christians call Messiah, was questioned about the personality of John the Baptist, he gave his hearers the simple answer: "If you are willing to accept it, he is Elijah who is to come" (*Matthew 11:14*).

## The Period of Reconstruction

From the fragmentary clues given above, we can see that life in Judah in the first half of the fifth century B.C. was a discouraged and discouraging affair. With no wall to repel attackers, Jerusalem was probably subjected to repeated raids from her hostile neighbors. In addition to this physical harassment, these neighbors did all they could to keep Judah in trouble with the imperial government by writing letters accusing the Jews of seditious behavior (*Ez. 4*). Under the stress of physical and political hardship, the moral and religious fiber of the community began to weaken. As Malachi made clear, the spiritual life of the community had deteriorated to a quite superficial level. The people had little real concern for anything deeper than getting enough money to live on. This kind of existence was hardly what one might have expected of the Golden Age the prophets had promised. All things considered, Judah was in serious need of extensive political, economical, social, and religious reform. These came with Nehemiah and Ezra.

### THE RELATIONSHIP BETWEEN NEHEMIAH AND EZRA

One of the major historical problems of the post-exilic period has to do with the relationship between Nehemiah and Ezra. On the surface, the Biblical account seems straightforward enough. Ezra is said to have

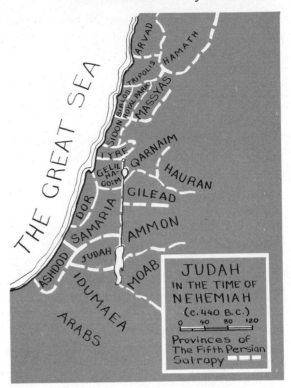

The Province of Judah in Nehemiah's time.

come from Babylon in the seventh year of Artaxerxes, or 458 (*Ez. 7:7*), and Nehemiah is said to have come in the twentieth year, or 445 (*Neh. 1:1*). The natural conclusion seems to be that Ezra came to Jerusalem thirteen years before Nehemiah, carried out his work of reforming Judah's religious life, and that Nehemiah followed this with a reformation of the political and social life of the community. A closer reading of *Ezra-Nehemiah*, however, will reveal the hazards of jumping to this "natural" conclusion too quickly. In fact, apart from these dates, most of the evidence from *Ezra-Nehemiah* suggests that Ezra followed Nehemiah, not the other way around.

Ezra is described as a man full of zeal for the Law of God. Jews have accepted this view and have considered him second in importance only to Moses. And yet, if he preceded Nehemiah, it is difficult to understand

333

how he got this reputation. Nehemiah was present at Ezra's first public reading of the Law (*Neh. 8:1–9*). If Ezra came to Jerusalem in 458, this means he waited at least thirteen years before reading the Law to the people. This, of course, is possible, but rather unlikely. Furthermore, if Ezra's reforms were carried out before Nehemiah's, we must conclude they were remarkably unsuccessful. Ezra moved the people to make a covenant in which they accepted the law of Moses as their rule of faith and practice. The climax of this renewal process came when all those who had married foreign women divorced them and disowned their children (*Ez. 9–10*). In *Nehemiah 13*, however, we are told that one of the abuses Nehemiah sought to correct was the high rate of marriages between Jews and foreigners. These mixed marriages infuriated Nehemiah (*Neh. 13:23–29*). He reminded the people of Solomon's sin in marrying foreign wives, but he did not mention the mass divorces that took place under Ezra's leadership. It is most unlikely he would have failed to mention that dramatic action if it had already occurred. If Ezra's reformation was such a monumental failure that Nehemiah could find almost no trace of it ten or so years later, it is hard to see how Ezra gained such a firm place in the heart of post-exilic Judaism. On the other hand, if he picked up what Nehemiah had already begun and successfully carried out a systematic reform based on the Law, both these narratives and the judgment of Jewish history make much better sense.

There are other arguments to support the view that Nehemiah preceded Ezra. In describing the early phases of his work, Ezra recalls his thankfulness that Jerusalem had a wall to protect her against her enemies (*Ez. 9:9*). It was Nehemiah, of course, who rebuilt the wall of Jerusalem in 445 B.C. If Ezra was talking about Nehemiah's wall—

and, it must be admitted, we cannot be absolutely sure he was—he must have arrived in Jerusalem not in 458, but sometime after 445. This verse also indicates that the city was operating under fairly stable conditions, presumably with an adequate population. In *Nehemiah 7:4*, we are told that when Nehemiah came to Jerusalem he found it virtually deserted. To remedy the situation, he set up a resettlement program under which ten per cent of the population of Judah moved into Jerusalem (*Neh. 11:1–2*). Unless we posit some unrecorded disaster that reduced the city from what it seems to have been when Ezra arrived to what it was when Nehemiah arrived, it is more reasonable to conclude that the political and social stability Ezra found was a result of Nehemiah's earlier efforts.

Other small items, such as a list of post-exilic leaders in which Nehemiah's name comes before that of Ezra (*Neh. 12:46*) are inconclusive by themselves, but add further weight to this view. But the fact remains that the Bible plainly says Ezra came to Jerusalem in the seventh year of Artaxerxes, which was thirteen years *before* Nehemiah arrived. What are we to make of this? No answer to this problem is entirely satisfactory, but Hebrew scholars have shown that it would be a simple matter for a scribe to have omitted part of the number in copying *Ezra 7:7*. In other words, instead of "seventh," the original manuscript may have had something like "thirty-seventh." It is risky to try to imagine what some scribe may have done over two thousand years ago, but, if Ezra did come from Babylon to Jerusalem in the thirty-seventh year of Artaxerxes, the problems we have raised above would be solved rather handily. We cannot, of course, be sure that this is what happened, but it seems to be the most workable solution available at present and is the one followed in the writing of this chapter. According to

A king's cupbearer. Only a person of unquestioned loyalty could attain this office.

this theory, Nehemiah came to Jerusalem in 445 B.C. He served as governor of Judah until 433, at which time he returned to the court of Artaxerxes (*Neh. 13:6*). After a short time, he went back to Jerusalem to serve a second term as governor. Then, probably about 428 B.C., Ezra came to Jerusalem to assist Nehemiah in the reconstruction of the moral and spiritual life of the community of God's people.*

### NEHEMIAH'S FIRST TERM

Nehemiah, although a Jew, was cupbearer to Artaxerxes king of Persia. The cupbearer was no ordinary servant. He was frequently the king's most trusted personal friend. Because he had daily access to the

*For a more detailed treatment of this problem and a fuller exposition of the above viewpoint, see John Bright, *History of Israel* (Philadelphia: Westminster Press, 1959), pp. 375-86.

king, it was necessary that he be a person of unquestioned loyalty. It is a tribute to Nehemiah's character and ability that he was chosen for this responsible position. In 445 B.C., the twentieth year of Artaxerxes (*Neh. 1:1*), Nehemiah was serving the king at Susa, the winter capital of Persia, when he received a visit from his brother Hanani, who had just come from Jerusalem. When Hanani told Nehemiah about the distressing conditions in Jerusalem, Nehemiah sat down and cried (*Neh. 1:4*). For several days he mourned and fasted and prayed. Eventually, the king inquired about the cause of his obvious sadness. Nehemiah knew Artaxerxes was a generous man, so he seized this opportunity to ask permission to go to Jerusalem to rebuild the ruined city.

Earlier in his reign, Artaxerxes had forbidden the Jews to rebuild Jerusalem (*Ez. 4:7–22*), but his trust in Nehemiah was so great that he not only gave him a leave of absence from the court, but appointed him governor of Judah and sent instructions to the satrap of the province "Beyond the River" (Palestine and Syria) to help Nehemiah secure whatever he needed for his project. Not long afterward, Nehemiah set out for Jerusalem under the protection of a royal bodyguard (*Neh. 2:9*).

*Rebuilding the Wall.* Three days in Jerusalem convinced Nehemiah that what was needed more than anything else was a wall that would give the people some measure of security. Without a wall, Jerusalem was wide open to any kind of raid or attack her enemies wished to make. Years of this kind of helpless existence had doubtless robbed the people of the self-confidence they so desperately needed. So, after a secret inspection of the burned and broken remnant of the old wall, Nehemiah called the leaders of the city together and told them of his plan to build a new wall. They readily accepted his leadership and his proposal, and

335

"strengthened their hands for the good work" (*Neh. 2:11–18*). Workers were called together, assigned a gate or a portion of the wall, and put to work (*Neh. 3*).

Not everyone was pleased with the news that Nehemiah was planning to rebuild Jerusalem. Almost immediately, a movement to thwart Nehemiah's plans began to develop. The leaders of the opposition were Sanballat, Tobiah, and Geshem. These men were not local roughnecks out to stir up trouble just for the fun of it. Sanballat was governor of the province of Samaria, Tobiah was governor of the province of Ammon in Transjordan, and Geshem was a powerful chieftain who governed the province of Arabia. Between the three of them, they controlled the territory to the North, West, and South of Judah. They were determined to oppose any action that might threaten their own position or deprive them of the luxury of bullying Judah at will. They had been displeased over Nehemiah's mission right from the start (*Neh. 2:10*). When they learned he was actually planning to rebuild the wall, they began immediately to try to stop him, using every tactic they could devise.

First, they tried to intimidate him with thinly-veiled accusations of rebellion against the king. Nehemiah was not impressed. He knew Artaxerxes would not believe any reports accusing him of disloyalty. Their next weapon was ridicule. Sanballat mockingly asked, "What are these feeble Jews doing? Will they revive the stones out of the heaps of rubbish, and burned ones at that?" Tobiah joined in, "Yes, what they are building—if a fox goes upon on it he will break down their stone wall!" (*Neh. 4:1–3*). Geshem does not seem to have been so clever, but he probably joined in the mockery as well as he could. Despite these taunts, the wall grew higher and higher, "for the people had a mind to work" (*Neh. 4:6*).

When words failed to daunt the Jews, their enemies decided to resort to force. Secretly, they plotted to attack the city by surprise and to kill the workers. But Jews who lived in enemy territory learned of the plot and warned Nehemiah. The news was disheartening, but Nehemiah rallied his people and stationed them at open places along the wall, armed and ready to fight. Then, like a true leader, he went from group to group, encouraging them with these words: "Do not be afraid of them. Remember Yahweh, who is great and terrible, and fight for your brethren, your sons, your daughters, your wives, and your homes" (*4: 14*). Nehemiah's defensive preparations frustrated the opposition and the Jews were able to start back to work. Still, they did not drop their guard. They divided the work force into crews. While one crew worked, the other stood guard, ready to pass out weapons and armor in case of attack. Each worker kept his hand weapon with him and a trumpeter stood ready to sound the alarm if he saw the enemy approaching (*Neh. 4: 15–23*). Nehemiah tells us they worked like this from dawn till dusk: "neither I nor my brethren nor my servants nor the men of the guard who followed me, none of us took off our clothes; each kept his weapon in his hand" (*4:23*).

Sanballat, Tobiah, and Geshem saw that nothing could stop the Jews as long as Nehemiah was there to spur them on. So, they tried to lure him to a meeting outside the city, planning to kill him (*Neh. 6:1–9*). Four times they invited Nehemiah to meet with them and four times he refused. Finally, Sanballat sent a letter accusing Nehemiah of planning to rebel against the empire. He also claimed he had heard Jewish prophets announce that Nehemiah had set himself up as king of Judah. Nehemiah's reply bristles with the contempt he felt for this transparently amateurish move by Sanballat: "No such things as you say have been done, for you are inventing them out of your own mind" (*Neh. 6:8*).

When the assassination plot failed, Sanballat and Tobiah tried to discredit Nehemiah before the people of Jerusalem. They hired a prophetess, Noadiah, to make fun of him and to warn him that he could not succeed (*Neh. 6:14*). Another hired agent, pretending to be his friend, told Nehemiah of a plot on his life and urged him to seek asylum in the temple. Nehemiah sensed the "friend" was trying to trick him into behaving like a coward. His reply shows he did not suffer from a lack of self-confidence: "Should such a man as I flee? And what man such as I could go into the temple and live? I will not go in" (*Neh. 6:11*).

Nehemiah had to rely mainly on himself and the support of his God in order to withstand this barrage of taunts, threats, and intrigue. He scarcely knew whom to trust, for many of the leading families of the city were related by marriage to Tobiah and kept the Ammonite ruler well supplied with information about every move Nehemiah made. But the governor of the Jews was a man of remarkable courage and fortitude who would not be stopped. In less than two months, Jerusalem had its wall, although the Jewish historian Josephus tells us they continued to strengthen it for over two more years.

*Economic Reforms.* The other major accomplishment of Nehemiah's first term in office was the reform of the economic life of Judah. A combination of famine, heavy taxes, and hard-hearted money-lenders had dragged Judah into the depths of economic depression. Many had mortgaged their land, their houses, and every stick of furniture they owned just in order to get enough food to live on. Things had finally gotten so bad that some were having to sell their sons and daughters into slavery to keep from starv-

ing. This incensed Nehemiah. If Judah was to survive, the people would have to forget their own selfish interests and pull together as brethren. He summoned the leaders of the financial community and harangued them for their lack of compassion toward their brethren. Heads hanging in shame, these men pledged under oath to stop taking interest on money they loaned, to cancel the mortgages they held, and to restore to their rightful owners all the property and goods they had taken (*Neh. 5:6–13*). Nehemiah himself set an unselfish example by refusing to take the food allowance the people customarily provided the governor (*5: 14–19*). Apparently, these measures had the desired effect, for Nehemiah compliments himself on all the good he had done for his people (*5:19*).

Coins of Judah, struck in the Fourth Century. These indicate a considerable amount of home rule under the Persians. Above: the daric (Ezra 2:69 RSV); below: a coin bearing the name Judah.

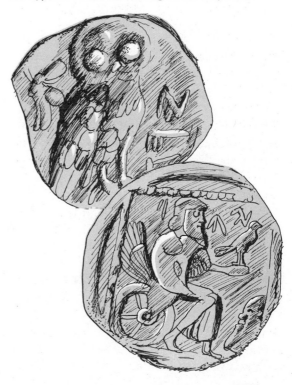

### NEHEMIAH'S SECOND TERM

After twelve years in Jerusalem, Nehemiah returned to the court of Artaxerxes, probably at the king's request (Cf. *Neh. 2: 6; 13:6*). We can imagine that, as loyal as he was, he could hardly put his heart into serving wine in the king's palace when he was needed so badly in Jerusalem. Finally, he persuaded Artaxerxes to let him return to the land of his fathers.

What Nehemiah found in Jerusalem appalled him. Eliashib the high priest had converted one of the rooms of the temple into an apartment for Tobiah—the same Tobiah who had tried to kill Nehemiah! Nehemiah wasted no time expressing his opinion of Eliashib's gesture of hospitality. He personally threw Tobiah's belongings out of the chamber, replacing them with the vessels and supplies that belonged there—but not until the room had been thoroughly cleaned to remove all traces of Tobiah's presence (*Neh. 13:7–9*).

As Nehemiah inspected the temple more closely, he saw that it was virtually deserted. Support for the Levites had been discontinued, forcing them to leave the temple to work in the fields to earn a living. First, Nehemiah rounded up the Levites and set them to work at their proper stations. Then he commanded the people to bring their tithes into the temple storehouses. Finally, he met with the city officials and set up a careful bureaucratic structure to make sure such a situation was not allowed to reoccur.

The arrival of the sabbath brought another shock for Nehemiah. The people had transformed it from a quiet day of worship and rest into a bustling market-day. Farmers and merchants from all over Judah came to Jerusalem on the sabbath to sell their products. Again, Nehemiah took decisive action. Late Friday afternoon, as the sabbath was beginning—the Jews counted their days from dusk to dusk, not midnight to midnight—he ordered his servants to shut the gates of the city and to keep them shut until the sabbath was over. The merchants came and camped outside the wall for one or two Saturdays, until Nehemiah threatened to arrest them if they showed up again. "From that time on they did not come on the sabbath" (*Neh. 13:21*).

These offences gave evidence that the Jews were losing their character as a peculiar and holy people and were taking on the characteristics of their heathen neighbors. This probably explains part of Nehemiah's intense opposition to marriages between the Jews and these neighbors. Intermarriage had become so common that Nehemiah found many children who spoke only "the language of Ashdod." It scandalized his patriotic soul to think that Jewish fathers could rear children who could not even speak Hebrew. His reaction was so violent as to be almost comical—"I contended with them and cursed them and beat some of them and pulled out their hair" (*Neh. 13: 25*). Nehemiah was convinced that the only way Judah could escape the wrath of Yahweh was to keep herself free from contamination by foreign elements. Solomon's foreign wives had turned him from the worship of Yahweh to the worship of idols. If it could happen even to wise Solomon what chance did an ordinary Jew have? The only safe course was to erect barriers of separation between Jews and non-Jews. To this end, Nehemiah forbade the people of Judah to contract any further marriages with foreigners (*13:23–27*).

To some, Nehemiah's attitude may seem excessively narrow. Nevertheless, it was this narrowness that kept the post-exilic community from being absorbed into its environment and enabled it to preserve the traditions that have shaped so profoundly the history of mankind.

## EZRA, THE FATHER OF JUDAISM

If the chronological scheme we have adopted is correct, Ezra arrived in Jerusalem about 428 B.C., shortly after the beginning of Nehemiah's second term as governor. The Chronicler describes Ezra as both a priest and a scribe, who was "skilled in the Law of Moses" and had "set his heart to study the law of the Lord and to do it, and to teach his statutes and ordinances in Israel" (*Ez. 7:6, 10*). Ezra was living among the exiles in Babylonia when he gained permission from Artaxerxes to return to Judah to reorganize the Jewish community on the basis of the Law of Moses. The decree of Artaxerxes authorizing this mission (*Ez. 7:11–26*) not only allowed Ezra the freedom to teach the law of Moses; it gave him legal authority to enforce the law—"whoever will not obey the law of your God and the law of the king, let judgment be strictly executed upon him, whether for death or for banishment or for confiscation of his goods or for imprisonment" (*Ez. 7:26*). Thus fortified, Ezra and those who chose to go with him set out for Jerusalem.

*Mixed Marriages Dissolved.* Shortly after Ezra arrived and made his plans known to the people, a group of troubled officials approached him about the problem of intermarriage. It may well be that they also approached Nehemiah at this time and that his tirade against those who had married foreigners was part of a joint effort between the two leaders.

Ezra was a less explosive man than Nehemiah, but he was equally appalled by the news "that the holy race has mixed itself with the peoples of the lands" (*Ez. 9:2*). Quickly, word was sent out that all the men of Judah were to come to Jerusalem. Three days later, they assembled in the square in front of the temple. A heavy rain was falling, but no one suggested calling off the meeting. When Ezra stood up to speak, he got to the point quickly: "You have trespassed and married foreign women, and so increased the guilt of Israel. Now then make confession to Yahweh the God of your fathers, and do his will; separate yourselves from the people of the land and from the foreign wives" (*Ez. 10:10, 11*). With one ashamed voice, the men admitted their guilt and agreed to do as Ezra said. But, they suggested, this was not the sort of thing that could be settled at a single meeting; too many people were involved—not to mention the fact they were all about to drown.

So, with their approval, Ezra set up a commission to investigate the matter thoroughly and to see to it that all mixed marriages were dissolved. In less than three months, all who had married foreign women and who wished to remain a part of the Jewish community had divorced their wives and sent them away with their children (*Ez. 10*). The first major hurdle on the path to a pure community had been cleared.

*Renewal of the Covenant.* Sometime during Ezra's first year, the people of Judah gathered in a large public square before the Water Gate in Jerusalem (see map) to hear him read from "the Book of the Law of Moses" that he had brought with him from Babylon. What a dramatic occasion this must have been! Ezra stood on a high wooden platform specially constructed for the occasion. As he opened the sacred book, the entire throng rose to its feet in reverence. Ezra then led a prayer of praise to Yahweh, and the people bowed their heads and lifted up their hands as they said, "Amen, Amen." Finally, Ezra began to read. From early in the morning until midday he read. And as he read, the Levites who were assisting him "gave the sense so that the people understood the reading" (*Neh. 8:8*).

It had been a long time since the people of God had given serious thought to the

339

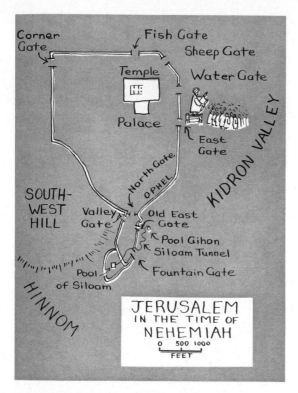

**Jerusalem in the time of Nehemiah.**

Law. Now, as they were reminded of God's mighty acts and the covenant of Sinai, and as they compared their lives with the life prescribed by the Law, they could not hold back the mingled tears of joy and guilt that welled up from their hearts. Nehemiah and Ezra and the Levites urged them to stop weeping and to think of the day as a time for rejoicing. Eventually, joy won out over sadness and the people disbanded to eat and to talk excitedly about what they had heard that morning (*Neh. 8:9–12*).

For seven days Ezra continued to read from the Book of the Law while the people kept the feast of tabernacles, in memory of the wilderness wanderings (*Neh. 8:13–18*). It was fitting they were observing this particular feast; for, after years of aimless existence, they, too, were about to emerge from a wilderness. Later that month, the people of Israel assembled to make a new covenant

with Yahweh. Following the pattern of the great covenant ceremonies of the past, Ezra recited the marvelous things Yahweh had done for his elect people. Then, in grateful response, Israel entered into a solemn agreement "to walk in God's law which was given by Moses the servant of God, and to observe and do all the commandments of Yahweh our Lord and his ordinances and statutes" (*Neh. 10:29*).

## The Hymnbook of the Second Temple

A major part of Ezra's work was to bring the worship of the second temple into strict accord with the rules of the Law. But there was more to this worship than legalism. We can get something of the rich flavor of this worship by reading the book of *Psalms*, for it was the hymnbook of the second temple. Many of the psalms, of course, were written long before the exile, but it was not until after the exile that the collection was completed and arranged in its present form. The Hebrew title of the book of *Psalms* is *sepher tehillim*, meaning "book of praises." The psalms deal with just about every facet of Israel's faith and life, but the praise of Yahweh is easily the dominant theme of the collection.

The backbone of the Psalter is a collection of psalms that bear the name of David: *Psalms 2–41* (except *31*), *51–72*, *108–110*, and *138–45*. This does not necessarily mean that David wrote all these psalms, since a psalm "of" David might mean it was written for him or dedicated to him. Still, David's importance in the development of Israel's musical heritage can scarcely be overestimated. David was Israel's musician *par excellence*. When he first came to the court of Saul as a boy, he served the troubled king by playing the lyre for him during his fits of madness (*I Sam. 16:23*). At the end of his life, when he turned his attention to the organization of Israel's worship, he appointed several Levitical families to lead in the instrumental and choral music of the temple service (*I Chron. 25*). Although we cannot be sure just how many of our psalms David actually wrote, his acknowledged musical ability and his rich and varied experiences as shepherd, warrior, king, parent, lover, and sinner certainly equipped him for the role Judaism and Christianity have traditionally accorded him, and we may be confident that many of these matchless pieces of devotional poetry came from the heart and pen of this great leader.

In addition to the psalms of David, there are two collections of Levitical psalms. *Psalms 12–49* are ascribed to the "sons of Korah" and *Psalms 73–83*, as well as *Psalm 50*, are attributed to Asaph, one of the leading musicians in the time of David and Solomon (*I Chron. 6:39; II Chron. 5:12; 29:30*, etc.). Some of the psalms are purely anonymous (e.g. *33, 84–89*). Others have a strong liturgical character, indicating the probability they reached their final form through a process of continued use in the worship service and cannot easily be assigned to any one author (e.g., *91–100*). Some of these liturgical psalms were thought to be particularly fitting for one or another of the special days of the religious calendar. Some were used primarily on the Sabbath while others were reserved for the Passover, the Feast of Tabernacles, or other Jewish holy days.

The *Psalms* are divided into five books: *1–41*, which witness particularly to David's life and faith; *42–72*, a group of historical psalms recalling Yahweh's treatment of Israel in the past; *73–89*, ritual psalms; *90–106*, reflecting pre-captivity sentiment and history; and *107–150*, which deal primarily with the captivity and the return from Jerusalem. There are psalms of affliction, lamentation, and penitence, as well as hymns of thanksgiving and trust. But whatever their origin or special purpose, the sublime poems of this sacred hymnbook transport us to the first and second temples and the days when Yahweh was "enthroned on the praises of Israel" (*Ps. 22:3*).

## The Age of Wisdom

Perhaps the chief characteristic of the post-exilic age was strict obedience to the Law of Yahweh. Through long experience, the Israelites had learned there could be no real happiness apart from a right relationship with God. But they did not feel that obedience, even of the strictest sort, automatically produced the good life in all its fullness. Obedience was a kind of ground rule. The truly happy life could be achieved only by the application of *wisdom* to the various practical matters that make up a man's life.

Wisdom was thought of as the ability to squeeze every drop of goodness out of life. It was gained by applying the principles of the Law to concrete situations, by reflecting on one's own experience, and by following the counsel of those recognized to be sages, or "wise men." The study of wisdom enjoyed great popularity in the post-exilic period, but it was by no means a new phenomenon. For many centuries, wisdom literature had flourished in the Ancient Near East, especially in Egypt and Mesopotamia. In Israel itself, Solomon was regarded as the founder of the wisdom movement. When Yahweh asked Solomon what special gift he desired, the great king asked not for wealth or a long life, but for "a wise and understanding heart" (*I Kings 3:5–13*).

Shortly after the gift was granted, two prostitutes came to Solomon. Both had borne children at about the same time. When one of the infants died during the night, both women claimed the remaining child. Solomon shrewdly suggested the child be cut in half and divided between the women. Naturally, the real mother could not bear to see her child slain and agreed to let the other woman keep him. Solomon immediately perceived which woman was behaving like a mother and ordered the child given to her. "And all Israel heard of the judgment which the king had rendered; and they stood in awe of the king, because they perceived that the wisdom of God was in him, to render justice" (*I Kings 3:28*).

In summing up the wisdom of Solomon, the writer of *Kings* tells us that

> God gave Solomon wisdom and understanding beyond measure, and largeness of mind like the sand on the seashore, so that Solomon's wisdom surpassed the wisdom of all the people of the east, and all the wisdom of Egypt. For he was wiser than all other men, wiser than Ethan the Ezranite, and Heman, Calcol, and Darda, the sons of Mahol; and his fame was in all the nations round about. He also uttered three thousand proverbs; and his songs were a thousand and five. He spoke of trees, from the cedar that is in Lebanon to the hyssop that grows out of the wall; he spoke also of beasts, and of birds, and of reptiles, and of fish. And men came from all peoples to hear the wisdom of Solomon, and from all the kings of the earth, who had heard of his wisdom.    —*I Kings 4:29-34*

This statement, though pertaining particularly to Solomon, reflects much about the wisdom movement in general. First, as we have already noted, it was an international movement. Men of all nations sought the good and happy life. In Israel, wisdom was interpreted in the light of the Law of Moses, but most of its counsel consisted of commonsense advice equally applicable in any nation. Secondly, there were definite leaders of the movement, men recognized for their own native wisdom and their knowledge of the wealth of wisdom literature that circulated in the Ancient Near East. Finally, this passage reflects the fact that most wisdom material was drawn from observations of nature and everyday life. This is perhaps the most distinctive feature of wisdom literature. Elsewhere in the Old Testament, the primary concern is with what is happening in the arena of history. Wisdom literature, in contrast, shows little interest in history. Its concern is not the welfare of the nation, but the happiness of the individual. Its counsels endure independently of the wider historical context.

Wisdom literature was of two general types. The first type consists of "proverbs" —short, epigrammatic sayings expressing a simple truth in a catchy, easily remembered form. As Solomon spoke of everything from "the cedar that is in Lebanon to the hyssop that grows out of the wall," so the topics dealt with by the ancient sages covered a wide range, from the benefits of faith in God to the disadvantages of a nagging wife. For the most part, the proverbs express the viewpoint that good will be rewarded and evil will be punished in a reasonably just manner. In the second type, the sage muses about the meaning of life, usually in a somewhat skeptical manner. In the Bible, the first type of materials is represented by *Proverbs,* the second by *Ecclesiastes* and the book of *Job*

### THE BOOK OF PROVERBS

The book of *Proverbs* was not compiled simply as a means of preserving some interesting wise sayings of Solomon and other wise men. It was designed to serve as a manual of instruction for young men. The reader is addressed as "son" (*Proverbs 1:8, 10,* etc.) and is urged to order his life according to the counsels of wisdom and the fear of the Lord. The sage advises his young pupil to keep the Law and to behave in a sensible, prudent manner. As suggested above, this class of wisdom lore was based on the assumption that good and evil were properly rewarded in this life. If a man were righteous, he would prosper. If he were evil, he would suffer—in this life. It was a simple, somewhat naive view. As the authors of *Ecclesiastes* and *Job* were to point out, it was too simple, too naive. But it was the orthodox position. Despite its shortcomings, it is full of keen observations about human nature, and an abundance of advice that is still useful in the quest for the good life.

Our book of *Proverbs* is not the only such collection of Hebrew wisdom. In the *Apocrypha,* the additional group of books found in Catholic Bibles and in some Protestant Bibles, two other such collections may be found: *Ecclesiasticus* and the *Wisdom of Solomon.* If the reader is particularly interested in this type material, he will do well to consult these books, but the average Bible student will probably find our canonical collection large enough to satisfy his thirst for wise sayings.

*Literary types.* The proverbs in our collection come in a wide variety of size and content. The most common is the simple "balanced" proverb, which forms a complete unit in itself and is independent of its neighbors. Like most Hebrew poetry, it is characterized by parallelism, in which the second half of a poetic unit may repeat the thought of the first half in different words (*synonymous parallelism*), or complete that thought with additional poetic imagery (*"climbing" parallelism*), or express a thought that is opposite to the thought of the first half (*parallelism of opposites*). By one of these three methods, the two halves are made to "balance." A glance at the *Psalms* or the poetic sections of the prophetic books will reveal that most Hebrew poetry falls into one of these three general categories. All three types are represented in *Proverbs*. Synonymous parallelism is seen in these familiar lines:

> A foolish son is a grief to his father
> and bitterness to her who bore him.
> —*Proverbs 17:25*

> A good name is to be chosen rather than
> great riches,
> and favor is better than silver or gold.
> —*Proverbs 22:1*

The following example represents the "climbing" type of parallelism:

> He who finds a wife finds a good thing,
> and obtains favor from the Lord.
> —*Proverbs 18:22*

Examples of the parallelism of opposites are even more common:

> The house of the wicked will be destroyed,
> but the tent of the upright will flourish.
> —*Proverbs 14:11*

> A soft answer turns away wrath,
> but a harsh word stirs up anger.
> —*Proverbs 15:1*

> A cheerful heart is a good medicine,
> but a downcast spirit dries up the bones.
> —*Proverbs 17:22*

In addition to the normal parallelism, there are numerous examples of striking similes, as in the following:

> Like a dog that returns to his vomit
> is a fool that repeats his folly.
> —*Proverbs 26:11*

> He who meddles in a quarrel not his own
> is like one who takes a passing dog
> by the ears.       —*Proverbs 26:17*

Another form the proverb frequently takes is the "better . . . than" form:

> Better is a dinner of herbs where love is
> than a fatted ox and hatred with it.
> —*Proverbs 15:17*

> Better is a dry morsel with quiet
> than a house full of feasting with strife.
> —*Proverbs 17:1*

Other poetic devices are also used. Several extended passages are constructed on a numerical scheme:

> There are six things which Yahweh hates,
>     seven which are an abomination to him:
> haughty eyes, a lying tongue,
>     and hands that shed innocent blood,
> a heart that devises wicked plans,
>     feet that make haste to run to evil,
> a false witness who breathes out lies,
>     and a man who sows discord among
>         brothers.            —*Proverbs 6:16-19*

> Four things on earth are small,
>     but they are exceedingly wise:
> the ants are a people not strong,
>     yet they provide their food in the summer;
> the badgers are a people not mighty,
>     yet they make their homes in the rocks;
> the locusts have no king,
>     yet all of them march in rank;
> the lizard you can take in your hands,
>     yet it is in kings' palaces.
>                     —*Proverbs 30:24-8*

To round out the stylistic variations, chapter *31*, the famous description of the "worthy woman," is written in acrostic form, each verse beginning with the succeeding letter of the Hebrew alphabet. Naturally, this does not show up in translation.

*Key Themes.* The proverbs include practical advice on a wide range of subjects, but the frequency with which certain themes keep popping up lets us see what the sages thought was most important for their young charges to learn. High on the list of virtues was diligence. Most of the students who studied with the wise men were probably from the middle and upper classes, since their fathers would be the only ones who could afford the cost of such instruction. It would be easy for young men of this status to fall into a life of leisure and fail to cultivate the habit of work. To counteract this temptation, the wise men warned:

> Go to the ant, O sluggard;
>     consider her ways, and be wise.
> Without having any chief,
>     officer or ruler,
> she prepares her food in summer,
>     and gathers her sustenance in harvest.
> How long will you lie there, O sluggard?
>     When will you arise from your sleep?
> A little sleep, a little slumber,
>     a little folding of the hands to rest,
> and poverty will come upon you like a
>         vagabond,
>     and want like an armed man.
>                     —*Proverbs 6:6-11*

Other temptations to which young men were, and are, especially vulnerable include wine and women. The pitfalls of strong drink are detailed in this passage:

> Be not among winebibbers,
>     or among gluttonous eaters of meat;
> for the drunkard and the glutton will come
>         to poverty,
>     and drowsiness will clothe a man with rags.
>
> . . . . . . . . . . . . . . . .
>
> Who has woe? Who has sorrow?
>     Who has strife? Who has complaining?
> Who has wounds without cause?
>     Who has redness of eyes?
> Those who tarry long over wine,
>     those who go to try mixed wine.
> Do not look at wine when it is red,
>     when it sparkles in the cup
>     and goes down smoothly.
> At the last it bites like a serpent,
>     and stings like an adder.
> Your eyes will see strange things,
>     and your mind utter perverse things.
>                     —*Proverbs 23:20-21, 29-33*

Against keeping company with loose women, these words were spoken:

> For the lips of a loose woman drip honey,
>     and her speech is smoother than oil;
> but in the end she is bitter as wormwood,
>     sharp as a two-edged sword.
> Her feet go down to death;
>     her steps follow the path to Sheol;

she does not take heed to the path of life;
   her ways wander, and she does not know it.
And now, O sons, listen to me,
   and do not depart from the words of my
      mouth.
Keep your way far from her,
   and do not go near the door of her house.
                              —*Proverbs 5:3-8*

The sages also gave their students advice about picking a wife. On the negative side, they warned them against choosing a contentious, nagging woman:

It is better to live in a corner of the housetop
   than in a house shared with a contentious
      woman.          —*Proverbs 25:24*

The famous Greek philosopher and sage, Socrates, is reputed to have had a nagging, shrewish wife. If the frequency with which this theme recurs in *Proverbs* is an accurate gauge, it may be that contentious women were an international occupational hazard of being a wise man. But not all the sages were anti-feminists. Even though the original source of *ch. 31* was a woman (*31:1*), the wise men who compiled *Proverbs* evidently endorsed its sentiments:

A good wife who can find?
   She is far more precious than jewels.
The heart of her husband trust in her,
   and he will have no lack of gain.
She does him good, and not harm,
   all the days of her life.

.  .  .  .  .  .  .  .  .  .  .  .  .

She rises while it is yet night
   and provides food for her household
   and tasks for her maidens.

.  .  .  .  .  .  .  .  .  .  .  .  .

She opens her hand to the poor,
   and reaches out her hands to the needy.

.  .  .  .  .  .  .  .  .  .  .  .  .

Strength and dignity are her clothing,
   and she laughs at the time to come.
She opens her mouth with wisdom,
   and the teaching of kindness is on her
      tongue.

She looks well to the ways of her household,
   and does not eat the bread of idleness.
Her children rise up and call her blessed;
   her husband also, and he praises her:
"Many women have done excellently,
   but you surpass them all."
                 —*Proverbs 31:10-12, 15, 20, 25-29*

But the good life consists of more than diligence, or sobriety, or purity, or even the getting of a good wife. The young man who seeks the fullness of life can find it only by following the path of wisdom. Hear what wisdom says to those who would be happy:

Does not wisdom call,
   does not understanding raise her voice?

.  .  .  .  .  .  .  .  .  .  .  .  .

Leave simpleness, and live,
   and walk in the way of insight.

.  .  .  .  .  .  .  .  .  .  .  .  .

Take my instruction instead of silver,
   and knowledge rather than choice gold;
I have counsel and sound wisdom,
   I have insight, I have strength.
By me kings reign,
   and rulers decree what is just.

.  .  .  .  .  .  .  .  .  .  .  .  .

I love those who love me,
   and those who seek me diligently find me.
              —*Proverbs 8:1; 9:6; 8:10, 14-15, 17*

In this classic passage in *Proverbs* 8, Wisdom is so exhalted that it is not only personified but is almost made a member of the Godhead:

Yahweh created me at the beginning of his
      work,
   the first of his acts of old.
Ages ago I was set up,
   at the first, before the beginning of the
      earth.          —*Proverbs 8:22-23*

"Get wisdom," the young men were admonished, "and whatever you get, get insight" (*4:7*). To the wise men of most of the Ancient Near East, the getting of "wisdom" and "insight" was largely a secular affair. And, to be sure, there is much in *Proverbs* that does not depend on a religious interpretation for its meaning. But the wise men of Israel made it clear they were not using "wisdom" and "insight" in a secular way. To them, as to the people of God in every age,

> The fear of Yahweh is the beginning of
>     wisdom,
>   and the knowledge of the Holy One is
>     insight. —*Proverbs 9:10*

### THE SKEPTICAL PREACHER: ECCLESIASTES

As we have already observed, *Proverbs* represented the orthodox aspect of the wisdom movement. According to this view, two ways are open to a man. If he chose the way of righteousness, he could count on a life of prosperity and happiness. If he chose the way of folly and evil, he was sure to reap the appropriate consequences: unhappiness, defeat, shortness of life. But, as has always been the case, there were those who challenged the orthodox view because it did not square with life as they knew it. The book of *Ecclesiastes* is a classic example of such a challenge. As a matter of fact, the views expressed in this book were considered so unorthodox that it was accepted into the Old Testament canon only after much opposition.

The central thought of Ecclesiastes is expressed in the phrase that occurs in slightly different forms throughout the book: "all is vanity and a striving after wind" (*Ecclesiastes 1:14; 2:17; 1:2; etc.*). To the Preacher (*1:1*), the easy arithmetic of traditional wisdom, in which good and evil reap exact balances of blessings and curses, was totally unacceptable. There is nothing that can assure a man a happy life. All the traditionally good things in life—laughter, wine, women, possessions, power, even wisdom itself—cannot guarantee contentment. The preacher knew this not because he had learned it from a wise man, but because he had tried all these things personally and knew from

his own experience that they could not deliver what they promised. The study of wisdom would help some, but one should not count on it too heavily. Its benefits were short term, applying only to the brief span of human life. When this was over, the wise man, like the fool and the dog, died, and no one could say what came after death. Notice the pessimism in these verses:

> The wise man has his eyes in his head, but the fool walks in darkness; and yet I perceived that one fate comes to all of them. Then I said to myself, "What befalls the fool will befall me also; why then have I been so very wise?" And I said to myself that this also is vanity . . . For the fate of the sons of men and the fate of beasts is the same; as one dies, so dies the other. They all have the same breath, and man has no advantage over the beasts; for all is vanity. All go to one place; all are from the dust, and all turn to dust again. Who knows whether the spirit of man goes upward and the spirit of the beast goes down to the earth?
> —*Ecclesiastes 2:14-15; 3:19-21*

Since this is the case, the Preacher reasons, the best thing for a man to do is to rest content with a sort of "high-grade muddling through," enjoying the relatively good things of life and being prepared to take the bitter with the sweet.

This is the way the Preacher sets the problem, but the problem itself goes much deeper than a simple fretting about the failures of certain activities to produce the expected dividends. The Preacher's real problem was the same one that troubles so much of modern society: What is the meaning of life? To be sure, there were certain "times" at which all the activities that occupy men between their birth and death are performed, and to this extent there is a measure of order in the world. But *order* is not the same thing as *purpose*. What is the good of an orderly arrangement if one does not know where things are leading, or indeed if they are leading anywhere? In expressing these cynical views, the Preacher is not speculating about whether there is a God, or whether that God is in control of the world and is dealing with it according to his purposes. He clearly accepts both of these ideas. Nevertheless, because he was unable to discover what these purposes were, this conviction made no practical difference in his life. Things still appeared to be absurd. Like some modern "philosophers of the absurd," the Preacher wonders aloud if there is any reason to prefer life to non-existence:

> I thought the dead who are already dead more fortunate than the living who are still alive; but better than both is he who has not yet been, and has not seen the evil deeds that are done under the sun.
>
> —*Ecclesiastes 4:2-3*

Virtually all of this most unusual book consists of this kind of gentle skepticism. Still, in the face of his doubts, the Preacher never surrenders his faith in God and the ultimate righteousness of his ways. He encourages his readers to lead lives of moderation, avoiding the extremes that inevitably lead to disappointment, to trust Yahweh, and to leave the final issue in his hands.

> Fear God, and keep his commandments; for this is the whole duty of man. For God will bring every deed into judgment, with every secret thing, whether good or evil.
>
> —*Ecclesiastes 12:13-14*

### THE IMPATIENT HERETIC: JOB

The second of the Biblical challenges to orthodox wisdom is the book of *Job*. *Job* is widely acclaimed as one of the greatest pieces of literature of all times. But even those who so regard it have frequently misunderstood its true nature. In the mind of the average person, *Job* is a book that deals with the problem of suffering in the context of a story about a man whose chief trait is a monumental patience. Actually, the problem of suffering is only of secondary interest in this remarkable book, and Job himself endured this situation with anything but patience. In fact, he expressed his displeasure with God in such strong terms that his "friends" regarded him as a heretic.

*Job* is unlike any other book in the Bible in that it is consciously a dramatic work. The principle characters are God, Satan, Job, and four of Job's friends. The author and date of composition are unknown and unimportant. The setting is the "Land of Uz," often thought to be a designation for some part of Edom. The non-Palestinian setting helps us to see that Job's problem is not just a problem of Jews, but a fundamental problem of the human condition. Still, we should not be too quick to identify Job with Everyman, since it is clearly presumed that Job was subject to the Law of Yahweh. Perhaps a more appropriate designation would be Everyjew.

Job is pictured as a man who had all that a man could want: seven sons, three daughters, and enormous wealth (*Job 1:1-3*). In addition, he was a pious man, scrupulous in his observance of all feasts and burnt offerings (*1:4-5*). After this introduction, the scene shifts to a heavenly council at which the "Sons of God" present themselves before Yahweh. Also in attendance is a figure called "the Satan"* or "the Adversary." The apparent function of this Adversary is not so much to tempt men to sin as it is to test their faithfulness to see if it is genuine. When Yahweh asked the Satan for his opinion about righteous Job, he asserted that Job's faithfulness was not the genuine article, that it was a form of insurance to induce Yahweh

---

*In most English versions, the text simply says "Satan," but the Hebrew text includes the article, making Satan (or Adversary) the description of a function rather than a proper name.

to continue to bless him. Take his children and possessions away from him, argued the Adversary, and Job's pious front would vanish with them. Yahweh responded to the challenge and gave the Satan permission to test his theory. A few days later, while Job was eating, messengers came to tell him his cattle, his servants, and his children had all perished in a variety of tragedies. On hearing this news Job tore his garment and shaved his head, the customary signs of mourning, and began to worship, expressing his feelings in these words:

> Naked I came from my mother's womb, and naked shall I return; Yahweh gave, and Yahweh has taken away; blessed be the name of Yahweh. —*Job 1:21*

"In all this, Job did not sin or charge God with wrong" (*1:22*). Job had passed the Satan's first test.

The Satan, however, was not convinced. A man can stand almost any loss, if he himself is not physically harmed. If Yahweh would let him hurt Job directly, his basic insincerity would surely show up then. So, with Yahweh's permission, the Satan "afflicted Job with loathsome sores from the sole of his foot to the crown of his head. And he took a potsherd with which to scrape himself, and sat among the ashes" (*2:78*). When Job's wife saw his miserable condition, she found it incredible that he could maintain his faith and candidly advised him to "curse God and die" (*2:9*). Job was not swayed by her words. He said to her, "You speak as one of the foolish women would speak. Shall we receive good at the hand of God, and shall we not receive evil?" (*2:10*).

In these first two chapters, and in the closing chapter, or epilogue, Job appears in his traditional role of patient suffering. But these brief prose sections merely provide the setting for the heart of the book, the poetic material in which the author devel-

ops the theme that is his primary concern: the nature of man's relationship to God.

The bulk of the poetic section is arranged in the form of dialogue between Job and his companions. When word of Job's misery spread, three of his friends—Eliphaz, Bildad, and Zophar—came to offer their condolences and comfort. They were shocked at his miserable condition, but even moreso by his bitter complaining. In his opening words to them, Job cursed the day of his birth:

> Let the day perish wherein I was born,
>   and the night which said,
> "A man-child is conceived."
>
> . . . . . . . . . . . . . .
>
> Why did I not die at birth,
>   come forth from the womb and expire?
>
> . . . . . . . . . . . . . .
>
> I am not at ease, nor am I quiet;
>   I have no rest; but trouble comes.
>                         —*Job 3:3, 11, 26*

The friends, who subscribed to the traditional dogma that a man gets what he deserves, took it upon themselves to lead Job to a more pious understanding of his plight.

Eliphaz, the first to speak, began cautiously by praising Job for his reputation for wisdom and implying gently that he apply some of the counsel he had given to others. Then, still in a tactful manner he asks:

> Think now, who that was innocent ever
>   perished?
> Or where were the upright cut off?
>                         —*Job 4:7*

The cause of Job's plight is obviously some serious blemish on his relationship with God. The remedy is just as obvious:

> As for me, I would seek God,
>   and to God would I commit my cause;
> who does great things and unsearchable,
>   marvelous things without number:
>
> . . . . . . . . . . . . . .
>
> Lo, this we have searched out; it is true.
>   Hear, and know it for your good.
>                         —*Job 5:8-9, 27*

Job had obviously thought of all these things before, and had decided that the orthodox view simply would not stand up in his case. He had every right to complain, because his punishment was out of all proportion to his sins. He rebukes his guests for their failure to support him in his time of affliction (*6:14-23*). If they had evidence that he has deserved such treatment, let them produce it (*6:24*). In the meantime, he would continue to complain (*7:11*). All he wants is for God to leave him alone. His sense of helplessness and perplexity in the face of the Divine Afflictor is expressed in these words:

> What is man, that thou dost make so much
> of him,
>     and that thou dost set thy mind upon him,
> dost visit him every morning,
>     and test him every moment?
> How long wilt thou not look away from me,
>     nor let me alone till I swallow my spittle?
> If I sin, what do I do to thee, thou watcher
> of men?
>     Why has thou made me thy mark?
>     Why have I become a burden to thee?
>         —*Job 7:17-20*

Bildad enters the conversation by describing Job's protests as "a great wind." He chides him for calling God's justice into question (*8:3*) and strongly implies that Job's children got what they deserved. God does not punish the innocent. Job's cynicism reaches a high point here. He would like nothing better than to be treated justly, he asserts, but God does not bind himself by standards of justice. Instead he operates solely on the basis of unlimited power. As a result, naturally, no mortal stands a chance against him.

> If it is a contest of strength, behold him!
>     If it is a matter of justice, who can summon
>     him?
> Though I am innocent, my own mouth would
>     condemn me;

> though I am blameless, he would prove me
> perverse.

. . . . . . . . . . . . . . . . . . .

> For he is not a man, as I am, that I might
>     answer him,
>     that we should come to trial together.
> There is no umpire between us,
>     who might lay his hand upon us both.
>         —*Job 9:19-20, 32-33*

If God would come down from his inaccessible reaches and enter into a courtroom where justice is respected, then Job would be happy to defend himself.

> Let him take his rod away from me,
>     and let not dread of him terrify me.
> Then I would speak without fear of him,
>     for I am not so in myself.   —*Job 9:34-35*

Since God would not do this, Job sees no reason to stop complaining and again picks up the familiar refrain in which he despises his life and asks to be left to die in peace (*ch. 10*).

Zophar tacitly admits that he cannot produce evidence of Job's guilt, but he does not therefore abandon the position of his colleagues. Job is able to silence men by his babbling, but if God would speak, he could trace Job's guilt in bold lines: "Know then," he tells Job, "that God exacts of you less than your guilt deserves" (*11:6*).

Job is irritated by the superior attitude of his friends, and replies sarcastically:

> No doubt you are the people,
>     and wisdom will die with you.
> But I have understanding as well as you;
>     I am not inferior to you.   —*Job 12:2-3*

In other words, he knows the arguments that are used to defend Wisdom's dogmas as well as they do. But he also knows from his own experience, that they do not always hold true. If they will just be honest with themselves and with the facts as they are, they will have to admit that it is impossible to confine God's dealings with men within the neat systems the sages had developed.

By insisting this is the case, they put themselves in the absurd position of lying to defend God (*13:1–12*). The problem is difficult enough without clouding it with deliberate lies.

By this time, Job has abandoned all hope of being dealt with according to his merits. He knows God will prevail in the end. But this is no longer important. All Job wants is a chance to prove his innocence, to vindicate his integrity in the face of his accusers.

> Behold, he will slay me; I have no hope;
> yet I will defend my ways to his face.
>
> .  .  .  .  .  .  .  .  .  .  .  .  .  .  .  .
>
> Behold, I have prepared my case;
> I know that I shall be vindicated.
> —*Job 13:15, 18*

Job, however, has little hope he will be granted his day in court. And so, he asks once again to be left alone. At best, life is a bad bargain—"of few days, and full of trouble" (*14:1*)—and when it is over there is no guarantee of life after death (*14:7–22*)*. Since this is the case, Job pleads, the least God could do would be to "look away from him, and desist, that he may enjoy, like a hireling, his day" (*14:6*).

In the remaining speeches between Job and his three antagonists—for this is what they had become—these same basic ideas are further elaborated. The three defenders of orthodoxy continue to berate Job for his impiety and to insist upon his guilt, and Job continues to contrast their fatuous arguments with reality and to insist that he would be vindicated if given a fair trail. In his final speech in this exchange, Job recalls his former blessed state, and the swiftness with which it was stripped from him (chs. *27, 29, 30*). Then, in a final summary for the defense (ch. *31*), he paints a picture of his

righteousness in terms that would shame his accusers. Their failure to reply is probably intended to suggest they knew in their hearts he was right. From a dramatic standpoint, of course, this serves to heighten the contrast between what Job deserved, according to orthodox standards, and what he got. On this final statement, Job is willing to rest his case.

At this point, a young man named Elihu entered the lists of Job's antagonists. Because of his youth, Elihu had listened respectfully while the older men contended with Job. But Job's self-righteous spirit and the failure of the three to prove him wrong were too much for Elihu. He could no longer contain the emotions and opinions that welled up within him (*32:1–22*). The thrust of Elihu's speeches is that Job is guilty of blasphemy for his assertions of God's injustice (ch. *34*) and that God is punishing him because he recognizes Job does not have a genuine, submissive attitude (ch. *35*). By complaining about his lot, Job was passing judgment on the action of God, a gross offense.

> The Almighty—we cannot find him;
> he is great in power and justice,
> and abundant righteousness he will not
> violate.
> Therefore men fear him;
> he does not regard any who are wise in
> their own conceit.     —*Job 37:23-24*

*The Speeches of Yahweh.* Now that each man has developed his position to his own satisfaction, in an attempt to put God in what he considered to be a proper-sized box, Yahweh decides to speak for himself. Speaking from a whirlwind and addressing himself to Job, Yahweh asks him a long series of questions designed to convince him of his utter impotence:

> Who is that that darkens counsel
> by words without knowledge?

---

*The author of *Ecclesiastes* also doubted there was any meaningful life after death (*Eccl. 3:19-22*).

THE RETURN TO JERUSALEM

Gird up your loins like a man,
   I will question you, and you shall declare
     to me.

Where were you when I laid the foundation
   of the earth?
   Tell me, if you have understanding.
Who determined its measurements—surely
   you know!
   Or who stretched the line upon it?
On what were its bases sunk,
   or who laid its cornerstone,
when the morning stars sang together,
   and all the sons of God shouted for joy?

. . . . . . . . . . . . . . . . . . .

Have you comprehended the expanse of the
   earth?
Declare, if you know all this. —*Job 38:2-7, 18*

And so Yahweh continues. Does Job know the origins of light and darkness? Does he know the location of the storehouses of snow and hail? Did he put the stars in the sky? Does he understand the secrets of the birds and wild beasts? Was it by his wisdom that the hawk soars, or the eagle flies? At the close of this devastating avalanche, Yahweh poses one further question:

Shall a faultfinder contend with the
   Almighty?
He who argues with God, let him answer it.
               —*Job 40:2*

Before, Job had recognized that Yahweh possessed great power but he had conceived of him as a sort of cosmic bully who uses his brute strength to push around defenseless men. Now, as he gets a glimpse of the actual magnitude of God's power, his protestations of innocence and integrity vanish like a vapor and he repents of his pride and self-righteousness in sackcloth and ashes.

Behold, I am of small account; what shall I
   answer thee?
   I lay my hand on my mouth.
I have spoken once, and I will not answer;
   twice, but I will proceed no further.

. . . . . . . . . . . . . . . . . . .

I know that thou canst do all things,
   and that no purpose of thine can be
     thwarted.
"Who is this that hides counsel without
   knowledge?"
Therefore I have uttered what I did not
   understand,
   things too wonderful for me, which I did
     not know.
"Hear, and I will speak; I will question
   you, and you declare to me."
I had heard of thee by the hearing of the ear,
   but now my eye sees thee;
therefore I despise myself,
   and repent in dust and ashes.
        —*Job 40:4-5; 42:2-6*

In the epilogue that follows this confession (*42:7–17*), the author tells us that Job's fortune was restored, that his wife (or wives) bore him an additional ten children, and that he lived to a ripe old age. But it would be a mistake to suppose that the point of the book is that if a man will admit his dependence on God, he will be richly blessed (in a material sense) in this life. As we have seen, this is precisely the viewpoint the author was challenging. It is not the epilogue, but Job's confession that provides the real conclusion to the book. By confessing his own weakness and ignorance and acknowledging God's boundless power and matchless glory, Job was admitting that he, like his accusers, had been arguing from the wrong premise. They were mistaken in maintaining they knew how God ran the world; Job was mistaken in maintaining he knew how God *ought* to run the world if he were truly just. Yahweh's speeches, however, had convinced Job that God could not be measured by human standards. Man's proper relationship to God is not one of trying to figure out what God will do or ought to do. It is one of admitting one's dependence on him, glorifying him, and humbly acknowledging that his ways are past finding out.

# 14

# Between the Testaments

*Internal tensions and external
pressures continue to shape
the character of Judaism*

MANY BIBLE STUDENTS have made the mistake of going directly from the Old Testament to the New Testament, dismissing the centuries between the close of the Old Testament period and the birth of Christ as "the period when there was no prophecy" or giving it some other title that indicates nothing really important went on during these years. Nothing could be farther from the truth. In the years between the work of Ezra and Nehemiah and the advent of Christ, the whole known world underwent fundamental changes that profoundly influenced the character of Judaism and the development of Christianity. Alexander the Great brought East and West together in a vast empire and initiated a program, carried on by his successors, to stamp Greek thought and culture on the whole. The Jews in Palestine and those scattered in foreign lands met this attempt in various ways, some with great enthusiasm, others with bitter resistance. Both attitudes left their mark upon the religion of Israel. In this period the Macca-

bees, about whom everyone has heard but few really know, waged their brave struggle against the tyrannical kings of the Seleucid empire. In this period arose the Pharisees and Sadducees, the Jewish sects so prominent in the New Testament. In this period Palestine fell under the rule of Rome. And in this period Judaism reached what we may call its normative stage. Indeed, far from being merely an interest of the specialist, it seems fair to say that a working knowledge of the intertestamental period is essential to a full understanding of the New Testament and its message.

### THE WORLD SITUATION FROM EZRA
### TO ALEXANDER THE GREAT

*The End of the Persian Empire.* Artaxerxes I, the Persian ruler who allowed Nehemiah to return to Jerusalem, died in 424 B.C. and was succeeded by his son Darius II (423-404 B.C.). Darius II maintained the *status quo* fairly well, and even improved the Persian position in Asia-Minor. He was succeeded by his son Artaxerxes II (404-358), who had a somewhat rougher time of it. Early in his reign, Egypt threw off the Persian yoke, but the most troublesome source of difficulty was Artaxerxes' own brother Cyrus (not to be confused with Cyrus the Persian).

Cyrus was crafty, treacherous, and ambitious—a dangerous combination. On the very day Artaxerxes II took the throne, Cyrus tried to kill him. Most men would have ordered him executed, but Artaxerxes forgave him and made him satrap of Asia-Minor. Remote from the eyes of the king, Cyrus gathered an army that consisted mainly of Greek professional soldiers and began the march toward Babylon. The two brothers met at Cunaxa, near Babylon, in 401 B.C. Cyrus was killed and the rebellion was over.* Artaxerxes reestablished control over Asia-Minor and Greece without undue difficulty, but his troubles in the West were far from over. The examples of Cyrus and Egypt inspired other satraps to try their hand at revolt. Before long, most of the Western rulers had formed a coalition to break free of Persian rule. Just when it appeared the attempt might succeed, Egypt had to withdraw because of internal problems and the revolt collapsed. Artaxerxes II moved swiftly and once again brought the rebels into line, but it was becoming increasingly clear that Persia's grip on the world was slipping.

When Artaxerxes II died, his son Artaxerxes III (358-338) took the throne, after first killing all his brothers and sisters in order to avoid any unpleasant family quarrels over who should be the rightful heir. Obviously, a man of this character was not to be toyed with. He ruthlessly crushed all rebellion and even managed to reconquer Egypt. To the casual observer, it must have looked as if the Persian Empire might roll on forever. But, as is frequently the case with power based on naked force, the rule established by Artaxerxes III was too brittle to

endure. In 338, his son Arses poisoned him and seized the throne. Arses held power for only two years (338-336) before he and his whole family were murdered. The next king called himself Darius III (336-331). It was during his rule that the Persian Empire came to an end.

For some time now, Philip, the king of Macedon (359-336), had been quietly extending his holdings. By 338, he controlled all of neighboring Greece. In 336, the same year Darius III came to the throne, Philip was murdered. But the Macedonian kingdom did not disintegrate, for Philip had groomed his son to take his place. The young man's name was Alexander. History knows him as Alexander the Great. We shall follow Alexander's brilliant career of world conquest shortly, but first let us notice what had been happening to the Jews during this period.

## Judaism in the Century after Ezra

Concrete information about the fortunes of the Jews in the late fifth and fourth centuries is almost non-existent, but it is possible to make some general statements about this period. For one thing, we may be sure that relations between Jews and Samaritans grew steadily worse. The anti-Samaritan sentiment that arose while the wall was being rebuilt was hardened into dogma by Ezra's prohibition of mixed marriages. Even though the Samaritans worshiped Yahweh, the Jews denied the acceptability of their religion and refused to allow them to worship in the temple in Jerusalem. It was probably at sometime during the fourth century that the Samaritans finally gave up trying to prove their orthodoxy and built their own temple on top of Mt. Gerizim, thus providing a permanent symbol of the schism.*

The Jews had taken Ezra's warnings

---

*The Greek historian Xenophon, who accompanied Cyrus on this march, gives a fascinating account of this battle in Book IV of his *Anabasis*. The title means "the going-up" and refers to Cyrus' march from Asia-Minor to Babylon.

*John 4:20 refers to this temple.

**Greek amphora found at Samaria.
As early as 500 B.C. Palestine
had begun importing Greek articles.**

against contact with foreigners seriously, but the impact of non-Hebraic culture continued as always to leave its mark. Aramaic, the official language of the Persian Empire, gradually replaced Hebrew as the everyday language of Judaism. Travelers from other parts of the empire injected their thought and culture into the stream of Jewish life. This created quite a tension in Judaism. On the one hand, there were those who stedfastly resisted everything that was non-Jewish. These drew upon the words of Ezra to support their position. But there were some who viewed the contact with other cultures in a positive light. Not only could the Jews enrich their national culture, they could share the blessings of their religion with other men. After all, had not the Captivity Oracles (*Isa. 40–66*) spoken of the days when men of all nations would flock to Jerusalem to worship Yahweh? Perhaps those days were now approaching. Would it

not be a mistake to hinder the process? These opposing views are represented by two Old Testament books that were probably composed at about the same time, *Esther* and *Jonah*.

### ESTHER

The book of Esther has long been a favorite with Jews and is still read aloud when the feast of Purim is celebrated. Esther was a beautiful Jewish girl who was reared by her older cousin Mordecai, an officer in the household of Ahasuerus—another name for the Persian ruler Xerxes. According to the story, Xerxes became angry with his queen, Vashti, and held a contest to find someone to take her place. Unaware of her race and parentage, Xerxes chose Esther to be his queen. Later, because of Mordecai's refusal to pay homage to Haman, a high official in the Persian government, Haman influenced Xerxes to issue a decree calling for the extermination of the Jews. Mordecai persuaded Esther to intervene, at the risk of her life, on the Jews' behalf. Esther found favor with the king and revealed Haman's plot. As a result, Haman was hanged on gallows he had built for Mordecai and Mordecai was given a place of high honor. Then, to counteract the decree of execution, the Jews were permitted to kill their persecutors.

In celebration of their deliverance, the Jews instituted the feast of Purim. The word *purim* means "lots" and refers to the lots Haman cast to determine the day the Jews were to be massacred. The story is repeated today primarily to remind Jews how the festival of Purim began, but it had far deeper significance in the fourth century B.C. Then, it reminded Jews of the pressures to conform to alien culture and of the dangers inherent in resisting this pressure. But it also asserted that true Jews had no choice in the matter and promised Yahweh would uphold those who stood firm—and separate.

### JONAH

The viewpoint of the book of *Jonah* is just the reverse of the narrow nationalism of *Esther*. The setting of the story of Jonah is sometime in the past, before the destruction of Nineveh. The author did not bother to provide a more specific date, because this had no real bearing on what he was trying to say. He was not writing simply to record an interesting bit of history in the life of one of God's prophets; he was writing to convince men that God is concerned for the welfare of all men, not just the Jews.

The story itself is one of the most familiar in the Old Testament. Jonah, a prophet of God, is called to deliver a message of repentance to Nineveh, the capital city of Assyria. For some reason, presumably because Assyria was Israel's chief enemy, Jonah tried to avoid his duty and boarded a large sailing vessel bound for Tarshish. In the midst of a great storm, Jonah was thrown overboard and swallowed by a large fish. After three days inside the fish, Jonah was cast up on the shore. He decided that if the Lord would go to that much trouble just to make his point, perhaps he ought to go to Nineveh after all. So, he went and preached and moved the city to repentance. Most preachers would have been gratified by the response, but Jonah was angered. He did not like Assyrians and he did not want them to share in the grace of God. In a sullen display of nationalistic self-righteousness, Jonah climbed a hill outside the city and sat down to pout over the rather sloppy way God was running things. For awhile, he had a gourd plant to protect him from the sun, and when God sent a worm to attack and kill the plant, Jonah complained that he was "angry enough to die" (*4:9*). Yahweh's response to this childish display contains the point toward which the whole story has been leading:

You pity the plant, for which you did no labor, nor did you make it grow, which came into being in a night, and perished in a night. And should not I pity Nineveh, that great city, in which there are more than a hundred and twenty thousand persons who do not know their right hand from their left?
—*Jonah 4:10-11*

These biting words form a sharp rebuke to the parochial attitude of those Jews who refused to admit that non-Jewish peoples could be recipients of the mercy and grace of Yahweh.

## The Hellenistic Period

"Hellas" is another name for Greece. The words "Hellenism" and "Hellenistic" are used to refer to the thought and culture that originated in Greece and spread over most of the known world after the conquests of Alexander the Great. Hellenism affected every facet of life that it touched—political, social, intellectual, religious. Perhaps no period in the world's long history has made a more lasting impact on the thought and behavior of humanity than the Hellenistic period.

### ALEXANDER THE GREAT

When Alexander of Macedon took the throne from his father Philip in 336 B.C., he was only twenty years old. But he had enjoyed certain advantages that prepared him better than most twenty-year-old youths. Whereas the well-educated youth of today must know something of the thought of Aristotle, Alexander was privileged to have Aristotle as his private tutor. We cannot say just how much influence Aristotle actually had on Alexander, but it would be most surprising if that matchless molder of the Western mind did not leave a profound and lasting impression on his young pupil. At any rate, Alexander developed a passion for "the Greek way" and determined to share it with the world.

Two portraits of Alexander the Great: above, fragment of a marble statue; below, a coin (enlarged) showing a lion skin on the hero's head.

The accounts of Alexander's fantastic concepts are heavily laced with legend, but his successes were real enough. Setting out in 334 B.C. he soon took all of Asia-Minor. This was impressive, but not totally convincing, since the occupation troops stationed in Asia-Minor were not really numerous enough to withstand a full-scale attack. How would Alexander fare against the main Persian army? The answer was not long in coming. The next year at Issus in Upper Syria, Alexander's disciplined troops met the best Darius III had to offer and thoroughly routed them. After this, the rest was easy. From Syria, he moved southward through Palestine, laying claim to that territory and to Egypt, which offered no resistance. With the West thus in hand, he resumed his eastward push. In 331, he crossed Mesopotamia to Arbela, where he crushed what remained of Darius' army. Persia was his. After receiving the homage of the people of Babylon, Susa, and Persepolis, the three major capitals of the Persian Empire, Alexander continued to march toward the East, laying claim to everything in his path. When he reached the Indus River in 327/6, according to a popular legend, he wept beause there were no more worlds left to conquer.

Now that the world belonged to him, Alexander resolved to unite it in the bond of Greek culture. Unhappily, he fell ill and died in 323 B.C., shortly before his thirty-third birthday. But his dream did not die with him. When Alexander died, no one man took charge of the vast empire he had created. Instead, it was divided among his leading generals. The most important of these generals were Selecus and Ptolemy. Selecus gained control of Mesopotamia and Syria, and established his capital at Antioch, in Syria. Ptolemy seized Egypt and established his capital at Alexandria, a new city built in honor of Alexander. Both Ptolemy and Selecus, as well as their successors,

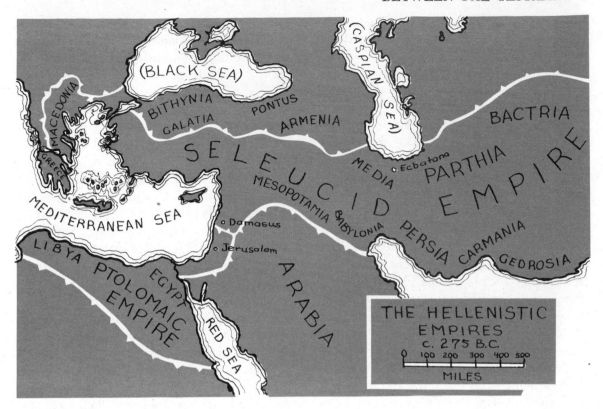

**The Hellenistic Empires.**

shared Alexander's dream of a world united by Greek culture. Antioch and Alexandria became great centers of learning and progress. In Alexandria, the greater of the two cities, the Ptolemies founded scientific research institutes, museums, centers for the arts, and one of the finest libraries the world has ever seen. In some ways, because it was so self-consciously Hellenistic, Alexandria was almost more Greek than Greece itself.

Once again, Palestine was a buffer zone between rival nations. Both the Ptolemies and the Seleucids sought to control her and, eventually, both did. For virtually all of the third century B.C., Palestine was a Ptolemaic province. During this century of Greek-Egyptian domination, thousands of Jews migrated from Palestine to Egypt. Great numbers of them settled in Alexandria; so many, in fact, that Alexandria soon

became one of the great world centers of Judaism and a large section of the city was recognized to be the Jewish quarter.

Greek was the official language in Ptolemaic Egypt. Soon, just as the Jews in Palestine had adopted Aramaic as their everyday language, so the Jews living in Egypt began to speak Greek. Before long, a large portion of Egyptian Jews were unable to read the Hebrew Scriptures. To meet this crisis, a translation of the Scriptures into Greek was made. This translation is called the *Septuagint,* from the Latin word for "seventy."* It

---

*In commentaries and other Bible study aids it is frequently designated by the abbreviation LXX, the Roman numeral for seventy. According to a popular —and largely fictional—story describing the work was done by about seventy scholars; hence, this unusual title. See "The Letter of Aristeas" in R. H. Charles, *The Apocrypha and Pseudepigrapha of the Old Testament,* Vol. II (Oxford: Clarendon Press, 1913).

would be difficult to overestimate the importance of the Septuagint. Not only did it enable Greek-speaking Jews to remain faithful to the Law; it gave them a valuable instrument for communicating their faith to the Gentile world.

The confrontation with Greek culture was not a severe problem during the reign of the Ptolemies. There were Jews who picked up Greek dress and manners rather easily and there were Jews who stoutly resisted any accommodation to the new patterns of life and thought, on the grounds that it would corrupt the purity of Judaism. The strictest of the holdouts were known as *Hasidim,* or "the pious ones." The sect of the Pharisees, the strict legalists whom Jesus attacked so vigorously, developed out of the Hasidim.

Despite their thorough-going Hellenism, the Ptolemies showed little interest in pressing their culture on the Jews. In fact, it appears they allowed them to run their affairs pretty much as they pleased, as long as they paid their taxes and stayed out of trouble. All this changed when the Seleucids gained control of Palestine.

## Persecution and Resistance

When Antiochus III, usually called Antiochus the Great, came to the Seleucid throne in 223 B.C. he inherited an empire that had dwindled to a shadow of its former self. After a quarter-century of vigorous campaigning, however, Antiochus not only regained the original holdings, but pushed the Ptolemies back into Egypt. In the process, Palestine became a Seleucid territory. As long as Antiochus lived, it appeared the Jews had gained by the shift of power. He went out of his way to win their support and confidence. He freed prisoners of war, temporarily cancelled taxes to hasten economic recovery, and financed the operation of the temple out of the royal treasury.

Unfortunately, this happy situation was short-lived. Antiochus failed to appreciate his limitations and hurled a challenge at the rising western power, Rome. Rome had gained a dominant position in the West by defeating Carthage (led by Hannibal) in 202 B.C. Antiochus correctly saw this as a threat to his own position and moved into Greece to discourage Rome from pushing further eastward. He never made a more serious mistake. With comparative ease, the Roman troops threw the Seleucid army back into Asia. Then, having seen that Antiochus could offer no real resistance, they marched in and crushed him on his home grounds. In 190 B.C., after a decisive victory at Magnesia, the Romans stripped Antiochus of most of his defenses and placed him under a crippling tribute. The heyday of the Seleucid empire was over almost before it had begun.

The financial burden Rome placed on the Seleucid kingdom was really more than it could bear, but Rome was inflexible and demanded it be paid. The effects of this harsh policy were felt throughout the kingdom, as the attitude of its rulers changed from one of benevolence to one of ruthless grasping. Nowhere was the change more disrupting than in Judah.

After Antiochus the Great was slain in 187 B.C. while plundering a temple in Elam to raise the tribute money—an act that would have repulsed him under different circumstances—his son Seleucus IV came to the throne. He reigned twelve years (187–175) before he was assassinated and succeeded by his brother, Antiochus IV (175–163), better known as Antiochus Epiphanes. The latter title was given him because he claimed to be the human *epiphany,* or manifestation, of Zeus, the high God of the Greeks. As might be expected of a man who claimed to be a Greek god, Antiochus Epiphanes had rather strong opinions about the worth of Greek culture and about his

A silver tetradrachma with a portrait
of Antiochus IV on one side and
Zeus on the other. Inscription: Antiochus,
the manifest god, bearer of victory.

royal authority. With regard to the first, he
was determined to press the Greek way on
all his subjects, partly because he believed
it was a superior way of life and partly because it would serve to unify his kingdom in
the face of the Roman threat. With regard
to the second, he demanded absolute submission to his will, not simply as a test of political loyalty, but as a sign of allegiance to
Zeus. For most of his subjects, homage to
Zeus would be no problem. It was a fairly
simple matter for them to add a new god to
the roster of those they were already worshiping. But for the Jews, there could be no
god beside Yahweh. To submit to the religious demands of Antiochus would be an
act of apostasy of the gravest sort. Given
this situation, conflict between Antiochus
Epiphanes and the Jews was inevitable.

Onias was High Priest in Jerusalem when
Antiochus seized the Seleucid throne. He
was a conservative man and had resisted the
influx of Hellenism. Also, he had foiled the
attempts of Seleucus to gain access to the
temple treasures. For these two reasons, he
was not exactly a favorite of the Seleucid
court. Shortly after Antiochus came to
power, Onias' brother Jason, a confirmed
Hellenizer, offered him a large sum of
money to oust Onias and appoint him High
Priest in his place. To sweeten the deal, he
promised to throw the full weight of the
High Priestly office behind Antiochus' programs of Hellenization. Antiochus gladly
sealed the bargain, and Jason was made
High Priest—the first who had ever bought
the office outright. Jason proved as good as
his word. Within a few months, he set up a
Greek-style gymnasium in Jerusalem and
encouraged young Jews, including priests of
the temple, to participate in its activities.

The reaction of faithful Jews was loud
and bitter. To appreciate their opposition, it
is necessary to remember that participation
in the activities of a Greek gymnasium involved much more than simply going down
to the local sports facility to shoot a few
goals. It involved paying homage to the
Greek gods who were believed to watch
over the gymnasium; in other words, it involved idolatry. The presence of such an establishment in Jerusalem was a gross scan-
dal to pious Jews. The fact that it had been
built by the High Priest himself was an out-
rage almost beyond belief. But this was only
a start. Three years after Jason bought the
high priestly office, another ambitious Jewish Hellenizer, Menelaus, bribed Antiochus
to turn the position over to him. For those
who blessed the day Moses had ordained
Aaron High Priest of Israel, this prostitution
of the sacred post could no longer go unchallenged. Riots broke out and Jason drove
Menelaus from the city. Menelaus felt he
was fully entitled to serve as spiritual leader

of the Jews—after all, he had paid for the privilege—and appealed to Antiochus to help him. Antiochus was furious that the Jews would dare to resist his order concerning Menelaus and hurried to help his new ally. The riots were quelled and Menelaus was given a firm grip on the high priesthood. Then, for good measure and to punish the Jews for resisting the royal policy, Antiochus plundered the temple. With this act of sacrilege, the lines were permanently drawn. Henceforth, Judaism and Antiochus Epiphanes were mortal enemies.

The latter events took place in 169 B.C. For two years, Antiochus left the task of Hellenizing the Jews to Menelaus and his assistants, some of whom were specially appointed for this purpose by the king. Then, apparently not satisfied with their progress, Antiochus once again took direct action. First, to lessen the chances of organized resistance, he launched a surprise attack on Jerusalem, slaughtering a sizable portion of the population and tearing down the walls. He followed this by building a fortress that would allow him to keep a garrison permanently stationed in Jerusalem, thus putting real teeth into orders that might otherwise be difficult to enforce. Then, assured that he could finish what he started, Antiochus began a frontal assault on Judaism itself, for it was the faith of Israel, not the wall of Jerusalem, that was the real obstacle to Antiochus' ambitions.

Antiochus missed no detail in his program to exterminate Judaism. All copies of the Law were to be destroyed. Some, of course, were preserved. Circumcision of children was forbidden. Feast days and Sabbaths were outlawed. Pagan altars were set up and Jews were forced to eat the meat of pigs that had been sacrificed on them. Failure to comply with these orders was punishable by death. Finally, as the capstone of offense, Antiochus Epiphanes set up an altar to Zeus within the holy temple itself and offered a pig as a burnt offering to the Greek deity. There could be no greater sacrilege than this. To pious Jews it was truly what the book of Daniel calls "the abomination of desolation" (*Daniel 11:31; 12:11; cf. 9:27*).

### THE BOOK OF DANIEL

The book of *Daniel* achieved great prominence during this period, because it contained thrilling stories of faithfulness under persecution and because it provided a hope in Yahweh's triumph over evil. *Daniel* is a classic example of what is called *apocalyptic literature,** a bizarre form of religious writing that was immensely popular in late Judaism and early Christianity. The New Testament book of *Revelation* is the only other major apocalyptic work in the Bible—in Catholic Bibles it is called the *Apocalypse*—but *Isaiah 24–27, Zechariah 12–14,* as well as several shorter passages, are composed in the same style. The identifying marks of apocalyptic literature are its imaginative, sometimes grotesque visions and symbols. As diverse and complex as these visions and symbols are, they all proclaim a similar message: despite the apparent dominance of the forces of evil, God is in absolute control of the historical process and is directing it toward its glorious consummation, at which time evil will be overthrown and the kingdom of God will be established among men. The Jews desperately needed something to rekindle the fires of devotion to the Law of the Lord and to bolster their courage in the face of severe tribulation. The book of *Daniel* met this need and provided them with a faith that carried them through the crisis.

Daniel was one of the great heroes of Judaism. Ezekiel ranked him alongside Noah and Job as an example of righteousness and wisdom (*Ezek. 14:14, 20; 28:3*). The stories

---

*(See p. 327)

told of him and his brave companions in *Daniel 1–6* were just the sort calculated to reassure those who were suffering under Antiochus that Yahweh would uphold and deliver those who refused to surrender their faith and their hope. Those who were tempted to succumb to Antiochus' demand that they eat the flesh of pigs would be strengthened by the story of the young men who refused to defile themselves with the rich food and wine that came from the table of the king of Babylon (*1:5–16*). As Shadrach, Meshach, and Abednego had chosen the fiery furnace rather than bow down to the golden image Nebuchadnezzar had set up for all his subjects to worship, so faithful Jews should be willing to face death rather than bow before the altar of Zeus Antiochus had erected in the temple (*ch. 3*). If any feared he would lose his life unless he renounced the Law of Moses, as Antiochus commanded, let him remember the deliverance of Daniel after Darius cast him into a denful of hungry lions for refusing to abandon his practice of daily prayer to Yahweh (*ch. 6*).

Pious Jews like the Hasidim drew great strength from these stories of God's faithfulness to those who did not succumb to the temptations of alien culture, even at peril of their own lives. But even more important to their morale were the dreams and vision found in *Daniel*. Their strange symbolism conveyed to the troubled Jews the conviction that the present order would soon be overthrown and replaced by Yahweh's eternal kingdom of righteousness and peace.

*Nebuchadnezzar's Dream.* The first of these symbolic passages is the account of Daniel's interpretation of Nebuchadnezzar's dream (*ch. 2*). Interpreting another person's dream is a tricky enough business under the best of circumstances, but Nebuchadnezzar presented his official wise men with a harder task than usual by demanding

an interpretation of a dream he could not even remember. Naturally, they were completely baffled. When Daniel learned what was going on, he offered to interpret the king's dream. Giving all the credit to Yahweh, Daniel reminded Nebuchadnezzar that he had dreamed of a large human-like image, with a head of fine gold, breast and arms of silver, belly and thighs of bronze, legs of iron, and feet of clay mixed with iron. As the image stood, a stone "cut out by no human hand . . . smote the image on its feet of iron and clay, and broke them in pieces." The pieces were carried away by the wind like chaff, "but the stone that struck the image became a great mountain and filled the whole earth" (*2:24–35*).

In Daniel's interpretation of the dream, each of the portions of the image represented a great world power. In the second century B.C., it was easy to recognize each kingdom. The head of gold represented the Babylonian empire, the chest and arms of silver symbolized the Median kingdom, the abdomen of brass was Persia, the legs of iron stood for the kingdom of Alexander, and the feet of iron and clay represented the reign of the Seleucids. The stone that brought this image down, of course, was the Kingdom of God which would never be destroyed (*2:36–45*).

In the last half of the book (chs. *7–12*), there occur several other visions in which the proud kingdoms of this world are brought low as the eternal purposes of the Lord of History move inexorably toward their conclusion. In the first of these visions (ch. 7), Daniel sees four beasts again representing the Babylonian, Median, Persian, and Greek empires. The ten horns of the fourth beast represent the Seleucid kings, and the little horn that sprouts among them is Antiochus Epiphanes. Daniel foresees that this beast will be slain and that "one like a son of man will take his place."

And to him [will be] given dominion
   and glory and kingdom
that all peoples, nations, and languages
   should serve him;
his dominion is an everlasting dominion
   which shall not pass away,
and his kingdom one
   that shall not be destroyed.
                    —*Daniel 7:14-15*

For any who may have missed the symbolism of the first vision, the record of the second vision (ch. 8) is accompanied by an explanation by no less a personage than the angel Gabriel (8:15–26). In this vision, the ram and the he-goat (8:1–8) stand for the Medo-Persian and Greek empires. The four horns (8:8) are the four divisions of Alexander's empire. The little horn that arises out of the four is unmistakably Antiochus Epiphanes. He is described as magnifying himself "even up to the Prince of the host," of overthrowing the sanctuary of the host (the temple), and of setting up "the abomination that makes desolate."

The third vision revolves around the interpretation of Jeremiah's prophecy that the desolation of Jerusalem would last seventy years (*Jer. 25:11; 29:10*). Actually, Jeremiah had said that Israel would remain in Babylonian captivity for seventy years, which was approximately, though not exactly, correct. But Daniel apparently felt the prophecy had not been fulfilled and was puzzled about it. In the interpretation offered by the angel Gabriel (9:20ff), the seventy years stand for seventy weeks of years, or 490 years. The day was not far off when 490 years would have passed since the fall of Jerusalem. At that time, Gabriel assures Daniel, "the decreed end [will be] poured out on the desolator" (9:27). The chief significance of this vision is the assurance that all of history is finally in the hands of Yahweh and is proceeding on schedule.

The final vision (chs. 11–12) contains a symbolic account of the history of the kingdoms of the South and North—the Ptolemaic and Seleucid kingdoms. The key aspects of Antiochus Epiphanes' actions against the Jews are described in 11:20ff. He is clearly the "contemptible person" (v. 21) who invades the land, sweeps away "the prince of the covenant," or high priest (v. 22), desecrates the temple (v. 31) and magnifies himself "above every god" (v. 36). This account of Antiochus' career not only describes the exact sequence of events in his profanation of the temple, but even notes that it followed a campaign against the kingdom of the South that was frustrated by a threat from "the ships of Kittim" (v. 30). Antiochus' climactic action against Jerusalem actually did follow a campaign against Ptolemaic Egypt in which the threat of Roman intervention (the ships of Kittim) forced him to withdraw.

As in the previous visions—and indeed, in all apocalyptic visions—the faithful are to be delivered. But here, something new is introduced. Some would die in their defense of the faith, but they could look forward to the time when "those who sleep in the dust of the earth shall awake, some to everlasting life, and some to shame and everlasting contempt" (12:2). This passage is the first clear reference to the resurrection in the Bible. By New Testament times, the concept was a prominent feature of Judaism, though not everyone believed in it.

In the description of Antiochus' violation of the temple, it is stated that "the people who know their God shall stand firm and take action" (12:32). Thus far, we have talked mostly about the villains of this piece. Now let us turn to the heroes, to those who stood firm and took action.

### THE REVOLT OF THE MACCABEES

The outrageous demands of Antiochus Epiphanes stirred feelings to the point of revolt all over Judah. These feelings broke into the open in Modein, a Judean village in the hill country northwest of Jerusalem. The flare-up occurred when a Seleucid officer came to Modein to force the villagers to offer pagan sacrifices. Mattathias the village priest, refused, and when a less courageous villager stepped forward to comply with the order, the old priest rushed out and slew both the villager and the royal officer. With this act, the revolt began. Now there could be no turning back. Mattathias fled to the hills with his five grown sons: John, Simon, Judas, Eleazar, and Jonathan. There they called "everybody who is zealous for the Law and stands by the covenant" to join them (*I Maccabees 2:27*).* Among those who joined were a number of the Hasidim, the pious Jews who had resisted Hellenism from the first.

The band of rebels that gathered in the hills was neither large nor really well-equipped, but they were brave and courageous men and quickly developed remarkable skill in guerilla warfare. As soon as they were well-organized, they began to strike at Seleucid troops and at groups of Jews who had sided with the persecutors. That these were not just a band of rag-tag ruffians spoiling for a fight is shown by the fact that hundreds of them were killed when they refused to fight on the Sabbath. As a practical necessity, however, Mattathias suspended the Sabbath regulations until the crisis was past (*I Macc. 2:29–41*).

Mattathias died in 166 B.C., a few months after the revolt began, but on his deathbed, he turned the leadership of the rebel forces over to his middle son, Judas. If any were

*The references in this section are not to the Bible proper, but to the books of *I and II Maccabees*, which appear in the Old Testament Apocrypha. These are not included in most Protestant Bibles, but are a valuable source of history for the intertestamental period and should be in the library of serious Bible students. See discussion on pp. 373-5.

surprised Mattathias did not name his oldest son to succeed him, they were quickly convinced his judgment had been correct. Judas was a bold and able leader and soon gained the nickname, "Maccabeus," frequently interpreted to mean "the hammer," symbolizing the swiftness and power of his attacks against the enemy. Judas was such an outstanding figure that the whole revolt is commonly called the Maccabean rebellion.

Judas' military talent and cunning were so marvelous that his exploits filled the Seleucid troops with awe. Hopelessly outmanned, he met and defeated the royal forces in a series of brilliant victories. These served not only to throw the enemy off balance, but to rally hesitant Jews to Judas' side. Because of campaigns elsewhere, Antiochus was not able to send his main army against the Jews, but he did dispatch a large and well-equipped force to Palestine in 165

The Maccabean period in Palestine.

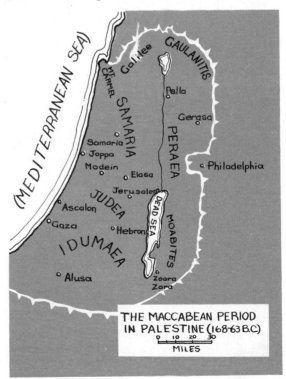

B.C. These troops camped south of Modein at Emmaus and sent a sizable force out at night to kill Judas. While the enemy forces were thus divided, Judas attacked the encampment and crushed the troops who had remained there, then met and defeated the group that had come out to search for him (*I Macc.* 3:42–4:25). The next year, Judas defeated an even larger army, thus opening the way for repossession of Jerusalem. In December, 164,* Judas established Jewish control of the Holy City and began to purify the temple. All the trappings of pagan worship were removed. The defiled altar was torn down and a new one built in its place. The Jews celebrated this occasion with joyous feasting. Modern Jews still commemorate this event December in the Feast of Hanukkah (Dedication).†

Antiochus Epiphanes died in 163 B.C. Philip, who succeeded him, quickly sent a large force against Judas. The strength of superior numbers finally won out and the brave Jews were defeated and scattered. The Seleucids were once more in control of Jerusalem. Alcimus, a disloyal Jew, was made high priest. He correctly saw Judas as a threat to his position and asked Demetrius, who had seized the Seleucid throne from Philip, to help him conquer the Maccabeans. The army that was sent terrorized Judea, but failed to capture Judas. Finally, Alcimus and the Seleucid general, Bacchides, managed to trap Judas between two large sections of their army. Judas beat back one group, but the other proved too much for his outnumbered men. In a last heroic gesture, Judas gathered his finest warriors about him and went down fighting, surrounded by literal heaps of slain enemies. As a striking tribute to his bravery, his body was released

to his supporters and returned to Modein, where he was buried beside his father. After Judas' death, his brothers Jonathan and Simon took their turns at the head of the Jewish community, serving both as political leader and high priest, a combination of offices that was eventually to have far-reaching implications. They widened what had been a rebellion into a fullscale war and not only gained independence but led Judah to a considerable measure of glory. Simon was succeeded by his son John Hyrcanus (135–105 B.C.), who proved to be a true son of the Maccabees. The Syrians (Seleucids) once again overran Palestine, but John finally managed to oust them and regain Jewish independence.

With the death of John Hyrcanus (105 B.C.), the day of the great Maccabeans was over. The decades that followed were scarred by intrigue and bloody infighting as men and women of questionable motives struggled to gain power. The final collapse of the Maccabean house came in 63 B.C. when Pompey led his Roman troops into Jerusalem. Pompey himself entered the Holy of Holies in the temple, an offence for which the Jews never forgave Rome. Not long afterward the hordes of Parthia overran Palestine and put its official political status in some doubt. Rome regained control in 37 B.C., with the aid of an Idumean prince who enjoyed the approval of Mark Antony and Augustus. In this prince, who became king of Judea, we have the bridge to the New Testament period, for he was none other than Herod the Great, the evil ruler who ordered the slaughter of Judean infants in an attempt to kill the baby some were calling the king of the Jews.

## Judaism at the End of the First Century B.C.

In the last historical books of the Old Testament, *Ezra* and *Nehemiah*, Judea was un-

---

*Or perhaps 165. There is a chronological uncertainty of one year on all dates in the Seleucid period.

†Another name for Hanukkah is the "Festival of Lights."

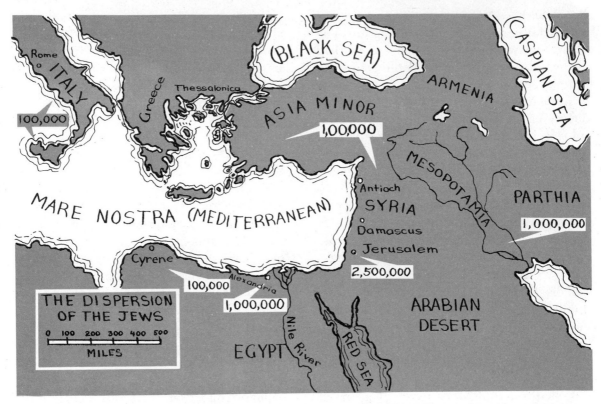

The Dispersion of the Jews in the First Century A.D., showing estimated population of Jewish settlements.

der Persian control. As the New Testament opens, Judea was ruled by one Herod, who had received his authority from Rome. The brief historical sketch presented above has enabled us to see, in a broad-stroke fashion, how this development took place. The faith and practice of Judaism, as reflected in the gospels, is also quite a different thing from what it was in the time of Ezra and Nehemiah. It will be helpful for our understanding of the New Testament if we have some idea as to the changes that occurred during this period and as to the general character of Judaism at the end of the first century B.C.

### THE DISPERSION

As we have already noted, the Jews were widely scattered before the time of Alexander the Great (356–323 B.C.). In the period of Ptolemaic domination of Palestine, thousands of Jews emigrated to Egypt. Philo Judeus, a Jewish philosopher and theologian who lived 20 B.C.–A.D. 40, estimated that in his day there were one million Jews living in Alexandria. The Seleucid persecution also drove many Jews from their homeland to various parts of the world. The map dispersion Greek geographer and historian Strabo is quoted as having said that it was hard to find a place in the habitable earth that "hath not admitted this tribe of men." It is this extensive scattering of Jews all over the known world that is commonly referred to as the *Diaspora,* or Dispersion.

Despite the wide geographical spread, the Jews of the Dispersion were remarkably united with Palestinian Judaism. All Jews who held on to their faith regarded the temple in Jerusalem as the focus of their religious life, and all who were able came to Jerusalem at the time of the great feasts. This unification of Jews, especially when com-

365

bined with strict religious views, posed a major problem for the Roman Empire. The manner in which the problem was worked out was a typical example of the genius for practical solutions that was a characteristic of Roman administration. Rome was always deeply concerned about the loyalty of her subjects and demanded certain external acts of obedience as tokens of this loyalty. Some of these, such as taking oaths in the name of Roman deities, were incompatible with Jewish religious beliefs. It soon became apparent that Rome would either have to punish the Jews for disobedience or grant them special privileges. Because the prospect of having Jews all over the empire organizing rebellions like that of the Maccabeans was an unpleasant one and because the Romans viewed culture different from their own with a more tolerant eye than did Antiochus Epiphanes and his successors, the latter course was chosen.

Jews throughout the empire were freed from the obligation to perform ritual acts that offended their consciences and were given full freedom to practice their own religion. The strict Sabbath laws were also respected, even though they caused some inconvenience to the Romans. According to an empire-wide decree, no Jew could be summoned to justice or pressed into forced labor on the Sabbath. If the day for payment of taxes fell on a Sabbath, an alternate day was arranged for Jews. Jews who served in the Roman army, and there were many, were not forced to march on the Sabbath. Jews of the Dispersion were allowed to send the regular temple tax to Jerusalem, although Roman practice ordinarily forbade the sending of money from one country to another. From a political standpoint, the most important concession the Romans made was to allow the high priest to act as the legitimate head and official representative of all Jews everywhere in the empire. In

Judea itself, great authority in both religious and political matters was invested in a governing body called the Sanhedrin. Under normal circumstances, the only power it lacked was the right to execute a death penalty. It was because of this limitation that Jews had to be taken before Pilate to receive the sentence of crucifixion.

The presence of these peculiar people throughout the empire drew considerable attention. Men grew curious about a people and a religion that was able to demand such special consideration from the powerful Roman government. As they investigated, many were attracted by the teachings of Judaism and by the pure lives of its adherents, and some wanted to live according to its tenets. Eventually, two classes of proselytes developed. The first class included those who submitted fully to the Law, including the dietary laws and circumcision. The second class was comprised of those the Jews called "God-fearers." These accepted the traditions and ethical standards of Judaism, and worshiped according to Jewish law, but did not submit to circumcision or the dietary laws and were unwilling to sever all their ties with the pagan world.

*The Synagogues.* Although the temple in Jerusalem remained the official and symbolic focal point of Judaism, the actual center of the individual Jew's religious life shifted to the institution known as the synagogue, which simply means "gathering-place." It is usually thought that the synagogues first began during the period of Babylonian exile, as a result of the desire of devout Jews to gather together to hear an exposition of the Law. Prayers and preaching were eventually added and the synagogue became the regular place of worship. A standard synagogue service consisted of a recitation of specific verses, reading of portions from the Law and the Prophets, prayers, a sermon, and the benediction. By

New Testament times, a regular hierarchy of synagogue officials had developed. The elders had jurisdiction not only over the affairs directly connected with the synagogue, but acted as a local tribunal with judicial authority over members of the congregation. The Ruler of the Synagogue was probably chosen from the elders; his duty was to appoint those who were to participate in the service and to act as a general overseer. The Ruler and the Learned Men of the Synagogue sat in the "chief seats," facing the congregation. Other functionaries of the synagogue included the "delegate of the congregation," who was chosen at each meeting to conduct the prayers; the interpreter, who translated the Hebrew scriptures into the everyday language of the people; and the "almoners" whose duty it was to collect and distribute alms for the poor.

*The Significance of the Dispersion for Early Christianity.* It would be difficult to overestimate the importance of the Dispersion for the widespread early successes of Christianity. The great literary monument of the Dispersion, the Septuagint, provided an invaluable avenue for interpreting the scriptures to a Greek-speaking world. The large numbers of Jewish proselytes and God-fearers were open to the new ideas that radiated out of Palestine. And, finally, the network of synagogues served as effective bases for launching Christian missions throughout the empire, as our study of the evangelistic efforts of the apostle Paul will make clear.

### PARTY MOVEMENTS WITHIN JUDAISM

In the period between the beginning of the Maccabean wars and the ministry of Jesus, there developed within Judaism several major parties, or sects. They all shared a deep concern about the direction Judaism would take in the future, but they differed over just what that direction should be.

*The Sadducees.* One of the most important of these parties was known as the Sadducees, frequently mentioned in the New Testament, usually in a derogatory manner. It is somewhat difficult to ascertain the true character of the Sadducees since virtually all the information we have of them comes from their opponents. Scholars generally agree that the name "Sadducees" is probably derived from the word Zadokite, which refers to the priests who were descended from Solomon's high priest, Zadok. As the name suggests, the Sadducean party centered around the priesthood. Because of the great temporal powers of the high priest in Maccabean times, landowners and other members of the secular nobility were closely allied with the priestly class. So, the Sadducees drew their support mainly from these levels of the Jewish community.

The primary goal of the Sadducees was the continuation of the temple services under the supervision of the "authorized" clergy. To attain this goal, they were sometimes more willing to collaborate with foreign rulers than stricter Jews thought they should be. On the other hand, they were also regarded, and regarded themselves, as strict and conservative because they insisted on taking only the written Law, or Torah, as their rule of faith. In the post-exilic period a group of religious leaders known as *Soferim,* or scribes, had made some attempt to apply the Law to the practical matters of life. For the most part these were very simple, and some felt a more elaborate method should be devised for adapting the Law to new customs and developments. From this desire came the *Midrash,* a body of material consisting of deductions from the Law in justification of current rules and customs. In addition, there developed the concept of "Oral Law;" that is, the position that not all of the Law had been written, but that some had been handed down orally from the Fathers and was to be considered as authoritative as the written law. Later (c. A.D. 200), this was embodied in a collection called the *Mishnah,* to provide authority for customs that had developed but could find no support in the written law. The Sadducees rejected these traditions outright. In the bargain, they rejected several others ideas that had gained prominence in the post-exilic era, including belief in angels and spirits and in the resurrection of the body. Part of this conservatism was undoubtedly based on genuine religious conviction, but it is highly probable that it was also motivated by the desire of the Sadducees to regulate custom and practice by priestly decree that could be issued and revoked at will. A large body of authoritative material not under supervision of the priests was a definite threat to this prerogative.

*The Pharisees.* Standing over against the Sadducees were the Pharisees. Most scholars agree that the party of the Pharisees was an offspring of the Hasidim, the pious Jews who had so stoutly resisted Hellenism, but the exact course of development is quite uncertain. Even the origin of the name "Pharisee" is an unsolved problem. It is generally agreed that it means "the separated ones," but this is somewhat indefinite, since the Pharisees could properly be spoken of as separating themselves from the king, the Sadducees, various sorts of impurity, and the *'am ha-aretz,* the "people of the land" who made little attempt at strict observance of the Law.

The Pharisees were drawn largely from among the ordinary people, in contrast to the aristocratic Sadducees, and therefore commanded wide influence with the masses. Consequently, they were able to force the Sadducees to follow their bidding on many matters, on pain of losing the support of the people. The Pharisees used their influence in an attempt to bring religion into the common life of the people. As a result of their efforts, the Sabbath and other holy days were endowed with greater sanctity, daily prayers were encouraged and practiced widely, divorces were made more difficult to obtain and the general status of women was greatly improved, the synagogue service was fully developed, and, eventually, the canon of Old Testament scripture was fixed. In contrast to the Sadducees they espoused and furthered the doctrines of angels and spirits and of the resurrection of the body.

The Pharisees eventually came to stress religious observance for its educational worth, believing it had great benefit in impressing upon the mind the truth behind the observance. Doubtless, this often resulted in genuine and profound piety. On the other hand, it also produced a legalistic spirit that could justifiably be charged with formalism and hypocrisy. It was against this narrow and exclusive element in Pharisaism that Jesus spoke so strongly. Despite the unfavorable picture presented in the New Testament, it should not be forgotten that the Pharisees represented much that was good in Judaism and performed a valuable service in protecting the worship of Yahweh against idolatrous innovations.

*The Zealots.* The Hasidim and their descendants, the Pharisees, had participated in the Maccabean wars, but they were never quite convinced that salvation for the people of God lay in revolution and warfare. Except in times of the most intense revolutionary activity, their interest in these things ran rather cool. They believed man's overriding responsibility was to keep the Law as carefully as possible. If the community gave its attention to this, Yahweh would preserve them and would establish the kingdom in his own good time. But not everyone felt this way. The Zealots, so-called because of their fiery nationalistic zeal, were not content to wait for God. They, like the Maccabeans,

Cave IV at Qumran where an Essene community stored part of its library.

saw the future of Judaism in terms of an independent Jewish state and jumped at the slightest opportunity to revolt against their overlords, whether Seleucid or Roman, fully trusting that Yahweh would come to their aid. Unfortunately, their zeal outdistanced their realism and eventually gave rise to rebellions (in A.D. 66–70 and A.D. 132–135) that led to the destruction of Jerusalem, and the dissolution of the Jewish state.

*The Essenes.* The remaining party of importance was the sect of the Essenes. For centuries, our chief sources of knowledge of the Essenes were the writings of Josephus[*] and Philo Judeus.[†] The widely-publicized discovery of the Dead Sea Scrolls in the late 1940's and early 1950's, however, has greatly

enriched our knowledge of this sect. These scrolls, discovered in cliffs near the north end of the Dead Sea, are from the library of a sectarian community that had its headquarters nearby, at a place called Qumran. The term "Essene" does not appear in any of the scrolls, but the faith and practice of the Qumran community so closely fits what we know of the Essenes from Josephus and Philo that most scholars agree Qumran was an Essene settlement.

No one knows how the Essenes got their name or what it means, or even if they ever used it to refer to themselves, although numerous suggestions have been made. It does seem clear that they, like the Pharisees, developed out of the Hasidim. They were the pious of the pious. To them, even the Pharisees were dangerously lax. So concerned were they about the degenerate state of Judaism that they refused even to take part in

[*]*The Jewish War*, II, viii, 2-13 and *Antiquities*, XVIII, 1, 5.
[†]*Hypothetica*, 11.1-18 and *Every Good Man is Free*, 12-13.

369

the services of the temple as long as "impure" men controlled it. The Essene party was active in Jerusalem until the end of the second century B.C. At some time in the next twenty-five years—the exact date is unknown—they became so distressed at the compromising policies prevalent in Jerusalem that they left the city and established the community at Qumran.

The overthrow of the Maccabean house by Herod the Great in 36 B.C. signalled a new era in Essene history. Herod's position was shaky at first, because of the lingering loyalty most of the people felt for the Maccabeans. To offset this undercurrent, Herod went out of his way to favor anti-Maccabean elements. Since the Essenes viewed the Maccabeans as a symbol of disloyalty to the covenant, they were singled out for special treatment. Perhaps at Herod's bidding, they left Qumran at this time and apparently occupied a section in the southern part of Jerusalem. For the remainder of Herod's reign, they engaged in extensive missionary work and established Essene communities in towns and villages all over Judah. At Herod's death, however, they once again abandoned Jerusalem for their Qumran retreat. There they remained until the outbreak of war with Rome in A.D. 66.

The Essenes saw themselves as the people of the New Covenant of which the prophets had spoken. They were already participating in this covenant by their strict adherence to the Law, but they expected the imminent arrival of the day when Yahweh would usher in the New Age of the Eternal Covenant. They also expected that, on the arrival of that day, they would be called upon to take part in the great battle against the armies of the Children of Darkness. This consciousness of the need to prepare for Holy Warfare combined with their scrupulous zeal for the Law to produce a communal life of striking discipline.

The Essenes were missionary-minded, but admission into their community involved far more than mere assent to the worth of their goals. A candidate for membership was placed on trial for one year, during which time he was obliged to follow a discipline placed on him by the community. This was a rigorous test, but satisfactory completion of this first year did not make the candidate a full member of the community; it merely qualified him for the more important two-year period of testing. It was only at the successful conclusion of this three-year period that the candidate was accepted into the society as a full-fledged member.

Life as a member of the Essene community was an austere affair. The younger members always submitted to the elders, or to a decision of the majority of the community. Sabbath regulations were rigorously observed. Laughter was frowned upon. Spitting in the midst of a group was forbidden. Marriage was strongly discouraged, though not absolutely prohibited.* If a member of the order was charged with a crime, he was given a fair trial by a large court, and if found guilty was cast out of the community.

One of the most striking features of Essene life was their common meal. At Qumran, archaeologists have excavated a dining hall large enough to seat about two hundred people. Next to it they found a smaller room stocked with hundreds of dishes and utensils that were used in the dining hall. According to Josephus, the Essenes took their noon and evening meals in this room. Before entering the hall, they purified themselves by bathing in cisterns of cold water. Then, dressed in white linen garments, they entered the great hall, where they took their meals in si-

*This attitude was probably based on the conviction that a family would be a hindrance when the war against the legions of evil broke out, rather than a belief that marriage was intrinsically sinful.

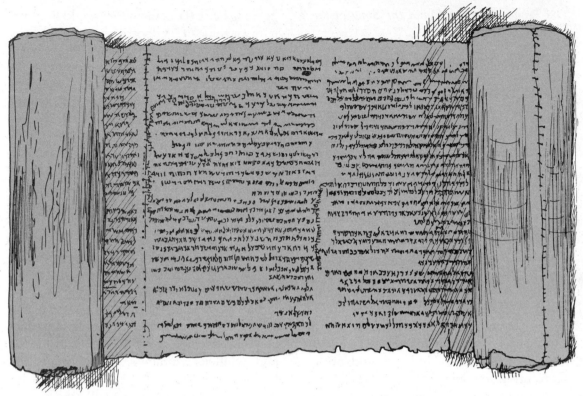

**The Isaiah manuscript found in Cave I at Qumran, copied and corrected by Essenes.**

lence regarded by outsiders as "an awful mystery." Based on evidence found in the Dead Sea Scrolls, most scholars feel that at least some of these meals were regarded by the Essenes as a foretaste of the banquets they would enjoy together after the coming of the Messiah.

When we say there were four major parties of Judaism, this does not mean that the Jewish community was divided into four neat packages, with no remainder. Just as is the case today with major religious groups or political parties, there were undoubtedly many who favored this or that party but who never formally identified with it. And, of course, there were many who never gave a thought to anything beyond the mundane problems of everyday existence. Still, these parties were the major focal points of Judaism and each played an important role in preparing the ground of Judaism for the coming of Christ and Christianity.

### THE APOCRYPHA

As most Bible students know, Roman Catholic Bibles contain several books not usually found in Protestant versions. This collection is known as the *Apocrypha* and contains the following works:

*I and II Esdras*
*Tobit*
*Judith*
*Additions to Esther**
*The Wisdom of Solomon*
*Ecclesiasticus,* or *The Wisdom of Jesus the Son of Sirach*
*Baruch*
*The Letter of Jeremiah†*

---

*Sometimes called *The Rest of Esther*.
†Actually a sub-division of *Baruch*.

371

*The Prayer of Azariah and the Song of the Three Young Men*
*Suzanna*
*Bel and the Dragon*
*The Prayer of Manasseh*
*I and II Maccabees*

Much of the historical material contained in this chapter was drawn from *I and II Maccabees*. In our discussion of Wisdom Literature, we mentioned *Ecclesiasticus* and the *Wisdom of Solomon* (p. 345). *II Esdras* is a work in the apocalyptic tradition. Other types of literature include the romantic stories of *Tobit* and *Judith*, sequels to the books of *Esther* (*Additions to Esther*), *Jeremiah* (*Baruch*), and *Daniel* (*The Song of the Three Young Men, Susanna,* and *Bel and the Dragon*), and the liturgical work, *The Prayer of Manasseh.*

The word "apocrypha" comes from a Greek word meaning "hidden" and originally referred to books that were kept secret from the general public for one reason or another, usually because they were thought to contain material that common men would be unable to understand. Eventually, the word came to mean "not genuine" or "heretical;" this is the sense in which it is applied to the collection of books under discussion.

The process of deciding which books were to be regarded as "scripture" and which were to be regarded as "outside books" began with the work of Ezra. It was brought to completion, as far as the Old Testament was concerned, at a historic council in the town of Jamnia in A.D. 90. After the fall of Jerusalem in A.D. 70, the rabbis were faced with a situation in which the vast amount of religious literature produced in the intertestamental period was more of a liability than an asset. On the one hand, the fall of Jerusalem had caused many Jews to repudiate the dreams of the apocalyptic writers and to return to the Law as the only reliable source of guidance. On the other hand, the bur-

geoning Christian movement could find support for some of its doctrines in these books. It would not do to dignify their efforts by allowing such books to stand on a par with the older orthodox writings. And so, at Jamnia, the rabbis fixed the Old Testament canon* for all time, at least as far as Jews were concerned. The books they accepted were those found in Protestant Bibles, although the order varies somewhat. The books now found in the Apocrypha were rejected—some because they were written after the time of Ezra, which was believed to be the time Yahweh had ceased to reveal himself to his people, others because they were written in Greek instead of Hebrew, and others because they were no longer popular.

The early Christian church had no uniform policy regarding these books. Some accepted them as a valuable source of history and religious guidance, while others followed the lead of the Jews in dismissing them as "outside books." Despite the opposition of some, however, early Christian writers continued to quote and allude to these books. Lists of the books that were to be regarded as Christian scripture often included several of these books. In the fourth century A.D., a Christian scholar named Jerome was commissioned by the Bishop of Rome to produce a Latin translation of the scriptures for use in the Western church. Jerome was obliged to include the apocryphal books in his translation, because they were being read so widely in the church, but he did so only after making it clear he did not regard them as canonical or as legitimate sources for the support of church doctrine. Over the

---

*The word "canon" is derived from a Hebrew term meaning "cane" or "reed." Since the reed was one of the first instruments of measurement used by man, the term carries with it the idea of a norm or pattern by which other things are measured. This is the sense in which it is commonly used to refer to the collection of writings that comprise our Bible and have come to be regarded as the authoritative and inspired word of God.

years, however, as this translation, called the Vulgate, became the official version of the Roman Catholic Church, most men forgot Jerome's qualifying statements and began to accord these books a canonical status. The Roman Catholic Church officially declared them to be canonical at the council of Trent in 1546, a decision later ratified by the Vatican Council of 1870.

Protestant opposition to these books grew out of the emphasis of Luther and other Reformation leaders on taking the Bible as the only rule of faith and practice. This policy necessitated a decision on the apocrypha, because of the always dubious position of the books, and because the Roman Catholic Church was using them to support some of the beliefs the Reformers opposed, such as the doctrine of purgatory. In Luther's 1534 translation of the Bible into German, he gathered the books together at the end of the Old Testament—previously, they had been scattered among the undisputed Old Testament books—and introduced them with a statement to the effect that they were useful books to read and study but were not to be regarded as scripture. Most subsequent translations of the Bible followed Luther's example until the early nineteenth century, when it became standard procedure to omit the books altogether from copies of the Bible. Now, after 150 years, Protestament versions of the Bible are once again appearing with the Apocrypha included.

Because of the dispute over the canonicity of these books, non-Catholics have often treated them with suspicion or hostility. There is really no reason for either attitude. In fact, every serious student of the Bible would do well to own a copy of the Apocrypha*, as it serves well to illuminate the period we have just been studying and to

---

*If one does not wish to have the books in the same volume with the Bible, they are available separately at nominal cost.

bridge the gap between the Old and New Testaments.

### LEGALISM: ITS STRENGTHS AND WEAKNESSES

In our study of the years following the return from Babylonian captivity, we have noticed again and again that the distinctive trait of post-exilic Judaism was its emphasis on strict obedience to the Law. Nebuchadnezzar's destruction of Jerusalem had finally convinced the Jews that their relationship to Yahweh was not unconditional, that it depended upon the seriousness with which they regarded the Law. This being the case, the only real hope for the future lay in turning all their attention to the proper observance of even the most minute regulations of the Law. They gave great attention to the Sabbath, the details of ritual and sacrifice, and the laws of cleanness and uncleanness, which governed a man's fitness to approach God in worship.

To Christians who experience their relationship to God as a joyous response to an unspeakable gift of grace, this kind of religion seems sterile and cold. But this harsh judgment is not wholly justified. In our discussion of the covenant of Sinai (pp. 69-70), we noted that the Ten Commandments were given *after* a recitation of God's mighty acts on behalf of Israel. In other words, the Law came *after* grace, as a response *to* this grace. To the Jew who understood this, the Law was not a burden. He gladly kept its precepts—even the apparently trivial ones— out of gratitude for what Yahweh had done in the past and could be counted on to do in the future. Unfortunately, not everyone understood this relationship between the Law and grace. By the time of Jesus, the grateful love for the Law as the expressed will of a caring God had degenerated into a calculating kind of legalism, which has always been "an abomination unto the Lord." Rituals became perfunctory and meaningless. Gratitude for election was perverted into self-righteous exclusivism and religious snobbery. Concern for the tithing of "mint, anise, and cummin" took precedence over what Jesus called "the weightier matters of the Law: justice, mercy, and faith" (*Matthew 23:23*). It was this legalistic attitude against which Jesus and Paul directed so much of their attention and energy. In the early church this heresy—for, surely, legalism was and is a heresy—threatened to undermine the missionary efforts of the apostle Paul. And even today, it frequently poses a positive hindrance to a genuine understanding and reception of the Christian gospel.

### CONCLUSION

These, then, were God's people and this was their religion at the beginning of the Christian era. Their history had begun two thousand years before when a wandering Aramean set out from Ur of the Chaldees, "not knowing whither he went." God had promised him he would be the father of a great nation and that through his seed all the nations of the earth would be blessed (*Genesis 12:1–3*). It seemed an incredible promise, but God had kept his word and had created a mighty nation out of a band of runaway slaves. Time and again he had crushed them as a potter crushes his clay, in an effort to mould them into a vessel that would be suitable for bringing the promised blessing to the nations. The vessel was not yet perfect, but God's eternal purposes could be delayed no longer. The fullness of time had arrived.

# PART FIVE

## *The Beginnings of Christianity*

# 15

# The Life of Christ

*The life and teachings of Jesus
of Nazareth,
who was the Christ*

Most of the civilized world orders and records its affairs according to a system of dating whose two chief divisions are represented by the familiar letters "B.C." and "A.D." These letters, and the system of dating they represent, are a tribute unparalleled in all history to the life and work of a man whose public career lasted less than three years. At other points in history, men have reckoned time from the birth or reign of this or that great figure, or from this or that momentous event. Inevitably, the passage of time has dimmed or erased these memories and the system of dating they inspired has been dropped. But the short career of the carpenter from Galilee made, and continues to make, such an impact on the history of individuals and nations that even those who do not believe the wondrous things his followers have said about him have had no choice but to divide the history of the world into the time "B.C." or "Before Christ"* and the time since "A.D." or "*Anno Domini* (the Year of our Lord)."

Our study thus far has brought us to A.D. 1, commonly reckoned as the year in which the birth of our Lord occurred.† Before we turn to the narrative of the life and teachings of Jesus, let us quickly review the major aspects of the political and religious situation in Palestine during his lifetime.

## The Historical and Political Background

### ROME FROM 44 B.C.–A.D. 37

Rome, of course, was mistress of the world throughout Jesus' lifetime. At the time of his birth, the great empire was in the midst of what is usually called the Augustan Age. After the assassination of Julius Caesar in 44 B.C., the republic of Rome had undergone a critical shake-up in its government. No one individual was powerful enough to assume the dictatorial role Julius Caesar had held. As a sort of compromise, the leadership of the republic was taken by the famous Triumvirate of Mark Antony, Ledipus, and Gaius Octavian, the eighteen-year-old stepson of Julius Caesar. The chief opposition to their rule came from Brutus and Cassius, who had engineered the assassination plot.

---

*Jews and other non-Christians frequently use the letters "B.C.E." to signify "Before the Christian Era."

†See the discussion of the chronology of Jesus' life beginning on p. 388-89.

This crumbled in 42 B.C. when both of the rebels committed suicide after Antony and Octavian defeated their armies at Philippi. Ledipus faded from the picture before long, leaving Antony in charge of the Eastern part of the empire and Octavian in command of the West, including Rome itself. In 36 B.C. Antony began his fabled affair with Cleopatra, the beautiful princess of Egypt. Probably, the Romans would have winked at the affair itself, but when Antony gave several Roman provinces in the East to Cleopatra's children, the Senate stripped Antony of his authority and declared war on Cleopatra. In 31 B.C. Octavian defeated Antony in the naval battle at Actium. Antony and Cleopatra retreated to Egypt and, the next year, committed suicide. Now every challenge to the leadership of Octavian was gone, and the Augustan Age of Rome was about to begin.

Because he was the stepson of Julius Caesar, and because Caesar had requested in his will that he should be his successor, Octavian possessed a decided advantage from the start in the struggle for the leadership of the republic. His position was enhanced even further when the triumvirate declared Julius to be a god, for the people naturally came to regard Octavian as a son of god. But more important than all these, Octavian possessed ability and strength of character in a quantity and combination such as the world has seldom seen. So far was he above the ordinary run of men that the Roman Senate gave him a title by which is commonly known—Augustus, a title signifying reverence for one who stands somewhere between man and God.

As soon as he gained what amounted to a free hand, Augustus set about to reform the empire. First, he drew more people into the governing process, realizing that some sort of consensus of the governed is necessary for a healthy political situation. This was no

mere gesture; it was a bold and genuine constitutional experiment that worked magnificently. He sought to replace an image of militarism with an image of piety. He placed curbs on luxury and encouraged a revival of religion. Statues and images on coins pictured him in priestly robes rather than the garb of a warrior. All these things enhanced the aura of divinity he enjoyed and eventually gave rise to the cult of emperor worship. Augustus made some show of discouraging sacrifice or worship offered directly to him, but it was clear that he received the homage of the people with deep satisfaction. It was not easy to be plain Mr. Octavian when in fact he was the ruler of the world.

Augustus had no direct contact with Christianity, for Jesus was but a youth during his reign (27 B.C.–A.D. 14), but the relative peace he created, the policies he established, the roads he built, the piety he encouraged—all played their role in preparing the world for the Christian gospel.

When Augustus died, the imperial mantle fell upon Tiberius Caesar, whom he had adopted and tutored for the role. Tiberius reigned A.D. 14–37, and was thus emperor at the time of Jesus' ministry. We need not concern ourselves with the details of his reign. It is sufficient to note that he continued, more or less, the policies of Augustus, and that no major upheavals threatened the empire during this period. With this larger background in mind, let us notice the effects of Roman rule of the provinces of Palestine.

### PALESTINE UNDER ROMAN RULE

In chapter 14, we noted that Rome had established control over Palestine in 63 B.C., in the campaign led by Pompey, and that Herod the Great served as king of Palestine, under Roman oversight, from 40–4 B.C. When Herod died, his territory was divided, according to his wishes, between his three

**A bust of the young Tiberius Caesar, successor of Augustus.**

sons. Philip was assigned the territories northeast of the Sea of Galilee, which he ruled until A.D. 26. Galilee and Perea (east of the Jordan) were given to Herod Antipas, the Herod who ordered the execution of John the Baptist and who allowed Jesus to be subjected to cruel mockery just before his crucifixion. Despite the unfavorable light in which the New Testament places him, Antipas was a capable administrator and ruled until A.D. 39, at which time his nephew Herod Agrippa I (the Herod of *Acts 12*) conspired with the new emperor, Caius Caligula, to have him removed and banished to Lyon. As might be expected, Agrippa I was granted control over his territory.

The last division of Herod's kingdom, which consisted of Samaria, Judea, and the northern part of Idumea, was assigned to Archelaus. Archelaus proved to be less ca-

pable than his brothers and was deposed in A.D. 6. When this happened, rather than try to choose a satisfactory ruler from among the Jews, the Romans decided to place Judea under the direct control of Roman governors known as procurators. From A.D. 26–36, this post was held by Pontius Pilate, the Roman official in charge of the crucifixion of Jesus.

The Roman yoke chafed and galled the Jews during this period. For a people whose whole history and faith was oriented around an act that brought freedom from bondage—the Exodus—the whole idea of direct Roman control was a constant, nagging irritant. It was true the procurators of Judea had moved their headquarters from Jerusalem, the natural location, to Caesarea on the Mediterranean coast, but they had left occupation troops in the city and whenever large crowds of Jews were expected in the city for a religious holiday, a situation that might possibly lead to rebellion, the procurators usually made it a point to be on hand. During these periods, they stayed at the palace of Herod the Great. This explains why Pilate was in Jerusalem at the time of Jesus' passion, since it occurred just before Passover.

In keeping with longstanding practice, the Jews were allowed to worship according to the Law of Moses, and were not forced to perform some of the oaths or ritual acts demanded of other citizens of the empire. Still, the high priest was little more than a puppet of the Roman government who could be appointed or fired at the discretion of the procurator. As a matter of fact, even the ceremonial robes of the high priest were kept under Roman lock and key. The jurisdiction of the Sanhedrin was reduced to the point that it really had very little authority over anything that was not strictly religious, and all its decisions had to be reported to the government.

379

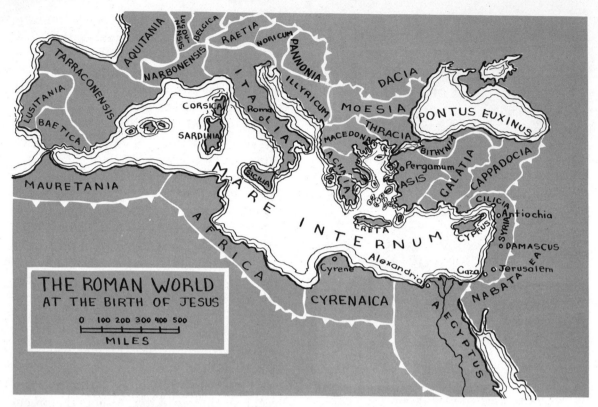

**The Roman World at the birth of Jesus.**

Roman taxation was another cause of real discontent in Palestine. By itself, the high tax rate would have been a burden, but its oppressiveness was compounded by the manner in which it was collected. The tax collectors, known as publicans, were neither elected by their constituents nor appointed on the basis of merit. Instead, they bought their office from the government. The government then assigned them an amount they were expected to collect in their district, with the understanding they collected in excess of that figure was theirs to keep. Naturally, this policy led to the grossest sort of abuse. Unscrupulous publicans, and this seems to have included the majority, gouged the people for all they could in order to fatten their own pocketbooks. Because of this practice, the publicans were hated bitterly, especially if they were

fellow-Jews, and were regarded as in the same moral category with prostitutes.

All these factors combined with general poverty and the usual irritations of living in territory occupied by a foreign power to produce a situation from which many devoutly wished to escape. These wishes fanned the flame of messianism to a white heat. Some still cherished the prophetic ideal of a Messiah who would usher in the glorious kingdom of God in which men of every nation would live in peace and unity. But admittedly, altogether too many thought in terms of a nationalistic hero who would throw off the Roman yoke and reestablish a triumphant Jewish state. A variety of hopes developed, and a variety of would-be saviors arose to capitalize on these hopes. Time after time, the movements they led died of their own accord or were crushed by the

Roman army. Then, on the day of Pentecost in the year A.D. 29,* a Galilean fisherman announced to a tremendous crowd assembled in Jerusalem that Messiah had come and that his life had fulfilled the things that were spoken by the prophets. The Jews had rejected him and arranged for his death by crucifixion. But, claimed the fisherman, God had not allowed his eternal purposes to be thwarted by their rejection. The Anointed One of God had been raised from the dead and exalted to a position of glory at the right hand of God, and there he reigned as the Risen Lord.

This announcement kindled a fire in the hearts of thousands. Smitten with their own guilt and convinced that the long-awaited Day of the Lord had at last arrived, they surrendered their lives to this Risen Messiah. Of those that gladly received Peter's word about this Christ,† God formed a remarkable community. It was more than just a community that remembered the mighty works of Messiah. It was a community that was filled with and moved by the living Spirit of its Risen Lord. Whereas other messianic communities had come and gone, this community would endure unto the end of the age, for not even the gates of hell could prevail against it. Before we trace the early history of this community, the New People of God, let us see what manner of man this was about whom the fisherman preached the good news.

## The Sources of Our Knowledge About Jesus

In the earliest period of the Christian community, the gospel, or "good news," consisted essentially of what Peter had declared on Pentecost: 1) Jesus had fulfilled the messianic expectations of the prophets,

2) God had borne witness to his ministry with "signs, and wonders, and mighty works," 3) he had been crucified by lawless men, according to God's divine plan, 4) God had raised him from the dead and exalted him at his own right hand, and 5) all men everywhere should repent and submit to his lordship, that they might receive forgiveness of their sins, for "there is salvation in no one else, for there is no other name under heaven given among men by which we must be saved" (*Acts 4:12*).

This was the heart of the Christian message. If men believed this and responded to it, they could be part of this marvelous fellowship that was forming. As the community developed, of course, there arose a need and desire for a fuller account of the career of Jesus. An effective witness among Jews demanded that some support be given the claim that Jesus' life had truly been lived "according to the scriptures." If the gospel was to be preached to people who had no previous knowledge of either the ministry of Jesus or the prophets, some of both would have to be provided. If God had confirmed the ministry of Jesus with signs and wonders, men would want to know something about them. If they chose to live as his disciples, they would want to know what he expected of them. As interpretations of the basic message arose that threatened to rob it of its saving power, some official standard was needed to protect the church from heresy. And of course, there was the quite natural desire of the early Christians to learn all they could about him to whom they had surrendered themselves.

It was in response to these needs that the four books that stand at the beginning of our New Testament came to be written. We commonly refer to these books as "the four gospels." There is no real harm in this as long as we understand that, really, there was only one gospel and that what we have

---

*See chronological discussion below (pp. 386-87).

†The words Messiah, Christ, and Anointed One are synonymous.

in these books is just what the traditional title suggests, the gospel, or good news concerning Jesus Christ, *according* to Matthew, Mark, Luke, and John.

It is universally agreed, by conservatives and liberals alike, that none of our four gospels was written until after the death of Paul, or at least thirty-five years after the Christian church came into existence. But this does not mean the early Christians had no knowledge of the material in these books. The apostles and other eyewitnesses to the life of Jesus had undoubtedly preserved all sorts of information about the Master. They remembered the miracles they had seen him perform. They recalled his sermons and his parables, and even the brief statements he had made as comments on something he observed or in response to questions by his disciples or his enemies. They remembered what they had seen or heard of such events as his birth, his baptism and temptation, and his passion. And they remembered many other things—so many that the writer of the fourth gospel said, "were everyone of them written, I suppose that the world itself could not contain the books that would be written" (*John 21:25*).

These traditions—remember, the word "tradition" simply means "that which is handed down" and in no way implies that the material is false or unreliable—were well-known and deeply cherished by the early Christians. In all probability, they circulated among the churches singly or with a group of traditions of the same general character. For example, the parable of the mustard seed may have been passed around the churches by itself, or with other parables on the same general subject of the Kingdom of God. Eventually, a sizable body of oral and written traditions developed. It was from this material that the gospel writers, inspired of God, chose most of that they included in their books.

Actually, the situation was not far different from what frequently occurs in modern times. When a great national or world figure dies, a rash of books and articles appear that record the things about the figure that were most meaningful to the authors. Some tell of his heroic deeds and great decisions. Others recall the way he behaved in person-to-person relationships. Others contain his finest speeches. And still others record examples of his humor, or his ideas on such subjects as religion or politics or art; these are usually drawn from his speeches, writings, and off-the-record remarks. Finally, some will undertake to write a comprehensive biography of the man which will include all these elements. Naturally, each of these accounts will differ somewhat, depending on the author's purpose for producing his work, the state of his knowledge, and such factors as his personality and style of composition. For the fullest possible picture, a reader will want to read several of these larger biographies, even though many of the basic facts and ideas are repeated.

In the same way, the finished products of these four great interpretations of the gospel differ somewhat in content, arrangement, and point of view, but they all proclaim the same essential message. By reading them all, we can gain the most comprehensive picture of the different ways in which the early church viewed Jesus.

### THE SYNOPTIC GOSPELS

The first three gospels are frequently referred to as the *Synoptic* gospels, because they provide a synopsis, or general view of the life and teachings of Jesus. The *Gospel according to John* was probably written near the end of the first century, a bit later than *Matthew, Mark, and Luke*. It is far more concerned to set forth an understanding of the life and ministry of Jesus that was particularly needed in its time than to present an orderly account like that of the other three. For this reason, we shall base our treatment of the life of Christ primarily, though not entirely, on the three Synoptic gospels, and postpone our discussion of the fourth gospel until a later chapter (see p. 492ff).

As we shall see momentarily, each of these three gospels differs from the others in some most significant respects. At the same time, however, there are a number of equally striking similarities. Basically, the situation is this:

1) Approximately ninety per cent of the material found in *Mark* also appears in *Matthew* and/or *Luke*. In almost every case, the order in which it occurs is the same as in *Mark*, although additional material is interspersed with it. Not only that, the actual phrases and words, even when these are unusual constructions in Greek, are frequently identical.

2) *Matthew* and *Luke* contain considerable material in identical or quite similar form, that does not appear in *Mark*.

3) And finally, both *Matthew* and *Luke* contain materials that are peculiar to them.

How are we to explain these similarities and differences? We do not doubt that these writers were inspired of God to perform their task, but if one will read the writings of Peter, Paul, James, John, and the other New Testament authors, it becomes clear that no respectable theory of inspiration can rule out the obvious fact that the Biblical writers wrote in their own words and that their writings reflect differences in outlook, emphasis, approach, and even the ability to handle the Greek language. For example, the Greek of *Revelation* is far inferior, from the standpoint of grammar, style, and beauty, to that found in the gospel according to Luke. In the face of this kind of evidence, it is all the more unusual that three writers who had such different purposes for

writing (see discussion below) should agree so exactly in some places while differing so widely in others.

Fortunately, it is possible to make a reasonably good guess as to what happened. In the prologue to his account of the gospel, Luke states that "many have undertaken to compile a narrative of the things which have been accomplished among us" (*Luke 1:1*). He goes on to say he had been collecting information from "eyewitnesses and ministers of the word" for some time and that he now felt qualified to set down "an orderly account" for the benefit of his friend Theophilus. In other words, Luke acknowledges the fact that he was indebted to a number of sources for the material he was including in his book. Based on the observation that virtually everything found in *Mark* is also found in *Matthew* and/or *Luke*, and that the order and even the wording of this material is either identical or quite similar, it seems reasonable to assume that both Matthew and Luke used Mark's gospel as one of their primary sources. Both would almost certainly have had ample opportunity to become familiar with Mark's work. For reasons given below, *Mark* is usually dated from A.D. 64-69, with general opinion favoring the early part of the period, while *Matthew* and *Luke* are usually dated from sometime just before A.D. 70 to about A.D. 85, with opinion leaning toward the latter. Mark's gospel probably received wide circulation and was recognized as a trustworthy narrative. In all likelihood, Matthew and Luke used it as the basic outline for their gospels, filling it in with additional material whenever it suited their purposes.

What about the material common to both *Matthew* and *Luke*, but not found in *Mark?* The most logical explanation seems to be that *Matthew* and *Luke* both had access to a body of oral or written traditions that Mark did not use, either because he did not know of it or because he did not feel it was pertinent to his aims.

The material that appears *only* in *Matthew* or *only* in *Luke* is easiest of all to explain. Obviously, this consists of traditions the other writers either did not know or did not care to use. No further theory is required. With these preliminary ideas in mind, let us note some of the particular factors involved in the production of each of these three gospels.

### THE GOSPEL ACCORDING TO MARK

It is generally agreed that the *Gospel according to Mark* was the first of the three to be written down. None of the gospels gives the name of its author, but early Christian tradition was unanimous in ascribing the second gospel to Mark, also called John Mark. Mark was a Palestinian Jew who was closely associated with the teachings of Jesus and the apostles. He was a companion of Paul and Barnabas on the early part of the first missionary journey, but left the party at Perga in Pamphylia (*Acts 13:13*). We do not know his reasons for leaving, but we do know that Paul did not think them good enough. When the time came for the second missionary tour, Paul and Barnabas came to a parting of the ways because Paul refused to allow Mark to make the trip (*Acts 15:36–41*). In later years, however, Mark managed to regain Paul's confidence and was singled out as being particularly useful to the apostle (*II Tim. 4:11*). Mark also enjoyed a good relationship with the apostle Peter, who had visited in his home in the early days of the church (*Acts 12:12–17*). In *I Peter 5:13*, written many years later, we learn that Mark was Peter's co-worker in "Babylon," which is almost certainly a code word for Rome.

These references make it seem probable that Mark was in Rome with Peter and Paul in A.D. 64-65, which was about the time both of them are believed to have been martyred. It was also the time of the first real persecution of Christians by the Roman government. The emperor was Nero (A.D. 54-68), a vain and cowardly man who fancied himself a musician and poet. In A.D. 64, a nine-day fire destroyed a great portion of Rome. Persistent tradition has it that Nero himself was responsible for starting the fire, as part of an early effort at urban renewal. Whether this is true or not, he shifted the blame to the Christians, who were already under suspicion simply because their religion was new and different from the standard Roman brands. As punishment for their alleged crime, Christians were covered with animal skins and thrown to wild dogs, who tore them apart. Others were dipped in pitch, tied to poles and set on fire, to serve as human torches for one of Nero's garden parties. The Roman historian Tacitus tells us that many respectable Romans were sickened by this ghastly spectacle and regarded the Christians as victims of the gluttonous cruelty of a warped monster in need of a scapegoat.

In all likelihood, the *Gospel according to Mark* was written for the benefit or persecuted Christians. This helps to explain why Mark puts so much emphasis on Jesus' struggle with the forces of evil. Jesus had had to face evil at every turn; surely, his disciples could not expect less. They, too, would have to be ready to travel the way of the cross. But if they remained steadfast in spite of all the senseless cruelties being visited upon them, they could expect untimate vindication at the hand of God.

The theory that Mark wrote for the Christians in Rome, many of whom were probably Gentiles, is also supported by the absence of any references to the Jewish Law and the presence of only one quotation from the Old Testament. In addition, Hebrew phrases and customs that might not be understood by Gentile readers are carefully explained.*

### THE GOSPEL ACCORDING TO LUKE

The second of the Synoptic gospels to appear in written form was probably that ascribed to Luke. Most of the evidence for the authorship of *Luke* is based on material found in *Acts*. It is generally conceded that the third gospel and *Acts of Apostles* are part of a two-volume work by the same author. Both are dedicated to an individual named Theophilus (*Luke 1:3; Acts 1:1*), and Acts *1:1* refers to a "former treatise" which would seem to point to the third gospel. The unanimous voice of the early church identified the author as Luke, "the beloved physician" who is known to have been one of Paul's faithful companions on his mission journeys (*Colossians 4:14; Philemon 24; II Timothy 4:11*).

In *Colossians 4*, Luke is grouped with Epaphras and Demas, in distinction from those "of the circumcision." This means that Luke was a Gentile. In many ways, *Luke* and *Acts* reflect their Gentile parentage. Theophilus, the individual to whom both the gospel and *Acts* are addressed, was apparently a Gentile, perhaps a new convert or a man on the verge of conversion, who wanted to learn more of the life and teachings of Jesus. It is quite possible he was a wealthy individual who was expected to serve as a patron for the books, introducing them to a larger circle of readers.

The approach Luke uses in writing his account of the gospel reflects a desire to set forth Christianity as a universal religion without racial limitations. He notes the Roman emperor and the governor at the time of Jesus' birth (*Luke 2:1–2*). He records Simeon's pronouncement that Jesus would be "a light to the Gentiles" (*2:32*). He

---

*See *Mark 3:7; 5:41; 7:2; 9:43; 10:46; 14:12, 36; 15:34, 42.*

traces the lineage of Jesus past Abraham all the way back to Adam to show that the Christ is related to all men and not just to the Jews (*3:23–38*). He pictures Jesus not merely as a Jewish Messiah, but as the Friend and Savior of all that believe him and receive him. He underlines Jesus' concern for sinners and outcasts. He (and he alone) preserves the moving story of neighbor-love in which the hero is not a priest or a Levite, but a Samaritan, one of the half-breeds so despised by the Jews (*10:29–37*). His gospel is the first half of a narrative (*Acts of Apostles* being the second half) that traces the origin, development, and advance of Christianity from Bethlehem to Jerusalem, to Antioch, to Macedonia, to Achaia, to Ephesus, and finally to Rome, the capital of the Western world.

### THE GOSPEL ACCORDING TO MATTHEW

When we turn from the writings of Luke to the *Gospel according to Matthew*, we cannot help but be struck by the difference in their approach and emphasis. Whereas Luke wrote primarily for a Gentile audience, *Matthew* is obviously directed toward a Jewish-Christian audience. In fact, an early tradition has it that it was originally written in the Hebrew language. There is no trace of a Hebrew original, however, and most scholars are convinced that the present gospel is not a translation, but was originally written in Greek, like all the other books of the New Testament.

Some have questioned whether Matthew was really the author of the gospel. The sum of the information the New Testament provides about Matthew, or Levi, as he was sometimes called, is that he was a tax collector whom Jesus summoned to be an apostle and that he entertained several of his friends at a banquet at which Jesus was the guest of honor (*Mk. 2:14–15*). Since the book does not name its author, there is no way to be certain on the matter, but it is difficult to see why the name of such an obscure person as Matthew became associated with the gospel unless he had a major role in its composition. It has been suggested, with considerable plausibility, that the book was designed to serve as a handbook for the guidance of a "school" or circle of Jewish-Christian disciples who gathered around Matthew. Whether or not this actually was the case, the rather neat and orderly arrangement of materials on various subjects that is characteristic of *Matthew* certainly would make it a useful manual for such a community.

The controlling purpose of the *Gospel according to Matthew* seems to be a desire to drive home the point that Jesus is indeed the Messiah for whom the Jews had been longing, that his life and death had fulfilled the prophecies of the Old Testament, and that the day was at hand when he would come again in glory to judge the nations of the world. Against this backdrop, *Matthew* contains an abundance of material that would be helpful to the church in interpreting its situation with respect to the Law of Moses, in dealing with problems that were likely to arise within the fellowship, and in preparing itself for the imminent return of the Messiah.

### CHRONOLOGY OF THE LIFE OF JESUS

The analogy with modern biographical works, suggested above, helps us to understand the process by which we got our gospels, but it is important to remember that, strictly speaking, the gospels were never intended to be biographies in our modern sense of the term. They are primarily theological writings that set forth the central features of the message of salvation within a broad historical framework that includes not only the major events of Jesus' life, but many examples of his religious and ethical

teaching, as well as accounts of his miracles. The authors were writing at a particular time, to a particular audience, and for particular reasons. All these factors influenced the way in which they handled their materials. Each had his own method of selecting and recording data, under the guidance of the Holy Spirit. One recorded things another chose to omit. There seems to have been little or no attempt to make certain the chronology of their writings coincided exactly with that of other writers, although the sequence found in Mark was the basic chronological scheme. For this reason, it is rather fruitless to construct intricate "harmonies" of the gospels in which all the minute details of Jesus' life are woven into one continuous strand. To do this is to miss the point of the gospels. It is possible, however, to construct a broad outline of the life of Jesus with some assurance of accuracy.

Although we commonly speak—indeed, we have so spoken in this chapter—of A.D. 1 as the birth of Jesus, careful investigation of the chronology of this period, the details of which will not concern us here, has shown that this date can hardly be accurate. Herod the Great is known to have died in the year commonly reckoned as 4 B.C. And yet, the Bible tells us the same Herod tried to kill Jesus when he was a baby, forcing Joseph to flee to Egypt with his family and to remain there until Herod died (*Matthew 2*). This means that Jesus was probably born in the year commonly reckoned as 7 or 6 B.C. This is somewhat confusing, but historians have felt it was easier to say that Jesus was born in 6 B.C., despite the apparent contradiction in terms, than to change all the dates in history.

According to this revised chronology, the ministry of Jesus is also shifted backwards, from A.D. 31–33 to A.D. 27–29. A broad outline of Jesus' life, strung between these two poles, looks something like this:

| | |
|---|---|
| 6 B.C. | Birth of Jesus<br>Flight to Egypt |
| 4 B.C. | Death of Herod the Great<br>Return of Joseph, Mary, and Jesus<br>to Nazareth |
| A.D. 6 | Jesus in the temple at age twelve |
| A.D. 27 | Ministry of John the Baptist<br>Baptism and Temptation of Jesus |
| A.D. 28<br>Spring<br><br>Summer<br>Fall<br>Winter | Death of John the Baptist<br>Ministry in Galilee<br>Ministry north of Galilee<br>Ministry in Judea and Perea |
| A.D. 29<br>Spring | Final visit to Jerusalem<br>Crucifixion, Resurrection, Ascension<br>Establishment of the church on<br>Pentecost |

With this outline in mind, let us turn at last to the record of the gospels themselves.

## Birth and Early Years of Jesus

*Mark* does not provide an account of the birth and early life of Jesus. For that matter, neither do *Acts* nor any of the epistles. It was his ministry and his death and resurrection that lay at the heart of the gospel, and these were what the early church emphasized. As time passed, however, men naturally wanted to learn the details of what had happened when God became man. As a result, Matthew and Luke have preserved for us some of the most beautiful stories that men have ever told.

### THE ANNUNCIATION TO ELIZABETH AND MARY

The central figure of the birth and infancy narratives is Mary, a maiden who lived in the Galilean town of Nazareth. Galilee was a prosperous region, a fact which made the Roman oppression seem worse to the Galileans than it did to their southern

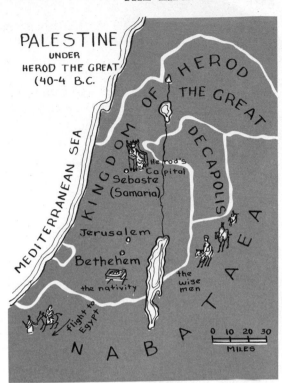

Palestine under Herod the Great.

countrymen who were accustomed to hard times, for Galilee was frequently the scene of rebellion against the Roman rule. In such an atmosphere, men are bound to have to spend a good deal of time talking and thinking about the promised Messiah who would come to liberate the nation and establish a kingdom of peace and justice that would endure forever. Mary herself may have reflected on this hope from time to time, even though she was a very young woman. But Mary was soon to be married to Joseph, a carpenter in Nazareth, and probably was not thinking about the Messiah on the day the angel Gabriel appeared to her to tell her that the hope of Israel was about to be fulfilled in a more marvelous way than she could ever have imagined.

When Gabriel greeted her with the words, "Hail, O favored one, the Lord is with you," Mary was puzzled about what he meant. Gabriel assured her she had nothing

387

to fear, for she had found favor with God. Then he told her she would conceive and bear a son, whose name would be Jesus, which means "Yahweh is salvation." Gabriel spoke of this promised child in a language that abounds with messianic imagery:

> He will be great, and will be called the Son
> of the Most High;
> and the Lord God will give to him the throne
> of his father David,
> and he will reign over the house of Jacob
> for ever;
> and of his kingdom there will be no end.
> —*Luke 1:32-33*

Mary was perplexed, since she was not as yet married, so Gabriel explained to her that

> The Holy Spirit will come upon you,
> and the power of the Most High
> will overshadow you;
> therefore the child to be born
> will be called holy,
> the Son of God.          —*Luke 1:35*

Mary scarcely knew where to turn. The logical person to tell was Joseph, but how would he react to such a fantastic story? And so, she hurried off to the hill country of Judea to visit her older cousin, Elizabeth. When Elizabeth heard her greeting, she was overcome by the Holy Spirit and cried out in joy: "Blessed are you among women, and blessed is the fruit of your womb! And why is this granted me, that the mother of my Lord should come to me?" (*Lk. 1:42–43*). Gabriel had told Mary that Elizabeth, who was well past the normal age of childbearing, would also bear a child. When she saw that Elizabeth was indeed pregnant and that she apparently knew something of the news Mary herself had just received, she too became ecstatic and broke into a beautiful hymn of praise to God.

> My soul magnifies the Lord,
> and my spirit rejoices in God my Savior,
> for he has regarded the low estate of
> his handmaiden.

> For behold, henceforth all generations
> will call me blessed;
> for he who is mighty has done great
> things for me,
> and holy is his name.
> And his mercy is on those who fear him
> from generation to generation. . . .
> He has helped his servant Israel,
> in remembrance of his mercy,
> as he spoke to our fathers,
> to Abraham and to his posterity for ever.
> —*Luke 1:46-50, 54-55*

Mary stayed with Elizabeth for about three months. At the end of that time, she went home to Nazareth to face Joseph. When Joseph learned she was pregnant, he was naturally shocked, but, because he was a kind man, he did not wish to subject her to public humiliation and made plans to divorce her quietly.* Before he could do this, however, an angel appeared to him in a dream and explained the situation. And so, Joseph accepted Mary as his wife.

### THE BIRTH OF JOHN THE BAPTIST

About this time, Elizabeth gave birth to her child. The birth of a son was always an occasion of rejoicing in Israel, but the birth of a son to a couple who had despaired of ever having any children of their own was doubly exciting. Elizabeth's neighbors and relatives flocked to her house on the day the child was to be circumcised and named. They naturally supposed he would be named after his father, Zechariah, but Elizabeth insisted he would be called John. Names meant a great deal more then than they do now, and since none of the relatives were named John, the guests could not understand why Elizabeth had chosen this name. They asked Zechariah what he

---

*In this period, the betrothal amounted to a marriage that had not been consummated, and was a far more binding arrangement than our modern practice of engagement.

wanted to call the child. The old man, who had been struck dumb when Gabriel told him he was to become a father, took a slate and wrote on it, "His name is John." Immediately "his tongue loosed" and he began to praise God. Filled with the Holy Spirit, he said of his precious son:

And you child, will be called the prophet
    of the Most High;
for you will go before the Lord to prepare
    his ways,
to give knowledge of salvation to his people
in the forgiveness of their sins,
through the tender mercy of our God,
when the day shall dawn upon us
    from on high
to give light to those who sit in darkness
    and in the shadow of death,
to guide our feet into the way of peace.
              *—Luke 1:76-79*

"And the child grew and became strong in spirit, and he was in the wilderness till the day of his manifestation to Israel" (*Lk. 1:80*).

### THE NATIVITY OF JESUS

"In those days a decree went out from Caesar Augustus that all the world should be enrolled. This was the first enrollment, when Quirinius was governor of Syria. And all went to be enrolled, each to his own city" (*Lk. 2:1–3*).

For a long time, many scholars doubted the accuracy of Luke's record, for it was believed that only one census took place while Quirinius was governor of the province of Syria and that it was several years after the birth of Jesus. In recent years, however, it has been established that there was an earlier census, and that it took place in the year 7–6 B.C., the year to which we have assigned the birth of Jesus. At that time, Augustus had decided to levy a new tax on the empire, and ordered every subject of the Roman government to register in his home city. Although Joseph lived in Nazareth, his family

**Caesar Augustus, from a full-length statue.**

was associated with Bethlehem in Judea, so he had no choice but to go there and to take Mary with him. It was a long, hard trip for Mary because the time had come for her child to be born. When they arrived in Bethlehem, they found the city packed with travelers and were unable to get a room at the inn, so they bedded down in the stable. During the night, Mary gave birth to her firstborn son and wrapped him in swaddling cloths, and laid him in a manger.

We have all viewed many representations of this scene, usually under circumstances that were most pleasant: in a store window after a happy shopping trip; in a churchyard with carols playing in the background; on Christmas cards in the cozy warmth of our homes. Because of this, most of us have become sentimental about it. It is entirely proper that this scene should fill us with joy and peace and goodwill, but it is also important to remember that the birth of Jesus

389

did not occur in a store window, or a church yard, or a cozy home, and that it was not attended with much romance. There is nothing lovely or charming about walking through dark streets with a pregnant wife looking for a room, or delivering a baby without a midwife in a cold and drafty cave or shed, or laying a two-hour-infant in a feeding trough because the only alternative is the dirty ground. And smiles do not come easily to a mother who wonders if the world has a place for her child.

In this little wooden feed trough in a stable out behind an inn lay the Savior of the world, and no one knew about it—at least not yet. But the angels around the throne of God knew, and before long they had spread the word to others. The first to hear the glad tidings were "shepherds out in the field, keeping watch over their flock by night." Suddenly, the glory of the Lord shone round about them and an angel said to them, "Be not afraid; for behold, I bring you good news of a great joy which will come to all the people; for to you is born this day in the city of David a Savior, who is Christ the Lord" (*Lk. 2:10–11*). Suddenly there was with the angel a multitude of the heavenly host praising God and saying:

> Glory to God in the highest,
> and on earth peace among men
> with whom he is pleased!
> —*Luke 2:14*

When the angel went away, the shepherds hurried to Bethlehem to see the child, and they told Mary and the others who had gathered what the angel had said about the infant. Luke tells us that "Mary kept all these things, pondering them in her heart" (*2:19*).

On the eighth day the infant was circumcised and given the name Jesus. On the fortieth day, his parents took him to the temple in Jerusalem for the ceremony of purification in which children were "presented" to the Lord. While they were at the temple; a man named Simeon came in. Simeon was a righteous man who had longed devoutly for the coming of Messiah. When he saw the holy infant, he took him in his arms and praised God and said:

> Lord, now lettest thou thy servant depart
> in peace,
> according to thy word;
> for mine eyes have seen thy salvation
> which thou hast prepared in the presence
> of all peoples,
> a light for revelation to the Gentiles,
> and glory to thy people Israel.
> —*Luke 2:29-32*

Joseph and Mary marveled at Simeon's words. He blessed them also; then, turning to Mary, he said:

> Behold, this child is set for the fall and rising
> of many in Israel,
> and for a sign that is spoken against
> (and a sword will pierce through your own
> soul also),
> that thoughts out of many hearts may be
> revealed.     —*Luke 2:34-35*

### THE VISIT OF THE MAGI AND
### THE FLIGHT TO EGYPT

Luke has given us an account of Jesus' infancy that is filled with joy and triumph, that brims with exultation over the knowledge that the Savior of mankind is born in Bethlehem. Except for the conditions of Jesus' birth, which he passes over in one verse (*2:7*), all he records glows with humility and gratitude and love for God. Matthew, however, introduces a note of intrigue and terror into the narrative (*ch. 2*).

In the ancient East and Near East, men were greatly concerned to arrive at the secrets of the universe, to discover the principles by which God (or the gods) runs the universe, and thus to be able to know what to expect of the future and to prepare for it accordingly. The wisdom movement, which flourished all over this area, was one attempt along these lines. By gathering and comparing the observations of sages from all nations, men hoped to be able to construct a blueprint for the good life. Some of these "wise men," especially those of Media, Persia, and Babylonia, branched out into the interpretation of dreams and the observation of the movements of the stars as a means of divining the will and purposes of God.

The wise men, or magi, who came to visit Jesus belonged to this latter class. As they searched the heavens for clues to the meaning of life, they had noticed one star that was unusually bright. They inferred from its brightness that a new king had been born in Judea and they came to pay homage to him. When Herod the Great heard this, he was troubled, as was most of Jerusalem. He gathered the chief priests and scribes together and asked them where the Messiah was to be born. They told him that Bethlehem was the expected place and cited the following passage from the prophet Micah in support of their claim:

And you, O Bethlehem, in the land of Judah,
are by no means least among the rulers
    of Judah;
for from you shall come a ruler
who will govern my people Israel.
            —Matthew 2:6; cf. Micah 5:2

Herod then sent for the wise men and asked them to let him know when they found the child, as he would like to go and worship him also.

Matthew tells us the wise men followed the star until they came to the house in Bethlehem where Joseph and his family were living. As Bethlehem was Joseph's native city, it seems likely that they had moved in with a relative or an old friend. When the magi saw the child, they worshiped him and offered him the fabled gifts of gold, frankincense, and myrrh. "And being

warned in a dream not to return to Herod, they departed to their own country by another way" (Mt. 2:12).

When Herod realized the wise men had tricked him, he flew into a furious rage and issued a decree that all male children under the age of two who lived in and around the city of Bethlehem should be slain, hoping, of course, to kill Jesus in the wholesale slaughter. This horrible scheme also failed, for Joseph had been warned in a dream that Herod would try to kill Jesus and he had fled with his family to Egypt. There they remained until the death of Herod in 4 B.C. Apparently, Joseph intended to settle in Judea, but when he learned that Herod's son Archelaus was ruling the province, he kept going until he reached Nazareth.

Matthew's assertion that this incident in Jesus' life fulfilled the prophecy found in *Hosea 11:1*—"Out of Egypt have I called my son"—is distressing to some readers, as are other examples of the use of Old Testament prophecies in the New Testament. In the context of the oracle in which it occurs, this phrase seems clearly to refer to the historical nation of Israel, for the next verse says, "The more I called him, the more they went from me; they kept sacrificing to the Baals, and burning incense to idols" (*Hos. 11:2*). This could hardly be said to refer to Jesus. And yet, the application of *11:1* to Jesus is meaningful because in him all that individualites and Israel as a nation were ever intended to be is summed up and perfectly personified. He was the first fruits of the New Creation to which the prophets had pointed. He would mediate a New Covenant, written on human hearts, to replace the Old Covenant written on tables of stone. It is thus understandable, and even perfectly fitting, that Matthew should see the act that created Israel—the exodus—as an antetype of this event in the life of Jesus, the Beginning of the New Israel.

### JESUS AS A YOUTH

It would be fascinating to have a fat volume entitled *Jesus and How He Grew*. It would tell us the kinds of food he liked, how he felt when he had to stay home from the synagogue service with the measles, or how his mother felt when a deadly epidemic swept through Nazareth. It would tell how he got along with his brothers and sisters, how he reacted when his dog died, how well he learned to use the tools in his father's carpenter shop. It would tell us what kind of games he was good at, and whether his playmates liked him. It would tell us how much time he spent reading the Old Testament and the literature produced by the rabbis, and what authors he may have read besides these—perhaps he, like young men today, knew and appreciated the classic tragedies of Aeschylus, Sophocles, and Euripides, or perhaps he chuckled at the comedies of Aristophanes.

Yes, such information would be fascinating, and if our gospels were biographies, as we usually conceive of biographies, they would surely contain considerable material dealing with the thirty-odd years between Jesus' infancy and his public ministry. But they were not, and they do not. Despite our disappointment, perhaps it is best they do not. For if they did, we might give more attention to these things than to the things that really matter. If we knew what foods Jesus liked, we might make a fetish of eating the same things, though our own diet may be tastier and more nutritious. If we knew what games he enjoyed, we might force our children to play them, which would be pointless, perhaps even unhealthy. If we knew what books he read, we might spend an unreasonable amount of time trying to figure out how much influence Aristophanes' play, *The Clouds*, had on Jesus' use of nature symbolism, or trying to solve some of the

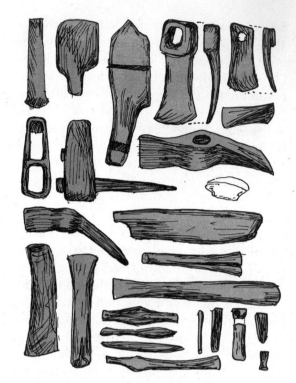

Ancient carpenter tools found in Palestine.

other problems that keep scholars out of mischief.

The Gospel writers preserve us from all these temptations by sticking to their task of producing not biographies, but what we have characterized as "theological writings that set forth the central features of the message of salvation within a broad historical framework" (*p. 388*). The period between the infancy and the beginning of the public ministry apparently contributed nothing of importance to this task, so the writers of our gospels almost completely ignored it.

The only event from this period of which we have any knowledge whatever is the well-known visit to the temple at the age of twelve. Joseph and Mary were devoutly religious parents. They traveled to Jerusalem every year to celebrate the feast of Passover. This particular year, they started home along with a large crowd of pilgrims. They knew, of course, that Jesus was not with them, but they supposed he was walking with relatives or friends in another part of the crowd and would join them when they stopped for the night. When they discovered he was not with the group at all, they hurriedly returned to Jerusalem, where they found him in the temple, "sitting among the teachers, listening to them and asking them questions; and all who heard him were amazed at his understanding and his answers". When Mary scolded him for causing them so much anxiety, Jesus calmy replied: "How is it that you sought me? Did you not know that I must be in my Father's house?" Luke tells us that again his parents did not fully understand the significance of what they were hearing, but "his mother kept all these things in her heart" (*Lk. 2:46–47*).

The remainder of Jesus' youth and early manhood is summed up by Luke in one short verse: "And Jesus increased in wisdom and in stature, and in favor with God and man" (*Lk. 2:52*).

## The Time of Preparation: John the Baptizer

In the fall of A.D. 27, "in the fifteenth year of the reign of Tiberius Caesar, Pontius Pilate being governor of Judea, and Herod (Antipas) being tetrarch in Galilee, . . . in the high-priesthood of Annas and Caiaphas, the word of God came to John the son of Zechariah" (*Lk. 3:1–2*).

In the closing words of his book, the prophet Malachi, speaking for Yahweh, had written: "Behold I will send you Elijah the prophet before the great and terrible day of the Lord comes" (*Mal. 4:5*). As the hope for a Messiah revived, the Jews began to look for the return of the fiery prophet of Israel. Elijah had been a rustic creature who lived in caves and hills and by the side of brooks, showing up in the city to deliver his words of doom and then disappearing into

the wilderness again. And so, it is not surprising that when this John suddenly appeared wearing a garment of camel's hair and a leather girdle around his waist and living on a diet of locusts and wild honey (*Mt. 3:4*), and declaring that the Day of the Lord was near, great crowds flocked out to hear him. Later, Jesus was to say that indeed John was the "Elijah they had been expecting (*Mt. 11:11–15*).

Matthew, Mark, and Luke all speak of John's ministry as the fullfillment of a prophecy found in *Isaiah 40:3*. Both of them quote this passage as it appears in the Septuagint, the Greek translation of the Hebrew scriptures: "The voice of one crying in the wilderness, 'Prepare the way of the Lord.'" In the original Hebrew text, however, the passage reads "A voice cries, '*In the wilderness* prepare the way of the Lord," or, to make the intention even more clear, "Prepare the way of the Lord in the wilderness." Our discussion of Israelite hopes during the period of the exile showed that the captives in Babylon were expecting Yahweh to lead them back to Jerusalem along a gloriously blooming pathway through the desert-wilderness. Thus, the Septuagint translation and the use of the text by the gospel writers alter the original meaning of the passage somewhat. Since the Septuagint was in common use and since its translation fit the situation better than the original text, it was natural they should use the passage in this way. This need not cause us any discomfort. The important thing was not the physical location of the voice or the path, but the news that the Lord was coming.

When the Israelites first began to expect the Day of the Lord, they apparently thought of it as a day when God would relieve Israel of all her misery and elevate her to a position high above the nations. Amos, however, launched a frontal attack on this self-centered smugness with these words:

Woe to you who desire the day of the Lord!
　　Why would you have the day of the Lord?
It is darkness, and not light; as if a man fled
　　from a lion, and a bear met him;
or went into the house and leaned
　　with his hand against the wall,
　　and a serpent bit him.
Is not the day of the Lord darkness,
　　and not light,
and gloom with no brightness in it?
　　　　　　　　　　　　—Amos 5:18-20

From the mid-eighth century B.C. onward, the prophets regularly balanced their descriptions of the glories of the Day of the Lord with a warning that it would also be a day of judgement on the wicked. John likewise sounded both these notes. At the Lord's coming in power, the valleys would be filled, the mountains brought low, the rough ways made smooth, and all flesh would see the salvation of God (Lk. 3:5–6). At the same time, though, the ax would be laid to the root of the trees, and the trees that did not bear good fruit would be cut down and thrown into the fire. The harvest of the fields would be separated, and the chaff would be burned with unquenchable fire. Even the religious leaders who came out to hear John were warned they could not expect automatic participation in the glories of the Lord's coming just because they were descendants of Abraham. God could make Jews out of stones. It was not their bloodline that would prepare them for the Day of the Lord, but a genuine repentance, a turning away from their sin to the paths of righteousness.

The sign and seal of this repentance was baptism, which John administered in the River Jordan. This baptism was a symbol of one's wholehearted willingness to do the will of God, and carried with it the assurance of pardon from past sins. It was also a preparation for the coming of him who would baptize with the Holy Spirit. Al-

though we have not heard of baptism previously in the Bible, it was not an altogether unfamiliar rite in first century Palestine. From other sources, we know that Gentiles who converted to Judaism were customarily baptized as a sign of their initiation into their new life. Also, ritual washings were a regular part of Essene life, as we have seen. In recent years, it has become fashionable in scholarly circles to suggest that John had spent some time among the Essenes before he began his ministry. In the present state of our knowledge, it is impossible to say whether or not this was the case, but the fact that John's baptism was a one-time occurrence, and not a regularly repeated act, and the fact that John did not require his disciples to undergo any formal program of candidacy makes it clear that he was not trying to duplicate what was going on in the Essene community at Qumran.

Some thought John himself was the Messiah, but he would have none of this. He was merely a forerunner, he insisted, and was not good enough to untie the shoes of the One who was to come.

### THE BAPTISM AND TEMPTATION OF JESUS

"In these days Jesus came from Nazareth in Galilee to be baptized of John in the Jordan" (Mk. 1:9). Jesus had not yet begun his ministry, and the Bible tells us nothing of any previous contact between the two, but John had at least some inkling of the nature and mission of this one who was presenting himself for baptism, for he objected to Jesus' request, saying, "I need to be baptized by you, and do you come to me?" But Jesus insisted, claiming that it was necessary for him to be baptized "to fulfill all righteousness" (Mt. 3:15). There has been much speculation as to exactly what Jesus meant by this. There is no way to be absolutely sure, but he apparently regarded it as the symbol of his wholehearted dedication to the purposes of God and therefore as a dramatic sign that his own ministry was about to begin. So John baptized him. As he arose from the water, he received divine ordination for his ministry, for "behold, the heavens were opened, and he saw the Spirit of God descending like a dove, and alighting on him; and lo, a voice from heaven, saying, 'This is my beloved son, with whom I am well pleased'" (*Mt. 3:16–17*).

Immediately after his baptism, the Spirit led Jesus into the wilderness to be tempted by Satan. The temptations were those he faced throughout life. Introducing them with the taunting "If you are the Son of God"—a taunt that followed Jesus everywhere, even to the cross (see *Lk. 23:35–39*)—Satan attempted to provoke Jesus into using his messianic powers: 1) to satisfy his own physical desires or those of his followers ("Command these stones to become loaves of bread"), 2) to impress the crowds that clamored for a sign ("Throw yourself down; for it is written, 'I will give the angels charge of you'"), and 3) to achieve earthly power and glory ("All these I will give you, if you will fall down and worship me"). In each case, Jesus answered with an Old Testament passage that expressed his repudiation of the popular notions concerning the Messiah. "And when the devil had ended every temptation, he departed from him until an opportune time" (*Lk. 4:13*).

### THE ARREST AND DEATH OF JOHN

With the baptism of Jesus, John's public ministry reached its climax. Shortly afterward, his preaching led to a decision by Herod Antipas to arrest him and lock him up. The gospel writers tell us Herod was irritated because John had publicly denounced his adulterous relationship with Herodias, who was his brother's wife (*Mk 6:17–29*). Josephus says that Antipas feared an uprising. Both could easily be true.

Copper Coins of Herod the Great (above) and Herod Agrippa II (below).

John apparently remained in prison for some time. Meanwhile, Jesus had begun teaching publicly and had attracted considerable attention with his mighty works. John heard of these wondrous deeds and sent his disciples to ask Jesus, "Are you he who is to come, or shall we look for another?" (*Mt. 11:2–3*). Jesus replied in the manner that was to become characteristic of him. So often during his ministry when he was asked a direct question, instead of giving a simple yes or no answer, he asked another question, or told a story, or made an oblique observation and left his audience to draw their own conclusion. To the question of John's disciples he said, "Go and tell John what you see and hear: the blind receive their sight and the lame walk, lepers are cleansed and the deaf hear, and the dead are raised up, and the poor have good news preached to them." Then, especially for John it seems, he added, "And blessed is he who takes no offense in me" (*Mt. 11:4–6*).

As John's disciples left, Jesus paid a mar-

395

velous tribute to this wilderness preacher. What had they expected when they went out to hear John? Had they thought they would find a glory-seeker who would bend with every wind of opinion to hold his following? Had they gone out to hear a polished orator in fine garments? If their purpose had been to have their ears tickled, then surely they must have been disappointed. But if they had gone out to see a prophet, that was a different matter, for "among those born of women there has risen no one greater than John the Baptist." As a matter of fact, said Jesus, John was the Elijah whom the Jews had been expecting since the days of Malachi. And yet, those who were ready for the kingdom to which John had pointed would receive power that not even this mighty prophet possessed (*Mt. 11:7–15*).

Had it been left to Herod Antipas, John might eventually have been set free, for Herod knew that John had done nothing to deserve death and had been careful not to harm him. It perplexed him to talk with John, "And yet," Mark tells us, "he heard him gladly" (*Mk. 6:21*). But Herodias, who did not like John's opposition to her adulterous marriage to Antipas, conspired to have him killed. At a birthday celebration for Antipas, Herodias' daughter, whom tradition has called Salome, danced for the king and pleased him so much that he asked her to name any gift she desired. At the urging of her mother, the girl asked for the head of John the Baptist on a platter. Herod Antipas feared the reaction of the multitude that followed John, but he had made a bold promise in front of a large assembly and could not back out. A soldier was sent to the prison to behead John. The gift was then presented to the girl, who gave it to her mother. What Herodias did with her grisly trophy we are not told, but when John's disciples heard what had happened, they came and took his body and gave it a decent burial. The task of the Forerunner had been accomplished; that of the Fulfiller was just beginning.

## The Beginning of the Galilean Ministry

In the spring of A.D. 28, shortly after Herod arrested John, "Jesus came into Galilee, preaching the gospel of God" (*Mk. 1:14*). The great bulk of Jesus' ministry occurred in his native region of Galilee. There he performed most of his mighty works and spoke most of his matchless parables. In every town and village, crowds flocked to the synagogue to hear him preach or brought their sick to his quarters to be healed. When he went into the wilderness to seek a bit of solace, they followed him. They recognized him to be a man of courage, gentleness, and wisdom that exceeded that of the scribes. And some recognized him to be even more than that.

At the outset of his public ministry, Jesus selected several men to assist him in spreading the good news about the coming of the Kingdom of God. One would expect that he would go to the synagogues to look for scribes and rabbis, but he did not. Professional religious men were not what he needed to communicate his message to the people of Galilee. Instead, he walked down by the Sea of Galilee and mingled with the fishermen. The first he chose were Andrew and his brother Simon, whom Jesus called Peter. They had been disciples of John and knew something of Jesus already (*John 1:40–42*). When Jesus approached them, they were casting their nets into the sea. With characteristic aptness he said to them, "Follow me and I will make you become fishers of men." So magnetic was the personality of this man who stood before them that without another word they left their nets and followed him. As he continued down the shore, he found James and Paul, the sons of Zebedee, mending their nets. He called them and they, like Andrew and Peter, immediately followed, leaving their father and his servants standing in the boats, probably staring in disbelief (*Mk. 1:16–20*). The next day, he found Philip, and Philip found Nathaniel, an Israelite in whom was no guile (*John 1:43–51*). Not long afterward, Jesus met a man named Levi, who is better known to most Bible students as Matthew. Levi was one of the hated class of Jews who had turned their backs on their countrymen to become tax collectors for the Roman government. One would scarcely think such a man would have an interest in the gospel, but when Jesus called him, he, like the others, arose and followed. In fact, Levi was so taken with Jesus that he held a banquet to introduce Jesus and his disciples to his fellow publicans (*Mk. 2:15f*). Eventually, Jesus chose twelve such special disciples whom he called apostles (*Mk. 3:13–19*). It has been suggested that Jesus chose twelve apostles to correspond to the twelve sons of Jacob and that he intended them to be the spiritual ancestors of the New Israel, as the Twelve Patriarchs had been of the old. It is impossible to say whether this was actually Jesus' intention, but the parallell is striking in any case.

With this band of unlikely associates who had forsaken all to follow him, Jesus began the ministry that changed the world.

## The Kingdom of God

As Mark points out in the passage quoted above, the central and controlling emphasis of Jesus' ministry was the imminent coming of the Kingdom of God. Unfortunately, there is no chapter in the gospels entitled *"The Theory and Practice of the Kingdom of God,"* so we have to piece together our understanding of the Kingdom from the great mass of direct and indirect statements about it that appear throughout the gospels. The task is not really an easy one, and there is no absolute guarantee that we will come out with the right answers, as few concepts in the Bible have been the subject of more debate and disagreement than this one. Still, we have no choice but to make the effort, for it is virtually impossible to make sense of the person and work of Jesus unless we have some understanding of what he thought about the Kingdom of God and his relation to it.

To begin, we should notice that the Greek word for "kingdom" (*basileia*) emphasizes the "kingly rule" or "reign" or "sovereignty" of God rather than the geographical territory of the Kingdom. Jesus was not proclaiming that Palestine was about to be wrested out of Roman hands and reorganized as some sort of Jewish super-state. He was saying that God's sovereignty over his creation would soon become—indeed, was already in the process of becoming—visibly manifest in the stream of history.* Jesus proclaimed the good news about this inbreaking of the Reign of God in both major aspects of his ministry, his mighty works and his public teaching.

### "MIGHTY WORKS, AND WONDERS, AND SIGNS"

One of the points we made in discussing the temptation was that Jesus refused to use his mighty powers and prerogatives to prove that he was the son of God, or to satisfy his or his disciples' physical needs, or to draw attention to himself by means of spectacular miracles. He was not a traveling magician with a bagful of extraordinary tricks which he used to gain a following. He was

---

*The alternative phrase, "Kingdom of Heaven," means the same thing. Because they feared they might unintentionally transgress the third commandment—"You shall not take the name of the Lord your God in Vain"—Jews frequently used expressions like "Heaven" to avoid direct reference to God.

the evangelist anointed by God to proclaim the gospel of the Kingdom. It is true that he performed many "mighty works, and wonders, and signs." It is also true that these did relieve physical needs, that crowds did flock to him when they heard about them, and that, as the gospel of John points out, they did provide evidence of his divinity (*John 20:30–31*). But these were by-products, and not the primary aim.

The mighty works that attended the ministry of Jesus were signs, given by God, that the grip of evil upon the world was being broken. When John sent from prison to find out if Jesus was really "he who is to come," if the Reign of God was really beginning, Jesus answered by pointing to the things God was doing through him—"the blind receive their sight and the lame walk, lepers are cleansed and the deaf hear, and the dead are raised up" (*Mt. 11:2–6*). Had he desired, he could have added that palsy and epilepsy and other diseases being cured, and withered hands restored, and fever removed, and hemorrhages stopped, and storms stilled.* All these bore witness to the fact that the long night of darkness was passing away and the day Israel had yearned for was about to dawn.

*Casting Out Demons.* The healing miracles of Jesus were impressive, but the acts that declared most decisively that the forces of evil were under all-out attack were his exorcisms of demons. In his Galilean ministry, Jesus cast out demons on many occasions, culminating in the spectacular case of the Terror of the Gerasene Graveyard, in which a "legion" of demons was expelled and sent into a large herd of swine, which then ca-

reened into the sea and drowned (*Mk. 5:1–20;* see also *Mk. 1:21–27, 39; Lk. 4:41; Mt. 9:32–33; 12:22,* etc.).*

Jesus' opponents could not deny that he had really performed some startling exorcisms. All they could do was impugn the source of his power to do it. In a bit of interesting logic, they charged that it was by the power of Beelzebul, the prince of demons, that he cast out demons. Jesus replied with an argument that not only unmasked the weakness of the charge, but explained the true significance of his exorcisms.

If, for the sake of argument, it were granted that he was in league with Beelzebul, this would mean that the Kingdom of Satan was divided against itself and could not stand; thus, even if their charge were true, it did not affect the growth of his proclamation that the reign of evil was being overthrown. On the other hand, if it were by the Spirit† of God that he was casting out demons, this was a sure sign the Kingdom of God had come upon them, for one cannot enter a strong man's house and plunder his goods unless the strong man is first bound. That is to say: It would not be possible to be wreaking such havoc with Satan's demons unless Satan's power had already been drastically reduced (*Mt. 10:22–32*). And

---

*Tables of Jesus' miracles often appear among the reference material found in the back of many Bibles. These help the student to see at a glance the different kinds of miracles Jesus performed and where they are recorded in the gospels. One such table is found in the appendix of *The Layman's Bible Encyclopedia* (Nashville, Tennessee: The Southwestern Co.), a helpful companion to this volume.

*Here and in other places in this chapter when reference is made to an event or teaching that is recorded in two or three of the gospels, the passage cited in the text will be the fullest account. When *Matthew* and/or *Luke* contain an account of an event or teaching that is identical or virtually identical to that found in *Mark*, the Markan passage will be cited, since *Mark* is believed to have been the earliest gospel and was probably a chief source of the other two (see discussion above, p. 383). Parallel passages may be found by consulting the center columns or footnotes of reference Bibles, or charts in the appendix of many Bibles that attempt to harmonize the four gospels, or such study aids as books in which the full texts of the gospels are arranged in parallel columns. If one remembers the warning against taking such attempts to harmonize the gospels too seriously (p. 386), these reference tools can be helpful in showing how each writer adapted (if he adapted) the basic material to serve the particular purposes of his account of the gospel.

†Luke says "the finger of God" (*Lk. 11:20*).

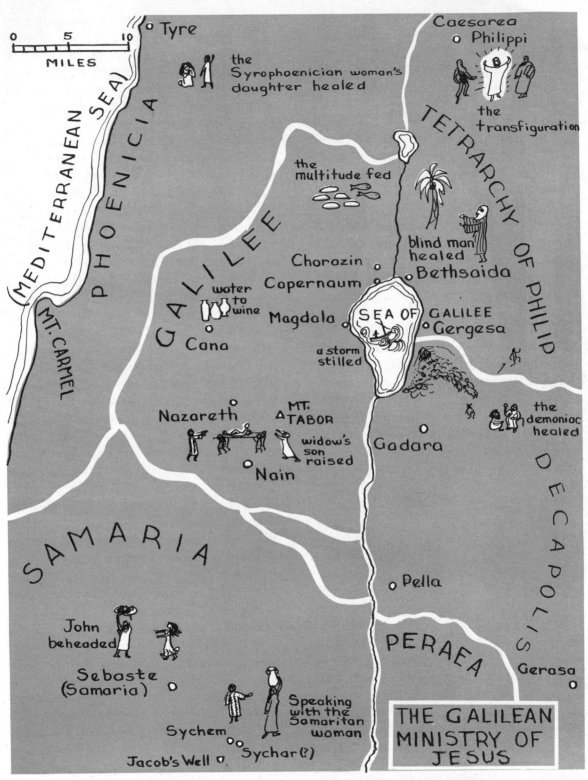

The Galilean ministry of Jesus: his power over diseases, demons, and the hearts of men.

this was exactly what the breaking in of the Reign of God signified.

Before passing on to Jesus' teaching about the Kingdom, some word about the whole matter of demons is in order. In New Testament times, the existence of demons was taken for granted. They were thought to be ministers of Satan, or Beelzebul (sometimes spelled Beelzebub), and were regarded as responsible for a wide variety of disease and disorder. It was therefore quite natural that the exorcisms performed by Jesus and his disciples should attract wide attention. All this talk of demons and exorcisms is somewhat troubling to many thoughtful modern readers. Did such spirits of the nether regions really exist in Jesus' time? If they did, do they exist now?

The usual solution to the problem is to conclude that first century men *interpreted* various physical and emotional disorders as the work of unseen spirits. At a later time in history, the "humours" were blamed for some of these same problems. Now, of course, we know (or believe) these disorders are caused by such things as unfortunate combinations of genes, hormone imbalance, germs, unsatisfactory relationships between parents and children, and other "natural" causes.

From a strictly rationalistic standpoint, this appears to be a rather simple, commonsense way out of the difficulty. But what are we to make of the apparently undeniable fact that Jesus seems to have shared the attitude of his first-century contemporaries toward demons? We may say that Jesus knew there were really no demons but that he used the familiar language in order to communicate with the common people. Or, we may contend that Jesus shared in the intellectual limitations of his age. We know he had physical and emotional limitations, for he grew hungry and weary, and was sometimes sad and depressed. It would not be

particularly surprising or inconsistent if he also believed in demons because everyone else believed in them, even though in fact no such beings actually existed. Or, we may conclude that demons did exist in the first century, that they did speak to Jesus in language that could be understood, and that they did change their place of residence from the Gerasene madman to a herd of swine. If we accept this viewpoint, we are faced with the question of whether demons still exist today. If they do, where do we find them? Are they the cause of emotional disturbances that seem difficult to account for on other grounds? Or have they disappeared from the scene, presumably as the result of the Reign of God?

Given our present state of knowledge and the lack of passages in the New Testament that make any real effort to explain a phenomenon that was taken for granted in the first century, each of these possible answers has its strong and weak points. The upshot of the matter is this: there seems to be nothing in our present experience that corresponds exactly to the phenomenon of demons as it is described in the New Testament. And yet, something dramatic was happening that had an enormous impact on the people who saw it happen. Whatever we may decide about the details of these accounts, it seems clear that men were receiving evidence—evidence that was meaningful to them—that what Jesus was saying about the coming of the Kingdom of God could not be lightly dismissed.

In these ways, then, the mighty works and wonders and signs that Jesus did bore witness to what God was doing on a cosmic level. Jesus seems to have thought it natural that those who saw them would repent and believe the gospel. If they did not, then judgment would fall upon their heads more heavily than if they had never seen them (*Mt. 11:21-24*).

### THE KINGDOM IN JESUS' TEACHING

Jesus' mighty works illustrated one facet of his proclamation about the Kingdom of God, namely, that it was already breaking into history. His oral teachings reinforce and add to this basic idea to give us a much fuller notion of his conception of the Kingdom.

Jesus taught in several ways. Like any traveling evangelist, he preached sermons and expounded on readings from the scripture. And when he taught, the people recognized that "he taught them as one having authority, and not as their scribes." He taught by the answers he gave to the questions of his disciples or to questions raised by his ememies in an effort to trap him into saying something they could use against him. And, of course, he taught them in parables. The great majority of Jesus' parables deal with some phase of the subject of the Kingdom of God. In a technical sense, a parable is a short, fictitious, and comparative narrative of something that might occur in real life, from which a moral or lesson can be drawn. In a broader sense, many of Jesus' similes, in which something he is discussing is said to be "like" something in another realm of human experience, could also be called parables. From the earliest times, Hebrew teachers had used parables, but Jesus brought this useful form of instruction to its highest development.

Parables were especially helpful in talking with people who had received no formal training in the scriptures and rabbinic theology, for even the most ignorant people could absorb and digest a parable, whereas direct language might prove to be beyond their comprehension. Many of Jesus' parables were of this simple, self-explanatory sort. But simplicity was not the only reason for using parables. In *Mark 4:10–12*, we are told that Jesus spoke in parables to confuse his opponents. His disciples would relate the parables to other things he had said, but his opponents would simply be puzzled and would have no opportunity either to trap him or to learn they were mistaken and join his following—apparently, Jesus knew their attitude was improper and did not want them for disciples. But this was a special use of the parables. To be sure, some are obscure, but when we see the simplicity of most of them, it becomes clear that their primary purpose was to reveal, not to puzzle.

It is difficult to put everything Jesus said into neat pigeonholes, but we can divide his teaching on the Kingdom into several broad categories.

*The Present Reality of the Kingdom.* The heart of Jesus' proclamation concerning the Kingdom, of course, was that it was at hand. This was basically what he came preaching. This was what his miracles were designed to show, as we have just seen. He also touched upon this theme in several of his parables. The Kingdom was already in their midst, he declared, but what they could see of it now was only a foretaste of what would develop. The Reign of God, he said, is like a tiny piece of leaven that is hidden in a lump of dough. It works quietly until it permeates the whole lump (*Mt. 13:33*). It is like a tiny mustard seed that grows in secret until it becomes a great tree so large that the birds of the air come and build their nests in its branches (*Mt. 13:31–32*). The seeds of the Kingdom were already being sown. Some would be too unconcerned, or too busy, or too fainthearted to accept it and allow it to bear fruit in their lives, but many would receive it and, in its own good time, it would issue in an abundant harvest (*Mk. 4:1–9, 14–20*). In all these ways, Jesus announced that the Reign of God was already operative and that its end results would be far out of proportion to its obscure and relatively unheralded beginnings.

*The Imminent Crisis.* Whereas John the Baptist had laced his sermons heavily with warnings of doom and calls to repentance, Jesus generally emphasized the brighter aspects of the coming of the Kingdom. Nevertheless, it was true that inseparable from the reign of God was the judgment that would fall on those who refused to acknowledge it. For them, the prospect of the consummation of the Kingdom constituted a real crisis. Those who tried to build their lives on shifting sands of self-righteous complacency instead of the solid rock of trust in God would be washed away in the floodtide of God's judgment (*Mt. 7:24–27*). Those who spent their time denouncing the imperfections of the "people of the land", who made little effort to keep the strict traditions of the Pharisees, were like men trying to remove a speck from the eye of another while the log in their own eyes was so great that it kept them from recognizing the signs of the Kingdom (*Mt. 7:3–5*).

The scribes and Pharisees should have had a natural advantage over their less scrupulous brethren because of their presumed acquaintance with the ways of God. But if they became more concerned with preserving what they had than with taking full advantage of that which was coming, they would be like men who made no effort to obtain advantage from the talent or pound their master had entrusted to their care. When he returned, they would be cast into outer darkness, where the only sounds are weeping and wailing and gnashing of teeth (*Mt. 25:14–30; Lk. 19:12–27*).

The time of this crisis was not far off. The present generation would not pass away before it came( *Mt. 24:34* etc.). As the leaves of a fig tree announce that summer is near, or a cloud in the west that a shower is coming, or a southwind that scorching heat will follow, so the signs of Jesus' ministry should make it clear that the Day was fast approaching (*Mk. 13:28; Lk. 12:54–56*). The banquet was being prepared. The first invitation would go out to the "righteous," but if they refused, they would be destroyed and their places taken by sinners and outcasts (*Mt. 22:2–14*).

*The Response to the Crisis.* If the Reign of God was to be an occasion of joy instead of a catastrophe of damning judgment, those who heard the word were called upon to repent and accept the gospel, with all its implications. The foremost sign of this repentance was to be thorough and abject humility. All who entered (or received) the Kingdom would have to become like little children (*Lk. 18:17*, etc,); that is, they would have to acknowledge their weakness and place their trust in their heavenly father rather than in themselves. In the parable of the laborers in the vineyard (*Mt. 20:1–16*), Jesus made it clear that those who counted themselves the righteous of Israel would have no advantage over anyone else who accepted the gospel. The blessings of the Kingdom were not bestowed because anyone earned them, because the Lord is gracious to those who trust in him.

Jesus spoke of the Kingdom as a magnificent treasure, a pearl of great value that was worth any price they had to pay to obtain it because of the great joy it would bring (*Mt. 13:44–46*). He promised that those who put the Kingdom first in their lives would not have to worry about food or raiment (*Mt. 6:25–33*). But he did not try to win disciples by promising them a life of ease. The cost of discipleship was high. Unless a man was willing to count and pay that cost, he would be better off not even trying to follow Jesus. There was no place in the field of the Lord's harvest for a half-finished or crooked furrow. No man should put his hand to the plow if he intended to look back (*Lk. 9:62*). No sensible man would start to build a tower unless he knew he could finish it, lest his friends mock him for his folly. No king would start a war with an army that was obviously inadequate. Neither should he attempt to enter the strait gate and walk on the narrow way unless he was prepared to renounce his claim on all that he had, including his property and his family, in order to follow Jesus (*Lk. 14:25–33*). This requirement of single-mindedness necessarily made it more difficult for a rich man to receive the gospel—"How hard it will be for those who have riches to enter the Kingdom of God! . . . It is easier for a camel to go through the eye of a needle" (*Mk. 10:23–25*). Rich men could be fools, thinking they could insure security by storing their treasures in magnificent barns, but these are of no avail in the face of death and judgment of God (*Lk. 12:16–21*). A poor man like Lazarus was more likely to inherit the riches of the Kingdom than the rich man at whose table he had begged (*Lk. 16:19–31*). The priests of the temple had extolled those who could make large contributions to the temple treasury, but Jesus ranked the two mites of a poor widow even higher, because she gave all that she had (*Mk. 12:41–4*).

Jesus did not mean that it was necessary for every disciple to sell all that he had and to abandon his wife and children as well, although that might be required of some. But he did mean that all these had to take second place to his relationship to the Kingdom. Nothing less than complete dedication to God would suffice. No man can attend to two treasures or serve two masters at the same time, for his heart will be with one and he will despise the other (*Lk. 12:33–34; Mt. 6:24*). To be acceptable, a man's life must be guided by the single principle of complete dedication to the purposes of God. This principle is like a sound eye or a bright lamp that guides a man and prevents him from stumbling (*Lk. 11:33–36*).

For some disciples there would doubt-less be heartbreak and persecution—father would turn against children and children would rise against their parents and conspire to have them put to death. Some, of course, would not stand firm, and these the son would deny before his heavenly father (*Mt. 10:17–33*). But those who did not hesitate to confess their faith in Jesus need have no fear, for the Spirit of God would stand by them and teach them how to answer their accusers. And those who lost their life for the sake of Christ would actually just be entering into life that is life indeed (*Mt. 10:17–39*).

*The Waiting Disciples.* Jesus professed not to know the precise day or hour of the coming of the judgment crisis (*Mk. 13:32;* see p. 402), but he admonished his disciples to wait for it in watchful alertness, as the friends of a bridegroom wait for him to come to the marriage feast (*Mt. 25:1–13*). The very attitude in which they waited would be a light to the unbelieving world (*Mt. 5:14–16*).

The identifying mark of the waiting disciples, the salt with which they flavored the human community (*Mt. 5:13*), would be their deep humility, for only "the poor in spirit" can receive the Kingdom of Heaven (*Mt. 5:3*). Again and again Jesus taught his disciples the absolute necessity of humility. In a story about a Pharisee and a publican, he hammered home the point that God prefers the humble and contrite to the self-righteous and arrogant (*Lk. 18:9–14*). In the parable of the marriage feast he illustrated the principle that "everyone who exalts himself will be humbled, and he who humbles himself will be exalted (*Lk. 14:7–11*). And when his beloved disciples, James and John, asked for a special place of glory when the Kingdom was fully come, he told them there was no place in the Kingdom for disputations over rank. If a man would be truly great, he must become a servant, for "whoever would be first among you must be slave of all" (*Mk. 10:35–45*). Jesus' most memorable instruction on humility, of course, came on the night of the Last Supper, when he took off his clothes and girded himself with a towel and washed his disciples' feet. This was a task usually performed by the humblest of servants. Lest any miss the point of this acted parable, Jesus said to his disciples after he had dressed and resumed his place at the table: "Do you know what I have done to you? . . . I have given you an example that you also should do as I have done to you" (*Jn. 13:3–17*).

The wellspring of this monumental humility was gratitude for the unspeakable gift of God's merciful forgiveness and for his hungry desire to accept and cherish those who would throw themselves upon him. The knowledge that they were totally undeserving of God's favor should lead them to avoid making harsh criticisms of the motives and actions of others (*Mt. 7:1–5*). It should also encourage a spirit of forgiveness and understanding of the shortcomings of others. A son who wasted his life but had been received into the loving arms of a father who was prodigal with his love should be able to show mercy and forgiveness to those who wronged him (*Lk. 15:11–32*). If a benevolent king forgave one of his servants a collossal debt and later learned that same servant had been harsh with a man who owed him a trifle, he would cast him into debtor's prison in anger. So, said Jesus, would God do to everyone of the disciples who did not forgive his brother from his heart (*Mt. 18:23–25*).

The crown that would mark the disciples as both servants and kings, of course, was to be love. As God had loved them, irrespective of their attitude toward him, so they were to love both their neighbors and their enemies, as much, even, as they loved themselves. A turned cheek, the gift of a cloak, a second mile, an open moneybag, a wounded man

being treated by a Samaritan—these were the symbols of the extent to which love might be asked to go (*Mt. 5:38–42; Lk. 10:30–37*). Even if a disciple were never slapped in the face, or forced by a Roman soldier to carry his equipment for a mile, or (less likely) approached by a neighbor for a loan, these striking examples would challenge his imagination whenever he was seeking the loving act.

So Jesus taught concerning the present and coming Reign of God.

## Jesus and Judaism

Wherever Jesus went, the crowds gathered to listen and ask him questions. Many were drawn by an earnest desire for a right relationship with God. Others came because they hoped to gain some material advantage from their association with this wonder-working prophet. Since Galilee was a hotbed of revolutionary activity, some saw Jesus as a potential leader for a new effort to throw off the Roman yoke. But in almost every crowd that gathered there were also some who saw Jesus as a threat to everything they stood for. Ironically, yet true to Israel's past record, these were not Roman officials who feared a rebellion, but religious leaders who feared a prophet. Throughout Jesus' ministry, he was harassed by scribes and Pharisees, priests and Levites. Finally, they succeeded in nailing him to the cross.

In some respects, this opposition to Jesus is surprising. After all, it was not as if he had come in the manner of a Hellenistic philosopher, speaking of things he had learned from Plato or Zeno or Epicurus (see p. 437ff). He dressed and spoke and behaved like a rabbi. He attended the synagogue services and observed the Jewish holy days. When he taught, he often quoted the Old Testament, which he regarded as the sacred and inspired record of God's revelation to men. He grounded his teaching on the same foundation that supported the Law of Moses: the goodness of God. He emphasized the value of prayer and instructed his disciples in its practice. Surely these were not the cause of the hostility toward Jesus. Neither should it have been particularly offensive for a Jewish religious teacher to announce that the Kingdom of God was at hand, since this theme held an honored place in the teachings of the prophets and in the soul of first-century Judaism. Why, then, did they challenge him and harass him and, finally, crucify him? It is always risky to try to account for a complex phenomenon in terms of a single underlying cause, but there is one factor that shows up again and again in Jesus' disputations with his opponents: the threat he represented to the traditions, and hence to the authority, of the scribes.

The scribes and Pharisees accused Jesus of blasphemy but what Jesus had called into question was not the will of God, but what the scribes and Pharisees had decided the will of God *ought* to be. In the long history of organized religion, it has been demonstrated countless times that men can forgive the former more easily than the latter.

Three classic examples of Jesus' challenge to the scribal traditions are his attitude toward the Sabbath, toward sinners and outcasts, and toward ritual defilement.

### THE SABBATH

There were few institutions more sacred to the scribes than the Sabbath. In the spiritual crisis produced by the Babylonian Exile (see p. 294ff), religious leaders had seized upon Sabbath observance as a concrete measure of piety. Devices like this are handy for religious leaders. It is a relatively simple matter to determine whether or not one keeps the Sabbath. He either does or he does not. No difficult evaluation of his motives or attitudes are necessary. If enough devices can be discovered, or manufactured, the whole problem of motive and attitude can be dismissed. In the process, of course, the soul becomes warped and brittle, and a proper relationship to God is rendered impossible. But the appeal of convenience and self-assurance too often obscures this fact, as it had done in the time of Jesus. When he broke with the "official" viewpoint regarding the Sabbath, Jesus placed himself in direct conflict with men who no longer felt any need of the grace of God, because their own rules declared them righteous. And among religious men, these are the worst kind.

According to the Law, no work was to be done on the Sabbath. Even such normal, everyday activities as kindling a fire, or lifting a heavy object, or gathering food were forbidden. Ingenious rabbis had discovered, or created, loopholes in the Sabbath regulations that allowed some latitude in applying them, but no latitude was given for open violation of a Sabbath rule. So when Jesus allowed his disciples to pluck and eat grain on the Sabbath (*Mk. 2:23–27*), and when he healed the sick and infirm on the Sabbath (*Mk. 3:1–6*, etc.), his actions appeared as willful and flagrant violations of the Law of Moses.

In defense of the action of his disciples in the grainfield, Jesus pointed out that David and his men had eaten the shewbread from the tabernacle (*I Sam. 21:1–6*). According to the letter of the Law, none but the priests were to eat this bread, but Abiathar the high priest recognized that human need took precedence over technical regulations. The Sabbath, Jesus pointed out, had been given to benefit man, to assure him of sufficient respite from his labors for relaxation and meditation. To turn it into a straitjacket that ignored his needs was to pervert its whole significance—"the Sabbath was made for man, not man for the Sabbath" (*Mk. 2:27*). This perversion was underscored when his opponents reprimanded Jesus for healing people on the Sabbath. Healing was "work," they argued, and it should be confined to the other six days of the week. Jesus observed that their laws allowed a man to rescue an animal that fell into a pit on the Sabbath. Surely the healing of a human being was of greater importance than the saving of an animal—"of how much more value is man than a sheep!" (*Mt. 12:11–12; Lk. 14:5*).

Jesus' appeal to the higher law of love and mercy silenced the legalists, but their silence was not an expression of agreement, for the gospel writers report that "the Pharisees went out, and immediately held counsel with the Herodians against him, how to destroy him" (*Mk. 3:6*).

### THE MINISTRY TO OUTCASTS

Jesus' apparent disregard of the Sabbath regulations irritated his opponents mightily, but it came up, at most, only once a week. Every day, however, he greatly offended their religious scruples by the kind of people with whom he persistently associated. He talked with immoral women and ate with sinners. One of his disciples was a hated tax collector; who knows what some of the rest of them may have been! Wherever he went, he was followed by crowds of *'am haaretz*, ("people of the land"), the common folk who made no real attempt to keep the Law. If he had used his influence to get them to straighten up and start living like good Pharisees, he might have been forgiven. But instead, he received them warmly and told them God loved them and desired their salvation. Wherever he went, he emphasized that he had come to seek and save the lost. He told stories of lost sheep and lost coins and lost boys (*Lk. 15*), all designed to express God's loving concern for sinners and his joy over those who repented and accepted his gracious offer of salvation. The "righteous" of Israel had been invited to

share in the messianic feast, but had refused the invitation. Not their places would be taken by "the poor and maimed and blind and lame" (*Lk. 14:15–24*). Even the Great Physician could not heal those who would not admit they were sick (*Mk. 2:17*).

### RITUAL DEFILEMENT

Directly related to his mission to the poor and outcast was Jesus' attitude toward the scribal traditions concerning ritual defilement. To a good Pharisee, failure to wash before a meal, or eating food of which a tithe had not been offered to God, or eating out of the wrong kind of vessel rendered a man ceremonially "unclean," which meant he had to go through a prescribed process of purification before he could approach God in worship. To them, these regulations were the bread of life. When they came to hear Jesus preach, they did not rejoice that the audience consisted of former adulterers and thieves who were now "hungering and thirsting after righteousness." They complained that not all of them washed their hands before sitting down to eat. Fed up with their hypocrisy, Jesus recalled the words of the prophet *Isaiah*:

> This people honors me with their lips,
> but their heart is far from me;
> in vain do they worship me,
> teaching as doctrines the precepts of men.
> —*Mark 7:6-7* (*Isaiah 29:13*)

Then he attacked the whole system of hedges and loopholes that enabled them to regard themselves as the Holy People while, in fact, they were missing the point of both the Law and the Prophets. "You have," he said, "a fine way of rejecting the commandments of God, in order to keep your traditions!" As an example, he referred to a regulation that required a man to let his parents remain destitute rather than provide for them from money (or other goods) that had been pledged, even rashly, to God. The fifth of the Ten Commandments specifically forbade the neglect of parents, but these holy hand-washers had set this commandment aside in favor of one of their own traditions, which had no basis in scripture. "And" charged Jesus, "many such things you do" (*Mk. 7:13*).

Purity, taught Jesus, is not a matter of washing hands, or boiling plates, or avoiding certain foods. What goes into a man from outside cannot defile him, since it enters not his heart but his stomach. On the contrary, it is what comes out of a man that defiles him—"For from within, out of the heart of man, come evil thoughts, fornication, theft, murder, adultery, coveting, wickedness, deceit, licentiousness, envy, slander, pride, foolishness. All these evil things come from within, and they defile a man" (*Mk. 7:21–23*).

Thus, in the early stages of his ministry, Jesus provoked a serious, and ultimately fatal, rift with the most powerful forces in Judaism. He had not sought it, but there had been no way to avoid it, for the gospel of God's grace was, and is, in basic conflict with Pharisaic legalism.

### THE LAST STAGES OF THE GALILEAN MINISTRY

Despite the opposition of the scribes and Pharisees, Jesus' work appeared to be going quite well. The crowds were growing and enthusiasm was running high. Eager to reap the plenteous harvest that was ripening, Jesus called the Twelve together. He conferred on them the power to heal and cast out demons and gave them detailed instructions as to how to conduct their ministry. Then he sent them forth* to preach the gospel of the Kingdom to "the lost sheep of the house of Israel" (*Mt. 9:35–11:1*).

---

*The familiar term by which the Twelve are known —"apostle"—is derived from the Greek word for "send forth."

We do not know just how long the mission of the Twelve lasted, but it seems to have been the most productive period of the entire Galilean campaign. When they rejoined Jesus to give him a report on their activities, there were so many people swarming in and out of his home that they were unable to talk. So, they took a boat to a deserted area across the sea of Galilee. Even there they found no privacy, for the people recognized them in the boat and raced around the lake to meet them. Jesus must have been growing weary of this sort of thing, but "he had compassion on them" because they reminded him of sheep without a shepherd. So he taught them and healed their sick.

The crowd numbered well over five thousand (*Mt. 14:21*). When evening came, the disciples grew worried because they knew the people had brought no food and it was already past the time when they should have started home. Jesus was not troubled. He asked how much food was available. The disciples checked and found a grand total of five loaves of bread and two fishes, scarcely a banquet for five thousand. But Jesus instructed the people to divide into groups of hundreds and fifties and distributed the food to them. Not only was there enough for all, but twelve baskets of scraps were left over (*Mt. 6:30–44*).

The feeding of the multitude—the only miracle recorded in all four gospels—marked the climax of the great Galilean campaign, but it also brought it to a swift and unexpected close. The Gospel according to John tells us why: "When the people saw the sign which he had done, they said, 'This is indeed the prophet who is to come into the world!' Perceiving then that they were about to come and take him by force *to make him king*, Jesus withdrew again to the hills by himself." There, on the spot, the crowd wanted to make him their king. Perhaps

407

Palestine at the time of Jesus' ministry.

Jesus sensed that their impulse stemmed more from a desire to have a king who could take care of their material needs or mount a successful rebellion than from a conviction that in him the Reign of God was being accomplished. In any case, he had no intention of becoming the king of Galilee. He realized, however, that once the idea spread, this scene would be repeated every time he appeared in public. And so, before they could start a clamor, he persuaded the multitude to go home and retreated into the hills to be alone.

## Jesus, the Messiah, and the Son of Man

After the incident with the multitude, Jesus left Galilee to go into the Phoenician territories of Tyre and Sidon. This was not a mission tour. On the contrary, Jesus did his best to keep his movements a secret (*Mk. 7:24*), that he might find time for quiet reflection on the events of the last few hectic months. Then, aften an unspecified time, he came back to Galilee. Almost immediately, the people again flocked to him with their sick and afflicted. During this brief period, he again fed a large multitude with a handful of loaves and fishes (*Mk. 7:31–8:9*). Then he and his disciples set out for Caesarea Philippi, north of the sea of Galilee.

### THE CONFESSION AT CAESAREA PHILIPPI

On the way, Jesus asked the disciples what the people were saying about him. Who did they think he was? They replied that the crowds generally seemed to feel he was some sort of special representative sent from God, but beyond that, there was little agreement. Some thought he was John the Baptist; others thought he was Elijah or one of the other great prophets come back from the dead. "But who do *you* say that I am?" he asked. And Simon Peter answered, "You are the Christ (or Messiah)."

This incident was a major turning point in Jesus' career. Never in all his preaching and teaching about the Kingdom had he openly identified himself as Israel's long-awaited Messiah. His concern had been to proclaim that the Kingdom of God was at hand, not to explain his relationship to it. When the five thousand tried to make him King, however, he realized he could no longer avoid this question. So, when Peter made his confession, Jesus accepted it, but he strictly charged the disciples not to tell anyone else that he was indeed the Messiah. He had no intention of conforming to popular ideas about the Messiah and did not want to be forced into revealing the true nature of his mission until "the time was fully come." From this point on, he began to explain to his disciples something of what the future held for him and for them.

### THE SON OF MAN

It is a striking feature of these explanations that Jesus carefully avoided saying, "*I, Jesus*, will do such and such." Instead, at almost every point at which we would expect a reference in the first person ("I"), he substitutes the peculiar phrase, "the Son of man." Why did he do this? Was it simply a sign of modesty? Or did he use it because it had some special significance? This question has received a number of answers, but the more we examine these passages in the light of the messianic and apocalyptic expectations that were current in this period, the clearer it becomes that Jesus' choice of this title as a self-designation was far from accidental.

The title had two distinct advantages. On the one hand, it had been associated in Jewish apocalyptic thought with a Messiah-like figure. In the vision of the four beasts in *Daniel 7*, a triumphant figure appears who is described as "one like a son of man" (*Dan. 7:13*). After the beasts are slain, this

409

son of man is presented to the Ancient of Days.

> And to him was given dominion and glory
> and kingdom,
> that all peoples, nations, and languages
> should serve him;
> his dominion is an everlasting dominion,
> which shall not pass away,
> and his kingdom one
> that shall not be destroyed.
>
> —*Daniel 7:14*

On the other hand, the title had not been so widely used that popular thought with regard to it had become as fixed as it had with regard to the title "Messiah." By referring to himself as the Son of man, Jesus was able to talk about the nature of the messianic mission in a way that he could never have done had he used the term Messiah, which automatically conjured up visions of a national hero who would drive out the Romans and reestablish the throne of David.

*The Future Glory of the Son of Man.* In keeping with the idea expressed in *Daniel* 7, Jesus taught that the Son of man was preeminently a figure of great authority and judgment. In "the last days," which, as we have seen (p. *404*), were thought to be fast approaching, he would come in clouds of glory to judge the world (*Mk. 8:38; 14:62*). The elect would be gathered from the four winds by his holy angels, to shine forever in the Kingdom of his Father. But the wicked would be plucked out and thrown into the furnace of fire. (*Mk. 13:26; Mt. 13:41–43*). This spectacular advent of the heavenly figure would come without warning (*Mt. 24:43–44*). The disciples, therefore, if they were not to be cast into the fire, would have to "watch at all times, praying [for] strength to escape all those things, and to stand before the Son of man" (*Lk. 21:36*).

*The Present Role of the Son of Man.* The full revelation of the Son of man, then, like that of the Kingdom in which he would

reign, was still to be accomplished. Yet, again like the Kingdom, he was already active in the world in the present age, seeking the lost (*Lk. 19:10*), sowing the seed of the Kingdom (*Mt. 13:37*), proclaiming his lordship over the Sabbath (*Mk. 2:28*), and, most significant of all, claiming and using his authority to forgive sins (*Mk. 2:10*).

*Victory through Suffering.* These aspects of Jesus' teaching about the Son of man probably gave the disciples little difficulty. They had heard him forgive sins and declare his lordship over the Sabbath. If he was truly the Son of man, then obviously these were things the Son of man did. Neither was it particularly difficult for them to accept his statements about the future glorious reign of the Son of man. After all, the book of *Daniel* had painted a similar picture. There was, however, the question of how the transition was going to be made from the present to the future activity of the Son of man. Was he going to continue preaching and healing and casting out demons until the world acknowledged his sovereignty? Or would he simply drop out of sight for a few days and suddenly reappear in the clouds? It was to answer these questions that Jesus began to teach his disciples that "the Son of man must suffer many things, and be rejected ... and be killed, and after three days rise again" (*Mk. 8:31*).

The disciples were totally unprepared for this announcement. Peter, in fact, refused to accept it and rebuked Jesus for talking this way. He had just announced his conviction that Jesus was the Messiah and now Jesus was saying things that went completely contrary to anything he had ever thought about the Messiah. Jesus fairly hurled his reply at Peter: "Get behind me Satan! For you are not on the side of God, but of man" (*Mk. 8:33*). Jesus realized it would be difficult for people who had envisioned a triumphant Messiah to begin thinking in terms of One who had come "not to be served but to serve, and to give his life as a ransom for many" (*Mk. 10:45*). That was surely part of the reason he had not discussed the subject until it was forced upon him. But he could not allow popular sentiment or the preconceptions of his disciples to turn him for his ordained course. The victory Peter had envisioned would still come, but it would come through suffering, suffering unto death.

### THE TRANSFIGURATION

About a week after Peter's confession and the announcement that the Son of man would have to suffer before the messianic hope could be fulfilled, Jesus took what has been called the "inner circle" of his disciples—Peter, James, and John—up on a high mountain, "and he was transfigured before them, and his garments became glistening, intensely white, as no fuller on earth could bleach them. And there appeared to them Elijah and Moses, and they were talking to Jesus." As the disciples stood overwhelmed, "a cloud overshadowed them, and a voice came out of the cloud, 'This is my beloved Son, listen to him.' And suddenly looking around they no longer saw any one with them but Jesus only" (*Mk. 10:3–8*).

The disciples scarcely knew what to make of this experience. Mark tells us that even Peter "did not know what to say," a novel reaction for Peter. But without doubt, that which they had seen must have redoubled their conviction that truly, this was the Christ, the Son of the Living God.

## In Judea and Beyond the Jordan

"When the days drew near for him to be received up, he set his face to go to Jerusalem" (*Lk. 9:51*).

After the dramatic days in the region north of Galilee, Jesus decided the time had come for him to go to Judea. Passing through Galilee and Samaria, he arrived in Jerusalem at the time of the Feast of Tabernacles (*Jn. 7:2, 10*). For the first two or three days of the eight-day celebration, Jesus stayed out of sight, but the news that he was in the city inevitably leaked out and touched off a flurry of discussion. While some said, "He is a good man," others said, "No, he is leading the people astray." About the middle of the feast Jesus went up to the temple and began to teach publicly. This fanned the flames of controversy even higher. The scribes and Pharisees wanted to kill him, but they dared not try, for fear of the reaction of the people, who were hanging on his every word. The crowds knew the scribes and Pharisees wanted to kill him and wondered if the reason they had not done so, now that he was appearing regularly in public, was that they knew he was the Messiah, or Christ (*Jn. 7:25–26*). Many believed he was the Christ because of the signs he did (*Jn. 7:31*). Others, who did not know the details of his birth, argued that he could not be, because he was from Galilee, and the scriptures taught that the Messiah was to come from Bethlehem. And so it went until the feast of Dedication two months later (*Jn. 10:22*).

At that time, the crowd found Jesus walking in the temple grounds, in the portico of Solomon, where Peter was to preach a famous sermon several months later (see *Acts 3:11ff*). They pressed him hard on the question of his role. "How long will you keep us in suspense," they asked. "If you are the Christ, tell us plainly" (*Jn. 10:24*). Jesus responded by pointing to his mighty works as evidence that the Father was with him. Then, in a statement unlike any he had ever made before, he said, "I and the Father are one." Understandably, this struck the Jews as outright blasphemy, and they immediately picked up stones to stone him for his sin. His attempts to defend himself only heightened their anger, but he somehow

411

managed to escape them, at least for the time being (*Jn. 10:25–39*).

After this narrow escape, Jesus and his disciples withdrew to Perea, the region east of the Jordan. Not long afterward, Jesus received an urgent message from Mary and Martha, two disciples who lived in the village of Bethany, a suburb of Jerusalem, and in whose home he had visited when he first came to Judea at the time of the Feast of Tabernacles. Lazarus, the brother of Mary and Martha, had fallen gravely ill, and the sisters wanted Jesus to know about it, in the hope that he could heal him. Jesus dearly loved Mary and Martha and Lazarus, but he did not immediately rush to Bethany. When he finally did arrive, Martha came out to meet him with the news that Lazarus had already been dead four days. She was brokenhearted and could not help expressing her sorrow that the Master had not come sooner. Jesus reassured her with the words that have reassured Christians throughout the ages: "I am the resurrection and the life; he who believes in me, though he die, yet shall he live, and whoever lives in me and believes in me shall never die" (*Jn. 11:25–26*). Then Jesus, after weeping in sympathy for Mary and Martha, went to the tomb and called for Lazarus to come out. And "the dead man came out" (*Jn. 11:44*).

In many ways, this was the most dramatic of all Jesus' miracles, and the people flocked to Bethany to see if Lazarus was really alive and to get a glimpse of Jesus. John tells us that the chief priests (who were Sadducees) and the Pharisees gathered the Sanhedrin together to discuss the implications of this excitement. Their primary fear was that the people would create such a stir over Jesus that the Romans would assume a rebellion was brewing and would step in and crush the whole nation. "So from that day on, they took counsel how to put him to death" (*Jn. 11:53*).

Once again Jesus withdrew beyond the Jordan, this time to the little village of Ephraim, about twenty miles northwest of Jericho. As Passover drew near, he once again "set his face for Jerusalem." It was on this trip, as he passed through Jericho, that he healed blind Bartimaeus (*Mk. 10:46–52*) and visited in the home of the "wee little man," Zacchaeus the publican (*Lk. 19:1–10*). Then, six days before Passover, he came to Bethany, to the home of Mary and Martha and their brother Lazarus.

## The Final Week

Passover, you will remember, was celebrated in commemoration of the event that had called the people of God into being, the exodus from Egypt. It was the greatest of all the Jewish holidays and Jews from all over the world poured into Jerusalem to celebrate it. We mentioned earlier that the Roman governor usually came up from his headquarters at Caesarea to be in Jerusalem on major feast days, to make sure no trouble arose. Passover was an especially critical time, since the whole celebration centered around God's bringing deliverance from a foreign oppressor, a theme that could easily be exploited by a shrewd nationalist leader. This particular Passover must have been regarded as even more of a threat than usual, since it was widely suspected that Jesus would be in the city. So, the governor at that time, Pontius Pilate, had come to Jerusalem to keep an eye on things.

### THE TRIUMPHAL ENTRY

The day after Jesus arrived in Bethany, he went into Jerusalem itself. It was not a secret entry, as on his last trip to the city. But neither was it an ordinary entry. It was a triumphant entry, and yet, it was not triumphant in a customary fashion. Jesus did not ride on a white charger or in a chariot of war at the head of a legion of soldiers, as a

Roman general might. Instead, he came riding upon a lowly ass, with borrowed garments for a saddle. As word traveled that he was coming, a large crowd lined the road. Most of them spread their garments before him in the path. Others cut branches from palm trees and laid them before him as a sign of praise and homage. As he passed, they shouted the words of a familiar psalm:

Hosanna to the Son of David!
Blessed be he who comes in the name of
　　the Lord!
Blessed be the King of our father David
　　that is come!
Hosanna in the highest!
　　　　　　　　　—Mk. 11:9; Mt. 21:9

It is doubtful that the crowd had much of an idea as to the true nature of Jesus' mission, but they clearly recognized him as someone in whom lay at least the possibility of fulfillment of the hopes of Israel. It is interesting to notice that Jesus made no claims or explanations regarding the demonstration. He did not deny that he was who the crowd seemed to think he was. On the other hand, he deliberately chose to enter the city riding upon an ass, a symbol of peace and humility, as a vivid illustration of the fact that his kingdom was not of this world.

### THE CLEANSING OF THE TEMPLE

When Jesus walked through the temple grounds in the large afternoon of the day of his triumphal entry, he was appalled by what he saw. A major section of the sacred temple grounds had been turned into a market place and a center for money-changers! The next day Jesus returned "and began to drive out those who sold and those who bought in the temple, and he overturned the tables of the money-changers and the seats of those who sold pigeons" (Mk. 11:15). He also forbade people to use the sacred areas of the temple as a shortcut (Mk. 11:16).

How one man managed to do this, we cannot say. Perhaps he was so dynamic that no one dared challenge him. Or it may be that he took the merchants by surprise and it was easier for them to get out of his way than to resist him. Whatever the case, it was a remarkable demonstration that would be remembered long after the tables and chairs had been righted and business resumed as usual.

There is little indication that Jesus' opponents were seriously upset by the triumphal entry. Luke tells us the Pharisees suggested that he rebuke his disciples for calling him a king (Lk. 18:38-9), but they do not seem to have thought he was doing anything that was particularly objectionable. After the cleansing of the temple, however, the priests and scribes began plotting against him. For a layman to call the temple "a den of robbers" and to take it upon himself to correct things was a direct slap in the face of those who had charge of the temple, since it implied that they either did not know or did not care how the affairs of the house of God ought to be conducted. If he were allowed to continue this sort of criticism of their effectiveness as ministers of God, they would soon lose their hold on the people. This, in turn, could lead to political catastrophe, for if the Romans could no longer count on the compromising priests to keep down anti-Roman sentiment, they might decide to destroy the nation (as they finally did in A.D. 66-70 and again in 132-135). And so, "they sought a way to destroy him, for they feared him" (Mk. 10:18).

### CONFLICTS IN THE TEMPLE

For most of the next day after the cleansing of the temple, Jesus and the leaders of the Jews were in almost constant conflict. They were trying to trap him into saying something that would discredit him before the crowds, and he was trying to expose

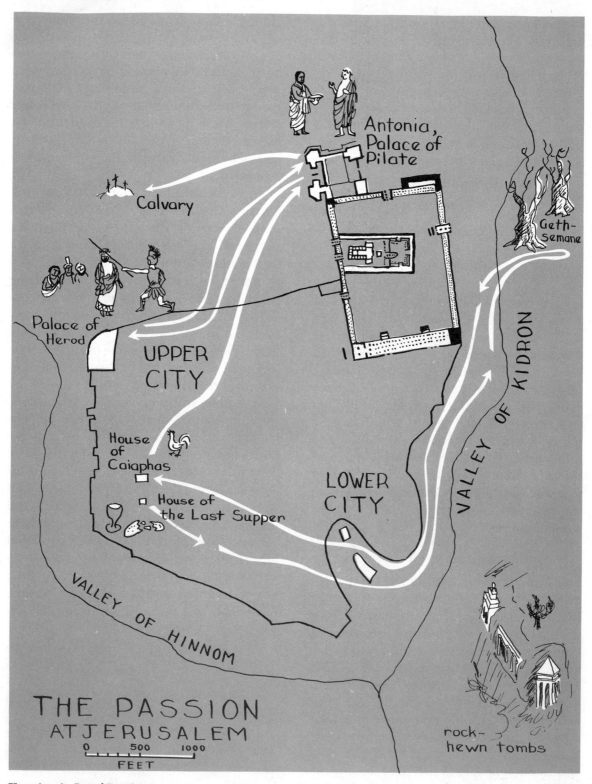

Antonia,
Palace of
Pilate

Calvary

Geth-
semane

Palace of
Herod

UPPER
CITY

VALLEY OF KIDRON

House
of
Caiaphas

House of
the Last Supper

LOWER
CITY

VALLEY OF HINNOM

THE PASSION
AT JERUSALEM

0    500    1000
FEET

rock-
hewn tombs

**Key sites in Jesus' Passion.**

their hypocrisy and utter incompetence as spiritual leaders.

*The Question of Authority.* When Jesus came back to the temple area on the day following the cleansing, several members of the Sanhedrin confronted him and demanded to know where he had received the authority to do the things he had been doing. Jesus would not be put on the spot by men of this caliber. Instead of giving them an answer they could twist and distort, he asked them to tell him by what authority John the Baptist had preached. This put them in a perfect dilemma. They could not say John received his authority from heaven, because they had not accepted his message and been baptized. Neither could they say he received it from men, because the people regarded John as a martyred prophet of God. So they had to answer, "We do not know." At this obvious evasion, Jesus declared he would not answer their question. If they did not know the answer to his question, they would not understand his answer to theirs (*Mk. 11:27–33*).

*Two Parables.* One might think that Jesus would go out of his way not to offend the Jewish leaders unnecessarily, now that he knew they were after him. But that was not his style. Instead, he related two parables whose sole intention was to further indict his opponents for their spiritual bankruptcy.

In the parable of the two sons (*Mt. 21:28–32*), he compared them to the son who piously agreed to do the will of his father, but made no effort to keep his word. The second son announced that he would not do what the father desired, but later repented and did it. This second son, said Jesus, represented the tax collectors and harlots, who, because they had listened to the preaching of John and repented, would go into the Kingdom of God before the self-righteous Sadducees and Pharisees.

In the second parable (*Mk. 12:1–11*), the priests and leaders are likened to wicked tenants whom a landlord had put in charge of his carefully prepared vineyard. Time and again the wicked tenants had slain the servants of the lord who had come to reap the fruits of the vineyard. Finally, the lord sent his beloved son, thinking that surely they would show him the honor due him. The tenants were more wicked even than he had supposed, for they took his son and killed him. "What will the owner of the vineyard do?" asked Jesus. "He will come and destroy the tenants, and give the vineyard to others."

The representatives of the Sanhedrin immediately perceived that he was talking about them and wanted to arrest him, but they realized they could not at this time, because of his popularity with the masses (*Mk. 12:12*).

*Three Hard Questions.* Thwarted and rebuked in their attempt to get a straight answer from Jesus, the leaders resorted to every device they could think of to lure him into a vulnerable position.

First, they sent a group of Pharisees and Herodians, both of whom were concerned with the whole question of the obligation of Jews to the Roman government. They asked him, "Is it lawful to pay taxes to Caesar or not?" They figured that if Jesus approved of paying the hated Roman tax, the people would turn against him. On the other hand, if he counseled them not to pay, the Romans could arrest him on a charge of sedition. Jesus' answer has become a classic in discussions of the relationship of Christians to their government: "Render to Caesar the things that are Caesar's and to God the things that are God's." There can be little organized society without government. As long as Caesar does not infringe on the rights of God, his demands may be considered legitimate (*Mk. 12:13–17*).

Next came the Sadducees. In reply to a

trick question regarding the resurrection (which the Sadducees denied), Jesus employed a bit of typical rabbinic interpretation to "prove" that the resurrection must occur: when God spoke to Moses, he introduced himself as the God of Abraham, Isaac, and Jacob: since God is the God of the living and not of the dead, it stands to reason that the resurrection is a fact. By strict standards of logic, Jesus' argument is less than completely satisfying, but it impressed the Sadducees sufficiently that they apparently abandoned their examination of him (*Mk. 12:18–27*).

The third questioner was a scribe who asked which of the commandments was most important. Without hesitating, Jesus answered, "The first is 'You shall love the Lord your God with all your heart, and with all your soul, and with all your mind, and with all your strength.' The second is this, 'You shall love your neighbor as yourself.'" If the scribe had been hostile when he asked his question, Jesus' answer had won his heart, and he acknowledged that Jesus had spoken wisely. And Jesus said of him, "You are not far from the Kingdom of God" (*Mk. 12:28–34*).

"And after that no one dared to ask him any question."

### JESUS TAKES THE ATTACK

After the attempts to ensnare him had failed so miserably, Jesus turned his perceptive and brilliant searchlight on his opponents. First he exposed the legalistic hypocrisy of the scribes and Pharisees. In one of the most biting attacks found anywhere in scripture (*Mt. 23*), he calls them hypocrites, blind guides, and whited sepulchres, who proselyte zealously and then make their converts twice as much a child of hell as themselves, who strain out a gnat and swallow a camel, who appear outwardly beautiful, but inwardly are full of dead men's

bones and all manner of corruption. Despite their ostentatious piety and rich gifts, they were spiritually inferior to the poor widow who gives her last penny. They had been given much, these wicked tenants "who devour widows' houses and for a pretense make long prayers," but they had betrayed their trust and, consequently, "they will receive the greater condemnation" (*Mk. 12:38–44*).

*Signs of the End.* As Jesus left the temple that day, one of his disciples, probably a Galilean who had never seen the temple before this trip, said to him, "Look, Teacher, what wonderful stones and what wonderful buildings!" And Jesus said to him, "There will not be left here one stone upon another, that will not be thrown down." This saying puzzled the disciples and when they were alone they asked him to explain his words more fully. Jesus' answer consisted of a vivid description of a calamitous situation in which war, earthquake, and famine would be regular features. And these were only the beginning. They would be followed by persecution and tribulation so severe that if the Lord had not already decided to shorten the appointed time of trial, none would be able to endure it. When all these things had taken place, then would come the Son of man in clouds of glory to gather his elect and judge the nations. All this, he told them, would take place before the present generation passed away (*Mk. 13:1–36*).

There are elements of this reply that are troublesome, especially the fact that the glorious return of the Son of man in the clouds did not occur within the announced time limit. But it was not the primary purpose of Jesus to provide a time table for the future. In fact, he admitted that he did not know just when the things he was describing would occur, for this was entirely in the hands of the Father. Whatever the explanation to these problems of interpretation, the

416

central truth of Jesus' teaching still holds good: "Take heed, watch; for you do not know when the time will come."

## The Sufferings of the Son of Man

It was now two days before the Passover and the feast of Unleavened Bread. The time of which Jesus had been speaking had come, the time when the Son of man would suffer many things.

### THE LAST SUPPER

On the first day of the Passover celebration, the day the passover lamb was killed and eaten, Jesus directed his disciples to go to a designated "upper room" and prepare the passover meal. When evening came, he joined them there and ate the passover meal with them.

In the course of the sacred meal that celebrated Israel's grateful reception of God's redeeming grace, Jesus took a piece of bread from the table and blessed it and broke it and gave it to the disciples, saying, "Take, eat; this is my body." Later, he took a cup of wine, presumably the red wine prescribed for passover use, and when he had given thanks, he gave it to them and they all drank of it. Of the cup he said, "This is my blood of the covenant, which is poured out for many. Truly, I say to you, I shall not drink again of the fruit of the vine until that day when I drink it new in the Kingdom of God" (*Mk. 14:22–25*).

To those of us who are Christians, these words and actions of Jesus are laden with rich meanings. As we participate in the Lord's Supper, or Holy Communion, or whatever we may choose to call the Church's reenactment of this event, our thoughts and emotions are shaped not only by the Biblical account, but by almost two thousand years of Christian history, by the words and prayers of him who administers the elements, by our relationship to those

The Wailing Wall, part of the enclosure which Herod the Great built around the temple. Here Jews still mourn the destruction of Jerusalem.

417

who are sharing with us in the holy meal, and by our own previous communion experiences. It is probably not possible to erase all these things from our minds—nor should we try, for they may all serve to deepen and enrich our communion with our Lord and with one another. But how did the disciples in the upper room understand these symbolic actions? It is, of course, impossible for us to answer this question with certainty, but there are several clues that may help us reach an approximate understanding.

A standard feature of Jewish messianic thought was the notion of a banquet at which the Messiah and those who were faithful to him would share in a glorious common meal. The communal meals of the Essene community at Qumran were almost certainly regarded as a foretaste of this banquet. Jesus was fully aware of this notion. Several times in his ministry, he had described the coming Kingdom in terms of a great feast or banquet. It has sometimes been suggested that the meal shared with the five thousand in the wilderness in Galilee may well have been a conscious attempt on the part of Jesus to foreshadow this messianic banquet. And when he gave the disciples the bread and the cup at the Last Supper, he referred to eating and drinking it anew in the fully-come Kingdom of God (*Lk. 22:16; Mt. 14:25*). We cannot say just what the disciples actually did think and feel about the Last Supper, but in the light of the above evidence, it seems quite likely that Jesus intended for them to regard it as a present participation in the glorious age to come.

The coming of this glorious age of the Kingdom, the great victory of God over Satan, was to be made possible, as Jesus had taught his disciples, by the sufferings of the Son of man. The Last Supper bore witness to these sufferings as well as to the Kingdom

itself. The bread symbolized Jesus' body, which was to be torn on the cross. The cup was his blood, poured out in payment of "the ransom for many" and sealing the New Covenant, as the blood of bulls and goats had sealed the old.

The early disciples, then, probably regarded the supper as a prelude to the sufferings that were necessary to usher in the New age (though they did not fully understand all that was involved) and as a participation-in-advance in the blessings of the Kingdom —a kind of down payment or first instalment of the messianic age.

*Announcement of the Betrayal.* While they were eating, Jesus startled the disciples with the announcement that one of them, one of the Twelve who had been with him throughout his ministry, was going to betray him. Naturally, each one of them asked anxiously, "Is it I?" According to the Synoptic gospels, all he would say was that the traitor was one of those who had dipped in the same dish with him, but John tells us that he announced that he to whom he would give a morsel of food would betray him, and that he then gave a morsel to Judas Iscariot. It seems doubtful, however, that this sign was as clear to the disciples as it is to us, for when Judas left the room after Jesus' famous directive, "What you are going to do, do quickly," John tells us that "no one at the table knew why he said this to him" (*Jn. 13:28; cf. Mk. 14:17–21; Mt. 26:21–25; Lk. 22:21–23*). In any case, Judas soon left the room and went out into the night.

### GETHSEMANE

After Judas left, according to the fourth gospel, which adds material not found in any of the Synoptics, Jesus told his disciples even more plainly that the time had come for him "to be lifted up," that he would soon be taken from their presence. He urged them to love one another and promised to send a Holy Comforter to be with them and to guide them in his absence (*Jn. 15–16*). Then, after a moving prayer on their behalf (*Jn. 17*), Jesus and the eleven sang a hymn and went out to the Mount of Olives. There he told them that his suffering and death would cause them all to desert him, as sheep desert a fallen shepherd. Peter, bold as usual, declared that this might be the case with the other disciples, but that he would never fall away. Jesus, however, had seen Peter run hot and cold before, and he told him, "Before the cock crows twice, you will deny me three times." Peter objected vehemently and insisted, "If I must die with you, I will not deny you." And they all said the same thing.

After receiving these fervent pledges of loyalty unto death, Jesus took Peter and James and John to a quiet section of an enclosed garden called Gethsemane. He asked them to keep watch for anything unusual— he must have been expecting Judas—and drew off about a stone's throw to pray. The picture of Jesus in the garden is not one of a fanatic bold in the face of death or a misguided man who seeks enduring fame through martyrdom, but of a man genuinely sad and even terrified by what lay before him. When he knelt to pray, he pleaded earnestly, "Father, if thou art willing, remove this cup from me; nevertheless, not my will, but thine, be done." Luke, who frequently observed details the other writers omit, notes that "being in agony he prayed more earnestly; and his sweat became like great drops of blood falling down upon the ground" (*Lk. 22:44*).

In the course of his torturous ordeal in the garden, Jesus returned several times to check on his disciples. Each time he found them sleeping. At first he seemed disturbed, but as the night wore on, his communion with his heavenly Father had enabled him to accept their weakness and to face what

lay in store for him with a spirit of quiet resignation (*Mk. 14:32–42*).

### THE ARREST AND TRIAL

While he was talking with his disciples there in the garden, Jesus saw a large crowd approaching in the night. The light from their lanterns and torches outlined their swords and clubs against the darkness. As they drew closer, Jesus could see that Judas was leading the mob. When Judas had left the upper room, he had gone to the temple and arranged with the Sanhedrin to turn Jesus over to them for thirty pieces of silver, the legal price of a slave. Because of the great stir Jesus had caused, the leaders of the Jews did not dare arrest him publicly, but they had been seeking a chance to catch him in an unguarded situation and gladly accepted Judas' offer.

In the darkness, it would be difficult for men who did not know Jesus well to recognize him, so Judas had told the mob that he would single Jesus out by kissing him. And so, the universal sign of love and respect became the instrument by which he who is worthy of all love and honor was betrayed into the hands of a band of cutthroats.

*Peter's Denial.* Jesus' captors led him first to the house of the high priest Caiaphas, where a number of scribes and elders had gathered to examine him. A crowd gathered outside in the courtyard to await news of what was happening inside. For the most part, the crowd probably consisted of those who had been in the mob that arrested Jesus, but Peter was also among them. As they sat warming themselves around a fire they had kindled, a maid pointed to Peter and said, "You were with Jesus of Galilee." The brash apostle who had pledged his loyalty to the Master with such fervor just a few hours before replied, "Woman, I do not know him." A little later someone else recognized him as one of Jesus' disciples, but again he denied it. Finally, after Peter talked with the people long enough for them to notice his accent, they said, "Certainly you are one of them, for you are a Galilean." At this Peter denied any association with Jesus again, only this time he made his denial even stronger by taking an oath in which he invoked some kind of curse on himself if he were not telling the truth. And immediately the cock crowed, and Peter remembered what the Lord had predicted. And he went out and wept bitterly.

*The Preliminary Examination.* Inside the high priest's house, the scribes and elders put Jesus through a grueling cross-examination. For several hours, they tried to uncover some piece of evidence that would prove him worthy of death. Several "witnesses" came in to testify against him, but their artificial charges were so absurd and distorted that no two of them could agree. Finally, Caiaphas asked Jesus if he had any reply to make to the charges that had been made against him, but Jesus said nothing. Then Caiaphas asked him point-blank, "Are you the Messiah?" Matthew reports that Jesus replied, "You have said so," which could be understood as Jesus' way of avoiding a direct answer (*Mt. 26:64*), but Mark reports his answer to have been a straightforward "I am." Whichever of these two versions of his reply is technically correct, the high priest obviously understood Jesus' words as an affirmative answer, for he tore his robes as a sign of his anger and indignation and hurled a charge of blasphemy at Jesus. This demonstration swayed any who may have had doubts and the group unanimously declared Jesus to be deserving of death. Then they made cruel sport of him, blindfolding him and mockingly challenging him to identify the ones who were spitting on him or striking him.

*Trial before the Sanhedrin.* The proceedings at Caiaphas' house had been an unoffi-

cial gathering. Before any kind of recommendation could be given to Pontius Pilate, who had to approve all death sentences, the entire Sanhedrin would have to convene and hand down an official decision. So, when dawn came, Jesus was led before the august council. This was something of a formality, since many members of the Sanhedrin had been present at the house of Caiaphas, but Jesus' accusers did manage to get Jesus to admit that he was the Son of God, an affirmation that was, to them, even more blasphemous than his admission that he was the Messiah. After a short consultation, they found him guilty and took him to the royal palace to stand before Pilate.

*The Trial before Pilate and Herod.* The Jews realized that Pilate would not be interested in the news that Jesus claimed to be the Son of man or the Son of God, so they portrayed their captive as a dangerous political criminal. He had, they charged, urged the people to withhold taxes to Caesar (the exact opposite of what Jesus had said) and was claiming to be the King of the Jews. Pilate was struck by the fact that Jesus made no attempt to defend himself. Surely no man who was deluded enough to think he could lead a successful revolt against the Roman Empire would receive such accusations so calmly. So he asked Jesus, "Are you the King of the Jews" and Jesus gave him the same kind of qualified affirmation he had given Caiaphas—"You have said so." Pilate quickly concluded that Jesus posed no real threat to the security of the province and announced to the crowd that had assembled, "I find no crime in this man." Grasping at straws, the chief priests insisted, "He stirs up the people . . . from Galilee to this place." When Pilate heard the word Galilee, he saw an opportunity to get out of a difficult situation. If Jesus was a Galilean, he was a subject of Herod. Since Herod was in town for the feast, why not turn Jesus over to him?

All through his Galilean ministry, Jesus had carefully avoided any direct confrontation with Herod. The King, of course, had heard of Jesus' mighty works and was delighted to see him in person, hoping Jesus would entertain him by performing a miracle or two—perhaps he would have promised him half his Kingdom, as he had to the daughter of Herodias. Jesus, of course, disappointed him on this score, and Herod was forced to get his amusement out of dressing him in royal robes and mocking him for pretending to be a king. When he had finished with him, Herod sent Jesus back to Pilate.

Pilate was unpopular with the Jews for several things he had done early in his term as governor and did not wish to offend them further. Still, he was a reasonably just man and did not wish to condemn an innocent man to death, either. At the time of Passover, he customarily set free, as a gesture of good will, any one prisoner the Jews named. He seized on this custom to get him out of his dilemma. He believed, with good reason, that the multitudes still supported Jesus and therefore offered to beat him, to please the Sanhedrin, and release him, to please the people. To his great surprise, the people, influenced by their leaders, refused the offer and demanded the release of one Barabbas, a notorious criminal. Pilate tried to reason with the crowd, but they drowned him out with cries of "Crucify him, crucify him." And so, after publicly washing his hands as a symbolic gesture of disavowal of any guilt in the matter, Pilate delivered Jesus up to be beaten and crucified.

## THE CRUCIFIXION

After the scourging, a beating so severe that it frequently cheated the cross of its victims, Jesus was led into the court of the palace, where the Roman soldiers dressed him in the garb of a king. To us he is a tragic figure in the robes of purple, with thorns for a crown and a reed for a scepter. But to the soldiers, he was little more than a clown. In mockery of the charge for which he was about to die, they knelt before him and "praised" him, saying, "Hail, King of the Jews." Then they spat on him and took the reed from his hand and beat him over the head with it. When they tired of their crude sport, the soldiers led Jesus outside the city to a hill called Golgotha (literally, "the place of a skull"), the customary spot for public executions. There they crucified him between two thieves.

Death by crucifixion was the most horrible form of punishment in the ancient world and was ordinarily reserved for the vilest of criminals. The victim was tied or nailed to a wooden cross and left to hang there until he died of starvation, exposure, and, sometimes, gangrene or blood poisoning. Frequently, the ordeal lasted several days, but Jesus was so physically and emotionally spent after a night of anguish and inquisition and a morning of harsh physical punishment and cruel mockery that he lasted less than six hours. In the garden the night before, he had committed himself to the purposes of his father. Still, the pain of his wounds and the agony of being deserted by his disciples in the hour of his suffering was so overwhelming that he could not restrain a pitiful cry of dereliction: "My God, My God, Why have you forsaken me?" A short while later, at about 3:00 o'clock in the afternoon, he cried again with a loud voice and "yielded up his spirit."

Since noon, the sky had been covered with darkness. At the moment of Jesus' death, the earth quaked and the curtain in the temple was torn in two, from top to bottom. When the Roman centurion who had supervised the execution saw these signs and noticed that Jesus was dead, he said, "Truly this man was a son of God" (*Mk. 15:39*).

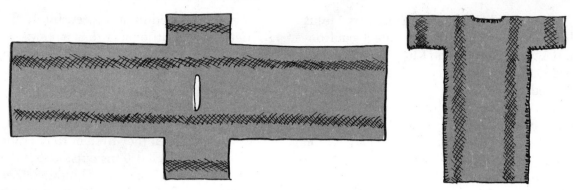

A tunic "without seam, woven from top to bottom" (John 19:23). Left: spread lengthwise; right: sewn together at the sides.

Because the Passover Sabbath would begin in a matter of hours, the Jews asked Pilate to complete the execution as quickly as possible so that the bodies could be removed and buried before the holy day began. Things had happened so fast that the family and disciples of Jesus must have wondered what they would do with his body. Perhaps someone suggested they take it to the tomb that belonged to the family of Lazarus, whom Jesus had raised from the dead. In any case, the problem was solved when a rich man of Arimathea, whose name was Joseph, asked and received permission from Pilate to allow him to bury Jesus' body in his own tomb, which was not far from Golgotha. Joseph's action must have been a great surprise to both the friends and enemies of Jesus, for he was a highly respected member of the Sanhedrin. But he was also, as Mark phrases it, "looking for the Kingdom of God." So, with the help of another respected ruler of the Jews, a man called Nicodemus (*Jn. 19:39;* see *Jn. 3*), he took the body and laid it in his own new tomb and rolled a large stone against the door.

### Christ Is Risen!

Christians have called the day of the crucifixion Good Friday, but it would not have been good, not is it likely we would have called it anything, if it had been the final page in the story of Jesus. But, it was not the end. Early on the first day of the week, just as the sun was rising, Mary Magdalene and Mary the Mother of James came to the tomb to complete the customary preparation of the body for burial, as there had not been time to do this on the afternoon of the crucifixion. On the way, they remembered that the tomb had been sealed with a large rock and wondered who would help them move it. When they arrived at the tomb, however, they were astonished to find the stone had already been rolled back. They were even more astonished when they looked in and saw that the body was gone. Sitting to one side was a figure in dazzling white robes who said to the women, "You seek Jesus of Nazareth, who was crucified. He is not here, for he is risen!" (*Mk. 16:6*).

It appears impossible to arrange the four accounts of the events of the resurrection morning into a single consistent pattern. John says Mary Magdalene came to the tomb while it was still dark (*20:1*); Mark says the two Marys came "when the sun was risen" (*16:2*). Mark and Matthew report one angelic figure inside the tomb (*Mk. 16:5; Mt. 28:5*); Luke says there were two (*24:4*). Mark says the women said nothing about what they had seen (*16:8*); Matthew says they ran immediately to tell the disciples (*28:8*).

These apparent discrepancies do not mean that the gospel writers concocted their accounts of the resurrection out of the air. They simply mean that the resurrection was an event of a different order from the crucifixion, which they reported with considerable agreement of details. The crucifixion was a public event, open to the world. Pilate's secretary, composing an official report of the execution, could have described it fully as well and accurately as the gospel writers. But the resurrection was not a public event. The Risen Christ did not appear on the mountaintop or in the temple, and no such disinterested account could have been composed. He manifested himself only to those who had acknowledged him as Lord.

The accounts of these appearances were not subject to the same kind of checking and verification as was true in the case of the traditions concerning the crucifixion. It may be that there are logical explanations for the differences in the four accounts and that if we had a few missing parts, we could fit them into a unified whole. But it really is of little consequence that we cannot do this, for it does not matter if there was one angel or two, or if he appeared to one woman or two, or if they kept silent or shouted their story from the housetop. What matters is that Christ was truly risen, was no longer dead but alive. This was the essence of the proclamation that called the church into existence or Pentecost. It was the unanimous conviction of the early church. And it has been the ground of the hope of Christian believers in every age since then. If the gospel writers had reported the resurrection in identical words, or if it could be established beyond the slightest doubt that the tomb was really empty when the disciples found it that memorable morning, this would still not prove the resurrection was real. Before his crucifixion, Jesus' life was open to the scrutiny of all. But the experience of the Risen Lord was, and is, open only to those with eyes of faith.

For forty days, the Risen Christ appeared to his disciples. At the end of this period, he called the eleven together and said to them, "Thus it is written, that the Christ should suffer and on the third day rise from the dead, and that repentance and forgiveness of sins should be preached in his name to all nations, beginning from Jerusalem. You are witnesses of these things and behold, I send the promise of my Father upon you; but stay in the city, until you are clothed with power from on high" ( *Lk. 24:47–49* ).

And when he had said this, as they were looking on, he was lifted up, and a cloud took him out of their sight.

# 16

# The Birth of
# The Christian Church

*The Spirit-filled church
prepares for its assault
on the world*

THE DISCIPLES left the Mount of Ascension in something of a daze. They went back into Jerusalem to ponder the strange things they had seen and heard in the past three years, especially the experiences of the last six weeks. They were not sad, because they knew their Lord was not dead but alive. But neither were they happy, for he was no longer with them. But he had given them a great commission and he had promised to provide the support they needed to discharge it. And so, they waited. While they waited, they worshiped and studied together. They also chose a man named Matthias to take the place of the traitor Judas. And, because they were good Jews, they got ready for Pentecost.

## The Pentecost Experience

The day of the feast came. Unaware of what was about to take place, the small band of disciples prepared to observe Pentecost in the customary manner. They crowded into the temple area in the early part of the morning, mingling with thousands of Jewish pilgrims from all over the empire. No one had any idea this was to be an extraordinary day.

Exactly what happened there is a mystery. The point is, something did happen. "Suddenly a sound came from heaven like the rush of a mighty wind, and it filled all the house where they were sitting. And there appeared to them tongues as of fire, distributed and resting on each one of them. And they were all filled with the Holy Spirit" (*Acts 2:2–4*). As the apostles spoke, each of those within earshot "heard them speaking in his own language" (*Acts 2:6*). The confusion and bewilderment that accompanied these strange occurrences amazed all the onlookers, and brought the charge from some that the apostles were drunk. Peter stood up to reply to this accusation, and before this uneducated fisherman had finished speaking, the Christian message of the Risen Lord had been proclaimed abroad for the first time.

It is hard to imagine that this Peter was

424

the same man who had denied his Lord only a few days before, but the Holy Spirit had come, and Peter was a new man. He demonstrated, through the testimony of the prophets and psalmists, that Jesus of Nazareth was truly the Anointed One, the Redeemer of Israel, the Son of God. His crucifixion had been the gravest of crimes. But God had raised him from the dead and he was now "exalted at the right hand of God" (*Acts 2: 33*). Peter further made it plain that his hearers were the very ones responsible for the crime. The Messiah had come. He had been rejected and executed by an unbelieving and lawless people, who now stood condemned in God's sight for their actions.

The message hit home. Now these same people, "cut to the heart" at what they were hearing, begged release from their sin. Peter then told them of a divine offer of forgiveness through this Messiah. Those who were touched by the sermon responded, and "there were added that day about three thousand souls" (*Acts 2:41*).

The Pentecostal experience, with the tongues of fire and the "rushing mighty wind" is not quite like anything that happens in our time. Certainly the proclamation of the gospel in many languages at once is foreign to us. The whole account sounds rather weird and unnatural. But the significant thing about all of this is that these spiritual manifestations provided visible and audible evidence that Jesus was indeed the Christ, and that he was bestowing his gift and power upon all who responded in his name. To the first Christians, a new age had dawned. They now experienced a triumphant relationship with their master, who was no longer a crucified carpenter but a Risen Redeemer. They preached that an acknowledgement of allegiance to him by faith, repentance, and baptism provided not only the forgiveness of sins but "the gift of the Spirit" (*Acts 2:32–38*).

## The Church in Jerusalem

The Jerusalem church, which began full-grown, grew rapidly. Many of the initial converts had been foreigners who had expected to be in Jerusalem only for the feast, after which they were to return home. Their conversion to Christ, however, meant that their stay was to be prolonged—and this created problems. They had no home, no source of income, and many had no acquaintances or relatives in the city. Out of these difficulties arose a group that had "all things in common" (*Acts 2:44*). Those who had took care of those who had not. Those with homes housed the homeless. From the experiences of that one day, a group was begun which shared meals, homes, problems, and joys. They immediately began referring to themselves as "the called." In all things, they saw the Holy Spirit leading them. They were happy—tremendously happy.

They observed special services regularly. They met in private houses daily, both to eat and to worship. The "breaking of bread" (*2:42*) served more than one purpose. In the first place, it provided a means of support for the needy. No one went hungry. Also, the partaking of a common meal strengthened the bonds of fellowship between all the members of the early church. Genuine love, concern, and unselfishness were natural products of such a situation. Finally, these meals united all the participants together in communion with their Lord. By now, the apostles had told them about that last supper in the upper room just before Jesus' death. Regularly, the disciples commemorated that meal; but now it had a deeper significance, for they were eating and drinking in the mystical communion of the Kingdom of God.

This is not to say that the church had no problems. On the contrary: the church, as a human community, faced the same difficulties that arise whereever people live together. There were even critical times. On one occasion, a certain group within the church felt that they were being treated unfairly, and had to register a complaint about it (6:1ff). Another time, a man and his wife (Ananias and Sapphira) lied about their giving and brought shame and reproach upon the whole church (5:1ff). Still, the general atmosphere of the Jerusalem congregation was one of peace, joy and love.

Organization was simple. The leadership of the church quite naturally fell to the twelve apostles. They remained responsible for the spiritual oversight of the entire group, while lesser tasks were delegated to specially chosen men. There was no tightly defined system of government. Each problem was dealt with as it arose, for these people trusted in the guidance of the Spirit. To them, that was sufficient. The church was yet in its infancy and it was still localized. Outside missionary activity had not yet begun—though it was only a short time before the preaching of Christ was heard throughout the land.

### THE BEGINNING OF OPPOSITION

From the time the apostles first stood up to preach on Pentecost, they never missed an opportunity to spread their message. During the week of the feast, they became prominent men in Jerusalem. Only a short while later, Peter and John healed a man in the temple in the name of Jesus Christ (3:1–10). These two, and the others, were constantly found in the midst of the city proclaiming their Lord. It was only natural that opposition would come soon—and it did. For one thing, their message itself was highly controversial. Many Jews remained as antagonistic toward the person of Jesus as they had ever been. They still saw him as a disturber and a criminal. To say that he was "the Son of God" and to assert that he was

now "exalted at the right hand" of the Father was to utter the most extreme blasphemy. Then, there were many who opposed this new way out of a fear for the future of their nation's faith—to them, it appeared that the disciples' disregard of historic ritual was a real threat of Judaism itself. Thus, wherever the disciples went, opposition went with them.

### THREE IMPORTANT INCIDENTS

Within the first few months of the life of the church, three incidents occurred that profoundly affected its destiny.

*The Problem of the Hellenists.* The first is mentioned in *Acts 6:1ff.* One of the initial problems to face the struggling congregation arose from the fact that its membership consisted of two major groups: "Hebrews" and "Hellenists." The "Hebrews" mentioned in *6:1* were Aramaic-speaking Palestinian Jews; the "Hellenists" were probably Greek-speaking Jews of the Dispersion who had been in Jerusalem for Pentecost and had become members of the new way at that time. The name "Hellenists" indicates that these people were more open to Greek influences than the more strict natives of Jerusalem.

According to Luke's account, a complaint arose that the Hellenist widows were being slighted in the daily distribution of food. Though this matter in itself was a minor one —one that a quick adjustment could correct —it generated charges of favoritism, and posed a threat to the unity of the church. At that point, there was a danger of the community's splitting into "Hebrew" and "Hellenist" factions.

There may have been factors other than the one mentioned behind the grievance. It is possible, for instance, that the Palestinians manifested an attitude of smugness and superiority toward their Greek-speaking brethren. Some of the local citizens may

An inscription from the Synagogue of the Freedmen, with whose members
Stephen was disputing just before his martyrdom (Acts 6:9).

have been arrogant in their dealings with
those who had been forced to rely upon the
hospitality of others. Whatever the source
of friction, an immediate solution was
needed, lest the bonds of love and unity be
broken. To meet the challenge the young
church, following the suggestion of the
twelve apostles, chose seven men to be in
charge of food distribution.

Had they been less wise, they might have
chosen a group of men whose names were
prominent in local circles. As it happened,
they did not. The significance of the action
taken does not lie in the mere fact that
"deacons" were appointed to serve tables.
The important thing to notice here is that all
seven of the men chosen bore Greek names.
This was a masterpiece of diplomacy. The
twelve men who led the church's spiritual
action were Palestinian Jews. Now the task
of administering to the daily needs of the

community was entrusted to Hellenists.
Apparently this was a satisfactory answer.
The Hellenists were thus awarded proper
recognition in the church, the Hebrews
were willing to compromise in the interest
of love, and harmony was restored.

*The Martyrdom of Stephen.* The second incident of major consequence was the
stoning of Stephen. It was a milestone in the
respect that Stephen was "the first Christian martyr"; but a far more widespread
effect of this action was what happened to
the church itself as a result of it. Stephen
was the first Christian preacher to emphasize the revolutionary character of the new
faith. Peter and John had spoken in strong
terms—but they emphasized the connection
between Jesus and the hope of the Jewish
nation. The speech of Stephen in *Acts* 7 emphasizes the continual disobedience of the
Jewish people and their repeated rejection

427

of divinely sent leaders. Perhaps Stephen (whose name was Greek) sought to detach the Christian community from Judaism altogether. In any case, his zeal, bluntness, and lack of tact brought forth an immediate reaction from his hearers. No sooner had he denounced the entire Jewish nation than he was set upon and killed.

Jewish action did not stop with the execution of Stephen. On the very day of his death, a local persecution was instituted, and many disciples were forced to leave the city. The effect of this persecution is summarized in *Acts 8:4:* "Those who were scattered went about preaching the word."

Up to this point, the church had confined its activity to the Jewish people. All of its members were Jews, and it was considered by most to be a branch of Judaism with a new emphasis. But with the scattering of the members of the group, the new faith began to confront the Gentile world as well. One of the seven who had been chosen to serve tables—a man named Philip—went to the city of Samaria and evangelized that area. This was extremely significant. While the Samaritans were "half-Jews"—that is to say, they observed the Law of Moses and practiced the rite of circumcision—the Jews had no dealings with them at all (see *John 4:9*). Pious Jews considered Samaritans no better than the most degenerate heathens. There was yet another direct consequence of the persecution following Stephen's speech: some of the "scattered" Christians went to Antioch and began preaching to Greeks there. Luke notes that "the hand of the Lord was with them, and a great number that believed turned to the Lord" (*Acts 11:21*). So it was that "Gentile Christianity" emerged.

*The Conversion of Cornelius.* A third major milestone in Christian beginnings was passed when Peter met Cornelius. This incident marked the "official" opening of the doors of the church to all believers every-where. Let the reader bear in mind that the Jerusalem church, of which Peter was a leader, was still completely Jewish. Bear in mind also that all previous mission efforts to non-Jews had taken place in distant cities, far from the great citadel of Jewish national hopes. And remember that the Jerusalem Christians themselves still retained all their notions that Jews were God's specially chosen people. They still identified their new path of commitment with the Mosaic covenant. They were Jews, and proud of it. Their way was a Jewish one, identified in every way with the hope of Israel.

It is impossible to say how long the situation would have remained this way had circumstances been different. But as things happened, one of the leaders of the Jerusalem church took the lead in broadening the scope of the Christian mission. Peter himself experienced a vision one day that indicated to him that the new way was not to be confined to the Jews. Almost immediately afterward, word came to him that a Greek military officer named Cornelius wished to speak to him. Peter responded to the request at once. While he visited in the home of Cornelius, the Holy Spirit fell upon this Gentile and his family. Peter, of course, was astonished, but he had the presence of mind to see that this truly meant that "God shows no partiality" (*Acts 10:34*). Cornelius and his family were immediately baptized into the apostolic community. Then Peter returned to Jerusalem to report that the barriers of race and nationality were broken down for all time.

We do not know whether Peter's action created a gulf between him and other Jerusalem Christians. We do know that the details of Christianity's relationship to Judaism were not worked for some time. Still, when Peter was later criticized for dining with Gentiles, he explained in detail what had happened. Luke reports that the brethren then "glorified God, saying, 'Then to the Gentiles also God has granted repentance unto life'" (*Acts 11:18*). From this point on, it was evident to the leaders of the church that Jesus' great commission had truly been a mandate to "make disciples of all nations" (*Matthew 28:19*). When this finally became clear to the disciples in Jerusalem, immediate steps were taken to evangelize the entire empire. This set the stage for the mission work of the Apostle Paul.

Before we turn to the story of Paul and his work among the Gentiles, let us notice the major features of the political, intellectual, and religious forces with which he had to contend.

## Understanding the Early Church

To understand the life of the early Christians, the Bible student must be aware of their heritage, their customs, and the world in which they lived. As we have seen, the church did not just happen; it made its appearance in a particular place at a particular time in history. Unfortunately, too many students of the Bible tend to think of Jesus, Peter, and Paul as men who lived in some unearthly, half-real dream world. Actually, nothing could be more harmful to a proper study of the New Testament than such a misconception. The Biblical accounts of what happened at Jerusalem, Damascus, and Athens will mean much more if we see that the early Christians grappled with many of the common, everyday problems and irritations that face men of every age. They had groceries to buy and taxes to pay. They wondered about such questions as: "How far does my relationship with the government extend?" "How shall I deal with those who misuse me?" "Am I obliged to pay taxes to support heathen institutions, and must I obey heathen laws?"

The point here is simply that Christianity was no dream scheme detached from reality.

Peter and Paul got hungry, they paid bills, and they thought about coats when the weather turned cold. As we understand this, we will see that Christians affected other people—and they, in turn, were affected by others. Every major influence upon the religious, political, and social structures of Palestine and Western Asia also had its impact upon Christianity, and Christianity exercised a definite influence of its own.

### THE NEAR BACKGROUND

In A.D. 29, the Roman empire extended throughout the civilized world—or at least throughout what was then known as "the civilized world"—and Rome ruled with a strong military hand. No rebellion against the government was tolerated at all. Indeed, the wise man knew better than to voice any strong criticism of Roman rule. The uprisings that occurred were dealt with quickly and severely, the insurrection was punishable by death. On the other hand, it should be noted that the government, which was certainly strict, was not extremely cruel to the people as a whole. Conquered nations (such as Israel) were definitely looked upon as conquered nations. As such, they were accorded an inferior status. But the people were not slaves, and we would perhaps be surprised to find out how much freedom they actually had.

In purely local matters, Rome usually delegated a certain amount of authority to a few specially approved citizens. In matters of religion, for instance, the Jews were given a good many special privileges. Also, the government encouraged such cultural factors as the interchange of scholarly thought and the construction of educational facilities. Then there were the road-building programs and the various commercial enterprises. All of these things tended to break down regional and provincial barriers. The Jews resented the impositions made upon

Ladies' hair styles of ancient Roman times.

them by the Roman government, but they did not go completely unbenefited in their contact with Rome. They were learning more and more about other nations and other cultures.

The times were complex, and Christianity was born into a world of many faces. Old orders had given way to new ones. The times were changing, and men's minds were changing with them. People were generally restless and insecure. Many felt as though they were lost in a world they did not understand. It was as if they were children or strangers in a totally new environment. Men were concerned about life, but in this particular age they worried a good bit about death, also. They asked themselves questions about the origin of life. They speculated about the possibilities of life after death. They worried about their problems—like all people—but they also spent a lot of time worrying about their sins. Everyone was asking hard questions, and there were many more questions than answers. To provide some answers, many different philosophies of varied nature were offered, and each had its following. For example, there were the various schools of philosophical thought that had originated in Greece; there were the mystery cults, which had recently been introduced from the East; and there was the budding movement of emperor worship, sponsored by Rome for political reasons. The emphasis, in many cases, was on the weird, the strange, the bizarre. Varying types of cults flourished. Mysticism was in fashion and anything that had a flavor of secrecy was bound to attract its share of followers.

The situation was confusing. The average man was unlearned, and had very little knowledge of these different movements. Therefore, educated men studied all of the questions that the people were asking. They made it their business to become acquainted with as many different philosophies of life as they could. Frequently, leaders of one type of thought attempted to incorporate everything worthwhile from another religion or philosophy into their own. One situation that reflected this attitude may be seen in *Acts 17:16ff.*

Because the world was confused, and because many were receptive to new ideas, Christianity was remarkably successful. In a very real sense, the gospel was received "gladly" simply because the Roman world was ready for it. Men's minds had been prepared psychologically, culturally, and philosophically. The whole atmosphere of the times was one that conditioned people for just such a message. The preached word and the zeal of the early preachers provided the power and the planters, but the soil was plowed and ready for the implantation of the seed.

## THE DISTANT BACKGROUND

It would be foolish to point to a specific spot in history and say, "This is where the background for a study of Christianity begins." The choice of a beginning-point is certainly arbitrary, and one cannot be imposed here. However, one generally accepted point of departure for a study of the New Testament background is the life of Alexander the Great.

As we noticed in chapter 14, Alexander changed the entire rule-book of political, economic, and cultural standards in each of the areas he conquered. With him, Greek civilization became the new yardstick of society. Previous to his time, men throughout the world had built their societies around the concept of the "city-state." Cities had been self-governing, self-contained, self-sufficient units, almost completely isolated from all other cities (which were similarly governed). For instance, if a man was born in Jerusalem, he was very likely to spend his entire life there and die there, knowing very little about any other city, province, or nation. With Alexander, all of this changed. He was firmly convinced that Greece and Greek institutions were superior to other nations and national customs. Furthermore, he intended to teach that superior mode of living to all men everywhere. Alexander spread his gospel—called "Hellenism," after "Hellas," the Greeks' name for their country—so effectively that it became the dominant factor in the Mediterranean world for hundreds of years.

Because Alexander was successful, century-old traditions of conquered nations were forced to give way to a new order. This not only meant that such nations as Syria, Egypt, and Israel found themselves becoming very "Greek" in a great many ways—it also meant that they were losing many of their Syrian, Egyptian, and Jewish charac-

teristics. Because of Alexander the Great, the "city-state" idea broke down altogether, and civilization became cosmopolitan for the first time. A man was no longer simply a Jew, or a Persian. He became a citizen of the empire, and shared in the empire's accumulated influence and learning. It he was educated, he learned two or more languages. A common culture flourished in the largest metropolitan centers, and East and West were joined for the first time. Such was the legacy of Alexander the Great.

But the old walls of tradition did not come tumbling down overnight. The East was Hellenized by evolution rather than revolution. Alexander might have wished to promote sweeping, wholesale changes, but he died before he had that chance. Instead, change came by the erosion of old ways and replacement with the new. As one might imagine, there was plenty of opposition to most of these changes. Not everybody wanted to be "Greek," and when the Hellenists pushed too strongly, there was sure to be a reaction. In fact, the entire Hellenistic period in Palestine was marked by uprisings and rebellions of one sort or another, such as the Maccabean revolt.*

During this time, several strange and bizarre systems made their appearance, and all had some impact upon the times. Cults of every sort abounded everywhere. The mystery religions filtered in from the East, and they appealed to many who felt lonely, out-of-place, and despondent. They invited the participant to align himself with the gods through sacrifice, ceremony, and mystical communion. The astrological cults claimed to find the meaning of life in a study of the stars. A number of different schools of philosophy arose, each purporting to have the key to the mysteries of man's existence. Of these, Stoicism and Epicureanism were the most outstanding, and probably the

*See pp. 362ff.

431

most influential. Around the time Jesus was born, there arose cults of emperor worship, and the Roman rulers were gradually exalted to a position of deity. It was with all of these—and with the cross currents of many other influences and pressures of the time—that Christianity was forced to compete when it made its entrance.

## Religions and Philosophies of the Hellenistic Age

When the religion of ancient Greece is mentioned, most people will almost automatically think of Zeus and the other mythological gods of Mount Olympus. It is true that Zeus and his pantheon dominated the Greek religious scene for several centuries—but this is only a part of the story. The full tale of Greek religion is far more complex than one might at first imagine.

As early as 600 B.C., the more advanced Greek thinkers were questioning the existence of these mythological deities. However, there were only occasional dissenters, and they were definitely in the minority. But as the years went by, more and more people came to doubt the traditional stories, and faith in Zeus and the other gods was seriously damaged—perhaps even crushed—by the Peloponesian War (431-404 B.C.). This was a terrible civil war of twenty-seven years' duration. The antagonists were the rival city-states of Athens and Sparta. By the time this war finally came to an end, the religious, social, and economic structures of Greece were in ruins. A whole generation fraught with savagery and desolation was enough to convince many Greeks that moral order had disappeared from the earth. In an earlier, more prosperous time, it had been fairly easy to envision a noble ideal of goodness, reason and order. Now, things were different. Many thinkers concluded that the whole structure of Greek religion was a case of fools listening to fools.

Because of repeated attacks upon them by the intellectuals, the gods gradually began to fall into disrepute. This does not mean that worship to them ceased. Indeed, the worship ceremonies and sacrifices resumed after the war, and for several centuries continued as before. But by now, the system had definitely been undermined, and many doubted the value of their worship. Men continued to pay homage to these various deities, but their hearts were hardly in it. They had seen to much evil to believe that the gods controlled men's actions.

During this period of disillusionment, men began to turn elsewhere for solace. There was little to be found. Fear and insecurity prompted the belief that "Tyche" (the Greek term for "Chance") ruled the destinies of men. In some places, Greeks personified Tyche, picturing "Chance" as a goddess, and erected temples and statues in

An altar to an unknown god, from Pergamum.

432

her honor. This sort of thing typified the confusion of an entire nation at its lowest ebb of fortune.

In a state of constant internal turmoil and confusion, there is a great possibility that men will turn to some strange or alien influence. When an individual, or a city, or a country begins to be bowed down by uncertainty and bewilderment, a search for something new begins. If no help appears on the immediate horizon, then the troubled person looks beyond the borders of the immediate for help—help of any kind. If anything looks promising, it makes little difference that it may be of a nature totally foreign to the past experience of the seeker. It simply amounts to this: help is needed, help is sought. For this reason, a multitude of people asked Peter and the apostles, "Brethren, what shall we do?" (*Acts 2:37*). For this reason, impoverished countries have turned to Communism in our century. For this reason, a disillusioned, disappointed nation of Greeks began to turn to foreign philosophies for answers that their own systems had failed to provide. In this way, the Hellenistic world became the crossroads for all types of philosophies. It was on this account that there came to be a meetingplace where "all the Athenians and foreigners who lived there spent their time in nothing except telling or hearing something new" (*Acts 17:21*).

So it was that the cults of astrology and the mysteries began to be introduced from the Orient, even at the time the old mythological religion was crumbling. Here, for the first time, the natives of Greece were introduced to a passionate longing for immortality. This appealed to them, for what they had experienced on earth was far from satisfying. Men who had once been content just to be Greeks and live "the good life" now chafed at the limitations of human existence. At this particular point in time, an awareness of the inadequacies of this life made its first real impact.

## ASTROLOGY

Astrology became immensely popular in the Roman world, and was perhaps at the peak of its popularity during Jesus' lifetime. Augustus Caesar was governing the empire at the time of Jesus' birth (*Luke 2:1*). During the time he ruled, much magic was practiced. Augustus attempted to curb it, but with little success. Just how unsuccessful he was may be seen from the fact that his successor, Tiberius, was himself an avid student of the movements of the stars. Everywhere there were magicians and sorcerers who specialized in "love potions," conjurations of spirits, hexing, and the like. Men feared the stars, which appeared to be gods or demons who could be appeased by sacrifices and prayers, or mastered by magic. Even the Jews, who so steadfastly opposed idolatry or magic in any form, were not immune to this sort of influence. Pious Jews everywhere wore phylacteries, or "prayer bands." Theoretically, these phylacteries were designed to remind their wearers of their ever-present obligation to the Law (see *Matthew 23:5*). Practically speaking, however, they frequently received the same kind of unspoken reverence that a charm might have evoked from a pagan. In any case, charms, amulets, and statuettes of various gods and goddesses were to be found throughout the empire. Careful Jews shunned any form of idolatry, of course, but many Greek and Roman businessmen made a good living through the manufacture and sale of these charms (see *Acts 19*). Omens were seen in any unusual act of nature. Dreams were commonly regarded as portents of the future. Oracles were consulted when one faced a major decision. All in all, the Hellenistic world was a highly superstitious one.

### THE MYSTERY CULTS

This superstition and fear, so prevalent everywhere, drove many into the arms of the mystery cults. Men felt little kinship with other men, and they had lost sight of anything divine. Human life was cheap in those days, and there was no real emphasis on the worth of the individual. With no one else to worry about them or care for them, men worried about themselves. The mysteries stepped in at that point and filled the unsatisfied needs of the people. Their initiation ceremonies made the individual feel that he was taking part in something holy—and was even sharing in its divinity. A closeness to other men, which was sorely lacking in everyday life, was provided here. However strange they might have been, the mysteries did partially satisfy the spiritual hunger that gripped so many.

It is easy to see how men in an age of skepticism and unbelief would seek such a refuge as the mysteries offered. Here men were presented with an answer which they could seek and find. Here participation was accomplished by free choice. There was no talk of helpless gods standing by, unable to correct the human condition. In the world of the mystery cult, no blind fate pulled the strings of life. Men were no longer at the mercy of the stars and the planetary conjunctions. Through the mysteries, they could participate in the initiation, be absorbed into the divine through intoxicating experiences, and enjoy the understanding that the cult promised.

Faith was once again restored to man through the mysteries. The participants believed that faithful observance of the proper rites enabled one to gain deliverance from the endless cycle of reincarnation. The appeal of the mysteries was simple, yet obvious: If there *is* an answer here, why not try it? If man *can* escape the misery of this

life and the nothingness of death by initiation, then why not do it?

The mysteries presented a strong attraction for such people as slaves who were offered, through participation in the cult, freedom in an afterlife. Those who had never enjoyed any real happiness in life, or those who were simply weary of living, were also drawn to them. To the member of such a cult, life took on new meaning. It was no longer an aimless striving after wind. Now there was a definite goal at which to aim, a specific prize to be won.

In a time of general religious inquisitiveness, the more weird aspects of the mysteries fit right in. Where men had once shunned such things, now there was a simple curiosity about the mysterious and the exotic. The ancient notion that a whole colony of gods ruled the world from the top of a mountain had given way to the idea that all of these gods were in reality one. Men felt their own ignorance and helplessness and desired enlightenment. To gain answers to their questions, many sought to be initiated into as many cults as possible. As the demand created the supply, new cults of varying natures continued to appear.

### THE GREEK MYSTERIES

In the unusual blend of the Greek heritage with the strange systems of the East, most cults were mixtures of both East and West. In some, the "Greek" side dominated; in others, the "Oriental" strains were more apparent. Of the Greek mysteries, three of the dominant ones may be taken as representative: the Eleusinian, the Dionysian, and the Orphic.

The Eleusinian system centered around Demeter, the goddess of the field; Kore, Demeter's daughter; and Hades, god of the dead. Adherents to this cult believed that autumn and winter occurred when Hades carried Kore to the underworld and kept her there for eight months of the year. The coming of spring heralded Kore's return from the realm of the dead. As nature was reborn in the spring, so by participation in the secret rites of Eleusis, men celebrated their own spiritual rebirth. The rites of spring also symbolized the worshiper's hope for a blissful immortality.

The cult of Dionysius was another important Greek mystery. Dionysius was originally a fertility god who later became known as the god of wine. In this latter role he was also called "Bacchus." The Dionysians were typical of those cults that completely threw off the bounds of restraint. In the sacred Dionysian rites, female worshipers danced themselves into a frenzy, tearing living animals to pieces and eating their raw flesh while they moved. This represented a partaking of the nature of deity. The devotees who witnessed the strange dances also ate of the flesh, and drank new wine with it. To them, this elevated them to a state of union with the divine, and provided them with a foretaste of the eternal life they anticipated.

The Orphic cults depicted the death and resurrection of Dionysius. Firm believers in the reality of life after death, members of this group produced vivid prophecies of the coming pleasure of the initiated in the life to come. They also envisioned horrible punishments that were due the wicked. Orphism stressed the sins and guilt of man, and showed the way to eternal salvation. The prescribed manner of life for these people involved strict diets, abstinence from all taboo foods, and repeated ritual purification.

### THE ORIENTAL MYSTERIES

The Oriental mysteries were generally even more imaginative than their Greek counterparts. Possibly the forerunner of all Oriental mysteries was the cult of the sibyls. Actually, there were several such cults. Greek in origin, they adopted many oriental ideas and characteristics, and paved the way for the later, more occult mysteries.

*The Sibylline Cults.* For centuries, Greeks had revered certain aged women as possessors of divine wisdom. These women—sibyls, as they were called—were considered inspired phophetesses. When they spoke, men heard and obeyed. Eventually the idea arose that the state should collect, preserve, and consult the oracles handed down by these women. By this means, the collection known as "The Sibylline Books" or "The Sibylline Oracles" originated. The pronouncements of the sibyls were introduced to Italy by Greek colonizers. Their acceptance there provided a means of access to Rome for the earliest mystery cults.

Following a famine in the fifth century B.C., a Sibylline oracle was obeyed, and a temple was built in Rome to Demeter, Dionysius, and Kore. An oracle was consulted in 205 B.C.—a time of war—and word was received that the enemy would not be defeated unless a Phrygian goddess was brought to Rome. In compliance with this decree, the Romans imported the holy stone of Cybele, "the great mother of the gods," who was worshipped as the source of all creation.

A cult legend told how Cybele loved the male god Attis. When Attis became unfaithful to her, she drove him mad. In his distraction, he emasculated himself under a pine tree and died. Then Attis was resurrected and made god of the underworld. Attis' death and resurrection were seen to be related to the annual death and resurrection of vegetation upon the earth. For years, the Phrygians had held an annual spring festival commemorating this. During this feast, the cult retold the story of Cybele and Attis, and accompanied the storytelling with wild orgies. Some of the male worshipers imitated Attis and emasculated themselves,

435

doubtless hoping to stimulate Cybele for the unending task of reproduction. Eunuchs who endured this ordeal and survived donned women's clothing and became priests of Cybele, called "Galli." As the cult developed, Attis eventually became more popular than Cybele.

*Osiris and Isis.* A popular cult of Egyptian origin was that of Osiris and Isis. A legend told of the god Osiris, the goddess Isis, and their son, Horus. Osiris allegedly died, rose again, and showed men how they could also attain immortality. As the cult was spread from Egypt into other countries, Isis came to be identified with other godesses. Finally she became something of a "representative goddess," and was revered as the greatest friend of women. Sometimes she alone was worshiped, as she was generally considered a composite of all other female deities.

The worship of Isis and Osiris became popular in many areas, and some of the most attractive aspects of this movement were connected with the priestly rites. Sacrifices were offered twice every day. Ritual was conducted with exactness, and was carried out with pomp and precision. Practices which demonstrated penitence and remorse for misdeeds were continually observed by members of the cult. Priests wearing black reminded the worshippers of the abiding presence of their three gods.

In late autumn, an annual festival was held in commemoration of the suffering, death, and resurrection of Osiris. This was probably the chief celebration for the group.

It is interesting to note that Isis and Osiris won great popular favor in Rome during the time of the emperors. Even the demented ruler Caligula (who ruled from A.D. 37-41) erected a temple to Isis in that city. Historical records further indicate that the cult of Isis and Osiris was a favorite with several of the Roman emperors.

Isis protecting Osiris with her wings, an Egyptian sculpture.

*Mithraism.* One of the most spectacular and widespread of the cults was that of Mithra. It was originally brought into the empire by Eastern sailors who introduced it in their ports of call. Apparently there were many attractive aspects of Mithraism, for it caught on immediately and spread like wildfire, probably through international commerce.

Followers of Mithra sought to resolve the problem of the origin of the world, and their theory was that creation resulted from several successive generations from the divine source. In one of these generations, the god Mithra supposedly sprang from a rock. At that time, the earth was young, and there was as yet no source of food, nor any real vegetation. Mithra, who came forth from the rock full grown, spied a bull grazing nearby. At that point, he received a divine decree to pursue and slay the bull. This he did, unwillingly, and after a chase he cornered the bull in a cave and slaughtered it. Then, as the animal's blood flowed, a miracle occurred. From its body, blood, and spinal chord sprang forth ears of corn, young plants, flowers, and vines. The forces of evil tried to prohibit the miracle from taking place, but they failed. Therefore, in its death, the bull became the father of creation, and from its blood and sperm came forth every species of useful animal and vegetable. After this great act of creation had occurred, Mithra was drawn up to the heavens, where he then made his dwelling, evermore to rule the affairs of men and combat the forces of the Evil One.

Initiation to the society of Mithra covered seven steps. The admission to each successive grade was marked by certain symbolic ceremonies. One such act was the offering of a crown to the initiate, who placed it upon his head, then immediately took it off and put it on his shoulder, saying that Mithra was his only crown. Other steps included a firewalk, where the neophyte, blindfolded and bound, was obliged to pass through or near flame. He was also given a blood-dripping sword, with which some sort of simulated murder had taken place.

The most widely publicized and the most spectacular of all Mithraic rites was the blood-bath (taurobolium). This was also practiced in the Sibylline cults and may have been borrowed from them. In this observance, the devotee was lowered into a pit, over the opening of which was placed some sort of lattice or grate. A cow or bull was then brought in, garlanded with flowers, and slain upon the grate over the pit opening. As the devotee stood below, he extended his arms and uplifted his face—and with mouth wide open, received the warm blood as it gushed from the throat of the newly sacrificed animal. To a member of the Mithraic cult, this was the most satisfying of all possible experiences, for it meant that his "waiting period" was over, that he had entered the realm of full fellowship with Mithra, and that the promise of a glorious immortality was now his.

After a rise in popularity which spanned several centuries, Mithraism reached its peak in the fourth century A.D. Shortly after the reign of the Emperor Julian, (C. A.D. 360), it began to decline rapidly and soon died away.

### SCHOOLS OF HELLENISTIC PHILOSOPHY

In the Hellenistic era just prior to the birth of Jesus, two Greek philosophies stood above all other schools of philosophical thought. They were Stoicism and Epicureanism. Each was constructed as an answer to the pessimism and skepticism that gripped the Mediterranean world. Both of them appealed to rational, educated men who no longer could believe in the mythologies, but who found total skepticism an equally displeasing alternative.

*Stoicism.* Stoicism was founded by an Athenian philosopher named Zeno (336-263 B.C.). A system that appealed to intellectuals and to the suffering, Stoicism taught that everything that happens is in complete accord with the changeless decrees of Necessity, or Providence. The Stoic asserted that when a man comes to the proper understanding of life, he realizes that "what will be, will be." With such an outlook, he stood in no awe of circumstance, nor in fear of the future, for he was fully prepared for anything, good or ill.

The true Stoic affirmed that every man had within himself a spark of the Divine Fire, which was distributed throughout all creation. This "Divine Fire" was God, or Pure Reason. All creation was believed to be of a single essence. By this unity, creation was held together and functioned as a gigantic machine. To be sure, it had many parts, but there was only one machine. All creation went together, and each part meshed with all the other parts.

The Stoic, like others of his time, asked the question, "How is man to live?" His answer went something like this: "Man's highest good is to live according to the workings of the universe. Behind the universe is Pure Reason, and that Pure Reason causes all that we see. Therefore, man's highest good is to live in accord with Nature, accepting good and bad alike; neither gloating over the good nor complaining about the bad. Each man contains a spark of that Pure Reason, and it is his duty to see that his particular spark works in concord with the Divine Fire that sustains him."

To the Stoic, then, the "good life" consisted in doing what was fated. Reason was always to be followed. The passions were never to be obeyed. As to the coming of good or ill, the Stoic would say: "Life is going to happen a certain way, regardless. So why not accept things the way they are?" But how can man detach himself from his passions? Again, the Stoic would answer, "By self-examination and restraint." To the Stoic, the truly wise and good man was he who sought to be wholly dependent upon Nature, and wholly independent of human desires and external things.

One might at first think that this fatalism led to a neglect of one's fellow man. In the case of Stoicism, it did no such thing. Reason told the Stoic that he ought to help his neighbor, that he ought to make himself as useful as possible. Perhaps through helping others, the Stoic was able to forget himself more easily. In any case, Stoic philosophers preached a message of concern for the unfortunate. Indeed, the Stoics were so interested in helping men to live better lives that they sent missionaries into all major cities of the empire. Their gospel was a gospel of action, and one of their keywords was "duty." The Stoic said, "It is man's *duty* to take part in public life; it is man's duty to bring others to the true understanding of Reality."

Some of the most prominent scholars of the late Hellenistic period were Stoics. Stoicism appealed to the intellectual, and this partially accounts for the emphasis Stoics placed upon the study of logic, physics, and ethics. It must be remembered also that they placed a premium upon excellence. The good man was one who exercised his capabilities to their fullest extent. The higher the degree of excellence in any undertaking, the more one's life was thought to be in accord with nature.

*Epicureanism.* Epicurus (342-270 B.C), the founder of the philosophy named for him, also lived in Athens. Like Zeno, he searched for a rational understanding of man's existence. He concluded that pleasure was the fulfillment of human existence; therefore, man should seek pleasure whenever it was available and avoid pain whenever possible.

It is easy to misunderstand what Epicurus meant. Actually, a popular conception of Epicureanism as a philosophy of gluttony and excessive self-indulgence does not fit at all. To say that this was simply a matter of "eat, drink, and be merry" is quite unfair. Epicurus *did* propose pleasure as the highest good, but it was a quiet, moderate pleasure. Epicurus never proposed that one should indulge himself excessively; rather, he insisted that the highest form of pleasure takes all probable consequences into account. In this way, the "good" became a carefully calculated pleasure, rather than the riotous overindulgence with which the philosophy is frequently associated.

What Epicurus really advocated was a "pleasure of the mind"—a genuine contentment, based on a lack of pain and fear. Because it was easily misrepresented and misunderstood, the opponents of Epicureanism did much to weaken its attraction by picturing it as a life of wanton abandon. The caricature alienated many, and Epicureanism never enjoyed an extensive influence among the people.

### GNOSTICISM

Gnosticism, one of history's most complex and most fascinating movements, took its name from the Greek word *gnosis,* meaning "knowledge." It is rather difficult to define the term with any precision, for dozens of different systems of thought come under this general heading. Most of these systems varied widely in nature and practice. Also, the Gnostic movement covered a span of several centuries. For these reasons, it is impossible to give one exact definition and say, "This is Gnosticism."

Generally, though, the name "Gnosticism" refers to those systems that promoted the doctrine of salvation by knowledge. In each of the sects that bore this label, the most important thing was some sort of secret knowledge that elevated its members above the commonplace world of other men. More specifically, when one today speaks of Gnosticism, he normally will be talking about certain movements of religious speculative thought that flourished in the early Christian era, especially the second century A.D.

The Gnostic movement was a strange melting-pot of all sorts of different religions and philosophies. It included notions and facets of the Persian religion, Babylonian religions, Egyptian myths, Judaism, Greek mythology and philosophy, and—in its fullest development—Christianity. This will help to explain why nobody knows exactly what it was, or when it started.

The membership of Gnostic circles consisted of an exclusive clientele. Gnostics considered themselves the initiated, the elect, the specially favored. They boasted of a secretly revealed knowledge of the hidden secrets of the universe. Since these secrets were too deep and too important for common men to understand, those who *did* know enjoyed a special status.

Gnosticism was a long time coming to maturity. Since it centered around certain Christian words and symbols in its mature stage, it may not be altogether proper to speak of a "pre-Christian Gnosticism." However, since many of the elements that later went into the full-grown doctrine were in existence long before Jesus' lifetime, this phrase is not entirely inappropriate.

What did the Gnostics teach? Again, we must recognize that there was a wide variation of thought in the Gnostic spectrum. Still, there were certain definitely recognizable features in most Gnostic groups, and those are noted here.

1) The Gnostics visualized creation in terms of two co-existent principles. One of these principles was good, the other bad. One was responsible for the spirit within man, the other for matter and everything material. One was the god of light, the other of darkness. The Gnostics paired nearly everything off in a "good vs. evil" scheme.

2) The universe was considered a vast prison, in which the souls of men had become enchained. The earth was the creation of an evil god, who had made it to advance his own wicked designs. The Supreme God, who could not have been responsible for an evil world, was above all creation. To the Gnostics, anything fleshly was the creation of the evil god, and was therefore to be shunned. Only that which could be considered "spiritual" was good. The true Gnostic was only a pilgrim or a stranger in this world, and he looked forward to the day when his spiritual enlightenment would enable him to throw off the yoke of the flesh.

439

3) Men were divided by the Gnostics into three classes. There were the "spiritual" men, who were predestined to salvation, the "men of the soul" who had the need for someone "spiritual" to reveal the truth to them; and there were the "fleshly" men, predestined to doom.

4) The goal of the Gnostic was release of the divine spark within him. To reach this goal, he had to gain and be possessor of the Gnostic secrets of "true knowledge."

5) The practical effects of Gnosticism were such that men who sought *gnosis* took two opposite extremes of living. Since they considered themselves above normal human concerns, they had no use for traditional human moral and ethical standards. They were a special brand of people; therefore, they had their own special rules for living. Some followed the path of extreme self-denial, refusing to have the least bit of interest in anything earthly. Others intentionally indulged in the most riotous conduct possible. This was to show their contempt of earthly standards, which had been initiated by the evil god. Whether a Gnostic was an ascetic or a libertine, he was living by his creed of nonconformity to "fleshly" patterns and "worldly" institutions.

### RULER WORSHIP

As the Roman empire grew in territory and in strength, its leaders prospered. The old Roman gods had slipped in popular favor, so there was a spiritual vacuum in the empire, even as there had been one in Greece. To supplant the old religious structure, the state attempted to institute a cult of emperor worship. This did not happen overnight. At first, the leaders were accorded honors for specific accomplishments. A general won a great victory in a battle, and he was acclaimed a public hero and a military giant. For a while, this seemed to be honor enough. Then, due to jealousy of po-

A portrait head of the Roman emperor, Nero, under whom both Peter and Paul suffered martyrdom.

sition, rapid changes in leadership, and the inordinate pride of the rulers, the magnitude of the homage increased. The extra praise and reward may not have been given with as much sincerity as the earlier honors, but they were gladly received anyway. Soon, this "extra" praise became a normal part of the system of etiquette and public relations. It was "good business" to flatter those in power. Not all of it was mere flattery. Early in the Roman empire, some leaders enjoyed popular favor because they did have some interest in the wishes of the people. Some of the honors bestowed upon these men doubtless were genuine expressions of gratitude. As time went on, however, the sincerity lessened and the pomp increased. What had begun as a ceremony of gratitude was rapidly becoming a display to win favor.

About the time of the birth of Jesus, the

cults of emperor worship were nearing the peak of their strength. In 27 B.C., Octavius Caesar had been given the title "Augustus." This had been a compromise between praising Caesar as a man and elevating him to the position of outright deity. By 12 B.C., the official Roman oath included a phrase saluting the "genius" of Augustus, and in 10 B.C. an altar to Caesar was dedicated, with four colleges of priests selected to perform annual sacrifices.

From there it was a short, easy step to the exaltation of Caesar to the rank of full deity. It was sometimes held that he was a god come to earth. As this idea developed, tolerance for those who failed to support the emperor-cults diminished. Whatever private opinions the members of the Roman court may have had, they gave public assent to the emperor-worshiping structure. Their homage was demanded, and they knew better than to withhold it.

What were the practical effects of these imperial cults? First of all, they gave the soldiers in the army a feeling of pride in the unity of the strength of the empire. From the standpoint of military morale and discipline, this was quite important. Secondly, they brought open conflict with Christianity, which was, at this point, in its infant stages. The idea that the emperor was some sort of a god was blasphemous to Christians. They openly refused to have anything to do with the exaltation of the ruler to a state of divinity. This alone was enough to make them suspect. But as they went about proclaiming that "Jesus is Lord," and as they urged other men to drop their idolatrous practices to walk in a new way, they began to sound a bit like traitors to the empire. And this is how the persecution of Christians by the Roman government began.

Lack of any genuine religious content was a major factor in the decline of the emperor cults. To those who were honestly searching for the truest, noblest way, disappointment was inevitable. The men they worshiped were frequently decadent, and the praise heaped upon them was only a mockery of religion. It is likely that many of the "worshipers" were actually performing their religious rites out of a desire to remain on the good side of the government. To fall from favor frequently meant to forfeit one's life. Another reason for the failure of emperor-worship was the fact that the emperors themselves acted in such a way that no thinking person could have been fooled by them. Some of the men worshiped as gods were inept, some were mentally deranged, and all showed normal human frailties. Their conduct betrayed their extravagant claims.

## The Apostle to the Gentiles

Early in the first century A.D., a child was born in Tarsus, a city of Cilicia, which was a district in the Southwest section of Asia Minor. The baby was named Saul—not an unusual name for Jewish boys in that period. Saul's father was a Jew who had probably rendered some meritorious service to the Roman government. In return, he had been given the right of free Roman citizenship. By imperial decree, this citizenship descended to all of his children. Thus the boy enjoyed at least one special privilege that most Jewish children did not possess. Other privileges came to him as he matured. The family was fairly well-to-do economically, which meant that young Saul escaped the poverty that beset so many Jews. Also, Tarsus was a leading educational center in those days. A good bit of the knowledge of Greek and Roman thought that Saul later demonstrated in speeches and letters may be traced to his early training. Because of his family's circumstances, he received the benefits of an excellent education. During his boyhood he also learned a trade. Though this was not necessitated by economic conditions, it was standard procedure for any young student of the law to take up a craft or trade. Later, when Saul became Paul the Apostle, he made use of this trade, which was the making of tentcloth and tents. This enabled him to be self-supporting in his mission work.

When Saul reached the proper age, he was sent to Jerusalem to study under the well-known teacher and scholar, Gamaliel. Gamaliel was a strict Pharisee, and one of the most influential scholars and religious leaders of the Jewish nation. Saul probably completed his formal theological training about the time of Jesus' death. We can imagine him as a young man, full of zeal for the Jewish faith, having nothing but contempt for the religious movement that was springing up around Jesus and his teachings. Perhaps Jesus' denunciations of the Pharisees had particularly irked him. At any rate, he was a leader in the early persecution of Christians by the Jews. He is mentioned in *Acts 7:58* and *8:1* as having a part in the stoning of Stephen.

### FROM PERSECUTOR TO PREACHER

The Pharisees eagerly anticipated the coming of the Kingdom of Heaven. In its coming, God was to restore freedom and supremacy to Israel. All the world was to see his salvation. The Pharisees taught that an essential condition of man's salvation—and participation in the Kingdom—was obedience to the Law of Moses.

The message of Christianity came in open and direct conflict with Pharisee beliefs. The Christians proclaimed God's mercy toward the sinful and the undeserving; they told of the Messiah who had come to be the friend of the lowly; they preached a message of salvation to "publicans and sinners."

This was a direct slap in the face of the Pharisees, who taught rigorous obedience to the law in every respect. It was outrageous for these common folk of Galilee to claim that they were "the New Israel," and that they were the recipients of all the blessings God had promised to the fathers by the prophets. Saul could see how Christianity, if given a chance, might undermine the very foundations of Jewish teaching. To him, Christianity was not "good news"; but an insult to the God of Moses and Elijah. It was a subversion of the law and the prophets. It was blasphemy.

Saul had studied the scriptures, and he knew about the promised Messiah. He was well-versed in the prophecies that told of Israel's hopes. This talk of a "suffering Savior" and a "crucified Messiah" was nothing more than a grotesque distortion of Israel's hope. Did not the scriptures themselves say, "cursed by every one who hangs on a tree" (*Deut. 21:23*)? Had not this "Messiah" of theirs been put to death in that very manner? To Saul, such a perversion of Israel's national hope seemed worthy of the severest punishment. There can be little doubt that Saul's persecution came from the highest of religious motives. As a strict Pharisee, he felt strongly that the Law should be protected at all cost. He further knew that the Law itself provided stern retribution for those who sought to tamper with it. For this reason, he aligned himself with those who were taking immediate and stringent steps to stamp out this blasphemous new movement.

The Christians had not only upset Jerusalem with their teachings; the movement was spreading, and now it had become obvious that only persecution could slow it down. Word had come to Saul that followers of Jesus were now actively promoting their message as far away as Damascus, a city some 200 miles northeast of Jerusalem.

Anxious to bring the Christian movement to a halt, Saul and a group of equally zealous companions received permission from the

442

High Priest to seek out the Christians in Damascus. They intended to arrest them and bring them back to Jerusalem to stand trial for heresy—and perhaps insurrection. On the way, however, a blinding light drove Saul to his knees. A voice asked "Saul, Saul, why do you persecute me?" The story is recorded in detail in *Acts 9*. Saul, blinded, was led into Damascus and remained there for three days, neither eating nor drinking. At the end of this time, a disciple named Ananias confronted him, told him what was expected of him, and baptized him.

Saul's conversion marked a complete reversal of all of his former convictions. Suddenly, he knew that he had been wrong. Following the experience on the Damascus road, it became clear to him that if Jesus had died for these Christians, to persecute them would compound his guilt. And if forgiveness was actually being offered to him, then the witness of Christians was "good news" indeed.

*Acts* makes it clear that the sole motivation for Saul's about-face was a vision of Jesus Christ in his risen glory. Paul himself later insists this was the source of his enlightenment. He had not reasoned his way from error to truth, nor had he accepted another man's teachings. Purely and simply, Jesus had made himself known in a vision— and had called Saul the Persecutor to be Paul the Apostle. It was a great victory for Christianity that its chief persecutor should become its foremost champion.

Though Saul's experience was certainly unique, we may notice that it contained the same basic elements that distinguished all the conversions recorded in *Acts*: a genuine conviction that Jesus Christ was *not* dead, but still alive; that he was the promised Messiah and man's only Savior; that he was God's power for salvation; and that Jesus, as risen savior and supreme Lord, was calling men to his service.

The Street called Straight in Damascus, which probably preserves the same line as the ancient street walked by the Apostle Paul.

After his conversion experience, Saul went through a period of training and preparation for his new mission of preaching. He apparently spent some time in Damascus preaching and debating with the Jews. It also seems that he made a trip to Arabia at this time. Probably, this was a period of retreat and contemplation. If so, this indicates that he knew fully the need for preparation for the great task that lay before him. The length of Saul's period of preparation is uncertain. After his period of withdrawal in Arabia, he apparently returned directly to Damascus. There he began preaching immediately to let others know he was a changed man. The churches in Judea heard the strange and joyful news that Saul of Tarsus was now preaching the very faith he had tried to destroy (*Galatians 1:23*).

Predictably, his old Jewish friends were

confounded and infuriated. When a plot to kill Saul was discovered he hastily made his exit from Damascus at night. Since the city gates were being watched, it was necessary for the disciples to lower him in a basket over the city wall. This must have been a humiliating experience for one who had been so zealous for the traditions of his forefathers! It is supreme irony that Saul had approached Damascus with orders from the High Priest to arrest Christians—and that he left it as a refugee from his brethren, and a Christian himself! When he returned to Jerusalem, he found that the Christians still feared him. Many apparently felt that he was some sort of a spy for the Jews. However they felt, the Christians generally received Saul with some suspicion until Barnabas took him to the apostles and explained to them the circumstances of his conversion.

From that point he was welcomed warmly, and thereafter was constantly seen in the company of the apostles.

Saul's first major task as a preacher of the gospel was a ministry in Syria and Cilicia which probably lasted ten or eleven years. With Barnabas as his partner, Saul plunged himself into his new calling. In A.D. 46, the area around Jerusalem suffered severely from a famine. At this time, Barnabas and Saul journeyed to Jerusalem to carry relief money from Christians at Antioch in Syria to their Jerusalem brethren. Returning to Antioch, Saul and Barnabas began making plans for their first missionary journey. It was about this time that Saul began to use his new name, Paul. That name has since become a synonym for zeal, courage, and perseverance—due to one handicapped man who changed the world in his lifetime.

# PART SIX

## The Expansion of Christianity

# 17

# The Mission to the Gentiles

*The ministry and
message of Christianity's
foremost missionary*

Bᴇɢɪɴɴɪɴɢ with chapter 13, *The Acts of the Apostles* becomes what we might call *The Acts of Paul*. From this point forward, Luke concentrates on the labors of Paul, and him alone. Yet even with the focus on one instead of many, the story is the same. It is still the account of the message of the risen Lord, who accomplishes his will through his chosen witnesses by means of the guidance of the Holy Spirit. Witness had been borne in Jerusalem, Judea, and Samaria (see *Acts 1:8*). Now this chosen apostle—along with others—was receiving power to proclaim the message to the ends of the earth.

*Acts 13–28* is, more than anything else, a travel narrative. As with a travelogue, Luke notes points of embarkation, ports of call, and the major incidents that occurred at each location. The itinerary is remarkably complete. No doubt Luke had his own travel diary for reference. Since he did not accompany Paul on all his travels, he relied on oral or written traditions to fill out his narrative. He did not, for example, go on the first missionary journey, yet he wrote the account of it in travel-diary style, as if he had been there. This means that the numerous speeches and anecdotes were supplied him by another. But the same pattern of composition is consistent throughout the book, whether Luke was present or not.

### CHRONOLOGICAL CONSIDERATIONS

Before we begin a detailed review of Paul's mission work, it will be helpful to notice the chronological timetable of his life. Many students of the Bible remain confused about when all this happened. Some events of Paul's life cannot be dated with certainty, but others can, and they provide us with fixed references for guidance.

In *Acts 18:12–18*, Luke mentions Paul's appearance before Gallio, proconsul of Achaia. Archaeologists have discovered an inscription that dates Gallio's period of oversight from July, ᴀ.ᴅ. 51 to July, 52. Other dates in Paul's life may be reckoned by figuring forward and backward from that time, employing notes of time and place in *Acts* and Paul's letters. This enables us to place Paul's conversion around ᴀ.ᴅ. 33–35, and his death during Nero's reign in ᴀ.ᴅ. 64–65. It also tells us that all of Paul's letters were written near the end of his life, within a comparatively brief period of time.

447

According to available evidence, the following chronological scheme seems to account best for the major periods and events of Paul's life:

Before A.D. 29   Birth in Tarsus
Schooling in Jerusalem under Gamaliel

29   Resurrection of Jesus
Beginning of the church

c. 32   Conversion of Saul
Visit to Arabia
Return to Damascus

35   First visit to Jerusalem
Ministry in Syria and Cilicia
In Antioch of Syria

40   Second visit to Jerusalem

49   First missionary journey
Jerusalem conference

49-52   Second missionary journey

52-56   Third missionary journey

56   Imprisonment in Jerusalem, Caesarea
Trip to Rome; imprisonment

?   Release from prison
Further mission efforts, including possible trip to Spain
Second imprisonment

c. 65   Martyrdom under Nero

## The First Missionary Journey

Paul's first mission voyage resulted in the opening of "a door of faith to the Gentiles" (*Acts 14:27*). As far as we know, this was the first church-sponsored mission. Barnabas and Paul were not simply free lance missionaries, as were Philip and the Hellenists (see *Acts 8*), but personal representatives of the Antioch congregation. This single church stood behind their work and supported the effort in every way. At the departure of Paul and Barnabas, the Christians at Antioch bid them godspeed and sent them

448

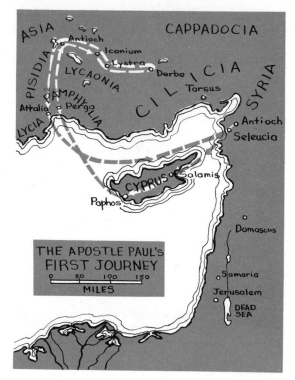

The Apostle Paul's First Missionary Journey.

forth with prayer, fasting, and the laying on of hands (*Acts 13:3; 14:26*).

The initial target of the mission tour was the island of Cyprus. Barnabas was a native of Cyprus, and he was anxious to bring the good news of his Lord to his own people (see *Acts 4:36*). The first highlight of this journey came when the proconsul of the territory, a man named Sergius Paulus, heard the word and believed. This was the first conversion of a Roman official, and Sergius Paulus is described as "a man of intelligence" (*Acts 13:7*). The missionaries were opposed on Cyprus by Bar-jesus, "a Jewish false prophet," but his opposition was swiftly and decisively overcome.

One fact that may go unnoticed to the general reader is a definite tendency on Luke's part to demonstrate exactly how it happened that the missions of these Jewish Christians turned out to be missions to the Gentiles. Notice that Paul went first to the synagogue when he entered the city. This was not just by accident. Paul and his brethren were convinced of the necessity that the Jews should be given first opportunity to hear. (See *Acts 13:46;* also *Romans 1:16; 9:1–5; 10:1*). To Paul, the Jews were still the people of God. They still had a very special place in God's plan. Since it was through the Jewish nation that the Savior had come, the Jews should take the lead in hearing and accepting the message. But notice also how the Jews continually rejected Paul and his teachings. This pattern repeats itself again and again through the book: Paul goes to the Jews; they oppose him violently; rejected, he turns to the Gentiles with his message, and they respond (see *Acts 13:40–51; Romans 10:18–21*). Throughout his life, Paul never gave up hope for the conversion of his Jewish brethren. He continually directed his message to them first (*Romans 1:16*). This gave them no grounds for complaining or excusing themselves. And when their opposition and unbelief forced Paul to go elsewhere, he consistently directed his preaching to the more receptive Gentiles.

Leaving Cyprus, Paul and Barnabas journeyed to Iconium, cities of the Phrygian region. Once again, Paul went first to the Jews. These particular Jews turned out to be highly emotional folk who responded to his message so violently that he and Barnabas barely escaped with their lives (*14:1–6*). When they came to Lystra, they met with a quite different reception. There they were welcomed as gods, and if Paul had permitted them to do so, the people would have offered sacrifice to them. This response was probably due to an old legend among the people that the Greek gods Zeus and Hermes had once visited the earth in disguise. On that visit, the gods were angered because of the poor hospitality they received. As a result, they destroyed the entire population of the city they had visited, except for two peasants who had treated them well. When Paul healed a man who had been crippled from birth, the people were convinced that Zeus and Hermes were back again. Determined not to repeat the mistake of their ancestors, they were about to go to hospitable extremes until Paul and Barnabas assured them it was a case of mistaken identity. Then Paul preached to them.

In his sermon, Paul did not quote scripture or argue the Law, for these were pagans, and scripture had little meaning for them. Instead, he reasoned from nature (*14:15–18*). For awhile, the people were attentive, until a delegation from Iconium came and convinced them that Paul and Barnabas deserved stoning, not sacrifice. The crowd, disillusioned and angered, stoned Paul and dragged him out of the city, fully believing they had killed him. But Paul was a man of amazing stamina, and the next day found him preaching in nearby Derbe. After a brief ministry there, the apostles returned to Lystra. In the face of what had happened just a few days before, this took considerable courage. Paul had that courage, and demonstrated it by spending time in Lystra and Iconium exhorting the disciples and proclaiming the gospel in word and deed. Before they left the area, they saw to it there was an organized community of believers. It is a tribute to the effectiveness of their preaching that they were able to appoint qualified elders in every church established during the first missionary journey. When this was accomplished, they returned to Antioch. There they reported to the brethren "all that God had done with them." All they had undertaken had been accomplished. The process of world-wide evangelism was underway.

### THE JERUSALEM CONFERENCE

Shortly after the first journey, a practical problem arose in the Antioch area. If the problem had been merely a local dispute, a strong church like that at Antioch could probably have solved it, but the point at issue was important enough for all the apostles to come together. The situation was this: certain Jewish Christians in the Jerusalem area had gone out among the churches insisting that all converted Gentiles should be circumcised according to the Jewish law. These "Judaizers," as they were called, insisted that salvation was dependent upon the physical act of circumcision. There could be no salvation without it, and baptism was no substitute for it.

On the surface, the dispute seemed trivial. Actually, there was far more at stake than just the problem of whether Gentiles should submit to circumcision. The Judaizers were insisting that all converts to Christianity should become Jews as well, and that they should keep the Mosaic law in every respect. This meant continuing the authority of the Jewish food laws. It meant continuing the Jewish distinctions of "clean" and "unclean." It meant that Gentiles would be compelled to live like Jews. Most important of all, it meant dividing the church into "first-class" and "second-class" Christians. An inevitable result of this kind of teaching would be Jewish supremacy and a tendency of Jewish Christians to lord it over their Gentile brethren.

Paul and some of his co-workers saw this, and knew that unless this teaching were stifled immediately, Christian communities would become hopelessly segregated. When that happened, the vision of the community in which Jew and Greek would be brethren would be no more than an empty dream. To complicate matters even further, there were some Jewish Christians who were not quite willing to bind the Mosaic law on Gentiles; neither, however, were they willing to allow them a full measure of fellowship. By refusing to eat with the Gentile brethren, these Jewish-Christians were guilty of insincerity. They spoke of equality and unity in the church, but their practices belied their words.

Paul saw the implications of the problem. He recognized that it was not just a matter of circumcision. The real problem was the one question most fundamental to the Christian message: on what does salvation rest? Does it rest on keeping the Mosaic tradition? Is it a reward for righteousness achieved in obedience to the Law? Or is it a free gift bestowed on "everyone that believes" (*Romans 1:16*)? In Paul's mind, the answer was clear: Christianity is a life of joyful and willing response through faith in the proclamation of Jesus Christ.

Paul knew that, if the Judaizing position were adopted, Christianity would never be anything more than a sect within Judaism. This would undermine everything he had done on his first missionary journey, and it would destroy everything the gospel of Christ had come to mean for him. How could he preach a message that would force Gentiles to become Jews before becoming Christians? This would not only set the mission to the Gentiles back; it would threaten the gospel itself. It emptied the cross and the resurrection of any saving power. If salvation could be won by obedience to the law, then Christ had died to no purpose!

These points were doubtless brought up when the brethren came together. Peter, Paul, James, and the others discussed the matter thoroughly. Finally, they concluded that circumcision ought not to be imposed. Speaking for the apostles, Peter laid heavy emphasis on the things he had learned just before the conversion of Cornelius (see *Acts 10, 11*). Once, he had been prejudiced; he had felt that Jews were better than Gentiles and more deserving of salvation. He had even held the opinion that salvation was solely for the Jews. But God had revealed to

Ruins of a Roman aqueduct at Antioch of Pisidia.

him in a vision that this was not the case. God had showed him that no person was deserving of partiality, and that honest believers were accepted by him regardless of nationality or heritage. Then Peter concluded, "If God has made no distinction, have Christians the right to do so?" (*Acts 15:6-11*). Following Peter's speech, Paul and Barnabas added their comments, appealing to the signs and wonders done among the Gentiles. The climax of the conference came with James' announcement that nothing but necessary things should be laid on the Gentiles. Circumcision was not among the list of "necessary things" for the Gentiles to observe. At this point, Judaizing resistance broke, and the Christian pattern was apostolically established.

This was a crucial point for Christianity, and when the conclusion had been established beyond doubt, three things were settled for all time: (1) Christianity was a movement in its own right, and not just another sect of Judaism; (2) the message of the cross had retained its supremacy, overcoming the possibility of being submerged in a system of laws; and (3) tradition and ritual practice had now given way to the witness of the Holy Spirit. The crucial question was echoed shortly thereafter by Paul, in his letter to the churches of Galatia: "Did you receive the spirit by works of the Law, or by hearing with faith?" (*Galatians 3:2*).

### THE EPISTLE TO THE GALATIANS

Paul had no systematic process of writing. The situation directed his correspondence. The crises of the moment influenced the content of his message. When he wrote, he apparently visualized his readers and anticipated their reactions. As he dictated his letters, his words became charged with feeling, for they reflected the heart of this great man.

The letter to the churches of Galatia—along with *Romans*—contains Paul's distinctive exposition of the gospel. One might call *Galatians* "the gospel according to Paul." This letter has been termed "the Magna Carta of Evangelical Christianity." If *Galatians* is the Magna Carta, *Romans* is its commentary. They deal with the same subject. *Romans* and *Galatians* together form the "Christian Declaration of Independence."

*Galatians* was written by Paul in hot indignation at certain circumstances that had arisen in the area. Probably, Paul wrote it shortly after the Jerusalem conference, for it deals with the problem of Judaizers and Judaizing. It also appears that some had challenged Paul's right to speak authoritatively. In this letter, he vigorously defends his right to speak as an apostle commissioned by the Lord Jesus Christ. With an open admission of the problems, he undertakes a refutation of all who would seek to bind the Jewish law upon Gentile Christians.

451

This letter is a treatise on Paul's independence of all human authority, the total sufficiency of the gospel, and the relation of the Christian to his Lord.

Many scholars place the date of the writing of *Galatians* around A.D. 56, during Paul's third missionary journey. This would mean that he probably wrote it from Ephesus, Corinth, or perhaps Antioch. This may be the case; however, it appears from the tone of the letter, and the sense of urgency in it, that the Judaizing problem is a rather recent one in the Galatian area. This would necessitate an earlier date. The most plausible solution appears to be to see *Galatians* as Paul's earliest letter, written soon after his first journey. This would coincide with the Judaizing problem at Antioch. Regardless of whether the letter was written early in Paul's ministry or at a later time, the meaning of it is the same. The importance and teachings of the epistle are in no way dependent upon the date of writing.

In Paul's day, the Roman province of Galatia included the old kingdom of Galatia proper, to the north, and also parts of Lycaonia, Pisidia, and Phrygia, which adjoined to the south. Since the letter clearly implies that the churches addressed were all founded in the same general period, Paul could not have been writing to both areas. It is now generally agreed that he was writing to the Southern Galatian churches; Lystra, Derbe, Iconium, Pisidian Antioch, and others in the vicinity.

Returning from his first journey, Paul had received word that these churches were suffering from serious defections as a result of Judaizing teachers. These men, attempting to bind circumcision and food laws upon Gentile converts, sought to bolster their position by claiming Paul had no right to speak as he did. They even pointed out that he had once advocated circumcision.

In reply, Paul tried to destroy the influence of the false teachers by defending himself against the attacks they had leveled at his apostleship. Then he set about to refute the Judaistic claims that insisted Christianity should be mingled with certain Jewish laws, notably circumcision. He asserted that this teaching and his authority to teach it were not derived from the older apostles but came directly from Jesus Christ. After having made these two basic points, he defended the faith by pointing out that the true function of the Law was not to rival Christianity, but to act as a servant to guide men to Christ. Christ, he said, has established a religious and social unity that recognizes no difference between Jew and Greek, free man and slave, male and female.

To convince those who would have argued that Paul was preaching a gospel different from that of the other apostles, Paul drove his clinching point home: there is but *one* gospel. All the apostles are in accord about this. Christ has come to abolish all artificial distinctions. In him, all men are one. *This* is the gospel. There is no other, "for neither circumcision counts for anything, nor uncircumcision, but a new creation." (*Galatians 1:15*).

After his opening affirmation that there is but one gospel, Paul then reviews his relations with the church at Jerusalem. He tells how he was converted and speaks of his "calling" as something that took place even before his birth. When the call came to him on the Damascus road, the purpose of his life was revealed.

Next, he turns his attention to the Law of Moses. Does it have any place in Christianity? This must be answered negatively. All who rely on the works of the Law to merit God's blessing are under its curse (*3:10*). God had promised Abraham that his posterity would bless the world. Jesus Christ was the subject of that promise, and he is the blessing (*3:14–16*). God's gift of the Law of

Moses did not nullify that promise( *3:17*). Then what was the purpose of the Law? The Law was provided to expose the sinfulness of the people of God. It was intended to remind them of their condition and thereby keep them dependent upon his gracious promise (*3:19–21*). As such, it could only be temporal and provisional. It was, in fact, a source of instruction and discipline designed to bring men to Christ (*3:24–25*). Now, those who believe in Christ are freed from its guidance; there is no more purpose for it. And if any man attempts to gain salvation through observance of it, he is leaving freedom and seeking bondage (*4:1–9*)! So, Paul asks, do you wish now to be enslaved again?

A transition of thought is made in *4:21*, where Paul develops an allegory on the story of Abraham's two sons (*Genesis 16, 21*). This is how he introduces the theme of freedom and slavery. Salvation by the Law and salvation through Jesus Christ are sharply contrasted here, and Paul emphasizes again that "we are not children of the slave but of the free woman." (*4:31*).

The remainder of the letter points out the responsible use of the freedom enjoyed in Christ. Those who are led by the Spirit are not under the Law; but they must not live lawlessly, or in any way abuse the freedom they have. If "freedom from the law" is interpreted as removal of all moral restraint, "the flesh" would be allowed to control one's life. Christians are therefore subject to a new law: "You shall love your neighbor as yourself" (*5:14*). This law of neighbor-love means that Christians, though free from the Law of Moses, are to be "servants of one another." (*5:13*). And how will the follower of Christ be able to follow this pattern? By surrendering to the guidance of the Holy Spirit (*5:16–18*)! The Spirit will lead; the Christian must follow, and make every effort to restrain his natural "fleshly" inclinations

(*5:16–24*). All virtuous characteristics are divine gifts, and not the result of self-cultivation.

The letter ends with a personal touch. Paul laments that a situation has arisen that demands such strong language. The reception these churches had given him earlier, contrasted with their present attitudes, causes him shame. He has had to be very blunt with them; he has had to assert himself strongly. The softer tone of the concluding portion of the letter indicates his intense desire for them to understand why this has been necessary.

## The Second Missionary Journey

Following the completion of the first missionary tour, Paul and Barnabas remained in Antioch for a while preaching and teaching. After a certain period of time, they decided to return to the churches they had established. A disagreement arose between the two over Barnabas' desire to have Mark accompany them. When neither could be persuaded to accept the other's point of view, they parted as brethren. In *Galatians 2: 11–14*, Paul charged that Barnabas and Peter had avoided table fellowship with their Gentile brethren. Apparently Paul and Barnabas had experienced this early disagreement, and perhaps the dispute over Mark just brought things to a head. Even so, there was no malice or rancor involved in this decision; just a disagreement among brethren in Christ. As they saw it, the best way to resolve the difficulty was for Barnabas to take Mark with him and go back to Cyprus. Silas would accompany Paul, and they would strengthen the churches Paul and Barnabas had previously established in Asia Minor.

Paul and Silas (whose Roman name was "Silvanus") began the second journey by retracing the steps of the first. They were joined by Timothy at Lystra. Timothy was

453

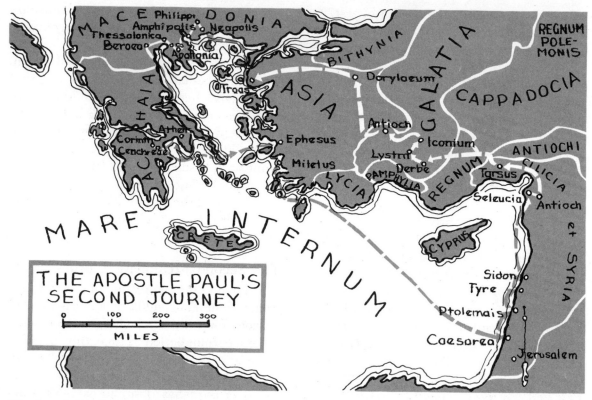

The Apostle Paul's Second Missionary Journey.

half Jewish. His father was a Gentile, but his mother and grandmother were devout Jewish women known to Paul. Timothy became one of Paul's most steadfast friends and companions. The three of them visited the churches in various areas. Some of their plans had to be abandoned because of the leadership of the Holy Spirit, who prevented their going into certain areas. Somewhere about this time, Luke joined the group. Eventually coming to the city of Troas, Paul experienced the vision in which a man begged him to "come over into Macedonia and help us." (*Acts 16:9*). It was a call that could not be resisted, and Paul made immediate plans to answer it.

The trip across the Aegean Sea from Troas to Neapolis and Philippi is not particularly lengthy—but in this case it was a highly significant one. For the first time, the gospel was being brought to the continent of Europe. Macedonia was a section of the Roman empire, of course, and in that time it would not have been considered a part of a different continent. The modern reader, however, may see in this journey the unfolding drama of the early church. Within a generation after Jesus' death, the news of his crucifixion and resurrection was being published throughout the entire empire.

*Philippi (Acts 16:12–40)*. The first European site of Christian missionary activity was Philippi, the principal city of Macedonia. Full of historic significance, Philippi had been the site of the crucial battle that had aligned Brutus and Cassius against Mark Anthony and Octavian, the avengers of Julius Caesar. After Octavian had won the battle, many soldiers settled at Philippi. Octavian, who shortly there-

454

after became "Caesar Augustus," rebuilt the city, gave it the rank of a royal colony, and made it a special military outpost of Rome. The inhabitants were granted special privileges by the government. Latin was the official language here, and the citizens were people of cultivated Roman manners. Philippi was an important crossroads of culture and commerce, and the city fathers remained in close touch with the imperial capital. Thus, Philippi was an excellent place to begin the westward missionary expansion of the church.

The first European convert to Christianity was a woman named Lydia. Apparently a person of high integrity, Lydia was a Gentile who had become sufficiently attracted to Judaism to become a worshiper of God. In Philippi the Jews met outside the city gate, by a river. Perhaps, though by no means certain, a synagogue was located here. At any rate, it was the accustomed site of worship, and Paul went there on the Sabbath day and spoke to the gathered women. A significant fact of Lydia's conversion is her occupation. Luke indicates she was a well-to-do merchant. Though the majority of Christian converts in this time were people of the oppressed classes, there were also some at the other end of the social scale who professed faith in Jesus.

In *Acts 16:16ff*, we find the interesting story of the healing of the mad slave-girl. Paul, Luke, and the others were on their way to prayer-meeting when this girl "who had a spirit of divination" began to follow them crying out, "These men who proclaim to you the way of salvation are servants of the Most High God." This girl was obviously insane, and insane people held a strange fascination in New Testament times. This particular girl heightened that fascination through her practice of soothsaying, an art that was rapidly making her masters wealthy. She trailed Paul's company for some time, shouting all the while. Finally, Paul grew irritated and commanded the demon that possessed her to come out of her.

When her owners saw their financial source had been taken from them, they dragged the missionaries in a fury to the city magistrates and demanded they be punished immediately. The fact that Paul and Silas were Jews probably heightened the hostility of the officials. In any case, the gathered mob immediately set upon them, beat them violently, and had them thrown into prison. They probably had no chance to make any protest; even if they had, it would likely have done little good.

The conduct of Paul and Silas in prison made quite an impression upon those in the building with them. Instead of moaning about their hard lot, they prayed and sang hymns. That night an earthquake—something not too uncommon in that region—occurred. Luke draws the reader's attention to the effect the action of Paul and Silas had upon their jailer. When he thought the prisoners entrusted to him had escaped, he was ready to commit suicide, and was prevented from doing so only by Paul's reassurance that they were still there. Brought to a sudden realization that these men had something he needed desperately, the jailer begged Paul and Silas to tell him what he needed to do to be saved. He could not have known much about Christianity yet, so we are not sure what he meant by that. But Paul and Silas had a ready answer, and they told him what to do. He responded immediately, and after attending to the wounds of his prisoners, was baptized. He had feared punishment from the officials, as he had assumed that all of the prisoners had escaped. Paul and Silas offered him a salvation that went far beyond mere deliverance from the punishment he dreaded.

For the sake of the gospel, and in order to spare the new Philippian Christians any embarrassment, Paul demanded an official public apology the next day. The city officials, having had time to think about the injustice of their treatment, were at first inclined to let Paul depart from the city quietly. This Paul refused to do. Public acknowledgement was then made, and Paul and his companions left Philippi after making sure the reputation of the gospel suffered no tarnishing.

*Thessalonica and Beroea (Acts 17:1–15).* The next stop on the journey was Thessalonica. This city, named for the step-sister of Alexander the Great, was the leading harbor of Macedonia. It stood on a hill overlooking a beautiful fertile plain in one direction and the Thermaic Gulf in the other. In both Greek and Roman times it was an important city, due to the harbor and the great Egnatian highway that ran through it. The missionary band spent only a brief period of time in Thessalonica, but they developed a strong bond of love and loyalty with their converts, of whom many were Gentile believers who "turned from idols to serve the living and true God" (*I Thess. 1:9*).

The Jews in Thessalonica felt threatened by the efforts of Paul and his associates. They hired a mob to bring false accusations against them and set the city in a general uproar. The city authorities intervened at this point and urged Paul to move on, to avoid further disturbance.

That night, Paul and Silas journeyed to Beroea, where they were more favorably received by the Jews. The people of the covenant who lived here were faithful students of the scripture. They examined the books of the Old Testament to see if this crucified Christ preached by Paul did indeed fulfill the prophecies. Finding this to be the case, many Bereans believed and accepted Jesus as their Lord. Some Jews from Thessalonica, however, who had heard of the success of Paul among these people tried to cause a

disturbance in Beroea similar to the one in their own city. This attempted persecution led to a temporary separation of Paul, Silas, and Timothy. Silas and Timothy remained in Beroea, while Paul—the chief target of the aroused Jews—went on to Athens.

*Athens (Acts 17:16–34).* Just outside the city of Athens there was a place called "Areopagus," or "Hill of Mars." This was a gathering place of scholars and spokesmen of the various philosophical schools of thought. Probably, it was a type of open forum where anyone could "mount a soapbox" and undertake some street-corner preaching. Many people spent entire days there doing nothing more than listening to the propagators of the various cults and philosophies. When Paul's turn to speak came, he presented the listeners with a way of life completely new to them. The very novelty of his ideas was enough to make them pay attention to what he was saying. No doubt the heightened their interest with his beginning remarks; and his knowledge of contemporary thought probably impressed more than a few.

In essence, what Paul said to the gathering was this: "I know that you are a religious group, for I have seen many statues here in the area. I also know that you are interested in ultimate questions, for your presence in such a place as this shows an inquisitiveness about religion. I have noticed one particular thing as I have visited your altars and shrines. There is one vacant altar that has no statue. It honors none of your ancient deities. And there is an inscription on it which has especially caught my attention. It says, "To an unknown God." Now, I suspect some of you here have knelt at that altar. I suspect some of you here have paid your respects to that deity of whom you had no knowledge. I would like to tell you about this "unknown God." You may have worshiped him in ignorance. Today I can tell you some things about him, for he has revealed himself."

The Areopagus or Mars Hill, where Paul delivered his sermon to the Athenians.
Above it are the ruins of the Acropolis, the fortified portion of the
city. Below are present-day dwellings.

From there Paul went on to tell about the God of the Universe, who had manifested himself through Jesus Christ his Son. This God was one—the Most High—and he was calling all men everywhere to come to repentance, to commit their lives to him in faith, and to live in hope of a resurrection from the dead.

This was certainly news to those who listened. To all, it was strange. To some, it was nonsense. To others, it was entertaining. To a few, it was good news. The response to Paul's sermon varied. Some of his hearers were so disgusted they made sport of him. Perhaps these were the sophisticated Epicurean and Stoic philosophers, who thought Paul was a "seedpicker." Others were confused, for they thought he spoke of certain foreign divinities about which they had not heard. Some said, "We will hear you again about this." That may have indicated genuine interest, or it may have meant simply, "Well, that's about as much as we need from you right now." Then there were the few who joined Paul and believed his message. This latter group included an aristocrat named Dionysius, a women named Damaris, and a few others.

We have no reference to the church in Athens in New Testament times. It seems that whatever positive results Paul achieved were only short-lived. Christianity did not make many converts here. Perhaps the general intellectual atmosphere was not conducive to an actively religious philosophy of life. Paul had called for commitment. This was apparently a foreign idea to the people of Athens where the premium was placed upon talk, not action.

*Corinth (Acts 18:1–17).* From Athens, Paul moved on to Corinth. There he awaited the arrival of Silas and Timothy, who were to rejoin him there. During the period of waiting, he busied himself with the preaching of the message that had become such a part of him. One of Paul's most outstanding characteristics was his eagerness to take advantage of every opportunity to promote Christianity. He never passed up a chance to proclaim the news of the risen Lord.

Another facet of Paul's personality—this one not quite so admirable, perhaps—is reflected in his actions in Corinth. Upon his arrival, he made the Jewish synagogue his temporary headquarters. "And he argued in the synagogue every Sabbath, and persuaded Jews and Greeks" (*Acts 18:4*). Naturally, it was not long before certain Jews began to oppose him bitterly. When this happened, he simply moved his pulpit from the synagogue to the house immediately next door. Paul was an opportunist, but he certainly was no master of tact! It is humorous to imagine the scowling Jews walking past this stubborn preacher as he proclaimed his message in the very shadow of the synagogue. On the other hand, what Paul lacked in tact he made up for in courage. Few men would have remained so stedfastly in the face of their adversaries as Paul did when these Jews continually "opposed and reviled him." (*Acts 18:6*).

Paul infuriated the Jews, but he never turned his back on them. They were his brethren, and he knew it. To the end of his life, he never lost hope that one day "all Israel shall be saved" (*Romans 11:26*). Perhaps this explains why he remained so close to the synagogue even in the face of the most stringent opposition. We notice that his efforts did not go completely unrewarded, for Crispus, the leader of the synagogue, believed and became a disciple of Jesus. This no doubt compounded the opposition Paul faced, and it must have irritated the Corinthian Jews no end to see Crispus walking into the home of Titius Justus to hear Paul preach. We may wonder that he escaped assassination in a situation such as that. As it happened, Paul himself had probably wondered if an attempt might be made on his life. He was reassured in a vision that no harm at all would come to him. And no harm came. He remained in Corinth preaching and teaching for a year and a half.

Paul did get into at least one scrape in Corinth. Several Jews banded together in a united attempt to get him arrested and out of the way. In an attempt to cast Paul in the role of lawbreaker, they brought a case before Gallio, the proconsul, charging him with disorderly conduct and lawlessness. But Gallio was no fool, and he saw through these trumped-up charges. He probably had little use for the Jews, anyway. Now they were bothering him, wasting his time, trying his patience, and straining his credulity. Probably more than slightly irritated, he bawled them out for trifling with the court and dismissed the case. The entire incident is rather humorous. Apparently there were a good many witnesses present. When Gallio shrugged off these Jewish charges, some of the onlookers decided to give Sosthenes, who had recently been appointed as the new ruler of the synagogue, a sound beating. Gallio seems to have been more amused than concerned over these proceedings, and the only reward Sosthenes got for his attempt was a good thrashing.

Just why Paul decided to leave Corinth is not actually known. Perhaps it was because he wanted to be in Jerusalem at the time of Passover. Whatever the reason, after a time he completed his work and sailed away to Syria. Before he left, though, he sent off two letters to the church at Thessalonica. These dealt with certain specific situations that had arisen relative to the Christians in that city. Many scholars consider the Thessalonian letters to be Paul's earliest. Whether they preceded the epistle to the Galatians is debatable, but they were certainly among his first epistles.

### THE FIRST LETTER TO THESSALONICA

Paul's visit to Thessalonica was a brief one. After his ministry to the Christians there, he frequently sought to return and visit them. However, for a variety of reasons, this desire was never fulfilled (*I Thess. 2: 18*). In his place, he sent Timothy to encourage and establish them further in sound doctrine. Also, he wanted an accurate report of their current spiritual condition, and he knew he could rely upon Timothy to provide that (*3:1–5*). At the time of the writing of the first letter, Timothy had brought back an encouraging report (*3:6–10*).

The first three chapters of the first epistle contain Paul's message of thanksgiving for this good report. Still, there were some disturbing elements. The reader may notice something of a defensive tone early in the letter. This is probably indicative of the fact that an element hostile to Paul had crept into the Thessalonian church. Perhaps someone in the church there had been actively attempting to undermine Paul's influence. Lest anyone be persuaded that Paul's motives were personal, he reminds them he was never any sort of a burden—financially or otherwise—during his labors in their city. He points out that he had provided his own support (*2:9*). While he was there, he had cared for them as a nurse looks after a child (*2:7*). Their relationship had always been a cordial one, and Paul is anxious that it remain that way.

There was another reason for writing. The Thessalonians were in need of additional teaching on the second coming. Paul had preached on it while among them. Since that time, some of them had obviously conceived some distorted ideas about the subject. They had grown concerned about some disciples of their number who had died since becoming Christians. Since they were expecting the second coming at any time, and since they knew that when Jesus came they would be caught up to meet him, they wondered about the fate of those who had now gone on. Would they be left out? Would they have no share in the glory?

Another aspect of the same problem had come to Paul's attention. When he had been with them, he had preached that the second coming would occur very soon. Because of this, many members of the Thessalonian church were neglecting the ordinary duties of life. They had literally dropped all responsibility in their anticipation of the Lord's return, and had fallen into the sins that often accompany idleness. *1 Thessalonians 4:13–18* is devoted to the correction of these misconceptions. Paul assures the brethren "by the word of the Lord" (*4:15*) that the dead in Christ are at no disadvantage. They shall fully share in the blessings of his coming.

The last two chapters of the first letter are full of admonitions against worldliness. This was always a serious problem in an idolatrous city like Thessalonica; therefore, he provides them with a series of exhortations to remain steadfast in the faith, that their entire "spirit and sole and body be kept sound and blameless at the coming of our Lord Jesus Christ." (*5:23*).

### THE SECOND LETTER TO THESSALONICA

The second letter to this church appears to have been written only a few weeks—or perhaps a few months—after the first. A new situation had arisen. The Thessalonians were now being taught that the Day of the Lord, for which Paul had urged them to be ready, had already arrived.

Paul shows some uncertainty as to the origin of this new idea (*II Thessalonians 2: 1–2*), and seems perplexed that such a notion could have arisen in the wake of his rather extensive teaching on the matter (*2:5*). He sets about to correct the misunderstand-

ing immediately. First, he reviews those things that he had taught them earlier; then he exhorts them to abide in these teachings, separating themselves from any who might promote a different doctrine.

In this brief letter, he attacks the current error by demonstrating that the hope of Israel has not yet been fulfilled; therefore no one can say that the Lord's coming has already taken place. Furthermore, they should realize that salvation through Christ is both a present reality and a future hope as well.

In *II Thessalonians*, Paul does not give any kind of full explanation of his views on the subject at hand. He has asked his readers to recall his earlier teachings, and he assumes they remember them clearly. His immediate purpose in writing is to help quiet down some of the excitement that had arisen as a result of this teaching that "the Lord has come." (*2:2*).

A problem to the current reader of *II Thessalonians* is the meaning of Paul's remarks on "the rebellion" and "the man of lawlessness" (*2:3*). What is he talking about? "The rebellion" probably refers to the belief, commonly held in Paul's time, that a general religious apostasy was to precede the coming of the Day of the Lord. It is more difficult to say what is meant by "the mystery of lawlessness already at work" (*2: 7*) and "the man of lawlessness, the son of perdition." (*2:3*). There are those who have claimed that "the man of lawlessness" is a reference to a Roman emperor. If this were the case, "the mystery of lawlessness" would be a phrase to be applied to the Roman government itself, and the corruption within it. Others have objected to this interpretation. They point out that Paul elsewhere (*Romans 13*) speaks very highly of the government's role in man's affairs, and that he traces the source of governmental power and authority to God. Seen from this perspective, the Roman government would be considered a deterrent to lawlessness; certainly not the cause of it. An alternate interpretation would have Judaism as "the mystery." Some Jewish leader would therefore be "the man of lawlessness."

It seems likely that Paul *did* have specific historical persons and occasions in mind as he wrote, but there is no certainty even of this. His full meaning is uncertain. Since the thought patterns of his day were considerably different from ours, those to whom he wrote were in a far better position to understand his words. Whatever this "mystery" was, the Gospel was holding it back—and Christ would eventually overcome it.

## The Third Missionary Journey

In *Acts 18*, Luke introduces Apollos, an "eloquent man, well versed in the Scriptures," who had a partial understanding of Christianity. We are told that "he knew only the baptism of John" (*Acts 18:24–25*). Some have suggested that this refers to a tradition, of which Apollos had heard, that John and Jesus were both preachers of repentance and heralds of the coming Kingdom of God. Apollos was a man of magnetic personality, ability, and learning. But his experience was limited, and he had not heard of the things that gave Christianity its true power. He was unaware of the resurrection of Christ, he was ignorant of the fact that a new age had dawned, and he had never been taught that those who were baptized in the name of Jesus were experiencing the abiding presence of the Holy Spirit.

Apollos, despite his learning, was receptive to new information. When a Christian couple named Priscilla and Aquila heard him, they took him aside "and expounded the way of God more accurately" (*Acts 18: 26*). Through their instruction, Apollos became acquainted with the living presence of Jesus, in addition to his knowledge of the historical carpenter from Nazareth.

*Ephesus.* Ephesus was the capital of the Roman province of Asia. It was a city of great prominence, both from the historic point of view, and from the fact that it was a thriving commercial center. Most of its inhabitants were Greeks, although the influx of immigrants from the East had given the city a sizable Oriental community. There were also large numbers of Jews in the area. Ephesus was a "free city," and in keeping with the special status Rome had given it, the people enjoyed an extra measure of self-government.

The primary feature of the city was a great temple to the ancient goddess Diana. This temple, located just outside the city, was one of the seven wonders of the ancient world. Because of it, the whole city enjoyed a sort of sacredness. Travelers from distant lands made pilgrimages to the shrine of Diana, so tourism was a major source of income. For this reason, many silversmiths made their living by fashioning small likenesses of Diana. There was always a market for miniature replicas of the goddess—both from travelers and natives. Therefore, silversmithing was one of the most lucrative occupations here.

A second architectural feature of the city was the great theatre on Mount Coressus. It supposedly seated around 25,000 people. Some have estimated the capacity as high as 50,000. It was to this theatre that the mob attempted to drag Paul following disturbances that had arisen over his preaching. (*Acts 19:28–29*).

When Paul arrived at Ephesus, on his third missionary tour, he evidently found it a fertile field for his preaching. We are told that he spent between two and three years here, preaching daily in the lecture hall of Tyrannus. Luke makes special mention of the fact that "a number of those who practiced magic arts brought their books together and burned them in the sight of all"

(19:19). This is an apparent reference to certain magic books called "The Ephesian Letters," mentioned by several Greek and Latin authors.

Three years in one place would be time enough for a man like Paul to make an impact upon any city. Ephesus was no exception. In the first place, we are told that "God did extraordinary miracles by the hands of Paul" (19:11). Second, the incident concerning the seven sons of the priest Sceva would have been broadcast widely (19: 11–16). In fact, Luke says that this very incident caused fear to fall "upon them all; and the name of the Lord Jesus was extolled" (19:17). Next, the spectacular book-burning recorded in 19:19 doubtless created considerable commotion.

Probably as a result of several incidents, Paul found himself in trouble with the Ephesian businessmen. His repeated attacks on idolatry had found many hearing ears, and the statuette trade obviously had declined considerably since his arrival. The silversmiths correctly blamed Paul for the fact that sales were down. Appealing to the patriotism of Ephesian citizens, they initiated a mob scene that lasted over two hours. What they were really worried about was their depleted income—not patriotic causes. Finally the uproar was quelled by the town clerk (19:28–40). Perhaps he was really fair-minded enough to fear that Paul's companions might suffer injustice. More likely, he feared the Roman government might intervene—and therefore restrict the city's self-government—if a serious disturbance of the peace should occur.

Shortly after this incident, Paul left Ephesus, spent some time in Macedonia and Greece, and eventually returned to Jerusalem. It was during this particular period—beginning with his stay in Ephesus—that Paul wrote several of his most important letters.

## THE CORINTHIAN CORRESPONDENCE

Up to this time, the church had drawn most of its members from lower, less educated classes of people. There were exceptions, of course, but this was certainly the general rule. These converts, many of whom had come from the most sordid of backgrounds, frequently found it difficult to shake off the influences of their pagan environment.

The first Corinthian letter (as we know it) was not actually Paul's first epistle to the Christians in the city of Corinth. In I Corinthians 5:9, he refers to another letter he had written earlier, and to a misunderstanding it had caused. Scholars have determined that Paul directed at least four letters to the Corinthians, and perhaps even more.

After leaving Corinth, Paul had gone on to Ephesus and had continued his ministry there. While in Ephesus, some unpleasant reports began coming to him concerning certain developments within the Corinthian church. One message came from members of Chloe's household (I Cor. 1:11), another from Apollos (I Cor. 16:12), and a third came in a visit to Paul by three Corinthian Christians (I Cor. 16:17). Upon learning of these developments, Paul wrote our "I Corinthians" from Ephesus (I Cor. 16:8). It is believed that Timothy was the messenger who delivered this epistle to the church. The date of writing has been set between A.D. 54 and 57.

Paul wrote one letter, then another shortly thereafter. I Corinthians was actually the second letter he sent. After that, things seem to have taken a turn for the worse, prompting a trip in person on Paul's part (II Cor. 2:1; 12:14; 13:1). This visit turned out to be unfruitful and even painful for Paul. Greatly disappointed by the reaction of the church, he returned to Ephesus and wrote the "severe" letter mentioned in

*II Cor. 2:3–11* (see also *II Cor. 7:5–16*). It seems likely he sent Titus with this letter, giving him instructions to return via Macedonia to meet him. Apparently this brought the desired result. Wishing to commend the Corinthian brethren for their change of heart, Paul promptly dispatched a fourth letter. This letter is all or part of our *II Corinthians*. In it, he expresses joy over their repentance and issues further exhortations to faithfulness.

We have no real knowledge about what happened to the "severe letter." Some think it is contained in *II Corinthians 10–13*. There is some merit in this conclusion, for this section reflects a real change of mood from chapter 9. Chapters *10–13*, much more stern in tone than the rest of the book, hardly seem like part of a thankful letter. It is possible that a part of Paul's "severe letter" was inserted in the fourth one (*II Corinthians*) when the letters of Paul were collected by the church. There is no manuscript evidence, however, that would substantiate this position, and hence no way to prove it.

The church at Corinth was seriously divided. It was divided over preachers, it was divided over views of marriage, it was divided according to wealth and social status, and it was divided concerning the resurrection of the body. Paul had hopes of healing these schisms, but one of the most pressing problems was the very fact that there were some in the Corinthian church who did not recognize his authority. In dealing with the situation, he did not analyze the opinions of the various groups, nor did he directly attack the leaders of the various functions. This might have widened the breaches even more seriously. Instead, he directed his attention to the schismatic spirit itself, pointing out its destructive nature. He had to make them understand that the church could not hope to survive, much less be an influence for good, if its members could not conduct themselves with harmony and charity.

### I CORINTHIANS

Paul begins this letter by pointing out that it had never been his intention to make "Paulinists" of people. All he had ever sought was to make them good Christians. True, he was the "father" of the Corinthian church in a very special way, in that he had helped establish it. Still, that did not make him the leader of a Corinthian faction. Even the few members whom he had personally baptized bore no special relationship to him. What matters is not who baptized whom, but one's wholehearted dedication to Christ. Paul is anxious for them to see that all Christians are fellow-workmen for God. In the Christian enterprise there is no room for church feuds.

Another problem that had infested the church at Corinth was an excessive emphasis on "knowledge." This was probably a result of the growing movement that later developed into "Christian Gnosticism." At any rate, there were those who had boasted that the knowledge they imparted was a powerful instrument for man's salvation. Paul refutes this notion by emphasizing that the gospel of the crucified and risen Christ is not to be compared with the "wisdom" taught by other religions and philosophies of the age. The Christian message itself is a very special kind of power and wisdom. It is a "mystery"—but it is a mystery revealed by the Spirit of God and not by any kinds of cultic secrets. Those who do not possess the Spirit cannot receive its gift. The truly spiritual man, on the other hand, is a humble one. A man who is filled with the Spirit has no basis for intellectual pride, for he knows that all that he has is a gift from God. Any jealousy or pride that arises over "knowledge" is of the flesh, and is a result of improper and unchristian thinking.

The next error to which Paul directed his attention was a notorious case of incest that, for some reason, the Corinthian church had condoned. Many factors at Corinth had combined to bring about this type of sexual laxity. For one thing, there were numerous brothels to accommodate the sailors who made port there. For another, there was a strong group of followers of Aphrodite, goddess of love. Paul had come into this environment insisting on sexual purity and self-discipline. While there were doubtless some who had been able to adapt themselves to the Christian view of sex, there were others who were unable to overcome the environmental handicap. Paul found it necessary to be quite stringent in advising the church in this matter. He called their attention to the fact that the church must keep a watchful eye on the conduct within the group, while God will judge those who are outside the body of Christ.

Another aspect of the sexual problem was evident in the attitude of certain members who thought in terms of "body" versus "spirit." In the minds of these people, what one's physical body did had no relation to the status of one's spirit. In other words, they thought that "soul" and "body" should be kept entirely separate, and the one not judged by the other. One can see how this led to a rationalization that could excuse any kind of sexual behavior. Paul fought this false idea by proclaiming the sanctity of the body. He pointed out that the new life of the Christian was purchased at great cost, and that the body of the Christian was the temple of the Holy Spirit.

There was also an opposite notion of sex that had its following in the Corinthian church. Equally erroneous, this was the ascetic view that the sex act was inherently immoral, and that spiritual men avoided marriage for this reason. Paul saw all kinds of dangers in this view, and sought to combat them by insisting that married Christians not deny their mates their sexual rights, except by mutual consent; and then only for a brief time of special religious devotion. Paul warned them of the advantage that Satan could take of married Christians who avoided the conjugal relationship. Still, he observed, if there *were* unmarried Christians who through special dedication wished to remain unmarried, they had a perfect right to follow that course. In fact, it might even be the best course possible, if the individual were equal to its demands. But the main thing Paul was concerned with was that Satan be given no opportunity to corrupt the follower of Jesus through illicit sexual relations. The general rule he offered to the Corinthians was that they maintain their current marital status, if they had any doubts about their own personal situation. His elevation of the celibate ideal was almost certainly due to his belief that the coming of Jesus was very near.

Animal sacrifice was practiced by other religious groups besides Judaism in the Roman world. In Corinth, for instance, many public and private sacrifices were made constantly. When such a sacrifice was made, it was customary for the priests to get a cut, with the remainder of the flesh being distributed among the worshipers. A wealthy pagan could throw a successful party or banquet by inviting friends to join him in sacrifice. Following the religious part, dinner would be served, with the sacrifice performing double duty as the main course of the meal.

When public sacrifices were arranged, it was customary for the sacrificial meat that had neither been burned nor given to the priests to be sold in the market place. This kind of situation gave rise to a practical problem in the Corinthian church: should a Christian buy and eat meat that has been sacrificed to heathen idols? The problem

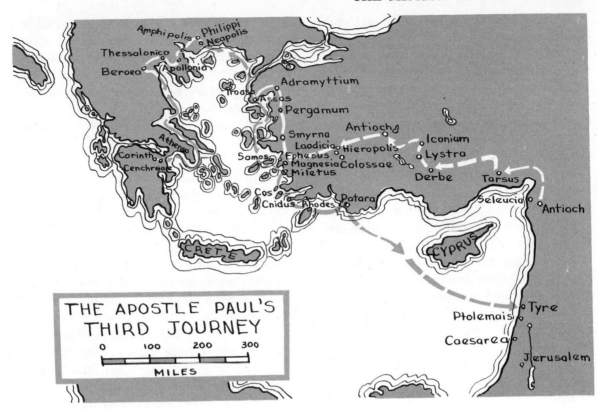

Paul's Third Missionary Tour.

was made more complex by the common notion that spirit powers possessed men through the eating of food.

Here is how Paul deals with that situation. First of all, he says, these heathen gods do not actually exist. In theory, then, there is nothing wrong with buying the meat as long as the Christian realizes this. Still, there is the matter of influence. What if a weak Christian, a recent convert, sees his stronger brother eating this sacrificed food? What will he think? Will it further weaken his faith? Might it renew his old beliefs? The practical aspects of the situation might demand that the strong Christian voluntarily abstain from the purchase of such meats— not that he sins by eating it, but that he might be a stumbling-block to a weaker brother. In other words, love dictates the action. No superior understanding or strength of conviction permits a man to violate the supreme principle of love. Christian liberty allows certain latitude, but it also imposes a certain amount of self-discipline for the sake of the brethren. This was Paul's message regarding the situation. He appealed to the example set by Christ, and called for imitation. He urged the Corinthians in this matter—as in all others—to avoid any conduct that would give offense.

Gross misunderstanding of the purpose and nature of the Lord's Supper had been responsible for some scandalous behavior on the part of certain Corinthians. It appears that some of the wealthier members had formed a habit of coming to the meetings of worship, indulging themselves with food and drink without waiting for the poor, and had generally formed picnic-cliques. The poorer Christians, who sometimes did not

465

even have enough to eat, were left completely out of the fellowship. Paul levels a scathing attack upon these greedy and callous people who have made a travesty of the Lord's Supper by their indifference to their brethren (*I Cor. 11*).

The lack of fellowship in the Corinthian church had led to still another deplorable situation. The spirit of strife and self-seeking so prevalent among them had caused a good many expressions or disorderliness. Their services of worship had degenerated into unintelligible shouting contests. Therefore Paul demanded that "all things be done decently and in order" (*I Cor. 1:40*). This would keep the church from being a laughingstock to outsiders, and would go a long way in the preservation of fellowship and unity. Each member should see to his own spiritual gift. Each gift should be mastered and used "for the common good" (*I Cor. 12:7*).

This subject leads directly into Paul's beautiful lyric description of love in chapter *13*. Pointing the Corinthians to the ideal that should ever be before them, Paul shows them "a more excellent way"—the way of love. Love, he says, "is patient and kind; love is not jealous or boastful; it is not arrogant or rude. Love does not exist on its own way; it is not irritable or resentful; it does not rejoice at wrong, but rejoices in the right. Love bears all things, believes all things, hopes all things, endures all things." (*I Cor. 13:4–7*).

Then he closes with a reminder of the essentials of the Christian faith. His concluding subject is an exposition of the Christian hope of the resurrection of the body. Some of the Christians at Corinth had evidently doubted the actuality of the resurrection; Paul makes it plain that without this, Christianity would be just another vain, hopeless philosophy. He declares that the validity of the entire structure of the Christian message rests upon one fact: that God has raised Jesus Christ from the dead. Paul gives assurance that Christ has triumphed over all the powers of evil through his resurrection; and that his victory has begun, his reign now continues, and that death itself will one day be destroyed.

## THE CORINTHIAN REACTION

Paul had sent his letter to Corinth in hopes of straightening out the many problems that had beset the church there. Timothy delivered the letter and probably stayed long enough to note its reception. When he returned, he regretfully told Paul that no improvement of the situation was evident. Soon afterward, Paul himself went to Corinth. This is what he called "the painful visit" (*II Cor. 2:1*). From the standpoint of what might have been accomplished, it was a complete failure. When Paul arrived and attempted to correct the various misdeeds and misunderstandings, at least one member rebelled, and the congregation as a whole acted defiantly. His hopes crushed, Paul returned to Ephesus in defeat.

Upon his return, he wrote a third time. This letter has not been preserved, unless it is a part of our *II Corinthians*. It was a particularly severe letter; it had to be. Paul sternly demanded that the rebel in the church be punished and apparently set forth other strict measures.

Paul sent his letter apparently by Titus while he was still seething with anger and disappointment. Later, he began to have second thoughts. Had he been too harsh? Had he spoken so strongly that there was a possibility the bonds of fellowship might now be broken? Pondering these things, he left Ephesus sooner than he had planned. While at Troas, he became so upset about the Corinthian situation that he was not even able to continue his work. So, he left Troas and journeyed along the Egnatian way, hoping to meet Titus with news from Corinth.

In time, Titus rejoined him, and met him with the happy word that the worst of the Corinthian crisis was now over. Paul's blazing language had shocked the Corinthians out of their indifference. In fact, it had grieved them and moved them to repentance. The offender had been disciplined. Apparently, the church had cast him out of its fellowship, though not all had agreed that this should be done (*II Cor. 2:6–11*).

### II CORINTHIANS

His spirits buoyed by this good news, Paul wrote a fourth letter to the church at Corinth. Writing in a far happier tone than he had been able to use previously, Paul reminisced over their common experiences. It is evident, however, that he had not completely overcome his anxiety and apprehension over their problems. Somewhat defensively, he encouraged the church to waste no time accepting responsibility and becoming active. The first action he urged was completion of the collection for the poor saints in Jerusalem. They had begun this collection a year earlier, but had suspended it when the dissension arose (*II Cor. 8:8–15*).

A good many different explanations have been given for Paul's cutting, somewhat bitter language in the closing chapters. No one is able to give a conclusive reason for this. It may have been just a momentary flare-up as he recalled the ill treatment he had received at their hands. Perhaps his temper got the best of him for a spell. In any case, no one can question Paul's genuine concern or his abiding love for his friends at Corinth. They had often made him suffer. They had not traveled the road to Christian maturity as far as he could have wished. Despite all this, his love had not dimmed, and his anxiety for their spiritual well-being had increased rather than diminished.

### The Epistle to the Romans

Paul had long wanted to go to Rome, but the entanglements of the immediate situation always seemed to prevent his doing so (*Romans 1:13*). A trip to Palestine was more important at the moment. If he could take care of that, then a trip to Rome might be his next move.

Following the uproar in Ephesus caused by Demetrius and the other silversmiths (*Acts 19:23–41*), Paul embarked upon a brief excursion into Macedonia and Achaia. Perhaps he felt a need for overseeing some of the young churches he had established; perhaps he needed to consult with other Christians about his coming trip to Jerusalem. Whatever his purpose in the journey, Paul spent a few months in these areas collecting money to provide relief for the poverty-stricken Jerusalem Christians. By this act, he hoped to cement the bond of fellowship between the Jewish Christians in Palestine and the Asian Gentile converts.

During this period, Paul stopped off in Corinth long enough to send a letter to the church at Rome. Indicating his concern for the saints in the imperial capital, he informed them of his wishes and prepared them in advance for the journey he hoped to make soon.

No book of the New Testament has had a stronger impact than Paul's letter to the Romans. No letter written anywhere has had more far-reaching implications. The total effect of this epistle upon the world—then and now—has been incomparable. *Romans* has been called the most profound book in existence, the "diamond of the Scriptures," and an understanding of history that is "an uninterrupted conversation between the wisdom of yesterday and the wisdom of tomorrow."

Whatever else it may be, *Romans* is surely Paul's most thoughtfully precise and systematic statement of the gospel. The influ-

**The Roman Colosseum, built by Titus and Diocletian, where countless Christians were martyred.**

ence it has had upon the thought of the church is beyond question. Statements are frequently made to the effect that *Romans* is the result of Paul's determination "to outline basic Christianity for all ages." Actually, such statements, well-meaning as they are, fail to reflect the fact that this is a genuine letter to a specific church with particular problems. While its value may be timeless, it was originally intended to deal with specific situations in the church of Paul's time. As such, then, *Romans* is not a theological treatise. Notice the introduction in *1:1–15* and the personal notes at the end, beginning with *15:14*. Paul's intentions had long been focused upon a trip to Rome. He longed to preach in the capital of the empire and follow that visit with a trip westward into Spain. Paul saw his own function as the work of a pioneer evangelist. He preferred to establish churches and help them in their initial struggle toward maturity, rather than to build upon the foundations of another's labors (*Romans 15:23*).

The church at Rome had been established by others, so his visit there would be an exception to his general rule. Still, his eyes were directed to Rome, and his strong compulsion to go there was delayed only by the necessity of going to Jerusalem first. After delivering the contribution of Asian churches to the poor Christians in Jerusalem, his wishes would be fulfilled.

What was Paul doing when he wrote this letter? It was not characteristic of him to spin theology off the top of his head or create conversations with imaginary people. We conclude that he was summing up the understanding of the gospel he had accumulated over years of active missions with churches in Asia. His words reflect a thorough understanding of the Jew-Gentile relation in Christianity—something that was still a problem in Palestine. They further mirror a knowledge of Christianity's most pressing problems in a pagan environment, such as faced the church in a place like Corinth. Out of the sum total of his ex-

468

perience as a Christian, Paul had developed deep and thorough insights as to what it meant to be a Christian. The book of *Romans* is the result of his studied reflections on that subject, and is directed to a church that can benefit from these insights.

Following the greeting, creedal statement and thanksgiving that open the letter to Rome, Paul begins his summary of the gospel. He acknowledges his own deep faith that this message has originated with God, contains the power necessary to change the lives of men, and is intended to be the principle by which men can live (*1:16–17*). To him, salvation is a future hope, but it is also anticipated and even apprehended in the present. The gospel is the power of God working towards salvation in every man having faith. The terms are equal for all. There is no favoritism.

Lest anyone wonder why he emphasizes the matter of "salvation" so much, he explains in detail why all men—Jew and Gentile alike—stand under the judgment of God (*1:18–2:24*). No one is righteous, all men are sinners (*3:10, 23*). But God has provided a corrective which has nothing to do with the Law. It is a righteousness which comes from God as a gift; which is bestowed upon men with faith, and which "has been manifested apart from law, although the law and prophets bear witness to it" (*3:21*). Chapters *1* and *2* contain Paul's arguments that demonstrate the need of all men for this righteousness. The Gentiles are indicted for idolatry, sexual perversion, and social vices. The Jews stand equally condemned for their failure to obey the Law that they knew to be of God. All are without excuse; the Jews, because they have willingly transgressed the Law of Moses, and the Gentiles because they have ignored the law of nature. Paul sums up his point in these words: "I have charged that all men, both Jew and Gentile, are under the power of sin" (*3:9*).

Having demonstrated that all men are sinners, Paul is now ready to develop his doctrine of justification. The believer, he says, must always be ready to acknowledge the fact that he *is* a sinner; and that he *is* therefore under God's judgment. There is room for no boasting on the part of anyone (*3:27*). However: once the believing sinner makes this admission, he is accepted by God in that very acknowledgement. His sins are no longer held against him. In the language of the courts of law, he is acquitted from his crimes (*3:22–28*).

The justified sinner is also redeemed by Jesus Christ, through the "expiation by his blood to be received by faith" (*3:25*). But what do these terms "redemption" and "expiation" mean? These two words originally referred to the act of buying back a slave and thereby transferring him from servitude to freedom; and the ancient practice of offering sacrifice to remove the burden of an offense against God. In context, here is what Paul is saying: "You became slaves to sinful ways because of your transgressions. As such, you were slaves in a very real sense. But now God has acted, and his son Jesus Christ has purchased your freedom. The price was high—it was his own life's-blood. But the act of the shedding of that blood was the divine means by which atonement was made for your sins."

"Redemption" and "expiation" therefore emphasize the "free gift" idea, and point to the historic deed by which deliverance from sin was accomplished. Both terms meant a great deal to the Jewish Christians at Rome, for both had special association with Israel's deliverance from Egyptian bondage by God's grace and power. Both terms equally meaningful to Paul's Gentile readers, for they were acquainted with the mystery cults that featured the shedding of blood as a means of removing guilt.

But how does the cross reveal what Paul

calls "the righteousness of God"? It does so by demonstrating God's wrath as a reaction to sin and judgment upon it. It also reveals God's righteousness in a more active way in that it shows the divine love that has provided for forgiveness. The cross leads men to an acknowledgement of their sin and their utter dependence upon God. Thus, through faith in Jesus, men have been restored to a right relationship with their creator. This deliverance by faith has removed all cause for pride in moral achievement. It has taken away any cause for interpreting God's favor to Israel as mere partiality. Instead of destroying the validity of the Law, then, God has established it by fulfilling it. To support this claim, Paul treats at length the case of Abraham, who was justified by faith and whose promise has been fulfilled in the coming of the Savior of mankind (ch. 4).

In chapter 5, we have one of the most interesting sections in the New Testament, a chapter regarded by many as the one passage central to a proper understanding of Christianity. It deals with two men: Adam and Christ. Paul asserts that sin existed in the world when the first man set himself against God. Through the transgression of the first man, all the evil and death in the world came into being. The effects continued and were compounded with the sins of all of Adam's descendants. But now Christ has come, and has repaired the damage done by Adam. Now those who have followed Adam into sin and enmity with God can be lifted into a new order of life. In this new order, established by Christ, goodness is more powerful than evil. The bad has been removed and supplanted by a good with limitless implications. In short, men have become a part of a whole new creation in Christ. Any evil that has been done by the "first Adam" and his followers has been more than counteracted by the "second Adam," Jesus Christ.

This raises an interesting question: if Christ can un-do anything that sin has done, why not just go ahead and sin—and let Christ take care of the forgiveness of it? Paul anticipates this very question. He asks it in this way: "Shall we continue in sin that grace may abound?" (6:1). The answer is an emphatic negative. When one believes in the saving power of Christ's redeeming act, he is brought to his knees and is made to repent of his sins. Upon this repentance, he is baptized into the death of Christ Jesus. As Christ's burial and resurrection marked a transition from Galilean carpenter to risen Lord of all creation, so the burial of baptism initiates a completely new life (6:3–4). The old man is put off, the new is put on. Therefore in baptism, the past and its ways have been renounced. The new life is one risen with Christ (6:4).

So Paul asks his hearers: "Do you understand this? Do you see the point? If we have risen to walk in a new life, it is unthinkable— even impossible—that we should even consider a return to the old way of living" (6: 1–4). "We know that our old self was crucified with him so that the sinful body might be destroyed, and we might no longer be enslaved to sin" (6:6). He concludes this line of argument with these words: "So you also must consider yourselves dead to sin and alive to God in Christ Jesus. Let not sin therefore reign in your mortal bodies" (6: 11–12).

*Romans 7* is a discussion upon the meaning of the Law of Moses and its place in the divine plan. The Law, though it was given to guide men in the right way, actually served as an enticement for wrongdoing (7:5). It was not due to any defect in the Law itself but things happened this way; rather, the fault lay in man's nature. Man knew the Law was good and beneficial to right living, but the inclination to sin was too strong, and the law became man's tool for compounding his own guilt (7:7–11). Since man tends to rebel against any sort of external restraint, the commandment against certain things actually made man desire them (7:7–8).

Of course, it occasionally happens that men find themselves able to obey certain laws—not all, but some. When this occurs, they become proud and self-righteous, and the law becomes an instrument for their own self-glorification. Paul concludes that man's salvation lies neither in the reforming of old laws nor in the making of new ones, but in the obedience of faith that is found in submission to God's power through the gospel (2:17–29; 10:1–4). When men commit themselves to the gospel in faith, they find the key to the meaning of life. They are no longer alone, no longer struggling to remain obedient to a law they cannot keep. Rather, they are aided in all things by the Spirit of God, who enables them to do that which they are unable to do themselves (8:26–27). And because that Spirit is always present, the Christian knows that "in everything God works for good with those who love him, who are called according to his purpose" (8:28).

In chapters 9–11, Paul deals with the tragic rejection of the gospel by the Jews. The whole history of Israel has been a process of getting ready for the coming of Christ and the good news concerning him. Christ's ministry was to them and the gospel had first been preached to them. Despite all this, however, the Jews refused to accept Jesus as the promised Messiah. In these chapters, Paul is at pains to assure his readers that this rejection was not really a surprise, nor would it frustrate God's eternal purposes. On the contrary, their disobedience, past and present, was a key instrument God was using to bring salvation to all men, Jew and Gentile alike. Paul's hope is that the triumphant power and love of God will find

a new response in the people of the covenant and that, through this response, "all Israel will be saved" (11:26).

The words of chapters 12–15 compose the nearest thing to a systematic ethic that we find in Paul. It is easy enough to see why a more thorough systemization was never attempted. For one thing, he was generally opposed to a development of a "Christian moral code." He would not even have liked such a phrase as that. Paul believed in being "led by the Spirit." Those who are led by the Spirit have no need of a code of laws, for their very lives will be actively responding to the grace of God. Still, there were always practical considerations to ponder. The gospel was not simply a theory or a plan—it was a way of life. And people who followed that way of life would inevitably have questions about these practical problems. This enables us to understand what Paul is doing here in chapters 12–15. He takes the Christian moral attitudes that he finds in the gospel; then he shows how these may be applied to conduct in the church, and also in the world as a whole.

Following the pattern set by the Old Testament prophets, Paul proclaims in this section that the only sacrifice acceptable to God is conformity to his will through a transformed mind (12:1–2). The Christian must learn to get along with others, inside and outside the body (12:3–18). He must not let his independence and freedom as a Christian lead to an irresponsible individualism or to an arrogant rejection of secular laws (13:1–7). Paul's advice to the Christian is to be led by the Spirit into transformation that renews the mind; to have the love that is necessary to "live peaceably with all men" (12:18); and to be self-forgetting enough to avoid anything that would cause a brother to sin (14:1–19). Christians are people of liberty, but not of irresponsibility.

In closing, Paul reminds his Roman friends, "I myself am satisfied about you, my brethren, that you yourselves are full of goodness, filled with all knowledge, and able to instruct one another. But on some points I have written to you very boldly by way of reminder . . ." (15:14–15). *Romans* is still the great "reminder" to Christians who seek to understand God's will and God's way for them.

### The Final Trip to Palestine

Paul had hoped to be in Jerusalem to celebrate the Passover feast. He did not make it by then, so he set his sights on arriving in time for the Pentecostal celebration fifty days later. En route, he stopped off at Miletus, only a short distance from the city of Ephesus. From there he sent a message to the elders of the Ephesian church, and they came down to meet him. Paul's farewell speech to these brethren is contained in *Acts 20:18–34*. He speaks of the privilege and responsibility that is theirs as church leaders. He enjoins them to be careful guardians of the flock God has entrusted to their care. In a touching conclusion, he reminds them of a statement Jesus himself had once made, "It is more blessed to give than to receive" (20:35).

He was apprehensive about his visit in Jerusalem, but made the journey anyway. Had Paul been of a different temperament, had he been a little less conspicuous, the trip might have been uneventful. As things happened, it was disastrous. The church situation in Jerusalem was a touchy one. There were still those in the church whose Jewish consciences were offended at Christianity's growing breach with its heritage. To pacify these brethren, and to show he still conducted himself as one within the Law, Paul decided to indulge in some church politics. He was probably talked into this procedure, and may have consented against his better

judgment. Whatever the case may have been, he paid the expenses of four men who had made the Nazirite vow—and he himself underwent the ceremonial purification required of participants in the feast. But he made the political mistake of being seen in the company of a Gentile near the temple area. This precipitated charges of temple desecration, blasphemy, and even insurrection against him. It is difficult to say whether Paul's enemies really thought he had brought a Gentile into the temple, or whether these were just trumped-up charges. But the very accusation brought the wrath of all Jerusalem down on his head and put him in grave danger of a death penalty.

If the crowd had had its way, Paul would have been put to death on the spot. He was rescued from this immediate danger by a tribune who thought him a dangerous criminal. When the tribune discovered his mistake, he gave Paul a chance to speak to the crowd, hoping this would ease the tension. Instead, it only got Paul into more trouble. As he made his defense before the crowd, he related his Damascus road experience and told how it happened that he was now a member of the group he had once persecuted (*Acts 22:1ff*). The crowd remained silent for a few minutes; then, when he spoke of Christ's sending him to the Gentiles, they burst into a flame of rage and hatred (*Acts 22:21–24*).

The tribune, who had witnessed all of this, no doubt wondered what had been said to drive these Jews into such a fury. There was much here he did not understand. What he could see was that Paul was obviously some sort of rabble-rouser who deserved punishment. So, he decided to flog him and was halted only when Paul revealed he was a Roman citizen. It was against the law for punishment of this nature to be administered to a Roman citizen, so Paul was mo-

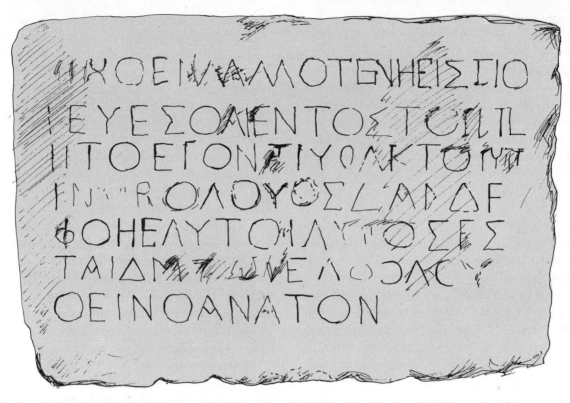

**An inscription from the Herodian temple at Jerusalem forbidding Gentiles to enter the courtyard. The penalty announced is death.**

mentarily returned to his prison cell to await further development.

On the next day, Claudius Lysias (this was the name of the tribune) called the Jewish Sanhedrin together for a hearing of Paul's case. Paul stood before them and began, "Brethren, I have lived before God in all good conscience up to this day" (*Acts 23:1*). Already he was in trouble again; his manner of speaking seemed to the Jews to be one of insolence. The high priest, standing nearby, commanded an aide to strike Paul across the mouth. This caused Paul to flare up in anger at the "whitewashed wall" who was standing in his judgment (*23:2–6*).

Realizing that he was in a situation of more than slight difficulty, Paul decided to try politicking again. At this point, he was fairly certain he would never get justice in such circumstances, so, his next move was to confuse the issue. One would think that an august group of judges would know better than to be sidetracked in such a way, but when Paul explained to them that he was on trial for his hope of the resurrection of the dead, the Sanhedrin immediately split into Pharisee and Sadducee camps. The Pharisees, you will remember, believed in the resurrection, but the Sadducees rejected this doctrine. By raising the issue in this way, Paul opened an old wound, and turned their hatred for him into hatred for one another. In the midst of the bitter squabble that followed, the bewildered tribune, no better informed than he had been the day before, led Paul back into the police barracks. That night the Lord appeared to Paul in a vision and told him he would "bear witness also at Rome" (*23:11*). This certainly supplied Paul with strength, and it came at

473

an opportune time, for he had probably begun to despair for his life.

The frustrated Jews concocted a plot to kill Paul, but this was thwarted when Claudius Lysias discovered it and transferred Paul into protective custody at Caesarea. Caesarea was the seat of the Roman government in Palestine, and was the city where the governor lived. Antonius Felix had charge of Judea from A.D.52-59, and it was to him that Paul was committed for official hearings.

Paul appeared before Felix, and the situation became even more confused. The prosecuting attorney cited a list of crimes Paul had allegedly committed, and "the Jews also joined in the charge, affirming that all this was so" (24:1–9). Felix, however, was unconvinced. The little man standing before him just did not appear to be capable of such misdeeds. And when he spoke, it was of his religious experiences and religious hopes. Felix could not bring himself to condemn Paul as a criminal. Some have wondered why Felix did not go ahead and free Paul. One answer is that Paul was a well-known personage, notorious among the Jews. Any further development in the case would have been reported to Jerusalem immediately. Had Felix released Paul to freedom, there might have been a Jewish uprising. Felix had the political sense to realize that the case had to be handled with discretion and caution; therefore, Paul remained in jail for two years. Even at that, Felix knew he was no common criminal, and for that reason he must have given him as much freedom as political expediency allowed.

Felix was replaced by Porcius Festus, and the arrival of the new governor meant a reopening of Paul's case. This gave Paul's enemies another opportunity to seek his conviction. A delegation from Jerusalem came to Festus requesting that Paul be returned to that city for trial. Meanwhile, an ambush was planned, and men were alerted to seize and kill Paul on the way. To Festus' credit, he immediately saw through this ruse. To send Paul back to the very place of his near-lynching was to ask for trouble. Festus replied by suggesting that all interested Jews who had authority in the matter come to Caesarea. This was done, and once again Paul stood to defend himself. Two years in prison had given him fairly careful insight into what was at stake. He knew very well what sort of case was being prepared against him. Again the Jews requested that the trial be moved to Jerusalem. When Festus suggested to Paul that this might be a good idea, Paul decided to appeal to Caesar. He knew no justice would be done in Jerusalem. His situation was desperate now, and his back to the wall. An appeal to Rome was his only real chance.

Festus granted the appeal, which meant there could be no turning back. There was one more hearing scheduled before Paul's departure to Rome for the appeal. This time he was to go before Agrippa II, the king of Palestine. Agrippa was a member of the Herod family which had ruled Palestine under the oversight of Rome. He was in the city of Caesarea at this time on a courtesy visit to the new governor. Since Festus had this interesting case to call to Agrippa's attention, he called for a new hearing and turned it into a state occasion.

The next day, the governor, the king, and the queen arrayed themselves in their royal garb and had Paul brought before them. Standing in chains, the apostle gave an impassioned defense of his actions and the truth he sought to promote. As Paul spoke, Festus interrupted him, thinking he was surely insane to be saying all these things. Agrippa also seems to have been momentarily dismayed. Was this Paul trying to make them all Christians? When Paul had finished speaking, the king and the governor rose and retired to another room. They had little use for Paul's views, but he had certainly convinced them that he was innocent of the crime of insurrection.

ON TO ROME

*Acts 27*, which tells of Paul's voyage to Rome, the storm, and the shipwreck, is one of the most exciting chapters in the Bible. From the standpoint of adventure narrative alone, it grips the reader. Yet there is more involved here than the mere telling of a shipwreck tale. Luke is attempting to show the reader how difficult it was for Paul to reach Rome. Like Jesus, Paul had been subjected to all sorts of indignities at the hands of his own people. Both Jesus and Paul had gone on trial before the governor, the high priest, and Herod. The storm and shipwreck further compounded the picture of darkness. Perhaps Luke meant for this scene to parallel that of Jesus' crucifixion. There was the same type of mistreatment, and the same type of injustice, and the same picture of gloom. Luke is intending to demonstrate that Paul, like his Lord, was a man of God. Paul, like Christ, was an instrument of God in fulfilling his purpose. Jesus' resurrection from the dead had been prophesied, and it had occurred. By the same token, Luke makes it clear that Jesus' promise to Paul (*Acts 23:11*) did not go unfulfilled.

After the shipwreck and three months on the island of Malta, Paul renewed his journey to Rome. This time he achieved his goal.

In Rome, Paul once again spoke "to the Jew first" (*Acts 28:17; Romans 1:16*). His theme was still the same: "It is because of the hope of Israel that I am bound with this chain" (*Acts 28:20*). The Jews had heard of Christianity, and they knew that it was generally regarded with disfavor. Yet they were willing to hear Paul speak for himself, and this was all he had ever asked. He used his two years in prison to preach every way he could within the limits of his confinement. He spoke to the Jews who came to see him from the Old Testament, trying to convince them that Jesus had fulfilled all the Messianic scriptures. The story ends triumphantly, as Luke intimates that the spread of Christianity was now too extensive to be stopped—ever. It is also clear that he intends for the reader to understand that Paul was primarily responsible.

## The Prison Epistles

"Paul, an ambassador and now a prisoner also for Christ Jesus . . ." *Colossians, Philemon, Ephesians,* and *Philippians* are sometimes called the *Prison Epistles* because all four mention that they are being written from prison. It has traditionally been assumed that these were composed during Paul's first Roman imprisonment. In the modern period of Biblical studies, however, many scholars have come to favor Ephesus as the source of these letters. As a matter of fact, a number of factors *do* favor Ephesus as the location. For example, many argue that *I Corinthians 15:30–32* and *II Corinthians 1:8–10* imply that Paul had been in prison in Ephesus, since both these letters were written from Ephesus and both seem to refer to a recent imprisonment. Also, Paul's allusions in the Prison Epistles to his companions indicate he was surrounded by Asian Christians. Their presence might be more easily explained if he were in Ephesus rather than in Rome. On the other hand, it is not unlikely that Paul would find himself in the company of old friends in practically any section of the evangelized world.

References to the "praetorium" (*Philippians 1:13*) and "Caesar's household" (*Philippians 4:22*) are used by some to argue that these letters originated in Rome. But "praetorium" was used to refer to the official residence of the government in *any*

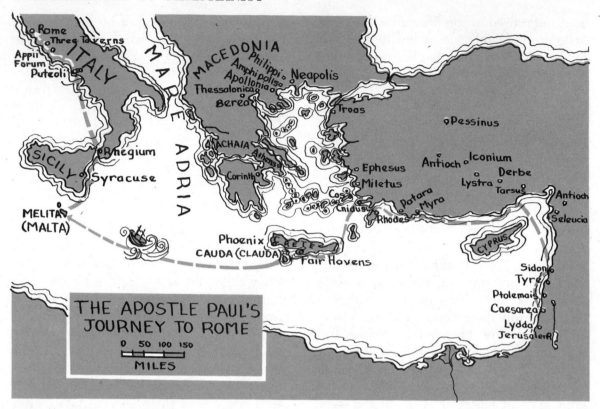

The Apostle Paul's Journey to Rome.

province, and "Caesar's household" might refer to all those who were attached to the personal service of the emperor, whether in Rome or elsewhere. This explanation is plausible, and could be true, but it appears somewhat artificial.

Finally, the presence of Onesinus, with whom the letter to Philemon is concerned, is cited as evidence for a non-Roman origin. The rationale here is that a runaway slave would not travel all the way to Rome, but would seek refuge in a neighboring city. But Rome was a favorite refuge for such individuals. A runaway slave frequently sought to get as far away from his master as possible. One could easily lose himself in the mass of humanity found in such a metropolis as Rome.

Although arguments for Ephesus as the place of writing of these epistles make sense,

Rome is favored because of Paul's discussion of his impending trial as a life and death affair. Such language could scarcely fit any place besides Rome, since Paul could always exercise his right of appeal from another city. Thus, the weight of evidence seems to be on the side of Rome as the site. Admittedly, there is merit for the non-Roman hypothesis, and several scholars favor it. For our purposes, however, we will conclude that Paul was imprisoned at Rome when he wrote these letters. Fortunately, the merit of the epistles is in no way dependent upon our figuring this out.

### COLOSSIANS

Colossae was a city of Phrygia located in the Lycus River Valley. It sat on the great highway leading from Ephesus down to the Euphrates basin. Two important neighboring cities, Hierapolis and Laodicea, were only a short distance away, and each of them, like Colossae, had churches. *Colossians 4:12–15* makes it plain that the churches in the area had been established by someone other than Paul. We are not told who the founder of these congregations was, but *Colossians 1:7* hints that it may have been Epaphras, who could have heard the gospel from Paul when he was in Ephesus, or some other city in the region. Paul had never visited Colossae. Epaphras had visited Paul in prison, bringing him news and greetings from the churches in the area. Naturally, he also brought a progress report with him, and Paul was undoubtedly interested in learning everything he could about the congregational situations.

The results in the Colossian church in its earliest stages were apparently satisfactory (*Col. 1:4–6*). At the time of the writing, however, the church was in danger of being misled by certain false teachers. It is difficult to determine the exact nature of the Colossian heresy, although it did bear more than passing resemblance to what later became Valentinian Gnosticism. It is fairly safe to conclude that the Colossian problem reflected the widespread efforts of the philosophies and cults to find the relation between man's inner life and the universe.

Whatever teachings were embodied in this heresy had the reputation of "wisdom." Christ was considered the greatest source of this wisdom. This in itself was not so bad, but the teaching was being promoted as something of an exclusive nature. It encouraged some measure of asceticism, as indicated by its teaching on foods (*2:16*). Its main error was that it apparently ignored much of the true doctrine of the nature of Christ. The role of Christ in the salvation of mankind was being minimized and the fact that he alone had obtained redemption for man's sin was being ignored.

There were other problems, too. A cult of angel-worship was involved. Much investigation has been made in an attempt to discover the origin of this cult. At this point, however, the only safe conclusion is that an angel-cult was present, and that it evidently found its origin in paganism.

But the Colossian heresy was not just a simple adoption of heathen ideas and practices. Elements of Judaism were involved as well. For example, the promoters of the doctrine advocated circumcision (*2:11*), and they had made demands on the church concerning the observance of certain aspects of Jewish law (*2:14–15*). Also involved was special reverence for certain days and certain seasons (*2:16*). Even with all of this information, however, it is virtually impossible, in our present state of knowledge, to assign the heresy to any particular group or school of thought. Whatever it was, it was in a relatively early stage and had not yet become a clearly defined movement.

A few crackpot ideas here and there might have been relatively harmless. The greatest danger of the heresy lay in its asserting the lack of sufficiency of Christ's work of redemption. The notion fostered here that made it a really grave error was that the work of Jesus was being supplemented, in the minds of these people, by the cult of angels. This robbed Jesus Christ of his sovereign rule. This was what really alarmed Paul, and this was the major target of his letter. The purpose of the Colossian epistle was to convince the readers that the problems to which they sought an answer could be resolved only by returning to the gospel and restoring the sufficiency to Christ.

Along with this major purpose, Paul took care of the more practical matters. In *Colossians* he informs his readers that they are free from all of this ceremonial observance, asceticism, and elements of pagan devotion. He tells them that the only safe tradition to

477

follow is the doctrine of Christ. In developing his argument, Paul speaks of the new life in Jesus Christ in which the believer experiences spiritual union with the risen Lord (*3:1–4*); separation from sin (*3:5–9*); and the putting on of a completely new and Christlike nature (*3:10–11*). Concerning the social life of the church, he commends to them brotherly affection and forgiveness (*3:12–14*); peace (*3:15*); mutual edification in word and song (*3:16*), and thankfulness to God in all things (*3:17*).

The Colossians were worried about the demonic "principalities and powers." Paul explains to them that they no longer need strive, through rigorous legalistic processes, to disarm these "principalities and powers" (*2:15*). This is of no value. It is unnecessary, for Christ has triumphed through his resurrection and robbed them of their power.

Paul concludes the epistle to the Colossians with a series of moral exhortations (*3:5–4:6*). First, he catalogues a list of vices that are to be avoided (*3:5–8*); then he issues a succession of virtues that should be cultivated (*3:12–4:6*). The things he says are practical in nature. In these exhortations he is not extremely original, since contemporary Jewish rabbis and pagan moralists issued similar injunctions. Paul charges all of it with new meaning, however, for he is not giving out a legal procedure to follow—he is characterizing life in Jesus Christ, and demonstrating the kind of conduct that life produces.

### PHILEMON

The second of these epistles to be considered was written not to a church but to an individual. The recipient was a well-to-do Christian named Philemon, who may have been an elder in the Colossian church. He was surely a leader among the Christians in Colossae, since the church met in his home

(*verse 2*). Paul was acquainted not only with Philemon, but with Apphia and Archippus, who were probably Philemon's wife and son. In the letter, Paul sends his personal greetings to all.

Indications are that Philemon was an unselfish steward of whatever wealth he possessed. He was known to be warmhearted and hospitable (*v. 7, v. 22*). He appears to have been Paul's close personal friend, having been with him in some former work, and having carried on a good work in the apostle's absence. (*v. 4–5*).

Onesimus was a former slave of Philemon who had run away, possibly with some money (*v. 18*). He had gone to Rome to seek refuge. While in that city, he had come in contact with Paul in some way, and had been brought to faith and repentance by the apostle. After his conversion, Onesimus had been a great source of comfort and strength to Paul. Although Paul appreciated Onesimus' aid and company, he felt the slave should be returned to his master. Knowing the case and feeling that Philemon would not be a hard and unforgiving master, Paul had persuaded Onesimus to return to the household of his rightful owner. According to ancient law, Philemon actually had the right to kill Onesimus, as he had committed one of the gravest of offences. So Paul, in this letter, serves as an advocate to insure the proper reception for Onesimus.

Notice that Paul does not ask for freedom for the slave. Onesimus is sent home for the service of the gospel. Philemon is expected to acknowledge a new relationship between master and slave, not merely within the church, but with respect to law and social custom. From this point on, Onesimus is to be more than a slave. He is, in fact, to be a brother to Philemon (*v. 16*). Observe also Paul's tact in vv. *17–20*. This is a sort of I.O.U. Paul probably does not intend for Philemon to take him entirely seriously here, but he is anxious to avoid offending this brother so dear to him.

This epistle shows how Paul behaved in little things. It demonstrates part of the reason for his great missionary success. His interest in this matter appears to be as great as his concern for the heresy that troubled the entire Colossian church. To show Philemon the importance he attached to it, he wrote with his own hand, filling the letter with evidence of his consuming love.

In this brief letter, we also have a beautiful picture of a first-century Christian family: the parents are well known for their hospitality and kindness, the son is a worker in the church, and the household is the center of the local congregation.

### EPHESIANS

The letter to the Ephesians, which deals with the relationship between Christ and the church, is a magnificent statement of Pauline theology. Here we see a treatise on the church: what it is, how it has been called, and what it is to accomplish.

Several historical problems present themselves in a study of this epistle. One is that of its original destination. Most scholars do not feel this letter was written for the church at Ephesus—or at least not exclusively so. There are two major reasons for this opinion. One is the fact that several of the best ancient manuscripts omit the words, "at Ephesus" (*1:1*). A second reason given is the conspicuous absence of personal greetings. Remember that Paul labored with the Ephesian church for a span of time covering between two and three years. It is almost a foregone conclusion that Paul would have many dear friends at Ephesus—yet no mention is made of any of them. Also, there are portions of the epistle that imply that Paul had never known these people personally; that they were acquainted only by reputation (*1:15; 3:1–10*).

A coin showing the temple and image of Diana (Artemis) and proclaiming Ephesus the "temple-keeper."

Several scholars have concluded that the letter originally had another destination, perhaps Laodicea (see *Colossians 4:16*). Or it may have been that it was not intended solely for the church at Ephesus, but for all the congregations in the general area. If it were a general letter, it might have been sent to Ephesus first and later passed around to the other churches.

The Ephesian letter is lofty and sublime in its style of language. In this it resembles *Colossians*. The sentences are long and complicated, and reflect careful thought, in contrast to an epistle like *Galatians*, which is intense in emotion and written in short, choppy sentences.

Throughout Ephesians, there runs the conviction that a predestined purpose works throughout history, and beyond it, toward some marvelous, all-embracing goal. Christ has revealed the mystery of the divine will

479

(1:9). Through Christ and his church, God is accomplishing an ultimate unity, and is putting back together all the broken and disruptive forces in the universe. God is spoken of as "our Father" (1:2). He is the prototype of all authority. His sovereignty is not just an abstract concept for philosophers to discuss—he relates to each of us personally. He is "our Father."

This is a statement of the grace of God extended to his church. The church, which is the body of Christ, draws its life from the divine head (1:22–23). It too plays a role in this divine plan, for the church is the primary stage in God's plan to unify the universe. Paul sees the church as a necessary complement of Christ; and it is Christ and he alone who gives the church life and meaning. As head of the church, Christ is the center of its activity and purpose. The church, as his body, brings to completion those things that Christ directs. Christ and the church are working together toward a common purpose. The purpose will be fulfilled when all things are one day united in him. To that end all activities, all ideals, all goals of the church are directed.

To help them to fulfill these expectations, Christians have been provided with the necessary spiritual gifts. They are to use these gifts to promote the corporate unity of the church, in order that each part of the body might work together in growth and in harmony. The overarching purpose behind every activity is to be the building up of the body of Christ in love (4:11–16).

The concluding paragraphs of the epistle consists of practical exhortations and injunctions. Paul directs his attention to the families. The ideal relationship, he says, is the union of Christ and his church. Husbands and wives are to look to this union for a pattern of their own marriage "for the husband is the head of the wife as Christ is the head of the church, his body, and is himself its Savior . . . Husbands, love your wives, as Christ loved the church and gave himself up for her . . ." (5:23–25).

Paul warns his readers against lapsing back into their former manner of life (5:3–13). Since the majority of the Ephesians (and other Asian Christians) had been converted from pagan backgrounds, such a warning made good sense. There was always a very real danger of this—a danger that should constantly be guarded against. The ethical section of the letter concludes with a brief table of household duties. Again, stress is placed upon the mutual love and subordination of husbands and wives. Once more marriage is seen as a profound symbol of the nature of the church.

In closing, Paul depicts the Christian life as one of relentless warfare against evil. The picture reminds the church that all the resources of the gospel are needed "to stand against the wiles of the devil" (6:11).

### PHILIPPIANS

Since the beginning of the church in Philippi on Paul's second missionary journey, the Philippian Christians had contributed generously to the support of missionary and benevolent programs (II Corinthians 8:1–5; Philippians 4:15–19). Even though this church occasionally had financial crises among its own members, its generosity never waned. Fifty years after this time, the church in Philippi was commended by Polycarp for the steadfastness it exhibited.

A number of motives for writing are seen in the letter to this church. An obvious one is Paul's desire to express his gratitude for the gift that had been sent to him by Philippians, and to inform them of the unselfish manner in which Epaphroditus had discharged his mission in ministering to Paul. He also used the epistle as an occasion of telling them his feelings for them and of his own personal condition. He informed them of the impending visit of Timothy and of the return of Epaphroditus, thus assuring both of a good reception (2:19–20). Finally, he wanted to warn them that they would suffer for the gospel (1:29) and to urge them to guard themselves against those who would seek to introduce false doctrines into the church (3:1ff). Philippians is a letter of joy, emanating from a heart full of love.

This church was perhaps closest to Paul's heart of any he established. When others had turned their backs upon him and forgotten him in his afflictions, these had stood by him faithfully. Twice they had sent supplies in support of Paul's mission projects. They had remembered him when he was in trouble, and now that the opportunity had again presented itself, they had once more come to his aid (4:14–16). It is no wonder Paul felt great affection for the Philippians and experienced joy at their progress in the faith. His only regret seems to be that his imprisonment had hindered a personal visit and He makes it plain to them that this letter was a poor substitute for the visit he would have liked to make.

If we assume Paul wrote *Philippians* from a Roman prison, certain problems of chronology present themselves. For one thing, it was a long way from Rome to Philippi—about a seven week trip. Yet this letter itself contains mention of four trips between the prison and Philippi. The sequence goes this way: when the Philippians received word that Paul had been cast into prison, they had sent Epaphroditus to see about it. Epaphroditus had become ill and Paul had sent word back of Epaphroditus' illness. Finally, another message was received from Philippi which told of the anxiety of the church there over Epaphroditus' condition. With Rome and Philippi about 800 miles apart, this certainly would have involved a lot of traveling. Still, it was possible. The roads were good, and frequently traveled.

Some seek to avoid this dilemma by positing an imprisonment in Ephesus. As we have already noted, allusions in Paul's letters to Corinth indicate that he might have been thrown into jail during his Ephesian ministry (1 Cor. 15:32; 2 Cor. 1:8ff, 11:23ff). Since only a ten to twelve day journey separated Ephesus and Philippi, all the visits are made possible. On the other hand, nothing is ever actually said about Paul's being in prison in Ephesus. Even if he were, it would not have been for any sustained length of time. In Paul's letter to Philippi, he has obviously been in jail for quite some time. Only the Roman hypothesis, which involves a long imprisonment, allows for all of the activities that have gone on.

But none of this is of really major importance, anyway. It would be good to know every circumstance under which these epistles were written. But the value of this letter is undiminished by our lack of knowledge of the situation. As with *Philippians*, so with the other letters. We could wish to have a full understanding of the circumstances; but even if we did, the content of the letters themselves would be the same.

Unlike his practice in other letters, Paul does not begin the Philippian epistle by calling attention to his apostleship. These people did not question his position. He simply mentions that he, along with Timothy, is a slave of Jesus Christ (1:1). The thanksgiving that follows reflects a deep feeling of affection for these people. Paul and the Philippians enjoyed a type of relationship that came only with years of common experience. They had rejoiced, they had mourned, they had been anxious together. Their hearts were combined in one great mutual interest. Paul's prayer for his friends was for their continued establishment in the gospel, "that your love may abound more and more, with knowledge and all discernment." (1:9).

Paul was confident that one day he would

be vindicated before God. Many people had made bitter and scathing attacks upon him; others had forsaken him in his moments of greatest distress; and there were some in the church who even rejoiced at Paul's imprisonment (*1:17*). Paul knew, though, that he had given his life to Christ, that every fibre of his being had been thrown into the proclamation of the gospel. And he knew that Christ waited to receive him at the proper time (*1:19–23*). He yearned to be with Christ. Given his own way, he would choose "to depart and be with Christ, for that is far better" (*1:23*). Still, he knew that he still had work to accomplish; and since his only desire was that Christ be glorified, he was perfectly willing to remain a while longer.

One of the loftiest passages found anywhere in scripture is the hymn of *Philippians 2:5–11*. Here, Paul was making use of a poetic version of the story of salvation. This was likely a hymn used by the early Christians to recite to each other the story of the coming of Christ. Paul probably used it here to unify the Philippians in a common bond of devotion and service.

The section found in *3:2ff* represents an angry attack by Paul upon certain Jewish propagandists. His words do not represent a slur on the Jewish nation as a whole, for he still loved his brethren and yearned for their salvation. But there had been Jews who, like scavenging animals, had preyed upon Paul's converts. For these he had no use, and his language indicates his contempt for them. Lest any of the Philippians be taken in by their reasoning, Paul warns them that there is no value at all in circumcision, which had no more religious worth than other mutilations of the flesh (*3:2–9*). Paul's glory is Christ, not the fact that he was circumcised as an infant. He hopes the Philippians will follow his example, so he cautions them against the extremes of legalism and license.

In conclusion, he mentions certain qualities that he wishes them to incorporate into their lives and offers the suggestion, "think on these things" (*4:8*). Then he ends the letter on a note contentment in Jesus Christ: "I have learned, in whatever state I am, to be content. I know how to be abased, and I know how to abound; in any and all circumstances I have learned the secret of facing plenty and hunger, abundance and want. I can do all things in him who strengthens me" (*4:11–13*).

\* \* \*

The remainder of Paul's career is obscure. Some scholars feel he remained in prison until his death. Others, including most conservative scholars, feel that he was released from prison shortly after the completion of the Prison Epistles and that he continued his evangelistic efforts for six or eight more years, years that may have included a trip to Spain. According to this theory, he eventually had another clash with the Roman government and once again landed in jail. Tradition has it that he was taken from prison a short while later, probably in A. D. 64 or 65, led out on the Ostran Way, and beheaded.

To some, the martyrdom of the great apostle may seem sad, but to Paul himself, death came as a release. At last, his burning desire to be with his Lord was to be fulfilled (*Philippians 1:23*). The courageous faith with which he met death is well expressed in these words:

> I am already on the point of being sacrificed; the time of my departure has come. I have fought the good fight, I have finished the race, I have kept the faith. Henceforth there is laid up for me the crown of righteousness, which the Lord, the righteous judge, will award to me on that Day, and not only to me but also to all who have loved his appearing. —*II Timothy 4:6–8*

These familiar lines form a fitting epitaph for the figure whose influence on Christianity has been second only to that of Jesus.

# 18

# The Second Generation
of Christianity

*A picture of Christianity
in the closing years
of the first century*

Wɪᴛʜ ᴛʜᴇ ᴅᴇᴀᴛʜ of the apostle Paul, Christianity entered a new era. Paul had given the gospel of Christ its essential shape and had transformed the Christian church from a sect of Judaism into a vital independent and international movement. In the decades that followed his death, the church occupied itself with the necessary task of deciding just what it was, how it was to regulate its own life, and how it was to meet the challenges and opportunities that lay before it. In this final chapter, we shall trace the main lines along which this effort proceeded.

### The Church: Heir of Israel
### —Bride of Christ—People of God

The christian church is viewed throughout the New Testament as the people of God, and therefore it is described in many ways as the continuation and fulfillment of previous convenants God has made with men. Almost all the New Testament descriptions of the church utilize concepts and images which in the Greek translation of the Jewish scriptures (the Septuagint) had been applied to God's people. This connection with Israel of old is made quite explicit, not only by Paul, who speaks of the church as the "Israel of God" (*Galatians 6:16*), but also by James (*1:1*) and John (*Revelation 7:4*) who address the church as the twelve tribes of Israel. And in the *Letter to the Hebrews*, the church is identified as the community that fulfills Jeremiah's prophecy of the establishment of a "new covenant" (*Jeremiah 31:31–34*), and as true sons of Abraham through repentance and faith. *Hebrews 11*, one of the great rhetorical masterpieces of the New Testament, traces the community of faith from the beginning to the end of history, including all who have lived by faith in God's covenant promises. This great and faithful "cloud of witnesses" (*Heb. 12:1*) surrounds the church and encourages steadfastness in the face of persecution, suffering, and martyrdom.

483

To call the church the "people of God" also clearly means that it is the society which God has chosen for his own possession (*I Peter 2:9; Revelation 21:3*), which he has created and brought into existence by his grace in the forgiveness of sins (*Heb. 2:17; I Peter 2:9*). It is a community held wonderfully together by its memory of deliverance (*Titus 2:14*) and its hope of promised inheritance (*II Peter 3:12*), being bound to God by a covenant written on each Christian's heart, a covenant that God will never repudiate (*Heb. 8:10–12*). On man's part, fellowship in this company is a matter of obedience, a matter of the heart's allegiance. For the church is the community of those who through faith have accepted enlistment as slaves, servants, stewards, ministers, witnesses, confessors, ambassadors, soldiers and friends.

The "people of God" understand themselves as the "slaves of God" (*I Peter 2:16, Rev. 7:3*), that is, as slaves to God rather than as slaves any longer to fear, to the Law, the flesh, the world, or Satan. Indeed, the slaves of Christ are his friends; they are not like chattels who do not know what their Lord is doing (*John 15:15–20*). To be a slave of Christ is to imitate his lowliness, humiliation, and suffering, to be his witness, to proclaim his gospel and his kingdom and to worship the one, true God (*Rev. 19–22*). Thus the life of God's people essentially involves glorifying God among the nations and extending the bounds of the covenant community to include men and women from every tribe, tongue and people (*Rev. 5:9, 10*). And from first to last, Jesus Christ is the shepherd and anointed king of this people; his rule is inseparable from his redemption of them through his death (*Titus 2:14*).

### THE PRIESTHOOD OF ALL BELIEVERS

Jesus is also the chief cornerstone and high priest of this community. He is the great high priest, appointed according to the order of Melchizedek (*Heb. 5*), "who in every respect has been tempted as we are, yet without sinning" (*Heb. 4:15*). So his people are called both living stones and priests. In fact, in *I Peter* the whole church is described as both a royal and a holy priesthood, whose corporate duty is the offering of spiritual sacrifices. Such sacrifices include proclaiming the wonderful deeds of him who called them out of darkness into his marvelous light, and demonstrating "good conduct among the Gentiles" so that they may see the church's good deeds and "glorify God on the day of visitation" (*I Peter 2:9–12*). In the *Revelation to John*, likewise, the church is a community of priests brought into existence as a fruit of the emancipating love, the atoning death, of God's Son; and therefore as a witnessing and worshipping society. Notice carefully that here the idea is neither that of a separate order of priests within the church nor that of the individual priesthood of each believer, but that of a shared priesthood in a community that receives power and life through its crucified and resurrected Lord.

The exceptional richness of understanding the church in terms of the "priest of all believers" has been obscured in our time by widespread misunderstanding. Perhaps this is a good place to attempt to clarify its meaning, especially in light of the far-reaching consequences that followed Martin Luther's "rediscovery" of the Biblical passages summarized above. Contrary to popular opinion, the "priesthood of all believers" does not mean that every man is to be his own priest and therefore has little real need of the community of faith. Of course, Luther did insist that every man has his own access to God in Christ, and this is true New Testament teaching. But by this he meant (with *I Peter* and *Hebrews*) that all Christians are "worthy to appear before God to pray for others and to teach one another the things of God." Negatively, Luther's rediscovery meant a rejection of the medieval conception of the priesthood as constituting a special class in the eyes of God with a special hierarchical power and a higher morality. Positively, it meant emphasizing that every Christian bears the responsibility of prayer and care for every other Christian, that each man is called to be a priest to every other, that every man is equally accountable before God.

Jesus Christ, the great high priest, became the access into the Holy of Holies, the very presence of God, providing by his self-offering the "altar" (*Heb. 13:10*) on which Christians are to present themselves as living sacrifices, with hymns of praise, good deeds and mutual sharing. Every Christian has been set in a place of maximum responsibility as a witness to God's goodness and mercy for the sake of his neighbor. The Biblical conception of the "priesthood of all believers" is thus rightly understood as the "mutual ministry of believers." And out of this mutual ministry goes forth a common ministry to the world.

### THE CHURCH—GOD'S FAMILY

As we have seen, many Old Testament concepts gain a new vitality when used by Christian writers to describe the surging center of God's new activity, Jesus the Christ and his people, the church. As in the Old Testament Israel is spoken of as a "house," so, too, in the New Testament the church is called the house of Israel, or of Jacob, of Moses, of David, and also "the house of God" (*Hebrews 3:2-6; I Peter 4:17*). Furthermore, Christians are adopted as "sons of God" who as sons and therefore brothers in God's family are to act like sons and brothers. As John says, "We know that we have passed out of death into life, because we love the brethren. He who does

not love remains in death. Anyone who hates his brother is a murderer . . . by this we know love, that he laid down his life for us; and we ought to lay down our lives for the brethren" (*I John 3:14–16*).

To be sons of God is to take seriously the discipline of the Lord (*Heb. 12:5–11*), to be sanctified and delivered from the fear of death, to be strengthened in the hour of extreme trial (*Rev. 21:7*), and to be purified by the glorious hope of Christ's appearing.

> Beloved, we are God's children now, it does not yet appear what we shall be, but we know that when he appears we shall be like him, for we shall see him as he is!
>
> (*I John 3:2*)

The determining picture of sonship and brotherhood, and therefore of the people of God, is thus provided by Jesus Christ himself, the elder brother who is not ashamed to call Christians his brethren, and who with them is dependent upon the Father's will.

This interdependence is also beautifully expressed in the striking Biblical image of God's people as the bride of Christ. Developing another aspect of Old Testament thought in which Israel had been visualized as the chosen bride of God in spite of her repeated adulteries (*Jeremiah 2, Ezekiel 16, Hosea*), New Testament writers present Jesus as the bridegroom and the church as his bride (*John 3:29*). By faithful obedience in difficult times the church prepares for the marriage that will be the sign of God's dwelling with men in the Holy City, Jerusalem (*Revelation 19–21*). In accord with this manner of thinking, the worship of God's people is movingly summarized by the prayer of the Bride: "Come, Lord Jesus" (*Rev. 21:17, 21*).

### THE NEW EXODUS

The richness and variety of these Old Testament images and events, which are given new life as pictures of the church, often surprises the casual reader of the Bible. Frequently Christians are described as exiles of the Dispersion, engaged in an ongoing struggle against the tyrannical captivity of Babylon (*James 1, I Peter 1, Rev. 16–18*). But most pervasive, subtle, and significant are the many ways in which the events of the Exodus are seen to be recurring in the life of the church. For example, in *I Peter* and *Hebrews* the church is pictured as the community of pilgrims and strangers, and in *Hebrews 3–4*, especially, as patient travelers toward the Promised Land. In this same book, elaborate comparisons are drawn between Moses and Jesus, between the old, earthly sanctuary and the new and eternal Holy Place, between the first and now "obsolete" covenant and the new covenant mediated by Christ. In the *Revelation to John*, the plagues in Egypt have become analogies to God's final judgment of the world (*Rev. 8, 15, 16*). And in the *Gospel according to John*, Jesus offers himself as the "true bread from heaven" in contrast to the bread the fathers had eaten in the wilderness. Jesus said: "I am the bread of life; he who comes to me shall not hunger, and he who believes in me shall never thirst" (*John 6:35*). The fathers ate manna in the wilderness and died there. But Jesus is the living bread, and "if any one eats of this bread, he will live for ever" (*John 6:51*).

### VINE AND SHEPHERD

Agricultural images, first used in the context of the wilderness wanderings, also play a very important role in the *Gospel according to John*. In chapter 15 Jesus is pictured as the "true Vine" upon whom all Christians are dependent. His father is the vinedresser who prunes and purges various branches in order to produce greater fruitfulness. And in the *Revelation*, a related tree, the Tree of Life, binds together the entire Biblical story, as the Garden of Eden is linked to the church as the New Jerusalem (*Rev. 2, 22, Genesis 3*).

In the most pervasive agricultural image, however, the church is portrayed as God's flock. The powerful smybolism of *Psalm 23* and *Ezekiel 34* is movingly magnified by the activity of Jesus Christ, the "great shepherd of the sheep" (*Heb. 13:20*), who even gives his life for the sheep (*John 10*), and who commands his apostles and elders to feed them (*John 21, I Peter 5*). Jesus' rule over his people, as well as over the nations, is sometimes described in terms of shepherding God's flock. And in a startling shift of imagery, Jesus is said to qualify as a Shepherd by giving his life as a Lamb (*John 10, I Peter 1, Rev. 5, 7*). In the words of John the Baptist: "Behold, the Lamb of God, who takes away the sin of the world" (*John 1:29*). Moreover, the *Revelation to John* speaks of the faithful multitude who have "washed their robes and made them white in the blood of the Lamb" (*Rev. 7:14*). It is the "Lamb in the midst of the throne" who "will be their shepherd, and he will guide them to springs of living water" (*Rev. 7:17*. Jesus is referred to as a Lamb twenty-seven times in this book). His sacrificial death becomes the source and standard of the concern which church leaders are to manifest to his flock; and he is a living example for the life of each of the sheep. He is the "good shepherd" who lays down his life for all sheep, for his flock extends beyond the bounds of Judaism. His sheep will heed his voice and, as there is but one Shepherd, "so there shall be one flock" (*John 10:16*).

As the people of God, then, the church has become heir to an astonishing array of conceptions and descriptions that pertained first in time to ancient Israel: slaves of God, living stones, a royal priesthood, the house of God, the sons of God, the faithful bride, exiles and pilgrims, the flock of the Great

Shepherd. And this list does not include the unique and exceedingly powerful Pauline description of the church as the body of Christ, nor such fresh New Testament metaphors for the church as "the realm of light," "the woman clothed with the sun," the "pillar of the truth," those who are "born again" and who constitute the first fruits of God's new humanity. Actually, no list could do justice to the inspiration or the vivid imaginative power or the vitality of these later New Testament writers. The actual, visible people of God were given many heavily lade words on every hand by which to understand themselves, in which they could rejoice, and through which they could grow and mature.

## Offices and the Spirit of God

In the later writings of the New Testament, the church is viewed as the people of God in the last days, the end time. This people is being gathered out of the nations by the redeeming work of the Messiah, to share in the new age that he inaugurated. This gathering of God's people spans all spaces and generations and fulfills all the covenants of the past. It is both a redeemed and a redeeming community, both a recipient and a channel of God's glory, fighting against Satan and inheriting the promises and the downpayment of the Holy Spirit. Thus no person became a member of this community without at the same time entering a personal ministry, equal to his calling and his ability. "As each has received a gift, employ it for one another, as good stewards of God's varied grace" (*I Peter 4:10*).

So between his resurrection and his return, Jesus Christ continues his ministry in and through the church by the Spirit. The Twelve whom he had chosen, and the wider circle of apostles, proclaimed to the world what God had done in Jesus of Nazareth and taught men what he had said. The expansion resulting from this missionary effort required new ministries for edifying the church, and by the end of the apostolic age the first lines of church organization come into focus. Men were needed to take special responsibility in preaching and explaining the Gospel, to see that all things were done "decently and in order," to care for the sick and distressed and to distribute assistance to the poor and unfortunate. In the earliest churches these ministries are characterized by spontaniety and variety, although a strong sense of unity seems to overshadow the entire development.

We have already noted the apostles' appointment of the Seven (p. 427), the commission of Barnabas and Paul as missionaries (p. 448), and the appointment of elders in the Pauline churches (p. 449). These events described in the *Acts* illustrate only a few of the terms used for the leaders in the early congregations. We may assume that following the practice of Jewish synagogues, the term translated "elder" ("presbyter") denoted both office and age, as it clearly does in *I Peter 5:1–5*. In the predominantly Gentile congregations, however, perhaps following the terminology of certain municipal officials and officers of various associations, the leaders are referred to as "overseers" or "bishops" (*episkopoi*) and "assistants" or "deacons" (*diakonoi*), as in *Philippians 1:2*. More general designations, such as the "leaders" mentioned for imitation in *Hebrews 13:7*, continued to be used long into the second century, as is clear from *I Clement* and the *Shepherd of Hermas*, Christian writings that appeared at the end of the New Testament period.

### ELDERS AND BISHOPS

The actual difference between "elders" and "bishops" during the last part of the first century A.D. was probably no more than one of terminology. Both titles evidently mean the leaders of the congregation. Here and there both titles were used for the same persons, as is evidenced with particular clarity in the so-called *Pastoral Epistles, I and II Timothy* and *Titus*, as well as in *I Clement.* Timothy and Titus were Paul's agents in Ephesus and Crete, whose task it was to supervise the good organization of the churches, selecting faithful men who could be entrusted with the gospel and who would in turn teach others also (*II Timothy 2:2*). Paul directed them to establish elders in their churches (*Titus 1:5, I Tim. 5:22*), as he himself had done. "Elder" seems to be the more familiar term in these letters. But when the qualifications for this office are spelled out, the functional term "overseer/ bishop" is used (*Titus 1:7, I Tim. 3:2*).

### IGNATIUS OF ANTIOCH

Probably the distinction in meaning between these two titles arose only when the outstanding leader among the elders began to assume special responsibility for hospitality to traveling Christians and for the preservation of traditional apostolic teaching against any deviation. Our earliest evidence for using these terms for two distinct offices comes the letters of Ignatius, bishop of Antioch, written about 110 A.D., while he was being conducted as a prisoner through Asia Minor on the way to martyrdom in a Roman wild-beast show. Ignatius' overwhelming concern, in response to the schisms and false teachings that ripped through the congregations in the second century, was for the *unity* of the church. He supports his preoccupation with the role of the bishop, not by an appeal to direct succession from an apostle, but by his exalted conception of the church as united, eternal and universal. And he sees the bishop as the earthly center of this unity in the local church (*Letter to the Philadelphians 3:2* and *To the Magnesians 6:2*).

Ignatius knew of no officers having power outside of the local church to which they belonged, although he appears to have thought that his approaching martyrdom gave him the special authority to write quite strong letters to congregations other than his own. No other evidence for the rule of a single bishop (often called "monarchial episcopate") appears until the end of the second century, a fact that emphasizes the uniqueness of Ignatius and further complicates our understanding of what was happening in the development of church offices during this crucial period.

Some scholars have suggested that James, the brother of Jesus, provided a model for Ignatius by his strong position of leadership among the elders of the Jerusalem Church (*Acts 15, 21*). But this theory is attractive primarily because of the absence of any other suggestions. To be sure, James was probably the most respected and authoritative leader in Jerusalem for most of the first Christian generation. But his special place was determined by two irrepeatable factors: he was a witness to the resurrection of Jesus Christ (*I Corinthians 15:7*); and he was, after all, the Lord's brother (*Galatians 1:19*), and such family connections carried much weight in the ancient Near East.

### BISHOPS AND DEACONS

In any event, Timothy and Titus were to look for men of irreproachable character, hospitable disposition, and sound doctrine. Such men in every town were to be appointed elders, and some of them were then to take up the work of preaching and teaching, services worthy of "double honor." More than likely this extra reward was thought of as additional pay rather than as the more "spiritual" esteem from the congregation (*I Tim. 5:17–22*). From this it is clear that the functions of elders differed somewhat, with ministers of the word in the pre-eminent place. All the elders appear to be paid, however, which suggests that they devoted at least part of their time, if not all of it, to their ministry.

Apparently, "assistants" or deacons were also to be selected. These men were expected to possess strong moral and practical qualities (*I Tim. 3:8–13*). Their duties are not clearly defined, but we may assume that they devoted themselves to "assisting" in the church according to their particular abilities. There may also have been an "order of widows" (*I Tim. 5:9–10*) as well as an order of "deaconesses" (*I Tim. 3:11*). But on the basis of these letters alone, it is impossible to know with any certainty just what role these women may have filled, if any, in the early church.

By the end of the first century, the special "apostles, prophets, pastors and teachers" often mentioned by Paul appear to have fulfilled their Spirit-directed tasks. "Bishops" and "deacons" of the types described in the *Pastoral Letters* appear to be serving the ongoing church in every way necessary. Yet in an early second century "church manual" called the *Didache* (or, *Teaching of the Twelve Apostles*), there is quite a distinct reluctance to abandon the idea that Christian leaders were to come forth spontaneously as called by the Spirit. Nevertheless, this same passage also warns against traveling "apostles" and "prophets" as potential charlatans to be tested (*Didache XI*). Any "prophet" who asked for more than two days free lodging or whose behavior betrayed his words was a "false prophet" to be ignored. Of course, any tested and true prophet was highly esteemed and well supported. But the bishops and deacons, who were "meek men, not lovers of money, truthful and approved," fulfilled the ministry of the wandering prophets and teachers whenever such men were absent from the congregation (*Didache XV*).

## ORDINATION

None of the available documents suggest the presence of any "automatic" guarantee of the Spirit in any particular leader or office of the church. Information regarding the ordination of ministers during this period is extremely sketchy probably because Christians of apostolic times had little interest in such matters in light of their hope for an early return of the Lord. To be sure, the Seven described in *Acts 6*, as well as Timothy (*I Tim. 4:14; II Tim. 1:6*) had apostolic hands laid upon them. And it seems to be taken for granted that Timothy will be involved in "the laying on of hands" on others (*I Tim. 5:22*). But this is all we can learn regarding this period. Apparently, not until the church was threatened by splits and false teachers was it important to be able to guarantee sound Christian teaching by tracing the succession of teachers back to one of the Twelve or Paul. But even this concern for successsion of the apostolic tradition did not lead to any immediate interest in the question of ordination.

## THE SPIRIT IN THE CHURCH

What we do find in the New Testament, is the people of God under the continuing leadership of the Spirit. This community is not a democracy, in the sense that the power is in the hands of the people who by free election delegate it to certain ministers. Nor is it an oligarchy, in the sense that the apostles or ministers freely appointed by the apostles are able to designate their own successors with authority. Rather, Christ is the head of the church, and he rules by his Spirit. The power belongs not to the ministers and not to the people, but to Christ.

## Worship and Prayer

Christian worship in New Testament times was centered around preaching, baptism, and the Lord's Supper. It was dominated by the church's faith in Jesus as the risen Messiah and the living Lord. The rich heritage of Jewish worship is evident on every hand. Indeed, the earliest Christians worshipped regularly in both temple and synagogue. Of course, the Christians abandoned the sacrificial system of the temple, regarding this system as obsolete since the death of Christ (see especially the principal argument of the *Letter to the Hebrews*). Temple sacrifice also ceased for the Jews in the first century of the Christian Era, but only because the temple was destroyed by the Romans in A.D. 70.

It was from the synagogues, the local centers of worship which developed in post-exilic Judaism, that the church got many features common in Christian worship services today: Scripture reading (especially the Law and the Prophets), exhortation, psalm-singing, and public prayer. Also, the celebration of the Lord's Supper was profoundly influenced by the home rituals surrounding the Passover meal as a time of thankful remembrance of God's mighty acts and of hopeful anticipation of the approaching consummation. Yet many aspects of Christian worship were new or distinctive.

### THE LORD'S DAY

John, the prophet of Patmos, informs his readers that his first vision came to him on the "Lord's Day" (*Revelation 1:10*). Sunday, the first day of the week, was the day of Christ's resurrection; and long before there was an annual celebration of this event on Easter, the church celebrated the resurrection weekly on Sunday. When John had his vision, he knew that Christians everywhere were gathering on that very day for worship, even the congregations in Asia Minor to which he addressed his book. Ignatius of Antioch and the writer of the *Didache* also refer to the "Lord's Day."

The Lord's Supper, or the "breaking of bread," was the climax of these Sunday services. *Jude 12* and Ignatius refer to this service in the context of a fellowship meal, the *agape,* that is, the "love feast." It is not clear just when the Lord's Supper began to be regularly celebrated outside of the context of this common meal. Before the meal itself, the Jewish Scriptures were read as the Scriptures of the church, which by the light of the gospel were found to testify gloriously to Jesus as the Christ. In the *Pastoral Letters,* Timothy is urged to "attend to the public reading of scripture, to preaching, to teaching" (*I Tim. 4:13*). The "sacred writings" with which he was acquainted from childhood were, of course, the Jewish Scriptures. And it was this book which was regarded as "inspired by God and profitable for teaching, for reproof, for correction, and for training in righteousness, that the man of God may be complete, equipped for every good work" (*II Tim. 3:16, 17*).

Other writings, some of which were later gathered in the book of the New Testament, were also read in these services, though of course at that time they were not viewed as having equal authority with the Scriptures (Old Testament). The first reference we have to the reading of Gospel tradition in such worship services comes from Justin Martyr, a Christian theologian who wrote about the middle of the second century A.D. He says that in Rome the "memoirs of the apostles" were read regularly along with the Old Testament.

The reading of the Scripture was usually followed by explanatory teaching and exhortatory preaching. A beautiful literary example of how this was done can be found in the *Letter to the Hebrews,* which bears more marks of a sermon or homily than it does of a letter. Based largely on *Psalms 2, 8, 95, 110* and on *Jeremiah 31:31–34,* the book develops along a fairly regular outline in which the Old Testament passage is cited and then interpreted by the light of the revelation in Christ. Then specific practical implications are drawn on the basis of which the Christian reader is exhorted to action.

### EARLY CHRISTIAN HYMNS

The joyous shout of psalms, hymns and spiritual songs was also a very important part of early Christian worship. Fragments from some of these hymns are imbedded in the New Testament itself. The hymn to Christ in *Philippians 2:5–11* has already been mentioned (p. 482). Another hymn to Christ is quoted in *I Timothy 3:16*:

> He was manifested in the flesh
> vindicated in the Spirit
>     seen by angels,
> preached among the nations,
> believed on in the world,
>     taken up in glory.

Recent research has also shown how much the form of the book of *Revelation* seems to be influenced by Christian worship. For example, "the song of the Lamb" in chapter *15* begins: "Great and wonderful are thy deeds, O Lord God the Almighty! Just and true are thy ways O King of the ages!" And in chapter *19* a great multitude in heaven crys: "Hallelujah! Salvation and glory and power belong to our God . . . Hallelujah! For the Lord our God the Almighty reigns."

### THE CHURCH AT WORSHIP

John's use of these hymns, hallelujah choruses, prayers, responses to prayers, and doxologies points toward the development of a distinctively Christian liturgy. The best example of this is found in *Revelation 4* and *5*. The "Call to Worship" opens chapter *4*, followed by "Holy, holy, holy is the Lord God Almighty, who was and is and is to come!" in vs. *11*. Chapter *5* begins with the "reading from scripture" which is fol-

lowed by a psalm at vs. *9*, a "congregational response" in vs. *12*, and a "doxology" to God and Christ in vs. *13*, concluding with the "Amen." And it is not strange that the book of *Revelation* should reflect Christian worship, for the core of John's message is the victory of God revealed in Christ, and in this cosmic drama he sees all the heavenly hosts worshipping God and Christ for this marvelous triumph.

Of course, more informal prayers were also important in public worship. Many varieties of prayer are mentioned in *I Timothy*: supplications, prayers, intercessions, thanksgivings, and the duty of prayers for rulers. Man are urged to pray, "lifting holy hands" (*I Tim. 2:8*). Elders are called upon to pray over the sick, while anointing them with oil in the name of the Lord (*James 5:13–15*). Mutual confession is encouraged (*James 5:16* and perhaps *I John 1:8, 9*). Unanswered prayer is said to result from wrong requests that seek selfish ends (*James 4:3*).

### CHRIST THE MEDIATOR

It is in *Hebrews*, however, that the distinctively Christian basis for prayer is made plain, grounded as it is in Jesus' experience. Because in obedience, Jesus was tried as we are tried, he can mediate our needs. This makes him a unique and definitive high priest. Prayer is thus "drawing near" to God in and through Christ. It is drawing near, not to the stormy mount of Moses, but to the heavenly realm dominated by Jesus as the mediator of the new covenant. Such prayer can be afforded with boldness and a true heart. The vital matter is simply to look to Christ, who as the Pioneer and Perfecter of the Christian's faith, is seated at the right hand of the throne of God (*Heb. 12:2*).

In the *Gospel according to John*, also, the heavenly intercession of the living Christ is the basis of Christian prayer. The Christian's organic union with Christ as the true Vine, leads him to ask for only what the Vine can supply. This is what is meant by praying in the name of Christ (*John 14:13; 16:23; I John 5:13–15*). Jesus' own life of prayer and concern for his disciples is summarized in the magnificent prayer in *John 17*. The essence of his utterance is that the oneness between God and himself be shared by the disciples with him and with each other (vss. *11, 21*). In this prayer, rooted in true communion with God and seeking that communion, Biblical prayer reaches its highest point.

### BAPTISMAL INSTRUCTION

The formal beginning of this communion with God through Christ occurred in Christian baptism. And *I Peter* may well be our first witness to the development of instruction given at the Sunday worship service to those just baptized into Christ. A baptismal sermon may be reflected in the definition of baptism as a sacrament of regeneration (*I Peter 1:3–12*) and the lengthy section of instructions regarding the character and conduct which God expects of the new Christian (*1:13–4:11*). Great concern over the fearful consequences of post-baptismal sin was expressed in *Hebrews 10:31*. If the new Christian was going to avoid such sin, it would be necessary to instruct him in righteousness. The first letter of Peter is a powerful document intended to serve that very purpose, and potent exhortation was needed, for to neglect the implications of one's baptism was to invite judgment and "a fury of fire" (*Heb. 10:26, 27*).

### PRIVATE DEVOTIONS

Little can be known from the New Testament about the private devotions of second generation Christians. The devout Jew prayed three times daily, and without doubt many Christians continued this spiritual dis-

cipline. The *Didache*, written early in the second century A.D., mentions threefold daily prayer, and the Christian is to say the "Lord's Prayer (*Matthew 6*) at each of these times. This prayer was thus the staple of private devotion, even though it does not appear in a public worship service until the fourth century A.D. Christians also fasted before significant events such as ordinations (*Acts 14:23*) and baptisms (*Didache 7*).

## Conflicts Within the Church

The Christian Church was born in the midst of conflict. Had not Jesus himself done his work in opposition to Jewish leaders who finally brought him into conflict with the Roman procurator? Did not the infant church struggle with Judaism from without and Judaizing Christians from within? During the second generation of the church, the principal opposition appeared in the disruptive activity of certain "false teachers." The church's struggle against them is reported in the *Pastoral Letters, II Peter, I, II, and III John, Jude,* and the *Gospel according to John.*

### GNOSTICISM

In our sketch of the backgrounds to Christianity in chapter 16, we discussed the important intellectual movement known as gnosticism (p. 439f). By the end of the first century A.D., gnosticism had gained a foothold in the Christian church and was threatening to destroy its very foundations. For the next three centuries, the leaders of the people of God had the mind-stretching task of fighting and refuting its teachings.

### DOCETISM

Influenced by the gnostic belief that "spirit" is good and "matter," or physical stuff, is bad, some Christians apparently began to refuse to acknowledge that Jesus had been flesh and blood. They thought, of course, that they were "improving" the Christian faith by making the Savior more "spiritual." Those who held this view were called "docetists," a term derived from the Greek verb, *dokeo*, meaning "to seem" or "to appear." Thus the docetists claimed that while Christ *seemed* to have flesh and bones, he really did not! How could the spiritual and heavenly redeemer have any real association with a body of flesh? It must have been that the spiritual Christ descended on the man Jesus at his baptism and left him just before his crucifixion.

*I and II John* were written precisely to put a stop to this kind of false teaching that denied the humanity of Jesus the Christ. The very first words of *I John* are loaded with anti-docetic ammunition:

> That which was from the beginning, which we have *heard* which we have *seen* with our eyes, which we have *looked upon* and *touched with our hands* concerning the word of life—the life was made manifest and we saw it, and testify to it.  —*I John 1:1-2*

The disciples had heard the voice of Jesus, looked into his face, and touched his hand. And John says that anyone who denies that the man Jesus is the Christ, or who denies the Father and the Son, is an antichrist (*I John 2:22*). All traveling prophets and teachers, therefore, were to be tested. If they teach that Jesus Christ has come in the flesh, they are of God; but if not, they are deceivers under the influence of the antichrist (*I John 4:2, 3; II John 7*). They are not to be believed!

No book in the New Testament is any harder to place in its original environment than the *Gospel according to John*. The one definite clue, however, is found in *John 1:14*: "And the Word became flesh and dwelt among us, full of grace and truth." This confession is the climax to John's introductory words in which he speaks of this "Word" as the agent of creation, as the true

light, as the source of power to become the children of God, as God! And while John does make some dualistic contrasts between "light" and "darkness" and "good" and "evil," the confession in *1:14* is the absolute negation of all gnostic thinking abous Jesus. The gnostics could say that the Word came "in the form of flesh." But John says the Word *became* flesh, altogether a human being. God had acted in history through the man Jesus of Nazareth, "the only Son from the Father."

## GNOSTIC FREEDOM

What was at stake in the conflict over the humanity of Jesus extended beyond theological discussion to the whole life of the people of God. For the radical dualism of the gnostics led them to make a sharp division between "spiritual" and "fleshly" men. They thought of themselves, of course, as "spiritual men," who therefore possessed secret traditions they claimed were passed down from Jesus, and who therefore could look down on all others as, at best, second-class Christians. In *I Timothy* these secret traditions, as well as the fantastic interpretations of the Old Testament that fascinated the gnostics, are derided as "fables and genealogies" and as "old wives tales." And against these spiritual snobs, both *I and II Timothy* repeatedly emphasize that love of the brethren is the very essence of the Christian life; where there is faith there must also be love.

Some gnostics felt as if they were beyond any law, even the law of love, because they were free from all sin. So against this false teaching John charges that if any man says he has no sin, he makes God a liar (*I John 1:10*)! And the little epistle of *Jude* vigorously attacks libertine Christians who live by their instincts like irrational animals. *II Peter 3:17* also warns against being carried away with the "error of lawless men," men

A fine red pottery plate found in Palestine, a luxury item imported from Italy.

who twist the scriptures to their own destruction. The gnostics promised men "freedom," but they themselves were slaves of corruption. "For whatever overcomes a man, to that he is enslaved" (*II Peter 2:19*).

### ASCETICISM

*I and II Timothy* were also written to put a stop to the opposite gnostic tendency: asceticism. The first letter argues against the "pretensions of liars whose consciences are seared, who forbid marriage and enjoin abstinence from foods which God created to be received with thanksgiving . . . For every thing that God has created is good and nothing is to be rejected if it is received with thanksgiving (*I Tim. 4:3, 4*). Timothy is to have "nothing to do with godless and silly myths" (*I Tim. 4:7*). Young widows are encouraged to marry again, and bishops are to have children. Contrary to gnostic teaching, God is both Creator of this world and Savior of all men (*I Tim. 4:10*).

### FAITH

One result of the fight for these doctrines was the special emphasis placed on the body of truths Christians had in common and which were indispensable for the defense of the Gospel, "the faith which was once for all delivered to the saints" (*Jude 3*). The word "faith" begins to refer doctrine rather than to man's relationship with God. In these later New Testament letters, then, "faith" is no longer so much a matter of trust and commitment to God in response to the gospel, as it is sound theology and ethics, the tradition from the apostles.

## Everyday Christian Living

Among our sources of knowledge for second generation Christianity are the so-called "General Epistles": *James, I and II Peter, I, II, and III John* and *Jude*. Because these writings were directed as open letters to the church at large, or at least to large groups of Christians, they give us our best window for

494

looking at "average" Christianity. That is, these letters do not seem to have been written with special problems of particular congregations in mind, but rather to more general Christian concerns. We refer to these writings, therefore, not according to their destinations as we do to Paul's letters, but according to their authors.

Paul and John stand as giants in the theology and piety of the early church. Such experiences of insight or heavenly transport as they enjoyed must have seemed miles beyond the "average" Christian in a small congregation anywhere in the Roman Empire. But *I Peter* seems to be addressed to just such "average" people who in this case were being disturbed by the unwelcome attentions of government officials and by the scorn and abuse of their non-Christian neighbors, to people who needed to be reminded of the rich resources of the Christian gospel and to be renewed in courage and hope in their daily lives. *I Peter* is thus a very appealing book and a favorite of many Christians today. As one scholar observed: "this gallant and high-hearted exhortation breathes a spirit of undaunted courage and exhibits as noble a type of piety as can be found in any writing of the New Testament outside of the gospels."

### IN HIS STEPS

The famous devotional novel, *In His Steps,* written in 1899 by Charles M. Sheldon takes its title from *I Peter 2:21:* " . . . Christ also suffered for you, leaving you an example, that you should follow in his steps." It is striking, however, that the "imitation of Christ" is not often stressed in the New Testament. There is a difference between being a disciple and trying to shape one's life in detail after that of Jesus. Clearly, many aspects of his life are unique and possess a "once-for-all" quality. The Christian cannot always ask, "what would

Jesus do in this particular situation?", because he knows Jesus would not have gotten himself into this or that difficult situation in the first place, because he would have made better decisions back along the path of life. The Christian has difficulty imagining Jesus in his own particular shoes, and he can hardly pretend to be able to put on the shoes of the Redeemer of the world.

Yet Jesus was a human being, and *Hebrews 2:18* assures the Christian that because Jesus himself has suffered and been tempted, "he is able to help those who are tempted." And it is in this special context of suffering and temptation that Christ's example of faithfulness and patience is so effectively pointed to in *I Peter* as a means of strengthening resolve and encouraging trust. For Christ is not only the example, but also the "Shepherd and Guardian of your souls" (*I Peter 2:25*). And if one suffers as a Christian, he is blessed by God and is not to be ashamed (*I Peter 4:14–16*).

### ETHICAL OPTIMISM

James, too, is concerned with trials. But his extremely infrequent references to Jesus Christ become immediately noticeable when he urges his readers to "count it all joy" when these trials come, not because of the sympathetic suffering of Jesus or the blessing of God, but because of the commonsense conclusion that "the testing of your faith produces steadfastness" (*James 1:3*). Like *I Peter,* James is concerned for everyday Christian living. But while Peter hoped to encourage the disheartened and suffering Christian, James was primarily concerned with exposing the moral sterility of Christians whose faith is nothing but talk. Thus James' working definition of pure and undefiled religion is: "to visit orphans and widows in their affliction, and to keep oneself unstained from the world" (*James 1:27*). He was scandalized by the special preference shown toward rich people in the gatherings for worship; for in the Christian fellowship, all men are "neighbors." And at the other end of the economic scale, James was distressed if a needy brother or sister was simply sent away with the words, "Go in peace, be warmed and filled," rather than with the needed clothes and food." This very practical concern is also expressed in *I John* where the question is asked: "If any one has the world's goods and sees his brother in need, yet closes his heart against him, how does God's love abide in him?" (*I John 3:17*)—a good question. In these later letters of the New Testament there is a kind of ethical optimism; the Christian life is difficult, but possible and desirable.

### APPLYING THE OLD TESTAMENT

Also in these letters we can find specific examples of the way in which the Old Testament was carefully read and used to meet specific situations in the second generation of the church. *Isaiah 40:6–9* ("All flesh is like grass . . . but the word of the Lord abides forever") is quoted in full in *I Peter,* and there it is applied to the gospel, which his readers had heard with joy. In *James 1:10, 11,* the same passage is obviously in mind, but here it is applied to the proud rich man, who like the grass, will "fade away in the midst of his pursuits."

Again, *I Peter 5:5* quotes *Proverbs 3:34* ("God opposes the proud but gives grace to the humble") in support of his exhortation to both young and old to act humbly toward each other. *James 4:6* quotes the same passage, but he uses it as a warning to resist the devil and to draw near to God. *1 Peter 4:8* perhaps paraphrases *Proverbs 10:12* while exhorting Christians above all to hold unfailing their love for one another, "since love covers a multitude of sins." James also quotes this saying, but he applies it specifically to the results of rescuing a sinner

from the error of his way. (*Jas. 5:20*).

Now all this somewhat detailed comparison of *I Peter* and *James* has been done to illustrate how the Jewish Scriptures were creatively used by the early Christians to assist them in understanding the specific events and problems of their lives. Perhaps the most elaborate and consistent use of the Old Testament in the New appears in the *Letter to the Hebrews.* A recent scholar's judgment that *Hebrews* is the least read of the major New Testament writings is no doubt correct, primarily because contemporary readers simply do not know their Old Testament. The Old Testament was all the Bible the early church possessed, however, and its thinking was permeated with its categories and cadences. From its manifold riches both comfort, challenge, creed, and courage took shape in the light of God's Messiah, Jesus the crucified.

## The Expectation of the End

From the beginning, the Christian community understood itself as the people of God living in the last days, near the end of history. Christians eagerly anticipated the time when Christ would return in glory and power, when God would complete the work of transforming his creation. Appropriately enough, the hope is most fervently expressed in the last book of the New Testament, the *Revelation to John.* Some of the special problems that surround the interpretation of this exceedingly powerful but difficult book are discussed below (pp. 499f). Here it is enough to say that John's words undoubtedly brought great comfort and encouragement to the Christian community in Asia Minor, where persecution was threatening and martyrdom was imminent.

In other parts of the empire, however, the hope of Christ's coming was being denied by some. According to *II Peter 3,* scoffers will come in the last days, chiding, "Where is the promise of his coming? For ever since the fathers fell asleep, all things have continued as they were from the beginning of creation." This skepticism is vigorously met by the affirmation of a radical transformation of the elements by the word of God, at both the creation and the day of judgment, "the Day of the Lord." Rather than emphasizing the immediacy of this last day, however, the author calls to mind *Psalm 90* and the teaching that God's time scheme differs from clock-time. The Lord is not slow about his promise; rather, he is forbearing so that all should reach repentance (*II Peter 3:8, 9*). Such forbearance by God is to be counted as salvation (*II Peter 3:15*).

### ETERNAL LIFE

This emphasis on salvation conceived as going on in the present is developed with magnificent power in the *Gospel according to John*. For example, "eternal life" is regarded less as a reward to be bestowed at some future time than as the present transforming possession of the believer in Jesus Christ. As a matter of fact, John makes this quite explicit in his explanation of why he became an author:

> Now Jesus did many other signs in the presence of the disciples which are not written in this book, but these are written that you may believe that Jesus is the Christ, the Son of God, and that believing you may have life in his name.     —*John 20:30-31*

The "signs" that are written in the *Gospel of John* are included in the so-called "Book of the Signs," (chapters 2–12). In contrast to the remainder of the book, which is written as a revelation to the community of faith, these early chapters describe Jesus' revelation to the world, his public ministry. Like the "signs" performed by the prophets of old, Jesus' actions were more than illustrations of ideas. Indeed, they all point to *the* forthcoming event—the death and resur-

rection of Jesus—which for John is the greatest of all the signs, the sign that reveals the meaning of all the others. For example, in *John 2:4,* Jesus' "hour" is really the "crucifixion, the moment of his deepest humiliation, but also of his glorification. This symbolic use of the term "hour" or "time" reappears throughout the gospel.

The entire dialogue with Nicodemus in chapter 3 makes sense only in light of the revelation of the entire gospel, that is of events described later in the book. What does it mean for the Son of man to be lifted up as Moses lifted up the serpent in the wilderness (*3:14*)? No doubt the phrase "lifted up" is doubly laden with meaning: the elevation of Christ on the cross (death) and the elevation of Christ to heaven (resurrection). And in the next phrase, John reveals the purpose of Christ's mission to the world: to bring eternal life to anyone who believes in him. God's love means eternal life now for those who are born "anew" ("from above"). Christ was not sent to judge the world, but in fact judgment has come by him to those men who love darkness rather than light, who do evil rather than what is true.

Throughout *John 3* we can feel the strong emphasis on the present reality of God's work in Christ, since eternal life has already entered into history with his coming; throughout this gospel, the signs and discourses testify to the new life in Christ open to all *now*. And in the first letter of John we find this test for the presence of this eternal life:

> We know that we have passed out of death into life, because we love the brethren.
>     —*I John 3:14*

Such a shift of emphasis to the present reality of salvation was bound to relax the tension created by the yet unfulfilled promise that the new age would come soon.

A relief showing Romans carrying the temple spoils of fallen Jerusalem, carved on the arch of Titus, who conquered the city.

### JOHN AND THE FUTURE

We should notice, however, the significant strand of future expectation that runs through John's gospel. There will still be a "last day," a day of resurrection and judgment (*John 5:29*). And at the very end of Jesus' public ministry he says: "He who rejects me and does not receive my sayings has a judge; the word that I have spoken will be his judge on the last day" (*John 12:48*).

It would seeem that neither disappointment over the failure of the end to come, nor various emphases that directed attention away from this failure, were able to alter the basic conviction of the people of God that when Jesus came the new age began, but that the full glory of that day was yet to be revealed and would be revealed. It would seem that the very sign that marked the church as the community of the last days, namely the marvelous presence of the Spirit of God, became the bridge by which the people of God confidently marched into history, into the future.

## God's People and the Taste of Victory

The message of the Gospel was sent into a Roman world which was as filled with differing religious beliefs and practices as our own. The recently discovered Dead Sea Scrolls (p. 369) have further emphasized the great variety of religious viewpoints within Judaism itself. Much of this variety is reflected in the books of the New Testament. To be sure, men became new creatures in Christ; their living and their thinking were transformed. Yet, their past continued to speak to them in a thousand ways, many of which finally had to be thrown out,

498

but some of which provided the alphabet from which the words of the Christian faith could be formed.

As we have seen, the Jewish Bible made new and glorious sense when read with the spectacles of the Gospel. The Holy Scriptures of the Jews became the Old Testament of the Christians. Testimony to Jesus as the Christ seemed to abound on almost every page of the Law, of the Writings, and especially of the Prophets. And the kind of apocalyptic thinking expressed in one of these prophets, Daniel (pp. 360ff), was transformed to convey the overwhelming yet often subtle message of the last book of the New Testament, the *Revelation to John.* This complex, mystifying and sometimes frightening book is a marvelous example of what we have called apocalyptic literature. In books of this type, which are frequently composed as reports of a heavenly vision, the opposing forces of good and evil are dramatically portrayed, and knowledge about the future is revealed. Daniel was the first of such books written among the Jews, and later examples include *II Esdras* (p. 371), the *Book of Enoch,* and the *Apocalypse of Baruch.* Certain facts and truths typical of these writings were not only accepted by John, but were glorified and transposed into a new key of joy in response to God's sure victory. There is much tragedy; but there is even more glory. And from this amazing book, we constantly hear bursts of rapturous, heavenly music.

The one great God has come to earth in Jesus Christ, who suffered the worst onslaught of all the evil in the world. He was finally nailed to the cross; but by the power of God he came forth alive, triumphant and now both Savior and Judge, before whom all other authorities and powers will finally disintegrate and pass away. He is the power and the authority forever! Men are either on his side or not. If they are not, the death sentence has already been proclaimed on their evil lives in which they seem so secure. Those who are for him are to share all the security of his own triumphant and glorious destiny.

This confidence was always smoldering in the heart of the entire church. In John of Patmos it broke forth into a blazing flame. And in a time of great trouble for many Christians, John was given the power to command the brilliant vocabulary of this astonishing apocalypticism, so that all who read the *Revelation* rejoice in the warm hope of ultimate Christian victory.

### EMPEROR WORSHIP

Most scholars, both ancient and contemporary, agree that the *Revelation to John* was written close to the end of the first century A.D., during the final phase of Emperor Domitian's rule (A.D. 81-96). A century before, Augustus Caesar had been worshipped as a god in the provinces of his empire, though somewhat unofficially (pp. 440f). Following his death, this emperor-worship was officially encouraged as a means of holding the empire together. It had been the custom in the eastern provinces to regard rulers as divine since the campaigns of Alexander the Great. In first-century Rome, however, the emperor cult was an innovation. Theoretically, it was the "genius" or divine double of the emperor—not the emperor in person—that was worshipped, but this subtle distinction between the human and the divine was greatly obscured in practice, and Domitian was addressed by his courtiers as Master and God as early as 89 A.D. This did not prevent his last years from being characterized by financial crises, however, and he began a "reign of terror" that was climaxed by a plot in which he himself was murdered.

During this tumultuous period, Domitian appears to have pressed worship of his office if not of himself in many places throughout the empire, and especially in Asia Minor. Both Christians and Jews were scandalized by his claim to be "God the Lord," which he had stamped on his coins. At Ephesus a huge marble statue of Domitian became the focus of emperor worship in Asia. The Christians did not receive the legal protection granted the Jews, because by now they were recognized as a sect that had broken away from Judaism. So when the Christians refused to worship the emperor, great troubles came to them, troubles that John of Patmos hoped to put in a dramatic, cosmic, hopeful, victorious perspective.

### CAESAR OR CHRIST?

For the Christian, Christ was the judge of both the empire and the emperor. And while they repeatedly stated that they could and did pray *for* the emperor, they could not possibly pray *to* him (*I Tim. 2:1–3.*) To John the issue was clear: allegiance to Christ and worship of the emperor were absolutely incompatible. John speaks of Pergamum as "Satan's throne" because it was a center of emperor worship; and he praised a certain Antipas who was martyred for the faith there (*Revelation 2:13*) as well as "those who had been beheaded for their testimony to Jesus and for the word of God, and who had not worshiped the beast or its image" (*Rev. 20:4*). In such days of testing, John's marvelous testimony must have encouraged countless Christians to be "faithful unto death." The Romans little suspected the tremendous power and conviction that this queer and "other-wordly" vision could gen-erate among Christians. For while the special apocalyptic "code" in which John wrote made wonderful sense to the believers, it must have been completely bewildering to a hostile Roman. Indeed, any serious attempt to interpret this book must reckon with the initial historical situation to which it was directed as well as with this "coded" quality of its apocalyptic expression.

### THE TASTE OF VICTORY

John made it clear to God's people that the reign of Christ was eternal. It was Rome that was passing away! The Christian martyr was completely victorious, even in the very hour of his seeming defeat. But those alone who were faithful to Christ had sure security in a universe where Christ reigned in victory over the powers of evil and death. So taste the victory of faithfulness to the end. A crown of life awaits!

This message of triumphant hope has never been expressed with more commanding authenticity or more ineffable glory than in *Revelation to John*. Yet it would be a mistake to see this book merely as a source of consolation for Christians experiencing persecution. For here the church is portrayed as at once the company of the saved (*3:5; 15:2–4*) and the redemptive agency by which God will both save and rule the world (*11:1–14; 3:21; 20:4–6*). The *total* picture in John's vision stresses God's ultimate saving purpose and the significant and meaningful part God's people are to play in its accomplishment. For these people were God's people!

# *Appendix*

## BIBLIOGRAPHY

### GENERAL

The following books and articles have been helpful to the author in his study of God's people and their book, the Bible, and are recommended to the discerning reader who desires instruction beyond the scope and intent of this book.

Albright, William Foxwell. *The Biblical Period.* Pittsburgh: Biblical Colloquium, 1950.

_____. "The Old Testament World," *The Interpreter's Bible,* I, 233–71. New York: Abingdon Press, 1952.

_____. *From the Stone Age to Christianity.* Second edition. Garden City, New York: Doubleday Anchor Books, 1957.

Anderson, Bernhard W. *Understanding the Old Testament.* Englewood Cliffs, N. J.: Prentice-Hall, Inc. 1957.

Black, Matthew, and Rowley, H. H. (eds.). *Peake's Commentary on the Bible.** New York: Thomas Nelson and Sons, Ltd., 1962.

Bright, John. *A History of Israel.* Philadelphia: Westminster Press, 1959.

_____. *The Kingdom of God.* New York: Abingdon Press, 1953.

Freedman, David Noel, and Campbell, Edward F., Jr. (eds.). *The Biblical Archaeologist Reader,* Vol. II.* Garden City, N. Y.: Doubleday Anchor Books, 1964.

*The Interpreter's Bible.** 12 vols. New York: Abingdon Press, 1952.

*The Interpreter's Dictionary of the Bible.** 4 vols. New York: Abingdon Press, 1962.

Kee, H. C., and Young, F. W. *Understanding the New Testament.* Englewood Cliffs, N. J.: Prentice-Hall, Inc., 1957.

Martin, William C. *The Layman's Bible Encyclopedia.** Nashville, Tennessee: The Southwestern Co., 1964.

McNeile, A. H. *An Introduction to the Study of the New Testament.* Second edition. Oxford: University Press, 1963.

Neil, William. *Harper's Bible Commentary.* New York: Harper and Row, 1962.

Price, James C. *Interpreting the New Testament.* New York: Holt, Rinehart, and Winston, 1961.

Pritchard, James B. (ed.). *Ancient Near Eastern Texts Relating to the Old Testament.** Princeton, N. J.: Princeton University Press, 1955.

Thomas, D. Winton. *Documents from Old Testament Times.* New York: Harper Torch Books, 1961.

Wright, G. Ernest. *Biblical Archaeology.* Philadelphia. Westminster Press, 1957.

_____, (ed.) *The Biblical Archaeologist Reader.** Garden City, N. Y.: Doubleday Anchor Books, 1961.

_____, and Fuller, Reginald H. *The Book of the Acts of God.* Garden City, N. Y.: Doubleday Anchor Books, 1957.

_____. "Bringing Old Testament Times to Life," *The National Geographic Magazine,* (December, 1957), 833–64.

_____. *The Old Testament Against its Environment.* Studies in Biblical Theology, #2. Chicago: Henry Regnery Co., 1950.

_____, and Filson, Floyd V. *Westminster Historical Atlas to the Bible.* Philadelphia: Westminster Press, 1945.

*The following abbreviations are used in this Bibliography:

| | |
|---|---|
| ANET — | *Ancient Near Eastern Texts* |
| BAR — | *The Biblical Archaeologist Reader* |
| BAR2 — | *The Biblical Archaeologist Reader, Vol. II.* |
| EB — | *Encyclopaedia Britannica,* 11th edition. |
| IB — | *The Interpreter's Bible.* |
| IDB — | *The Interpreter's Dictionary of the Bible* |
| LBE — | *The Layman's Bible Encyclopedia* |
| PCB — | *Peake's Commentary on the Bible* |

# REFERENCES BY CHAPTERS

## Introduction: The Task Before Us

Bentzen, Aage. *The Books of the Old Testament.* Vol. II of *Introduction to the Old Testament.* Copenhagen: G. E. C. Gads Forlag, 1949.

Nielsen, Eduard. *Oral Tradition.* London: SCM Press, Ltd., 1954.

Wright, G. Ernest, and Fuller, Reginald H. *The Book of the Acts of God.*

Wright, G. Ernest. *God Who Acts.* London: SCM Press, 1952.

_____ . *The Old Testament Against Its Environment.*

## 1. The Prehistory of Israel

Bowie, Walter Russell. "The Book of Genesis (Exposition)," *IB,* I, 439–848.

Bright, John. "Has Archaeology Found Evidence of the Flood?" *BAR,* 32–40.

"The Creation Epic," *ANET,* 60–72, 514.

Driver, S. R. *The Book of Genesis.* Westminster Commentary Series. New York: Edwin S. Gorham, 1904.

Frankfort, H. and H. A. et. al. *The Intellectual Adventure of Ancient Man.* Chicago: The University of Chicago Press, 1946.

"The Gilgamesh Epic," *ANET,* 72–9, 514–5.

von Rad, Gerhard. *Genesis: A Commentary.* Trans. John H. Marks. Philadelphia: Westminster Press, 1961.

Simpson, Cuthbert A. "The Book of Genesis, Introduction and Exegesis," *IB.* I, 439–848.

## 2. The Patriarchs

"The Code of Hammurabi," *ANET,* 163–80.

Driver, S. R. *The Book of Genesis.* New York: Edwin S. Gorham, 1904.

Gordon, Cyrus H. "Biblical Customs and the Nuzu Tablets," *BAR2,* 21–33.

Mendenhall, Geo. E. "Mari," *BAR2,* 3–21.

"Mesopotamian Legal Documents," *ANET* 217–222.

Pedersen, Johannes, *Israel, Its Life and Culture, I-II.* London: Oxford University Press, 1926.

## 3. The Exodus

Bodenheimer, F. S. "The Manna of Sinai," *BAR,* 76–80.

"Egyptian Historical Texts," *ANET,* 227–262.

McNeile, A. H. *The Book of Exodus.* London: Methuen and Co., 1908.

Poole, Reginald Stuart, and Griffith, Francis Llewelyn. "Egypt, History, Ancient," *Encyclopedia Britannica,* °11th edition. IX, 80–90.

Rylaarsdam, J. Coert. "The Book of Exodus, Introduction and Exegesis," *IB,* I, 833–1097.

## 4. The Covenant

Albright, William Foxwell. "What Were the Cherubim?" *BAR,* 95–97.

Davies, G. Henton. "Tabernacle," *IDB,* IV, 498–506.

"Egyptian and Hittite Treaties," *ANET,* 199–206.

Martin, William C. "Leviticus," *LBE,* 906–7.

Mendenhall, George E. *Law and Covenant in Israel and the Ancient Near East.* Pittsburgh: Biblical Colloquium, 1955.

Mickelm, Nathan. "The Book of Leviticus, Introduction and Exegesis," *IB,* II, 3–136.

## 5. Forty Years of Wandering

Marsh, John. "The Book of Numbers, Introduction and Exegesis," *IB,* II, 137–311.

Wright, G. Ernest. "The Book of Deuteronomy, Introduction and Exegesis," *IB,* II, 311–540.

## 6. The Conquest of Canaan

Bright, John. "The Book of Joshua, Introduction and Exegesis," *IB,* II, 541–676.

"Poems about Baal and Anath," *ANET,* 129–42.

von Rad, Gerhard. *Studies in Deuteronomy.* Trans. David Walker. London: SCM, 1948.

Wright, G. Ernest. "The Book of Deuteronomy, Introduction and Exegesis," *IB,* II, 311–540.

_____ . "The Literary and Historical Problem of Joshua 10 and Judges 1," *Journal of Near Eastern Studies,* V, 2 (April, 1946), 105–114.

## 7. The Time of the Judges

Meyers, Jacob M. "The Book of Judges, Introduction and Exegesis," *IB,* II, 677–826.

## 8. Rise of the Monarchy in Israel

Cross, Frank M., Jr. "The Priestly Tabernacle," *BAR,* 201–228.

Stinespring, W. F. "Temple, Jerusalem," *IDB,* IV, 534–60.

Wright, G. Ernest. "The Last Thousand Years Before Christ," *The National Geographic Magazine,* (December, 1960), 813–53.

_____ . "The Temple in Palestine-Syria," *BAR,* 169–84.

Yadin, Yigael. "New Light on Solomon's Megiddo, *BAR2,* 240–7.

## 9. The Divided Kingdom

Albright, William Foxwell. "Review of James A. Montgomery Commentary on the Book of Kings," *Journal of Biblical Literature,* LXXI (1952), 245–53.

"Babylonian and Assyrian Historical Texts," *ANET,* 274–87.

Bright, John. *The Kingdom of God.* New York: Abingdon Press, 1953.

Cross, Frank Moore, Jr. Unpublished chronological charts on the period of the monarchy.

Herbert, A. S. "I and II Chronicles," *PCB*, 357–69.

Mauchline, J. "I and II Kings," *PCB*, 338–56.

"The Moabite Stone," *ANET*, 320–21.

Oppenheim, A. Leo. "Sargon," *IDB*, IV, 222–4.

"The Sargon Chronicle," *ANET*, 266.

Wright, G. Ernest. "The Last Thousand Years Before Christ," *The National Geographic Magazine,* (December, 1960), 813–53.

## 10. Judah Under Assyrian Rule

"Babylonian and Assyrian Historical Texts," *ANET*, 287–300.

Barrois, G. A. "Siloam," *IDB*, IV, 352–355.

Bright, John. "Isaiah – I," *PCB*, 489–515.

_____. *The Kingdom of God.* New York: Abingdon, 1953.

Herbert, A. S. "I and II Chronicles," *PCB*, 357–69.

Mauchline, J. "I and II Kings," *PCB*, 338–56.

Scott, R.B.Y. "Isaiah, chs. 1–39, Introduction and Exegesis," *IB*, V, 151–380.

"The Siloam Inscription," *ANET*, 321.

## 11. Judah's Last Days

"Babylonian and Assyrian Historical Texts," *ANET*, 307–8.

Bright, John. *Jeremiah.* Garden City, N. Y.: Doubleday Anchor Books, 1965.

Brockington, L. H. "Obadiah," *PCB*, 626.

Hyatt, James Philip. "The Book of Jeremiah, Introduction and Exegesis," *IB*, V. 777–1142.

"The Lachish Ostraca," *ANET*, 321–2.

Oppenheim, A. Leo. "Nebuchadrezzar," *IDB*, III, 529–30.

Wright, G. Ernest. "Judean Lachish," *BAR2*, 301–12.

## 12. Life in Exile

"Aramaic Papyri from Elephantine," *ANET*, 222–3.

"Babylonian and Hittite Historical Texts," *ANET*, 308–17.

Freedman, David Noel. "Slave of Yahweh," *Western Watch*, X (March 1, 1959), pp. 1–19.

Gray, Geo. Buchanan. *The Forms of Hebrew Poetry.* London: Hodder and Stoughton, 1915.

Herbert, A. S. "Lamentations," *PCB*, 563–67.

Howie, C. G. "Gog and Magog," *IDB*, II, 436–7.

"Letters of the Jews in Elephantine," *ANET*, 491–4.

May, Herbert G. "The Book of Ezekiel, Introduction and Exegesis," *IB*, VI, 41–338.

Meyer, Eduard. "Media," *EB*, XVIII, 20–22.

Muilenburg, James. "Ezekiel," *PCB*, 568–90.

North, C. R. "Servant of the Lord," *IDB*, IV, 292–4.

Oppenheim, A. L. "Nabonidus," *IDB*, III, 493–5.

## 13. Return to Jerusalem

Ackroyd, P. R. "Haggai," *PCB*, 643–45.

"Babylonian and Hittite Historical Texts," *ANET*, 305–15.

Brockington, L. H. "Joel," *PCB*, 614–6.

_____. "Malachi," *PCB*, 656–8.

Browne, L. E. "Ezra and Nehemiah," *PCB*, 370–80.

Burrows, Millar. "Jerusalem," *IDB*, II, 843–66.

Meyer, Eduard. "Cambyses," *EB*, V, 99–100.

_____. "Cyaxares," *EB*, VII, 680–1.

_____. "Cyrus," *EB*, VII, 706.

_____. "Darius," *EB*, VII, 832–3.

_____. "Persia," *EB*, XXI, 187–224.

_____. "Xerxes," *EB*, XXVIII, 887.

Muilenburg, James. "The Book of Isaiah, chs. 40–66, Introduction and Exegesis," *IB*, 381–776.

Pfeiffer, R. H. "Nehemiah," *IDB*, III, 533–4.

Pope, M. H. "Job," *IDB*, II, 911–25.

Rankin, O. S. "The Book of Ecclesiastes, Introduction and Exegesis," *IB*, V, 3–90.

Ryder, E. T. "Ecclesiastes," *PCB*, 458–67.

Rylaarsdam, J. Coert. "The Proverbs," *PCB*, 444–57.

Terrien, Samuel L. "Job, Introduction and Exegesis," *IB*, III, 877–1198.

Wolf, C. U. "Cupbearer," *IDB*, I, 749.

Xenophon. *The First Book of the Anabasis.* London: Macmillan and Co., Ltd., 1960.

## 14. Between the Testaments

Barrett, C. K. *The New Testament Background: Selected Documents.* London: S.P.C.K., 1958.

Black, Matthew. "The Development of Judaism in the Greek and Roman Periods," *PCB*, 693–8.

Burrows, Millar. *The Dead Sea Scrolls.* New York: Viking Press, 1955.

_____. *More Light on the Dead Sea Scrolls.* New York: Viking Press, 1958.

Cross, Frank Moore, Jr. *The Ancient Library of Qumran and Modern Biblical Studies.* Garden City, N. Y.: Doubleday Anchor Books, 1957.

*Josephus, Flavius, The Life and Works of.* Philadelphia: Universal Book and Bible House, 1949.

Rowley, H. H. "Apocalyptic Literature," *PCB*, 484–8.

Sundberg, A. C. "Sadducees," *IDB*, IV, 160–3.

## 15. The Life of Christ

Bowie, Walter Russell. *The Story of the Bible.* New York: Abingdon, 1934.

Bowman, J. W. "The Life and Teaching of Jesus," *PCB*, 733–47.

Burrows, Millar. "Jerusalem," *IDB*, II, 843–66.

Dodd, C. H. *The Apostolic Preaching and Its Development*. New York: Harper and Brothers, 1962.

_____. *The Parables of the Kingdom*. New York: Chas. Scribners, 1961.

Evans, O. E. "Kingdom of God," *IDB*, III, 17–26.

Gaster, T. H. "Demon, Demonology," *ID*, I, 817–24.

Grant, Frederick C. "Jesus Christ," *IDB*, II, 869–96.

Jenni, G. "Messiah, Jewish," *IDB*, III, 360–5.

Jeremias, Joachim. *The Parables of Jesus*. New York: Chas. Scribners, 1962.

Johnson, S. E. "Christ," *IDB*, I, 563–71.

_____. "Son of Man," *IDB*, IV, 413–20.

Knox, John. "Caesar," *IDB*, I, 478.

Lampe, G. W. H. "Luke," *PCB*, 820–43.

Martin, William C. "Herod," *LBE*, 317–20.

_____. "Jesus," *LBE*, 393–404.

_____. "John the Baptist," *LBE*, 414–7.

_____. "Kingdom of God," *LBE*, 446–7.

Operti, Piero. "Rome," *Encyclopedia Americana*, 23, 658–72d.

Perry, Alfred M. "The Growth of the Gospels," *IB*, VII, 60–74.

Richardson, Alan. *An Introduction to the Theology of the New Testament*. New York: Harper and Brothers, 1958.

_____. "Kingdom of God," *A Theological Word Book of the Bible*, 119–21. New York: Macmillan, 1960.

_____. Sandmel, S. "Herod (Family," *IDB*, II, 585–94.

Schweitzer, Albert. *The Quest of the Historical Jesus*. London: A. and C. Black, 1910.

Stendahl, Krister. "Matthew," *PCB*, 769–98.

Streeter, B. H. *The Four Gospels*. London: Macmillan, 1930.

## 16. The Beginnings of the Christian Church

Barrett, C. K. *The New Testament Background: Selected Documents*. London: S. P. C. K., 1958.

Dodd, C. H. The Apostolic Preaching. New York: Harper and Bros., 1962.

Enslin, Morton Scott. *The Literature of the Christian Movement*. Part III *of Christian Beginnings*. New York: Harper Torch Books, 1938.

Grant, Frederick C. (3d). *Hellenistic Religions*. New York: The Liberal Arts Press, 1953.

Macgregor, G. H. C. "The Book of Acts, Introduction and Exegesis," *IB*, IX, 3–352.

Nock, A. D. *Early Gentile Christianity*. New York: Harper Torch Books, 1964.

## 17. The Spread of Christianity

Craig, C. T. The First Epistle to the Corinthians, Introduction and Exegesis," *IB*, X, 3–262.

Dodd, C. H. *The Epistle to the Romans*. New York: Harper, 1932.

Filson, Floyd V. "The Second Epistle to the Corinthians, Introduction and Exegesis," *IB*, X, 265–425.

McNeile, A. H. *An Introduction to the Study of the New Testament*. Second Edition. Oxford: University Press, 1953.

Nock, A. D. *Early Gentile Christianity*. New York: Harper Torch Books, 1964.

## 18. Christianity in the Second Generation

*The Apostolic Fathers*. Trans. and ed. by Kirsopp Lake. 2 vols. Cambridge: Harvard University Press, 1959.

Barnett, Albert E. "The Second Epistle of Peter, Introduction and Exegesis," *IB*, XII, 163–206.

Cullmann, Oscar. *The State in the New Testament*. New York: Charles Scribner's Sons, 1956.

Easton, Burton Scott. "The Epistle of James, Introduction and Exegesis," *IB*, XII, 3–74.

Gealy, Fred D. "The First and Second Epistles to Timothy and the Epistle to Titus, Introduction and Exegesis," *IB*, XI, 343–551.

Hunter, A. M. "The First Epistle of Peter, Introduction and Exegesis," *IB*, XII, 77–159.

Kee, H. C. and Young, F. W. *Understanding the New Testament*. Englewood Cliffs, New Jersey: Prentice-Hall, Inc., 1957.

Menoud, P. H. "Church, Life and Organization of the," *IDB*, I, 617–26.

_____. *Images of the Church in the New*

Minear, Paul. "Church, Idea of," *IDB*, I, 607–17. *Testament*. Philadelphia: Westminster Press, 1960.

Richardson, C. C. "Worship in New Testament Times, Christian," *IDB*, IV, 883–94.

Rist, Martin. "The Revelation of St. John the Divine, Introduction and Exegesis," *IB*, XII, 347–614.

Shepherd, M. H., Jr. "Ministry, Christian," *IDB*, III, 386–92.

Smith, C. W. F. "Prayer," *IDB*, III, 857–67.

Wilder, Amos Niven. "The First, Second, and Third Epistles of John, Introduction and Exegesis," *IB*, XII, 209–313.

# INDEX